HANDBOOK ON THE ECONOMICS OF WOMEN IN SPORTS

T0313920

Handbook on the Economics of Women in Sports

Edited by

Eva Marikova Leeds
Moravian College, USA

Michael A. Leeds
Temple University, USA

Edward Elgar
Cheltenham, UK • Northampton, MA, USA

Published by
Edward Elgar Publishing Limited
The Lypiatts
15 Lansdown Road
Cheltenham
Glos GL50 2JA
UK

Edward Elgar Publishing, Inc.
William Pratt House
9 Dewey Court
Northampton
Massachusetts 01060
USA

A catalogue record for this book
is available from the British Library

Library of Congress Control Number: 2012953527

This book is available electronically in the ElgarOnline.com
Economics Subject Collection, E-ISBN 978 1 84980 939 9

ISBN 978 1 84980 938 2 (cased)

Typeset by Servis Filmsetting Ltd, Stockport, Cheshire
Printed and bound in Great Britain by T.J. International Ltd, Padstow

Contents

List of contributors   vii
Acknowledgments   xii

Introduction: women, sports, and economics   1
Eva Marikova Leeds and Michael A. Leeds

PART I   WOMEN AND SPORT IN CONTEXT

1   Women's attendance at sports events   21
    Sarah S. Montgomery and Michael D. Robinson
2   Participation in women's sport in Australia   40
    Ross Booth and Michael A. Leeds
3   Individual decision-making in a social context: the sociological
    determinants of female sports participation   56
    Judith Stull

PART II   PERFORMANCE AND REWARDS IN WOMEN'S
          PROFESSIONAL SPORTS

4   Gender and skill convergence in professional golf   73
    Stephen Shmanske
5   Gender differences in responses to incentives in sports: some
    new results from golf   92
    Keith F. Gilsdorf and Vasant A. Sukhatme
6   Earnings and performance in women's skiing   115
    XiaoGang Che and Brad R. Humphreys
7   Understanding the WNBA on and off the court   132
    David J. Berri and Anthony C. Krautmann
8   The goals and impacts of age restrictions in sports   156
    Ryan M. Rodenberg

PART III   WOMEN IN INTERCOLLEGIATE SPORTS

9   The economics of Title IX compliance in intercollegiate
    athletics   175
    Susan L. Averett and Sarah M. Estelle

10   Revenues and subsidies in collegiate sports: an analysis of
      NCAA Division I women's basketball   213
      Robert W. Brown and R. Todd Jewell
11   The impact of increased academic standards of Proposition
      16 on the graduation rates of women and men in Division IA
      intercollegiate athletics   233
      B. Erin Fairweather
12   Gender differences in competitive balance in intercollegiate
      basketball   251
      Jaret Treber, Rachel Levy and Victor A. Matheson
13   Coaching women and women coaching: pay differentials in
      the Title IX era   269
      Peter von Allmen

PART IV   WOMEN IN OLYMPIC AND INTERNATIONAL
           SPORTS

14   Gender differences in competitiveness: empirical evidence
      from 100m races   293
      Bernd Frick and Friedrich Scheel
15   Do men and women respond differently to economic contests?
      The case of men's and ladies' figure skating   319
      Eva Marikova Leeds and Michael A. Leeds
16   International women's soccer and gender inequality:
      revisited   345
      Joshua Congdon-Hohman and Victor A. Matheson
17   The economic impact of the Women's World Cup   365
      Dennis Coates
18   An economic analysis of the sudden influx of Korean female
      golfers into the LPGA   388
      *Young Hoon Lee, Ilhyeok Park, Joon-Ho Kang and
      Younghan Lee*
19   Media coverage and pay in women's basketball and netball in
      Australia   410
      Ross Booth

Index   427

Contributors

Susan L. Averett is the Charles A. Dana Professor of Economics at Lafayette College in Easton, PA, USA. She has written dozens of academic articles and book chapters on a wide array of topics in labor and health economics. Her current research includes adolescent risky behavior, the effect of marriage on health, and the causes and consequences of obesity. She is the co-editor of the *Eastern Economic Journal* and serves on the board of the Committee on the Status of Women in the Economics Profession.

David J. Berri is Professor of Economics at Southern Utah University in Cedar City, UT, USA. He has published extensively on consumer demand, competitive balance, and worker productivity in professional sports. His work has been featured prominently in the popular press. He is a past president of the North American Association of Sports Economists and a member of the editorial board of the *Journal of Sports Economics* and the *International Journal of Sport Finance*.

Ross Booth is a Senior Lecturer in the Department of Economics at Clayton campus of Monash University in Melbourne, Victoria, Australia. He received a Dean's Teaching Award in 2005. His research has focused on the economics of professional sports leagues, especially the Australian Football League. Since 1988, he has been a commentator for the Victorian Football League on ABC TV. He is a life member of the Victorian Amateur Football Association (VAFA) and was a Board member from 1986 to 2010.

Robert W. Brown is Professor of Economics at California State University San Marcos, CA, USA. He has published papers on such topics as estimating the marginal value of college athletes, NCAA academic policies, discrimination in sports, and revenue sharing in college football. His other research interests are regional land use, environmental recreation, and housing economics.

XiaoGang Che is a Post-doctoral Fellow in the Department of Economics at the University of Alberta, Edmonton, Canada. He earned his PhD from the University of Sydney, Australia, in 2012. His research interests include applied game theory and sports economics.

Dennis Coates is Professor of Economics at the University of Maryland – Baltimore County in Baltimore, MD, USA. His published work has analyzed topics ranging from the voting behavior of legislators to the economic effects of stadiums and professional sports franchises. He is a past president of the North American Association of Sports Economists and the Book Review Editor for the *Journal of Sports Economics*.

Joshua Congdon-Hohman is Assistant Professor of Economics at the College of the Holy Cross in Worcester, MA, USA. His research is primarily in the fields of labor and public economics, and he has a strong interest in topics involving sports economics.

Sarah M. Estelle is Assistant Professor of Economics at Hope College in Holland, MI, USA. Her research interests span labor, public, and health economics and include the economics of education, families and parenting, and adolescent risky behavior. Her research examines the influence of parents and the home environment on early elementary academic outcomes, the effectiveness of parental communication about sex on adolescent sexual activity, and the returns to for-profit collegiate attainment.

B. Erin Fairweather is an economics lecturer in the New York metropolitan area. She has taught at several universities, including Rutgers, Temple, and CUNY. Her research interests include experimental economics, the unintended consequences of public policies, and the impact of race and gender on educational and professional achievements. She has spent over seven years providing consulting services in high-profile litigation matters with top firms such as Duff & Phelps in New York City.

Bernd Frick is Professor of Organizational and Media Economics and a Vice President at the University of Paderborn, Germany. He is also Director of the Institute of Labor and Personnel Economics at Mobile Life Campus of Volkswagen AG in Wolfsburg and Research Associate at the Institute for Labour Law and Industrial Relations in the European Community at the University of Trier. His research interests are in organizational and personnel economics, industrial relations, and sports economics.

Keith F. Gilsdorf is Associate Professor of Economics at Augsburg College in Minneapolis, MN, USA. Previously, he spent several years as a regulatory economist for the State of Minnesota, analyzing regulatory policy in the natural gas and electric utility industries His research interests are in compensation systems and sports labor markets, public utility regulation, and the determinants of market structure. He has published articles on the utility industry and on tournament incentives in men's and women's tennis.

Brad R. Humphreys is Professor in the Department of Economics at the University of Alberta, Edmonton, Canada, where he holds the Chair in the Economics of Gaming. His research on the economic impact of professional sports, the economics of gambling, and the financing of the Olympic Games has been published in numerous scholarly journals. He is a past president of the North American Association of Sports Economists and is currently editor of *Contemporary Economic Policy* and associate editor of the *International Journal of Sport Finance*.

R. Todd Jewell is Professor of Economics and department chair at the University of North Texas in Denton, TX, USA. He has published extensively in the economics of sports, with a recent focus on aggressive play in professional sports. He has also published in the areas of the economics of immigration and health economics.

Joon-Ho Kang is Professor of Sport Marketing and Director of the Center for Sport Industry at Seoul National University in Seoul, Republic of Korea. His research interests include sport sponsorship, sport consumer behavior, sport industry, and sport development. He has been an editorial board member of the *Journal of Sport Management*, the *International Journal of Sport Finance*, and the *International Journal of Sport and Health Science*.

Anthony C. Krautmann is Professor of Economics at DePaul University in Chicago, IL, USA. He has published many papers on topics ranging from wage determination of professional athletes, to competitive balance in sports leagues, to the potential disincentives associated with long-term labor contracts. He is a past president of the North American Association of Sports Economists.

Young Hoon Lee is Professor of Economics at Sogang University in Seoul, Republic of Korea. He has published widely on team efficiency measurement, temporal variations in competitive balance, and the uncertainty of outcome hypothesis. He has been a member of the editorial board of the *Journal of Sports Economics* and the *International Journal of Sport Finance*.

Younghan Lee is Assistant Professor of Sport Management in the Isenberg School of Management at the University of Massachusetts in Amherst, MA, USA. His research centers on the practical implementation of marketing theory and business strategy in sport. It includes strategic sport marketing, customer relationship marketing and management, management efficiency, and ticket pricing strategy.

Eva Marikova Leeds is Professor of Economics at Moravian College in Bethlehem, PA, USA. She has written on privatization and mortgage markets in transition economies. Her work in sports economics includes the application of event analysis to stadium naming rights and finding determinants of national success in sports.

Michael A. Leeds is Professor of Economics and Director of Graduate Studies in Economics at Temple University in Philadelphia, PA, USA. His recent research includes work on the economics of baseball in Japan and gender differences in the response to economic contests. He is co-author with Peter von Allmen of the textbook *The Economics of Sports* and is President-elect of the North American Association of Sports Economists.

Rachel Levy is a client account manager for Bessemer Trust in Washington, DC, USA. She played on the varsity basketball team at Kenyon College and was a captain for two years. Her senior thesis explored the economics of women's intercollegiate basketball.

Victor A. Matheson is Associate Professor of Economics at the College of the Holy Cross in Worcester, MA, USA. He has published extensively on the economics of collegiate and professional sports, including the impact of sports stadia and events on the local economy. He has also worked as a top-level soccer referee, officiating national team and professional women's matches as well as over 150 Division I intercollegiate women's games.

Sarah S. Montgomery is Professor Emerita of Economics at Mount Holyoke College in South Hadley, MA, USA. She has a longstanding interest in the economics of the arts.

Ilhyeok Park is Associate Professor of Physical Education at Seoul National University in Seoul, Republic of Korea. His research focuses on measurement theory, applied statistics, as well as the analysis of exercise, health, and sports data. He is a member of the editorial board of several journals, including *Measurement in Physical Education and Exercise Science* and the *Journal of Sport Management*.

Michael D. Robinson is Professor of Economics at Mount Holyoke College in South Hadley, MA, USA. He has published on topics in labor economics, including gender and racial earnings differentials. He has recently worked with Professor Sarah Montgomery on several papers on the economics of the arts and on the attendance patterns at arts and sports events.

Ryan M. Rodenberg is Assistant Professor of Sport Management in the College of Education at Florida State University in Tallahassee, FL, USA. Previously, he was associate general counsel at Octagon, Washington, DC. His research interests include sports law analytics and forensic sports law.

Friedrich Scheel is a PhD student at the University of Paderborn in Paderborn, Germany, where he works as a research assistant with Professor Bernd Frick. An active sportsman and current national university champion in squash, he studies gender differences in competitive sports settings.

Stephen Shmanske is Professor Emeritus of Economics at California State University, East Bay in Hayward, CA, USA. He is the Director of the Smith Center for Private Enterprise Studies at the same campus. He has written extensively on sports economics, especially the economics of golf.

Judith Stull is Associate Professor of Sociology at LaSalle University in Philadelphia, PA, USA. She is also is a Senior Research Associate at Temple University in the Institute for Schools and Society. Her research has focused on improving the educational achievement of at-risk students and the use of educational technology.

Vasant A. Sukhatme is Edward J. Noble Professor of Economics at Macalester College in St. Paul, MN, USA. He has received the Excellence in Teaching Award and the Thomas Jefferson Award for lifetime teaching, research, and service contributions to Macalester College. His research includes work on agricultural markets in India and tournament incentives in men's and women's tennis.

Jaret Treber is Associate Professor of Economics at Kenyon College in Gambier, OH, USA. He has published in economic history on topics in healthcare and housing construction. His more recent work has focused on occupational regulation and the economics of sports.

Peter von Allmen is Professor of Economics at Skidmore College in Saratoga Springs, NY, USA. His research has focused on compensation mechanisms, incentives, and monopsony power in professional sports. He has also published in the area of family labor supply and post-secondary pedagogy. He is co-author with Michael Leeds of the textbook *The Economics of Sports* and serves on the editorial board of the *Eastern Economic Journal*.

Acknowledgments

This volume began with a casual conversation with Tara Gorvine, acquisitions editor at Edward Elgar, whose patience and persistence has helped bring a once-vague idea to fruition. The project would not have been completed without her. This book is a creation of the many authors whose knowledge and creativity make this volume a genuine contribution to the literature. We thank them for their diligence and responsiveness to our comments.

We also thank Lauren Banko, a PhD student at Temple University, for her very efficient editorial assistance in finalizing the chapters. Finally, we are grateful to Alison Hornbeck, assistant editor at Edward Elgar, who checked our manuscript for consistency and accuracy.

Introduction: women, sports, and economics
Eva Marikova Leeds and Michael A. Leeds

The economics of sports has given rise to a rapidly growing literature. General-interest journals publish an increasing number of articles devoted to sports economics, and two journals (*the Journal of Sports Economics* and *the International Journal of Sport Finance*) are now devoted to the field. Edited volumes on the economics of sports in general or on the economics of specific sports (such as baseball or soccer) have also become increasingly popular (see, for example, Fizel et al., 1996; Andreff and Szymanski, 2007; Humphreys and Howard, 2008; and Kahane and Shmanske, 2011). It is therefore surprising that so little has been written about the economics of women in sports. From 2009 through 2011, *the Journal of Sports Economics* published 102 feature articles. Despite the openness of the editorial staff to topics outside the 'big four' of baseball, basketball, football, and hockey, none of these articles was specifically devoted to women and only seven focused even partly on women. Instead, the lack of attention reflects a surprising dearth of interest among economists in women's sports.

On one level, this lack of interest is surprising. An important reason for studying sports is that they provide a 'laboratory' in which to study larger socioeconomic issues (Kahn, 2000). Readily available data on performance and compensation allow researchers to analyze phenomena ranging from the incentive effects of salaries to racial and ethnic discrimination. Sports seem to be a natural vehicle to evaluate whether women behave differently from men or whether society treats women differently.

On another level, the lack of interest is natural. Sports economists, like all social scientists, tend to follow their personal interests when they perform research. As a result, research on sports economics has tended to focus on professional team sports, particularly in the United States. Women, however, have had relatively few opportunities in professional team sports. Women's professional softball came and went without arousing much notice, and two women's soccer leagues struggled for a few years before folding. Only the Women's National Basketball Association (WNBA) has managed to survive for more than a few years. In contrast to team sports, women have thrived in individual sports, such as tennis, golf, or figure skating. However, these sports receive relatively less attention from researchers than baseball, football, basketball, hockey, and soccer. Over 75 percent of the 102 *Journal of Sports Economics* articles from 2009 through 2011 dealt with those sports. Because women's sports neither make much of an impression on the American psyche nor have a significant economic impact, few economists have felt compelled to investigate them.

Economists have largely left the field of women's sports to the other social sciences. Judith Stull shows in Chapter 3 of this volume that there is already an extensive literature on women and sports in both sociology and psychology. As was true with the study of discrimination, which – as several chapters in this volume note – plays a significant role in the study of women in sports, economics has lagged behind the other social sciences in the study of women's participation in sports, despite having much to contribute to the topic.

The chapters in this volume correct the lack of attention to women's sports in three ways. First, the research to produce them has stimulated some of the leading scholars in the economics of sports to turn their attention to this topic. The research makes a genuine contribution to our understanding of women's sports and of how the behavior and treatment of female athletes reflect broader economic forces. Second, this handbook will help future researchers. In some cases, this takes the form of showing how a theoretical or empirical structure applies to sports, as when Young Hoon Lee et al. (Chapter 18) apply the theory of immigration and self-selection to women's golf or when Robert Brown and Todd Jewell (Chapter 10) apply quantile regression to women's intercollegiate basketball. In other cases, authors provide an introduction to sports that have not yet been treated in economics – as when XiaoGang Che and Brad Humphreys (Chapter 6) examine downhill and giant slalom skiing – so that future researchers can gain a basic understanding of the history and institutional structure of the sports they will analyze. At times, as in Ross Booth's (Chapter 19) discussion of netball, they may introduce researchers to sports they have never heard of. Finally, this volume is a valuable resource to instructors and students in the areas of sports economics, sports management, and women's studies.

Researchers and students need to understand both what theoretical and econometric tools to apply and what broader legal and social forces define and constrain the sphere in which female athletes operate. Thus, this volume contains a variety of approaches to the subject matter. Some chapters, such as Erin Fairweather's (Chapter 11) analysis of how academic requirements for college recruits affect graduation rates, are highly technical econometric studies. Others, such as Ryan Rodenberg's (Chapter 8) discussion of age limits in professional sports, probe the institutional and legal structures of sports. The particular approach of each chapter depends on the demands of the subject matter.

Part I, 'Women and Sport in Context', offers a setting for the next three parts of the book, which examine specific aspects of women in sports. While most of this volume focuses on women as participants in sports, two of the chapters in this section, 'Women's attendance at sports events' and 'Participation in women's sport in Australia', provide insight into women as consumers of sport. The former shows what motivates women's attendance at sporting events and the latter explains what sports women choose as recreational activities.

In their study of attendance, Sarah Montgomery and Michael Robinson extend and update their earlier work on attendance at sporting events (Montgomery and Robinson, 2006 and 2010). They draw an analogy between being a sports fan and being a patron of the arts. Both activities require a specific form of human capital that enables individuals to appreciate what they see. Individuals can acquire 'sports capital' first-hand, by participating in sports, or second-hand, by being married to someone with sports capital. Montgomery and Robinson find that the increasing participation of women in sports has increased their sports capital. This, in turn, has caused women's attendance at sporting events to approach that of men. Using data from the Survey of Public Participation in the Arts (SPPA), which contains data on attendance at sporting events, Montgomery and Robinson show that individuals who participate in sports also attend more sports events.

Montgomery and Robinson also find that marriage affects sports attendance, with married women attending more sports events than single women and with married men attending fewer events than single men. However, they find little evidence for the 'battle of the sexes', in which one spouse attends an event only because s/he prefers being with the spouse to being alone. Instead, they find evidence of assortative mating, in which individuals with similar amounts of sports capital are attracted to one another.

While Montgomery and Robinson analyze overall attendance rates, Ross Booth and Michael Leeds (Chapter 2) use data compiled by the Australian Bureau of Statistics (ABS) to examine how men and women differ in their attendance and participation in specific sports. The data show that women are more likely to engage in solitary physical activities, such as walking, while men are more likely to take part in social activities, such as golf. These choices are consistent with the different motivations men and women have for participating in sports. According to the ABS, women are likely to undertake physical activity for their health and physical well-being. Men, on the other hand, participate in athletics for the socialization and competition involved.

Booth and Leeds use these findings to formulate a theoretical model of physical activity. In the model, individuals maximize their utility by working and by undertaking leisure activities. Different activities increase utility in different ways, such as by promoting health, providing competitive outlets, or by enhancing earnings (such as by discussing business on the golf course). Using the values revealed by the ABS survey, it is easy to show how men and women are attracted to different sports.

In the final chapter of Part I, Judith Stull (Chapter 3) presents a sociologist's view of female athletes. She pays particular attention to the images that the surrounding culture has of these women and to the images that they form of themselves. This chapter provides economists with the concepts and terminology that they will need to understand the much broader sociology literature surrounding women in sports.

Stull begins her analysis by noting that female athletes operate in a much different context from their male counterparts. Specifically, women are subject to 'cultural lag', the disparity that sometimes arises because people's actions change more quickly than their value systems. Because female athletes must try to reconcile their roles as athletes with their traditional roles as women, female athletes are much more likely than male athletes to experience role strain. They are also more subject to role conflict, which results when the two roles cannot be reconciled. These conflicts often play out over perceptions of the female athletes' bodies. Women in 'non-lean' sports, such as softball or basketball, in which success depends upon physical strength, are often viewed as unfeminine or even sexually deviant. Women in 'lean' sports, such as gymnastics, are often pushed in the opposite direction, wearing form-fitting or highly revealing uniforms. Women in the 'lean' sports – and in sports divided into weight classifications – are particularly subject to eating disorders.

Great though the pressures on female athletes in Western countries have been, they are far less than those on female athletes from Islamic cultures. Although the Qu'ran contains no specific restrictions on physical activity by women – and can even be interpreted as encouraging fitness among women – many Muslim women face restrictions that prevent them from competing effectively. These often take the form of 'modest' attire that inhibits movement or even strictures against any physical activity in the presence of men.

The chapters in the remaining three parts of the book are generally devoted to analyzing specific professional and amateur sports. The studies in part II examine the reward structures present in women's professional sports and analyze how women respond to the resulting incentives. Only one of the five chapters in this section pertains to team sports, reflecting the dominance of individual sports at the professional level. Two of the chapters on individual sports analyze how women respond to tournament settings. This is because tournament theory plays a large role in determining the compensation of professional athletes in individual sports. The last chapter spans individual and team sports, as it investigates the role and impact of age restrictions in women's sports in general.

Stephen Shmanske (Chapter 4) analyzes the impact of incentives on driving distances in golf. Using data from the Ladies Professional Golf Association (LPGA), the Professional Golf Association (PGA), and Champions (formerly Seniors) Tours for 1992 through 2010, Shmanske examines two aspects of driving. First, he measures the male–female differential in driving distance and tests whether it has changed over time. Second, he performs Granger causality tests on driving distance and purse size for men and women to determine whether larger purses 'cause' driving distance to increase (for example, by enabling greater investments in training and equipment) or whether driving distance 'causes' purses to grow (for example, by increasing attendance and media ratings).

Shmanske accounts for gender difference in two different ways, running separate regressions for the three tours and using a pooled dataset with dummy variables that indicate the different tours. He consistently finds that women's drives are 37–40 yards shorter than men's drives. Year dummies show that both men's and women's drives have increased between 1992 and 2010 but that the rate of increase – and the gender difference – has been inconsistent over time.

The Granger test results also differ by gender. Shmanske finds that one can reject the hypothesis that higher purses cause men's driving distance to increase but that one cannot reject the hypothesis that greater driving distance causes the purses of men's tournaments to increase. Exactly the opposite holds for the women's Tour. Thus, it appears that fans and sponsors might be attracted to the men's Tour by prodigious drives, but that fans of the women's game are not interested in such displays of power. It appears that women's driving distance responds to larger purse sizes, perhaps because of greater access to training or technology. Men's driving distance, however, shows no response to larger purses.

Rank-order tournaments (ROTs) are at the center of the chapters by Keith Gilsdorf and Vasant Sukhatme (Chapter 5) and XiaoGang Che and Brad Humphreys (Chapter 6). ROTs were first proposed by Lazear and Rosen (1981), who used them to explain why small differences in performance often lead to large differences in compensation. This has given rise to a growing set of experimental studies, summarized by Croson and Gneezy (2009), that have found significant differences in how men and women (and boys and girls) respond to tournament settings.

Gilsdorf and Sukhatme provide a valuable extension to Croson and Gneezy's review by summarizing the literature devoted to gender differences in responses to incentives in sports. In the second half of their chapter, Gilsdorf and Sukhatme test the hypothesis that women respond differently from men to tournament settings, using data they compiled from the 2009 PGA TOUR and LPGA Tour in professional golf. They directly extend the work of Ehrenberg and Bognanno (1990a and 1990b) by estimating how men and women respond to differences in overall purse size (the total reward to be divided among all golfers in a given tournament) and the spread in prizes (how much of the total purse goes to the golfers who finish first, second, and so on).

Their results largely contradict those of the experimental literature. Gilsdorf and Sukhatme find that, when looking at total scores, women and men respond similarly to incentives. Looking specifically at final round scores, they find that female golfers respond more positively to incentives than male golfers do.

XiaoGang Che and Brad Humphreys apply ROT theory to alpine skiing, a new setting for this research. They analyze the impact of total prize money and the spread in prizes on performance. Like the National Association for Stock Car Auto Racing (NASCAR), skiing has a much flatter reward gradient than golf. Che and Humphreys speculate that this could be due to the greater danger attached to reckless performance in skiing. The flatter gradient means that the reward structure in skiing differs systematically from that in golf.

Che and Humphreys study the performance of female downhill and giant slalom skiers in the Fédération Internationale de Ski's Alpine World Cup Tour. The two events differ systematically. Downhill is a 'speed' event, in which the skier makes relatively few turns over a course that has a steep vertical drop. Giant slalom is a 'technical' event, in which the skier makes many turns on a course that has a shallower vertical drop.

Che and Humphreys use pooled OLS on an unbalanced panel, with data covering the 2001–02 season through the 2010–11 season. They generally finding that greater differences in prizes lead to faster times. This result does not hold, however, for all specifications of the prize gradient. In addition, they find that events with larger total purses yield faster times in the downhill but not in giant slalom results. Whether this difference is due to differences in the nature of the events or in the skiers who take part in them and whether these results also apply to men await further study.

David J. Berri and Anthony C. Krautmann (Chapter 7) examine the one women's sports league that has had any measure of success in the United States: the WNBA. Berri and Krautmann begin by piecing together evidence – data on the WNBA are much harder to find than data for the NBA – that the WNBA's revenue stream is very low. The WNBA's low revenues make it unlikely that WNBA teams have been profitable, despite labor costs that are a small fraction of those in the NBA.

The bulk of Berri and Krautmann's chapter consists of adapting the model of wins produced in the NBA outlined in Berri (2008) and elsewhere to the WNBA. They show that most of the factors that contribute to wins in the NBA have very similar effects in the WNBA. The one significant exception is assists, which contribute much more strongly to wins in the WNBA. The NBA and WNBA are also alike in that decision makers in both leagues overstate the value of scoring. While scoring contributes to wins, it fails to account fully for wins. Players who on average score many points per game but who do not contribute to other aspects of the game tend to receive more accolades and more playing time in both the NBA and the WNBA than their contributions to wins merits.

Ryan Rodenberg (Chapter 8) examines the motivation for and impact of minimum-age restrictions on female athletes. Perhaps because of the different physical demands in different sports, young women face a wide variety of age restrictions when they seek to enter professional or elite-level competition. Indeed, one of Rodenberg's most significant contributions is his compiling the first comprehensive set of age restrictions facing young women in sports competition in an Appendix to the chapter. He then provides detailed explanation of the restrictions imposed by the Women's Tennis Association (WTA), the WNBA, the LPGA, and the International Gymnastics Federation (FIG) in the body of the chapter.

While age restrictions differ from sport to sport, they share a common motivation – the protection of young female athletes from injury and abuse. In tennis alone, a dazzling array of adolescent girls (Tracy Austin, Martina Hingis, and Jennifer Capriati, to name a few) burst on the scene in the 1980s and 1990s, only to have their careers cut short by injuries and personal problems. There was also a growing fear that young girls were subject to physical, emotional, and sexual abuse while pursuing professional or Olympic success. Still, not everyone agrees with the need for age restrictions. Opponents of age restrictions have challenged them on antitrust grounds. By restricting who can participate at a sport's highest level, age restrictions appear to violate the Sherman Antitrust Act.

Finally, Rodenberg surveys the economic literature on the impact of age restrictions on performance in tennis. He concludes that there is little evidence that the age restrictions imposed by the WTA in the mid-1990s resulted in longer careers for female tennis players. He also finds little support for the claim that the restriction affected player performance, as reflected in rankings. Rodenberg stops short of condemning age restrictions, however, noting that the results of these studies could stem from limitations on the available data.

Part III turns to intercollegiate athletics. Thanks largely to Title IX, the last 40 years have seen massive increases in the number of girls and women participating in interscholastic and intercollegiate athletics and in the quality of play by women at all levels. The chapters in this part explicitly compare female and male student-athletes and, in one case, coaches. They chart how far women have come since Title IX and how far they have to go.

The 2012 London Olympics have rightly been declared the 'The Women's Olympics'. A record 44 percent of the participants were women, including two representatives from Saudi Arabia, which had never before sent women to any international competition. The representation of women was particularly great in the US delegation. For the first time, American women formed a majority of the team (269 women to 261 men). They also far surpassed the men on the podium, winning 58 medals – 29 of them gold – to only 45 medals (17 gold) for US men (Chappell, 2012; for a precise medal count, see '2012 Medal Standings', 2012). Much of the Olympic success of US women – and most of their achievements in athletics for over a generation – has been attributed to Title IX (see, for example, Anderson, 2012 and Shapcott, 2012).

Susan Averett and Sarah Estelle (Chapter 9) begin their analysis of Title IX by summarizing its history, interpretation, and application. They pay particular attention to how the courts have defined compliance with Title IX. Compliance is also at the heart of the second portion of the chapter, as they use six samples, drawn from all post-secondary schools that receive federal funds, to analyze whether schools comply and their degree of compliance or noncompliance.

The degree of compliance seems to be a greater issue for economists than for the courts, as no school has ever lost federal funding for noncompliance despite the many complaints that have been filed against colleges and universities that are clearly noncompliant. As a result, only 15 percent of the institutions actually met the standards of compliance between 2003 and 2010. Averett and Estelle identify many issues that hinder compliance, most importantly the size and importance of football programs, which have no equivalent women's sport. Despite the role of football in thwarting proportionality, they find that non-NCAA (National Collegiate Athletic Association) schools and Division III schools are more likely to be noncompliant than NCAA Division I schools, which are associated with 'big-time' football. They also note that compliance is more difficult when schools have disproportionately large female undergraduate enrollment, small endowments, low admissions standards, and a small student body. In addition, schools from the South and Midwest are more likely to be noncompliant.

The failure to comply with Title IX may stem in part from the rising proportion of women seeking tertiary education and colleges' challenge to increase the number of programs accordingly. It may also reflect the lower desire of the average woman to participate in sports. An inquiry into these factors is beyond their study. Nevertheless, Averett and Estelle stress that the lax enforcement of Title IX by the Office of Civil Rights provides schools with very weak incentives to comply with Title IX.

The growth of women's sports on college campuses has drawn women into the broader debate over whether college athletes should be paid. Robert W. Brown and R. Todd Jewell (Chapter 10) contribute to this discussion by investigating the impact of star female basketball players on the athletic revenues of the university. They define a star woman basketball player as a college player who is eventually drafted in the WNBA. Since star players have both direct and indirect effects on revenues, Brown and Jewell use three kinds of revenue in their estimation: ticket, direct, and total revenues. Their data on team revenues for the 2004–05 NCAA basketball season were made available by the Equity and Athletic Disclosure Act.

Brown and Jewell analyze their data using quantile regression (QR) techniques. QR has become popular because it is more appropriate than OLS for regressions with dependent variables, such as athletic revenue, that have skewed distributions. While OLS estimates the conditional mean of the dependent variable, quantile regression can estimate any percentile of the conditional distribution, for example the median; it computes coefficients by computing the least absolute deviation of points above or below a given percentile, conditional on the values of the explanatory variables. QRs are thus less sensitive to the presence of outliers in the data.

An earlier study by Brown and Jewell (2006) used aggregate revenue from the 2000–01 season to show that a star player generates about $300,000 per year in revenues, but the contribution of star players in the best basketball programs can be much larger. In Chapter 10, they show that a star player raises the median expected revenue of a university (given the independent variables) by approximately $100,000. For total revenues, this effect falls just short of statistical significance at the 10 percent level. The impact of star players is much larger at the 80th percentile, as a star player raises direct revenues by $200,000. However, even this large contribution is not enough to make women's basketball self-sustaining, and the programs at virtually all schools are subsidized from other sources at the university. This makes the issue of payment of athletes much more complicated and practically intractable.

As women's athletics has assumed a greater role on college campuses, some worry about whether the ills that plague men's athletics, from doctored high-school transcripts to illegal recruiting practices, will appear in women's intercollegiate athletics. There appears to be no such worry about graduation rates. For example, women who play on basketball teams that reach the NCAA tournament's 'Sweet 16' almost uniformly graduate at rates well above those of men whose teams reach the 'Sweet 16' (see Leeds and von Allmen, 2010). One would therefore expect policies aimed at improving graduation rates to have a greater impact on men than on women.

Erin Fairweather (Chapter 11) analyzes the impact of one particular NCAA reform, Proposition 16, on the graduation rates of men and women. 'Prop 16' increased the requirements facing high-school seniors who desired athletic scholarships. It was implemented in two stages. The NCAA increased the number of required high-school core courses for students who sought to enter college in 1995–96 from 11 to 16. The following year, the NCAA replaced a straight 700 SAT score requirement (for the verbal and quantitative portions combined) with a sliding scale that depended on the student's grade point average. While racial differences in the impact of Prop 16 (and earlier reforms) have received much attention, Fairweather's is the first systematic study of gender differences in its impact.

It might seem that one could measure the impact of Prop 16 on the graduation rates of student-athletes by simply including a dummy variable that captures the years following the reform's implementation. Unfortunately, such a procedure would fail to account for the possibility that secular changes in graduation rates could have caused all graduation rates – of athletes and non-athletes (who were unaffected by Prop 16) – to rise. Fairweather accounts for such potential bias by performing difference-in-differences (DiD) estimation. DiD compares the changes over time of the treatment group (in this case student-athletes) with those of a control group (non-athletes).

Fairweather uses university-level data on graduation rates obtained from the NCAA (more disaggregated data are not available because of privacy laws) to obtain the DiD estimates of the impact of Prop 16. Because the dependent variable is limited to lie between 0 and 1, she uses logit estimation. She finds that, as expected, Prop 16 had no impact on the overall graduation rate of female student-athletes. Surprisingly, she also finds that there is no impact on male student-athletes.

While most studies of competitive balance focus on professional sports, competitive balance is also an important issue for collegiate sports. Because studies show that spectators prefer closely contested matches in which the outcome is not a foregone conclusion, leagues have adopted policies that equalize team revenue in order to maximize profits. The issue of competitive balance in intercollegiate sports is even more fundamental. If fans become disenchanted with unbalanced play of women's teams, for example, then women's basketball may never become widely popular and the nascent WNBA may forever stay nascent.

Jaret Treber, Rachel Levy, and Victor Matheson (Chapter 12) use two different measures to compare competitive balance in men's and women's intercollegiate basketball in the United States. They measure within-season balance using the results of NCAA tournament games and find that women's games result in fewer upsets and larger point differentials than men's games. They measure between-season balance by computing the Herfindahl–Hirschman index (HHI) of the concentration of NCAA championships for men's basketball (1985–11) and women's basketball (1995–11). They then compute the ratio of each HHI to the 'ideal' HHI that would prevail in a world of perfect competitive balance and find that the ratio is twice as large for women as for men, implying that championships are far more highly concentrated among women's teams.

Treber et al. analyze the gender differences in competitive balance by appealing to Gould's (1986 and 1996) explanation for the disappearance of the 0.400 hitter in baseball. Gould claimed that several factors, including the breaking down of the color line, the internationalization of the game, and the increasing return to baseball skills, has attracted many more players to the game. This, in turn, has compressed the distribution of skills in MLB and shifted it to the right. The tighter distribution of skills makes it harder for any one player to stand out. Treber et al. claim that this observation also holds for men's basketball. On the team level, the 'mass' of exceptional players broadly ensures competitive balance. This compression has yet to occur in women's basketball, and the relatively low pay of women in the WNBA may not attract enough young women to create the same level of competitive balance in women's intercollegiate basketball.

The participation of women in college athletics has markedly increased since the passage of Title IX. One would expect this increase to expand the number of women coaches as well. In fact, the opposite is true. Peter von Allmen (Chapter 13) finds that the percentage of women coaches has steadily declined since the passage of Title IX. In 1972, 90 percent of women's teams had women coaches, while in 2010, only 40 percent of women's teams did. Von Allmen notes three possible explanations for this decline: a lack of desire to coach, which keeps women from exploiting the expanding opportunities; discrimination against women by athletic departments; and lower productivity by women as coaches.

Determining which of the above explanations is correct has important policy implications. If women are the victims of discrimination, then the

NCAA or the legal system can and should address this problem. If women face social obstacles that discourage them from coaching or if they lack the skills to be good coaches, we face a more complex problem that is very difficult to resolve.

Von Allmen first establishes that the salaries for coaching men's teams exceed the salaries for coaching women's teams. At Division IA schools, they are three times higher. Much of this inequality is caused by the presence of football. To see if this result can be attributed to coaching skill, von Allmen examines the records of Division I softball programs. He finds that women coaches are just as successful as men coaches. Specifically, carefully holding other factors constant, the gender of the coach does not affect the ranking of the team during the 2007 season. Von Allmen concludes that women are just as good at coaching as men and that skill does not explain their lower salaries.

Finally, von Allmen finds a novel setting to examine the effect of gender on salary. In golf, which is not a revenue-generating sport for either gender and is very similar for both genders, coaches of men's teams (all of whom are men) earn about $11,100 more than coaches of women's teams at Division I schools. Regression results attribute the salary of coaches of men's teams to 'the size of the institution and the performance of the team as measured by rank'. Intriguingly, a regression of salaries of women's team coaches indicates that the presence of football and the rank of the team both raise salaries and that woman coaches, *ceteris paribus*, earn about 13 percent more than men coaches. Based on these results, von Allmen urges administrators to make the coaching work environment more inviting for women. This could stem the declining percentage of women's teams that are coached by women and to let them shine.

Most of the chapters in the volume thus far have focused on sports in the United States. In contrast, Part IV focuses explicitly on the wider world. Four of the chapters, two about soccer, one about 100 meter sprints, and one about figure skating, treat sports that are inherently international, often explicitly pitting one country against another. Another chapter asks why Korean women have come to the United States to play golf. Finally, a chapter examines netball – a sport most Americans have never heard of – and explains how this linear descendant of the version of basketball that women played in the nineteenth century can coexist with the modern version of women's basketball, which closely resembles the men's game.

Much of the sports literature on how women respond to economic contests contradicts the experimental literature. Bernd Frick and Friedrich Scheel (Chapter 14) find one area of agreement. Rather than ask whether men and women respond 'positively' to the incentives of rank-order tournaments, Frick and Scheel build on the work of Booth and Nolen (2012), who conducted an experiment to see whether women sought to avoid tournament settings entirely. Frick and Scheel use data from international and German 100-meter sprinters to show that women enter races strategically to avoid confronting other elite runners; something men either will not or cannot do. This finding is consistent with Frick's earlier work on distance runners (Frick, 2011a and 2011b).

Frick and Scheel detect evidence of avoidance behavior among female sprinters by appealing to three unique datasets. The first was created and has been maintained by former runners. This dataset allows Frick and Scheel to compare the top 100 times by male and female sprinters for each year from 2001 to 2010. They also use a similar dataset assembled for the 50 best 100m times for German men and women over the same period. Finally, they use the five fastest times in the 100m finals at regional, national, and international championships (where the regional and national events refer to Germany).

Comparing the coefficient of variation and using OLS and quantile regressions, Frick and Scheel find that the percentage differential between men's and women's times at a given rank rise as the rank number rises (worsens). This implies a faster drop-off in women's performance as one moves down the rankings. Frick and Scheel take this as indirect evidence that the top women avoid competing with one another. This result supports Frick's earlier work on distance runners. Contrary to the earlier studies, this chapter finds that the gender gap has risen over time. While a firm conclusion is beyond the scope of this chapter, the authors speculate that the rising gender gap might be due to improved policing of the use of performance-enhancing drugs.

Eva and Michael Leeds (Chapter 15) shed new light on gender differences in responses to tournament settings by analyzing performances in men's and women's figure skating. They choose figure skating because it provides more control over outside forces, such as weather conditions or the performance of other participants, than other sports do. They use data from the 2009–10 figure skating season to estimate how male and female skaters' performances in the Free Skate respond to the incentives they face.

The structure of figure skating competitions presents both advantages and disadvantages in modeling the incentives facing skaters. On the one hand, skaters enter the final round of a competition, the Free Skate, knowing where they stand relative to other skaters and how much their performance is likely to affect their final standing. On the other hand, many of the competitions do not have an official monetary award, though some, such as the Olympics and the World Championships, are clearly more meaningful than others.

Leeds and Leeds find that female skaters respond more strongly to incentives than male skaters. A woman skates better in the Free Skate when she is closer to the leader and when she skates in a more prestigious competition. Men show no response to either set of incentives. Their results thus contradict the findings of the experimental literature in which women respond poorly to tournament incentives relative to men. They also find, unlike Gilsdorf and Sukhatme (2008a and 2008b), that favored skaters are not more dominant in more prominent competitions. Finally, unlike the experimental work of Booth and Nolen (2012) or the non-experimental work of Frick (2011a and 2011b), they find no evidence that women avoid competition more than men do.

There is a burgeoning literature on the standing of nations in international sport competitions, such as Olympic medal counts. Because of soccer's popularity and the availability of FIFA rankings, much of this literature focuses on the World Cup and performance in international soccer. Joshua Congdon-Hohman and Victor Matheson (Chapter 16) expand upon earlier attempts to examine national standings in women's soccer. Their focus on women enables them to rethink the received wisdom and to introduce new explanations for national success.

Congdon-Hohman and Matheson start by reviewing the history of women's soccer leagues around the world. Women began to play soccer almost as early as men, especially in England, but formal international competition did not start until the 1980s, and women's soccer has remained a largely amateur sport. The lack of professionalism suggests that success in women's soccer might stem from different sources than in the men's game.

To explain the FIFA ranking of women's national teams, Congdon-Hohman and Matheson employ traditional explanatory variables, including traditional ones, such as GPD/per capita, as well as new ones, such as the female share of members of parliament and the FIFA ranking of the country's men. To put their results in context, they run analogous regressions for men. They find that female representation in parliament has a positive impact on both men's and women's regressions and suggest that this variable likely captures the level of development in the country, which is reflected in sports institutions and success of women in soccer. Ultimately, they conclude that sports are a stage on which men and women can exhibit their potential and that sport success itself is an indicator of human development.

The maturity of women's soccer is also reflected in the growing size and popularity of the Women's World Cup. Dennis Coates (Chapter 17) documents the ebb and flow of attendance at the Cup finals and then analyzes the motivations that countries have for hosting them. He tests whether expanded international trade or economic growth could be one such motivator. Using a framework adapted from Rose and Spiegel (2011) as well as from Barro and Sala-i-Martin (1999), Coates shows that the Cup affects neither trade nor the growth of GDP per capita.

While the Cup offers a temporary boost to women's soccer leagues, it has yet to produce a fully professional women's league anywhere in the world. Coates presents national leagues in the US, England, France, Germany, Sweden, and Japan, and he describes their semiprofessional status. He also finds that success in the World Cup has had a limited impact on endorsement opportunities for the players. Coates demonstrates that soccer players lag far behind tennis players in income and argues that most endorsement opportunities for World Cup stars come from the fashion industry rather than from sports.

Asian women have come to dominate the LPGA like few other sports. In 2012, all four of the major LPGA golf tournaments were either held by Asians or being defended by Asians.[1] While Asian men have steadily improved their performance on the PGA TOUR, they are far from rivaling the success of Asian women. In Chapter 18, Young Hoon Lee et al. explain how and why Asian women – particularly Korean women – now play such a leading role in the LPGA.

After documenting the dramatic rise in the number and quality of Korean women on the LPGA Tour since the mid-1990s, Lee et al. adapt the work by George Borjas on immigration (Borjas 1987, 1990, 1994) to explain why Korean women have been so successful. Borjas does not believe that migrants accurately reflect the skills and motivations of their countrymen because they are a self-selected group. In particular, they have skills or other personal traits that are more highly valued in their host countries than in their home countries. These characteristics make them better adapted to the host labor market than the typical worker in either the home or host country.

Lee et al. show that highly talented Korean golfers have been attracted to the LPGA because the average prize is higher in the US than in Korea and because the prize structure is more highly skewed to the right in the US. However, growing rewards on the Korean LPGA (KLPGA) Tour suggest that this trend will slow and may eventually reverse itself. Their model also provides two reasons why Japanese women and Korean men have been less likely to move to the US Tours. Japanese women are deterred by the lack of a large Japanese community in the US, which increases the cost of migration, and by the success of the Japanese Tour, which offers high prizes without the cost of migration. Korean men have been less likely to move to the US because far more men than women participate in professional golf, which reduces both the expected earnings and the variance of earnings on the men's Tour. This argument echoes

Stephen Gould's model of athletic performance (Gould, 1986 and 1996), as discussed by Treber et al. in their chapter on women's basketball.

Finally, Lee et al. explain why Korean women are good enough to expect such high rewards. Using data from the LPGA Tour from 2004 through 2010, they find that Korean women do not drive for distance as well as non-Koreans (a factor that could help explain Shmanske's finding that women's driving distance has failed to keep pace with men's). However, their greater drive accuracy and better approach play allow them to reach 'greens in regulation' at the same rate as other women. Once on the green, Korean women show a distinct superiority, which has led to their better overall performance.

In the final chapter of this volume, Ross Booth (Chapter 19) contrasts two sports that have grown out of the original game of women's basketball, which was conceived by Senda Berenson in 1891. One version would be familiar even to an observer who has never watched women's sports, as it is virtually indistinguishable from the men's game and shares the name 'basketball'. The other sport, netball, would look vaguely familiar but suddenly move in unexpected directions, with players restricted to specific parts of the court and having narrowly defined functions. Until the early 1970s, this unfamiliar variant was what most of the world knew as 'women's basketball'.

Booth traces the history of the two sports and explains why Australia has maintained a strong international presence in both. This contrasts sharply with most other countries, including the United States, which abandoned the older version of the game when women were allowed to adopt men's rules. The few countries that have maintained netball, mostly members of the (formerly British) Commonwealth, have generally failed to establish a presence in the newer version of the sport.

Booth also contrasts both the media coverage of the two sports and the salaries earned by the players. He places this analysis in context by contrasting coverage and pay in women's basketball and netball with other women's sports in Australia and with the coverage and compensation in the men's sports. He finds that netball has generally fared better than its younger sister, though both fall far short of men's basketball, which ironically has not enjoyed the international success of either of the women's teams.

NOTE

1. The tournaments and golfers are: the Kraft-Nabisco Championship (Sun Young Yoo – Korea), the US Women's Open (Na Yeon Choi – Korea), the RICOH Women's British Open (Yani Tseng – Taiwan), and Wegman's LPGA Championship (Shanshan Feng – China).

REFERENCES

'2012 Medal Standings' (2012), *London 2012*, online at: http://www.nbcolympics.com/medals/2012-standings/index.html (accessed August 17, 2012).

Anderson, Kelli (2012), 'The Power of Play', *Sports Illustrated*, May 7: 49.

Andreff, Wladimir and Stefan Szymanski (2007), *Handbook on the Economics of Sport*, Cheltenham, UK and Northampton, MA, USA: Edward Elgar.

Barro, Robert and Xavier Sala-i-Martin (1999), *Economic Growth*, Cambridge, MA: MIT Press.

Berri, David J. (2008), 'A Simple Measure of Worker Productivity in the National Basketball Association', in Humphreys and Howard (eds), vol. 3, pp. 1–40.

Booth, Alison and Patrick Nolen (2012), 'Choosing to Compete: How Different Are Girls and Boys?', *Journal of Economic Behavior and Organization*, **81**(2), February: 542–55.

Borjas, George J. (1987), 'Self-Selection and the Earnings of Immigrants', *American Economic Review*, **77**(4), September: 531–53.

Borjas, George J. (1990), 'Self-Selection and the Earnings of Immigrants: Reply', *American Economic Review*, **80**(1), March: 305–08.

Borjas, George J. (1994), 'The Economics of Immigration', *Journal of Economic Literature*, **32**(4), December: 1667–17.

Brown, Robert W. and R. Todd Jewell (2006), 'The Marginal Revenue Product of a Women's College Basketball Player', *Industrial Relations*, **45**(1): 96–101.

Chappell, Bill (2012), 'Year of the Woman at the Games? For Americans, it's True', *The Torch*, online at: http://www.npr.org/blogs/thetorch/2012/08/10/158570021/year-of-the-woman-at-the-london-games-for-americans-its-true (accessed August 10, 2012).

Croson, Rachel and Uri Gneezy (2009), 'Gender Differences in Preferences', *Journal of Economic Literature*, **47**(2), June: 448–74.

Ehrenberg, Ronald G. and Michael L. Bognanno (1990a), 'Do Tournaments Have Incentive Effects?', *Journal of Political Economy*, **98**(6), December: 1307–24.

Ehrenberg, Ronald G. and Michael L. Bognanno (1990b), 'The Incentive Effects of Tournaments Revisited: Evidence from the European PGA Tour', *Industrial and Labor Relations Review*, **43**(3), February: 74–88.

Fizel, John, Elizabeth Gustafson and Lawrence Hadley (1996), *Baseball Economics: Current Research*, Westport, CT: Praeger.

Frick, Bernd (2011a), 'Gender Differences in Competitiveness: Empirical Evidence from Professional Distance Running', *Labour Economics*, **18**(3), June: 389–98.

Frick, Bernd (2011b), 'Gender Differences in Competitive Orientations: Empirical Evidence from Ultramarathon Running', *Journal of Sports Economics*, **12**(3), June: 317–40.

Gilsdorf, Keith F. and Vasant A. Sukhatme (2008a), 'Tournament Incentives and Match Outcomes in Women's Professional Tennis', *Applied Economics*, **40**: 2405–12.

Gilsdorf, Keith F. and Vasant A. Sukhatme (2008b), 'Testing Rosen's Sequential Elimination Tournament Model: Incentives and Player Performance in Professional Tennis', *Journal of Sports Economics*, **9**: 287–303.

Gould, Stephen J. (1986), 'Entopic Homogeneity Isn't Why No One Hits .400 Any More', *Discover Magazine*, **7**(8), August: 60–66.

Gould, Stephen J. (1996), *Full House: The Spread of Excellence from Plato to Darwin*, New York: Three Rivers.

Humphreys, Brad and Dennis Howard, (2008), *The Business of Sport*, Westport, CT: Praeger.

Kahane, Leo and Stephen Shmanske (2011), *The Oxford Handbook of Sports Economics*, Oxford: Oxford University Press.

Kahn, Lawrence (2000), 'Sports as a Labor Market Laboratory', *Journal of Economic Perspectives*, **14**(3), July: 75–94.

Lazear, Edwin and Sherwin Rosen (1981), 'Rank-Order Tournaments as Optimum Labor Contracts', *Journal of Political Economy*, **89**(5), October: 841–64.

Leeds, Michael A. and Peter von Allmen (2010), *The Economics of Sports*, Boston, MA: Addison-Wesley.

Montgomery, Sarah S. and Michael D. Robinson (2006), 'Take Me Out to the Opera: Are Sports and Arts Complements? Evidence from the Performing Arts Research Coalition data', *International Journal of Arts Management*, **8**(2), Winter: 24–37.

Montgomery, Sarah S. and Michael D. Robinson (2010), 'Empirical Evidence on the Effects of Marriage on Male and Female Attendance at Sports and Arts', *Social Science Quarterly*, **91**(1) March: 99–116.

Rose, Andrew K. and Mark M. Spiegel (2011), 'The Olympic Effect', *Economic Journal*, **121**(553), June: 652–77.

Shapcott, Susan (2012), 'Make No Mistake, Wins for Gabby Douglas and U.S. Women's Soccer Teams Were Also Gold Medals for Title IX', *New York Daily News*, online at: http://www.nydailynews.com/sports/olympics-2012/mistake-wins-gabby-douglas-u-s-women-soccer-teams-gold-medals-title-ix-article-1.1136101 (accessed August 14, 2012).

PART I

WOMEN AND SPORT IN CONTEXT

1.   Women's attendance at sports events
Sarah S. Montgomery and Michael D. Robinson

1.1   INTRODUCTION

Attending sports events is a major leisure activity in the United States. A 2004 study by the Performing Arts Research Coalition (PARC) reports that, on average, respondents attend sporting events seven times per year, choosing roughly an equal number of amateur and professional events (PARC, 2004). This compares with four visits to the performing arts and 15 to movies, clubs, and popular concerts, combined. The study notes some stereotypical differences between men and women. Men are more likely to go to sports events and clubs, while women more often attend the performing arts and the movies.

Although economists have not devoted much attention to the determinants of individual choices to attend sports, they have studied factors that affect decisions to attend the performing arts. One of the main findings of this research is that arts socialization and education are important determinants of attendance (Seaman, 2006). To fully enjoy the arts, one must have a certain level of understanding of the art form. We adapt this methodology to explore in some depth the impact of what we call 'sports capital' on sports attendance.

Enjoying sports, like appreciating the performing arts, requires some understanding of the performance in question. We use sports participation (playing some kind of sport) as a crude measure of sports capital. Our results show that women and men who play sports are much more likely to attend sporting events. Applying these findings to the declining difference between men's and women's attendance indicates that as much as a third of this decline can be attributed to increasing sports participation on the part of women.

Finally, we examine the impact of marriage on the sports attendance of women. Again adapting research from the economics of the arts, we argue that women married to men with sports capital are more likely to attend sports events. The same is true for men married to women with sports capital. This leads to a more complex understanding of the impact of marriage on attendance than that provided by game theory's battle of the sexes. Rather than attending a sporting event only because they prefer the company of their husband, it is possible that women are more likely to attend sporting events when they acquire sports capital from their husband, which adds to their understanding and enjoyment of the event. The impact of sports capital does not, however, deny a role to the battle of the sexes, as we find that one spouse's attending more sports events leads the other spouse to attend more events as well, even when one controls for sports capital. However, the battle of the sexes occurs less frequently than might be presumed. Individuals engage in assortative mating, finding partners with similar sports interests. For those who are married to a partner with different sports capital, the attendance effects of the differences are quite large.

Our results show that women's choices are affected by the same factors that determine men's choices: age, education, and income. Specifically, younger, more-educated persons with higher incomes are more likely to attend sports. Overall, however, women are less likely to attend sporting events than are men. These demographic factors, though, explain little of the difference in men's and women's attendance.

The next section reviews the literature regarding attendance at sporting events. In Section 1.3 we construct an empirical model of attendance at sports events with particular attention to the impact of sports capital. Section 1.4 presents the dataset that we use, the Survey of Public Participation in the Arts (SPPA). It also contains an overview of men's and women's attendance at sports events, using data for 1992, 2002, and 2008 from the SPPA (National Endowment for the Arts, 1983–2008). In Section 1.5, we present our results. Not surprisingly, we find that women attend sports at lower rates than men, though the difference has declined substantially over time. We also find that both sports capital and the battle of the sexes play a role in sports attendance. Section 1.6 concludes.

1.2   PREVIOUS RESEARCH

Analyses of attendance at sports events seldom focus on gender. However, several studies employ national datasets to examine attendance and distinguish between male and female spectators. White and Wilson (1999) use Canadian data from the General Social Survey of 1992. Employing multiple classification analysis (MCA), they investigate the relationship of social class to spectatorship, holding age, language, and region constant. They find that the proportion of men in attendance at professional and amateur events was more than that for women and that income and education were significant predictors for both sexes.

Thrane (2001) uses data from three surveys conducted in 1996/97 by ACNielson – one each for Denmark, Norway, and Sweden. He employs multivariate logistic regression analysis to estimate the probability of annual sports attendance based on demographic variables, including gender and a measure of sports participation. Approximately two-thirds of the respondents in each country attend an amateur or professional sports event. Men are 18 percent more likely than women to be spectators in Sweden, 14 percent more likely in Denmark, and 11 percent more likely in Norway. The measure of sports participation is highly significant for each country.

Lera-López et al. (2011) investigate Spanish sports attendance. Fifty-five percent of their respondents were spectators at an amateur or professional event in 2006. Controlling for age, education, income and household characteristics, they find men approximately 19 percent more likely than women to attend a sporting event.

Montgomery and Robinson (2006 and 2010) use data for the United States from the Arts Participation Surveys completed in 2002 by PARC. In the first paper, we examine the relationship between attendance at arts, sports, and popular culture events and the demographic characteristics of various audiences. We find that attending amateur and professional sports are the closest substitutes for each other and that the two are both positively correlated with attending dance, theater, movies, rock concerts, live comedy, and nightclubs. Sports attendance had no relationship with attending orchestra or opera. Forty-three percent of those surveyed attended a combination of at least one sport, one performing art, and one popular cultural event in the survey year. Another 18 percent attended a sport and a popular cultural event, while 1 percent were in audiences for only sports and performing arts. In regressions that control for other demographic traits, the effect of gender on attendance varies widely among types of events. Women's attendance is larger at movies, theater, and dance, and men's is larger at rock concerts and night clubs. The biggest effects of gender are on sports attendance, with men attending 26 percent more professional contests and 17 percent more amateur contests.

In the second paper, we employ the same 2002 data to study differences in the behavior of single and married men and women. On average, women attended 2.4 professional sporting events, while men attended 4.3 events. For singles, the average was 2.3 a year for women and 4.4 for men. We estimated four separate Tobit models (for single and married women and men) that controlled for other demographic variables. Oaxaca decomposition results derived from these regressions show a positive marriage effect of between zero and 4 percent for women, and between 6 and 10 percent for men.

Sports economists tend to focus almost exclusively on total or average team attendance rather than the characteristics of individual attendees at sporting events. Villar and Guerrero (2009) review over 80 empirical papers on attendance, all focused on some measure of total team attendance with only two that deal with women's attendance. Gauthier and Hansen (1993) study female spectators at professional golf tournaments. Respondents to their questionnaire said that seeing the best players and live action were important reasons for attending. Gauthier and Hansen also find that the respondents' age and the frequency with which they played the sport affected their likelihood of attending the event. Hofacre (1994) briefly considers why the indoor soccer audience is atypically female. One of several suggested reasons is that women have been very involved in the growth of youth soccer as players, coaches, and parents.

A few articles in psychology and sociology analyze audiences at particular athletic events. James and Ridinger (2002) ask a sample of those who attended four basketball games to rate themselves as fans of the game and of the teams involved and to answer a series of questions aimed at discovering their motivations for attending. They find that, although the most important motivations (action and escape) were the same for men and women, men reported stronger fan ratings and were significantly different from women in the importance of other motives. Schurr et al. (1988) examine the characteristics of sophomores who did and did not attend two Ball State basketball games. As part of their study, they cross-tabulate personality and demographic traits with attendance. They find that women are less likely to attend than men. Men with business-oriented majors are the most likely to attend, while women from other majors are the least likely to do so.

1.3   A MODEL OF SPORTS ATTENDANCE

We begin with a standard neoclassical utility-maximization model. Consumers make sports attendance decisions based on their preferences, conditional on income and prices. Both income and time constraints are relevant for sports attendance. Because the dataset we employ has data only for whether one attended a sports event, our dependent variable is a dummy variable (ATT_i) equal to 1 if the respondent attended a sports event, at least one athletic event. On the right-hand side, we include income (Y_i) and a number of demographic variables designed to measure preferences and tastes, many of which are included in previous studies. We are particularly interested in the impact of gender (GEN_i) on attendance, so we express it separately from the other demographic variables (X_i) in equation (1.1):

Table 1.1   *Sports attendance by men and women, 1992 to 2008 (%)*

	Men	Women	Difference
	Attend	Attend	
SPPA			
1992	44.1	29.2	14.9
2002	39.7	28.7	11.0
2008	35.5	27.7	7.8
PARC			
2002	53.2	46.8	6.4

$$ATT_i = \beta_0 + \beta_1 Y_i + \beta_2 GEN_i + \gamma' X_i + \varepsilon_i. \qquad (1.1)$$

Because we expect sporting events to be normal goods, the pure income effect should be positive. However, higher incomes are frequently associated with higher hourly pay, which increases the opportunity cost of leisure. From the aggregate data and previous research, we expect to find that, all else equal, women are less likely to attend sports than men. This is consistent with data from the SPPA, as seen in Table 1.1.

The vector of demographic variables includes controls for age, education, urban residence, race, and marital status. Lera-López et al. (2011) report that age has generally been found to have a negative or insignificant impact on attendance. Also following Lera-López et al., we include education. We want to know whether college graduates have higher sports attendance given the prominence of intercollegiate sports in the United States. We include an urban/rural status dummy variable primarily as a control on the supply of sports because it is likely that there is a greater availability of events in urban areas. We also include a dummy variable equal to one if the respondent is white to see if race affects sports attendance. Finally, in our base model we control for marital status. We refine this set of controls in the next subsection.

1.3.1   'Sports Capital' and Attendance at Sports Events

In many ways, sports should mirror the arts. Seaman suggests that supply factors that have been listed for the performing arts, '(1) liveliness, (2) joint audience–performer presence, and (3) concern for the skilled presentation of created works with the labor contribution being the essential feature of the final product', could describe sports activities (Seaman, 2003, 82). The venues and experiences are quite similar in sports and the arts, so,

Table 1.2   Sports attendance by sports participation (total, male and female)

	Total		Male		Female	
	Participate	Don't participate	Participate	Don't participate	Participate	Don't participate
1992	59.8	21.3	64.5	24.2	53.6	19.6
2002	64.1	20.9	66.6	23.2	60.8	19.5
2008	59.7	21.4	62.6	22.1	55.5	20.8

Table 1.3   Men and women participating in sports, 1982 to 2008 (%)

	Men	Women	Difference
1982	48.9	31.3	17.6
1985	50.3	31.1	19.1
1992	49.2	28.3	20.8
2002	38.1	22.4	15.7
2008	33.3	20.1	13.1

analogous to the arts, the pleasure received from watching a sporting event may depend on one's knowledge of the sport. Being able to identify a strikeout, home run, base hit, or an error and knowing its significance are instrumental to the enjoyment of baseball. Upright (2004) calls knowledge of the arts 'cultural capital'. We adapt his language and study the impact of a person's sports capital. Sports capital is the acquired knowledge that allows one to fully enjoy attendance at sporting events. We expect sports capital to be an important determinant of sports attendance.

In the arts literature, childhood or adolescent training in the arts is typically used as a proxy for cultural capital. While we do not have similar data on the sports activities of one's youth, we believe that current, active participation in sports is a good proxy. Fortunately, the SPPA includes a question about such activity: 'During the last 12 months, did you participate in any sports activity, such as softball, basketball, golf, bowling, skiing, or tennis?'. Table 1.2 shows the relationship between sports participation and sports attendance. In 2008, 60 percent of those who participated in sports also attended sports events. In contrast, only 21 percent of those who did not engage in sports attended a sports event. Similar results are found for other years for both men and women. However, Table 1.3 shows that men have much more sports capital than women. Individuals' sports participation can be viewed as their investment in sports. Playing, even at an amateur level, can increase appreciation and understanding for spectators. In order to explore the impact of sports capital on sports attendance more fully we expand our base model by adding a dummy variable for sports capital ($SCAP_i$) to equation (1.1):

$$ATT_i = \beta_0 + \beta_1 Y_i + \beta_2 GEN_i + \beta_3 SCAP_i + \gamma' X_i + \varepsilon_i. \qquad (1.1a)$$

1.3.2   Marriage and Attendance at Sports Events by Women

In previous research using the PARC data, we document that married women attend more sporting events than single women (Montgomery and Robinson, 2010). We posit two reasons why marriage affects the attendance of women. The 'Battle of the Sexes' is a standard game-theoretic approach to a situation in which each player would like to coordinate his or her behavior, but the payoffs to each player differ across choices. In a common, eponymous version of this game, the players are a married couple who would like to attend either a sporting or an arts event together. However, the husband's payoff is higher from sports and the wife's is higher from the arts. Since we have seen that men attend more sports events than women, this situation is likely to be relevant. One possible solution to this type of game is a variant of the tit-for-tat strategy, in which the agents take turns attending sports and art events. (This solution is not without its flaws, as Woody Allen makes clear in *Manhattan Murder Mystery* when he leaves the opera early after making Diane Keaton sit through a hockey game.) If this is the solution adopted by many or all of the married couples, we might observe that marriage has a positive impact on the sports attendance of women while lowering that of men.

The second way in which marriage affects sports attendance is through the sports capital of one's spouse. This approach was adopted by Upright (2004) in analyzing the effect of one spouse's art knowledge on the art attendance of the other. We expect spouses who have no playing experience to learn and gain sports capital from those who are active players and therefore attend more sporting events. Because we have seen that men have more sports capital than women, this might be more important for married women than for married men. Attendance patterns, however, may result from household maximizing decisions that combine the now-enhanced combined sports capital of the couple with the battle of the sexes. In this case, the attendance of the partners with more sports capital may decrease at the same time that the attendance of their spouses increases. This implies that our model must control for whether both, one, or none of the marriage partners has sports capital. In this specification, the sports capital variable, $SCAP_i$, now indicates the presence of sports capital for an unmarried individual. Married couples have a series of dummy variables that show whether the husband ($SCAP_i^H$), wife ($SCAP_i^W$), or both ($SCAP_i^B$) have sports capital. This transforms equation (1.1a) into:

$$ATT_i = \beta_0 + \beta_1 Y_i + \beta_2 GEN_i + \beta_3 SCAP_i + \beta_4 SCAP_i^H + \beta_5 SCAP_i^W$$
$$+ \beta_6 SCAP_i^B + \gamma' X_i + \varepsilon_i. \tag{1.2}$$

In regressions that use data for only men or women, we delete the gender variable (GEN_i).

1.4   DATA

We use the SPPA (National Endowment for the Arts, 1983–2008), which is conducted periodically as an add-on to other US government surveys. In addition to providing standard demographic data, the survey asks respondents whether, with the exception of youth sports, they attended professional or amateur sports events during the previous 12 months. Unfortunately, prior to 1992, the sports attendance question did not exclude youth sports, so we focus on the surveys from 1992, 2002 and 2008. The survey conducted in 1997 had very few questions on demographic characteristics so we cannot use its data to estimate our models.

1.4.1   Women's Attendance at Sporting Events

As noted earlier, Table 1.1 shows SPPA data on the proportion of men and women attending sports events from 1992 to 2008 and PARC data on attendance at professional sports events from the 2002 survey. Not surprisingly, women attend sports events at lower rates than men. In the 2008 SPPA, 36 percent of men report attending sports events, compared to only 28 percent of women. It is likely that the difference in average number of events attended is greater than the difference in the percent of individuals attending at least one event. (In the PARC data, men attend four professional sporting events a year, while women attend only two.) Throughout this period, the percentage of both men and women attending sports events declines. However, the decline for women is substantially smaller. As a result, the gap in the percentage of male and female attendance declines by nearly 50 percent between 1992 and 2008.

While we do not have data to determine the cause of this convergence, we can speculate about two possibilities. Title IX, passed in 1972, has increased women's sports opportunities at the high-school and collegiate levels. This greater access to sports may have increased relative female

Table 1.4   Sports attendance by sex and marital status (%)

	Men		Women		Difference	
	Single	Married	Single	Married	Single	Married
1992	49.3	41.3	26.0	31.7	23.3	9.6
2002	40.6	39.2	26.5	30.6	14.1	8.6
2008	35.1	35.8	24.8	30.1	10.3	5.7

interest in attending other sports events. Second, the large rise in popularity of women's professional and collegiate sports over this time period may have increased the relative attendance of women. Examination of overall attendance, however, tells us little about why men and women attend sports at different rates and whether this difference can be explained by other demographic characteristics.

1.4.2   Marriage and Attendance at Sporting Events

Table 1.4 reports sports attendance of men and women by marital status. Consistent with our previous research, the data show that married women attend more sports events than single women, while married men attend fewer events in two of the three years for which we have data. Table 1.4 also shows that there is considerable convergence in men's and women's sports attendance for married men and women. In 2008, the single male/female difference in attendance is 10.3 percentage points, while the married male/female difference is a little more than half as large, at 5.7 percentage points. We have reported similar results using PARC data (Montgomery and Robinson, 2006). Aggregate data, however, fail to account for the sports capital in marriage.

In order to study the role of sports capital more closely, we use couples in the SPPA data to determine the sports attendance and sports activity of each person's spouse for the 2002 SPPA. To construct this dataset for married couples, we identify the reference person for each household and then match that person with his/her spouse. In order to facilitate comparisons with single individuals, our dataset contains all the respondents who were reference persons, whether single or married. It is less nationally representative than the full SPPA dataset used to construct our earlier tables because that includes all individuals.

Using these data, we identify six different types of family structures, four for married partners and two for single individuals. Couples can be in marriages in which one, both, or neither of the partners has sports

Table 1.5   Sports attendance for men and women, by marital status and own and spouse's sports capital* (%)

Marital status/sports capital	Men attending	Women attending
Single/none	19.6	20.3
Single/yes	71.4	67.5
Married/both	67.5	62.8
Married/male only	63.4	42.0
Married/female only	40.8	52.0
Married/neither	22.5	15.4

Note: * Sports capital defined as playing a sport.

capital. We distinguish between couples in which only the man and only the woman has sports capital. Single individuals make up the final two household types based on whether they have or do not have sports capital. Table 1.5 compares couples and singles with and without sports capital. Only 20 percent of both single women and single men without sports capital attend sports, while 68 percent of single women and 71 percent of single men with sports capital attend. Men and women who engage in sports when married to a spouse who also participates have almost as high rates of attendance as singles who participate in sports. The attendance patterns of individuals whose spouse differs in sports capital are less extreme than those of single persons. The spouse without sports capital is more likely to attend than a single person without sports capital and the spouse with sports capital is less likely to attend than a single person with sports capital. Only 20 percent of single women without sports capital go to sporting events (as noted above), but 42 percent of those married to a man with it do. In contrast, 68 percent of single women with sports capital attend sporting events, but only 52 percent of those whose partner lacks it do. In the final version of the model we include a series of dummy variables for the type of family in terms of sports capital.

1.5   ECONOMETRIC RESULTS

Table 1.6 reports the marginal effects for probit estimation of equation (1.1a) using data from the SPPA for 1992, 2002, and 2008. We find that age lowers the probability of attendance for both men and women but that the probability increases with income and education. The probability increases for men and women for each income class beyond $24,000 a year.

Table 1.6 SPPA regressions controlling for sports capital (marginal effects)

Variables	1992			2002			2008		
	Both	Female	Male	Both	Female	Male	Both	Female	Male
Age 18 to 24	0.272***	0.309***	0.204***	0.182***	0.236***	0.115***	0.158***	0.160***	0.158***
	(0.032)	(0.043)	(0.048)	(0.020)	(0.027)	(0.030)	(0.025)	(0.033)	(0.039)
Age 24 to 34	0.241***	0.244***	0.220***	0.153***	0.197***	0.102***	0.122***	0.127***	0.122***
	(0.026)	(0.036)	(0.039)	(0.016)	(0.022)	(0.024)	(0.020)	(0.027)	(0.031)
Age 35 to 44	0.191***	0.232***	0.126***	0.138***	0.176***	0.0963***	0.114***	0.114***	0.115***
	(0.027)	(0.036)	(0.039)	(0.016)	(0.022)	(0.023)	(0.020)	(0.027)	(0.029)
Age 45 to 54	0.127***	0.146***	0.0939**	0.0868***	0.117***	0.0544**	0.0869***	0.105***	0.0678**
	(0.029)	(0.039)	(0.043)	(0.016)	(0.022)	(0.023)	(0.019)	(0.026)	(0.029)
Age 55 to 64	0.0647**	0.116***	-0.00459	0.0477***	0.109***	-0.0195	0.0449**	0.0559**	0.0332
	(0.030)	(0.040)	(0.046)	(0.017)	(0.024)	(0.025)	(0.020)	(0.026)	(0.030)
Income 25 to 49	0.0920***	0.0694***	0.112***	0.0713***	0.0741***	0.0647***	0.101***	0.0978***	0.104***
	(0.017)	(0.022)	(0.027)	(0.013)	(0.016)	(0.020)	(0.017)	(0.022)	(0.027)
Income 50 to 74	0.135***	0.124***	0.139***	0.174***	0.164***	0.180***	0.177***	0.150***	0.208***
	(0.026)	(0.034)	(0.039)	(0.015)	(0.020)	(0.022)	(0.019)	(0.026)	(0.029)
Income 75 up	0.196***	0.172***	0.207***	0.213***	0.220***	0.201***	0.228***	0.211***	0.248***
	(0.032)	(0.043)	(0.045)	(0.015)	(0.020)	(0.022)	(0.019)	(0.025)	(0.028)
White	0.0624***	0.0741***	0.0354	0.111***	0.120***	0.0918***	0.0488***	0.0711***	0.0187
	(0.021)	(0.023)	(0.036)	(0.012)	(0.014)	(0.019)	(0.014)	(0.018)	(0.023)
Married	-0.00968	0.0121	-0.0463*	-0.0291***	-0.0361***	-0.0311**	-0.0285**	-0.0284*	-0.0277
	(0.016)	(0.020)	(0.026)	(0.010)	(0.012)	(0.015)	(0.012)	(0.015)	(0.018)
Urban	0.0426***	0.0178	0.0705***	0.0630***	0.0386***	0.0903***	0.0362***	0.0316**	0.0408**
	(0.016)	(0.019)	(0.025)	(0.010)	(0.013)	(0.015)	(0.012)	(0.016)	(0.019)

31

Table 1.6 (continued)

Variables	1992			2002			2008		
	Both	Female	Male	Both	Female	Male	Both	Female	Male
Some College	0.0886***	0.104***	0.0594**	0.0528***	0.0514***	0.0475*	0.0614***	0.0627***	0.0566*
	(0.019)	(0.023)	(0.030)	(0.016)	(0.019)	(0.025)	(0.019)	(0.024)	(0.030)
College	0.107***	0.0969***	0.110***	0.0962***	0.0816***	0.107***	0.118***	0.0920***	0.149***
	(0.023)	(0.030)	(0.035)	(0.012)	(0.016)	(0.018)	(0.015)	(0.019)	(0.022)
Graduate	0.0857***	0.102***	0.0690*	0.0689***	0.0536**	0.0797***	0.0987***	0.103***	0.0928***
	−(0.0268)	−(0.0366)	−(0.0393)	−(0.0158)	−(0.0209)	−(0.0232)	−(0.0193)	−(0.0266)	−(0.0281)
Sports Participant	0.282***	0.249***	0.317***	0.337***	0.318***	0.356***	0.296***	0.261***	0.326***
	(0.015)	(0.021)	(0.022)	(0.009)	(0.014)	(0.013)	(0.012)	(0.018)	(0.017)
Female	−0.0855***			−0.0558***			−0.0299***		
	(0.014)			(0.009)			(0.010)		
Observations	5,223	2,948	2,275	14,508	7,908	6,600	9,026	4,795	4,231

Note: Standard errors in parentheses. *** $p < 0.01$, ** $p < 0.05$, * $p < 0.1$.

Some college, a college degree, and graduate study all increase the likelihood of attendance. For men, a college education has the largest effect of the educational variables. Because we control for income, we suspect that the impact of college attendance reflects the high value placed on athletics in the collegiate setting. Marriage generally has a negative effect on the attendance of both men and women.

The estimated marginal effects of sports capital are very large. Overall, sports participation increases attendance by about 30 percent, even after controlling for age, education, income and the other demographic variables. Table 1.6 also shows the marginal effects of being female, which decreases from 9 percent in 1992 to 3 percent in 2008. In models that do not control for sports participation (not shown here but available from the authors), the gender difference in attendance is about twice as large as in these results. This indicates that lower levels of sports capital account for around half of the gender difference in attendance. An interesting manifestation of this is found in Hofacre (1994), who attributes women's relatively high percentage attendance in the early years of indoor soccer to the fact that neither men nor women were familiar with this sport.

We now use these estimates to calculate to what extent sports participation has contributed to the overall decline in the gap in sports attendance between men and women. We saw in Table 1.3 that between 1992 and 2008 the gender gap in sports participation fell from 21 to 13 percent. A marginal effect of sports participation on attendance of 30 percent implies that 2.4 percent of the decline in the gender difference in attendance stems from the decline in the gender difference in sports participation. This accounts for over a third of the 7.1 percent decline in the difference between men's and women's attendance at sporting events. Further analysis of either the overall decline in sports participation or the convergence in men's and women's sports participation is beyond the scope of this chapter. However, one must at least acknowledge the potential role of Title IX. By providing young women with more opportunities to play sports at a young age, Title IX probably has contributed to the convergence in sports attendance.

Tables 1.7 and 1.8 give the marginal effects for probit estimates of equations (1.1a) and (1.2) using the SPPA matched samples. We estimate four models. Each model contains standard demographic measures as independent variables along with a measure of sports capital. This measure takes two forms. In columns 1 and 4, we use a general indicator of whether the individual participated in sports, as appears in equation (1.1a). In columns 2 and 3, we use the vector of dummy variables that appears in equation (1.2) and captures each of the household types of sports capital. The set of dummy variables includes indicators for single persons who participate in sports, couples in which both spouses participate, and couples

Table 1.7   Women 2002 matched sample (marginal effects from Probit model on attendance)

Variables	1	2	3	4
Age 18 to 24	0.189***	0.143***	0.120***	0.133***
	(0.04)	(0.04)	(0.041)	(0.041)
Age 24 to 34	0.115***	0.0767***	0.0587**	0.0680**
	(0.026)	(0.026)	(0.027)	(0.027)
Age 35 to 44	0.0887***	0.0607**	0.029	0.0351
	(0.025)	(0.025)	(0.025)	(0.025)
Age 45 to 54	0.0296	0.0156	0.013	0.0173
	(0.025)	(0.025)	(0.025)	(0.026)
Age 55 to 64	−0.0213	−0.0255	−0.0219	−0.02
	(0.032)	(0.032)	(0.034)	(0.034)
Urban	0.0387**	0.0311*	−0.00053	0.00316
	(0.017)	(0.017)	(0.018)	(0.018)
Some College	0.107***	0.0952***	0.0837***	0.0853***
	(0.019)	(0.019)	(0.02)	(0.02)
College	0.131***	0.113***	0.105***	0.110***
	(0.023)	(0.023)	(0.024)	(0.024)
Graduate	0.0963***	0.0768***	0.0537*	0.0591**
	(0.03)	(0.029)	(0.03)	(0.03)
Income 25 to 49	0.0986***	0.0902***	0.0695***	0.0754***
	(0.024)	(0.024)	(0.024)	(0.024)
Income 50 to 74	0.199***	0.181***	0.122***	0.129***
	(0.028)	(0.029)	(0.029)	(0.029)
Income 75 up	0.264***	0.233***	0.159***	0.165***
	(0.029)	(0.03)	(0.031)	(0.031)
White	0.113***	0.109***	0.0841***	0.0875***
	(0.019)	(0.019)	(0.02)	(0.019)
Married	−0.0631***	−0.108***	−0.290***	−0.312***
	(0.023)	(0.028)	(0.031)	(0.027)
Both participate		0.406***	0.272***	
		(0.024)	(0.028)	
Male only		0.227***	0.0706***	
		(0.024)	(0.024)	
Female only		0.359***	0.369***	
		(0.038)	(0.041)	
Single participant		0.403***	0.412***	
		(0.037)	(0.038)	
Participate	0.320***			0.292***
	(0.018)			(0.02)
Spouse attends			0.492***	0.501***
			(0.018)	(0.017)
Observations	4,422	4,425	4,425	4,422

Note: Standard errors in parentheses. *** $p < 0.01$, ** $p < 0.05$, * $p < 0.1$.

Table 1.8   Men 2002 matched sample (marginal effects from Probit model on attendance)

Variables	1	2	3	4
Age 18 to 24	0.146***	0.227***	0.180***	0.117**
	(0.05)	(0.048)	(0.051)	(0.051)
Age 24 to 34	0.157***	0.211***	0.159***	0.116***
	(0.028)	(0.027)	(0.029)	(0.03)
Age 35 to 44	0.139***	0.176***	0.137***	0.108***
	(0.026)	(0.025)	(0.027)	(0.027)
Age 45 to 54	0.0781***	0.0964***	0.0641**	0.0499*
	(0.026)	(0.026)	(0.028)	(0.028)
Age 55 to 64	0.0498	0.0364	0.0428	0.0526
	(0.032)	(0.032)	(0.035)	(0.035)
Urban	0.0866***	0.0750***	0.0790***	0.0901***
	(0.018)	(0.018)	(0.019)	(0.019)
Some College	0.0595***	0.0372*	0.0341	0.0539**
	(0.021)	(0.021)	(0.022)	(0.022)
College	0.123***	0.105***	0.0748***	0.0952***
	(0.024)	(0.024)	(0.025)	(0.026)
Graduate	0.0952***	0.0686**	0.0693**	0.0930***
	(0.029)	(0.029)	(0.031)	(0.031)
Income 25 to 49	0.110***	0.0892***	0.0715***	0.0868***
	(0.025)	(0.025)	(0.026)	(0.026)
Income 50 to 74	0.202***	0.186***	0.143***	0.155***
	(0.028)	(0.028)	(0.03)	(0.03)
Income 75 up	0.233***	0.226***	0.146***	0.147***
	(0.029)	(0.029)	(0.031)	(0.031)
White	0.120***	0.118***	0.0790***	0.0800***
	(0.024)	(0.024)	(0.026)	(0.026)
Married	−0.0279	0.0524	−0.02	−0.197***
	(0.024)	(0.045)	(0.047)	(0.025)
Both participate		0.363***	0.246***	
		(0.022)	(0.025)	
Male only		0.304***	0.260***	
		(0.03)	(0.033)	
Female only		0.110***	−0.0034	
		(0.0343)	(0.0358)	
Single participant		0.449***	0.463***	
		(0.039)	(0.037)	
Participate	0.350***			0.295***
	(0.016)			(0.018)
Spouse attends			0.534***	0.518***
			(0.017)	(0.017)
Observations	4,314	4,344	4,344	4,314

Note: Standard errors in parentheses. *** $p < 0.01$, ** $p < 0.05$, * $p < 0.1$.

in which only the man or only the woman participate. Couples in which no one participates is the default for married couples, and single persons who do not participate is the default for singles.

Finally, we append to equation (1.2) a dummy variable that controls for whether one's spouse has attended one or more sporting events. The coefficient estimates provide a direct test of the battle of the sexes, as it shows whether one's spouse's behavior affects one's own behavior independent of sports capital. The results appear in columns 3 and 4.

In almost every case, either one's own participation or the participation of one's spouse increases sports attendance. The one exception is men without sports capital who are married to a woman with sports capital in the model that controls for spouse's attendance. Both one's own and one's spouse's sports capital are positively related to attendance. When both partners have sports capital, women are 40 percent more likely to attend than singles without sports capital, and men are 36 percent more likely to attend. When only one partner has sports capital, the effect is much smaller and depends on which partner has the capital. A woman (man) with sports capital who is married to a man (woman) without capital is more likely to attend than a woman (man) without sports capital married to a man (woman) with sports capital. The probability of attendance for couples with differing amounts of sports capital is lower than for singles with capital and higher than for single persons without capital. This suggests that some bargaining occurs over attendance choices for these couples that resembles what is predicted by the battle of the sexes. Unlike the traditional battle of the sexes story in which only men are interested in sports, this is true for both men and women with sports capital married to a partner without it.

The spousal attendance variable, which appears in columns 3 and 4 of Tables 1.7 and 1.8, has a large effect, increasing the probability of attending a sports event by about 50 percent. When this variable is included, the effects of sports capital remain large and significant except for the attendance of men when only their wife has sports capital. This suggests that the results for the battle of the sexes still hold when one accounts for the presence of sports capital.

Given the impact of one's spouse's capital on sports attendance, we wondered if assortative mating might be taking place. Individuals with sports capital might be inclined to marry other individuals with sports capital and likewise for those without it. The data suggest that a substantial amount of assortative mating occurs. Table 1.9 reports the distribution of couples by sports capital. In the 2002 SPPA, 76 percent of all couples were matched on sports capital. Neither spouse had sports capital in 60 percent of marriages, while both had it in 16 percent of marriages. Only 23 percent of the couples were mismatched. In 18 percent of marriages,

Table 1.9   Participation patterns of married couples (%)

Neither participates	60.2
Only male participates	18.4
Only female participates	5.0
Both participate	16.4

Participation rates for partners (%)	
	Participation rate of wife
Male participant	47.2
Male non-participant	7.7
	Participation rate of husband
Female participant	76.6
Female non-participant	23.4

only the husband had it, and in 5 percent of marriages only the wife had it. Thus, while the stereotypical battle of the sexes scenario, in which the husband has sports capital but the wife does not, is by no means common, it is about three times as likely to occur as the case in which the woman is the more active sports participant. Cutting the data another way, we see that 77 percent of the women who participated in sports were married to a man who also participated in sports, and 47 percent of the men who played sports had a wife who played sports. As Table 1.5 has shown, attendance mirrors these choices. When both partners have sports capital, 68 percent of husbands and 63 percent of wives attend sporting events. If neither spouse has sports capital, only 23 percent of men and 15 percent of women go to sports events.

The data reported here are consistent with the predictions of the battle of the sexes model and with the model of the transfer of sports capital combined with household maximizing decisions. Particularly striking is the convergence found in Table 1.5 when we compare singles with and without sports capital to those in a marriage to a partner with a different amount. We offer strong evidence for the general result of the battle of the sexes that couples attend events together. Our data also support the view that sports capital acquired from a spouse helps to determine an individual's attendance decisions.

1.6   CONCLUSIONS

We find that the stereotypical view of married couples – that women are art patrons while men watch sports – is inaccurate. When we look closely at women's behavior, we see that they attend sporting events in great numbers and that the factors affecting their attendance are very similar to those influencing men. We find that younger individuals attend more sports events than older ones. Income and education both positively impact sports attendance for men and women. Active participation in sports has a large effect on the attendance of both women and men and on that of their spouse. The majority of women who play sports are married to men who also participate: these couples have higher rates of attendance than other married couples. The attendance patterns of married individuals who differ widely in sports capital are more alike than those of single individuals with different levels of sports capital. A spouse with sports capital is less likely to go, while his/her partner's probability of attending increases. Thus, marrying someone with a different level of sports capital moderates one's behavior.

Whether or not either spouse plays sports, individuals are much more likely to go to sports if married to someone who attends. This result is consistent with the standard result of the game-theoretic battle of the sexes. While married individuals' attendance at sporting events draws closer to that of their spouse, women still attend fewer sporting events than men. Moreover, this gap cannot be explained by differences in the demographic variables we include in this model. We find that the male–female differences are related to the lower levels of women's active participation in sports and that that these differences have diminished over time.

REFERENCES

Gauthier, Roger and Hal Hansen (1993), 'Female Spectators: Marketing Implications for Professional Golf Events', *Sports Marketing Quarterly*, **2**(4), December: 21–8.
Hofacre, Susan (1994), 'The Women's Audience in Professional Indoor Soccer', *Sports Marketing Quarterly*, **3**(2), June: 24–7.
James, Jeffrey D. and Lynn L. Ridinger (2002), 'Female and Male Sport Fans: A Comparison of Sport Consumption Motives', *Journal of Sport Behavior*, **25**(3), September: 260–78.
Lera-López, Fernando, Manuel Rapún-Gárate1 and María José Suárez (2011), 'Determinants of Individual Sports Consumption in Spain', *International Journal of Sport Finance*, **6**(3), August: 204–21.
Montgomery, Sarah S. and Michael D. Robinson (2006), 'Take Me Out to the Opera: Are Sports and Arts Complements? Evidence from the Performing Arts Research Coalition Data', *International Journal of Arts Management*, **8**(2), Winter: 24–37.
Montgomery, Sarah S. and Michael D. Robinson (2010), 'Empirical Evidence on the Effects of Marriage on Male and Female Attendance at Sports and Arts', *Social Science Quarterly*, **91**(1), January: 99–116.
National Endowment for the Arts (1983–2008), 'Survey of Public Participation in the Arts. 1983–2008' [MRDF], Washington, DC: National Endowment for the Arts (producer), Princeton, NJ: Cultural Policy and the Arts National Data Archive.
Performing Arts Research Coalition (PARC) (2004), 'The Value of the Performing Arts in

Ten Communities: A Summary Report', Washington, DC: Performing Arts Research Coalition.

Schurr, K. Terry, Arno F. Wittig, Virgil E. Ruble and Arthur S. Ellen (1988), 'Demographic and Personality Characteristics Associated with Persistent, Occasional, and Non-attendance of University Male Basketball Games by College Students', *Journal of Sport Behavior*, **11**(1), March: 3–17.

Seaman, Bruce A. (2003), 'Cultural and Sport Economics: Conceptual Twins?', *Journal of Cultural Economics*, **27**(2), May: 81–126.

Seaman, Bruce A. (2006), 'Empirical Studies of Demand for the Performing Arts', in *Handbook of the Economics of Art and Culture*, edited by Victor A. Ginsburgh and David Throsby, Amsterdam: North-Holland, pp. 415–72.

Thrane, Christer (2001), 'Sport Spectatorship in Scandinavia: A Class Phenomenon?', *International Review for the Sociology of Sport*, **36**(2), June: 149–63.

Upright, Craig Barton (2004), 'Social Capital and Cultural Participation: Spousal Influences at Arts Events', *Poetics*, **32**(2), April: 129–43.

Villar, Jaume Garcia and Placido Rodriquez Guerrero (2009), 'Sports Attendance: A Survey of the Literature 1973–2007', *Rivista di Diritto ed Economia Dello Sport*, **5**(2), September: 111–51.

White, Phillip and Brian Wilson (1999), 'Distinctions in the Stands', *International Review for the Sociology of Sport*, **34**(3), September: 245–64.

2. Participation in women's sport in Australia

Ross Booth and Michael A. Leeds

2.1 INTRODUCTION

The health and social benefits from regular participation in sport and physical recreation activity are well known. Only recently, however, have economists begun to analyze the motivations and constraints that determine an individual's allocation of time to sport and exercise. For example, Humphreys and Ruseski (2009 and 2010) analyze the economics of physical activity in the United States and Canada, respectively, while Farrell and Shields (2002) do the same for England.

Governments at all levels in Australia have become increasingly active in encouraging people to adopt physical activities as a regular part of their lifestyle. However, there has been little formal study of what factors govern individual choices involving physical activity. This chapter uses data compiled by the Australian Bureau of Statistics (ABS) to motivate a simple model of how Australian men and women decide whether to undertake physical activity, and, if they do, how they choose which activity to pursue.

The data, contained in the report 'Women in Sport' (ABS, 2009), detail the differences in how men and women allocate their time across a variety of physical activities and how these choices change over the life cycle.[1] The survey population starts at age 15, and the survey defines a 'sport participant' as a person who physically undertakes the activity. Hence, individuals in non-playing roles, such as coaches or referees, are not regarded as participants. The survey also documents both why people choose to exercise or not to exercise. We use these reports of individual choices and motivations as a jumping-off point for creating a model of how a typical individual allocates his or her time. The model provides insights into individual behavior and can serve as the basis for future empirical studies based on micro-level data.

In Section 2.2, we present some key findings of the 2009 study. In Section 2.3, we construct a model of time allocation based on these findings and show how the data allow us to reach some basic conclusions regarding men's and women's behavior. We also briefly discuss the role of women as spectators of sports in Australia. Section 2.4 describes some institutional barriers to growing participation by women in Australian sport. Section 2.5 concludes.

2.2   PATTERNS OF SPORTS AND PHYSICAL RECREATION ACTIVITIES IN AUSTRALIA

Australian women differ significantly from men in their choice of recreational activities. One of the most notable differences is that women participate in a few highly popular activities, while men participate in a wider array of options. According to figures compiled by the ABS for 2005–06, the majority of female participants who were at least 15 years old (58 percent or 3.1 million women) undertook just one sport or physical recreation activity, with 25 percent participating in two activities and 17 percent participating in three or more. The most popular physical activity for women in 2005–06 was walking for exercise, with 2.7 million women (33 percent) participating. This accounted for almost half of all women who undertook any activity. Walking was also the most popular activity for men, with a participation rate of 17 percent (1.3 million men). However, men's activities were more widespread, so walking accounted for only a quarter of all men who exercised at all. This finding conforms to results of Humphreys and Ruseski (2009), who found that walking was by far the most popular sport in the US in terms of total participation.

Aerobics/fitness was the second most popular activity for both men and women. Aerobics was also dominated by women, with 16 percent (1.3 million women) participating, while only 9.4 percent of men (or 744,500) participated. This pattern continues, as eight of the 10 most popular activities for women also appear among the 10 most popular activities for men. The two activities that are not in the top 10 for men are yoga and netball.[2] The latter result is hardly surprising, as netball is generally regarded as a 'women's sport' in Australia.

Figure 2.1 illustrates the different patterns in sporting activities in which Australian men and women participate. Women are far more likely to engage in walking and aerobics than are men. Men are much more likely to be involved in cycling and golf than women.

Women are more likely than men to participate regularly in physical activity, where we define 'regular participation' as engaging in an activity more than twice a week. About 32 percent of all Australian women participate in a physical activity, while only about 27 percent of men do.[3] These figures are far lower than Humphreys and Ruseski report for the US. They

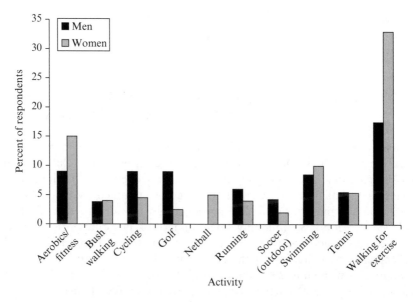

Source: *Participation in Sports and Physical Recreation, Australia, 2005–2006.*

Figure 2.1   *The 10 most popular sports and physical recreation activities by gender*

claim that over 50 percent of the US population participate regularly in some sport.

Figure 2.2 shows that men's and women's participation in physical activity changes over the life cycle. Women participate more in sport and physical recreation as they get older. Their participation rate peaks at 74 percent for the 25–34-year-old age group and then slowly declines until age 64. There is a discrete drop in the last category, but even then almost half the women aged 65 and over report participating in physical activity (48 percent or 652,900 women). The figure also shows that the changes in men's participation rates over the life cycle are highly correlated with women's rates, as they differ only slightly by gender.

The survey also provides insights into the motivation for physical activity, as women and men who participated in sports and physical recreation activities 13 times or more in the 12-month period prior to being interviewed also reported their reasons for participating. The vast majority of participants claimed that they participated for health/fitness reasons. About half did so for enjoyment and slightly under half did so for a sense of well-being. Other major reasons included social or family reasons and weight loss. Less than 10 percent of the women surveyed reported that

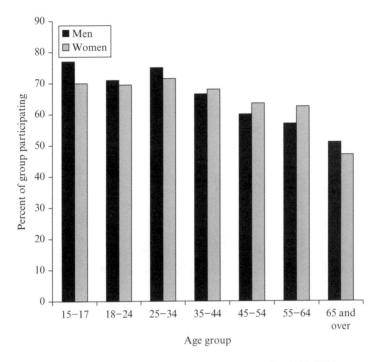

Source: *Participation in Sports and Physical Recreation, Australia, 2005–2006.*

Figure 2.2 *Participation in sports and physical recreation by age and gender*

they exercised for the competition or challenge involved. To put that figure in perspective, more women reported exercising in order to walk the dog than for the competition or challenge. Figure 2.3 shows the reasons given for each physical activity by men and women.

Early studies of reasons for athletic participation, such as McDonald and Thompson (1992), found clear differences between men and women, as women were much more likely to exercise to control their weight than men were. More recent studies – such as Strelan and Hargreaves' survey of Australian men and women (Strelan and Hargreaves, 2005) – found that men and women were equally likely to cite weight loss as a reason to exercise.

The ABS survey finds that the pattern of responses men gave for why they exercised closely resembles the pattern for women, though there are some differences. Women were more likely to cite health and well-being than were men, while men were more likely to cite enjoyment and social

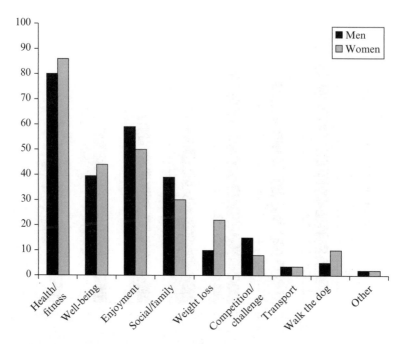

Source: Participation in Sports and Physical Recreation, Australia, 2005–2006.

Figure 2.3   Reasons for participating in sports and physical recreation

or family reasons. However, the percentages of men and women report-ing these reasons differed only slightly. Only two reasons for exercise differed significantly. Contrary to Strelan and Hargreaves, women were about twice as likely as men to report weight loss as a reason for exercise. Men were about twice as likely as women to cite competition or challenge as a reason for exercise or sport. The pattern of responses was generally consistent with the stereotypical image of male behavior. Only the greater tendency of men to cite the social aspect of physical activity surprised us.

The people who either did not participate at all in sports and physical recreation or who had participated only 1–12 times in the previous 12 months gave a variety of reasons for their lack of participation. The most common reasons they cited related both preferences – a lack of interest in exercise or sport – and constraints – a lack of time to participate because of their need to work or study or because of family obligations and the physical constraint of old age. Figure 2.4 illustrates the reasons men and women gave for not engaging in physical activity.

With two major exceptions, men and women hardly differed at all in

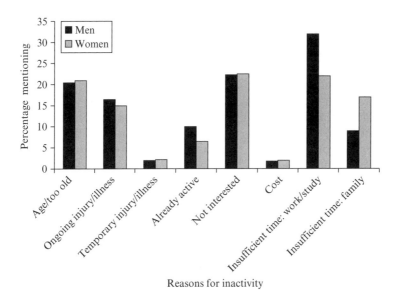

Source: *Participation in Sports and Physical Recreation, Australia, 2005–2006.*

Figure 2.4 *Reasons for not participating in physical activity*

the constraints they cited as preventing them from engaging in physical activity. The first exception was that men were over one-third more likely than women to cite work and study as reasons for not participating. The second exception was that women were almost twice as likely as men to cite family duties.

2.3   A SIMPLE MODEL OF PARTICIPATION IN PHYSICAL ACTIVITY

In this section, we gain deeper insight into the reasons for differences in the behavior of Australian men and women by extending the model presented by Downward and Riordan (2007). Downward and Riordan, in turn, extend Becker's (1965) model of the allocation of time by hypothesizing that different leisure activities bring unique rewards. Distinguishing between the value of different leisure activities allows us to analyze people's participation in sports because engaging in sports is part of their broader labor–leisure trade-off. For example, people might enjoy greater utility from participating in a sport because it improves their health (see, for example, Humphreys et al., 2011). Other possible sources of utility are success in the activity and the social interaction associated with the activity. Social interaction could overlap with labor supply in cases where engaging in a sport allows one to engage customers, suppliers, or coworkers.

To construct a simple model of engaging in sports activity, we assume that a person maximizes a utility function that is defined over consumption of a composite commodity (C), health (H), competition (Z) and social interaction (S). We define 'competition' as the enjoyment that comes from participation in an activity that has a clear winner and loser. The individual thus maximizes the utility function:

$$U = U(C, H, Z, S). \tag{2.1}$$

Consumption of the composite commodity, C, requires either income that is gained by time spent working for the wage w (T_L) or time spent in home production (T_p). Since, for simplicity, we ignore autonomous income, the budget constraint becomes:

$$C = w*T_L + f(T_p). \tag{2.2}$$

The function $f(T_p)$ can be thought of as the 'home production function' with $f' > 0$ and $f'' < 0$. Substituting equation (2.2) into equation (2.1) allows us to express consumption of the composite commodity in terms of the time variables and the wage. Health and social interaction come from time spent in either of two physical activities, A_1 and A_2. Individuals maximize (2.1) subject to the time constraint:

$$T = T_L + T_P + T_1 + T_2 \tag{2.3}$$

In equation (2.3), T_L is the time spent working for pay, T_P is the time spent in home production, T_1 is the time spent on physical activity A_1, and T_2 is the time spent on physical activity A_2. We assume that the amount of health, competition, and social interaction the individual consumes is a linear function of the time spent on the two activities, where α_j^i is the contribution of an additional hour spent in activity j to his/her consumption of health, competition, and social interaction $(i = H, Z, S)$:

$$H = \alpha_1^H * T_1 + \alpha_2^H * T_2, \tag{2.3a}$$

$$Z = \alpha_1^Z * T_1 + \alpha_2^Z * T_2, \tag{2.3b}$$

$$S = \alpha_1^S * T_1 + \alpha_2^S * T_2. \tag{2.3c}$$

Restating equation (2.2) in terms T, T_P T_1 and T_2, and combining equations (2.1)–(2.3c) yields:

$$U = U[w*(T - T_1 - T_2 - T_P) + f(T_P), \alpha_1^H * T_1 + \alpha_2^H * T_2, \alpha_1^Z * T_1 +$$

$$\alpha_2^Z * T_2, \alpha_1^S * T_1 + \alpha_2^S * T_2]. \tag{2.4}$$

Maximizing equation (2.4) with respect to T_1, T_P, and T_2 yields the first-order conditions:

$$\frac{\partial U}{\partial C} * w = \frac{\partial U}{\partial H} * \alpha_1^H + \frac{\partial U}{\partial S} * \alpha_1^S + \frac{\partial U}{\partial Z} * \alpha_1^Z$$

$$= \frac{\partial U}{\partial H} * \alpha_2^H + \frac{\partial U}{\partial S} * \alpha_2^S + \frac{\partial U}{\partial Z} * \alpha_2^Z$$

$$= \frac{\partial U}{\partial C} * f'(T_P). \tag{2.5}$$

The equality of the left-most and right-most terms of equation (2.5) yields the familiar result that the marginal value of home production equals the wage (see Gronau, 1980). The equality of $[(\partial U)/(\partial C)] * w$ with the remaining terms results from the fact that engaging in physical activity comes at the cost of earning income and thus of consumption. Similarly, the amount of time one spends on physical activity i depends on the activity's per unit contribution to health, success in competition, and social interaction as well as on these factors' contribution to the marginal utility of both of these activities. For example, an individual who places a low marginal value on social interaction and a high marginal value on health might engage in a lot of swimming, which is very good exercise but does not involve much interaction with one's fellow swimmers. Someone who has the opposite sentiments would choose to spend little time swimming and more time on an activity that allows for greater socialization, such as walking.

We can now use this simple framework to explain the gender differences in physical activities as well as the changing pattern of activities over the life cycle. Figure 2.1, for example, shows that aerobics and walking, two healthful activities that are not at all competitive, are much more popular among women than among men. In contrast, the more competitive activities of cycling, golf, and running are much more popular among men. This could reflect the fact that, as Figure 2.4 shows, women are more motivated than men by health-related factors, while men are more motivated by competition and 'enjoyment' of the sport itself. Thus the different choices in activities might be traced to differences in the marginal value of health or competition to men and women. The popularity of golf, particularly among men, might be traced to its social value, a factor that is especially important among men. We shall explore another reason for golf's popularity below.

The model also provides insight into why some people do not participate in physical activity. Men commonly cite work responsibilities as a reason for not engaging in sport. In terms of our model, a high wage increases the opportunity cost of sport, causing the individual to allocate more of his/her time toward work and less to leisure activities. Looking beyond the immediate context, the model also helps explain why people who live in subsistence societies do not engage in sport. Such people have very low hourly pay, but this is offset by a very high marginal utility of consumption $[(\partial U)/(\partial C)]$. This, again, causes people to allocate their time to work instead of recreation.

According to the Equal Opportunity for Women in the Workplace Agency (EOWA), Australian women earn almost 17 percent less than men (EOWA, 2011). If labor supply curves are upward sloping, lower wages lead to a lower quantity of labor supplied. As a result, we expect women to list work obligations as a binding constraint on their physical activity less frequently than men do. Given the continued prevalence of traditional sex roles, it is no surprise that household duties are far more of a factor for women. In terms of our model, traditional gender roles in the family dictate that the marginal product of home activity (f') is generally greater for women than for men, leading to home production being more of an obstacle to physical activity than work outside the home.

One final insight comes from modifying the model to account for interactions between work and play. People attribute such an interaction to golf, for example, as business deals are often closed on the fairway. Such interactions are denied to women through formal and informal restrictions at country clubs and golf courses. These restrictions – and their implications for business dealings – are summarized by the term 'grass ceiling' (*Golf Today*, 2011). We supplement the model by assuming that activity A_2 can be combined with work so that additional time spent at it increases consumption of the consumption commodity by $r_2 T_2$. This changes the first two first-order conditions:

$$\frac{\partial U}{\partial C} * w = \frac{\partial U}{\partial H} * \alpha_1^H + \frac{\partial U}{\partial Z} * \alpha_1^Z + \frac{\partial U}{\partial S} * \alpha_1^S$$

$$= \frac{\partial U}{\partial H} * \alpha_2^H + \frac{\partial U}{\partial Z} * \alpha_2^Z + \frac{\partial U}{\partial S} * \alpha_2^S + \frac{\partial U}{\partial C} * r_2. \quad (2.5a)$$

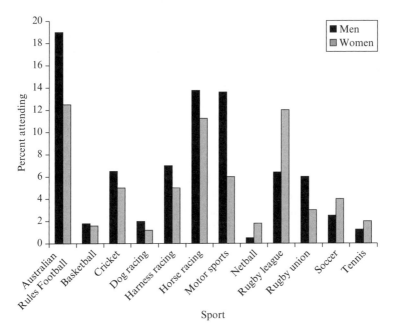

Source: *Participation in Sports and Physical Recreation, Australia, 2005–2006.*

Figure 2.5   *Attendance patterns at Australia's main sports*

Because activity A_2 now has an additional, positive term, an allocation of time that would have generated equilibrium in equation (2.5) now has too little time devoted to activity A_2. As a result, people will devote more time to activities that contribute to their business dealings as well as bring personal benefits, *ceteris paribus*. This helps explain the observation in Figure 2.1 that golf is more than twice as popular among men as among women.

In addition to participating in sports activities, large numbers of men and women watch others participate.[4] In 2005–06, 37 percent of Australian women aged 15 and older (about three million women) and 52 percent of Australian men aged 15 and older (about 4.1 million men) attended one or more sporting events, excluding junior and school sport (ABS, 2010). Figure 2.5 shows attendance patterns of men and women at Australia's most popular spectator sports.

Women's attendance patterns deviate substantially from those of men. Women are less than half as likely as men to attend either motor sports or cricket, and they are only about half as likely to attend a rugby match. Women are also far less likely to attend an Australian Rules Football match than men. The difference, however, is less pronounced for Australian Rules Football than for the above sports. Moreover, Australian Rules Football is the most popular spectator sport among women. The attraction of Australian Rules Football for women is not new. Hess (2000) notes that women attended football matches in large numbers – by some accounts, as much as 50 percent of the crowd – from the very beginning of the sport in the 1850s. This stands in sharp contrast to other sports, such as rugby, which have always catered to a more uniformly male clientele.

Only two sports, tennis and netball, draw more women than men. Again, the relative popularity of netball among women is to be expected, as it is played almost exclusively by women. Similarly, tennis might draw more women because so many women participate in the events and because many women play tennis recreationally.

Basketball and Australian Rules Football are far less popular in Australia than basketball and American football are in the United States. The percentage of American men who claim to be professional football fans ranges from 64 percent for 18–34-year-olds to 52 percent for those over age 55. (All US figures are from Clotfelter, 2011, p. 235.) The figures for American women range from 37 to 33 percent. Football is thus almost twice as popular among American women as it is among Australian men. One might discount this disparity, as Australian Rules Football is largely confined to the area around Victoria, which is in the southern part of the country. Such regionalism does not apply to basketball, but the same disparities between the US and Australia exist. The popularity of professional basketball in the United States ranges from 36 percent for 18–34-year-olds to 24 percent for 35–54-year-olds, with those older than 55 reporting at 26 percent. Basketball is only a little less popular among American women, with 20–22 percent claiming to be fans. Again, the figures for Australians are much lower, with 2–3 percent of both men and women reporting that they are fans.

The terms of the model developed above also have natural interpretations when we add a third activity (A_3), time spent watching sports. Being a spectator or a fan of a particular athlete or team should have no direct health benefits. The sedentary nature of spectating could even lead to poorer health outcomes. As a result, $\alpha_3^H \leq 0$ for activity A_3. Because the impact is likely to be small, we simplify the analysis by assuming $\alpha_3^H = 0$. Spectating could, however, have a large impact on socialization and on competitiveness, vicariously through the success of one's favorite team. As a result, α_3^S and α_3^Z could be large positive numbers. Finally, to the degree that businesses use sporting events to entertain clients or close business deals, spectating could also have a sizable financial return, as denoted by a large r.

We can also use the model to explain gender differences in spectator behavior. The fact that women engage in so much less spectating than men is consistent with the findings of the ABS that women place much greater emphasis on the health benefits of sport. Spectating holds little appeal for people who are attracted to sport because of its contribution to their physical well-being. Men, on the other hand, stress the social and competitive aspects of sport. For men, being a spectator provides an alternative way to satisfy their desire for socialization and competition. It is also likely that the pecuniary rewards from being a spectator, in the form of closing business deals at an event or a sports bar, are greater for men than for women. Given this, it is no surprise that men spend far more time as spectators at sporting events than women do. It also helps to explain why men have lower participation rates in physical activity than do women. Being a spectator might actually be a more efficient way for men to maximize their utility than participating in sports.

2.4   LOWERING BARRIERS TO PARTICIPATION

While Australian women participate broadly in physical activity, their participation has not translated into leadership positions in sport or into well-developed professional leagues for women. The lack of women as leaders and role models may present a barrier to further growth in physical activity among women in Australia. Already, participation rates appear to have stalled.

According to the Australian Sports Commission (ASC), the governmental body responsible for distributing funds and providing strategic guidance for sporting activity in Australia, there has been very little change over the past 10 years in the participation of women and girls in all aspects of sport. It notes that there has been a major shift away from participation in organized sport towards participation in informal activities. The ASC also notes that women remain underrepresented at all levels in coaching, officiating, and leadership.

The representation of women at the national level has been rising slowly, but it remains very low. Only 19 percent of the national sporting organizations (NSOs) are headed by women, and women comprise only 23 percent of all NSO board membership. The ASC has identified the promotion of women in leadership roles in sport as a key priority, believing that growth in the number of women on Australia's sporting boards will help to promote inclusive cultures that support women in sport (ASC, 2011a).

The underrepresentation of women also extends to the Australian Olympic Committee (AOC). Jeffrey (2011) reports on the dissatisfaction of AOC president John Coates, who argues that having only two of 15 AOC board positions occupied by women is not acceptable. It is particularly disturbing in light of the performance by Australian women at recent Olympic Games. For example, Australian women won 56 percent of the team's medals at the 2008 Beijing Olympic Games, despite their making up only 44 percent of the team. The representation of women on the AOC is roughly proportional to the representation of women on corporate boards in Australia. However, with most members of the AOC executive board elected rather than appointed, Coates cannot make unilateral decisions, and change will undoubtedly take time.

Coates also wants more women in senior management positions in Australian sport, and more women on the AOC executive committee. While the AOC's 2010 annual report states that 69 percent of the AOC's staff are women, only 40 percent of senior management positions are held by women. Coates said the gender imbalance was more marked in the management teams of the AOC's 32-member sports. Only six presidents and seven chief executives of the 32 national federations are female.

According to the ASC, five barriers prevent women from assuming a greater leadership role. First, women do not have enough role models and champions who are willing to foster the talents of women in their sport and its governance. The lack of mentors prevents women from receiving the same contacts and career advice that their male colleagues receive. This disparity can prevent even talented, ambitious women from attaining leadership roles ('A Word from Your Sponsor', 2012).

Second, the boards of the NSOs too often comprise volunteers with unlimited tenure. This perpetuates an 'old-boy network' in which mostly male volunteers recruit future members from among their own ranks. Lacking such connections, women have no way to break into this unending chain.

The third problem starts at the local level. Women remain a minority in the membership of many individual sports clubs. Thus, leadership candidates who advocate policies desired by women have a difficult time getting elected. Women therefore find it hard to move into leadership positions there and later into regional or national positions, which traps them in a vicious circle of underrepresentation.

The underrepresentation of women might stem from the fourth problem cited by the ASC, the inhospitable 'macho' culture of many of the local sports clubs. Many local organizations fail to accommodate the needs and desires of their women members. Some openly discriminate against women, which discourages them from participating at the grassroots level.

The final barrier is the family-unfriendly demands that participation in sports clubs poses. Even if women are encouraged and supported by their local organizations, women's role as primary care-giver in most Australian families may preclude them from greater participation because the care-giver role frequently imposes commitments that conflict with the nature and timing of sports events. For women to increase their representation in sports clubs, the clubs will have to go beyond simply permitting women to take roles; they will have to reshape leadership roles to accommodate the needs of its female members, something that has yet to happen on a large scale.

In 2002, the ASC implemented two programs to address the above barriers: the Sport Leadership Grants and Scholarships for Women Program, and the Women in Sport Leadership Register (ASC, 2011b). Since 2002, the Sport Leadership Grants and Scholarships for Women Program has provided A$3.3 million in funding for educational and development opportunities for over 16,000 women. Unfortunately, as the figures at the beginning of this section suggest, this initiative has had only limited success in increasing the representation of women. Any substantial improvement will occur over a long period of time.

2.5   CONCLUSION

The survey carried out by the ABS shows that there are clear similarities and differences in how much men and women engage in sport and physical recreation activities, the activities in which they choose to participate and their reasons for engaging in those activities. Women and men are roughly equally likely to engage in physical activity, but men's preferences are more widely spread than women's. While walking is the most popular physical activity for both women and men, about 33 percent of women who exercise engage in walking, while only 17 percent of men do. The reasons for exercising also differ. Women cite weight loss as their primary motive for exercise in contrast to men, who cite competition or challenge and socialization as leading motives. Men and women also play very different roles as spectators of professional or amateur sports.

We take these observations and provide a coherent model that explains how individuals allocate their time. Our model is based on Downward and Riordan's extension of Becker's theory of the allocation of time. We show that the different levels and types of physical activity are consistent with the results of a model of individual behavior in which the individual maximizes a utility function that is defined over consumption and different aspects of leisure, subject to income and time constraints. We also show that this model leads naturally to the conclusion that men participate much more as passive spectators at sporting events than do women because men can satisfy their desires for competition and socialization but women cannot satisfy their desire for fitness or weight loss by watching a sport. With sufficient micro data, this model could serve as a paradigm for a study that looks more closely at the individual characteristics that lead a person to engage in sport either as an active participant or as an observer.

While the degree to which women participate in physical activity and spectatorship is roughly equivalent to that of men, the same cannot be said about women's representation in Australia's sport leadership. Women are badly underrepresented in leadership roles in Australian sport. We detail five of these barriers. The Australian government has attempted to increase the representation of women in leadership roles in sport, but – until it addresses the five barriers we have listed – women will continue to be underrepresented. Lacking role models and encouragement at the highest levels will limit the participation of women in organized sport, particularly at the highest levels.

NOTES

1. The 2005–06 Multi-Purpose Household Survey and the data were published in *Participation in Sports and Physical Recreation, Australia, 2005–06* (cat. no.4177.0). The survey was to be conducted again in 2009–10, with the results published in early 2011.
2. Netball is played by two teams of seven players. It developed from early versions of basketball that began in England in the 1890s. Games are played on a rectangular court with raised goal rings at each end. Each team attempts to score goals by shooting a ball through its goal ring. Players are assigned specific positions, which define their roles within the team and restrict their movement to certain areas of the court. A player with the ball can hold onto it for only three seconds before shooting for a goal or passing to another player. For more on netball, see Booth, Chapter 19 in this volume.
3. A detailed definition of the participation regularity categories can be found in *Participation in Sports and Physical Recreation, Australia, 2005–06* (cat. no.4177.0).
4. For a deeper analysis of women as spectators, see Montgomery and Robinson, Chapter 1 in this volume.

REFERENCES

'A Word from Your Sponsor' (2012), *The Economist*, June 16: 75.

Australian Bureau of Statistics (ABS) (2009), 'Perspectives on Sport', Feature Article 3, Women in Sport, Canberra, online at: http://www.abs.gov.au/AUSSTATS/abs@.nsf/Prev iousproducts/4156.0.55.001Feature%20Article3May%202009?opendocument&tabname= Summary&prodno=4156.0.55.001&issue=May%202009&num=&view= (accessed May 29, 2011).

Australian Bureau of Statistics (ABS) (2010), 'Spectator Attendance at Sporting Events, 2009–2010', online at: http://www.abs.gov.au/ausstats/abs@.nsf/mf/4174.0 (accessed December 21, 2010).

Australian Sports Commission (ASC) (2011a), 'Get Involved', online at: http://www. ausport.gov.au/participating/women/get_involved (accessed October 8, 2011).

Australian Sports Commission (ASC) (2011b), 'Sports Leadership', online at: http://www. ausport.gov.au/participating/women/get_involved/sport_leadership (accessed October 8, 2011).

Becker, Gary S. (1965), 'A Theory of the Allocation of Time', *Economic Journal*, **75**(299), September: 493–517.

Clotfelter, Charles (2011), *Big-Time Sports in American Universities*, Cambridge: Cambridge University Press.

Downward, Paul and Joseph Riordan (2007), 'Social Interactions and the Demand for Sport', *Contemporary Economic Policy*, **25**(4), October: 518–37.

Equal Opportunity for Women in the Workplace Agency (EOWA) (2011), 'Pay Equity Statistics', *Equal Pay-day*, online at: http://www.eowa.gov.au/Pay_Equity/Files/PE_ STATS.pdf (accessed November 6, 2011).

Farrell, Lisa and Michael A. Shields (2002), 'Investigating the Economic and Demographic Determinants of Sporting Participation in England', *Journal of the Royal Statistical Society*, **165**(Part 2): 335–48.

Golf Today (2011), 'Women Encounter a "Grass Ceiling" in Golf', online at: http://www. golftoday.co.uk/news/yeartodate/news03/women.html (accessed November 6, 2011).

Gronau, Reuben (1980), 'Home Production: A Forgotten Industry', *Review of Economics and Statistics*, **62**(3), August: 408–16.

Hess, Rob (2000), 'Ladies are Specially Invited: Women in the Culture of Australian Rules Football', *International Journal of the History of Sport*, **17**(2–3): 111–41.

Humphreys, Brad R., Logan McLeod and Jane E. Ruseski (2011), 'Physical Activity and Health Outcome: Evidence from Canada', University of Alberta Department of Economics Working Paper 2011-06, Edmonton, Alberta.

Humphreys, Brad R. and Jane E. Ruseski (2009), 'Estimates of the Dimensions of the Sports Market in the US', *International Journal of Sport Finance*, **4**(2), May: 94–113.

Humphreys, Brad R. and Jane E. Ruseski (2010), 'The Economic Choice of Participation and Time Spent in Physical Activity and Sport in Canada', University of Alberta Department of Economics Working Paper 2010-14, Edmonton, Alberta.

Jeffrey, Nicole (2011), 'Coates Calls for More Women', *The Weekend Australian Sport*, **43**, May: 14–15.

McDonald, Karen and J. Kevin Thompson (1992), 'Eating Disturbance, Body Image Dissatisfaction, and Reasons for Exercising: Gender Differences and Correlational Findings', *International Journal of Eating Disorders*, **11**(3), April: 289–92.

Strelan, Peter and Duane Hargreaves (2005), 'Reasons for Exercise and Body Esteem: Men's Responses to Self-Objectification', *Sex Roles*, **53**(7/8), October: 495–503.

3. Individual decision-making in a social context: the sociological determinants of female sports participation
Judith Stull

3.1 INTRODUCTION

In the fall of 2011, Pinckney Community High School experienced the most unusual homecoming football game in its history. Barely an hour after being crowned homecoming queen, Pinckney senior Brianna Amat kicked the winning field goal in a 9–7 victory over rival Grand Blanc High School (Maynard, 2011). At halftime, Brianna appeared on the field with her court. The courtiers were dressed in long gowns, while the queen appeared in her football uniform. For one evening, at least, Ms Amat and the community in which she lived were able to bridge the worlds of femininity and athleticism.

Unfortunately, while such accounts are inspiring for many, they are relatively rare. Girls and women still need to navigate conflicting social expectations. Among the ways in which girls and women 'get to understand their roles' is through parental expectations, peer pressure, and the media. Indeed, girls and women are not only the object of these pressures; they in turn participate in their enforcement as well.

Female athletes are particularly subject to societal pressure because of cultural lag. The concept of cultural lag was first developed by William Ogburn (1922) and later elaborated by Woodard (1934). Ogburn saw cultural lag as the result of conflict between a society's material and non-material culture. At some risk of oversimplification, material culture refers to the physical resources that help provide a collection of individuals with a unifying identity. The material culture of the United States includes objects ranging from shopping malls and houses of worship to i-pads. Non-material culture consists of the ideas, belief structures, and institutions that help those individuals provide meaning to their physical resources. Cultural lag exists because the material culture typically changes and evolves more quickly than the non-material culture. When this occurs, people change their behavior more quickly than they change their ideas as to what is right or appropriate.

Cultural lag results in a period of conflict or maladjustment at the individual level when individuals obtain objects or engage in activities that they feel are somehow wrong. It is reflected at the social level when one portion of a group tries to repress the behaviors of another. This conflict between material goods and beliefs was popularized in Thomas Friedman's *The Lexis and the Olive Tree* (Friedman, 2000). A similar conflict is currently occurring with respect to girls' and women's participation in sports and exercise. While this conflict occurs throughout the world, it expresses itself in different ways and with different intensities in different societies.

This chapter explores the cultural conflicts that have accompanied the growing participation of women in organized sport and physical activity. In Section 3.2, I present sociological concepts to analyze the problems faced by female athletes. Because this volume is intended for economists, many of whom have little or no background in sociology, I provide background and define terms that are unfamiliar to economists. In Section 3.3, I apply these tools to the issue of conforming to a socially desired body image, which is a general problem that women confront. In Section 3.4, I use the concepts from Sections 3.2 and 3.3 to explain the pressures faced by female athletes in the United States and other Western cultures, especially those competing at the elite level. In Section 3.5, I turn to the conflict surrounding women who wish to participate in sports in an Islamic society or in an Islamic subgroup of a Western society. Section 3.6 concludes.

3.2   THEORETICAL PERSPECTIVE: ROLES AND STATUSES

To put this discussion in context it is necessary to understand how an individual's life is structured and how it functions. First, expectations as to appropriate attitudes and behaviors are complex and evolving. At any one moment in time, a person participates in many social groups, such as family, friends, and co-religionists. Each of these groups can affect that person by imposing explicit and implicit expectations. The individual's behavior can, in turn, affect the larger system. The constant interplay between the group and its individual members thus forms a dynamic process.

Individuals have differing time and emotional commitments to the groups to which they belong. Some of these commitments reinforce one another, while others conflict. Figure 3.1 illustrates the nature of these commitments. The largest circle in the figure represents the society within which an individual functions. The smaller circles are of varying size and represent subcultures within the larger culture. As noted earlier, some of

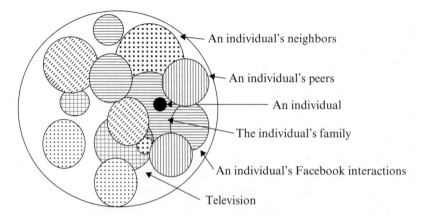

*Figure 3.1   Representation of some of an individual's status/role
obligations*

these subcultures overlap one another. In fact, some subcultures might
be entirely contained within larger subcultures. Being necessarily static in
nature, the figure fails to capture the dynamics of the system. In reality,
the circles continually grow, shrink, and move relative to one another,
reflecting the interaction of the components of the umbrella culture with
one another and with the umbrella culture as a whole.

The two basic dimensions of social behavior are the content of the
culture and the structure of the culture. Values and norms define a culture's content. Values are the theoretical and emotional underpinnings
of a culture. Unfortunately, they are difficult to measure. While individuals may hold on very strongly to their value systems, they frequently are
reluctant or unable to reveal or explain them to outsiders. For example,
they might respond as they think the researcher desires or expects them to
respond. This can be a particularly acute problem when studying youth
sports, as the subject is frequently a student who is responding to a faculty
member (see, for example, Walseth and Fasting, 2003; Walseth, 2006).
Indeed, Garfinkel (1984) claims that people reveal their values only by
violating them. Norms, the rules of social behavior, run the gamut from
folkways that informally regulate everyday social encounters to rigidly
enforced religious or secular laws. Unlike values, norms can be measured
by observing people's behavior because people's behaviors reflect their
norms.

The structure of a culture is determined by statuses and roles. At any one
point in time, individuals hold many 'statuses', that is positions, in their
social lives. Some of these statuses are *ascribed* to the individuals, as they

neither created them nor volunteered to hold them. Examples of ascribed statuses are 'woman', 'daughter', or 'Asian'. Other statuses are *achieved* in that the individual had to do something to attain them. Examples of achieved statuses are 'athlete', 'college graduate', or 'accountant'. Thus, because Elizabeth II became Queen of England because she was the first-born child of King George VI, her position as queen is an ascribed status. In contrast, Barack Obama's position as President of the United States is an achieved status because he successfully sought election to the post. An individual's menu of statuses changes over time, as is the case with age, which progresses through infancy, early childhood, middle childhood, adolescence, and adulthood.

A role is associated with each status that an individual holds. A role is composed of the rights and responsibilities that attach to a specific status. Roles therefore dictate how an individual behaves. Charles Cooley (1902) and later Crosnoe and Muller (2004) explained that an individual learns the appropriate behaviors associated with a role by appealing to what they call the 'Looking-Glass Self Model'. In this model, individuals internalize societal roles in order to meet with approval:

> According to reflected self-appraisal (part of the 'looking-glass self'), individuals' self-concepts are socially constructed through the judgment of others. Although some might react to negative judgments by nullifying them (e.g., changing themselves, avoiding likely critics) or counterbalancing them (e.g., eliciting positive judgments through other outlets), the more general tendency is for individuals to internalize these social judgments, including negative ones, into their self-concept. (p. 394)

In trying to meet one's role responsibilities an individual might encounter two different types of problems: role strain and role conflict.

Role strain occurs when an individual feels uncomfortable with one or more of the rights or obligations that are attached to a role (Goode, 1960). For example, an individual might like the freedoms and rights of being a college student and the lower expectations for material goods that are associated with this status, but might not like the time commitment to studying that being a student requires. A girl or woman who enjoys being highly competitive might also undergo role strain, as her competitive impulses pull against the traditionally defined role of girls and women, who are expected to assume supportive roles. The role strain represents an internal conflict within individuals that is caused by cultural lag. The old values are not yet fully in line with the material changes that are occurring. Role strain is less for those individuals who have already adjusted their values, though their behavior is often viewed by the surrounding culture as 'deviant'.

Unlike role strain, which reflects the tensions created by a specific status, role conflict occurs when the responsibilities of one role make it difficult or impossible to fulfill the responsibilities of another. This external conflict is inherent in human existence, especially for ambitious individuals with many statuses, such as parents who work and want to be community leaders as well. Role conflict is a common problem for the female student-athlete. A student's instructors expect her to attend class regularly and to be diligent in her studies. These obligations can sometimes clash with the obligations placed on her as an athlete. In this role, her coaches expect her to spend as much time as possible practicing, exercising, and performing at events. The obligations imposed by these two roles conflict when the student-athlete has to miss classes or assignments because of travel to an athletic event, or she has to miss practice in order to participate in a lab or take an exam. At these times, the woman's role responsibility as an athlete conflicts with her role responsibility as a student.

Visions of beauty and perceptions in general develop through socialization, a lifelong process that starts with the individual's role and status within her family and is reinforced in the educational sector and then wider influences, such as the media. The attitudinal component and the behavioral component are functions of the degree to which the socialization agents – individuals and institutions that help integrate a person into the existing social order – are in harmony. When socialization agents conflict – for example, when a girl receives opposing messages from her teachers and her parents – the girl must resolve the conflicting roles of student and daughter. Merton (1957) comments that a person resolves conflict by either assimilating and accepting the role desired by the broader culture or by rejecting the broader culture and embracing a 'deviant' role.

In an ethnographic study, Hills (2006) describes the process whereby girls learn about the complexities of being athletic and being female as they negotiate their way through adolescence. Lance (2004) notes that women generally feel role conflict as student-athletes much more than men do. However, this does not necessarily extend to money sports, as female basketball players report less conflict than male basketball players.

3.3   BODY IMAGES: VISUAL REPRESENTATION OF STATUS

In addition to the role and the associated rights and responsibilities that male and female status entails, an individual's status also has visual representation. In the United States, casual observation of a typical shopping mall or other heavily congested public places reveals many different body

types and clothing. Extreme appearances are concentrated among teenagers and young adults. Both male and female idealized body images are
discernible by their clothing. Adolescent and young women frequently
wear very tight and figure-revealing clothing because they regard thin as
beautiful. In contrast, adolescent and young men exaggerate their actual
or potential large body size with oversized clothing as a large, muscular
body is the ideal for them. As people age, the possibility of attaining these
idealized body types, thin for women and muscular for men, decreases,
and clothing styles become less exaggerated for most. This occurs in part
because the status of a young adult differs from the status of an older
person.

In this section, I identify the source of the conceptions of the ideal body
type in the contemporary United States. The analysis is complicated by
wide variations in what is deemed appropriate within a single culture at a
moment in time and by changes in social judgments over time. An example
of cross-sectional variation comes in differences in the ideal body image
among African Americans, Hispanics, and whites. In the United States,
the ideal body types for African American and Hispanic women are typically larger than they are for whites. The difference could be caused by a
number of factors, including systematic differences in the groups' current
and historical social class.

While society's vision of an ideal body image lags behind people's
actions, it does evolve over time. A body that contemporary Americans
regard as undesirably fat symbolized wealth at the turn of the twentieth
century and still does in some African countries today. In addition to
changing over time, ideal body images vary by subculture and social class.

The change in beauty standards over time is best captured by the term
'Rubenesque.' Based on the appearance of idealized women in the paint-
ings of the Flemish Baroque painter Peter Paul Rubens, the term has come
to mean an attractive but corpulent woman. This standard is perhaps best
exemplified in Rubens' masterpiece, *The Judgment of Paris*. In this paint-
ing, three full-figured Greek goddesses vie to be named the most beautiful
woman on earth.

In contemporary American society, most people would consider such
women to be far too heavy to be considered beautiful. However, at a
time when starvation was a common occurrence, extra weight was seen
as a desirable feature. As recently as the twentieth-century, American
standards of beauty idealized such sex-symbols as Mae West and Marilyn
Monroe, who were far heavier than their American counterparts are
today. Societies in which malnutrition persists continue to idealize a larger
body type.

3.4   ATHLETICS, ROLE STRAIN, AND ROLE CONFLICT IN THE UNITED STATES

In this section, I discuss the relationship between body image and sports participation, and I explain the reactions by girls and women to the ideal body perceived by the broader culture. Research on the impact of sport on girls and young women appears to yield highly contradictory findings. Some studies find that young women who participate in athletics feel better about themselves and their bodies, and – as a result – engage in more constructive behavior, from better eating and study habits to fewer unanticipated pregnancies (Miller et al., 1999; Marten-DiBartolo and Shaffer, 2002; Videon, 2002; and Leeds et al., 2007). Other studies find that athletics lead to negative self-images and self-destructive behaviors, such as disordered eating (for example, anorexia nervosa and bulimia) and excessive exercise (Krane et al., 1997).

One reason for the discrepancy in findings is the difference in the sample these studies use. For the average young woman, sports participation appears to provide a wide array of benefits with relatively few drawbacks. For example, disordered eating among high-school athletes is roughly in line with national averages (Thompson and Sherman, 2010). In contrast, many of the problems associated with sports activity have been found in studies of elite athletes. This dichotomy might result from the greater rewards for success, greater intensity of effort, and greater pressure that exist at the elite level. With less at stake at the elementary- and high-school level of competition, superior performance generally leads to higher self-esteem (Shaffer and Wittes, 2006). Tiggemann and Pickering (1996) also argue that involvement in sports can lead to a positive body image for women, but they find that the percentage of women with a poor body self-image increases at higher competitive levels.

One important change that occurs as an athlete moves from inter-scholastic athletic participation to intercollegiate and elite status is the narrowing of her peer group. At the high-school level, sports provide an important mechanism for the individual to share in the broader culture. A recent study of male high-school football players (Steinfeldt and Steinfeldt, 2010) argues that participation in sports has a positive effect on boys, as it solidifies subgroup memberships, a finding supported by O'Neil (2008). Thanks to the success of Title IX, girls can now benefit from such affiliations as well. Today, one of every 2.5 high-school girls plays a sport (as opposed to one in 27 prior to Title IX) (Daniels and Leaper, 2006: 875). Participation in sport thus provides a broad-based peer group for high-school-aged girls.

At higher levels of competition, the peer groups become much smaller and more homogeneous, with identity increasingly defined by the sport itself. This can be important for the girl's self-image and resulting behavior, as Daniels and Leaper (2006) show that peer acceptance is an important mediator between sport and self-esteem. There is an increasing risk that these mediators could work in a perverse way as athletes move to higher levels of competition. Parsons and Betz (2001) recognize this fluidity, as they find that participation in sports and physical activity is associated with higher scores on body shame subscale, indicating greater internalization of cultural standards of female beauty. However, '[o]verall, research on the relationship of sports participation to eating disorders has been inconclusive, with findings varying by sport, athletic performance level' (p. 210).

The problems faced by female athletes at the elite level depend crucially upon the sport in which they participate. At some risk of oversimplification, one can divide women's and men's sports into 'lean' and 'non-lean' sports.[1] Lean sports typically involve either weight classes, as in rowing or wrestling, or activities in which added weight presents a disadvantage. The disadvantage could be bio-mechanical, as in distance running. It could also create a subjective disadvantage in judged sports, such as figure skating or gymnastics (Borgen and Corbin, 1987; and Thompson and Sherman, 2010). Women's lean sports are frequently – but not uniformly – more overtly feminine than the non-lean sports, with young women often carefully made up and wearing dresses or leotards. These sports therefore involve less role strain than the non-lean sports, as they place women in roles that match their traditional role in society.

The danger facing young women in the lean sports comes not from role strain or conflict but from their complete acceptance of their roles and the images associated with their status. They internalize the pressure placed on them to stay thin. In a nationally representative sample of over 7,000 girls, Crissey and Honea (2006) found that those involved in stereotypically female sports, like gymnastics or ice skating, were more likely to report feeling overweight, to attempt to lose weight, and to use multiple weight-loss strategies than those who were non-athletes. A recent study by Arthur-Cameselle and Quatramoni (2011) finds that attempts to lose weight often resulted from pressure by coaches or parents to stay thin. Because of the surrounding competitive pressure, even something seemingly trivial, such as negative comments about an athlete's weight, can set off disordered eating behavior. Muscat and Long (2008) find that eating disorders are positively related to the number of criticisms girls and young women received about their bodies. Even the uniforms they wear contribute to the pressure to lose weight. These uniforms are often so tight and revealing that, in the words of one track athlete, 'You feel completely naked . . . your butt's right there' (Krane et al., 2004: 321).

Women participating in lean sports are much more likely than the overall population to fall prey to the combination of disordered eating and overly intense exercise that combine to form 'low-energy availability' (LEA). LEA, which is formally defined as caloric intake that is insufficient 'to fuel . . . physical activity and support normal bodily processes of growth and development' (Thompson and Sherman, 2010: 21) is one leg of what has been termed the 'Female Athletic Triad', a combination of three interrelated conditions that endanger female athletes. The other two conditions, which stem from LEA, are disrupted menstrual cycle and low bone density. These three disorders are dangerous to the health and – in extreme cases – to the life of the female athlete. Even if these disorders do not cause immediate harm, they can cause severe problems later in life.

Although young women who participate in non-lean sports do not feel the same pressure to lose weight, they are more subject to cultural lag, in which the belief structure of a society fails to keep pace with material changes. In this case, the growing participation of women in sports – 'from 294,015 girls in 1971, the year before Title IX came into existence, to 2,784,154 girls in 2001' (Dworkin and Messner, 2002: 348) a figure that has since risen to over 3 million (Anderson, 2012: 49) – has not been accompanied by changes in the perception of how girls or women should behave or look. While Weiss and Barber (1995) find that there is greater social acceptance of female athletes than there was in the 1970s, perceptions continue to lag behind participation. Thus, 'it is not surprising that questions continue to be raised about the potential role conflict that may be experienced by women who, having chosen to participate in the traditionally defined male domain of competitive athletics, must balance the roles of female and of athlete' (Goldberg and Chandler, 1991: 213).

According to Kornblum (2011), girls fill a particular role in society. They are expected to be compassionate and understanding, to be cooperative rather than competitive, to assume supportive as opposed to leadership roles, and to vicariously enjoy the success of the males in their environment. In effect, they are expected to be cheerleaders rather than athletes. Gender distinctions are reinforced on a daily basis. For example, in a content analysis of magazine advertisements, O'Barr (2006: 163) found, 'Masculine images typically convey power, strength, virility, athleticism, and competitiveness whereas feminine images show beauty, submissiveness, nurturance, and cooperation'. Such behaviors conflict with the independence and assertiveness athletes need to be successful. In the words of one athlete, 'You lose all femininity when you put on a hockey uniform' (Krane et al., 2004: 319).

The behavioral conflict is reinforced by differences between the ideal body type for most non-lean sports and the societal ideal of the thin woman described above. Young women recognize the conflict between the requirements of their sport and 'hegemonic femininity'. Female athletes have coped with this conflict in several ways. One particularly notice-able coping mechanism has been an effort to compensate for their body type and behaviors by overtly feminine displays during competition. As a result, one often sees women paying particular attention to their hair and make-up before competing in track, hockey, or even boxing (Krane et al., 2004; Kauer and Kane, 2006).

Some researchers specifically cite the conflict an athlete faces as being between having the body shape required for athletic success and having the ideal 'White' or 'Western' body. This argument implicitly assumes that there is no clash of ideals in other cultures (see Krane et al., 2004: 315; and Kauer and Krane, 2006: 44), but the problem appears to be universal. In the words of Amantle Montsho, Botswana's first world-class woman runner, 'Women in Botswana don't like sports. . . . They don't like the look of muscles' (Pilon, 2012).

We no longer live in an era when women confront scientific 'evidence' that intense exercise will prevent them from bearing children or turn them into men (Millar, 1999), but cultural lag can make young women question their female identity. Female athletes recognize that their participation in sports, particularly in such non-lean sports as softball and basketball, causes them to be perceived as 'jock girls' or lesbians (Kauer and Krane, 2006). Some (for example, Wright and Clarke, 1999) regard the stigmati-zation of lesbianism as a broader assault on women's sports. They claim that trivializing and sexualizing women's sport is a way to deny power to women who participate in non-traditional sports.

Women in other cultures, however, face more than just trivialization. For example, Longman (2011) points out that officials and the general public sometimes question the sexuality of women athletes. In the run-up to the 2011 Women's World Cup, Nigerian officials accused Equatorial Guinea of using men on their women's soccer team 'because of their sup-posed masculine appearance'. It has also led to an extreme fear of lesbian-ism on women's teams. This fear has caused players of suspect sexuality to be dismissed from the Nigerian team and, in South Africa, to incidents of physical and sexual violence against women soccer players.

3.5   BARRIERS IN ISLAMIC CULTURE

While the conflict between athleticism and femininity is present every-where, it is most pronounced in Muslim cultures. In addition, Muslim women often face explicit as well as implicit pressure. While sociological analyses of sport often cite the implicit pressure of 'hegemonic femininity' on women in Western cultures, women in Muslim cultures or subcultures often face explicit limitations placed on them by family, nation, and mosque. In some instances, the state has imposed restrictions on female athletes. For example, Saudi Arabia agreed – almost literally at the last minute – to send two women to the 2012 Summer Olympics. This about-face came only after extraordinary pressure from the International Olympic Committee, which included a possible ban of its male athletes (Cesari, 2012). Saudi Arabia's policy goes beyond the Olympics. It pro-scribes physical education for girls in public schools and has even refused to let women participate in the Islamic Women's Games (ibid.; Clarey, 2012). Even in the absence of official restriction – often in relatively per-missive Western societies – Muslim women are still subject to considerable pressure. This pressure often comes from the household, as parents place limits on their children, particularly their daughters, to stay within the reli-gious and cultural norms of the subgroup and not to take on the identity of the broader society (Kay, 2006; Walseth, 2006).

Islam places no restriction on physical activity by women *per se*. In fact, many believe that Islam encourages it. In a series of interviews with female Egyptian university students, Walseth and Fasting (2003) find that even deeply observant Muslim women believe that 'Islam encourages women to participate in sport' and that sport is 'a positive activity for them' (p. 53). In a popular hadith (saying of the Prophet Mohammed), the Prophet's youngest wife, Aisha, competes with him in a race and wins (Nakamura, 2002: 22). Many religious Muslims conclude from this hadith that 'taking care of the body through exercise is . . . an Islamic duty' (Kay, 2006: 358).

The barriers to sports participation arise from two conditions that strict interpretations of Islam might place on female athletes. Both of these con-ditions stem from the emphasis on modesty and the proscription of actions that could arouse the opposite sex. It is no surprise that some Saudi bloggers have referred to the country's two female participants – both of whom were completely covered (in one instance over the objections of the International Judo Federation) – as prostitutes who 'do not represent the chaste Muslim women' (Council on Foreign Relations, 2012). Although similar provisions of modesty apply to men's dress and behavior, men typically ignore such restrictions without arousing comment.

Some Muslim women are willing – or permitted – to compete publicly but only if they dress appropriately. Such dress ranges from the *hijab*, which covers the head, to the *krimar*, which covers the head, neck, and torso, to the full face and body covering of the *nikab*. This attire makes it increasingly difficult for women to participate in competitive sports, as even the *hijab* severely handicaps women who wish to participate in sports involving motion, such as track or gymnastics (Kay, 2006: 359).

For some, even modest attire is not enough. In the words of one young woman, 'Running is not OK in front of men. You should only run if there is a danger. Your body shakes when you run, and men can be attracted' (Walseth and Fasting, 2003: 54). For such people, women can participate in sport only if there is complete separation of the sexes. Thus, only the opening ceremonies of the Women's Islamic Games are open to the general public. All other activities take place 'in a completely female environment allowing women, who would not normally access similar competition due to religious and cultural sensitivities, to experience the thrill and privilege of representing their country at high-level competition' (Muslim Women's Sports Foundation, 2012).

Cultural lag in Muslim countries, such as Saudi Arabia and Iran, is strongly pronounced. The values of the ruling classes are purposefully held constant while the material culture surrounding them has changed. Muslim women are supposed to have no public body image at all. Many women are experiencing role strain as they struggle to adapt to the expectations placed on them. While this strain is most pronounced in the Muslim communities in Western cultures (Walseth, 2006), changes may soon move to majority-Muslim nations. The Muslim world is experiencing a revolution (the 'Arab Spring'), part of which might redefine the status of women in society and the accompanying roles they will take on.

3.6   CONCLUSION

This chapter presents a framework within which to analyze and understand the sports participation of women and the associated behavior of women athletes. People's behavior is influenced by the roles that follow from their statuses. Cultural lag sometimes presents an outdated set of behaviors associated with specific roles. For the individual, this leads to the internal struggles of role strain, which occur when the behavior associated with their roles no longer fully corresponds to the surrounding material culture. Role conflict occurs when a person holds multiple statuses that imply different rights and responsibilities.

The body image is a visual representation of the status of women. The ideal image changes over time and can differ among the many subgroups of society. The adoption of the image by women comes in several stages and its success depends on the harmony between different socializing agents.

In Western society, some women do not suffer from role strain but from the opposite problem of trying too hard to conform to the roles and statuses that confront them. Close identification with the thin ideal women can lead to many problems. Especially in lean sports, where lower weight improves performance, it can set off eating disorders, excessive exercise, and other behaviors that lead to low energy availability. The problem in non-lean sports is a less dangerous role conflict of woman versus athlete. Many athletes respond by exaggerating their body image to compensate for their athleticism. This general problem of conflict between the ideal image and athleticism seems to be universal.

The precarious position of women athletes in the Muslim world is not necessarily a function of religious doctrine. There is nothing intrinsically hostile to women sports participation in Islam, but the current status of women in the Muslim world is a result of cultural lag. The strict interpretation of Islam is in conflict with changing material culture and creates both role strain and role conflict for women in this culture.

NOTE

1.   While I focus specifically on women, men are also subject to many of the same pressures. There are many accounts of wrestlers or jockeys who have become ill or even died as a result of attempts to lose weight. See, for example, Thompson and Sherman (2010).

REFERENCES

Anderson, Kelli (2012), 'Nine for IX', *Sports Illustrated*, May 7: 49.

Arthur-Cameselle, Jessyca and Paula Quatramoni (2011), 'Factors Related to the Onset of Eating Disorders Reported by Female Collegiate Athletes', *Sport Psychologist*, **25**(1), March: 1–17.

Borgen, Jorunn and Charles Corbin (1987), 'Eating Disorders among Female Athletes', *Physician and Sports Medicine*, **15**(2), February: 88–95.

Cesari, Jocelyne (2012), 'Saudi Women Going to Games Is a Sham', *CNN Opinion*, online at: http://www.cnn.com/2012/08/01/opinion/cesari-saudi-women-sports/index.html (accessed August 1, 2012).

Clarey, Christopher (2012), 'Ban Urged on Saudi Arabia over Discrimination', *New York Times*, February 15, online at: http://www.nytimes.com/2012/02/16/sports/olympics/olympic-ban-on-saudi-arabia-is-urged-over-lack-of-female-athletes.html (accessed May 24, 2012).

Cooley, Charles (1902), *Human Nature and the Social Order*, New York: Scribner's.

Council on Foreign Relations (2012), 'The Symbolic Victories of Saudi Arabia's Female Olympians', *The Atlantic*, online at: http://www.theatlantic.com/international/archive/2012/08/the-symbolic-victories-of-saudi-arabias-female-olympians/260998/ (accessed August 11, 2012).

Crissey, Sara and Joy Honea (2006), 'The Relationship between Athletic Participation and Perceptions of Body Size and Weight Control in Adolescent Girls: The Role of Sport Type', *Sociology and Sport Journal*, **23**(3), September: 248–72.

Crosnoe, Robert and Chandra Muller (2004), 'Body Mass Index, Academic Achievement, and School Context: Examining the Educational Experiences of Adolescents at Risk of Obesity', *Journal of Health and Social Behavior*, **45**(4), December: 393–407.

Daniels, Elizabeth and Campbell Leaper (2006), 'A Longitudinal Investigation of Sport Participation, Peer Acceptance, and Self-esteem among Adolescent Girls and Boys', *Sex Roles*, **55**(11–12), December: 875–80.

Dworkin, Shari and Michael Messner (2002), 'Gender Relations in Sports', *Sociological Perspectives*, **45**(4), Winter: 347–53.

Friedman, Thomas (2000), *The Lexus and the Olive Tree*, New York: Farrar, Straus, & Giroux.

Garfinkel, Harold (1984), *Studies in Ethnomethodology*, Cambridge: Cambridge University Press.

Goldberg, Alan and Timothy Chandler (1991), 'Sport Participation among Adolescent Girls: Role Conflict or Multiple Roles?', *Sex Roles*, **25**(3/4), August: 213–24.

Goode, William (1960), 'A theory of role strain', *American Sociological Review*, **25**(4), August: 483–96.

Hills, Laura (2006), 'Playing the Field(s): An Exploration of Change, Conformity, and Conflict in Girls' Understandings of Gendered Physicality in Physical Education', *Gender and Education*, **18**(5), September: 539–56.

Kauer, Kerrie J. and Vikki Krane (2006), '"Scary Dykes" and "Feminine Queens": Stereotypes and Female Collegiate Athletes', *Women in Sport and Physical Activity Journal*, **15**(1), Spring: 42–55.

Kay, Tess (2006), 'Daughters of Islam: Family Influences on Muslim Young Women's Participation in Sport', *International Review for the Sociology of Sport*, **41**(3–4), December: 357–73.

Kornblum, W. (2011), *Sociology in a Changing World*, Belmont, CA: Wadsworth/Cenage Learning.

Krane, Vikki, Precilla Choi, Shannon Baird, Christine Aimar and Kerrie Kauer (2004), 'Living the Paradox: Female Athletes Negotiate Femininity and Muscularity', *Sex Roles*, **50**(5–6), March: 315–29.

Krane, Vikki, Christy Greenleaf and Jeannine Snow (1997), 'Reaching for the Gold and the Price of Glory: A Motivational Case Study of an Elite Gymnast', *The Sport Psychologist*, **11**(1), March: 53–71.

Lance, Larry (2004), 'Gender Differences in Perceived Role Conflict Among University Student-Athletes', *College Student Journal*, **38**(2), June: 179–90.

Leeds, Michael, Cristen Miller and Judith Stull (2007), 'Interscholastic Athletics and Investment in Human Capital', *Social Science Quarterly*, **88**(3), September: 729–44.

Longman, Jere (2011), 'Homophobia Still an Obstacle in African Women's Soccer', *New York Times*, June 23: B11.

Marten-DiBartolo, Patricia and Carey Shaffer (2002), 'A Comparison of Female College Athletes and Nonathletes: Eating Disorder Symptomatology and Psychological Well-being', *Journal of Sport and Exercise Psychology*, **24**(1), March: 33–41.

Maynard, Michelene (2011), 'The Kicking Queen', *New York Times*, October 4: B13.

Merton, Robert (1957), *Social Theory and Social Structure*, Glencoe, IL: Free Press.

Millar, Stuart (1999), 'How the Bearded Lady Spoiled Sport', *The Guardian*, March 30, online at: http://www.guardian.co.uk/uk/1999/mar/31/stuartmillar (accessed May 24, 2012).

Miller, Kathleen, Don Sabo, Michael Farrell, Grace Barnes and Merrill Melnick (1999), 'Sports, Sexual Behavior, Contraceptive Use, and Pregnancy among Female and Male High School Students: Testing Cultural Resource Theory', *Sociology of Sport Journal*, **16**(4), December: 366–87.

Muscat, Anne and Bonita Long (2008), 'Critical Comments about Body Shape and Weight: Disordered Eating of Female Athletes and Sport Participation', *Journal of Applied Sport Psychology*, **20**(1), January: 1–24.

Muslim Women's Sports Foundation (2012), *Islamic Games*, online at: http://www.mwsf. uk/islamic_games.html (accessed May 25, 2012).

Nakamura, Yuka (2002), 'Beyond the Hijab: Female Muslims and Physical Activity', *Women's Sport and Physical Activity Journal*, **11**(2), Fall: 21–48.

O'Barr, William (2006), 'Representations of Masculinity and Feminity in Advertisements', *Advertising and Society Review*, **7**(2), online at http://muse.jhu.edu/journals/asr/indexb.html (accessed September 14, 2006).

O'Neil, James (2008), 'Summarizing 25 Years of Research on Men's Gender Role Conflict Using the Gender Role Conflict Scale: New Research Paradigms and Clinical Implications, *The Counseling Psychologist*, **36**(3), May: 358–445.

Ogburn, William (1922), *Social Change with Respect to Cultural and Original Nature*, Oxford: Delta Books.

Parsons, Elizabeth and Nancy Betz (2001), 'The Relationship of Participation in Sports and Physical Activity to Body Objectification, Instrumentality, and Locus of Control among Young Women', *Psychology of Women Quarterly*, **25**(3), September: 209–22.

Pilon, Mary (2012), 'The Footprints on a Path to Gold', *New York Times*, April 22, online at: http:/www.nytimes.com/2012/04/22/sports/olympics/amantle-montsho-overcomes-obstacles-to-become-a-track-champion.html?pagewanted=all (accessed May 12, 2012).

Shaffer, David and Erin Wittes (2006), 'Women's Precollege Sports Participation, Enjoyment of Sports, and Self-esteem', *Sex Roles*, **55**(3–4), February: 225–32.

Steinfeldt, Jesse and M. Clint Steinfeldt (2010), 'Gender Role Conflict, Athletic Identity, and Help-seeking among High School Football Players', *Journal of Applied Sport Psychology*, **22**(3), July: 262–73.

Thompson, Ron and Roberta Trattner Sherman (2010), *Eating Disorders in Sport*, New York: Routledge.

Tiggemann, Marika and Amanda Pickering (1996), 'Role of Television in Adolescent Women's Body Dissatisfaction and Drive For Thinness', *International Journal of Eating Disorders*, **20**(2), September: 418–31.

Videon, Tami (2002), 'Who Plays and Who Benefits: Gender, Interscholastic Athletics, and Academic Outcomes', *Sociological Perspectives*, **45**(4), Winter: 415–44.

Walseth, Kristin (2006), 'Young Muslim Women and Sport', *Leisure Studies*, **25**(1), August: 75–94.

Walseth, Kristin and Kari Fasting (2003), 'Islam's View on Physical Activity and Sport: Egyptian Women Interpreting Islam', *International Review for the Sociology of Sport*, **38**(1), March: 45–59.

Weiss, Maureen and Heather Barber (1995), 'Socialization Influences of Collegiate Female Athletes: A Tale of Two Decades', *Sex Roles*, **33**(1/2), July: 129–40.

Woodard, James (1934), 'Critical Notes on the Culture Lag Concept', *Social Forces*, **12**(3), March: 388–98.

Wright, Jan and Gill Clarke (1999), 'Sport, the Media and the Construction of Compulsory Heterosexuality', *International Review for the Sociology of Sport*, **34**(3), September: 227–43.

PART II

PERFORMANCE AND REWARDS IN WOMEN'S PROFESSIONAL SPORTS

4. Gender and skill convergence in professional golf

Stephen Shmanske

4.1 INTRODUCTION

In golf, brute strength is not as important as it is in many other sports. Consequently, all else equal, women might be expected to compete effectively with men. However, with very few exceptions (for example, Babe Zaharias, Annika Sorenstam, and Michelle Wie) women have competed separately in women-only events. It is possible that separate competitions are an artifact of antique social mores that are slowly changing. As women, and society in general, become accustomed to the idea of women competing directly with men, women will be more willing to practice to develop the level of skills to compete in gender-neutral tournaments at the highest level. Many golf fans, including this author, eagerly await this day. However, Shmanske (2000, 2012) has shown that, at their current skill levels, women can earn more money by competing in women-only tournaments sponsored by the Ladies Professional Golf Association (LPGA) than they can by competing in the tournaments on the Professional Golfers' Association Tour (PGA TOUR), which are open to both genders.

Competitive professional golf in the United States is organized into annual 'Tours', in which the golf associations schedule tournaments. The associations determine which golfers are eligible to compete, and they negotiate with the golf courses and corporate sponsors for the right to stage the event. The PGA TOUR and its forerunner, the Tournament Players Division of the PGA of America, have organized the Tour since the 1930s, before which a less formal structure of the Tour was in place.

The LPGA was established in 1950, taking over from a short-lived association of women professional golfers called the Women's Professional Golf Association (WPGA), which staged the first professional Women's Open Championship in 1946. Although amateur women's golf had important women-only competitions as early as 1895, when the United States Golf Association (USGA) sponsored the first US Women's Amateur Championship, professional women's golf barely existed before the end of the Second World War. The WPGA ran the Women's Open for a few years; the LPGA took over in 1950, and the USGA took over in 1953.[1]

One other major Tour, the Champions Tour (formerly called the SENIOR PGA TOUR), organizes competitions for participants over the age of 50. This Tour was formalized in 1980, at which time the PGA TOUR recognized that older golfers could not compete effectively on the regular Tour but still had the ability to attract fans and television coverage owing to their name recognition. There are also European and other foreign and 'minor' Tours. These have also been studied, but data have been most readily available for the three major North American professional Tours, which are the basis for this study.

This chapter compares men's and women's skill levels over the last 20 years by focusing on the skill of driving distance. Even though the skills of chipping, putting, and overall accuracy are also important, driving distance is especially interesting for three reasons. First, if women can catch up to men in driving distance, the skill most likely to be affected by overall size and brute upper-body strength, they can, with practice, match men in the other skills. The other skills require touch, hand–eye coordination, flexibility, balance, and timing, all developed by practice, and all theoretically gender neutral. Women's performance relative to men in driving distance should, therefore, be a prime determinant of women's ability to compete with men.

Second, the skill of driving distance has evolved rapidly with the growth of technology in golf equipment. Advances in materials and design for both balls and clubs have led to an increase in driving distance for golfers of all ages and abilities. If these new materials and designs differentially advantage women over men or men over women, they may advance or forestall, perhaps indefinitely, the day when women achieve parity with men.

Third, it is obvious to even casual observers of the sport that the skill of driving distance characterizes professional golfers. Even mediocre amateurs will occasionally have a great round, sink a long putt, chip in from off the green, or make a birdie, but most will never hit a drive over 300 yards. Even though more astute fans and more accomplished amateurs recognize that professionals are perhaps even farther ahead in the areas of spin rate, trajectory control, and consistency, than they are in pure distance, these more subtle aspects of the game lack the 'wow' factor that long drives engender. As the old adage says, 'Drive for show, putt for dough'. Because of the fans' appreciation of the prodigious distances that professionals can hit the ball, there are important linkages extending from driving distance to prize funds to professional golfers' earnings and back to the incentive to increase driving distance. These linkages may differ systematically between the PGA TOUR and the LPGA.

The remainder of this chapter is divided into four sections. Section 4.2

sets the stage for this research by reviewing the previous literature on professional golfers' earnings and the golf production function. The two following sections describe and carry out two separate analyses of the gender differences in driving distance. Section 4.3 examines whether women are catching up to men in the skill of driving distance. Section 4.4 performs a Granger (1969) causality test to determine the extent to which increasing prize funds bring forth greater driving distance, and the extent to which increases in driving distance provide fan enjoyment, ultimately leading to larger purses. Section 4.5 concludes.

4.2 LITERATURE REVIEW: THE GOLF PRODUCTION FUNCTION

The literature on women's golf is not as extensive as that on men's. There are only a few studies, and most of them do not statistically analyze a formal relationship between the input of the golfer's skills and the output of the golfer's score or earnings. For example, Shin and Nam (2004) examine a player's race and nationality, focusing on Korea, while Kalist (2008) looks at performance before and after childbirth. Early on, Marple (1983) compares men's and women's earnings in golf and tennis, showing that women might have been catching up but have a long way to go. More recently, Matthews et al. (2007) examine the link between purse size and performance, and Tiruneh (2010) compares age and earnings profiles across gender. None of these studies estimates a production function *per se*.

At the simplest level, golfers use their skills in a variety of dimensions as inputs to earn prize money based on rank-order performance in tournaments. This suggests estimating a production function as a reduced-form regression of golfer earnings on a vector of skills, such as: driving distance, driving accuracy, accuracy with approach shots, putting proficiency, and ability to play from sand bunker hazards. Numerous studies of this relationship have been undertaken, differing slightly based on the year and Tour of the sample, the format of the dependent variable, the functional form, and the skill and control variables included on the right-hand side.

Early studies (Davidson and Templin, 1986 and Nix and Koslow, 1991) came from the exercise, sport, and body mechanics literature, as opposed to the economics of sports. Using data from 1983 and 1987, respectively, these researchers were interested in discovering which skills were statistically important in determining earnings, but they did not systematically control for other determinants of earnings. Therefore, they used stepwise regression and dropped multiple dimensions of skill from the analysis. The results confirm the importance of several golf skills, but they are hard to generalize due to the *ad hoc*, stepwise nature of the statistical calculations.

A paper from the exercise and sport literature (Shaffer et al., 2000) expands this analysis to include the top 50 golfers from the Champions Tour, the LPGA, and the PGA TOUR for the 1998 season. This chapter confirms that driving distance is important, but I do not estimate the full golf production function.

The earliest economic study is Shmanske (1992), who uses data on 60 top money earners in 1986. He regresses levels and natural logarithms of earnings per year and earnings per tournament on the five skills mentioned above, a calculated measure of short game skill, and a measure of experience. In the levels specification, the coefficient estimates are interpreted as value of the marginal product (VMP) of the various skills. Thus, an additional yard of driving distance is worth $6,775 per year or $341.10 per tournament. Shmanske also uses survey data on the golfers' practice routines to develop an estimate of the VMP of practice for each skill. He finds a return of between $200 and $300 per hour for practice on driving and a return of $300–$600 per hour for practice on putting.

Sommers (1994) uses the full set of 183 PGA TOUR golfers for 1992. The dependent variable is the natural logarithm of earnings per tournament. He finds that one yard of driving distance increases earnings by 3.8 percent. See Table 4.1 for a listing of the various parameter estimates for driving distance that appear in the economics literature, as well as a transformation of these estimates into elasticities for ease of comparison. For example, in this case, the average driving distance was 260.4 yards, so one additional yard is actually an increase in driving distance of $1/260.4 = 0.384$ percent. Transforming these calculations yields an elasticity of earnings per tournament with respect to driving distance of 9.90.

Several other studies examine variations on the above theme. They use different samples or include different control variables in addition to the usual five skills of driving distance, driving accuracy, greens in regulation, sand saves, and putts per green. Moy and Liaw (1998) develop separate estimates of the parameters for the PGA TOUR, the Champions Tour, and the LPGA for the 1993 season. Driving distance is statistically significant on the PGA TOUR and the Champions Tour but not in the LPGA Tour. Nero (2001) uses the highest 130 earners in 1996 to estimate a parameter that implies an elasticity of earnings per year with respect to driving distance of 13.34. Alexander and Kern (2005) use 10 years of PGA TOUR data in an unbalanced panel to track changes in the VMPs of golfer skills over the 1992–2001 period. The return to driving distance roughly tripled over this period, almost exactly matching an approximate tripling in purse sizes.

Table 4.1 Studies of professional golf production and earnings

Author and date	Sample	Descriptive statistics[a]	Impact of 1 added yard	Elasticity[b]
Nix and Koslow (1991)	PGA TOUR 1987	$267,000/year 263.4 yards	Estimates not reported	
Shmanske (1992)	PGA TOUR 1986	$256,000/year 262.1 yards	$6,775**/year	6.94
Sommers (1994)	PGA TOUR 1992	260.4 yards	0.038***ln$/event	9.90
Wiseman et al. (1994)	PGA TOUR 1992	70.9 strokes/round	−0.18*strokes/rd	−0.66[c]
	SPGA[d] 1992	261 yards	Estimates not reported	
	LPGA 1992		Estimates not reported	
Moy and Liaw (1998)	PGA TOUR 1993	$265,000/year 260.2 yards	Reports elasticities	9.28***
	SPGA 1993	$329,000/year 254.1 yards		3.14**
	LPGA 1993	$91,000/year 226.9 yards		4.07
Berry (1999)	PGA TOUR 1999	71.84 strokes/round 272.2 yards	−0.175strokes/rd	−0.66[c]
Shaffer et al. (2000)	PGA TOUR 1998 SPGA 1998 LPGA 1998		Estimates not reported	

Table 4.1 (continued)

Author and date	Sample	Descriptive statistics[a]	Impact of 1 added yard	Elasticity[b]
Shmanske (2000)	PGA TOUR 1998	$623,000/year 271.25 yards	0.036***ln$/event	9.76
	LPGA 1998	$139,440/year 236.6 yards	0.016ln$/event	3.79
Rishe (2001)	PGA TOUR 1999	$923,000/year 273.2 yards	0.015ln$/event	4.10
	SPGA 1999	$567,000/year 265.9yards	0ln$/event	0
Nero (2001)	PGA TOUR 1996	$433,000/year 266.9 yards	0.05***ln$/year	13.34
Fried et al. (2004)	PGA TOUR 1998	$18,806/event 270yards	$1,583/event	22.73
	SPGA 1998	$17,749/event 262 yards	$257/event	3.79
	LPGA 1998	$5,598/event 237 yards	$434/event	18.37
Alexander and Kern (2005)	PGA TOUR 1992–2001	$306,600/year[e] 268.19 yards	$11,728***/year 0.04*** ln$/year	10.26 10.73
Pfitzner and Rishel (2005)	LPGA 2004	$10,370/event 249.8 yards	Reports elasticities	4.95***

Callan and Thomas (2007)	PGA TOUR 2002	$953,000/year 280 yards	Reduced form: $12,257/year	3.60
			Multi-equation: $5,892/year	1.73
Shmanske (2008)	PGA TOUR 2006	$71,258/event 289.1 yards	Reduced form: 0.0326***ln$/event	9.42
			Structural model: 0.016 ln$/event	4.63
Kahane (2010)	PGA TOUR 2004–07	$52,020/event[f] 288.6 yards	OLS: $926**/event	5.14
			Median: $407*/event	2.26
			90th% $1,602*/event	8.89
Shmanske (2012)	PGA TOUR 2008	$71,323/event 288.0 yards	0.017ln$/event	4.90
	LPGA 2008	$19,299/event 248.1 yards	0.018ln$/event	4.47

Notes:
*, **, *** denote statistical significance of estimate at 0.10, 0.05, and 0.01 levels where reported in original paper.
a. Sample averages for earnings are measured in current dollars per golfer per year (or per event) unless otherwise noted. Sample averages for driving distance are those reported in the cited paper.
b. Implied elasticity of earnings (per year or per event) with respect to driving distance unless otherwise noted.
c. Elasticity of strokes per round with respect to driving distance.
d. SENIOR PGA TOUR or Champions Tour.
e. Constant dollars 1982–84.
f. Constant dollars 2007.

Shmanske (2000) applies the parameter estimates to compare the PGA TOUR to the LPGA for the 1998 season using the decomposition method of Oaxaca (1973). In a result of particular importance to this volume, the decomposition of the 1998 earnings gap between men and women in professional golf indicates that 32 percent of the gap is due to the higher return to the skill of driving distance on the PGA TOUR[2] and that 68 percent of the gap is due to the higher level of this skill exhibited on the PGA TOUR. In variations on this approach, Rishe (2001) decomposes the age-based earnings gap between the Champions Tour and the regular PGA TOUR using data from 1999, and Shmanske (2012) uses 2008 data to re-examine the gender-based earnings decomposition of his earlier study. By 2008, the higher return to driving distance on the PGA TOUR disappeared, and the portion of the gender gap in earnings due to the higher performance of men with respect to driving distance decreased to 45 percent.

Others have followed Shmanske (1992) in estimating a production function for women's golf. Pfitzner and Rishel (2005) use 2004 data from the LPGA and find a relatively low elasticity of earnings with respect to driving distance. Fried et al. (2004) use data envelopment analysis with 1998 data to define a frontier production function. They obtain very high elasticities of earnings with respect to driving distance for both the PGA TOUR and the LPGA.

Others presage or follow Scully's (2002) suggestion to estimate a structural model because golf skills do not directly produce earnings. Rather, skills produce scores in competitions that generate earnings according to a rank-based distribution of prizes. Wiseman et al. (1994) estimate the first half of the structure with 1992 data. They find that driving distance has a significant impact only on the PGA TOUR. One yard of distance decreases scores by 0.18 strokes per round. This translates to an elasticity of strokes per round with respect to driving distance of −0.66.

Using 2002 data, Callan and Thomas (2007) extend Scully's insight by estimating a three-step structural model in which skills produce scores, scores produce ranks in tournaments, and ranks in tournaments generate earnings. Combining the results of three equations, they estimate that increasing driving distance by one yard increases yearly earnings by $5,892. This is less than half of their reduced form estimate of the same VMP, $12,257 per year, which they calculate for comparison.

Each of the above papers has used the yearly averages of earnings and skills as the basic units of analysis. Other work has attempted to improve upon the measurement of the skills or the calculation of the coefficients. Berry (1999) recognizes that the skills may be interdependent in his study of PGA TOUR data from the first 28 tournaments of 1999. For example, the measure of sand saves depends upon how good a putter one is, the measure of greens in regulation depends on how long and accurate one's drives are, and, because of interaction, the value of driving distance depends on driving accuracy. Berry constructs new measures of each skill and includes the interaction term between driving distance and driving accuracy in his regression. Thus, one additional yard of driving distance reduces strokes per round by 0.067 directly and by another 0.108 indirectly when evaluated at the mean level of driving accuracy.

Shmanske (2008) follows the top 100 PGA TOUR earners from 2005 during the 2006 season to gather data on a tournament-by-tournament basis and offers two refinements. First, the measurements of the skills are adjusted for course characteristics. Second, instead of having only the year-end average skill level, a distribution of skills (from which mean, variance and skewness are calculated) is captured for each golfer. Then, following Scully's two-step suggestion, the distribution of skills produces a distribution of scores which, in turn, produces earnings per tournament. In the reduced-form estimation, one yard of driving distance increases earnings per tournament by 3.26 percent, whereas in the complex structural model one yard of driving distance affects mean, variance, and skewness of the scoring distribution for a combined effect on earnings of 1.6 percent, less than half of the reduced-form estimate.

Kahane (2010) further improves our understanding of the golf production function and the value of driving distance by estimating a quantile regression and contrasting these results with OLS estimates. He uses data from the PGA TOUR from 2004 to 2007 and controls for all the usual skills. His OLS estimates indicate that one additional yard increases earnings by \$926 per tournament. In the quantile regression, controlling for the other skills, at the median of the conditional earnings distribution, one additional yard leads to only an additional \$407 per tournament. At the 90th percentile, one extra yard leads to \$1,602 per tournament of extra winnings distribution. The return to driving distance is quantitatively higher as one moves up in the distribution of earnings, conditional on the explanatory variables. As expected, the typical, nonlinear prize distribution favors those at and near the top.

The most recent innovation in the estimation of a golf production function comes from using microdata collected by an army of PGA TOUR volunteers who track every shot by every golfer in every tournament. Thus, over time, the unit of observation has gone from yearly averages, to per tournament averages, and finally to individual shots. Results from studies using these new data are starting to arrive. Fearing et al. (2011) focus on putting performance based on the absolute distance of each putt. Recognizing that the contour of the green is also important, Stockl et al. (2011) measure the putting skill from each location on a single green. Work along these lines on distance and accuracy from every spot on the golf course will be a focus of continued future research on the golf production function.

4.3   RECENT TRENDS IN DRIVING DISTANCE

Table 4.1 confirms that the average driving distance of professional golfers has increased over the period in which economists have been studying the golf production function. A deeper look at the papers indicates that there has not been a marked increase in the other skills over the same period. This is true for both genders, although the LPGA has been studied less, and the evidence is spottier. This section examines the trends in driving distance for men and women over the last two decades to ascertain whether women are catching up or falling farther behind in this skill.

I have collected data on the age and yearly average driving distance of 694 male and 630 female professional golfers on the PGA TOUR, the LPGA, and the Champions Tour from 1992 to 2010. I use the data for women to estimate the following equation:

$$DRIVDIST = \beta_0 + \beta_1 AGE + \beta_2 AGE^2 + \beta_3 1993 + \ldots + \beta_{20} 2010 + \varepsilon.$$
$$(4.1)$$

I have suppressed i and t subscripts indicating the golfer and year of the individual observation. The dependent variable, $DRIVDIST$, is the yearly average distance in yards of the golfer's tee shots. AGE and AGE^2 capture an expected inverted-U shape age profile of the skill. The years are dummy variables that control for recent improvements in the skill, whether due to increased practice or improvements in technology, without imposing a specific functional form. The dummy variable for 1992 is omitted so that the β_3 through β_{20} coefficients measure the improvement over the base year of 1992.

I also estimate a variation of this equation for men with the addition of a dummy variable, $CHAMP$, for golfers on the Champions Tour. Finally, I pool both genders and add the dummy variables, $CHAMP$ and $PGATOUR$, to separate the men's distance on the regular and senior tours from the women's distance on the LPGA. The results appear in Table 4.2.

The constant terms in the first two columns show that men out-drive women over this period by about 40 yards. This result is corroborated by the coefficients on $CHAMP$ and $PGATOUR$ in the pooled regression, which indicate that drives are 37 yards longer on the Senior Men's Tour and 38 yards longer on the PGA TOUR than they are on the LPGA

Table 4.2   *Coefficient estimates (and* t-*statistics) of the determinants of driving distance*

Dependent variable: DRIVDIST

Sample / Variable	Women	Men	Pooled
Constant	229.647 (84.06)***	269.803 (105.05)***	227.118 (120.35)***
AGE	0.021 (0.14)	−0.102 (−0.73)	0.129 (1.25)
AGE^2	−0.006 (−2.86)***	0.005 (−2.63)**	−0.007 (−5.12)***
CHAMP		−1.635 (−2.07)**	37.258 (54.38)***
PGATOUR			38.138 (173.14)***
1993	1.706 (1.66)*	−0.002 (−0.00)	0.932 (1.39)
1994	2.677 (2.60)***	1.868 (2.25)**	2.339 (3.47)***
1995	7.842 (7.71)***	3.524 (4.30)***	5.902 (8.87)***
1996	9.354 (9.22)***	6.649 (8.16)***	8.120 (12.24)***
1997	12.992 (12.03)***	8.183 (10.13)***	10.318 (15.14)***
1998	13.502 (12.54)***	11.215 (13.81)***	12.171 (17.83)***
1999	12.679 (11.00)***	12.929 (16.08)***	12.612 (18.07)***
2000	14.800 (13.76)***	14.029 (17.58)***	14.225 (21.05)***
2001	18.060 (16.77)***	20.003 (25.11)***	18.946 (28.05)***
2002	23.476 (21.83)***	20.232 (25.79)***	21.434 (32.05)***
2003	24.689 (24.39)***	26.621 (33.66)***	25.525 (39.07)***
2004	23.766 (23.48)***	27.189 (34.53)***	25.334 (38.88)***
2005	21.643 (21.20)***	29.068 (37.31)***	25.321 (38.91)***
2006	23.016 (22.55)***	29.333 (37.46)***	26.092 (40.02)***
2007	23.151 (22.44)***	28.930 (37.18)***	26.038 (39.86)***
2008	21.692 (21.03)***	27.497 (35.47)***	24.585 (37.73)***
2009	24.352 (22.94)***	28.053 (36.09)***	26.176 (39.61)***
2010	21.660 (20.32)***	28.127 (36.55)***	25.095 (38.15)***
adj. R^2	0.428	0.641	0.835
n	3823	4115	7938

Tour. These coefficients also show that, after controlling for age, there is only a one- or two-yard difference between the regular PGA TOUR and the Champions Tour. This result is confirmed by the small size of the *CHAMP* variable in the men's regression.

Comparing the *AGE* and *AGE*^{2} coefficients shows an increasing falloff of driving distance as age increases, essentially forming the latter half of an inverted-U shape age profile; there is no evidence of the upward-sloped part of an inverted-U. The result is consistent across gender.

Both men and women have gained distance over the period. Women have gained over 20 yards, and men have gained close to 30 yards, but the pattern and timing of the gains differ by gender. Early in the period, women gained more than men, closing the distance gap by almost five yards by 1997. However, from 1997 until 1999, women's distances leveled off while men continued to gain, both ending up about 12 yards longer than in 1992. Both genders made large gains in the three years following 1999, with women adding another 11 yards for a total gain of over 23 yards compared to 1992, while men added eight yards for a total gain of 20 yards. So from 1992 to 2002, women gained three more yards on their drives than men did, making a small inroad on closing the gender gap in driving distance. Men started from a higher base in 1992, so the diminishing gap in driving distance is consistent with the convergence of skill levels.

Skill convergence disappeared after 2002, as women's driving distance leveled off while men's driving distance rose by more than six yards from 2002 to 2003 before leveling off. By 2010, men's drives were 28 yards longer than in 1992 while women's drives added less than 22 yards. The comparative pattern of gains to driving distance over the period is shown graphically in Figure 4.1. The first half of the top panel (a) can be

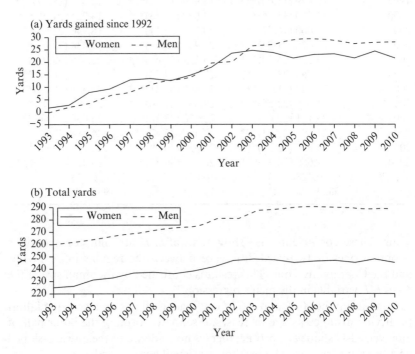

Sources: PGA, LPGA, and Champions Tour websites.

Figure 4.1   Driving distance

construed to indicate that women's driving distance was converging to the men's driving distance, but the second half of the top panel shows that the gains were lost. The bottom panel (b) puts into perspective the relatively unchanged gender gap into perspective.

4.4   PURSES, DISTANCE, AND GRANGER CAUSALITY

Both driving distance and prize funds have increased dramatically over the past two decades. Causality could run in both directions between these two time series, or both series could move together in response to an exogenous influence. For example, the growth in prize funds means that there is a greater incentive to practice all golf skills, thus supporting the argument that increases in prize funds cause increases in driving distance. At the same time, increases in driving distance may attract more fans, thus allowing tournament promoters to offer higher purses. Additionally, an outside factor may be causing both trends. For example, the arrival of popular and charismatic golfers, such as Tiger Woods and John Daly, who also happen to be long drivers, may simultaneously lead to increases in purses and average driving distances in professional golf.

It is beyond the scope of this chapter, and possibly beyond the limitations of the available data, to sort out all the possible directions of causality in a fully specified simultaneous equation model. It is possible, however, to get a sense of the timing of the growth in the related time series by applying a Granger causality test. The simple intuition is that if long drives, perhaps from technological innovations, stimulate fan interest and lead to higher prize funds, then the long drives should appear before the increases in the prize funds. Alternatively, if the increased prize funds create the incentive to practice more to develop higher skills, then the prize funds should increase first.[3] In reality, causation might run in both directions so that there is no clear cause and effect. Furthermore, recognizing the *post hoc ergo propter hoc* fallacy, causality cannot be determined from a simple comparison of the timing of effects in the time-series data. What is discoverable from this type of analysis is Granger causality, which I explain more fully below. Granger causality can never prove causality for the same reasons that statistical correlation can never prove actual causation. A Granger causality test can show whether the data are consistent with causality.

Despite the above concerns, it is interesting to compare the results obtained for the LPGA to those for the PGA TOUR. Thus, I run separate causation tests for the PGA TOUR and the LPGA. On the one hand, it is possible that the 'wow factor' of long drives leads to higher purses on the PGA TOUR, where the drives are longer, but not in LPGA tournaments. Women professionals still impressively outdrive casual amateur golfers, creating considerable entertainment value for the fans of the sport, which may lead to increases in prize funds for the LPGA. However, the effect of women's driving distances on purse size may pale in comparison to those of men.

I also run separate Granger causality tests in the other direction because there may be a gender-based difference in the impact of prize money on driving distance. One could argue that the higher prize funds on the open-to-all-genders PGA TOUR supplies the same incentive to both men and women to develop longer tee shots. However, the *marginal* impact of purse size on driving distance could be higher in LPGA events. In theory, any pattern of causality could be uncovered, making it important to analyze the data.

The Granger test has two parts. First, each data series is differenced, and these first differences are regressed on their own lagged values to determine the statistical lag structure. Second, keeping the significant own lags (time-series 'A') on the right-hand side, the lags of the other time series (time-series 'B') are added to see if they add significant explanatory power. If they do, then series A is Granger-caused by series B. If none of the lagged differences of B is significant, then there is no evidence that B Granger-causes A. The Granger test is thus a negative test – of non-causality. Because series B cannot cause series A if B does not occur first, we can only rule out the possibility that B causes A; we cannot definitively conclude that A causes B because other factors might have caused both B and A. The Granger causality tests were performed separately for men and women on the time series of average driving distances and yearly total purses. The results are in Table 4.3.

The columns in the bottom panel of Table 4.3 report the results of four regressions. The first column reports whether purses can Granger-cause distance for men. First, regressions not reported indicate that for the change in driving distance for men, the second own lag was significant but not the first. Using this lag structure, the lagged change in purses is not statistically significant. Thus, changes in purses do not Granger-cause changes in driving distance for men.

The second column shows whether changes in driving distance Granger-cause changes in purse size for men. In regressions not shown here, only the first-lagged change in purses was significant. With this lag structure, the lagged change in driving distance is statistically significant. Thus, driving distance Granger-causes purse size for men.

Table 4.3   Granger tests of purses and driving distance

Variable	Descriptive statistics			
	Mean	Standard deviation	Minimum	Maximum
DRIVDIST:[a] men	275.6	10.01	260.2	286.9
DRIVDIST:[a] women	239.3	8.51	223.5	248.8
Purses:[b] PGA TOUR	167.9	88.5	49.4	279.4
Purses:[b] LPGA	38.2	12.0	20.4	63.2

	Coefficient estimates (*t*-statistics)			
Sample	Men		Women	
Dependent variable	ΔDRIVDIST	ΔPurse[c]	ΔDRIVDIST	ΔPurse[c]
Constant	0.27	6.86E+05	0.74	3.16E+05
	(0.44)	(0.39)	(1.04)	(0.39)
ΔDRIVDIST$_{-1}$		1.15E+06*	0.19	3.76E+04
		(1.76)	(0.68)	(0.12)
ΔDRIVDIST$_{-2}$	0.47*			
	(1.88)			
ΔPurse$_{-1}$	7.8E-08	0.52**	4.8E-07*	7.81E-04
	(1.01)	(2.57)	(1.90)	(0.00)
Adj. R^2	0.29	0.41	0.09	0.00
n	16	17	17	17

Notes:
*, **, *** denote statistical significance at the 0.1, 0.05, and 0.01 levels.
a.   In yards.
b.   In undeflated millions of dollars.
c.   In deflated (1982–84) dollars.

These inferences are reversed for women. In the third column, the lagged change in purse size influences the change in driving distance, even after controlling for the (insignificant) first-lag effect in driving distance. So there is evidence consistent with the hypothesis that the increased prize funds for women have spurred efforts to increase the length of their tee shots, and that the efforts have paid off.

Column four shows that the increased length of women's tee shots does not seem to be a factor in the growth of prize money for women. There is virtually no explanatory power for the first difference in purses from either lagged changes in driving distance or lagged changes in the purses themselves.

Overall, these results are hampered by the small sample size.

Unfortunately, the comparable statistics on golfer skills do not go back far enough in time. Nevertheless, a coherent story emerges from the data. For men, the prodigiously increased length of tee shots, whether from technological innovation or practice, has been a factor in the fast-growing prize funds on the PGA TOUR. The 'drive for show' part of the old adage is in operation, as the popularity of long drivers, such as Tiger Woods, Phil Mickelson, and John Daly, has fueled the growth in purses. The same, however, is not true for women in LPGA events.

Meanwhile, on the incentives side, the purse growth does not seem to be a factor in bringing about longer drives for men. Perhaps men have already been maximizing their efforts in this dimension of the game. Most of the increased length of drives could then be attributable to technology.[4] But for women, the increased purses may be bringing about extra practice and effort to increase driving distance in the desire to cash in on the higher prizes. Curiously, higher prizes have always been available to women on the men's Tour if they wanted to compete directly against men. However, this has not brought the women's driving distance up to the men's level. The fact that there is a higher dollars per-yard return on the PGA TOUR than in LPGA events is irrelevant to women because they almost never play in PGA TOUR sponsored events. As a result, the relevant marginal increase in prize money occurs in LPGA events. It is reassuring that auxiliary regressions (not shown here) testing for Granger causality from men's distance to women's purse growth or from men's purse growth to women's driving distance show no correlations. Nor is there evidence that men's purses Granger-cause women's purses or that any women's variables Granger-cause any men's variables. These regressions are statistically insignificant, which provides a robustness and consistency check on the regressions reported in this chapter.

4.5 CONCLUSION

Most of the skills in golf do not necessarily depend upon brute strength or physical size, but driving distance may be the exception.[5] Therefore, if women's and men's skills converge in this dimension, golf may become gender neutral. An examination of driving distance indicates that both men's and women's driving distances increased from 1992 to 2010, probably due to innovations in club and ball designs and materials. Unfortunately, although women started to catch up to men in the 1990s, the gains were transitory. As a result, women are unlikely to compete against men in golf in the foreseeable future.

Although women and men typically compete on distinct Tours, the separation is not based on *de jure* segregation. Men are precluded from entering LPGA-sponsored events, but the PGA TOUR is explicitly non-discriminatory. Even though purses are lower in LPGA events, women self-segregate. When women compete with other women, they have higher expected returns, conditional on their skills, than on the PGA TOUR. Women might be motivated to improve their driving distance by prize levels in LPGA events, but they are not further motivated by the even higher purses on the PGA TOUR. Thus, women are motivated more by the attainable lower prizes in LPGA events than by the much higher prizes on the PGA TOUR.

In contrast, men are not motivated by increases in prize funds to increase their driving distances in terms of Granger causality. Given the already high prize funds in 1992, perhaps men were already practicing to the point of sharply diminishing returns so that the extra motivation supplied by the increases in prizes did not lead to a measurably significant increase in practice. There does, however, seem to be Granger causality from driving distance to prize funds. Spectators enjoy the long distances of professional golfers' drives, and purse increases have followed driving distance increases that result from technological innovations in golf-club and golf-ball design.

The impact of driving distance on overall performance and on purse size creates a vicious cycle for women's golf. Their shorter drives keep women from succeeding on the men's Tour. At the same time, shorter driving distances make women's golf less attractive to audiences and sponsors, increasing the difference in rewards on the two Tours. Separate and unequal golf Tours will thus persist.

NOTES

1. Historical information was gleaned from the following websites: www.uswomensopen.com/2002/history; www.usga.org/champnewsarchive.aspx; www.pgatour.com; www.lpga.com. Another good source is Crosset (1995).
2. There is a higher return to putting and reaching greens in regulation in LPGA-sponsored tournaments.
3. If the increased prize funds are anticipated, then the driving distance skill could be developed beforehand thus leading to contemporaneous increases, but there seems to be little reason to increase the skill *because of the money* even before the money arrives.
4. Technology growth may have been continuous over the period in question, but the application of the technology is also subject to the rules-making bodies in professional golf. Interestingly, driving distance appears to have leveled after 2002, at about the same time when rules were adopted limiting certain technical aspects of golf-ball and golf-club design. See Stachura (2002).
5. For a different perspective on the value of specific skills to performance in golf, see Chapter 18 in this volume.

REFERENCES

Alexander, Donald and William Kern (2005), 'Drive for Show and Putt for Dough? An Analysis of the Earnings of PGA Tour Golfers', *Journal of Sports Economics*, **6**(1), February: 46–60.

Berry, Scott M. (1999), 'Drive for Show and Putt for Dough', *Chance*, **12**(4): 50–55.

Callan, Scott J. and Janet M. Thomas (2007), 'Modeling the Determinants of a Professional Golfer's Tournament Earnings: A Multiequation Approach', *Journal of Sports Economics*, **8**(4), August: 394–411.

Crosset, Todd W. (1995), *Outsiders in the Clubhouse: The World of Women's Professional Golf*, Albany, NY: State University of New York Press.

Davidson, James D. and Thomas J. Templin (1986), 'Determinants of Success Among Professional Golfers', *Research Quarterly for Exercise and Sport*, **57**(1), March: 60–67.

Fearing, Douglas, Jason Acimovic and Stephen C. Graves (2011), 'How to Catch a Tiger: Understanding Putting Performance on the PGA TOUR', *Journal of Quantitative Analysis in Sports*, **7**(1), January.

Fried, Harold O., James Lambrinos and James Tyner (2004), 'Evaluating the Performance of Professional Golfers on the PGA, LPGA, and SPGA Tours', *European Journal of Operational Research*, **154**(2), April: 548–61.

Granger, Clive W.J. (1969), 'Investigating Causal Relations by Econometric Models and Cross-Spectral Methods', *Econometrica*, **37**(3), July: 424–38.

Kahane, Leo H. (2010), 'Returns to Skills in Professional Golf: A Quantile Regression Approach', *International Journal of Sport Finance*, **5**(3), August: 167–80.

Kalist, David E. (2008), 'Does Motherhood Affect Productivity, Relative Performance, and Earnings?', *Journal of Labor Research*, **29**(3), September: 219–35.

Marple, David (1983), 'Tournament Earnings and Performance Differentials between the Sexes in Professional Golf and Tennis', *Journal of Sports and Social Issues*, **7**(1), March: 1–14.

Matthews, Peter Hans, Paul M. Sommers and Francisco J. Peschiera (2007), 'Incentives and Superstars on the LPGA Tour', *Applied Economics*, **39**(1), October: 87–94.

Moy, Ronald L. and Thomas Liaw (1998), 'Determinants of Professional Golf Tournament Earnings', *The American Economist*, **42**(1), Spring: 65–70.

Nero, Peter (2001), 'Relative Salary Efficiency of PGA Tour Golfers', *The American Economist*, **45**(1), Fall: 51–6.

Nix, Charles L. and Robert Koslow (1991), 'Physical Skill Factors Contributing to Success on the Professional Golf Tour', *Perceptual and Motor Skills*, **72**(3c), June: 1272–4.

Oaxaca, Ronald (1973), 'Male–Female Wage Differentials in Urban Labor Markets', *International Economic Review*, **14**(3), October: 693–709.

Pfitzner, C. Barry and Tracy D. Rishel (2005), 'Performance and Compensation on the LPGA Tour: A Statistical Analysis', *International Journal of Performance Analysis in Sport*, **5**(3), December: 29–39.

Rishe, Patrick James (2001), 'Differing Rates of Return to Performance: A Comparison of the PGA and Senior Golf Tours', *Journal of Sports Economics*, **2**(3), August: 285–96.

Scully, Gerald W. (2002), 'The Distribution of Performance and Earnings in a Prize Economy', *Journal of Sports Economics*, **3**(3), August: 235–45.

Shaffer, Thomas L., Daniel P. Connaughton, Ronald A. Siders and John F. Mahoney (2000), 'An Analysis of the Most Significant Variables for Predicting Scoring Average and Money Won per Event in Professional Golf', *Research Quarterly for Exercise and Sport*, **71**(1), March: 119A–20A.

Shin, Eui Hang and Edward Adam Nam (2004), 'Culture, Gender Roles, and Sport: The Case of Korean Players on the LPGA Tour', *Journal of Sport and Social Issues*, **28**(3), August: 223–44.

Shmanske, Stephen (1992), 'Human Capital Formation in Professional Sports: Evidence from the PGA Tour', *Atlantic Economic Journal*, **20**(3), September: 66–80.

Shmanske, Stephen (2000), 'Gender, Skill, and Earnings in Professional Golf', *Journal of Sports Economics*, **1**(4), November: 400–415.

Shmanske, Stephen (2004), *Golfonomics*, River Edge, NJ: World Scientific.

Shmanske, Stephen (2008), 'Skills, Performance, and Earnings in the Tournament Compensation Model: Evidence from PGA Tour Microdata', *Journal of Sports Economics*, **9**(6), December: 644–62.

Shmanske, Stephen (2012), 'Gender and Discrimination in Professional Golf', in Shmanske and L. Kahane (eds), *The Oxford Handbook of Sports Economics, Volume 2: Economics through Sports*, New York: Oxford University Press, pp. 33–54.

Sommers, Paul M. (1994), 'A Bread and Putter Model', *Atlantic Economic Journal*, **22**(4), December: 77.

Stachura, Mike (2002), 'About-Face: The USGA's Final Edict on COR Should End the Confusion Over Which Drivers Conform and Which Do Not', *Golf Digest*, **53**, October.

Stockl, Michael, Peter F. Lamb and Martin Lames (2011), 'The ISOPAR Method: A New Approach to Performance Analysis in Golf', *Journal of Quantitative Analysis in Sports*, **7**(1).

Tiruneh, Gizachew (2010), 'Age and Winning in Professional Golf Tours', *Journal of Quantitative Analysis in Sports*, **6**(1), January.

Wiseman, Frederick, Sangit Chatterjee, David Wiseman and Neil S. Chatterjee (1994), 'An Analysis of 1992 Performance Statistics for Players on the U.S. PGA, Senior PGA, and LPGA Tours', in A.J. Cochran and M.R. Farrally (eds), *Science and Golf: II. Proceedings of the World Scientific Congress of Golf*, London: E & FN Spon, pp. 199–204.

5. Gender differences in responses to incentives in sports: some new results from golf

Keith F. Gilsdorf and Vasant A. Sukhatme*

5.1 INTRODUCTION

Women and men make very different labor market decisions, which lead to different employment rates, employment patterns, and earnings. For example, women are underrepresented in many high-profile jobs, including those in academia and public administration. Research in psychology has reported that women and men gravitate toward different incentive systems; men are eager to compete, but women shy away from competition. More than men, women prefer to work under piece-rate systems in which rewards are based on absolute performance as opposed to tournament pay systems in which rewards depend on relative performance.

Some of the early literature on this issue concluded that the earnings differences were caused by gender discrimination (Goldin and Rouse, 2000). Others claimed that women self-selected into jobs that did not demand large investments in human capital because they anticipated lower returns to such investment because they would leave the labor force (at least temporarily) after having children (Polachek, 1981). Over the last decade or so, economists and other social scientists have examined other hypotheses, among them the proposition that part of the gender pay gap arises from different reactions to prize incentives. Croson and Gneezy (2009) review experimental evidence on preference differences between men and women, focusing on three factors that have been extensively studied: risk preferences, social preferences, and reaction to competition. They find that women are more risk averse and more competition averse than men.

Several papers examine why men and women respond differently. Gneezy et al. (2009) argue that cultural factors play an important role in explaining gender differences in competitiveness, while Buser (2009) focuses on biological factors. Other scholars argue that differences in incentive structures lie at the root of the gender differences in competitiveness (Manning and Saidi, 2008).

The first objective of this chapter is to survey the work that has addressed the different responses men and women have to incentive structures and competitiveness in sports. While we focus on sports, we also selectively survey gender differences in experimental settings. Second, we use data from the 2009 men's and women's professional golf Tours to report new findings of the effects of prize money on player performance. Section 5.2 reports the outcomes of research focusing on gender differences in completing various tasks, such as solving mazes or math problems in experimental settings. Section 5.3 surveys the sports economics literature that addresses differences in men's and women's responsiveness to total prize money and prize spreads in tournaments. Section 5.4 reports our estimates of gender differences in professional golf. This work draws on a unique dataset that has several interesting features. Our data include 28 PGA (Professional Golf Association) and 16 LPGA (Ladies Professional Golf Association) tournaments in 2009, and we use objective measures of course difficulty and opponent and player performance. These features allow us to examine gender differences in response to financial incentives. Section 5.5 reports the results of our estimation. We find that larger tournament purses increase both women's and men's total scores, but the effect is slightly greater for women. Focusing on final round scores only, women improve their performance under several alternative specifications that we considered while men's scores worsen in all circumstances. Section 5.6 concludes and suggests further work on this important issue.

5.2   GENDER DIFFERENCES IN EXPERIMENTAL STUDIES

Gneezy et al. (2003) and Gneezy and Rustichini (2004) are the first experimental studies that examine the interaction of gender and competition. Gneezy et al. find that men react positively to tournament-style incentives while women react positively only when they compete against other women. Gneezy and Rustichini find essentially the same result using an experimental setting in which nine- and 10-year-old schoolchildren race against each other without any monetary rewards involved. Children ran alone and then in pairs with varying gender compositions. Boys run faster than girls when competing against someone else, regardless of the competitor's gender, but both boys and girls perform the same when they run alone.

Ivanova-Stenzel and Kubler (2005) examine the role of gender in teamwork. Their experiment looks at group incentives and productivity, focusing on the relevance of gender for the optimal composition of a team. They conclude that performance depends on both the incentive scheme and the genders of the group members. Holding the incentive scheme fixed, they find that the gender composition of the team matters for teamwork but not for team competition. Men perform worst when the benefits are shared with other men in a cooperative environment. Men's performance increases when women are present or when the environment is competitive, or both. In contrast, women do best when competing against men but reduce their work effort when paired with men in the case of team pay. Ivanova-Stenzel and Kubler also observe that there is a significant gender difference in performance in mixed teams that is not present in single-sex teams. These findings are broadly consistent with the findings of Gneezy et al. even when the former come from teamwork and team competition and the latter from individual performance.

Niederle and Vesterlund (2005) find that there is no difference between the performances of men and women in a competitive environment, but women are less willing than men to compete in tournaments when given the opportunity to work under piece rates. Dohmen and Falk (2006) confirm this finding. Their experimental approach consists of having subjects complete a series of arithmetic computations that vary in difficulty. Before subjects start to work, they are offered a variable pay contract and a fixed-payment contract. The chosen contract determines how subjects are paid for the output they produce in the work period. There are three types of variable pay schemes: piece-rate, tournament, and revenue-sharing contracts. Their results show that women are 15 percent less likely to enter a variable pay scheme than men when the alternative is a fixed payment. Sorting, therefore, offers a channel for gender differences in occupational choice, career choice, and ultimately wages.

Datta-Gupta et al. (2005) consider whether women and men make different choices because they have different attitudes toward competition. In their experimental setting, subjects choose between a tournament and a piece-rate reward scheme *before* they perform a real task. Men choose the tournament significantly more frequently than do women. Risk matters less for men when they choose their payment scheme than for women whose choices of payment schemes are more heavily influenced by their degree of risk aversion.

In a follow-up paper, Niederle and Vesterlund (2007) examine whether men and women of the same ability differ in their selection of a competitive environment. Their experimental subjects complete a real task first under a non-competitive piece rate scheme and then under a competitive tournament scheme. Participants then select one of the two compensation schemes to apply to their next performance. They find that the majority of men select the competitive tournament, whereas the majority of women select the non-competitive piece rate. Further, low-performing men enter tournaments more frequently while high-performing women enter less frequently than is warranted from a payoff-maximizing perspective. The gender gap in tournament theory can be explained in part by men's being more confident than women about their relative rank, and by men and women having different attitudes toward competition.

Niederle et al. (2008) use experimental methods to examine how affirmative action affects entry into tournaments. They find that when women are guaranteed equal representation among winners, more women and fewer men enter competitions. Affirmative action, which affects tournament entry through changes in the probability of winning, is one of several factors that affect entry. The authors investigate a quota-like affirmative action environment in which women must be at least equally represented among those hired. They find that affirmative action encourages women to enter while discouraging men from entering. They speculate that the mere mention of affirmative action changes the decision to enter a tournament. Their experimental design allows them to characterize how the composition of the applicant pool changes with affirmative action. They find that, prior to affirmative action, only a few high-performing women chose to compete and thus rarely won tournaments.

As noted in the introduction, Gneezy et al. (2009) study the impact of nurture on attitudes toward competition by investigating two distinct societies, the patriarchal society of the Maasai tribe of Tanzania and the matriarchal society of the Khasi tribe of India. The authors conducted a field experiment in which members of each tribe were given the opportunity to compete in a contest that consisted of tossing a tennis ball into a bucket. The authors find that, in the patriarchal society, women are less competitive than men. In the matriarchal society, women are more competitive. Moreover, Khasi women are more competitive than Maasai men. The authors claim that their results provide a link between culture and behaviors that affect economic outcomes.

Booth and Nolen (2009) examine the role of nurture in explaining the stylized conclusion that women shy away from competition. They use a controlled experiment in which the subjects are students just below age 15 who attend publicly funded single-sex and coeducational schools in the UK. Their evidence suggests that a girl's environment plays an important role in explaining why she chooses not to compete: girls from single-sex schools behave more competitively and more like boys than do girls from co-educational schools.

The studies summarized use experimental settings in which subjects complete tasks such as adding up sets of numbers or solving mazes or racing relatively short distances. In these settings, men and women react differently to prize incentives depending on whether the experiments involve single-sex or mixed gender competitions. We now turn to how tournament settings affect performance in sports.

5.3   GENDER DIFFERENCES IN SPORTS

Empirical research on the effects of financial incentives on individual performance in sports tournaments began with the seminal work on golf by Ehrenberg and Bognanno (1990a and 1990b), who studied the 1984 PGA TOUR and 1987 European PGA TOUR. They tested the predictions of tournament theory from two perspectives: (a) whether a tournament's total prize money affects a golfer's total score after four rounds, and (b) changes in marginal returns to effort in the tournament's final round affect a golfer's final-round score. Their findings in both studies found support for tournament theory predictions. A $100,000 increase in total prize money reduces total scores by about one stroke on the PGA TOUR and three strokes on the European Tour. In the final round, a one standard deviation increase in marginal returns lowers scores by one to three strokes, with the upper end of that range reflecting performance on the European Tour. They also find that prize money differences have a larger incentive effect in the final two rounds than in the first two rounds of the tournament. Finally, they show that players perform better when participating in major tournaments and when facing a less competitive field.

In contrast, Matthews et al. (2007) find no positive incentive effects for women on the 2000 LPGA Tour. They use the top 50 money winners for that year in their sample and find that higher total prize money actually increases total scores. Their results do not change when the sample includes only the top 20 or 35 money winners. Based on their estimates, a $100,000 increase in total prize money increases a player's golf score by 0.28 strokes. Their results also indicate that major tournaments have no effect on player scores. Finally, like Ehrenberg and Bognanno, they find that women's scores improve as the mean scoring average of the field increases, suggesting that players perform better as the opponents' ability level declines.

Matthews et al. offer several possible explanations for their results: (a) financial incentives may not affect concentration and effort levels for female golfers; (b) financial incentives affect performance but only over a long period of time; (c) LPGA prize money levels are much lower and may not change effort levels appreciably, even in lower-paying tournaments. The authors also suggest a superstar effect of Karrie Webb during the 2000 season. Webb's presence in a tournament may have adversely affected the responsiveness of other golfers to financial incentives and caused their scores to increase. However, excluding tournaments entered by Webb also causes the opponent's ability and par variables to reverse sign, indicating that women perform better when facing superior opponents and more difficult courses.

Other research on golf provides mixed evidence regarding tournament theory. Orszag (1994) re-examines Ehrenberg and Bognanno's PGA (1990a) study by using their total score model on data from the 1992 PGA Tour. He finds that total prize money has no significant effect on total golf scores and that players' scores are higher in major tournaments, contrary to tournament theory predictions. He suggests that substantially higher purses in 1992 may have increased player nervousness and caused more people to 'choke' under greater pressure. The other possibility is simply that prize money does not significantly affect effort or concentration over four rounds in a tournament.

In the spirit of Gneezy et al. (2003), Cotton and Price (2006) study the performance of male and female golfers ages 12–17 participating in American Junior Golf Association (AJGA) tournaments. They examine the existence of a 'hot hand', that is, whether the probability that an individual succeeds in the current period depends on whether the individual succeeded in previous periods. They find that women are more prone to experiencing performance streaks than men. Further, they find that hot hands occur in the first year of AJGA tournament competition but that they virtually disappear by the third year of tournament play. Cotton and Price interpret their results as being consistent with the broader literature, which has shown that men and women respond differently to competition. However, their preferred explanation for the initial gender difference is that men are more likely to have had competitive experience prior to joining the AJGA tournament than women. When women accumulate enough tournament experience, the gender difference virtually disappears.

Ehrenberg and Bognanno's research has sparked other studies of sports tournaments, including professional bowling, car racing, foot racing, and professional tennis. Most of these studies have focused on men's rather than women's sports. As von Allmen (2006) states, evidence on gender differences in competitive environments is limited, especially in professional sports, but there are several exceptions. We focus here on the responses of men and women to incentives in foot racing and tennis.

Maloney and McCormick (2000) analyze the effect of average prize levels and prize money spreads on race times in open invitational foot races held in the southeastern United States from 1987 to 1991. They find that larger overall prize levels attract better racers, and larger prize spreads increase effort and lower individual race times, consistent with tournament theory. The authors also separate out gender effects and find that faster women have a greater response to overall prize levels, but men respond more to larger prize spreads.

Frick and Prinz (2007) argue that Maloney and McCormick's study inappropriately combines all distance-type races and focuses only on regional races that do not attract a large number of elite racers. Instead, Frick (2011a) mentions two earlier studies that he conducted of professional marathons. Those earlier results indicate that increases in purse size and prize distribution reduce women's finishing times more than men's, but that bonus payments have no impact. Frick explains this by arguing that the distribution of ability is more homogeneous among male elite marathon runners than among female elite marathon runners. Therefore, women do not need to exert additional effort in response to bonus payments because they can win with less than maximal effort.

Frick (2011a) extends his analysis on road racing by analyzing finishing time differentials between men and women covering the 200 best finishes in races ranging from 3,000 meters to marathons. The dependent variable in his analysis is the percentage difference in finishing time between female and male runners by race type and runner rank. He argues that if women exhibit a lower degree of competitiveness, the percentage difference in finish times should increase with rank. For all race types, he finds that the percentage difference in finish times increases quickly at first and then rises at a diminishing rate.

Frick finds that gender differences have declined considerably over time, especially in races that offer greater financial rewards. He computes the coefficient of variation (variance divided by mean) for the top 200 performances by men and women in races of varying lengths and finds that the coefficients of variation for the two genders are strongly correlated. He also finds that the average ages of the men and women with the top-200 times at varying distances are correlated. He concludes that women and men respond similarly to financial incentives.

Frick (2011b) finds similar results for ultramarathons. The percentage difference between men and women's finish times increases with rank, first at a decreasing rate and then at an increasing rate, yet the difference appears to have fallen over time and to have fallen more significantly in the more lucrative 100km races. In addition, he reports that the variance in the top 100 performances of both men and women is smaller in the races with higher prizes and a larger pool of runners.

Deaner's (2006a) results for men's and women's performance in distance running are similar to those of Frick (2011a). He shows that gender differences in world-class running performances have stabilized at 10–15 percent across all races from 3,000 meters to marathons. Using gender-specific world records as a baseline for comparing performance across sexes, Deaner finds that, among elite US runners, two to four times as many men as women run fast relative to sex-specific world-class standards. Deaner (2006b) examines whether this sex difference also holds for the non-elite participants of road races that offer equivalent prizes for men and women. For the 20 largest 5,000-meter road races and marathons held in the USA in 2003, proportionally more men run close to sex-specific world-class standards than women. Deaner concludes that the potentially elite US runners are disproportionately male.

Several studies have also examined the responsiveness of men and women to monetary incentives in tennis. However, these studies focus either on the men's or the women's professional tennis tours, making direct comparisons difficult. Lallemand et al. (2008) and Gilsdorf and Sukhatme (2008a) found that women respond to prize money incentives. Using data from the final two rounds of WTA (Women's Tennis Association) tournaments from the 2002–04 Tours, Lallemand et al. find that doubling the prize spread increases the number of games won in a match by between 0.7 and 1.

Lallemand et al. also attempt to distinguish between the incentive effect and the capability effect of differences in player abilities. According to the incentive effect, greater differences in ability reduce effort and performance of both the underdog and the favorite. The capability effect suggests that the underdog exerts less effort but the favorite plays better. Their results indicate that larger ability differences reduce the number of games won by underdogs but increase games won by the favorites beyond what one would expect from ability differences alone. In addition, the margin of victory reflected in the difference in games won also increases by about 0.55 games with a doubling of ability differences. The authors argue that these findings suggest that the capability effect dominates in professional women's tennis. In contrast, Sunde (2009) finds that the incentive effect outweighs the capability effect for professional men's tennis.

Gilsdorf and Sukhatme (2008a) use data from the 2004 WTA Tour and test whether higher prize money differentials increase the probability that the favored player wins the match. After controlling for player- and tournament-specific characteristics, their findings support Rosen's (1986) elimination tournament model. An increase in the prize differential from the 25th percentile to the mean ($25,700 to $161,580) increases the favorite's probability of winning the match by 1.8 percentage points. The authors also conduct a similar study of the 2001 men's professional tennis tour (Gilsdorf and Sukhatme, 2008b) and find that an increase in the prize differential from the 25th percentile ($50,280) to the mean ($241,960) increases the favorite's probability of winning by about 1.9 percentage points. However, given the different sample period and model specifications, any direct comparisons of responsiveness should be made with caution.

Paserman (2010) analyzes data from the 2005–07 Grand Slam tennis tournaments to see if performance declines as pressure increases during a match. His preferred measure of performance measure is the probability of winning a point. In a match between players of equal ability, the one who can maintain performance at the most critical points of a match can increase the probability of winning from 50 to 80 percent. His results indicate that there is no significant gender difference in the probability of winning the point even while women make more unforced errors. He notes that both men and women adopt strategies that cause both the probability of making unforced errors and the probability of hitting winners to rise. Thus, he states that women, in this context, do not behave differently from men as competitive pressure rises.

5.4   A NEW MODEL OF INCENTIVES IN GOLF

Our work contributes to the literature in several ways. First, we address the contradictory findings of Orszag (1994) and Matthews et al. (2007) regarding the sensitivity of effort to prize money in professional golf. Second, we extend the literature on gender differences in economic contests to professional golf. We collect 2009 data for both the PGA and the LPGA tournaments, which allows us to test for gender differences in the effect of incentives on player performance. Third, our data are from single-sex tournaments and include individuals who voluntarily participate in a highly competitive environment, reducing the complications associated with using both mixed and single-sex groups. In their survey of differences in gender preferences, Croson and Gneezy (2009) cite numerous studies that find women respond more to the experimental setting than men do.

We adopt the total score methodology employed by Ehrenberg and Bognanno (1990a and 1990b), Orszag (1994), and Matthews et al. (2007). We also follow Ehrenberg and Bognanno's final-round score approach using marginal prize variables based on the players' rank after the third round.

In our empirical model, a player's total score depends on the tournament's total purse, player ability, the ability of the opponents, and tournament-specific characteristics. Specifically, the baseline model to be estimated is:

$$TSCORE_{ij} = \beta_0 + \beta_1 RRANKPT_{ij} + \beta_2 RCCUTSM_{ij} + \beta_3 RTOP10_i$$
$$+ \beta_4 FRACT20_j + \beta_5 OPPRANK_j + \beta_6 PRIZE_j$$
$$+ \beta_7 RDIST_j + \beta_8 PAR_j + \beta_9 MAJOR_j + u_{ij}, \qquad (5.1)$$

where ij represents player i in tournament j. The variables are:

$TSCORE_{ij}$	=	total score after four rounds for player i in tournament j;
$RRANKPT_{ij}$	=	player i's official world ranking points per event prior to tournament j divided by ranking points per event for the 150th officially ranked player prior to tournament j;
$RCCUTSM_{ij}$	=	player i's career cuts made through 2008 divided by the mean number of career cuts made through 2008 by the top 150 money winners in 2009;
$RTOP10_i$	=	player i's career number of top 10 finishes through 2008 divided by the mean number of career top 10 finishes through 2008 by the top 150 money winners in 2009;
$FRACT20_j$	=	the percentage of players who made the cut in tournament j that were ranked in the top 20 of the official world rankings prior to the tournament;
$OPPRANK_j$	=	mean official world-ranking points per event prior to tournament j of players who made the cut in tournament j divided by the ranking points per event of the 150th officially ranked player prior to tournament j;
$PRIZE_j$	=	total published prize money for tournament j measured in thousands of dollars;
$RDIST_j$	=	total course yardage of tournament j divided by the mean yardage of all four-round tournaments on the respective tour;
PAR_j	=	the par for tournament course j; and
$MAJOR_j$	=	a dummy variable equal to 1 if tournament j is a major tournament and 0 otherwise.

Our sample includes players who ranked among the top:

1. 150 money winners for 2009;
2. 150 in scoring average for 2009; and
3. 300 in official world rankings just prior to the tournament entered.

This leaves 142 women and 132 men in the sample. By restricting our sample to the top golfers, our results might be subject to self-selection bias. Specifically, our results might not be generalizable to all golfers on the respective Tours. For example, amateurs who receive exemptions to participate in PGA or LPGA events are not included in the samples.

Our data come from four-round tournaments with a player cut after the first two rounds. We include 28 of the 37 regular-season PGA tournaments and 16 of the LPGA's 29 regular-season tournaments, resulting in 1,204 and 1,060 observations for the PGA and the LPGA tournaments, respectively. Like Ehrenburg and Bognanno, we dropped the British Open from our sample for men, though we include it for women.

The PGA and LPGA websites provide much of the data, including player scores, career cuts made, career top 10 finishes, course yardage, par, and prize money. The websites also provide links to official world-ranking statistics for the top 300 men and women golfers during the season. Table 5.1 lists the PGA and LPGA tournaments included in the study along with their respective published prize money, par value, and course yardage. The average prize money for the PGA and LPGA tournaments is $5,700,000 and $1,948,785, respectively. If we include the British Open, the average PGA purse is $5,800,000, almost three times more than the LPGA average.

Based on tournament theory, we expect performance to improve as the prize and pressure increase, that is, we expect the coefficients for *PRIZE* and *MAJOR* to be negative. We also expect the coefficients for *RRANKPT*, *RCCUTSM*, and *RTOP10* to be negative since each variable measures a player's relative ability. Higher relative ranking points earned per event, career cuts made, and career top 10 finishes all suggest higher ability levels and therefore lower total scores. *RDIST* and *PAR* measure course difficulty, so we expect their coefficients to be positive. Finally, Ehrenberg and Bognanno (1990, 1990b) suggest that *FRACT20* and *OPPRANK* have positive coefficients because facing better opponents reduces the probability of winning and therefore lowers incentives to increase effort.

5.5   EMPIRICAL RESULTS

Table 5.2 lists the means and standard deviations of our variables. Using OLS, we estimate equation (5.1) separately for PGA and LPGA data. Table 5.3 reports the coefficient estimates and *t*-statistics, as well as gender differences in the coefficient estimates and their *t*-statistics. Tests not shown here indicate the presence of heteroskedasticity, so we report *t*-statistics using White's heteroskedasticity corrected standard errors. The

Table 5.1   *Sample tournaments, prize money, par, and course distance*

PGA				LPGA			
Tournament	Prize money	Par	Distance (yards)	Tournament	Prize money	Par	Distance (yards)
Legends	3,000,000	72	7,451	CVS	1,100,000	72	6,185
Puerto Rico	3,500,000	72	7,569	Corona	1,300,000	73	6,539
Mayakoba	3,600,000	70	6,923	Navistar	1,300,000	72	6,460
US Bank	4,000,000	70	6,759	Jamie Farr	1,400,000	71	6,428
John Deere	4,300,000	71	7,183	J Golf	1,500,000	72	6,711
Canada Open	5,100,000	72	7,222	Corning	1,500,000	72	6,223
Buick Open	5,100,000	72	7,127	State Farm	1,700,000	72	6,746
Wyndam	5,100,000	70	7,130	Kraft Nabisco*	2,000,000	72	6,673
Buick Invitational	5,300,000	72	7,569	Sybase	2,000,000	72	6,413
Sony Open	5,400,000	70	7,044	McDonalds*	2,000,000	72	6,641
Transitions	5,400,000	71	7,295	Wegmans	2,000,000	72	6,365
Honda	5,600,000	70	7,241	British Open*	2,158,550	72	6,492
St. Jude	5,600,000	70	7,244	Michelob	2,200,000	71	6,853
Shell	5,700,000	72	7,457	Canadian Open	2,585,007	71	6,427
Verizon	5,700,000	71	6,973	US Open *	3,187,000	71	6,740
FBR Open	6,000,000	71	7,216	Evian Masters	3,250,000	72	6,344
Arnold Palmer	6,000,000	70	7,239				
Travelers	6,000,000	70	6,820				
AT&T National	6,000,000	70	7,255				
Valero	6,100,000	70	6,896				
Northern Trust	6,300,000	71	7,298				
Zurich	6,300,000	72	7,341				
Quail Hollow	6,500,000	72	7,442				
HP Byron	6,500,000	70	7,166				
Masters *	7,000,000	72	7,435				
US Open*	7,500,000	70	7,445				
PGA * Championship	7,500,000	72	7,674				
The Players	9,500,000	72	7,215				

Note: * Major tournaments on the Tours.

coefficients for *RDIST*, *PAR*, and *RRANKPT* have the expected sign for both men and women. The effect of the course difficulty is statistically different for the PGA and the LPGA tournaments. A 1 percent increase in relative distance raises scores by almost one full stroke for men but only 0.3 strokes for women. The opposite occurs for *PAR*, as a one-stroke

Table 5.2   Means and standard deviations of key variables

Variable	PGA		LPGA	
	Mean	Std dev.	Mean	Std dev.
TSCORE	280.34	7.35	285.57	7.95
RRANKPT	1.72	1.42	4.32	4.28
RCCUTSM	1.03	0.83	1.05	0.99
RTOP10	0.98	1.10	1.14	1.57
FRACT20	0.09	0.07	0.18	0.05
OPPRANK	1.62	0.49	4.56	0.70
PRIZE	5,894.7	1,276.2	1,920.4	610.26
RDIST	1.00	0.03	1.00	0.03
PAR	70.94	0.89	71.81	0.52
MAJOR	0.09	0.29	0.23	0.42

Table 5.3   OLS results for LPGA and PGA regressions

Variable	LPGA		PGA		Coefficient difference	t-statistic
	Coefficient	t-statistic	Coefficient	t-statistic		
RRANKPT	−0.54***	−9.21	−0.58***	−3.59	0.035	0.20
RCCUTSM	0.61	1.56	0.29	0.66		
RTOP10	−0.28	−1.13	−0.21	−0.55		
FRACT20	−55.16***	−5.16	3.84	0.57	−59***	−4.66
OPPRANK	3.94***	4.07	−1.36	−1.01	5.30***	3.20
PRIZE	0.004***	8.26	0.001***	7.39	0.003***	4.62
RDIST	30.84***	4.05	95.92***	11.66	−65.08***	−5.81
PAR	4.49***	12.10	1.57***	6.80	2.92***	6.69
MAJOR	6.20***	9.20	3.64***	3.79	2.56**	2.18
Constant	−82.50***	−2.79	66.97***	5.35		
Adjusted R^2	0.42		0.42			
Observations	1,060		1,204			

Note: *Significant at 10 percent level; **Significant at 5 percent level; ***Significant at 1 percent level.

increase raises women's scores by almost 4.5 strokes but only about 1.5 strokes for men.

The *RRANKPT* coefficients for both the PGA and the LPGA tournaments are similar and statistically indistinguishable. A 1 percent increase in rank points per event relative to the 150th-ranked player reduces the total score by about 0.005 strokes for both men and women. The average

RRANKPT is 4.32 for women and 1.72 for men. A player with this relative ranking would have a total score about 1.8 and 0.41 strokes lower than the 150th officially ranked player, respectively.[1] Neither of the ability variables, *RRCUTSM* and *RTOP10*, is statistically significant for either the PGA or the LPGA tournament.

The coefficients for the opponent ability variables, *FRACT20* and *OPPRANK*, conflict with one another in the LPGA sample. A 1 percent increase in the number of players ranked in the top 20 reduces scores by a little over half a stroke, but a 1 percent increase in the average ranking point per event relative to the 150th-ranked player increases scores by approximately 0.04 strokes. However, the estimates are insignificant for men. *FRACT20* and *OPPRANK* are highly correlated in both samples, suggesting that multicollinearity could be an issue. In an estimation not shown here we drop *OPPRANK* from the men's equation. When we do this, *FRACT20* becomes negative but remains statistically insignificant.

Finally, the *PRIZE* and *MAJOR* coefficients are positive for men and women. A $100,000 increase in prize money increases total scores by 0.38 strokes for women and 0.15 strokes for men. In addition, playing in a major tournament raises a player's total score by about 6.2 and 3.7 strokes for women and men. Gender differences in both *PRIZE* and *MAJOR* coefficients are also statistically significant. The *PRIZE* findings support the results found by Matthews et al. (2007) for the women's tour but conflict with Ehrenberg and Bognanno's (1990a, 1990b) earlier findings on the men's tours and, to some degree, with Orszag's since he found no significant relationship between prize money and performance. Our results for *MAJOR* are consistent with Orszag but differ from Matthews et al., as they found this variable to be insignificant.

One concern with our specification is that par and course distance may not adequately capture course difficulty. Ehrenberg and Bognanno (1990a) use course rating as well as par to measure course difficulty. They obtain ratings measures from a representative from the Metropolitan Golf Association and various state golf associations. We do not have official course rating measures for the actual PGA and LPGA tournaments. Instead, we obtained course rating measures for all but two PGA and two LPGA tournaments from the websites of state and regional golf associations or the tournament course website. We choose the highest published course rating associated with each gender's tee box. Excluding the two PGA and LPGA tournaments for which we have no ratings from our sample reduces the number of observations to 1,134 for men and 949 for women.[2] Equation (5.1) thus becomes:

$$TSCORE_{ij} = \beta_0 + \beta_1 RRANKPT_{ij} + \beta_2 RCCUTSM_{ij} + \beta_3 RTOP10_i$$
$$+ \beta_4 FRACT20_j + \beta_5 OPPRANK_j + \beta_6 PRIZE_j$$
$$+ \beta_7 RDIST_j + \beta_8 PAR_j + \beta_9 MAJOR_j$$
$$+ \beta_{10} RATING_j + u_{ij}, \tag{5.2}$$

where $RATING_j$ is the course rating for tournament j. We also estimate a variant of equation (5.2) in which we replace PAR_j with dummy variables representing the par values for the courses. We do this because the tournament courses in each tour have only three possible par values. The dummy variables are:

PAR70	=	1 if the course has par equal to 70 and 0 otherwise;
PAR71	=	1 if the course has par equal to 71 and 0 otherwise;
PAR73	=	1 if the course has par equal to 73 and 0 otherwise.

Table 5.4(a) presents the results when using the *PAR* dummies and 5.4(b) reports the results for equation (5.2).

The results in Table 5.4(a and b) are very similar, with almost all coefficients being of the same sign and significance across the two specifications. *OPPRANK* has the only coefficient that differs. It is positive and significant for women in Table 5.4(a) but insignificant in Table 5.4(b) (though, with a t-statistic of 1.47, it comes close). In addition, the results in these two tables largely mirror those of Table 5.3.

RCCUTSM remains insignificant in Table 5.4(a and b) for men, but it has a positive effect for women. This is the opposite of what we expected since a higher value suggests greater ability and, thus, a lower total score. However, the change from Table 5.3 to Table 5.4(a and b) is statistically and economically insignificant. The coefficients are very similar in magnitude and are statistically indistinguishable. Moreover, the t-statistic for *RCCUTSM* is 1.57 for women in Table 5.3.

The course rating variable has the expected signs, as a one-point increase in course rating increases total scores by about 0.4 strokes for women and 0.5 strokes for men, although the difference is not statistically significant. The omitted par value for the par dummy variables is 72, so we expect negative coefficients for *PAR* values below 72 and positive for those above 72. Our results match these expectations, and the coefficients are statistically significant except for *PAR73*, probably because only one tournament course had a par of 73. Interestingly, the *PAR71* dummy for the LPGA Tour suggests that total scores would be almost seven strokes less than on a par 72 course, holding all else constant. This is much larger than any of the par dummy variables for men, so perhaps this par variable is capturing some other element unique to the

Table 5.4   LPGA and PGA regressions

(a)   *Course ratings and par dummies included*

Variable	LPGA		PGA		Coefficient difference	t-statistic
	Coefficient	t-statistic	Coefficient	t-statistic		
RRANKPT	−0.56***	−8.87	−0.56***	−3.50	0	
RCCUTSM	0.88**	2.22	0.30	0.68		
RTOP10	−0.33	−1.25	−0.21	−0.56		
FRACT20	−51.82***	−4.37	−2.40	−0.33	−49.42***	−3.54
OPPRANK	3.61***	3.24	−1.48	−1.06	5.09***	2.85
PRIZE	0.005***	9.59	0.002***	7.71	0.003***	6.25
RDIST	28.97***	3.61	81.01***	7.00	−52.04***	−3.70
PAR70			−2.33***	−5.03		
PAR71	−6.90***	−13.36	−0.96**	−1.99		
PAR73	1.33	1.47				
MAJOR	2.81***	3.60	4.34***	4.47	−1.53	−1.23
RATING	0.42***	4.06	0.50**	2.21	−0.08	−0.35
Constant	211.77***	17.76	156.5***	12.67		
Adjusted R^2	0.41		0.42			
Observations	949		1,134			

(b)   *Course ratings only*

Variable	LPGA		PGA		Coefficient difference	t-statistic
	Coefficient	t-statistic	Coefficient	t-statistic		
RRANKPT	−0.56***	−8.76	−0.56***	−3.50	0	
RCCUTSM	0.85**	2.09	0.31	0.70	0.54	0.89
RTOP10	−0.29	−1.11	−0.21	−0.57		
FRACT20	−28.49**	−2.54	−3.11	−0.43	−25.38*	−1.90
OPPRANK	1.53	1.47	−1.42	−1.02		
PRIZE	0.005***	9.84	0.002***	7.71	0.003***	6.56
RDIST	20.18***	2.63	80.07***	6.82	−59.89***	−4.27
PAR	5.18***	12.47	1.17***	5.01	4.01***	8.40
MAJOR	4.44***	6.20	4.33***	4.47	0.11	0.09
RATING	0.20**	2.12	0.52**	2.29	−0.32	−1.32
Constant	−132.29***	−4.14	71.47***	4.76		
Adjusted R^2	0.39		0.42			
Observations	949		1,134			

Note: *Significant at 10 percent level; **Significant at 5 percent level; ***Significant at 1 percent level.

LPGA courses. The coefficients for PAR rise by over a half a stroke when course rating is added.

Finally, the tournament theory variables, *PRIZE* and *MAJOR*, continue to be positive with high *t*-statistics in both specifications, contrary to

Ehrenberg and Bognanno's (1990a, 1990b) results and tournament theory predictions. Moreover, the difference between *PRIZE* coefficients for men and women increases and remains significant. Based on the par-dummy model's estimates, a $100,000 increase in prize money raises women's scores by about 0.5 strokes while men's scores rise by approximately 0.16 strokes, roughly the same as in the previous estimation.

One other addition to our PGA model involves recognizing that some players receive an exemption for qualifying in the following season's tournaments. Nonexempt players, on the other hand, face the added pressure of performing well enough to qualify for tournaments in the following year. Therefore, nonexempt players do not necessarily respond as much to prize differentials as exempt players do. Nonexempt players must maintain high effort to enhance their chances to gain exempt status, and Ehrenberg and Bognanno's (1990a, 1990b) results support this view. Therefore, we added a dummy variable for exempt PGA players (*EXEMPT*) and an interaction term between prize money and exempt players (*PREXEMP*) to the par-dummy model. The results, not presented here, show little change in coefficient magnitudes and no change in their statistical significance. In addition, the *EXEMPT* dummy is negative, perhaps indicating greater ability levels for exempt players not fully captured by ranking point differences. However, the interaction between *PREXEMP* and *PRIZE* is positive, contrary to Ehrenberg and Bognanno's (1990a, 1990b) findings.

In sum, our results using total prize money as a proxy for the marginal returns to effort consistently show that prize money raises total scores for both men and women golfers, with a slightly greater increase for women. These findings contradict Ehrenberg and Bognanno (1990a and 1990b) and agree with results from Matthews et al. (2007) and Brown (2011). Brown investigates superstar effects on the PGA TOUR and finds that higher prize money raises first-round scores and total scores, although the effect is small. She argues that the total prize money variable may capture unmeasured differences in course difficulty because course rating and distance may not fully reflect the degree of course difficulty on the Tour.

We now investigate whether larger marginal prize money levels affect the players' final round scores. Utilizing Ehrenberg and Bognanno's approach, we specify an equation in which the final-round score is a function of the player's scores in the first three rounds (*RD1*, *RD2*, *RD3*) and a marginal prize money variable. Like Ehrenberg and Bognanno, we include several alternative marginal return measures in the regression. UP1POS represents the estimated increase in prize money if the player's final rank improves by one step relative to the third-round rank. *DN1POS*, in a similar way, measures the estimated decrease in prize money if the final rank falls one spot below the third-round rank. *UP1STROKE* and *UP2STROKE* are the

Table 5.5   Means and standard deviations of marginal prize variables

Variable	PGA		LPGA	
	Mean(000's)	Std dev.	Mean(000's)	Std dev.
UP1POS	35.693	153.22	5.720	25.18
DN1POS	39.645	152.42	6.929	30.56
UP1STROKE	52.737	148.19	7.621	23.65
UP2STROKE	125.050	259.23	19.049	43.28

estimated increases in prize money if the player's final score improves relative to the field by one stroke and two strokes, respectively.

The first step in obtaining these alternative measures involves estimating the share of a tournament's total purse that would be paid to players at their final rank. Using data from all players who received prize money in the tournaments included in our sample, the following equations were estimated for the PGA and the LPGA tournaments:

$$\ln PGAPCT = -1.1558 - 1.2989 \ln \text{Rank} \qquad (5.3)$$
$$(0.004) \quad (0.014) \qquad \text{Adjusted } R^2 = 0.975$$

$$\ln LPGAPCT = 1.054 - 1.5389 \ln \text{Rank} \qquad (5.4)$$
$$(0.006) \quad (0.019) \qquad \text{Adjusted } R^2 = 0.967.$$

PGAPCT and *LPGAPCT* measure the share of the purse a player receives, given the final rank. Standard errors appear in parentheses. We use these estimates to calculate the predicted prize money that would have been paid to players at the end of the third round. The difference between the payments to players in adjacent ranks is the marginal return. Table 5.5 shows the means and standard deviations of the marginal prize variables for both tours.

Ehrenberg and Bognanno (1990a, 1990b) also argue that endogeneity is a concern in the model because a player's performance in each round (*RD1*, *RD2*, *RD3*) depends on player ability, opponent ability, prize money incentives, and tournament characteristics. In addition, the marginal prize money in the final round depends on the player's performance in the first three rounds. Hausman specification tests showed that the null hypothesis of exogeneity was rejected in both samples for all specifications. Therefore we use two-stage least squares (2SLS) to estimate the final round equations. The exogenous variables used to derive instruments for the endogenous variables include those listed in Table 5.4(a) (excluding *PRIZE*) as well as the following:

- *RD1AVG* and *RD2AVG* = a player's scoring average in rounds 1 and 2, respectively, during the 2009 Tour;
- Moneyrank = a player's official prize money rank at the end of 2009 Tour;
- Age = the player's age;
- Underpar = the player's percentage of rounds finished under par in 2009; and
- Girpct = the player's percentage of greens made in regulation for 2009.

Table 5.6 presents both OLS and 2SLS final-round score results for the PGA and LPGA samples, respectively, using the marginal prize money

Table 5.6   Final-round score results for both PGA and LPGA tournaments (t-statistics in parentheses)

Variable	PGA OLS	PGA 2SLS	LPGA OLS	LPGA 2SLS
RD1	0.23 (5.70)	0.04 (.22)	0.23 (5.99)	0.06 (0.30)
RD2	0.25 (6.50)	0.54 (2.61)	0.14 (4.19)	0.12 (0.59)
RD3	0.17 (5.16)	0.51 (2.88)	0.12 (3.78)	0.31 (1.38)
UP1POS	0.002 (2.87)	0.001 (.35)	0.002 (0.60)	−0.14 (−4.31)
Constant	25.60 (6.36)	−5.23 (−0.61)	36.36 (10.13)	37.38 (4.24)
Adjusted R^2	0.10		0.09	
RD1	0.25 (6.32)	−0.01 (−0.03)	0.24 (6.19)	−0.04 (−0.23)
RD2	0.28 (7.18)	0.57 (2.81)	0.15 (4.34)	0.03 (0.15)
RD3	0.18 (5.60)	0.54 (3.04)	0.13 (4.00)	0.44 (2.27)
DN1POS	0.003 (5.14)	0.01 (2.45)	0.01 (1.83)	−0.08 (−4.11)
Constant	20.84 (5.03)	−6.49 (−0.75)	34.65 (9.41)	41.77 (5.07)
Adjusted R^2	0.12		0.10	
RD1	0.23 (5.70)	0.05 (0.22)	0.23 (5.91)	0.15 (0.91)
RD2	0.26 (6.65)	0.42 (1.61)	0.14 (4.09)	0.06 (0.36)
RD3	0.18 (5.51)	0.73 (3.05)	0.12 (3.67)	0.28 (1.37)
UP1STROKE	0.002 (3.29)	0.02 (2.92)	−0.001 (−0.19)	−0.11 (−4.34)
Constant	24.30 (5.94)	−15.19 (−1.31)	37.05 (10.29)	37.729 (5.03)
Adjusted R^2	0.11		0.09	
RD1	0.24 (6.12)	0.14 (.68)	0.22 (5.74)	0.11 (0.73)
RD2	0.27 (7.02)	0.35 (1.53)	0.13 (3.81)	−0.09 (−0.61)
RD3	0.19 (5.91)	0.68 (3.46)	0.11 (3.36)	0.53 (3.13)
UP2STROKE	0.002 (4.86)	0.01 (3.42)	−0.004 (−1.57)	−0.04 (−4.47)
Constant	21.00 (5.04)	−11.87 (−1.25)	38.83 (10.51)	33.28 (4.88)
Adjusted R^2	0.12		0.10	

variables calculated using equations (5.3) and (5.4). For men, coefficients for all four marginal return variables are positive and significant in all but one case.

Like the previous findings in this chapter, these results conflict with Ehrenberg and Bognanno (1990a, 1990b). However, our results for women offer some support for tournament theory. All the 2SLS estimates of the marginal prize money coefficients are negative, suggesting that female golfers respond to financial incentives and improve their performance. Ehrenberg and Bognanno (1990b) point out that one can calculate the effect of a change in the marginal prize variable on player performance. If the marginal prize variable is one standard deviation above the mean, the effect is found by multiplying the marginal prize variable's standard deviation by the estimated regression coefficient for that marginal prize variable. For example, if a player faced an *UP2STROKE* one standard deviation above its mean, a player's score may be about 1.7 ($= 43.28*(-0.04)$) strokes lower on the final round. This is less than the 3.4 to 4.5 stroke estimates found in Ehrenberg and Bognanno (ibid.).

Several words of caution are in order. First, the explanatory power of the final-round score equations is much lower than that of the total score approach. Additional work on model specification would improve the model's predictive performance. Second, as noted above, we restrict our dataset to the best players on the two tours. Using a broader sample might yield different results.

5.6   CONCLUSION

Many economic studies have examined the impact of incentives on player performance in sports, but most of these studies have considered only men. The results of experimental work on differences in gender preferences suggest that female athletes might respond differently to prize structures than male athletes do. We analyze the impact of incentives on the performance of men on the PGA TOUR and women on the LPGA Tour. We find mixed evidence regarding the predictions of tournament theory in general and for gender differences in particular.

Using the total score approach, our results do not support tournament theory's predictions for either gender. Larger purses increase a player's total score for both men and women, slightly more for women. Final-round score equations bring a different perspective. Using alternative marginal return measures, we find that women improve their performance as prize money differentials increase while the men's scores worsen to some extent. When one accounts for endogeneity, women react to marginal prizes in the manner predicted by tournament theory, while men do not.

There are also significant gender differences in responsiveness to opponent ability. The tournament field had no significant effect on men's performance while, for women, it has a mixed effect. Women perform better when elite competition joins the field, as reflected by the *FRACT20* coefficient, but they do less well if the general field quality improves, as measured by *OPPRANK*.

Future work can extend and refine our work by considering alternative specifications of final round score equations and accounting for sample selection bias. Further, considering the potential for superstar effects and weather, such as in Brown (2011), may well be fruitful. Also, expanding the dataset to include several years and employing a fixed-effects model will better account for differences in ability between players and tournament-specific characteristics that are not being completely captured by course rating, par, and distance.

NOTES

*   The authors thank the editors of this volume, Jagre Walley (Augsburg College) and participants at the 2011 Western Economic Association meetings, especially Ross Booth and Michael Leeds, for many helpful comments on earlier versions of this chapter.

1.   Tiger Woods and Lorena Ochoa had the highest *RRANKPT* in the sample, with 11.6 and 28.94 in the PGA Championship and Sybase tournaments, respectively. Our estimates imply that Woods' score would be about six strokes less than the 150th-ranked player while Ochoa's score would be about 15 strokes less, holding all else constant.
2.   The tournaments for which we could not find course ratings were Legends and Wyndam on the PGA TOUR and the British Open and Evian Masters on the LPGA Tour. In addition, for the Masters course in Augusta, we used a course rating estimate published in the April 2010 issue of *Golf Digest*.

REFERENCES

Booth, Alison L. and Patrick J. Nolen (2009), 'Choosing to Compete: How Different Are Girls and Boys?', IZA Discussion Paper No. 4027, Institute for the Study of Labor, Bonn.
Brown, Jennifer (2011), 'Quitters Never Win: The (Adverse) Incentive Effects of Competing with Superstars', *Journal of Political Economy*, **119**(5), October: 982–1013.
Buser, Thomas (2009), 'The Impact of Female Sex Hormones on Competitiveness', Tinbergen Institute Discussion Paper 082.
Cotton, Christopher and Joseph Price (2006), 'The Hot Hand, Competitive Experience, and Performance Differences by Gender', online at: http://mpra.ub.uni-muenchen.de/1843 (accessed May 20, 2011).
Croson, Rachel and Uri Gneezy (2009), 'Gender Differences in Preferences', *Journal of Economic Literature*, **47**(2), June: 448–74.
Datta-Gupta, Nabanita, Anders Poulsen and Marie-Claire Villeval (2005), 'Male and

Female Competitive Behavior: Experimental Evidence', IZA Discussion Paper No. 1833, Institute for the Study of Labor, Bonn.

Deaner, Robert (2006a), 'More Males Run Relatively Fast in U.S. Road Races: Further Evidence of a Sex Difference in Competitiveness', *Evolutionary Psychology*, **4**: 303–14.

Deaner, Robert (2006b), 'More Males Run Fast: A Stable Sex Difference in Competitiveness in U.S. Distance Runners', *Evolution and Human Behavior*, **27**(1), January: 63–84.

Dohmen, Thomas and Armin Falk (2006), 'Performance Pay and Multi-Dimensional Sorting: Productivity, Preferences and Gender', IZA Discussion Paper No. 2001, Institute for the Study of Labor, Bonn.

Ehrenberg, Ronald G. and Michael L. Bognanno (1990a), 'Do Tournaments Have Incentive Effects?', *Journal of Political Economy*, **98**(6), December: 1307–24.

Ehrenberg, Ronald G. and Michael L. Bognanno (1990b), 'The Incentive Effects of Tournaments Revisited: Evidence from the European PGA Tour', *Industrial and Labor Relations Review*, **43**(3), February: 74–88.

Frick, Bernd (2011a), 'Gender Differences in Competitiveness: Empirical Evidence from Professional Distance Running', *Labour Economics*, **18**(3), June: 389–98.

Frick, Bernd (2011b), 'Gender Differences in Competitive Orientations: Empirical Evidence from Ultramarathon Running', *Journal of Sports Economics*, **12**(3), June: 317–40.

Frick, Bernd and Joachim Prinz (2007), 'Pay and Performance in Professional Road Running: The Case of City Marathons', *International Journal of Sport Finance*, **2**(1), February: 25–35.

Gilsdorf, Keith F. and Vasant A. Sukhatme (2008a), 'Tournament Incentives and Match Outcomes in Women's Professional Tennis', *Applied Economics*, **40**(18), September: 2405–12.

Gilsdorf, Keith F. and Vasant A. Sukhatme (2008b), 'Testing Rosen's Sequential Elimination Tournament Model: Incentives and Player Performance in Professional Tennis', *Journal of Sports Economics*, **9**(3), June: 287–303.

Gneezy, Uri, Kenneth L. Leonard and John A. List (2009), 'Gender Differences in Competition: Evidence from a Matrilineal and a Patrilineal Society', *Econometrica*, **77**(5), September: 1637–64.

Gneezy, Uri, Muriel Niederle and Aldo Rustichini (2003), 'Performance in Competitive Environments: Gender Differences', *Quarterly Journal of Economics*, **118**(3), August: 1049–74.

Gneezy, Uri and Aldo Rustichini (2004), 'Gender and Competition at a Young Age', *American Economic Review*, **94**(2), May: 377–81.

Goldin, Claudia and Cecilia Rouse (2000), 'Orchestrating Impartiality: The Impact of "Blind" Auditions on Female Musicians', *American Economic Review*, **90**(4), September: 715–41.

Ivanova-Stenzel, Radosveta and Dorothea Kubler (2005), 'Courtesy and Idleness: Gender Differences in Team Work and Team Competition', IZA Discussion Paper No. 1768, Institute for the Study of Labor, Bonn.

Lallemand, Thierry, Robert Plasman and François Rycx (2008), 'Women and Competition in Elimination Tournaments: Evidence from Professional Tennis Data', *Journal of Sports Economics*, **9**(1), February: 3–19.

LPGA Tour, website: http://www.lpga.com.

Maloney, Michael T. and Robert E. McCormick (2000), 'The Response of Workers to Wages in Tournaments: Evidence from Foot Races', *Journal of Sports Economics*, **1**(2), May: 99–123.

Manning, Alan and Farzad Saidi (2008), 'Understanding the Gender Pay Gap: What's Competition Got to Do with it?', CEP Discussion Paper No. 898, Center for Economic Performance.

Matthews, Peter Hans, Paul M. Sommers and Francisco Peschiera (2007), 'Incentives and Superstars on the LPGA Tour', *Applied Economics*, **39**(1–3), January–February: 87–94.

Niederle, Muriel and Lise Vesterlund (2007), 'Do Women Shy Away from Competition? Do Men Compete Too Much?', *Quarterly Journal of Economics*, **122**(3), August: 1067–101.

Niederle, Muriel, Carmit Segal and Lise Vesterlund (2008), 'How Costly is Diversity? Affirmative Action in Light of Gender Differences in Competitiveness', NBER Working Paper No. 13923, National Bureau of Economic Research, Cambridge, MA.

Orszag, Jonathan M. (1994), 'A New Look at Incentive Effects in Tournaments', *Economics Letters*, **46**(1), September: 77–88.

Paserman, M. Daniele (2010), 'Gender Differences in Performance in Competitive Environments: Evidence from Professional Tennis Players', Manuscript, 1–58.

PGA TOUR, website: http://www.pgatour.com.

Polachek, Solomon William (1981), 'Occupational Self-selection: A Human Capital Approach to Sex Differences in Occupational Structure', *Review of Economics and Statistics*, **63**(1), February: 60–69.

Rosen, Sherwin (1986), 'Prizes and Incentives in Elimination Tournaments', *American Economic Review*, **76**(4), September: 701–15.

Sunde, Uwe (2009), 'Heterogeneity and Performance in Tournaments: A Test for Incentive Effects Using Professional Tennis Data', *Applied Economics*, **41**(25), November: 3199–208.

von Allmen, Peter (2006), 'The Economics of Individual Sports: Golf, Tennis, Track, and NASCAR', in John Fizel (ed.), *Handbook of Sports Economics Research*, New York: M.E. Sharpe, pp. 149–69.

6. Earnings and performance in women's skiing

XiaoGang Che and Brad R. Humphreys

6.1 INTRODUCTION

Economic research on the performance of individual professional athletes has grown substantially over the last 20 years. The first reason for the growth is the substantial increase in the earnings of professional athletes. In 1968, the first prize for winning the US Open tennis tournament was $14,000, or about $91,200 in 2011 dollars. The winner, US Army Lt. Arthur Ashe, was an amateur and could not collect the check. Virginia Wade won the women's title and earned $6,000, about $39,000 in 2011 dollars. In 2011 Novak Djokovic and Samantha Stosur each collected $1.8 million dollars for winning this tournament. The second reason for the increase in research on the performance of individual professional athletes is the seminal work on the effects of rank tournaments on labor supply and effort by Lazear and Rosen (1981). They show that rank-order tournaments, where only the order of finish affects earnings, coupled with a nonlinear payoff in the tournament, can produce the same level of profit as a compensation mechanism that pays all workers their marginal revenue products. The crucial advantage of the Lazear and Rosen framework is that the employer does not have to observe the marginal product of the worker.

Lazear and Rosen set out to explain observed compensation in corporations, envisioning the firm's managers as competitors in a tournament for the position of CEO, a position that typically pays much more than other corporate positions. However, the effort or output of individual employees in corporations is rarely observable. Analogously, competition in individual sports is typically a rank-order tournament with nonlinear payoffs. Many athletic tournaments, like professional golf, tennis, bowling, and foot races, are rank-order competitions with nonlinear payoffs. These provide an ideal setting for testing the predictions of the model developed by Lazear and Rosen.

Most tests of the Lazear and Rosen model that use data from professional sports confirm that the effort supplied by participants responds to the prize structure in a way consistent with the model. However, most of these tests use data from men's individual professional sports, starting with Ehrenberg and Bognanno (1990a, 1990b), who analyzed outcomes in professional golf tournaments. Much of the subsequent work is summarized in Szymanski (2003).

Relatively little research has focused on outcomes in women's professional individual sports. Coate and Robbins (2001) analyzed the earnings and career length of men's and women's professional tennis players over the 1984–94 period. Maloney and McCormick (2000) investigated the outcome of foot races involving both men and women over the 1987–91 period. Lallemand et al. (2008) examined outcomes in Women's Tennis Association (WTA) Tour tennis matches over the 2002–04 period. Gilsdorf and Sukhatme (2008) studied the outcomes of matches on the WTA Tour in the 2004 season while Frick (2011) analyzed outcomes of male and female runners in professional distance running events over the 1973–2009 period. No previous research has focused on outcomes in women's professional alpine skiing.

Recent research on gender differences in preferences heightens interest in understanding differences in the performance of male and female professional athletes. Croson and Gneezy (2009) recently surveyed developments in the literature on gender differences in preferences. Economists have observed systematic gender differences in economic decisions in consumption, investment, and labor markets. An emerging literature attributes these differences to underlying differences in the preferences of men and women. In particular, recent research suggests that men and women have significant differences in risk preferences, social preferences and, most important for this chapter, preferences for competition. Croson and Gneezy conclude from recent research that 'women are more averse to competition than are men' (p. 1), that 'women are more reluctant than men to engage in competitive interactions like tournaments' (p. 17), and that 'men's performance, relative to women's, is improved under competition' (p. 17). All of the evidence discussed by Croson and Gneezy comes from experimental settings; none is based on evidence from the field. The emerging evidence about gender differences in preferences increases the need for research on how women respond to competitive forces, including the performance of female professional athletes.

In this chapter, we analyze the performance of female professional Downhill skiers in the Fédération Internationale de Ski (FIS, or International Ski Federation) Alpine Ski World Cup. To test the predictions of tournament theory, we use data from Word Cup skiing competitions, which is the top international circuit of alpine skiing competitions. The individual races that make up the FIS Alpine Ski World Cup are rank-order tournaments that have a relatively large, nonlinear payoff structure. The participants in these events can supply a variable amount of effort in the contests by choosing to ski faster or slower. Tournament theory predicts that the effort supplied by participants in a tournament will respond to the size and spread of the prize distribution.

Like Ehrenberg and Bognanno (1990a and 1990b), we find that professional athletes respond to a tournament prize structure in a way consistent with the Lazear and Rosen model. In particular, we find that the greater the spread of the prize distribution, the more effort female skiers exert. Differences in gender preferences may also play an important role in this setting, which could lead female skiers not to respond strongly to tournament incentives; we have weak evidence that this may take place.

Section 6.2 explains the history and structure of the FIS Alpine Ski World Cup competition. Section 6.3 places this chapter in the context of the broader literature applying rank-order tournaments to professional sports. Section 6.4 describes the data used in the analysis, and Section 6.5 presents and estimates the empirical model. Section 6.6 concludes.

6.2   THE FIS ALPINE SKI WORLD CUP

The FIS was founded in 1924 in Chamonix France. Its creation was part of 'International Winter Sports Week', an event that was later declared to be the first Winter Olympic Games. Today, the FIS sets rules for and oversees world championships in the Olympic ski disciplines of cross-country, ski jumping, Nordic combined, alpine, freestyle, and snowboarding, as well as in a variety of non-Olympic events, such as speed skiing, grass skiing, and telemark (FIS, 2012).

The FIS Alpine Ski World Cup (hereafter 'World Cup') began competition in 1967. Today, it is the world's premier international alpine ski competition. In its first season, the World Cup staged 18 races for men and women in three alpine skiing events: Slalom, Giant Slalom, and Downhill. The men's world champion in the first two seasons was Jean-Claude Killy of France, who won 12 of the 18 races in the inaugural season; the women's world champion in the first two seasons was Canadian Nance Greene. World Cup races are part of a tour that travels to famous ski resorts in the European Alps, Scandinavia, North America, and Asia over a season that runs from late October until mid-March.

The World Cup currently consists of five alpine skiing events: Slalom, Giant Slalom, Super-G, Downhill, and Super-combined, a composite event that consists of one short Downhill run and one Slalom run. Alpine skiing events take place on courses that are defined by gates formed by pairs of poles that alternate in color. The tips of both skis and the skiers' feet must pass between the poles that make up each gate, or the skier is disqualified from the race. Slalom and Giant Slalom races consist of two runs each. The skier with the lowest combined times for the two runs is the winner of the race. The Super-G and Downhill have only one run each.

The events are distinguished by the number of gates that make up each course and the vertical drop of the course. In general, events with larger vertical drops and fewer gates have faster speeds. FIS has detailed rules for the design of the course for each alpine event (see FIS 2012 for details).

Slalom and Giant Slalom are 'technical' events with many gates placed close together, requiring the skier to make many rapid, tight turns. The many turns, combined with a relatively small vertical drop, result in slower speeds. A Slalom course has 55–75 gates for men, 40–60 gates for women, and it has no vertical drop requirement. Slalom gates have a width of 4–6 meters. A Slalom race consists of two runs on two different courses. A Giant Slalom course has a vertical drop of 250–400 meters, and it has 56–70 gates for men and 46–58 gates for women. Giant Slalom gates have a width of 4–8 meters and must be at least 10 meters apart. Speeds are faster on the Giant Slalom than on the Slalom because the vertical drop is greater and the gates require less turning.

Super-G and Downhill are considered 'speed' events. A Super-G course has a vertical drop of between 400 and 650 meters for men and between 400 and 600 meters for women, with gates that are 6–8 meters wide. A Downhill course has a vertical drop of between 800 and 1,100 meters for men and between 450 meters and 800 meters for women and only a few gates. As a result, the speeds on the Super-G and especially the Downhill are far greater than on the Slalom or Giant Slalom, with speeds on the Downhill sometimes exceeding 90 miles per hour.

While the design of the course strongly influences the skiers' speeds, FIS rules clearly assume that individual athletes have some control over how fast they go. For example, the FIS rules for the Downhill state: 'It must be possible to ski the Downhill course from the start to the finish with different speeds. The athlete adapts speed and performance to his ski technical skills and to his individual self-responsible judgment.' A skier's speed in these races is, to some degree, under the control of each participant, and the courses are designed in a way that allows participants to alter their speed, depending on their skills and preferences.

An FIS World Cup race consists of five events held at the same ski resort over a period of 2–3 days. Each event has a cash reward, paid in euros or Swiss francs to the top finishers in the event. The size and spread of these awards vary across events and across races. Since the 1991–92 season, the top 30 competitors have also earned points based on the order of finish in each event. The winner gets 100 points, the second-place finisher gets

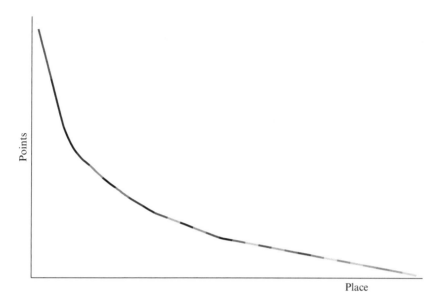

Figure 6.1   FIS World Cup scoring system

80 points, and the third-place finisher 60 points. Nonlinearities set in with the fourth-place finisher, who gets 55 points. Points then fall by four points for the 5th through 7th place, by three points for 8th through 12th place, two points for 13th through 21st place, and one point for 22nd through 30th place. As Figure 6.1 shows, the prize structure is piecewise linear with the penalty for a lower finish decreasing as one moves down the leader board. Total points are added for all events in the racing season, and the man and woman with the highest point total in each event wins the World Cup Championship for that event. In 2011, the first-place finisher in the season-long World Cup competition won 40,000 Swiss francs (CHF), the second-place finisher 25,000 CHF, the third-place finisher 15,000 CHF, the fourth-place finisher 10,000 CHF, the fifth-place finisher 6,000 CHF, and the sixth-place finisher 4,000 CHF. Like point totals, monetary prize differentials steadily decrease as a skier's placement worsens.

6.3   TOURNAMENT THEORY AND PROFESSIONAL SPORTS

Tournament theory dates back to Lazear and Rosen's (1981) seminal article. Initially applied to corporate labor markets, it has since been applied to a variety of sports. (See Frick, 2003, for a good survey of this literature.) Tournament theory posits that participants possess endowments of ability and choose an optimal amount of effort, given the ability and talent of their competitors and the prize structure of the tournament, which is known in advance. The contest is rank-ordered, so prizes are based only on relative performance, which depends on both the optimal effort of the participants as well as a random component attributed to luck and other stochastic factors outside the control of contestants. Later work (such as O'Keeffe et al., 1984, and Brown, 2011) has acknowledged that competitors might have different levels of talent and ability. As a result, the optimal choice of effort depends on the distribution of talent and ability across competitors, the expectation of effort made by other participants, and the prize structure.

Three testable predictions emerge from tournament theory. The optimal degree of effort depends

1. positively on the size and spread of the prize distribution;
2. negatively on the marginal cost of effort; and
3. positively on the degree to which an increase in individual's effort affects the probability of winning the contest.

Most research applying tournament theory to sports focuses on tests of prediction (1) because we can observe the contest features required to test the hypothesis. Since the marginal cost of effort cannot be easily observed in many settings, prediction (2) is difficult to test. Prediction (3) is also hard to test, as tournament theory provides no guidance as to the form of the relationship between effort and the probability of winning. Thus, we test prediction (1).

Most empirical tests of prediction (1) focus on the relationship between the size and structure of the prize pool and the effort made by contestants. Sporting events represent a natural setting for testing the predictions of tournament theory because both the contestants' effort and the size and structure of the prize pool are easily observed. In general, researchers identify an observable variable as a proxy for effort that varies across participants, and they explain observed variation in that effort proxy with variables reflecting the size and spread of the prize pool, event-specific characteristics, and participant-specific characteristics. Studies using data from golf and bowling typically use measures of previous performance to control for players' underlying ability and game or round scores as proxies for effort. Studies using foot races or car races use race time, and studies using data from tennis typically estimate probit models of the probability that a player wins a given match.

Maloney and McCormick (2000) performed one of the first tests of tournament theory that used data on female athletes. They analyzed the outcomes of 1,426 open foot races of various distances held over the 1987–91 period in the southeast US. These races were relatively low stakes events; the average prize was just $300 to $400, and the maximum payoff was $4,000 for women and $8,000 for men. They pooled races across different distances from one mile to marathons (26 miles), introducing a great deal of heterogeneity in the competitors. The dependent variable was average time per mile run in the race. The estimated parameter on both prize spread and average prize was negative for all models estimated, suggesting that both male and female runners respond to the prize structure consistent with the predictions of tournament theory. The bigger the prize and the larger the spread in the prize distribution, the more effort supplied by contestants and the faster they ran, given their abilities.

Coate and Robbins (2001) analyzed data from professional tennis, but they did not analyze effort. Instead, they examined factors that explain why players drop out of the top 250 places in the world tennis rankings, which effectively means that they retired from professional tennis. They found no evidence that women retire earlier than men, suggesting that they provide equal effort in professional tennis contests.

Lallemand et al. (2008) analyzed outcomes in women's professional tennis. Their effort proxy was the number of games won by a player in a match in tennis tournaments over the 2002–06 period. They calculated the difference in prize money that would be earned if the player won the match compared to the amount that she would have earned if she had lost. The estimated parameter on this prize differential was positive and significant in all models estimated, suggesting that the bigger the spread in prizes, the more effort the player made in a tennis match. The dependent variable in the analysis is limited by the number of sets played, which sets an upper bound on the participant's ability to increase effort.

Gilsdorf and Sukhatme (2008) examined match outcomes in women's professional tennis in the 2004 season. Their effort proxy was a dummy variable equal to one if the higher-ranked player won the match. Their prize spread variable was the difference between the top prize in each tournament and the prize the player would win if she lost the current match. The estimated parameter on this prize spread variable was positive and significant in all models estimated. This result implies that the bigger the spread in prizes in a match, the more likely the higher-ranked player was to win that match, which, in turn, suggests that the player provided greater effort.

Frick (2011) analyzed outcomes in 5k, 10k, half marathons, and marathons over a 40-year period. This paper explicitly compared the performance of female to male runners. The effort variable reflected the percentage difference in women's finishing times relative to men's in the same race for runners with the same world ranking. Explanatory variables included the rank of the participants in world rankings and their rank squared. Frick found that the difference in the relative performance of men and women of the same rank increases as their rank improves. He concluded that highly ranked women did not have to put in as much effort as highly ranked men to win their races. He also found that the performance gap narrowed considerably over time, suggesting that the gender gap has been closing in distance running. Clearly, this narrowing gap in performance cannot be attributed to changing preferences.

All of these papers found that female professional athletes respond to tournament incentives in a way that is consistent with the predictions of Lazear and Rosen's (1981) model. The bigger the prize and the larger the spread of the prize distribution, the more effort female professional athletes supply in these sports. Croson and Gneezy (2009) point out that gender differences in preferences for competition may be manifested in decisions to participate and not necessarily in effort supplied in competitions. If the most competitive females self-select into the competitions analyzed, then these studies might yield biased estimates because they fail to take account of self-selection. Thus, tests of the predictions of tournament theory in other settings involving female athletes are needed.

6.4   DATA

We obtained data on the outcomes of all FIS World Cup women's events for the 2001–02 season through the 2010–11 season from the FIS. We analyze outcomes for two events: the Downhill and the Giant Slalom. Recall that the Downhill is a 'speed' event, that involves few turns, and the Giant Slalom is a 'technical' event that involves many turns, so speeds are much faster for the Downhill than the Giant Slalom. The number of events held each season varies because some events are canceled due to weather conditions, such as ice, snow, and high temperature.

We have data on course characteristics, prize structure, and race outcomes. Course characteristics are captured by the vertical drop of the course and the number of gates. The prize structure of each race is defined by the amount awarded to each finisher and the total amount of prize money awarded in the event. Regardless of the event's location, prizes are paid in either euros or Swiss francs. To compare the prize structures in the events, we convert all prizes that are awarded in Swiss francs to euros at the current exchange rate. We also deflate the prize money to constant 2010 dollars using the harmonized index of consumer prices, which serves

Table 6.1   Summary statistics

Variable	Downhill				Giant Slalom			
	Mean	S.D.	Min	Max	Mean	S.D.	Min	Max
No. of entrants	54.00	9.71	12.00	71.00	61.62	15.64	26.00	81.00
Race time, seconds	97.47	11.80	69.12	126.41	142.64	13.92	96.96	214.90
Vertical drop, meters	711.08	76.27	451.00	800.00	364.17	32.11	270.00	416.00
No. of gates	37.26	5.21	23.00	50.00	47.00	4.99	31.00	59.00
Total prize*	89,335	18,457	49,991	112,360	87,129	18,057	49,311	112,360
No. of events	63				65			

Note: *Average total prize is calculated in euros.

the same basic role for the eurozone that the consumer price index (CPI) plays for the United States. Race outcomes are the total time each skier accumulated for each event, the total number of skiers who entered each event, and the total number of skiers who finished each event.

Table 6.1 shows summary statistics for the Downhill and Giant Slalom. There were an average of 54 entrants in each of the 63 Downhill races, and an average of 61 entrants in each of the 65 Giant Slalom races. Table 6A.1 in Appendix 6A contains a list of the events. Race time is our measure of effort. Recall that the Downhill, consisting of a single run down the mountain, is a long race with large vertical drops, few turns, and high speeds. In contrast, the Giant Slalom, consisting of two runs, is a shorter race with a smaller vertical drop and many turns. In addition to having more turns, the turns in the Giant Slalom are sharper because the gates are narrower and much closer together than in the Downhill. As a result, the gates in the Giant Slalom force the skier to move across the mountain much more than in the Downhill, causing the skier to move more slowly down the course.

The effort variable (that is, race time) has a relatively large standard deviation in both events. In part, this could reflect variation in the vertical drop of the races because the vertical drop determines both the maximum attainable speed and the danger of crashing during the race. The permissible range of vertical drops for each event is set by the FIS, but race organizers have some discretion. However, the standard deviation in vertical drop and the resulting coefficient of variation is much smaller for the vertical drop than it is for race time. This, in turn, suggests that the contestants, through differences in ability or effort, might have significant control over their times in the events.

Table 6.2   Prize distribution

Place	Event: Downhill			Event: Giant Slalom		
	Prize (€)	Difference (€)	% Difference	Prize (€)	Difference (€)	% Difference
1	51,825	16,970	48.69	60,613	24,674	68.66
2	34,855	11,141	46.98	35,939	13,539	60.44
3	23,714	8,085	51.73	22,400	7,250	47.85
4	15,629	4,521	40.70	15,150	5,238	52.85
5	11,108	2,550	29.80	9,912	2,886	41.08
6	8,558	1,881	28.17	7,026	1,923	37.68
7	6,677	1,153	20.87	5,103	1,142	28.83
8	5,524	1,081	24.33	3,961	1,068	36.92
9	4,443	1,217	37.72	2,893	953	49.12
10	3,226			1,940		

The key economic variable is the spread of the prize distribution in each event. The prizes awarded vary across events, race venues, and seasons; they appear in Table 6.2 in euros. Note that we converted Swiss francs to euros at current exchange rates for the empirical analysis. Even though most events have prizes paid in Swiss francs, we converted them to euros because of the availability of a price index for the eurozone over the sample period. For each event, the first column shows the average prize award for each of the first 10 places, the second column shows the absolute difference between the prize for each place, and the third column shows the percentage difference for the events with prizes awarded in euros.

The prize distribution is nonlinear, as the decrease in percentage terms is larger at the top of the distribution than at the bottom. The prize structure thus resembles that offered by such other sports, such as golf and bowling. All events awarded prizes to the first 10 finishers, but some races awarded prizes to lower finishers as well. We show the first 10 prizes here to save space, but when calculating measures of the prize distribution spread we use all of the prizes awarded.

The prize distribution in some of these events is not as nonlinear as found in other individual sports, especially for the Downhill events with prizes paid in euros. In sports like golf, tennis, and running, dropping from first to second place almost always brings a decline in prize money of more than 50 percent. Tournament theory is silent on the desired convexity of the prize gradient; it predicts only that a nonlinear prize distribution is needed to induce maximum effort from contest participants.

The prize gradient for skiing more closely resembles that for NASCAR

(National Association for Stock car Auto Racing), whose gradient is even flatter. Von Allmen (2001) explains that NASCAR penalizes lower finishers relatively little because it fears the negative externalities associated with trying 'too hard'. In particular, it fears that overly aggressive driving could result in crashes that endanger the driver and other drivers. FIS limits the prize structure for a similar reason. Skiers who approach the course very aggressively face a significant risk of crashing or missing a gate and not completing the race. The risk of crashing or missing a gate clearly increases with effort supplied by skiers. While many crashes and missed gates do not endanger other skiers, too many disqualifications might undermine a race's credibility. Race organizers may not set highly nonlinear prize distributions to reduce the number of participants who crash during the events.

6.5 EMPIRICAL ANALYSIS

We follow the standard procedure used in the literature for testing the predictions of tournament theory. We estimate a reduced-form empirical model of the determination of the speed of each competitor in the event, a proxy for effort supplied by the contestants. We explain observed variation in effort with a vector of characteristics of the specific contests and with a variable reflecting the spread of the prize distribution. The empirical model estimated is:

$$e_{ijkt} = \alpha_1 \mathbf{A_t} + \alpha_2 \mathbf{B_k} + \beta_1 \mathbf{CC_{jk}} + \beta_2 PS_{jkt} + \mu_{ijkt}, \tag{6.1}$$

where e_{ijkt} is the effort made in each event, captured by the total seconds raced by competitor i in event j at race location k in season t. The empirical model does not control for individual heterogeneity in ability using random or fixed effects; instead, we use OLS on a pooled sample of race participants.

$\mathbf{A_t}$ is a vector of indicator variables for each World Cup season in the sample. This vector controls for unobservable heterogeneity in seasons due to variation in equipment requirements and other factors that are constant within one racing season but change systematically across race seasons.

$\mathbf{B_k}$ is a vector of indicator variables for each venue at which the World Cup races take place. This vector controls for unobservable heterogeneity in the venues that might result from idiosyncratic conditions at each venue, such as topography.

$\mathbf{CC_{jk}}$ is a vector of variables capturing event-specific characteristics. This vector includes the vertical drop of the course, the number of gates on the course, and the number of entrants in the event. As noted earlier, we expect times to be inversely related to the number of gates. The impact of the vertical drop is theoretically ambiguous. The course effect itself should reduce times, as a steeper course over a relatively fixed distance will cause skiers to go downhill more quickly. However, this might be offset by the behavior of skiers, who must slow down to maintain control and avoid crashing or missing gates.

PS_{jkt} is our measure of the spread of the prize distribution in event j at venue k in season t. This is the key explanatory variable because it captures the incentive effects generated by the prize distribution in each event at each venue. We use two alterative measures of the spread of the prize distribution: the standard deviation of the prize distribution and the interquartile range of the prize distribution. The interquartile range is the difference between the prize value at the 75th percentile of the prize distribution and the value at the 25th percentile. In one model, we replace the spread of the prize distribution with the total prize money awarded, as tournament theory also predicts that the total size of the prize pool can affect effort supplied. The above models are consistent with the standard methodology used in the field.[1] While prize spread affects only effort, total purse can affect both entry decisions and effort decisions, which could reduce effort. Because of these offsetting effects, most empirical analysis estimates separate models for purse and spread. Tournament theory predicts that the greater the spread in the prize distribution, and the larger the prize pool, the more effort contestants supply. This implies that the sign of the parameter estimate on the prize distribution spread and prize pool variables should be negative. More effort supplied means faster times in each event.

The random error term μ_{ijkt} is unobservable and captures all other factors that affect race outcomes and effort supplied by contestants, which we assume to be randomly distributed across skiers. We also assume that this error term is mean zero and identically and independently distributed. We allow the variance to vary across both venues and events.

Parameters α_1, α_2, β_1 and β_2 are unobservable and must be estimated. We use STATA to perform OLS estimates of these parameters and estimate separate equations for the Downhill and Giant Slalom races. We correct the standard errors for clustering at the event level, since the measure of the spread of the prize distribution and the course characteristics vary only over events, and not over contestants. We also correct for heteroskedasticity in the equation error term using the standard White–Huber 'sandwich' correction.

Table 6.3 lists the parameter estimates and regression diagnostics for the two ski events we analyze. The three columns on the left are for the Giant Slalom (GS); the three columns on the right are for the Downhill (DH). Standard errors are in parentheses. Again, all empirical models control for

Table 6.3   OLS regression results

Variable	GS1	GS2	GS3	DH1	DH2	DH3
Std dev.	−0.228**	–	–	−0.202***	–	–
	(0.102)			(0.031)		
IQR	–	0.044	–	–	−0.181***	–
		(0.061)			(0.026)	
Total prize	–	–	−0.011	–	–	−0.31***
			(0.010)			(0.004)
No. of	0.014	0.012	0.013	0.088***	0.088***	0.091***
entrants	(0.014)	(0.014)	(0.014)	(0.009)	(0.009)	(0.009)
Vertical	0.206***	0.231***	0.211***	0.139***	0.139***	0.139***
drop	(0.015)	(0.015)	(0.015)	(0.001)	(0.001)	(0.001)
No. of gates	1.390***	1.341***	1.354***	0.447***	0.449***	0.463***
	(0.106)	(0.103)	(0.103)	(0.022)	(0.022)	(0.023)
R^2	0.94	0.95	0.95	0.98	0.98	0.98
Contestants	1,789	1,789	1,789	2,997	2,997	2,997
Races	65	65	65	63	63	63

Notes:
Standard errors in parentheses.
** Significant at 5% level; *** Significant at 1% level.
All models contain season- and venue-specific effects. Standard errors corrected for
clustering at the event level.

a season-specific effect and a venue-specific effect to capture unobservable
heterogeneity. These controls help explain the high R^2s in Table 6.3 but do
not appear there.

The parameter estimates on the number of entrants are positive and
significant in all Downhill and Giant Slalom specifications. Other things
equal, the more skiers in a field, the slower the times. This probably
reflects the fact that race course conditions deteriorate somewhat with
each run. Each participant that skis the course leaves ruts and other imper-
fections in the course, especially along the optimal path. As expected, the
parameter estimates for the number of gates is positive and significant.
Turns slow down the skier, and these results indicate that the more turns
the skier must make, the slower the speed. The effect of an additional gate
is smaller on the Downhill than on the Giant Slalom because turning is less
important in the Downhill.

The estimated parameter on the vertical drop variable is also positive
and significant in all model specifications. This suggests that the skiers'
behavior more than offsets the gravitational forces inherent in a larger
vertical drop. As explained above, a course with a larger vertical drop will
naturally lead to greater speeds, but it will also cause skiers to be more

cautious, leading to slower speeds. The positive sign on this parameter indicates that the crash avoidance motive dominates in these races.

The parameter estimates of greatest interest are those on the measures of the spread of the prize distribution in each event. Recall that we use two measures of this spread, the standard deviation of the prize distribution and the interquartile range. In three of the four model specifications, the parameter estimates are negative and significantly different from zero at conventional levels. This indicates that the greater the spread of the prize distribution, the more effort supplied by women in World Cup competitions. Female professional skiers respond to tournament incentives. The sole exception is the Giant Slalom when the spread of the prize distribution is captured by the interquartile range. Here, the estimated parameter on the spread variable is not statistically different from zero. This result may suggest that female skiers do not always respond to tournament incentives, or it could simply reflect differences in the two races; the Giant Slalom might not provide enough variability in times for the effect of the prize spread to be easily detected. Alternatively, this lack of a relationship suggests that some racers, in some events, do not ski faster when there is a larger spread of the prize distribution. This could reflect aversion to competitiveness, as discussed by Croson and Gneezy (2009).

The parameter estimate on the total prize variable is negative, but it is statistically significant only for the Downhill. In the Downhill, the more money awarded in a race, the faster the competitors ski, other things equal. In addition to – or even instead of – incentive effects, the lower times in races could reflect entry effects. In their study of road racing, Lynch and Zax (2000) and Frick (2003) find that better runners enter competitions that offer larger prizes. That could happen here as well. Higher prize pools could induce more high-quality skiers to enter a race, lowering the average time in the race. Moreover, the stronger incentive effects that we find for the Downhill might actually show that the entry effect is stronger for the Downhill. Unfortunately, we cannot address endogenous entry by professional female skiers since we lack an instrument that can explain entry decisions. As a result, identifying whether our results stem from incentive or entry effects is beyond the scope of this chapter.

6.6   CONCLUSIONS

A large, growing body of literature that tests the predictions of tournament theory in sports-related settings has emerged over the past two decades. The main question in these empirical investigations asks whether the relative performance of contestants will improve if a larger spread in prizes is offered in a contest. The results of these studies are mixed, with some supporting tournament theory and others contradicting it.

We build on this literature by estimating the incentive effects of prize structure on alpine skiing. We use a unique dataset from FIS World Cup women's professional events that includes details on race conditions and race outcomes across 10 racing seasons (2001–11). Our analysis focuses on two events, the Downhill and the Giant Slalom, which separately reflect the 'speed' and 'technical' features in women's professional skiing races. Generally, our results show that the two measures of the spread of the prize distribution, the standard deviation and interquartile range, are significantly and negatively associated with racing time. We interpret this as demonstrating that the greater the prize spread, the greater the effort by female skiers. This new empirical evidence provides further support for the predictions of tournament theory.

It is possible that the chance of a greater prize might simply attract better skiers. Maloney and McCormick's (2000) finding that the quality of the field in road races varies with the size of the purse might apply to ski events as well. The better times might therefore reflect self-selection rather than changes in effort. One cannot firmly identify incentive effects until one has fully accounted for such entry effects. Developing an accurate measure of skier quality is also important because it would make unobserved heterogeneity, a potential problem for OLS estimation, less of a factor.

However, female skiers may not always respond to tournament incentives. The results for the Giant Slalom show that the estimated parameter value of the spread of the prize distribution represented by interquartile range does not differ significantly from zero. This result can be connected to the argument by Croson and Gneezy (2009) that women are reluctant to engage in competitive activities. This natural tendency in preferences could explain the ambiguity in our results. Alternatively, the Giant Slalom may not be a race in which competitors can easily increase effort, due to the many turns and gates in this race.

In addition to accounting for self-selection, this chapter suggests three future directions for research. First, one can test whether the findings for Downhill and Giant Slalom extend to the Slalom and Super-G as well as nordic races. Second, as noted above, race order could affect times. Ideally, one would include each racer's starting position for each race. Finally, this chapter is one of the few settings in which research on women has gone beyond the research on men. Estimation of incentive effects for male skiers would allow for an analysis of gender differences in preferences among professional skiers, since men and women compete in the FIS World Cup.

NOTE

1. Lynch and Zax (2000), Gilsdorf and Sukhatme (2008), Lallemand et al. (2008), and Frick and Humphreys (2011) take a similar approach.

REFERENCES

Brown, Jennifer (2011), 'Quitters Never Win: The (Adverse) Incentive Effects of Competing with Superstars', *Journal of Political Economy*, **119**(5), October: 982–1013.
Coate, Douglas and Donijo Robbins (2001), 'The Tournament Careers of Top-Ranked Men and Women Tennis Professionals: Are the Gentlemen More Committed than the Ladies?', *Journal of Labor Research*, **22**(1), Winter: 185–93.
Croson, Rachel and Uri Gneezy (2009), 'Gender Differences in Preferences', *Journal of Economic Literature*, **47**(2), June: 1–27.
Delfgaauw, Josse, Robert Dur, Joeri Sol and Willem Verbeke (2009), 'Tournament Incentives in the Field: Gender Differences in the Workplace', Discussion Paper 4395, Institute for the Study of Labor, Bonn.
Ehrenberg, Ronald G. and Michael A. Bognanno (1990a), 'Do Tournaments Have Incentive Effects?', *Journal of Political Economy*, **98**(6), December: 1307–24.
Ehrenberg, Ronald G. and Michael L. Bognanno (1990b), 'The Incentive Effects of Tournaments Revisited: Evidence from the European PGA Tour', *Industrial and Labor Relations Review*, **43**(3), Special Issue: 74–88.
Fédération Internationale de Ski (FIS) (2012), 'Inside FIS', online at: http://www.fis-ski.com/uk/insidefis/fisoffice.html (accessed January 17, 2012).
Frick, Bernd (2003), 'Contest Theory and Sport', *Oxford Review of Economic Policy*, **19**(3), Winter: 512–29.
Frick, Bernd (2011), 'Gender Differences in Competitiveness: Empirical Evidence from Professional Distance Running', *Labour Economics*, **18**(3), June: 389–98.
Frick, Bernd and Brad R. Humphreys (2011), 'Prize Structure and Performance: Evidence from NASCAR', University of Alberta Working Paper, Edmonton, Alberta, August.
Gilsdorf, Keith F. and Vasant A. Sukhatme (2008), 'Tournament Incentives and Match Outcomes in Women's Professional Tennis', *Applied Economics*, **40**(16–18), August–September: 2405–12.
Lallemand, Thierry, Robert Plasman and François Rycx (2008), 'Women and Competition in Elimination Tournaments: Evidence from Professional Tennis Data', *Journal of Sports Economics*, **9**(1), April: 3–19.
Lazear, Edward P. and Sherwin Rosen (1981), 'Rank-order Tournaments as Optimum Labor Contracts', *Journal of Political Economy*, **89**(5), October: 841–64.
Lynch, James G. and Jeffrey S. Zax (2000), 'The Rewards to Running: Prize Structure and Performance in Professional Road Racing', *Journal of Sports Economics*, **1**(4), November: 323–40.
Maloney, Michael T. and Robert E. McCormick (2000), 'The Response of Workers to Wages in Tournaments: Evidence from Foot Races', *Journal of Sports Economics*, **1**(2), May: 99–123.
O'Keeffe, Mary, Kip W. Viscusi and Richard J. Zeckhauser (1984), 'Economic Contests: Comparative Reward Schemes', *Journal of Labor Economics*, **2**(1), January: 27–56.
Szymanski, Stefan (2003), 'The Economic Design of Sporting Contests', *Journal of Economic Literature*, **41**(4), December: 1137–87.
von Allmen, Peter (2001), 'Is the Reward System in NASCAR Efficient?', *Journal of Sports Economics*, **2**(1), February: 62–79.

APPENDIX 6A

Table 6A.1   FIS races in the sample

Downhill	Giant Slalom
Altenmarkt-Zauchensee (Austria)	Adelboden (Switzerland)
Åre (Sweden)	Alta Badia (Italy)
Aspen (United States)	Altenmarkt-Zauchensee (Austria)
Bad Kleinkirchheim (Austria)	Arber-Zwiesel (Germany)
Bansko (Bulgaria)	Åre (Sweden)
Bormio (Italy)	Aspen (United States)
Chamonix (France)	Bad Kleinkirchheim (Austria)
Cortina d'Ampezzo (Italy)	Berchstegaden (Germany)
Crans-Montana (Switzerland)	Bormio (Italy)
Garmisch-Partenkirchen (Germany)	Copper Mountain (United States)
Groden (Italy)	Cortina d'Ampezzo (Italy)
Haus im Ennstal (Austria)	Flachau (Austria)
Innsbruck Path (Austria)	Garmisch-Partenkirchen (Germany)
Kitzbühel (Austria)	Hafjell (Norway)
Lake Louise (Canada)	Hinterstoder (Austria)
Lenzerheide (Switzerland)	La Molina (Spain)
Lillehammer (Norway)	La Villa-Alta Badia (Italy)
Saalbach-Hinterglemm (Austria)	Lienz (Austria)
San Sicario (Italy)	Lenzerheide (Switzerland)
Santa Caterina (Italy)	Lillehammer (Norway)
Sestriere (Italy)	Maribor (Slovenia)
St. Anton (Austria)	Ofterschwang (Germany)
St. Moritz (Switzerland)	Panorama BC (Canada)
Tarvisio (Italy)	Park City (United States)
Val d'Isère (France)	Kranjska Gora (Slovenia)
Vail/Beaver Creek (United States)	Santa Caterina (Italy)
Val d'Isère (France)	Schladming (Austria)
Val Gardena-Groeden (Italy)	Sestriere (Italy)
Veysonnaz (Switzerland)	Sierra Nevada (Spain)
Kvitfjell (Norway)	Sölden (Austria)
Wengen (Switzerland)	Špindlerův Mlýn (Czech Republic)
Whistler, BC (Canada)	St. Moritz (Switzerland)
Zauchensee (Austria)	Val d'Isère (France)
	Vail/Geaver Creek (United States)
	Whistler/Vancouver (Canada)
	Yongpyong (Korea)
	Zwiesel (Germany)

7. Understanding the WNBA on and off the court

David J. Berri and Anthony C. Krautmann

7.1 INTRODUCTION

The creation and evolution of a sports league give sports economists an opportunity to examine the nature of institutions that they otherwise accept as given. One new league to enter the sports entertainment business is the Women's National Basketball Association (WNBA). Motivated by the gold medal won by the US women's basketball team in the 1996 Olympics, the league began organizing in 1996 and playing in 1997. The original league was composed of eight teams – four of which have since folded. Expansion, relocations, and bankruptcies have all followed in the subsequent 14 years. In 2011, the WNBA consisted of 12 teams located in markets all across the United States.

Not surprisingly, the league has experienced considerable growing pains. Obtaining reliable data on the profitability of any sports franchise is always difficult, but according to *USA Today* the typical WNBA club was losing about $1.5 to $2 million per year in 2006 (Steeg, 2007). Thus, the league was still losing millions of dollars per year as recently as 2007. While the WNBA was finally expected to turn a profit in 2009 (TVNZ, 2009), it has yet to publicly confirm that it has done so.

Many of the WNBA's claims about its finances appear overly optimistic. For example, while the league claimed that its most recent long-term broadcast contract would be worth 'millions and millions of dollars', it refused to disclose any details of its financial impact on teams (Evans, 2007). Data on attendance (and the resulting gate revenues) may be a misleading indicator of fan demand because teams frequently give away free tickets to boost the popularity of the franchise. These ongoing difficulties raise the question of whether the league is just continuing to experience growing pains or whether the league's business plan is unsustainable.

In Section 7.2, we use information from blogs, WNBA.com, and news websites to describe the basic economics of this league. In Sections 7.3 and 7.4 we describe competitive balance and the labor market in the WNBA before turning our attention to the game on the court. In Section 7.5, we model wins produced in a season by a team. In Section 7.6, we use tools from Berri et al. (2006) and Berri and Schmidt (2010) to develop a metric of the value of players in the WNBA. We find that the underlying determinants of this metric are remarkably similar to those underlying the metric for the National Basketball Association (NBA). In Section 7.7, we also find that the decision makers in the WNBA make the same mistakes as their counterparts in the NBA in that they overvalue players who score a lot of points. Section 7.8 concludes.

7.2   PROFITS, ATTENDANCE, AND REVENUE

All WNBA teams were originally owned and subsidized by the NBA.[1] In large part due to the WNBA's reported $12 million annual losses, the NBA sold its interest in the WNBA, mostly to the NBA teams in the same cities. Currently, nine of the 12 teams have a close partnership with the local NBA franchises.

The WNBA's questionable finances indicate that NBA owners did not expect WNBA franchises to be stand-alone profit centers. Risk diversification is also unlikely to be a motivation for owning a WNBA team; as Figure 7.1 shows, attendance per game in both the NBA and

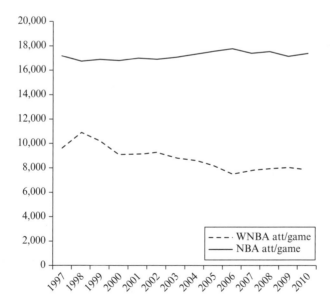

Sources: NBA and WNBA websites.

Figure 7.1   Attendance per game, WNBA vs. NBA

WNBA has been fairly flat throughout the last decade. In addition, the lack of rival leagues suggests that the motive is not to deter entry through product proliferation. However, owning both an NBA and a WNBA team might provide cost complementarities, which result in economies of scope. Greater utilization of the basketball arena, which would otherwise sit idle during the NBA's off-season, could provide an important cost saving. Further complementarities result from joint utilization of the NBA team's departments, such as marketing, legal, and public relations.

While information about the value of WNBA franchises is sparse, one team stands out. In 2006, owner Jerry Buss sold the Los Angeles Sparks to an ownership group for $10 million. Since the Los Angeles Sparks is one of the more successful and visible teams in the league, the $10 million sales price may be an upper bound on the value of a WNBA franchise. Nevertheless, this sales price is far short of the $370 million value of a typical NBA team. One reason for the low sales price is the limited revenue of the WNBA, whose primary sources are ticket sales and broadcast contracts. In contrast to the NBA, which has an average ticket price well over $50, the average price for a WNBA game is only about $15 (see Table 7.1).

Attendance at WNBA games has fluctuated over the league's short history. Per game attendance peaked in the league's second year of operation, and it has since declined to around 8,000 (see Figure 7.1). Assuming that about three-quarters of the gate attendance is paid admission, the typical team has gate revenue of about $90,000 per game. For 17 home games per season, the annual gate revenue for a typical WNBA team is around $1.5 million.[2] This translates to about $18 million for the entire league, which is just over half the $35 million revenue that a typical NBA team brings in.

Broadcast coverage of WNBA games is provided by ABC, ESPN, and NBA TV. In 2007, the league signed an eight-year contract with ESPN, guaranteeing the network a minimum of 18 broadcasts each season, as well as the rights to season-opening and All-Star games. While this contract is the first to pay rights fees to a women's professional sports league, the WNBA has never revealed what the fees are. In addition to the national broadcast contract, several WNBA teams have contracts with local television and radio stations and with Sirius Satellite Radio. Finally, the league recently initiated WNBA LiveAccess, a webcast of more than 200 live games available on-demand on WNBA.com.

Although most sports leagues in North America have avoided corporate branding on team jerseys, the WNBA has sought out this additional source of revenue. The league recently signed a long-term deal with Boost

Table 7.1   Attendance and ticket prices

Team*	Average attendance** (1997–2010)	Price range tickets (2011 season)		Metropolitan population (2003)
		Lowest	Highest	
Atlanta*	7,710	$12	$125	4,250
Charlotte	6,950		–	1,650
Chicago*	3,840	$15	$225	9,100
Cleveland	8,890		–	2,150
Connecticut*	7,150	$16	$200	260
Detroit	8,460		–	4,450
Houston	9,590		–	4,720
Indiana*	8,260	$24	$90	1,700
Los Angeles*	9,050	$10	$55	12,370
Miami	8,560		–	2,010
Minnesota*	7,500	$10	$175	2,700
New York*	11,930	$10	$250	18,320
Orlando	7,930		–	2,030
Phoenix*	9,440	$10	$195	3,250
Portland	8,320		–	2,170
Sacramento	8,290		–	2,080
San Antonio*	8,160	$9	$110	1,990
Seattle*	7,890	$10	$46	3,040
Tulsa*	4,810	$10	$115	900
Utah	7,330		–	1,100
Washington*	12,320	$17	$125	4,800
League average	8,200	$13	$140	

Notes:
*   Current teams in 2011.
**   Team-specific average attendance obtained from Womensbasketballonline.com.

Mobile that puts the cellphone company's logo on most teams' jerseys.[3] Without disclosing the terms of the deal, the front office of the WNBA said that it was the richest branding contract in the league's history.

7.3   COMPETITIVE BALANCE IN THE WNBA

Within-season competitive balance is often measured by the variation in winning percent across all teams in a given season. Figure 7.2 compares the Noll–Scully ratio of the standard deviation of winning percentage to the standard deviation of a perfectly balanced league for both the NBA

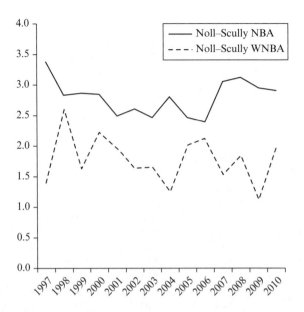

Note: The Noll–Scully ratio is the ratio of a league's actual standard deviation in winning percent to the corresponding standard deviation of a perfectly balanced league. For example, a value of *R* equal to 1.9 means that the standard deviation of winning percent in the league that season is 1.9 times larger than that of a perfectly balanced league.

Figure 7.2   Noll–Scully ratio (R)

and the WNBA.[4] It shows that the WNBA is significantly more balanced than the NBA, whose ratio was about 2.8 over the same time period.

Measures of competitive balance across seasons focus on the frequency of playoff appearances (Depken, 1999; Owen et al., 2007; Fort, 2011) or the distribution of playoff appearances (Leeds and von Allmen, 2011). Inter-seasonal balance for the WNBA is obscured by a number of factors (see Figure 7.3). First, the WNBA has experienced much turnover – it has had the same number of teams in successive seasons only four times. The rise in the number of playoff slots from four (from 1997 to 1998) to six (in 1999) to eight (since 2000) further complicates computations of inter-seasonal balance.

There does not appear to be a significant large-market effect on playoff appearances. The Los Angeles Sparks (in a city of 13 million) have appeared in 10 out of the 12 playoffs since 2000, but the Chicago Sky (in a similar city of 9 million) have not yet made the playoffs. At the opposite end of the spectrum, the Connecticut Sun (in Uncasville, a city of merely 20,000) has made the playoffs seven out of the nine years since the team

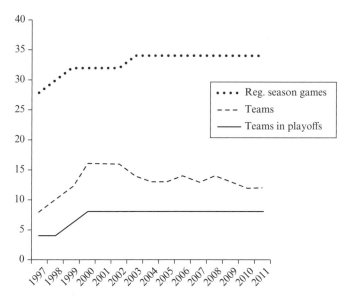

Source: WNBA website.

Figure 7.3 History of the WNBA

moved to the state. Table 7.2 reports the ratio of playoff appearances to the number of years each franchise has been in existence since 2000.[5] Using all current and former teams (listed in Table 7.2), the correlation between playoff appearances per year and population is only 0.11. The distribution of team championships is highly concentrated in both the NBA and WNBA. Seven NBA teams and seven WNBA teams won the 15 championships from 1997 through 2011.

7.4 THE LABOR MARKET IN THE WNBA

Rookie talent is allocated to teams primarily through a reverse-order draft similar to that found in other North American sports leagues. The WNBA draft lasts for three rounds. Expansion teams and teams that failed to make the playoffs in the previous season have the top picks in a lottery mechanism similar to that used in the NBA.[6] A special dispersal draft allocates players on teams that fold.

Free agency in the WNBA is defined by the collective bargaining agreement (CBA). The current CBA specifies three types of players: Reserved Players, Restricted Free Agents, and Unrestricted Free Agents. A player

Table 7.2   Playoff appearances

Team*	Team tenure	Playoff appearances (since 2000)**		Metropolitan population (2008)
		Playoffs/year	Percent	
Atlanta*	2008–	3/4	75	5,400
Charlotte	1997–06	3/4	75	1,700
Chicago*	2006–	0/6	0	9,600
Cleveland	1997–03	3/4	75	2,100
Connecticut*	2003–	7/9	78	260
Detroit	1998–09	7/10	70	4,400
Houston	1997–08	6/9	67	5,700
Indiana*	2000–	8/12	67	1,700
Los Angeles*	1997–	10/12	83	12,900
Miami	2000–02	1/3	33	5,400
Minnesota*	1999–	3/10	30	3,200
New York*	1997–	9/12	75	19,000
Orlando	1999–02	1/2	50	2,100
Phoenix*	1997–	5/12	42	4,300
Portland	2000–02	0/3	0	2,200
Sacramento	1997–09	8/10	80	2,100
San Antonio*	2003–	5/9	56	2,000
Seattle*	2000–	9/12	75	3,300
Tulsa*	2010–	0/2	0	900
Utah	1997–02	2/3	67	1,100
Washington*	1998–	6/12	50	5,400

Notes:
*   Current teams in 2011.
**   Playoff appearances/years in existence (2000 to 2011).

with three or fewer years of service is a Reserved Player and can sign only with her current team. Any team that drafts a rookie can exercise the Fourth Year Option, which allows the team to retain the player for a fourth year.[7]

A player with four or five years of experience is a Restricted Free Agent and may sign an offer sheet with any team. The offer sheet commits the player to the new team unless her current team matches the offer within 10 days. Unrestricted Free Agents can negotiate a new contract with any team. No compensation is required of a team that signs either type of free agent.

Teams can designate one player on their roster who would otherwise be a Restricted or Unrestricted Free Agent as a 'core player'. Teams retain exclusive negotiating rights to core players and must offer them a one-year, guaranteed contract at the maximum salary (explained below). During the negotiations, the team and player may agree to a multi-year contract. The Core Player designation lasts for the duration of the new contract unless the player is traded.

The league has used a number of mechanisms to control costs, including limited roster sizes, a sliding salary scale, and a salary cap. While the NBA allows teams to sign and practice with up to 15 players (of which 12 are allowed to play per game), the WNBA limits each team to 11 players. The CBA sets the salary scale based primarily on experience and draft position, with small increments that reward winners of player-of-the-year awards (for example, Most Valuable Player or Rookie of the Year). The minimum and maximum salary depends on the player's years of experience. In 2013, the minimum salary for players with 0–2 years of experience was $37,950, and for players with three or more years of experience, the minimum salary is $55,000. Similarly, the maximum for players with up to five years of experience is $105,000; and for players with more than six years of experience, this maximum is $107,500. All figures have been rising at approximately 2 percent per year. As a result WNBA salaries have risen about 10 percent over the last five years, which is slightly lower than the almost 11 percent increase in the NBA.

Each team also has an overall salary cap, which sets a maximum and minimum payroll. Unlike the NBA, which has a soft cap, the WNBA has a hard cap.[8] In 2008, the minimum team payroll was $750,000 and the maximum was $772,000. The minimum has been increasing at 3 percent, while the maximum has been rising slightly faster at 3.4 percent. Thus, in 2013, WNBA payrolls could range from $869,000 to $913,000.

7.5   MODELING WINS PRODUCED IN THE WNBA

The NBA and WNBA have market inefficiencies similar to that described by Michael Lewis in *Moneyball* (Lewis, 2004). Because most teams emphasize scoring, when evaluating players, teams that determine the true value of players can succeed relatively cheaply. We develop a method for evaluating players in the WNBA that closely follows the 'wins produced' methodology proposed by Berri (2008) for the NBA.[9] A player's wins produced shows how many of her team's wins result from her overall performance. Our findings for the WNBA closely resemble those for the NBA, and the differences are consistent with differences in the style of play exhibited by the two leagues.

We start from the observation that a team wins when it scores more points than its opponent. Over the course of a season, the difference between total points scored and total points allowed explains most of the variation in wins among teams. Points scored are a function of how many times a team gains possession of the ball and how efficiently it uses each possession. Because each team has roughly the same number of possessions in a game, a team's performance depends on its offensive and defensive efficiency. Offensive efficiency is the frequency with which a team converts possessions into points. Defensive efficiency consists of making the opponent's offense inefficient.

Using the above reasoning, we estimate the number of wins by team i in season t as a function of points scored (*PTS*) and points allowed (*opp.PTS*).

$$WINS_{it} = \alpha_0 + \alpha_1 PTS_{it} + \alpha_2 opp.PTS_{it} + \varepsilon_{1it}. \qquad (7.1)$$

We estimate equation (7.1) using team data for the WNBA from 1997 (the year it began) to 2011 and for the NBA from the 1987–88 season to 2010–11. The R^2s show that these two factors explain 81 percent of the variation in wins in the WNBA and 94 percent of the variation in wins for the NBA. The difference in the explanatory power of the two regressions stems from the fact that the WNBA season (34 games) is much shorter than the NBA season (82 games).

A player's value comes from how much she adds to her team's points and how much she limits the other team's points. A player's contribution is thus much more than the points she scores.[10] To determine what factors other than scoring explain a player's value, we take a step back and ask what determines how many points a team scores.

A team's score is determined by how many shots it takes and how often those shots go in the basket. If we know a team's shooting efficiency from the field – its points-per-shot (*PPS*) – and how many field goals it attempts (*FGA*), we know how many points the team scored on shots from the field. The same is true for a team's free throw percentage (*FTper*) and the number of free throw attempts (*FTA*). The identities in equations (7.2) and (7.3) show how many points a team scores and how many points it surrenders:

$$PTS = PPS*FGA + FTper*FTA \qquad (7.2)$$

$$opp.PTS = opp.PPS*opp.FGA + opp.FTper*opp.FTA, \qquad (7.3)$$

where $PPS = [(PTS - FTM)/FGA]$ and $FTM =$ free throws made. According to equations (7.2) and (7.3), wins are determined by eight statistics (*PPS, FTper, FGA, FTA, opp.PPS, opp.FTper, opp.FGA, opp.FTA*).

Before a team can take a shot, it must first gain possession of the ball. A team gains possession of the ball if it forces a turnover (*opp.TOV*), if it rebounds a missed shot by the opponent (defensive rebounds (*DRB*) or team rebounds (*TMRB*)), or if the other team scores.[11] Because not all foul shots result in a change of possession – as, for example, when the opposing team makes only the first of two foul shots and rebounds the second – we count only a fraction (b_1) of opponents' free throws made. All of the above add up to possessions acquired (*PA*):[12]

$$PA = opp.TOV + DRB + TMRB + opp.FGM + b_1{}^*opp.FTM. \quad (7.4)$$

When a team gains possession of the ball, it can attempt a field goal, shoot a free throw (*FTA*) because the other team has committed a foul, or commit a turnover (*TOV*).[13] If a team misses a shot, it can take more shots by making an offensive rebound (*ORB*). Thus, the number of field goals a team attempts is given by the identity in equation (7.5):[14]

$$FGA = opp.TOV + DRB + TMRB + opp.FGM + b_1{}^*opp.FTM$$
$$- TOV + ORB - c_1{}^*FTA. \quad (7.5)$$

As noted earlier, points scored are determined by possessions acquired and offensive efficiency. Hollinger (2002) and Oliver (2004) note that a team can 'employ' a possession in three ways: shooting a field goal, taking a foul shot, or committing a turnover. Possessions employed (*PE*) are thus given by:

$$PE = FGA + c_1FTA + TOV - ORB. \quad (7.6)$$

We subtract offensive rebounds because an offensive rebound extends a given possession and allows additional shots, free throws, and turnovers. Because each possession acquired is a possession employed (*PE* = *PA*), we express points scored as:

$$PTS + PTS/PE^* PA \quad (7.7)$$

$$opp.PTS = opp.PTS/opp.PE^* opp.PA. \quad (7.8)$$

Because both teams have roughly the same number of possessions in a game, a team's *PA* is about equal to its opponent's possessions employed (*opp.PE*). The game's outcome is therefore determined by how many points each team scores per possession, by its offensive efficiency (*PTS/PE*) and by its defensive efficiency (*opp.PTS/opp.PE*). These

Table 7.3   Determinants of winning percentage in the NBA and WNBA

Independent variable	NBA	WNBA
Offensive efficiency	3.152	2.391
	(82.11)	(18.26)
Defensive efficiency	−3.134	−2.450
	(73.35)	(17.37)
Constant	0.481	0.556
	(8.70)	(4.09)
R^2	0.94	0.81
Number of observations	681	196

Note: Model is estimated with team data from 1987–88 to 2010–11.

simplifications allow us to replace both *opp.PA* and *opp.PE* with *PA* in equation (7.8). Substituting equations (7.7) and (7.8) into equation (7.1) yields:

$$Wins_{it} = \delta_0 + \delta_1 * PTS_{it}/PE_{it} - \delta_2 * opp.PTS_{it}/PA_{it} + \varepsilon_{9it}. \qquad (7.9)$$

We compute *PA* and *PE* using the identities developed above:

$$PE = FGA + 0.44 * FTA + TOV - ORB \qquad (7.9a)$$

$$PA = opp.FGM + 0.44 * opp.FTM + DRB + opp.TOV + REBTM. \qquad (7.9b)$$

Estimates of equation (7.9) with data from the NBA and the WNBA appear in Table 7.3. We then calculate the marginal values of the individual components of the explanatory variables in equation (7.9). The results, which appear in Table 7.4, show that the marginal values of the statistics are very similar across the two leagues.

Three factors – personal fouls, blocked shots, and assists – are not part of the above calculations, but, as we show below, they all contribute to *PE* or *PA*. Personal fouls increase an opponent's free throws. Thus, Lindsay Whalen, a point guard for the 2011 WNBA champion Minnesota Lynx, was called for 64 (10.6 percent) of the team's 603 personal fouls. If we apply the same percentage to opponents' free throws, Whalen was responsible for 10.6 percent (50.9) of 480 free throw attempts by opponents. Blocked shots reduce scoring by an opponent. Regressing an opponent's made shots on a team's blocked shots and the opponent's field goal attempts reveals that each blocked shot reduces the opponents' field goals

Table 7.4   Value of points and possessions for the NBA and WNBA

Variable	Label	Marginal value for the NBA	Marginal value for the WNBA
Points scored	PTS	0.033	0.032
Possessions employed	PE	−0.034	−0.030
Points surrendered	opp. PTS	−0.032	−0.032
Possessions acquired	PA	0.033	0.031

by −0.618. Since each two-point field goal by an opponent – as noted below – costs a team 0.034 wins, a blocked shot by a WNBA team is worth 0.021 (0.618*0.034) wins.[15]

Assists contribute to wins produced by affecting a team's shooting efficiency. To show this, we regress each player's shooting efficiency on the number of assists per minute accumulated by her teammates (*TAPM*) and a set of controls.[16] (Results are available on request.) The estimated coefficient for assists reveals a key difference between the WNBA and NBA. For the WNBA, a one-unit change in *TAPM* leads to a 1.58-unit change in a player's adjusted field goal percentage. For the NBA, a one-unit change in *TAPM* leads to a 0.72-unit change in adjusted field goal percentage. This result suggests that assists are more important in the WNBA than in the NBA.

To see how assists affect wins produced, consider the contribution of the Lynx's assists to Lindsay Whalen's scoring in 2011. Whalen's baskets per shot are the product of *TAPM* (0.072) and its coefficient (1.58). To convert baskets to points, we multiply this product by two. We convert points per shot to overall points due to assists by multiplying this number by the number of shots Whalen took. Finally, we multiply by 0.032 because each additional point adds 0.032 to a team's wins. This calculation shows that over 1.2 wins produced by Whalen in 2011 can be traced to her teammates' assists. Doing this for every player on the Lynx and taking the sum yields the overall number of wins that are attributable to assists.

In this section, we have linked the performance of individual players to the number of games their team wins. We started by noting that the difference between total points scored and total points allowed explains most of the variation in wins among teams. Because both teams have roughly the same number of possessions in a game, the team that uses its possessions most efficiently will win. We then determine the contribution of individual performance measures to a team's offensive and defensive efficiency and hence to a team's wins.

Table 7.5   Value of player and team statistics in the NBA and WNBA

Variables	Marginal value in the NBA	Marginal value in the WNBA
Player		
Three-point field goals made (*3FGM*)	0.064	0.065
Two-point field goals made (*2FGM*)	0.032	0.033
Free throws made (*FTM*)	0.017	0.019
Missed field goals (*FGMS*)	−0.034	−0.030
Missed free throws (*FTMS*)	−0.015	−0.013
Offensive rebounds (*ORB*)	0.034	0.030
Defensive rebounds (*DRB*)	0.034	0.031
Turnovers (*TO*)	−0.034	−0.030
Steals (*STL*)	0.033	0.031
Opponent's free throws made (*opp.FTM*)	−0.017	−0.019
Blocked shots (*BLK*)	0.020	0.021
Team		
Opponent's three-point field goals made (*opp.3FGM*)	−0.064	−0.066
Opponent's two-point field goals made (*opp.2FGM*)	−0.031	−0.034
Opponent's turnovers (*opp.TOV*)	0.033	0.031
Team turnovers (*TMTO*)	−0.034	−0.030
Team rebounds (*TMRB*)	0.033	0.031

7.6   MEASURING WINS PRODUCED IN THE WNBA

To illustrate how we calculate wins produced, we again use the performance of Lindsay Whalen. We first calculate Whalen's baseline production of wins in 2011 (*PROD*) by multiplying values in Table 7.5 by Whalen's performance in each category:

$$
\begin{aligned}
PROD = {}& 17*0.065 + 162*0.033 + 89*0.019 + 171*(-0.030) \\
& + 33*(-0.013) + 30*0.030 + 89*0.031 + 75*(-0.030) \\
& + 37*0.031 + 50.9*(-0.019) + 5*0.021 \\
= {}& 4.26.
\end{aligned}
$$

However, this figure requires several adjustments. First, because wins produced varies with the number of minutes played, we must normalize *PROD* and compute wins produced per 40 minutes (*P40*), the length of a standard WNBA game. For Whalen:

$$
P40 = (PROD/\text{Minutes played}) * 40 = (4.26/956) * 40 = 0.178.
$$

Second, Table 7.5 contains five factors that are not attributable to offensive or defensive efficiency. Three factors are actions by the opposing team: two-point field goals, three-point field goals, and turnovers.[17] The other two refer to overall team statistics that are not attributable to a particular player: team turnovers and team blocks.

We allocate the team defensive factors to individual players in proportion to the minutes they play. This allows us to differentiate players on good and bad defensive teams but not among players on a given team. The team defense adjustment (again normalized to 40 minutes) applies team data to the marginal values from Table 7.5:

$$\text{Team defense adjustment per 40 minutes} = \{[opp.3FGM^*(-0.066)$$
$$+ opp.2FGM^*(-0.034) + opp.TOV^*0.031 + TMRB^*0.031$$
$$- TMBLK^*0.021]/\text{Minutes played}\}^*40.$$

Using the data for the Minnesota Lynx, we find their defensive adjustment is −0.003. We then take the difference between each team's defensive adjustment and the average adjustment for the entire league. For the Lynx, this is:

$$\text{Lynx } DEFTM40 = (-0.003) - (-0.023) = 0.020.$$

We add *DEFTM40* to each player's *P40* to compute her adjusted wins produced per 40 minutes (*Adj.P40*).

Whalen's *Adj.P40* is more than twice that of the average WNBA player (0.374 versus 0.172). However, such a blanket comparison might be unfair. Table 7.6 shows that the average value of *Adj.P40* varies systematically by position, with centers contributing the most, and shooting guards contributing the least. Because basketball teams need players at all positions, players should be evaluated relative to their position averages.

Identifying most players' positions is easy, but it can be a challenge for a few players, as play in basketball can be highly fluid, so assigning

Table 7.6   Value of Adj.P40 *across positions*

Position	Average *Adj.P40*
Point guards	0.170
Shooting guards	0.117
Small forwards	0.149
Power forwards	0.193
Centers	0.230

Table 7.7   Link between actual wins and wins produced for each team in 2011

Team	Actual wins	Summation of wins produced	Difference in absolute terms
Minnesota Lynx	27	27.3	0.3
Connecticut Sun	21	22.1	1.1
Phoenix Mercury	19	21.9	2.9
Indiana Fever	21	20.6	0.4
San Antonio Silver Stars	18	19.9	1.9
Atlanta Dream	20	19.5	0.5
Seattle Storm	21	19.0	2.0
Chicago Sky	14	17.1	3.1
New York Liberty	19	16.8	2.2
Los Angeles Sparks	15	12.3	2.7
Washington Mystics	6	6.4	0.4
Tulsa Shock	3	1.2	1.8
Average error			1.6

a position can sometimes be arbitrary. We based a player's position on the designation found at WNBA.com and her height and weight (when reported). Because the website did not separate point guards from shooting guards, we also considered each guard's assists per minute and assumed that the guards on a team with the most assists are point guards.

We next calculate a player's performance relative to the league-wide average at her position. Whalen's relative performance is 0.204 above the average for point guards, which means that she produced 0.204 more wins per 40 minutes than the average point guard. Given that Whalen played 956 minutes, she produced 4.9 more wins than the average point guard.[18]

Finally, we calculate a player's wins produced per 40 minutes (*WP40*) and her wins produced. As noted in Berri et al. (2006), to move from relative wins to absolute wins we need to know the average number of wins produced by a player per 40 minutes. The average team wins 0.500 times per game. Since a team employs five players per 40 minutes, the average player produces 0.100 wins per 40 minutes. Because teams occasionally play overtime games, the actual figure is 0.099 wins per 40 minutes. Thus, Whalen produced 0.303 wins per 40 minutes (0.204 + 0.099) in 2011. Multiplying this figure by Whalen's total minutes played and dividing by 40 yields 7.2, Whalen's total wins produced for 2011.

The sum of wins produced by all players on a team should roughly equal the team's win total. Table 7.7 reports the wins produced for all WNBA teams in 2011. The average difference between wins produced and actual wins – in absolute terms – is very small (1.6), which supports the validity of our metric.

This section adjusts the wins produced statistic that we developed in the preceding section. We account for playing time by normalizing the statistic to a per 40-minute basis. We then adjust the statistic for defensive contributions. Because some defensive statistics are team based rather than individually based, we cannot distinguish the defensive contributions by individual players on a given team. We also account for position-specific effects by comparing players to the average player at their position.

7.7   PERCEPTIONS OF PERFORMANCE IN THE WNBA

Continuing our example using the Minnesota Lynx, we find that 19 of the Lynx's 27 wins are attributable to Lindsay Whalen, Rebekkah Brunson, and Maya Moore, while only 3.7 are attributable to the team's leading scorer, Seimone Augustus. This leads to two important insights: a small number of players on each team account for most of its wins, and players who score a lot of points might not be particularly valuable. However, the perceptions of both the media and decision makers in the WNBA are often at odds with our findings.

Berri and Schmidt (2010) reveal that the Pareto principle – 80 percent of outcomes can be linked to 20 percent of people – applies to the NBA. The majority of wins in the WNBA are connected to relatively few players. Of the 142 players who played in the WNBA in 2011, only 40 – 28.2 percent of the league – produced 163.2 (80 percent) of the league's 204 wins.

In addition to showing that only a few players account for most a team's wins, our measure also shows the undue weight given to scoring. Table 7.8 shows the 40 best players in the WNBA in 2011 according to our wins produced metric. It shows that the WNBA's 2011 Most Valuable Player (MVP), Tamika Catchings, produced 8.0 wins in 2011, the most in the WNBA and more than three times those produced by the WNBA's leading scorer, Angel McCoughtry. Using our metric of wins produced, McCoughtry was only the sixth most productive player *on her own team*, the Atlanta Dream. However, the sports media covering the WNBA saw little difference between the two players, as McCoughtry was second to Catchings in the voting for the All-WNBA team.

While the All-WNBA teams and the league MVP awards are granted by the media, one might expect more nuanced evaluations from the league's decision makers. Unfortunately, we do not have access to salary data

Table 7.8 Top 40 players in the WNBA in 2011 (ranked by wins produced)

Rank	Player	Team	Position	Minutes	Voting points for All-WNBA teams	Votes WNBA MVP	WP40	Wins produced
1	Tamika Catchings*	Indiana Fever	SF-PF	1,040	187	292	0.308	8.0
2	Sylvia Fowles**	Chicago Sky	C	1,175	150	148	0.254	7.5
3	Lindsay Whalen*	Minnesota Lynx	PG	956	164	104	0.303	7.2
4	Penny Taylor**	Phoenix Mercury	PF-SF	864	82	10	0.311	6.7
5	Rebekkah Brunson	Minnesota Lynx	PF	938		1	0.268	6.3
6	DeWanna Bonner	Phoenix Mercury	SF	857			0.263	5.6
7	Becky Hammon	San Antonio Silver Stars	PG	1,050		18	0.198	5.2
8	Sue Bird**	Seattle Storm	PG	1,123	123	106	0.177	5.0
9	Candice Dupree	Phoenix Mercury	C-PF	1,075			0.183	4.9
10	Armintie Price	Atlanta Dream	SG	797			0.244	4.9
11	Tina Charles*	Connecticut Sun	C	1,136	166	209	0.167	4.8
12	Maya Moore	Minnesota Lynx	SF-PF	951		1	0.194	4.6
13	Kara Lawson	Connecticut Sun	SG-PG	832			0.221	4.6
14	Ticha Penicheiro	Los Angeles Sparks	PG	807			0.216	4.4
15	Renee Montgomery	Connecticut Sun	PG	991			0.168	4.2
16	Katie Douglas	Indiana Fever	SF-SG	940			0.173	4.1
17	Cappie Pondexter**	New York Liberty	SG-PG	1,151	94	9	0.138	4.0
18	Tiffany Jackson	Tulsa Shock	PF-SF	1,152			0.133	3.8
19	Kalana Greene	Connecticut Sun	SG-SF	781			0.188	3.7
20	Seimone Augustus**	Minnesota Lynx	SG-SF	997	69	33	0.147	3.7

148

21	Michelle Snow	Chicago Sky	PF	821			0.178	3.7
22	Alison Bales	Atlanta Dream	C	687			0.212	3.6
23	Danielle Robinson	San Antonio Silver Stars	SG-PG	786			0.185	3.6
24	Lindsey Harding	Atlanta Dream	PG	1,037			0.134	3.5
25	Diana Taurasi*	Phoenix Mercury	SG-SF	965	168	65	0.143	3.5
26	Candace Parker	Los Angeles Sparks	C	555			0.246	3.4
27	Tanisha Wright	Seattle Storm	SG-PG	953			0.143	3.4
28	Nicole Powell	New York Liberty	SF-PF	935			0.135	3.1
29	Swin Cash	Seattle Storm	PF-SF	1,128			0.110	3.1
30	Sheryl Swoopes	Tulsa Shock	SG	879			0.140	3.1
31	Taj McWilliams-Franklin	Minnesota Lynx	C	966			0.120	2.9
32	Sancho Lyttle	Atlanta Dream	PF	577			0.191	2.8
33	Crystal Langhorne	Washington Mystics	PF-C	1,063			0.102	2.7
34	Le'coe Willingham	Seattle Storm	SF	649			0.167	2.7
35	Sophia Young	San Antonio Silver Stars	PF-SF	1,043			0.101	2.6
36	Erin Phillips	Indiana Fever	PG-SG	689			0.153	2.6
37	Kia Vaughn	New York Liberty	C-PF	955			0.108	2.6
38	Erika de Souza	Atlanta Dream	PF-C	877			0.111	2.4
39	Tully Bevilaqua	San Antonio Silver Stars	SG	494			0.196	2.4
40	Angela McCoughtry*	Atlanta Dream	SF-PF	921	172	70	0.104	2.4

Note:

* Selected by members of the media to first team of the All-WNBA team.

** Selected by members of the media to the second team of the All-WNBA team.

for the WNBA. We do know, though, how the coaches allocate minutes on each team. To examine this decision, we estimate the determinants of minutes played per game (MGM_{it}):

$$MGM_{it} = \alpha_0 + \alpha_1 relPTS_{it} + \alpha_2 relTRB_{it} + \alpha_3 relSTL_{it} + \alpha_4 relAST_{it}$$
$$+ \alpha_5 relBLK_{it} + \alpha_6 relPF_{it} + \alpha_7 AdjFG_{it} + \alpha_8 FTper_{it}$$
$$+ \alpha_9 TOper_{it} + \alpha_{10} dTRADE_{it} + \alpha_{11} AGE_{it} + \alpha_{12} SQAGE_{it}$$
$$+ \alpha_{13} DftPos_{it}*XP1_{it} + \alpha_{14} DftPos_{it}*XP2_{it}$$
$$+ \alpha_{15} DftPos_{it}*XP3_{it} + \alpha_{16} DftPos_{it}*XP4_{it}$$
$$+ \alpha_{17} DftPos_{it}*XP5_{it} + \varepsilon_{10it}, \qquad (7.10)$$

where:

relPTS	=	points per minute, relative to the position average;[19]
relTRB	=	rebounds per minute, adjusted for position played;
relSTL	=	steals per minute, adjusted for position played;
relAST	=	assists per minute, adjusted for position played;
relBLK	=	blocks per minute, adjusted for position played;
relPF	=	personal fouls per minute, adjusted for position played;
AdjFG	=	adjusted field goal percentage;
FTper	=	free throw percentage;
TOper	=	turnover percentage;
dTRADE	=	equal to 1 if player was traded during the season;
AGE	=	player's age;
SQAGE	=	age squared; and
DftPos* XPi	=	the player's draft position multiplied by a dummy variable equal to one if she is in her *i*th year in the WNBA.

The results in Table 7.9 show that a player's minutes increase when her relative scoring, steals, assists, and blocked shots increase. They fall when her personal fouls and turnovers increase or when she has been traded. While our model of win production highlighted the importance of shooting efficiency and gaining possession of the ball, Table 7.9 shows that rebounds and shooting efficiency do not affect playing time.

To further highlight the similarity between the WNBA and NBA, we estimate the determinants of minutes played for a sample from the NBA. The results in Table 7.10 tell the same story. As in the WNBA, decision makers in the NBA give more minutes to players who score more points. While shooting efficiency affects playing time in the NBA, its impact is relatively small. In both the WNBA and NBA, assists

Table 7.9   Determinants of minutes per game in the WNBA: 1997–2011

Variable	Coefficient	Standard error	t-stat	p-value
*relPTS**	22.866	2.431	9.408	0.000
relTRB	−2.012	4.618	−0.436	0.663
*relSTL**	34.879	12.676	2.752	0.006
*relAST**	53.111	6.461	8.220	0.000
*relBLK**	38.414	12.040	3.190	0.001
*relPF**	−81.303	6.980	−11.648	0.000
AdjFG	5.340	3.782	1.412	0.158
FTper	−1.236	2.026	−0.610	0.542
*TOper***	−0.102	0.051	−1.979	0.048
*dTrade**	−2.777	0.894	−3.106	0.002
*AGE**	1.559	0.549	2.839	0.005
*SQAGE**	−0.026	0.010	−2.689	0.007
*DftPos*XP1**	−0.174	0.036	−4.764	0.000
*DftPos*XP2**	−0.101	0.033	−3.065	0.002
*DftPos*XP3*	−0.054	0.038	−1.415	0.157
*DftPos*XP4*	−0.062	0.038	−1.643	0.101
*DftPos*XP5*	0.021	0.032	0.653	0.514
Constant term	−4.404	7.894	−0.558	0.577
R-squared	0.490			
F-statistic*	53.9			
Observations	938			

Note: * Significant at the 1% level; ** Significant at the 5% level.

per minute have a smaller impact on minutes than personal fouls and scoring do. The impact of assists in the WNBA, though, appears to be larger. Thus, assists matter more in the WNBA than in the NBA, both according to our metric of wins produced and according to coaches' decisions.

Tables 7.9 and 7.10 also show the impact of draft position on minutes played. Consistent with studies of the NBA by Camerer and Weber (1999) and Staw and Hoang (1995), we find that a player's draft position affects minutes played in the WNBA, even after controlling for performance. The effect appears to last for only two years in the WNBA, about half the time it lasts in the NBA. We conclude that WNBA decision makers let go of their preconceived notions much faster.

This section has shown that decision makers in the WNBA make some – but not all – of the mistakes that their counterparts in the NBA make. As in the NBA, coaches place too much weight on points scored per game when allocating playing time. The lack of comprehensive salary data

Table 7.10   Modeling minutes per game for the NBA: 1999–00 to 2007–08

Variable	Coefficient	Standard error	t-stat	p-value
*relPTS**	22.788	1.234	18.469	0.000
*relTRB**	20.610	2.710	7.606	0.000
*relSTL**	34.186	11.016	3.103	0.002
*relAST**	36.941	4.362	8.469	0.000
*relBLK**	26.164	6.642	3.939	0.000
*relPF**	−136.380	4.958	−27.505	0.000
*AdjFG**	7.744	2.572	3.010	0.003
*FTper**	11.823	1.236	9.562	0.000
*TOper**	0.106	0.039	2.722	0.007
*dTrade**	−1.228	0.383	−3.211	0.001
*AGE**	2.431	0.331	7.334	0.000
*SQAGE**	−0.049	0.006	−8.058	0.000
*DftPos*XP1**	−0.142	0.015	−9.578	0.000
*DftPos*XP2**	−0.127	0.015	−8.336	0.000
*DftPos*XP3**	−0.105	0.015	−6.851	0.000
*DftPos*XP4**	−0.074	0.014	−5.136	0.000
*DftPos*XP5***	−0.030	0.016	−1.931	0.054
Constant term	−20.488	4.634	−4.421	0.000
Adjusted R-squared	0.646			
F-statistic*	248.8			
Observations	2,339			

Note: * Significant at the 1% level; ** Significant at the 5% level.

for the WNBA keeps us from determining the monetary value of scoring in terms of player salaries. We find, however, that WNBA teams are not as wedded to their top draft picks and are willing to disregard sunk costs much more quickly than NBA teams are.

7.8   CONCLUSION

A new league provides sports economists a wealth of information about the economic viability of the sport as well as new insights into the factors that make it viable. At this time, the jury is still out as to whether the WNBA will attain self-sustaining profitability. While the Los Angeles Sparks recently sold for $10 million, this price tag falls far short of the sales prices of its NBA brothers. In fact, it is unclear whether any WNBA franchise makes positive economic profits.

The WNBA's profits are limited by the dearth of non-ticket revenues, particularly broadcast revenues, as well as attendance, which peaked in the league's sophomore season and has not recovered since. This has, in turn, limited the league's ability to compensate its players. The WNBA has held down salaries by imposing a hard cap that, unlike the NBA's soft cap, does not allow exceptions.

The WNBA shows much more intra-seasonal balance than the NBA. In contrast, the NBA and WNBA have similar levels of inter-seasonal balance. Furthermore, whatever inter-season imbalance exists in the WNBA cannot be traced to any advantage held by franchises in larger cities.

In terms of individual play, we find that basketball – whether in the NBA or the WNBA – is essentially the same game. As a result, the marginal values of almost all offensive performance measures are roughly the same for each position. Assists are the one major exception. Our estimates indicate that they are much more important in the WNBA than in the NBA.

Finally, we find that coaches and other team officials in the WNBA make the same mistakes as their NBA counterparts when evaluating player performance. Coaches in both leagues place too much weight on points scored per minute when they allocate minutes to their players despite the fact that shooting efficiency and gaining and keeping possession of the ball (that is, rebounds, turnovers, and steals) primarily determine the outcomes of games in both leagues. The disconnect between perception and reality – which has been documented in a number of studies of the NBA – also appears in our study of the WNBA.

NOTES

1. The WNBA was approved by the NBA Board of Governors on April 24, 1996.
2. Under the current collective bargaining agreement (CBA), WNBA teams share 10 percent of their gate when league revenues hit an agreed-upon benchmarks. In 2008, this benchmark was $2.5 million.
3. The Phoenix Mercury and San Antonio Silver Stars already have separate deals with cell-phone companies and were excluded from the deal.
4. In a perfectly balanced league, games are decided by chance, and the variance in winning percentages is $(0.5/\sqrt{G})$, where G is the number of games in a season.
5. We focus on the past decade as that was when the WNBA expanded to eight playoff slots.
6. The WNBA adopted a version of the NBA's draft lottery, which was a response to claims that bad teams intentionally lost at the end of the season. For a review of the literature, see Price et al. (2010).
7. To exercise the Fourth Year Option, the team must declare its intention during the rookie's second year of service. A player bound by this option receives an automatic 15 percent increase in her base salary for her second and subsequent years.
8. The NBA's soft cap contains significant exceptions that allow teams to exceed the

maximum. Under very limited conditions, teams in the WNBA can exceed the limit by 4 percent without penalty.

9. See Berri et al. (2006) and Berri and Schmidt (2010) for a less technical version of this model.
10. Berri (2008) built a wins model for basketball, and Gerrard (2007) did the same for soccer.
11. Team rebounds are an accounting device. The number of missed shots should equal the number of rebounds. However, if a missed shot goes out of bounds or if a player misses the first of two free throws, a rebound cannot be credited to anyone. These events are called team rebounds. We include only team rebounds that result in a change of possession and treat all team rebounds as defensive rebounds (see Berri, 2008).
12. The percentage of free throws that result in a possession (b_1) is about 0.44. See Berri (2008).
13. We find that $0.44*FTA = FGA$ in both the NBA and WNBA.
14. The value of c_1 is about 0.44 in both the NBA and WNBA. This value is determined by calculating free throws that change possessions. For details see Berri (2008). Berri and Schmidt (2010) report that, even ignoring team rebounds that change possession, these statistics explain 98 percent of a team's field goal attempts in the NBA. Furthermore, the estimated impact of $opp.TOV$, DRB, $opp.FGM$, TOV, and ORB on a team's field goal attempts is approximately 1.0. This means that each time a team gains (loses) possession of the ball, it has gained (lost) the ability to take one field goal attempt.
15. Similar results hold for the NBA. Each blocked shot in the NBA reduces the opponent's made shots by 0.637. Hence, a blocked shot is worth 0.020 wins in the NBA.
16. The controls were the player's adjusted field goal percentage in the previous season, her age and age-squared, the percentage of games in which she played in the previous two seasons, her teammates' adjusted field goal percentage, and a dummy variable for each year). For the NBA, the equation also included measures of roster stability, dummy variables for playing under a new coach and a new team, and dummies for position played.
17. Only turnovers not attributable to steals by individual players are included in this calculation.
18. For players who played multiple positions, we calculate a weighted average of $Adj.P40$ using the minutes our analysis suggests the player played at each position as weights.
19. The calculation of a player's relative per-minute performance begins by determining the per-minute average performance of players at each of the five positions. These position averages are then subtracted from each player's per-minute performance. We then add the overall per-minute league average for that statistic. For example, Tina Charles had 0.329 rebounds per minute in 2011. The league average for a center in the WNBA was 0.240, while the average for all players was 0.166. So Charles's $RELTRB$ was: $(0.329 - 0.240) + 0.166 = 0.256$. These steps were followed for all variables statistics except those expressed as percentages.

REFERENCES

Berri, David J. (2008), 'A Simple Measure of Worker Productivity in the National Basketball Association', in *The Business of Sport*, edited by Brad Humphreys and Dennis Howard, vol. 3, Westport, CT: Praeger, pp. 1–40.

Berri, David J. and Martin B. Schmidt (2010), *Stumbling on Wins: Two Economists Explore the Pitfalls on the Road to Victory in Professional Sports*, Princeton, NJ: Financial Times Press.

Berri, David J., Martin B. Schmidt and Stacey L. Brook (2006), *The Wages of Wins: Taking Measure of the Many Myths in Modern Sport*, Stanford, CA: Stanford University Press.

Camerer, Colin and Roberto A. Weber (1999), 'The econometrics and behavioral economics of escalation of commitment in NBA draft choices', *Journal of Economic Behavior and Organization*, **39**(1), May; 59–82.

Depken, Craig II (1999), 'Free Agency and the Competitiveness of Major League Baseball', *Review of Industrial Organization*, **14**(3), May: 67–75.

Evans, Jayda (2007), 'WNBA Gets Its First TV Rights Fee', *Seattle Times*, July 16.

Fort, Rodney (2011), *Sports Economics*, 3rd edn, Boston, MA: Prentice-Hall.

Gerrard, Bill (2007), 'Is the Moneyball Approach Transferable to Complex Invasion Team Sports?', *International Journal of Sports Finance*, **2**(4), November: 214–28.

Hollinger, John (2002), *Pro Basketball Prospectus 2002*, Washington, DC: Brassey's Sports.

Leeds, Michael and Peter von Allmen (2011), *The Economics of Sports*, Boston, MA: Addison-Wesley.

Lewis, Michael (2004), *Moneyball: The Art of Winning an Unfair Game*, New York: W.W. Norton.

Oliver, Dean (2004), *Basketball on Paper: Rules and Tools for Performance Analysis*, Dulles, VA: Potomac Books.

Owen, P. Dorian, Michael Ryan and Clayton Weatherston (2007), 'Measuring Competitive Balance in Professional Team Sports Using the Herfindahl–Hirschman Index', *Review of Industrial Organization*, **31**(4), December: 289–301.

Price, Joseph, Brian Soebbing, David Berri and Brad Humphreys (2010), 'Tournament Incentives, League Policy, and NBA Team Performance Revisited', *Journal of Sports Economics*, **11**(2), April: 117–35.

Staw, B.M. and Ha Hoang (1995), 'Sunk Costs in the NBA: Why Draft Order Affects Playing Time and Survival in Professional Basketball', *Administrative Costs Quarterly*, **40**(3), September: 474–94.

Steeg, Jill (2007), 'New Owners Stake Claim in Overhauling WNBA', *USA Today*, June 7.

TVNZ (Television New Zealand Limited) (2009), 'NBA Getting Through Tough Times', online at: tvnz.co.nz/basketball-news (accessed January 16, 2012).

Womensbasketonline.com (2011), 'Attendance', online at: http://womensbasketballonline.com/wnba (accessed January 11, 2012).

8. The goals and impacts of age restrictions in sports
Ryan M. Rodenberg

8.1 INTRODUCTION

> They shouldn't make those kinds of rules. I've been practicing my whole life to play. And I'm . . . just waiting right now. For what, I don't know.
> Anna Kournikova (Roberts, 1997)

Chronological age is frequently used as a proxy of convenience for maturity and competency (Sowell and Mounts, 2005; McCann and Rosen, 2006). Non-sport examples include laws mandating a minimum age for alcohol consumption, automobile driving, military service, and voting rights (Miron and Tetelbaum, 2009). Similarly, in the sports industry, eligibility is often determined according to one's age. Sports provide a near-ideal laboratory to study the interaction between precocity and minimum age rules, as Bernhardt and Heston (2010) generally found that 'sports settings provide abundant clean data' (p. 14). Kahn (2000) posited that there 'is no research setting other than sports where we know the name, face, and life history of every production worker and supervisor in the industry' (p. 75). Kahn also observed that 'professional sports leagues have experienced major changes in labor market rules and structure – such as the advent of new leagues or rules about free agency – creating interesting natural experiments that offer opportunities for analysis' (p. 75). The imposition of minimum age rules in sport creates a quasi-natural experiment.

Precocity has long been an issue in sports, especially in women's sports, as young women typically mature physically earlier than young men do. Professional tennis provides several examples. Steffi Graf earned a world ranking at age 13 and won 22 Grand Slam titles during her long career. In addition to Graf, a veritable 'who's who' of top female players emerged on the elite-level professional tennis scene during their mid-teens and went on to win multiple Grand Slam singles titles, including Tracy Austin, Monica Seles, Jennifer Capriati, Venus Williams, and Martina Hingis. Each player started her professional career before the Women's Tennis Association (WTA), the leading governing body of professional tennis worldwide, adopted its more restrictive minimum age rule in 1995. Outside of tennis, young women also compete in golf, gymnastics, figure skating, and other women's sports. In September 2011, 16-year-old Alexis (Lexi) Thompson became the youngest golfer ever to win an LPGA (Ladies' Professional Golf Association) event when she finished first in the Navistar LPGA Classic. Ironically, Thompson was not a member of the LPGA at the time because she was too young. The exploits of such precocious athletes have been a fixture in several popular press books about tennis (Stabiner, 1986; Mewshaw, 1993; Wertheim, 2001), golf (Cook, 2008), and gymnastics and figure skating (Ryan, 2000).

Age restrictions have become particularly relevant in women's sports. They have been imposed in response to the growing domination of many women's sports by adolescent and preadolescent girls who trained at levels that one would associate with professional athletes (see, for example, Grenfell and Rinehart, 2003). Moreover, David (2005) claims that because young athletes are often removed from normal childhood surroundings and become dependent on their coaches, they are particularly vulnerable to overwork, physical abuse, and sexual abuse.

While numerous mainstream anecdotes have appeared in the popular press about the effect of age restrictions in sport, academic research has only recently begun to emerge, primarily from legal and economic standpoints. This chapter provides an overview of current age-based restrictions in sport (Section 8.2) and summarizes the legal status of age rules (Section 8.3). It also discusses the economic impact of age restrictions on both individual athletes and the labor markets in which they operate (Section 8.4), a particularly important point given the description of the relationship between age and ability as 'one of the most basic in all of economics' (Sowell and Mounts, 2005: 79). Section 8.5 concludes.

8.2   AN OVERVIEW OF AGE-BASED RESTRICTIONS

Table 8A.1 in Appendix 8A provides a summary of age eligibility rules in a number of women's sports. The underlying rationale for age-based eligibility rules is complex, combining ethical issues and health concerns pertaining to participation in professional sports by teenagers and pre-teens (Doherty, 1999; Rowland, 2000; Warren and Perloth, 2001; Merten, 2004).

In this section, I discuss the minimum age rules in four prominent women's professional sports, as they show how their governing bodies manage and administer age limits. The four governing bodies are: the Women's Tennis Association (WTA), the Women's National Basketball Association (WNBA), the Ladies Professional Golf Association (LPGA), and the Fédération Internationale de Gymnastique (FIG).

8.2.1   Tennis

Modified at least twice since its adoption, the current incarnation of the WTA Tour's age rule was promulgated in 1995 (Rodenberg, 2000). McGuire (2007: 248–9) states:

> Before the age eligibility program was put into effect, young stars in women's tennis burned out or suffered career-ending injuries with troubling frequency; by the time they were twenty-one, Tracy Austin, Andrea Jaeger, Jennifer Capriati, and Martina Hingis had all been forced out of the game for these reasons.

The International Tennis Federation (ITF), the rule-making body for tennis, created an Age Eligibility Commission in 1994 '[i]n response to concerns about the well-being and career longevity of individuals competing in women's professional tennis' (ibid.: 207). The WTA Tour's age rule appears in the governing body's rulebook and is structured as a sliding scale from the age of 14 to 18. Girls younger than 14 years old cannot compete at all in professional tennis events. Starting at the age of 14, girls are phased in. Fourteen-year-olds may play in up to seven ITF events and may obtain a 'wild card' to participate in one WTA Championship. They are allowed to play in an increasing number of tournaments each succeeding year and have the opportunity to play in tournaments carrying greater prize money, ranking points, and prestige. Women 18 and older can qualify via their ranking to play in an unlimited number of tournaments. Players who fail to comply with the WTA Tour's age rule can be fined, suspended, or have their tournament results (and accompanying ranking points) removed from their records.

After the age rule in tennis was enacted, commentary on the new rule was generally positive. For example, one commission member, Jim Loehr, said that 'all the data shows us that the longer . . . we delay stardom, the better the players' chances are of sustaining a successful career' (Finn, 1999: D1). Years later, Livengood et al. (2008) described the WTA Tour's age rule as a policy that 'aims to guide players to minimize the stressors associated with women's professional tennis and to promote their safety, career longevity, and performance' (p. 10). One person who felt the reform to be inadequate was Larry Scott, the former CEO of the WTA. He was particularly concerned about the ability of players under the age of 18 to circumvent age restrictions at 'grand slam' events, such as the Australian Open, because they are not sanctioned by the WTA. He also worried about the growth of the 'Junior Tour' and its lack of limits on the participation of women younger than 18 (Kaplan, 2004).

8.2.2 Basketball

The eligibility rule for American-born basketball players seeking to compete in the WNBA is unique among the regulations considered in this chapter in that it contains both age restrictions and education requirements. The WNBA has thus followed in the footsteps of the NBA (National Basketball Association), though its restriction goes much farther than the NBA's current restriction that players cannot enter the league until one year after their class has graduated from high school. The WNBA's rule requires players to be at least 22 years old or to have completed four years of college to be eligible for the annual draft (Edelman and Harrison, 2008). In contrast to tennis, golf, and gymnastics, all individual sports in which the athletes compete as independent contractors instead of employees, WNBA basketball is a team sport in which the athletes are members of a government-recognized labor union, the Women's National Basketball Players' Association (WNBPA). The age/education rule was specifically negotiated by the WNBA and the WNBPA, and it is codified in the collective bargaining agreement between the two entities.

Although Edelman and Harrison find the WNBA rule open to legal, cultural, and ethical criticism, they identify three potential social benefits from the WNBA policy. First, positioning its players as both scholars and athletes has helped the WNBA promote them as role models. Second, the policy 'helps to prepare . . . players for non-basketball careers upon personal retirement or league dissolution' (p. 25). Third, the rule is easy to understand and enforce.

Finally, the eligibility rule is far less binding for women than for men. Salaries in the WNBA are a small fraction of those offered in the NBA, so the incentive to challenge the ruling and jump to the professional ranks is much lower for women than for men.[1] As a result, college graduation rates for members of prominent women's basketball teams are typically higher than those of women who are not varsity athletes and much higher than for members of prominent men's basketball teams (see, for example, Lapchick, 2011).

8.2.3 Golf

Unlike the sliding scale adopted by the WTA Tour in women's tennis, the LPGA Tour's 'bright line' age eligibility rule requires full-time tour members to be 18 or older. However, players from the age of 15 through 17 may petition the governing body for early permission by 'demonstrating . . . their capacity to assume the professional and financial responsibilities required' (Rodenberg et al., 2009: 107). The LPGA Tour's rule was adopted in the 1970s. At least three underage players have been granted early permission to play professional golf full-time – Aree Song in 2003, Morgan Pressel in 2005, and Alexis (Lexi) Thompson in 2011. Moreover, despite needing special permission to join the tour – a decision that might have been made easier by the lack of prominent Americans on the LPGA Tour – Thompson is no stranger to LPGA tournaments. Having received sponsors' exemptions, she played in three US Women's Opens by the time she was 14, when she made the cut for the first time, and she tied for 10th in the US Women's Open as a 15-year-old (Elliott, 2011). The case-by-case determination of an early entry applicant considers a youth's 'playing ability, intelligence, maturity, and financial stability' (Rodenberg et al., 2009: 113). The literature is silent on the rationale for the rule's enactment.

8.2.4 Gymnastics

The FIG's age rules have moved in three phases (Rodenberg and Eagleman, 2011). Prior to 1980, gymnasts were required to be at least 14 years old. In 1980, the minimum age was increased to 15. In 1997, the minimum age was increased to 16, where it remains today. The restrictions came in response to a perceived trend toward 'adolescents who are usually less than 1.5 meters [4′11] tall and weigh less than 40 kilos [88 lbs]' and a fear that '[a]rtistic ability and femininity have given way to extremely difficult jumps and moves that can only be performed by girls whose bodies are kept artificially small' (David, 2005: 65). The current age rule has several justifications: the facilitation of healthy muscular and skeletal development, which is particularly likely for adolescents (Daly et al., 2001), the prevention of burnout, and the promotion of a better public image (Paul, 2010).

An unintended consequence of the FIG's move to increase its minimum age policy has been the increase in documented cases of age fraud among individual gymnasts and national-level federations, with China and North Korea having the most egregious cases (Rodenberg and Eagleman, 2011). The FIG-led investigation uncovered long-term systematic corruption among national governing bodies in both countries. FIG found that they had actively facilitated the fabrication of athlete ages to gain a competitive advantage.

8.3 THE LEGAL STATUS OF AGE RESTRICTIONS

The extensive literature on the legality of minimum-age rules in the sports industry spans many sports. In addition to the age policies in the women's sports detailed above, minimum-age rules exist in high-profile men's sports, including the National Football League (NFL), the NBA, Major League Baseball (MLB), the National Hockey League (NHL), men's professional golf on the PGA TOUR, and men's professional tennis on the Association of Tennis Professionals (ATP) World Tour. Like the WNBA, the NFL has an eligibility rule with both an age restriction and an education requirement, as a player may not enter the league until at least three years after he graduated from high school. The NBA's 2005 collectively bargained rule requires American players to be no less than 19 years old and at least one year removed from high school. The education-related portion of the NBA's rule does not apply to non-Americans. Eligibility rules in MLB, the NHL, the PGA TOUR, and the ATP World Tour are related only to age and include no minimum education requirements.

Examples of legal analyses of age restrictions that have focused on the NBA and NFL include Rosner (1998), Jones (2005), Cimino (2006), Pensyl (2006), Pitts (2008), Rodenberg (2008), and Shaffer (2008). Such legal analyses usually turn on whether the age eligibility rule in question violates antitrust and/or labor law, with experts split on the issue of whether such rules violate the law. Those who support the legality of minimum age rules in the sports industry usually point to the collectively bargained nature of the rules and the accompanying non-statutory labor exemption that likely shields the rules from antitrust liability. In contrast, critics of the age policies often point out that, under antitrust law's rule of reason, there is a dearth of evidence supporting any pro-competitive qualities and emerging evidence illustrating the rules' anti-competitive effect.

The Sherman Antitrust Act of 1890 (Sherman Act), the most prominent federal antitrust statute, prohibits '[e]very contract, combination . . . or conspiracy, in restraint of trade or commerce among the several states' (15 U.S.C. § 1, 2010). The Sherman Act was interpreted in *Standard Oil v. United States* (1911) as outlawing contracts, combinations, or conspiracies that 'unreasonably' restrain trade (p. 63). In *Chicago Board of Trade v. United States* (1918: 238), the Court set out the applicable antitrust rules:

> The court must ordinarily consider the facts peculiar to the business to which the restraint is applied; its condition before and after the restraint was imposed; the nature of the restraint, and its effect, actual or probable. The history of the restraint, the evil believed to exist, the reason for adopting the particular remedy, the purpose or end sought to be attained, are all relevant facts.

The Sherman Act's intersection with sports started over 90 years ago. In 1922, the Supreme Court decided *Federal Baseball Club of Baltimore v. National League of Professional Baseball Clubs*, a dispute between rival baseball leagues. It found MLB to be exempt from antitrust scrutiny. The ruling resulted from the Court's finding that professional baseball did not constitute interstate commerce. The Supreme Court revisited the issue in *Flood v. Kuhn* (1972) and alluded to the *Federal Baseball* decision as 'an aberration' and 'an anomaly', but did not explicitly overrule the case even though it found MLB to be 'a business [that] is engaged in interstate commerce' (p. 282). The *Flood* case turned on whether MLB could enforce the then-applicable reserve clause, a long-entrenched rule that mandated, among other things, that players be tied to the team that initially drafted them even after the player's contract expired. *Federal Baseball* notwithstanding, other sports have been deemed generally subject to federal antitrust laws: basketball (*Haywood v. National Basketball Association*, 1971), football (*Radovich v. National Football League*, 1957), hockey (*Philadelphia World Hockey Club, Inc. v. Philadelphia Hockey Club, Inc.*, 1972), boxing (*International Boxing Club v. United States*, 1958), and tennis (*Volvo North American Corp. v. Men's International Professional Tennis Council*, 1988). Although none of the preceding cases pertained to sport industry age rules, their disposition demonstrated that courts are willing to analyze whether the actions of sports leagues, tours, and teams comply with antitrust law.

A recent high-profile lawsuit evidences the contentiousness and practical importance of minimum age rules in sports. In 2003, former Ohio State University running back Maurice Clarett filed an antitrust lawsuit in federal court challenging the NFL's age rule. Following a stellar freshman season, in which he helped the team to a college national championship, Clarett sought to continue his football career in the NFL despite not meeting the league's eligibility rule. Clarett's move was also precipitated by looming sanctions that may have rendered him ineligible to play college football as a member of the Ohio State team. Among other things, Clarett claimed that the NFL's rule denied him the chance to earn a living as a professional football player. The case resulted in two published judicial decisions. Clarett prevailed at the district court level, but the NFL obtained a reversal upholding its eligibility rule on appeal (*Clarett v. National Football League*, 2004). Clarett's subsequent appeal to the United States Supreme Court was denied.

The basis for the Court's decision was the NFL's non-statutory labor exemption. This exemption frequently applies in the presence of a collective bargaining agreement. The exemption was created to protect a union's right to bargain on behalf of its membership, an action that inherently conflicts with the rights of individual workers to contract with the firm. The rationale for the exemption is that individual workers would not be able to bargain effectively with their employers in the absence of a union.

Thus, the right of a union to bargain collectively trumps antitrust considerations. Because the NFL's age restriction is part of a collective bargaining agreement between the NFL and the NFL Players' Association, the Court ruled that antitrust considerations did not apply, and the NFL's eligibility rule thus remains intact.

The status quo also holds in other sports. In 1997, female tennis player Mirjana Lucic unsuccessfully challenged the WTA Tour's age eligibility rule in an Australian court. There have been no legal challenges in American courts to age restrictions in women's professional sports in tennis, basketball, golf, or gymnastics.

8.4   THE ECONOMIC IMPACT OF AGE RESTRICTIONS

Outside of sports, economists have studied child labor for some time. Grootaert and Kanbur (1995) offer an analysis of child labor, discussing topics such as the determinants of child labor and the role of policy interventions. Lleras-Muney (2002) tracks the change in child labor laws from 1915 to 1939 and finds that an increase in the minimum age required to obtain a work permit, coupled with compulsory school attendance policies, resulted in increased educational attainment. Moehling (1999) tests the impact of minimum-age limits in the manufacturing sector from 1880 to 1910 and finds that they contributed little to the precipitous drop in child labor during the time period. Baland and Robinson (2000) provide a formal model of the efficiency of child labor.

In the subfield of sports economics, Sowell and Mounts (2005) use data from the Ironman Triathlon World Championships to analyze the relationship between age and ability. They use stochastic frontier analysis to determine the efficiency of male and female triathletes at transforming underlying talent into performance. They find that, while men reach peak efficiency in their late twenties, women reach peak efficiency in their early thirties but women's performance then declines more quickly than men's. These results, however, are of limited value for the sports considered in this chapter, as the triathlon events (running, swimming, and cycling) use 'slow-twitch' muscles, while the sports considered in this chapter rely much more on 'fast-twitch' muscles, which might age differently.

Rodenberg and Stone's (2011) investigation into the effects of the WTA Tour's age restriction on career success is the most in-depth empirical examination to date. Their data consist of all players who finished in the top 50 of the WTA Tour singles rankings for the first time between 1989 and 2000. Because the age rule was implemented at the mid-point of the time period (1995), a natural experiment results in which one can test the impact of the rule change. A dummy variable denotes whether a player was subject to the age restriction. In particular, the variable equals 1 when the player was born after December 31, 1977 and first played in a WTA main draw tournament after January 1, 1995.[2] The authors test the null hypothesis that the age rule has had no effect on the short- and long-run career success of elite female tennis players. With no single metric universally considered as the best measure of tennis success, Rodenberg and Stone use 'a variety of dependent and independent variables, adopt different sample restrictions, and show that the main results are robust to varying model specification' (p. 186).

All their models use a combination of the following six independent variables: age rule status, handedness, height, socioeconomic background, birth month, and career-best year-end ranking (as a proxy for talent and ability). To estimate any short-run effects of the 1995 age rule, they use ordinary least squares (OLS) regression with the dependent variable equal to the player's average WTA Tour singles ranking when 19 and 20 and no longer constrained by the age rule. Regression results do not 'evidence any systematic beneficial short-run effect of a player's [age rule] compliance status on the mean rank when young' (p. 191).

To investigate the long-run impact of tennis' age rule, Rodenberg and Stone select three dependent variables to capture the quantity and quality aspects of the rule's intended effect: the number of years a player is ranked, the number of years a player is ranked in the top 50, and the number of years a player is ranked in the top 10. Using OLS across the different specifications and among the three dependent variables, the authors do not find systematic evidence of the age rule's having any effect on player outcomes.

One reason for the age restriction was a desire to reduce early, career-ending injuries. To capture this, Rodenberg and Stone estimate two probit models with binary dependent variables that denote early career retirements (those occurring before age 26) and serious injuries of six months or more during the first nine years of a player's career after breaking into the rankings top 50. Neither being subject to the age restriction nor any other control variable affected premature retirement. In contrast, players who were affected by the age restriction had a higher rate of serious injury than those who were not. Although this result suggests a negative and unintended outgrowth of the minimum age rule, its importance is mitigated by the lack of any other corroborating evidence and could result from a relatively small sample that did not include the player's age.

Finally, the authors use panel data methods to exploit the dataset's player-level annual ranking time-series and control for time-varying effects. For these models, Rodenberg and Stone use binary dependent variables analogous to the three left-hand-side variables adopted in the long-run analysis described above. With the player-specific age rule dummy variable constant from year to year, they use a random-effects estimator instead of a fixed-effects estimator. The authors also assume that none of the explanatory variables is correlated with other time-invariant, unobservable characteristics, particularly the player's ability. Linear probability regression results from the panel data analysis, particularly the impact of the age restriction, were largely insignificant, like those of the long-run OLS regressions summarized above. In sum, using a variety of methods, Rodenberg and Stone find 'very limited evidence that the [WTA Tour age rule] has had any systematic beneficial effect on players' career longevity or success' (p. 181).

These findings suggest that the rule changes have failed to protect younger players and to promote longer, more successful careers. Further analysis, however, is required before drawing a firm conclusion. For example, the findings might reflect self-selection among tennis players. By looking at highly ranked players, Rodenberg and Stone are actually testing the impact of the rule change on the very best players. It is possible that these players have the physical and emotional tools needed to succeed even at a young age. It is possible that the age restriction extends and improves the careers of lower-ranked players. Such a result cannot be captured by this dataset.

Basketball is one of the few sports that have been the focus of economic analyses of age limits. The NBA's recently enacted minimum age rule, a policy similar in content and form to the numerous eligibility rules in women's sports, has been put under the economic microscope in a number of ways. Rosenbaum (2003) explains how collective bargaining agreements in the 1990s increased the opportunity costs of attending college for elite basketball players and, in turn, precipitated the 'flood' of high-school students who have been declaring themselves eligible for the NBA. McCann (2004) claims that 'high school players who have declared [for the draft] have encountered more success than has any other age cohort' (p. 197). Rodenberg and Kim's (2011) NBA-specific findings support McCann. They 'analyze the role of precocity on labor market outcomes of elite-level NBA players and, indirectly, test the on-court efficacy of the NBA's age rule' (p. 2186). Using a data set of all first-round draft picks from 1989 to 2000 and including a host of player-specific control variables, Rodenberg and Kim find evidence that 'players who enter the NBA at a relatively younger age have more successful on-court careers' (p. 2188).

As was the case for the study of tennis, the data underlying the findings for basketball might generate biased estimates due to self-selection. By considering only high draft choices, the studies leave out players who declare for the NBA but who are selected in the second round or are not selected at all. Not being a first-round draft pick has serious implications for a potential player, as only first-round picks receive guaranteed contracts. There is, moreover, some evidence that first-round picks are treated differently by their teams long after the draft even when one controls for the player's performance (see Staw and Hoang, 1995, and Camerer and Weber, 1999). The economic implications of age limits thus remain uncertain as they await correction for self-selection.

8.5   CONCLUSION

Table 8A.1 in Appendix 8A shows that age eligibility rules are common in a variety of women's sports. However, the formulation, enactment, and management of such rules is challenging from both a legal and economic perspective. The difficulties in administering age eligibility rules and the potential for inconsistency and unfairness are articulated by Weiss (2005):

> Chronological age is not equivalent to social, emotional, cognitive, and ana-
> tomical age. We need age eligibility rules, but we also know that chronologi-
> cal age, while we use it as a main index for classifying athletes, is not reliably
> associated with these other age or maturity levels. Two adolescents of the same
> age can be widely different in terms of social and emotional types of maturity.
> (p. 2)

Weiss also speculates that rules based solely on chronological age could be improved:

> The implication of this idea is that age eligibility rules and policies need to con-
> sider the wide variety of individual differences in these various age indices and
> strategize ways of ensuring that the adolescent phenom is ready for the transi-
> tion to professional. This might be done through other kinds of interviews and
> other kinds of standards than just age. (p. 2)

Asking whether age rules can be improved begs the question of whether the rules are effective – or even desirable. Fortunately, as noted in the introduction to this chapter, the plethora of performance and reward data in sports combined with the presence of exogenous changes in structure and rules mean that sports readily generate natural experiments (see Kahn, 2000). As aptly observed by Sowell and Mounts (2005: 92), such a 'controlled experiment [is] something rare' in academic research. One example, the WTA Tour minimum age rule promulgated in 1995, lends itself well to the 'before and after' analysis of the type found in Rodenberg and Stone (2011).

In an ideal experiment, the WTA Tour would have prospectively tested the age rule's efficacy for a number of years prior to mandating its compliance for all new players. The WTA Tour could have done this through randomization, like the clinical trials of pharmaceutical companies, given that '[t]he most credible and influential research designs use random assignment' (Angrist and Pischke, 2009: 11) in the process of making an informed decision. For a number of legal, ethical, and pragmatic reasons, sport governing bodies do not pursue randomization, a fact contributing to the sometimes contentious and controversial nature of minimum age rules in various sports. While there is a dearth of *ex ante* analysis, there are still opportunities for research *ex post*, after the age-based policies have been in effect for several years.

NOTES

1. Berri and Krautmann provide a detailed comparison of salaries in the NBA and the WNBA in Chapter 7 in this volume.
2. Thus Venus Williams, who was born in 1980 and did not enter the WTA Tour top 50 until 1997, was not subject to the age restriction because she had competed in the main draw of a WTA Tour tournament in 1994 as a 14-year-old. As a result, she was coded as a 0. Note that the dummy variable identifies players who were *potentially* restricted. Some players might have qualified at exactly 18 years of age in the absence of a restriction.

REFERENCES

Angrist, Joshua D. and Jörn-Steffen Pischke (2009), *Mostly Harmless Econometrics: An Empiricist's Guide*, Princeton, NJ: Princeton University Press.
Baland, Jean-Marie and James A. Robinson (2000), 'Is Child Labor Inefficient?', *Journal of Political Economy*, **108**(4), November: 663–79.
Bernhardt, Dan and Steven L. Heston (2010), 'Point Shaving in College Basketball: A Cautionary Tale for Forensic Economics', *Economic Inquiry*, **48**(1), January: 14–25.
Camerer, Colin F. and Roberto A. Weber (1999), 'The Econometrics and Behavioral Economics of Escalation: A Re-examination of Staw and Hoang's NBA Data', *Journal of Economic Behavior and Organization*, **39**(1), May: 59–82.
Chicago Board of Trade v. United States, 246 U.S. 231 (1918).
Cimino, Kevin J. (2006), 'The Rebirth of the NBA – Well, Almost: An Analysis of the Maurice Clarett Decision and its Impact on the National Basketball Association', *West Virginia Law Review*, **108**(3), Spring: 831–71.
Clarett v. National Football League, 306 F. Supp.2d 379 (S.D.N.Y. 2004), reversed in part, vacated in part, remanded by, 369 F.3d 124 (2nd Cir. 2004).
Cook, Kevin (2008), *Driven: Teen Phenoms, Mad Parents, Swing Science and the Future of Golf*, New York: Gotham Books.
Daly, Robin M., Shona L. Bass and Caroline F. Finch (2001), 'Balancing the Risk of Injury to Gymnasts: How Effective are the Counter-measures?', *British Journal of Sports Medicine*, **35**(1), February: 8–20.
David, Paulo (2005), *Human Rights in Youth Sport*, New York: Routledge.

Doherty, Eryn M. (1999), 'Winning Isn't Everything . . . It's the Only Thing: A Critique of Teenaged Girls' Participation in Sports', *Marquette Sports Law Review*, **10**(1), Fall: 127–60.
Edelman, Marc and C. Keith Harrison (2008), 'Analyzing the WNBA's Mandatory Age/ Education Policy from a Legal, Cultural, and Ethical Perspective: Women, Men, and the Professional Sports Landscape', *Northwestern Journal of Law and Policy*, **3**(1), Winter: 1–28.
Elliott, Mick (2011), 'Calm Down, Lexi Thompson Will Get Her Wish', *ESPNW*, September 21, online at: http://espn.go.com/espnw/news-opinion/7001638/calm-lexi-thompson-get-wish (accessed December 27, 2011).
Federal Baseball Club of Baltimore v. National League of Professional Baseball Clubs, 259 U.S. 200 (1922).
Finn, Robin (1999), 'Fourteen Year-old May Sue Over Locked Pro Courts', *New York Times*, D1.
Flood v. Kuhn, 407 U.S. 258 (1972).
Grenfell, Christopher C. and Robert E. Rinehart (2003), 'Skating on Thin Ice: Human Rights in Youth Figure Skating', *International Review for the Sociology of Sport*, **38**(1), March: 79–97.
Grootaert, Christiaan and Ravi Kanbur (1995), 'Child Labour: An Economic Perspective', *International Labour Review*, **134**(2), January: 187–203.
Haywood v. National Basketball Association, 401 U.S. 1204 (1971).
International Boxing Club v. United States, 358 U.S. 242 (1958).
Jones, Andrew M. (2005), 'Hold the Mayo: An Analysis of the Validity of the NBA's Stern no Preps to Pros Rule and Application of the Nonstatutory Exemption', *Loyola of Los Angeles Entertainment Law Review*, **26**(3), March: 475–522.
Kahn, Lawrence M.(2000), 'The Sports Business as a Labor Market Laboratory', *Journal of Economic Perspectives*, **14**(3), Summer: 75–94.
Kaplan, Daniel (2004), 'I.D. Please: WTA Tour CEO Pushing Grand Slams to Raise Age Limits', *Street and Smith's Sports Business Journal Daily*, April 19–25, online at: http://www.sportsbusinessdaily.com/Journal/Issues/2004/04/20040419/This-Weeks-Issue/ID-Please-WTA-Tour-CEO-Pushing-Grand-Slams-To-Raise-Age-Limits.aspx (accessed December 27, 2011).
Lapchick, Richard (2011), 'Keeping Score When It Counts: Sweet 16 Men's and Women's Teams. A Look at Their Academic Success', The Institute for Diversity and Ethics in Sport, March 23, online at: http://tidesport.org/Grad%20Rates/2011_Sweet_16_FINAL.pdf (accessed December 28, 2011).
Livengood, Thomas, Ashley Keber and Kathy Martin (2008), 'Introduction to PRO U Player Orientation', *Science and Medicine in Tennis*, **13**(2): 10–12.
Lleras-Muney, Adriana (2002), 'Were Compulsory Attendance and Child Labor Laws Effective? An Analysis from 1915 to 1939', *Journal of Law and Economics*, **45**(2), October: 401–35.
McCann, Michael A. (2004), 'Illegal Defense: The Irrational Economics of Banning High School Players from the NBA Draft', *Virginia Sports and Entertainment Law Journal*, **3**(2), Spring: 113–98.
McCann, Michael A. and Joseph S. Rosen (2006), 'Legality of Age Restrictions in the NBA and the NFL', *Case Western Reserve Law Review*, **56**(3), Spring: 731–68.
McGuire, Bartlett H. (2007), 'Age Restrictions in Women's Professional Tennis: A Case Study of Pro-competitive Restraints of Trade', *Journal of International Media & Entertainment Law*, 1(2), Winter/Spring: 199–251.
Merten, Jenna (2004), 'Raising a Red Card: Why Freddy Adu Should not be Allowed to Play Professional Soccer', *Marquette Sports Law Review*, **15**(1), Fall: 205–25.
Mewshaw, Michael (1993), *Ladies of the Court: Grace and Disgrace on the Women's Tennis Tour*, New York: Crown Publishers.
Miron, Jeffrey A. and Elina Tetelbaum (2009), 'Does the Minimum Legal Drinking Age Save Lives?', *Economic Inquiry*, **47**(2), April: 317–36.

Moehling, Carolyn M. (1999), 'State Child Labor Laws and the Decline of Child Labor', *Explorations in Economic History*, **36**(1), January: 72–106.

Paul, Jennifer (2010), 'Age Minimums in the Sport of Women's Artistic Gymnastics', *Willamette Sports Law Journal*, **7**(2), Spring: 73–90.

Pensyl, Tyler (2006), 'Let Clarett Play: Why the Nonstatutory Labor Exemption Should Not Exempt the NFL's Draft Eligibility Rule from the Antitrust Laws', *University of Toledo Law Review*, **37**, Winter: 523–50.

Philadelphia World Hockey Club, Inc. v. Philadelphia Hockey Club, Inc., 351 F.Supp. 462 (E.D. Pa. 1972).

Pitts, Jack N.E. (2008), 'Why Wait? An Antitrust Analysis of the National Football League and National Basketball Association's Draft Eligibility Rules', *Howard Law Journal*, **51**(2), Winter: 433–78.

Radovich v. National Football League, 352 U.S. 445 (1957).

Roberts, Selena (1997), 'Kournikova: Part Phenom, Part Press Agent's Dream', *New York Times*, 26 August.

Rodenberg, Ryan M. (2000), 'Age Eligibility Rules in Women's Professional Tennis: Necessary for the Integrity, Viability, and Administration of the Game or an Unreasonable Restraint of Trade in Violation of Antitrust Law?', *Sports Lawyers Journal*, **7**, Spring: 183–212.

Rodenberg, Ryan M. (2008), 'The NBA's Latest Three Point Play: Age Eligibility Rules, Antitrust, and Labor Law', *Entertainment and Sports Lawyer*, **25**(4), February: 14–17.

Rodenberg, Ryan M. and Andrea N. Eagleman (2011), 'Uneven Bars: Age Rules, Antitrust, and Amateurism in Women's Gymnastics', *University of Baltimore Law Review*, **40**(4), July: 585–605.

Rodenberg, Ryan M., Elizabeth A. Gregg and Lawrence W. Fielding (2009), 'Age Eligibility Rules in Women's Professional Golf: A Legal Eagle or an Antitrust Bogey?', *Journal of Legal Aspects of Sport*, **19**(2), Summer: 103–20.

Rodenberg, Ryan M. and Jun Woo Kim (2011), 'Precocity and Labor Market Outcomes: Evidence from Professional Basketball', *Economics Bulletin*, **31**(3), July: 2185–90.

Rodenberg, Ryan M. and Daniel F. Stone (2011), 'Short and Long Run Labor Market Effects of Age Eligibility Rules: Evidence from Women's Professional Tennis', *Journal of Labor Research*, **32**(2), April: 181–98.

Rosenbaum, Dan T. (2003), 'How the NBA Turned a Trickle of Underclassmen Leaving School Early into a Flood', unpublished working paper, Department of Economics, University of North Carolina, Greensboro, NC.

Rosner, Scott R. (1998), 'Must Kobe Come Out and Play? An Analysis of the Legality of Preventing High School Athletes and College Underclassmen from Entering Professional Sports Drafts', *Seton Hall Journal of Sport Law*, **8**(2): 539–74.

Rowland, Thomas W. (2000), 'On the Ethics of Elite-level Sports Participation by Children', *Pediatric Exercise Science*, **12**(1), February: 1–5.

Ryan, Joan (2000), *Little Girls in Pretty Boxes: The Making and Breaking of Elite Gymnasts and Figure Skaters*, New York: Warner Books.

Shaffer, Brian (2008), 'The NBA's Age Requirement Shoots and Misses: How the Nonstatutory Exemption Produces Inequitable Results for High School Basketball Stars', *Santa Clara Law Review*, **48**(3), January: 681–707.

Sherman Antitrust Act, 15 U.S.C. § 1 (2010).

Sowell, Clifford B. and Wm Stewart Mounts Jr. (2005), 'Ability, Age, and Performance: Conclusions from the Ironman Triathlon World Championships', *Journal of Sports Economics*, **6**(1), February: 78–97.

Stabiner, Karen (1986), *Courting Fame: The Perilous Road to Women's Tennis Stardom*, New York: Harper & Row.

Standard Oil Co. v. United States, 221 U.S. 1 (1911).

Staw, Barry M. and Ha Hoang (1995), 'Sunk Costs in the NBA: Why Draft Order Affects Playing Time in Professional Basketball', *Administrative Science Quarterly*, **40**(3), September: 474–94.

Volvo North American Corp. v. Men's International Professional Tennis Council, 857 F.2d 55 (2d Cir. 1988).

Warren, Michelle P. and N.E. Perloth (2001), 'The Effects of Intense Exercise on the Female Reproductive System', *Journal of Endocrinology*, **170**(1), July: 3–11.

Weiss, Maureen (2005), 'Successful Transitions: Strategies and Programs', oral presentation at the 'Phenoms to Professionals: Successful Transitions' forum hosted by the Ladies Professional Golf Association, Daytona Beach, FL, December.

Wertheim, L. Jon (2001), *Venus Envy: A Sensational Season Inside the Women's Tennis Tour*, New York: Harper Collins.

APPENDIX 8A

Table 8A.1   Age restrictions and governing bodies for selected sports

Women's sport	Minimum age*	Governing bodies
Archery	None	International Archery Federation
Badminton	19 'recommended'	Badminton World Federation
Biathlon	21	International Biathlon Union
Bobsled	18	Fédération Internationale de Bobsleigh et de Tobogganing
Body Building	21	International Federation of Bodybuilding & Fitness
Bowling	16	Fédération Internationale des Quilleurs
Boxing	17	International Boxing Association
Canoeing/ Kayaking	None	International Canoe Federation
Cricket	19	International Cricket Council
Cycling	Road = 19; BMX = 16	Union Cycliste Internationale
Diving	14	Fédération Internationale de Natation
Football	18	Independent Women's Football League
Fencing	13	Fédération Internationale d'Escrime
Field Hockey	None	International Hockey Federation
Ice Hockey	18	International Ice Hockey Federation
Ice Skating/ Ice Dancing	15	International Skating Union
Judo	15	International Judo Federation
Karate	None	World Karate Federation
Luge	15	Fédération Internationale de Luge de Course
Mixed Martial Arts	18	International Sport Combat Federation
Pentathlon	17	Union Internationale de Pentathlon Moderne
Polo	None	Federation of International Polo
Powerlifting	14	International Powerlifting Federation
Racketlon	None	International Racketlon Federation
Rowing	18	Fédération Internationale des Sociétés d'Aviron
Rugby	18	International Rugby Board
Sailing	None	International Sailing Federation
Shooting	16	International Shooting Sport Federation

Table 8A.1   (continued)

Women's sport	Minimum age*	Governing bodies
Skeleton	16	Fédération Internationale de Bobsleigh et de Tobogganing
Skiing	Snowboard/ Alpine/Freestyle: 15 Nordic/Cross-Country/Jumping: None	Fédération Internationale de Ski
Softball	None	International Softball Federation
Speed Skating	15	International Skating Union
Squash	None	World Squash Federation
Swimming	None	Fédération Internationale de Natation
Synchronized Swimming	15	Fédération Internationale de Natation
Table Tennis	15	International Table Tennis Federation
Taekwondo	18	World Taekwondo Federation
Track and Field	14	International Association of Athletics Federations
Volleyball	None	Fédération Internationale de Volleyball
Water Polo	None	Fédération Internationale de Natation

PART III

WOMEN IN INTERCOLLEGIATE SPORTS

9. The economics of Title IX compliance in intercollegiate athletics

*Susan L. Averett and Sarah M. Estelle**

> Those of us in the business know that universities have been end-running Title IX for a long time, and they do it until they get caught.
>
> University of Miami President Donna Shalala (Quoted in Thomas, 2011a)

9.1 INTRODUCTION

Gender equality in intercollegiate athletics has been the subject of numerous articles in the popular press and the economics literature. In this chapter, we examine what is arguably the most-studied topic in women's sports: Title IX. This law bans sex discrimination in schools and has opened a myriad of academic and sports opportunities for women at the interscholastic, intercollegiate, and – indirectly – professional levels. The idea of providing equal opportunities to women and girls in education has been met with little disagreement, but the policies that have been implemented in pursuit of this ideal, particularly in the realm of intercollegiate athletics, are very controversial. While sports is not its sole focus, Title IX (described in detail below) requires gender equality in athletic participation as well as funding for women's and men's sports.

For decades, athletic directors and colleges and universities in general have struggled to comply with the law, which they argue is unrealistic at best. Many critics of the legislation contest that it has led to reverse discrimination – that schools have slashed opportunities for men in order to demonstrate equal participation as stipulated by the law. Detractors also assert that Title IX ignores gender differences in athletic interests and ability to play varsity sports. Proponents of women's rights point to both the lack of progress towards compliance and the bloated budgets of men's football teams and the disproportionately high salaries paid to the coaches of football and men's basketball. They assert that, even if the law is unfairly stringent in its requirements, there is still room for progress toward gender equality in intercollegiate sports.

In the heat of this debate, colleges remain mired in a complex reality. Each institution must balance compliance with the law against budgetary pressures. Athletic departments must field teams that bring their institutions prestige, revenue, and the athletic participation opportunities consistent with their students' interests. While the National Collegiate Athletic Association (NCAA) first opposed Title IX, today the NCAA and its member schools proclaim their commitment to it, stating that the only impediment is money (Zimbalist, 1997).

Although the Title IX regulations were promulgated in the mid-1970s, mechanisms to monitor compliance have been put in place only relatively recently. A recent exposé in the *New York Times* revealed the extremes to which schools go in order to comply, including counting male practice players as women, allowing men to be on the rosters of women's teams, and putting students who are not even interested in competing on team rosters (Thomas, 2011a).

Despite the reliance of some schools on legerdemain, Title IX has had a real impact. The fact that athletic opportunities for women have increased since 1972 is doubtless due in large part to the passage of Title IX. In 1971, there were only 29,977 women on intercollegiate athletic teams, compared to 170,384 men (Monks, 2005). By the 2009–10 academic year, those numbers had climbed to 193,232 women and 256,344 men (Irick, 2011).

An economic analysis of Title IX compliance is both relevant and necessary to provide an understanding of the challenges that policy makers and colleges face. In Section 9.2, we provide an overview of the legislation, its history, and the evolution of its interpretation and enforcement. In Section 9.3, we review the literature pertaining to the economics of Title IX compliance, and in Section 9.4 we develop a model of institutional response to Title IX. Using data from 2000–01 to 2009–10, we conduct an empirical analysis of Title IX compliance. Our analysis differs from previous studies in that we include both NCAA and non-NCAA athletic programs, whereas previous studies have focused on the former. While a majority of schools and students belong to the NCAA, about 350 colleges belong to the National Association of Intercollegiate Athletics (NAIA) alone. We find scant evidence of any progress toward compliance over the last decade. More disturbingly, when schools do comply, the compliance is usually transitory. We find robust evidence, consistent with the existing literature, that institutions with a larger percentage of female enrollment or a football program are less likely to comply, while schools with larger total undergraduate enrollment are more likely to comply or come closer to compliance. In Section 9.5 we suggest extensions and improvements of the current literature that would aid in assessing the economics behind Title IX.[1] Section 9.6 concludes.

9.2   HISTORY AND OVERVIEW OF THE LAW

9.2.1   Title IX at Its Inception[2]

In contrast to the uproar it later incited, Title IX began as a rather insignificant supplemental provision in an executive order. After the passage of the 1964 Civil Rights Act, President Lyndon Johnson issued an executive order prohibiting employer discrimination on the basis of 'race, color, religion, or national origin' by employers receiving federal funds. Between 1970 and 1972, the Nixon administration proposed a series of amendments to the Civil Rights Act that extended the workplace discrimination regulations to educational facilities (Terry and Ramirez, 2005). While the focus was on neither sexual discrimination nor athletics at the time, Congress was in the midst of holding hearings on sexual discrimination in education (Suggs, 2005). Based on findings from these hearings, Congress included an amendment that would address sexual discrimination in education. Thus the regulations on intercollegiate athletics that are part of Title IX were enacted on June 23, 1972, and signed into law by President Richard Nixon.

Vast ambiguities in the law led to a variety of interpretations, which made its implementation virtually impossible. The final version of the law stated, 'No person in the United States shall, on the basis of sex, be excluded from participation in, be denied the benefits of, or be subjected to discrimination under any educational program or activity receiving federal financial assistance'. The phrase 'educational program or activity receiving federal financial assistance' was intended as an umbrella term for admissions and recruitment, educational programs and course offerings, counseling, financial aid, employment assistance, housing and facilities, insurance benefits, scholarships, and, of course, athletics (Terry and Ramirez, 2005). The only further clarification provided was that both public and private schools from kindergarten through the graduate level had to comply with the law. However, there was no mention at all of how to measure compliance, and it would be many years before compliance standards were outlined and adopted. As we document later in this chapter, as recently as 2009, the most common metric of compliance shows that the majority of US institutions of higher learning were not in compliance with Title IX.

9.2.2   Evolution of the Law

The failure to specify how to determine compliance with the new law caused a great deal of controversy. Universities and their athletic programs wanted to know if and when they would be held accountable, which led to court cases disputing the many interpretations of the law. These court decisions, in turn, helped mold the statute into the more coherent version to which institutions of higher education are held today.

In the immediate aftermath of the law's passage, between 1974 and 1979, a flurry of amendments to limit the jurisdiction of Title IX poured in. Perhaps the most important one was the Tower Amendment of 1974, which would have exempted any sport that was deemed 'revenue-producing' from Title IX (Zimbalist, 1997; Wushanley, 2004; Suggs, 2005; Terry and Ramirez, 2005). Had the amendment passed, schools would have found it significantly easier to comply with the law since many schools could have ignored participation in football and men's basketball in determining compliance. An alternative to the Tower Amendment, the Javits Amendment, passed in 1974 (Wushanley, 2004; Terry and Ramirez, 2005), attempted to clarify the applicability of the law. It stated that Title IX regulations would have to include reasonable provisions that took into account the nature of different sports (Terry and Ramirez, 2005). This meant that valid non-gender-related differences between sports (for example, equipment costs) could not be considered discrimination when assessing whether a school was practicing athletic discrimination based on sex.

In the meantime, the first few Title IX complaints against athletics programs at the University of Michigan, the University of Wisconsin, and the University of Minnesota were filed in 1974 (Suggs, 2005). It was not long before it became evident that for the law to be properly enforced, a clarification of its interpretation was in order. In 1979, the then Department of Health, Education and Welfare established a framework for compliance that encompassed three major categories: accommodation of student interests and abilities, athletic financial aid, and other program areas (Zimbalist, 1997). The first category has been the focus of the greatest attention and the source of most litigation activity. Within this category, a school can demonstrate compliance in one of three ways. Under this 'three-prong test', schools are deemed compliant with Title IX's requirements for equal participation opportunities if they satisfy any of the following criteria:

- provide a composition of athletic opportunities to men and women that is proportional to the gender composition of the student body (substantial proportionality);
- demonstrate consistent program expansion for women (continued expansion); and
- show accommodation of student interests or abilities (accommodation of interests) (Suggs, 2005; Terry and Ramirez, 2005).

The three-prong test was the major clarification that made the law enforceable, and it is still used to gauge compliance. Because the first prong is easily measurable, most schools choose to focus on substantial proportionality. Since it has been the most-studied, substantial proportionality is also the focus of the remainder of this chapter.[3] 'Substantial proportionality' does not imply perfect proportionality. Instead, it allows a 'proportionality gap' that is not 'too large', an issue we address later. To understand the proportionality gap, consider a university with an undergraduate student body that is 50 percent female but fills only 35 percent of all varsity athletic opportunities with women. This implies a proportionality gap of 15 percent.

In 1980, the newly established Department of Education was given oversight of Title IX. It set about enforcing the law through the Office for Civil Rights (OCR). Shortly thereafter, though, Title IX suffered a significant setback in the courts. In 1984, the US Supreme Court ruled in *Grove City College v. Bell* that Title IX applied only to specific programs that directly received federal funding (Terry and Ramirez, 2005; Mitchell and Ennis, 2007). This effectively eliminated most of the law's jurisdiction (Zimbalist, 2003) because, while almost all colleges and universities directly receive federal funding, few of their athletic programs do. Therefore, this case rendered the law largely powerless, and over the next four years Title IX remained moribund.

The law regained its effectiveness only after the passage of the Civil Rights Restoration Act in 1988. The Act restored the jurisdiction of Title IX to all educational institutions and activities receiving any type of federal aid (Zimbalist, 2003; Terry and Ramirez, 2005; Mitchell and Ennis, 2007). A critical factor in making enforcement easier was the 1994 passage of the Equity in Athletics Disclosure Act (EADA). EADA requires any co-educational institution of higher education that participates in any federal student financial aid program and that sponsors an intercollegiate athletics program to disclose information about its athletics program in an annual report, which must be publicly available.

Currently, Title IX is still formally enforced by the OCR. Institutions found to be noncompliant may lose their federal funding. If OCR receives a Title IX complaint, it first conducts an investigation to determine if the alleged discrimination took place. If so, it has several enforcement options ranging from a settlement agreement to a referral to the Department of Justice. Title IX can also be enforced through the court system, and the NCAA has the ability to provide compliance incentives for its member institutions. As of 2012, no institution of higher education has lost its federal funding due to a Title IX violation.

9.3   PREVIOUS EMPIRICAL WORK ON TITLE IX

In recent years, a handful of economic studies have investigated the factors influencing Title IX compliance and the effects of Title IX on women's and men's sports offerings. These studies have mainly used data from the mid-1990s or later because institutions subject to Title IX were required to disclose their data annually only with the advent of the 1994 EADA. In this section, we present the methodologies and results of the key studies, focusing on three topics: the economic determinants of proportionality compliance, the effects of proportionality compliance on sports offerings, and the effectiveness of changing compliance rules and enforcement. While numerous court cases and other, less formal complaints over the decades have argued that proportionality might not be an effective measure of compliance with Title IX, proportionality is still the prong most often used, largely because it is measurable (Anderson and Cheslock, 2004; Stafford, 2004).

Stafford (2004) and Anderson et al. (2006) examine the determinants of proportionality compliance. The former explains a binary outcome – compliance versus non-compliance, allowing a 5 percent proportionality gap – while the latter focuses on the magnitude of the proportionality gap among institutions with positive proportionality gaps. An advantage of analyzing compliance status is its direct applicability to the concerns of the OCR and judicial system since, in practice, compliance is an either–or determination, not one of varying degrees. However, in understanding what brings some schools to the compliance/noncompliance margin, the binary approach discards much potentially useful information in that some schools are much closer to compliance than are others. Another key difference between these studies is their scope: Stafford focuses on NCAA Division I institutions, while Anderson et al. analyze all NCAA member institutions. Both papers use compliance data for the 1995–96 and 2001–02 academic years.

Stafford finds a greater probability of compliance for large institutions with relatively few women and no football program. She also finds that large athletic programs do worse in terms of compliance but improved more than schools with smaller programs from 1995–96 to 2001–02, and that Southern institutions fare worse by both criteria. Finally, she considers the effects of what she terms four 'enforcement mechanisms', which vary by school, on the probability of being in compliance. These mechanisms are (i) whether the school has been subject to any NCAA sanctions since 1992; (ii) whether the school is currently on NCAA probation; (iii) whether the school was certified by the NCAA prior to 2001; and (iv) how many years the school has been NCAA certified.[4] Each of these variables is posited to influence compliance with Title IX, albeit in different ways. For example, a school that is currently on NCAA probation may want to increase its compliance as a part of a public relations campaign to improve its image. However, such a school may be less able to comply with Title IX if the probation affects its ability to earn revenues from athletic events. Including these four variables in the models of whether a school reaches proportionality allows her to ascertain whether sanctions or probation is useful in nudging schools closer to compliance. There is little empirical evidence that sanctions ensure that schools are in compliance.

Anderson et al. come to many of the same conclusions with respect to the determinants of the magnitude of the proportionality gap. Institutions located in the South and Midwest exhibit larger proportionality gaps than institutions in the Northeast and West. Institutions that exhibit low selectivity, little financial wealth, large populations of female undergraduates, and smaller overall student bodies, also have larger proportionality gaps, holding all else constant. Their results indicate that generally smaller Division II and III schools exhibit higher proportionality gaps than otherwise observationally equivalent Division I schools.

Another strand of literature exploring the effects of proportionality requirements has arisen in response to criticisms that Title IX may lead schools to cut men's sports opportunities in order to achieve compliance.[5] Carroll and Humphreys (2000) explain changes in team offerings among NCAA Division I schools between 1990–91 and 1995–96 using many school-specific characteristics. They use a multinomial logit model of change in the number of men's sports teams (increase, stay the same, decrease) as a function of a number of factors including expenditures on men and women's sports, number of women's teams, number of undergraduates, the type of institution (public or private), the subdivision (that is, Division I, II, or III), and the gender ratio as a proxy for proportionality. Carroll and Humphreys do not include an actual measure of proportionality in the model due to the lack of data, and they do not control for exogenous variables related to the institution, such as geographical location or racial demographics of the institution. They also look at changes in the number of teams rather than the number of participant slots. As a result, both their theoretical and empirical models neglect the full range of policies an athletic director has to pursue compliance with Title IX. Overall, their results show that large institutions with high enrollment and institutions with large athletic programs for men were more likely to cut men's opportunities to be in compliance. The authors also find that the greater the prestige of the athletic department as indicated by the expenditures per athlete and the presence of a Division IA football program, the less likely directors were to cut men's teams. Finally, they determine that institutions with high-quality women's programs and high ratios of women to men in the student body were less likely to cut men's sports.

Anderson and Cheslock (2004) update and improve upon Carroll and Humphreys by using more recent data that include explicit measures of schools' proportionality gaps. This allows them to examine the relationship between proportionality compliance within an institution and opportunities for male athletes. Specifically, they can test whether a school's proportionality gap in 1995–96 had a significant effect on the number of men's and women's teams in 2001–02. Using data on all NCAA divisions, Anderson and Cheslock separately estimate models predicting 2001–02 changes in the number of men's teams, women's teams, male participants, and female participants between the two time intervals for each school. In addition to their main explanatory variable of interest, the 1995–96 proportionality gap and its square (the quadratic form of the proportionality gap allows for nonlinear variation of Title IX pressures across the level of noncompliance), they control for other, potentially confounding factors, including whether the institution is public or private, undergraduate enrollment, region of the country, an indicator for historically black college or university, financial wealth measured by endowment assets per student, dollars donated per student, tuition and fee level and state appropriations per student (set to zero of it is a private institution), athletic division and selectivity factors (as measured by Barron's).

The estimates on the proportionality gap in both the models indicate that institutions were more likely to add women's teams and/or participants rather than to cut opportunities for men between 1995–96 and 2001–02. However, a school's probability of cutting men's opportunities increases with the magnitude of the proportionality gap. Their results indicate that, rather than solely adding opportunities for women or solely cutting opportunities for men, most schools pursued a policy of moderate 'give and take', with greater emphasis on giving.[6]

Deciding which sports to offer at a school is a complex process, involving many constituencies, including the president, athletic administrators, and board of trustees (Cheslock, 2008). Such decisions are based on a host of considerations, including trends in high-school sports. Lacrosse and soccer, for example, have become increasingly popular in the US over the past decade and have grown at the collegiate level as a result. Also, health-care costs may make dangerous sports prohibitively expensive to institutions with particularly acute budget constraints. Reduced funding by state governments means that universities are increasingly looking for students who can play sports, are academically qualified, and can afford high tuition.

In contrast to previous work, Monks (2005) examines whether Title IX has had the unintended consequence of leading to a preference for men in the college admissions process. He notes that, although the enrollment of women in higher education predates the passage of Title IX and has continued to grow, schools can achieve compliance under proportionality simply by reducing the proportion of women in their student body.[7] Monks specifies and estimates a model of admission preferences as a function of the lagged proportionality gap. He reasons that '[a]n institution that provides preference for male students, for whatever reason, in admissions is more likely to be in compliance with the proportionality measure, holding the mix of athletes constant, while an institution providing preference for female students in admissions is less likely to be in compliance' (p. 14). Using an instrumental variables approach to account for the potential endogeneity between admission preferences and the proportionality gap, he finds evidence that men are favored in admissions and concludes that Title IX may have the unintended consequence of lowering the probability that a woman is admitted to college.

A substantial amount of research has also been devoted to analyzing the possible effects of changing compliance standards. In particular, one strain of the literature analyzes the exemption of football from Title IX as a candidate policy. This research is an appropriate follow-up to the numerous findings that schools with football programs are more likely to be out of compliance (as gauged by proportionality) and hints at the potential impact of the Tower Amendment had it succeeded (Zimbalist, 2003). Leeds et al. (2004) investigate the role that college football plays in subsidizing other sports, particularly women's sports, and the effect that Title IX has on this role. Using data from the *Chronicle of Higher Education*'s 1995–96 Division I institutional data, *Peterson's Guide to Four-year Institutions*, and the NCAA, they model women's athletic expenditures in Division I schools as a function of selectivity indicators, type of institution, proportion of female undergraduates, enrollment figures in athletic programs and in general, football expenditures, and men's non-football athletic expenditures as well as net revenue from football in order to determine whether football helps subsidize women's sports. They do not include a measure of the proportionality gap or compliance. Their results indicate that football expenditures come at the expense of spending on women's programs. Only profitable football programs tend to subsidize women's sports and then only minimally.

Rishe (1999) also investigates the role of college football in schools' compliance with the proportionality prong of Title IX. Rather than using a single OLS regression like Leeds et al., Rishe estimates a model of male expenditures simultaneously with women's expenditures using two-stage least squares, based on the hypothesis that athletic departments are aware of how much must be allocated to male and female athletes to comply with Title IX. He controls for demographic composition of the school and the region in which it is located, but he does not include any direct measure of proportionality. Rishe's overall findings indicate that, while football programs, especially more profitable ones, are positively associated with expenditure per female athlete, they are negatively related to the proportion of overall expenditures allocated to women athletes.

Sigelman and Wahlbeck (1999) consider how compliance with the proportionality prong of Title IX among Division I schools would fare under various policy scenarios. They use data from the NCAA 1995–96 participation survey as a baseline and calculate the number of participation slots that would have to be added for women or dropped for men in order to achieve proportionality (defined in their research as a proportionality gap of 5 percent or less) at each school. They find that the median Division I school is very far from compliance and would have to drop many opportunities for men and add many opportunities for women before achieving compliance. They then consider three counterfactual scenarios: exempting football from Title IX, imposing the Big Ten's 60–40 intermediate scenario,[8] and placing caps on football rosters. They calculate that exempting football would substantially increase compliance across all divisions. The authors estimate that, in order for the median Division I school to reach the 60–40 quota, it would have to replace 10 men's varsity athletic slots with 10 slots for women. They also determine that most Division I institutions would have little trouble reaching the 40 percent target through such a reallocation of athletic opportunities. However, the only way to pull the Division I schools with football into compliance would be to rely on two very unlikely scenarios – either limiting football rosters to 50 from the current 85[9] or exempting football from Title IX, as in the failed Tower Amendment.

The literature has reached a consensus on several major points. Schools with football have the most difficulty complying with Title IX. In addition, compliance with the proportionality prong of Title IX's three-prong test is more difficult for schools that have a high percentage of female undergraduates, little financial wealth (as often measured by endowments), low selectivity, a small student body, and a Southern or Midwestern location.

The literature has yet to reach a consensus on *why* most of these factors play an important role in determining proportionality compliance. The factor that, at first glance, seems most obvious simply based on the math – the proportion of female undergraduate enrollment – is also not so straightforward. Schools with larger proportions of female students have to have larger proportions of female athletes to comply with the proportionality prong of the test and thus face more challenges. However, why cannot schools with more women simply fill more slots? One economic explanation is steeply diminishing marginal returns in women's athletics. It is possible that the prestige, revenue, or compliance benefits that additional women's varsity sports opportunities provide diminish swiftly at the margin or are smaller at the margin than for men's athletics. If this is so, then schools with particularly large female enrollment may find it more difficult to continue to add opportunities for women beyond some level. Another explanation is that women have less interest or ability to play at the collegiate level (Beveridge, 1996). This, of course, raises the possibility of discrimination at the high-school level or even earlier, when girls' interest and ability in sports is first nurtured.

Considerable research shows that sports participation is a laudable goal. It is associated with many positive outcomes, such as lower teenage pregnancy rates, better grades, and higher self-esteem (President's Council on Physical Fitness, 1997; Miller et al., 2000; Findlay and Bowker, 2009; Fox et al., 2010; Habel et al., 2010; Taliaferro et al., 2010). But whether there is a causal relationship between participation and these desirable outcomes was unclear until recently. The positive 'outcomes' may simply reflect self-selection; unobservable factors that make a particular girl more likely to play sports may also make her less likely to become a pregnant teenager or earn poor grades. Because she may already be ambitious and have a supportive family, it may not be sports, *per se*, that cause these outcomes.

Recently, two economists have addressed the problem of self-selection. Their results suggest that there is a causal relationship between participating in sports as a student and higher earnings and better health. Stevenson (2010) identified the causal effect of female athletic participation by focusing on variation by state in the speed at which Title IX compliance in high-school sports was achieved to show that women's sports participation increases women's college attendance, labor force participation, and the probability of entering occupations that were traditionally male dominated. In a similar analysis, Kaestner and Xu (2006) demonstrate that expanding athletic opportunities for girls leads to lower rates of obesity and greater physical activity.

While the literature makes it clear that there are benefits to women's athletics participation, the majority of postsecondary institutions still fall far short of compliance with Title IX, as measured by the first prong, more than 30 years after the passage of the law. This compliance is unlikely to be achieved soon. To achieve compliance, university athletic budgets will have to increase enough for them to continue to expand opportunities for women, a scenario that seems unlikely in the current economic environment. Alternatively, football would have to be exempted from Title IX, which is also unlikely.

9.4 A THEORETICAL MODEL OF INSTITUTIONAL RESPONSE TO TITLE IX

In this section, we present a theoretical model of an institution's response to Title IX. For ease of exposition, we assume that an athletic administrator maximizes his/her utility by choosing some combination of opportunities for men and women, as measured by the number of athletic slots available for each, S_m and S_w. For example, the appropriate choice of these variables could increase the athletic department's revenue and the university's prestige. Providing athletic slots comes at a cost, which, along with the budget allotted to the administrator, forms the budget constraint. At the highest levels of competition, the number of slots and the number of athletes are essentially the same, as few Division I athletes play more than one sport. In the lower divisions, this might not be the case, but schools report the number of athletes for purposes of Title IX.

Our model can be enriched by adding choice variables and constraints. For example, athletic administrators seldom make unilateral choices but instead respond to direction or pressure from the institution's President and Board of Trustees. In addition, athletic administrators must choose more than the number of slots available to men and women. They must choose the number of teams (subject to division-specific minima for NCAA-affiliated schools), the precise sports in which the school participates, and the quality of inputs allocated to each program. Our simpler model demonstrates why institutions may remain noncompliant with Title IX, even in the face of sanctions for noncompliance.

We begin by modeling the athletic administrator's choice in a world without Title IX. Figure 9.1 illustrates the utility-maximizing choice by an administrator with a budget E who faces prices P_m and P_w for men's and women's sports opportunities. These per-athlete prices include the cost of such items as coaching staff salaries, equipment, travel, and facilities. For reference, we add a line representing the combinations of S_m and S_w that are proportional to enrollment, which we call the 'compliance line'. For example, if the student body is a 50/50 mix, the compliance line is the 45-degree line. In the absence of any constraint other than the athletic budget, an administrator with indifference curves as shown in Figure 9.1 will choose Point *a* to maximize his utility subject to the budget constraint, settling on a distribution of athletic opportunities more heavily weighted toward men than the institution's enrollment mix would imply. In general, administrators with steeper indifference curves, representing a relative preference for male sports, will choose a gender mix of athletic opportunities to the southeast of the compliance line.

How an athletic administrator responds to Title IX depends on the

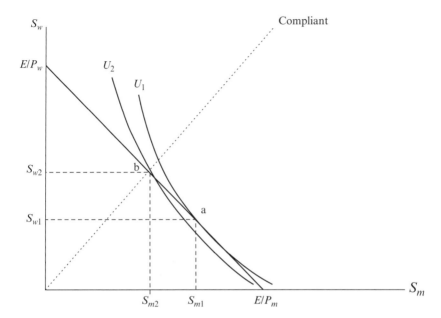

Figure 9.1   Noncompliance as a utility-maximizing choice

optimal ratio of women's to men's sports. In particular, if proportionality is mandated, most schools will be forced to move northwest along their constraint, reducing men's opportunities and increasing women's opportunities. While schools that offer 'too many' athletic opportunities to women could face an analogous constraint, such a situation does not seem likely in the foreseeable future. Throughout our analysis, we assume that noncompliance is punished only if the ratio of female to male athletes is less than the analogous enrollment ratio. If athletic departments cannot exist at combinations off the compliance line, the administrator illustrated in Figure 9.1 would choose Point *b* on the lower indifference curve (U_2), causing a decrease in men's slots from S_{m1} to S_{m2} and an increase in women's slots from S_{w1} to S_{w2}.

Previous empirical work and the results we present below show that the majority of postsecondary institutions are not in compliance with Title IX, even 40 years after the law's passage. Treating Title IX as a mandate in practice, thus, is too restrictive and leads to the prediction that every school complies, which is inconsistent with reality.

Instead of treating Title IX as a mandate in the sense that the school faces an infinite price of noncompliance, we assume that Title IX imposes a new price regime on athletic departments. We further assume that athletics

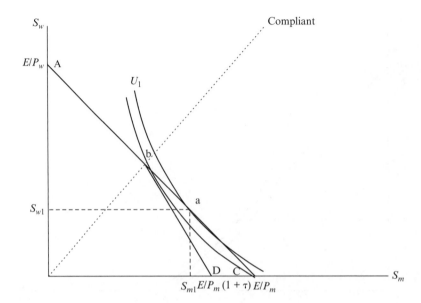

Figure 9.2   The impact of penalties on noncompliance

administrators consider the trade-offs associated with noncompliance when formulating their optimal choices of athletic opportunities. If administrators face financial penalties, additional legal expenses, or costs of effort to avoid detection (manipulating numbers, arranging for male practice players, or otherwise 'gaming the system') because of noncompliance, the athletic budget, E, can produce fewer athletic opportunities. In particular, we expect this cost to be increasing in the school's degree of noncompliance, so segment AbD in Figure 9.2, showing the new budget constraint faced by the athletic administrator, swivels in. (The original, non-Title IX budget constraint is AbC.) The kink in the budget constraint occurs at the compliance line because punishment occurs only when the gender ratio falls below that proportion. (Since schools that are very close to proportionality are not punished, compliance more likely requires $S_w = (1 - \varepsilon)*$(no. of women enrolled/no. men enrolled)$*S_m$ where $1 > \varepsilon > 0$.)

If the overall penalty for noncompliance is increasing in the degree of noncompliance, the lower portion of the new budget constraint is steeper. In effect, there is a per-unit tax, $\tau > 0$, on men's athletic opportunities so that the relevant price ratio is now $P_m(1 + \tau)/P_w$ rather than P_m/P_w. (Again, we assume that there is no penalty for having greater than proportional female representation in sports, but nothing in our model precludes this change to the budget constraint.)

The inward swivel of the lower portion of the budget constraint causes both substitution and income effects for noncompliant institutions. The substitution effect leads administrators to replace men's slots with women's slots because men's sports have become relatively more expensive. If women's slots are normal goods, the net effect of the penalty on women's slots is theoretically uncertain and the net effect on men is unambiguously negative. If women's slots are inferior goods to athletic administrators, then more women's sports will be offered since the income effect reinforces the substitution effect.

When the cost of noncompliance is less than infinite, an administrator could have a utility function that generates indifference curves that keep the institution noncompliant. As the cost rises, segment bD becomes steeper, and the school moves closer to compliance at point b. Even if the cost of noncompliance were infinite, effectively making segment bD vertical, the school could, under some circumstances, stay noncompliant. One limitation of our model is the assumption that the athletic budget, E, is given and is not a function of the athletic department's policies or behaviors. The fact that men's sports opportunities have not decreased in most cases since Title IX was implemented suggests that the constraint is not fixed for most athletic departments. If supporters of highly visible men's programs respond to the pressures of Title IX by increasing their giving, segment bD of the budget constraint an administrator faces would shift to the right. If these contributions were not subject to the mandate, schools would move off the 45-degree line and back out of compliance.

9.5 DATA AND ESTIMATION

Our goal in this section is to update existing work by using data from the 2009–10 academic year and to place recent trends in perspective by comparing them to the preceding decade of data. We rely on two data sources from the Department of Education: information submitted by athletic departments as required by the EADA as well as the more comprehensive Integrated Postsecondary Education Data System (IPEDS), which provides information on broader institutional characteristics.

EADA requires all coeducational postsecondary schools receiving federal funding through Title IV – the law that provides federal student aid through grants, loans, and work study – to submit annual data on their intercollegiate athletics programs. These data include participation by gender in each sport, expenses, scholarships, and employment of coaches. We use the EADA data chiefly for its participation information. We focus on the total *unduplicated* count of participants by gender rather than summing the participants by sport, which would result in double-counting of athletes involved in multiple sports.

Before 2003–04, colleges were not asked to report unduplicated counts of student athletes, so EADA published estimates of how many athletes in each sport participated in multiple sports. In 2002–03, even these estimated unduplicated counts were not made available. In 2003–04, the EADA survey began asking explicitly for unduplicated counts. According to the survey's user's guide, '[u]nduplicated count means a head count of all of the participants on at least one varsity team, by gender' (US Department of Education Office of Postsecondary Education, 2010). Elsewhere on the data collection website, agents of the athletic department are advised: 'Another way to look at this is to imagine that all of your varsity team student athletes are standing in the gym. How many males are there? How many females are there?' We use these data, rather than duplicated counts, because they represent more closely the spirit of equal opportunity. We also use EADA's data on each institution's classification as NCAA (including division) or non-NCAA. (We describe the distinctions in these classifications below.)

IPEDS, collected annually by the National Center for Education Statistics, comprises data from all postsecondary institutions participating in Title IV federal student financial aid programs, which are required by law to complete a series of surveys. With this wealth of information on institutions over time, we are able to both correct and amend the EADA data. Following the work of Cheslock and Eckes (2008), we use IPEDS enrollment figures, which are submitted by the institution rather than an agent of the athletic department, to calculate undergraduate enrollment figures by gender. We also append from IPEDS a number of other institution-specific variables (described below) that might affect compliance. Our use of IPEDS data is straightforward, but we discuss the variable definitions in more detail if they are unique to discussions of Title IX.

9.5.1 Sample Selection

We restrict our sample to degree-granting institutions that report their athletic data through EADA and are neither predominantly male nor predominantly female (no less than 10 percent of either male or female students). That restriction leaves 1,990 schools nationwide, 1,743 of which have complete data for the decade. We also define subsamples of the data as follows. Since we later focus on 2009–10, the most recent academic year for which data were available at this writing, we classify schools according to their status in 2009–10 to keep the composition of the subsamples unchanged over time.[10] We define six subsamples that, while not mutually exclusive, allow various comparisons across groups. We divide the sample into NCAA schools and non-NCAA institutions, comprising mostly the NAIA, the National Christian College Athletic Association (NCCAA), and the National Junior College Athletic Association (NJCAA).

Like previous work on Title IX, we focus on the NCAA because of its prominence in the policy debate. However, we also provide summary statistics for non-NCAA schools, as they represent almost half of the institutions and about 46 percent of undergraduate students in our data, yet they have been the subject of little analysis. Our final three subsamples are defined by membership in NCAA Divisions I, II, or III. The main distinction between NCAA divisions is that Divisions I and II can offer athletic scholarships while Division III schools cannot. Another distinction is size, as larger institutions generally belong to Division I and smaller institutions to Divisions II and III. Finally, the classification of a school's football program further narrows its classification. Within Division I there are two (non-exhaustive) football subdivisions, the Football Bowl Subdivision and the Football Championship Subdivision, known as Division IA and Division IIA, respectively, prior to 2006.

9.5.2 Time Trends in Proportionality and Compliance

The proportionality gap compares the percentage of athletes who are women with the percentage of students who are women. Specifically,

$$\text{Proportionality gap} = (\text{Percent female enrollment} - \text{Percent female participation}) \times 100.$$

Positive numbers denote underrepresentation of women in athletics. As discussed earlier, substantial proportionality, while not explicitly defined by the law, has been operationalized through investigations and court cases as a proportionality gap that is less than a given benchmark. In practice, the gap ranges from 3 to 5 percent, so we define the indicator of noncompliance as a dummy variable, Y_G. $Y_G = 1$ if the proportionality gap exceeds G, where $G = 3$ or 5 percent, and $Y_G = 0$ otherwise.

Figures 9.3 through 9.8 illustrate the changes in various measures of compliance over time. Each line represents a different subset of our data. The vertical line in each figure separates the years when unduplicated counts were estimated by the EADA (2000 and 2001) from years when unduplicated counts were collected explicitly (2003–10).[11] (No unduplicated figures were provided in the 2002 EADA data.) We focus our discussion on the trends after the EADA began asking for unduplicated counts of athletes. In Figure 9.3, on average, the proportionality gap has

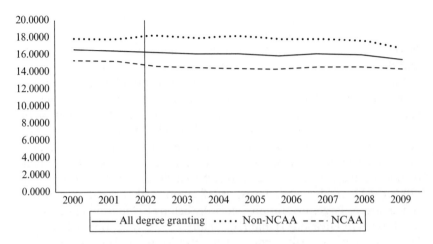

Figure 9.3   Proportionality gap by NCAA membership

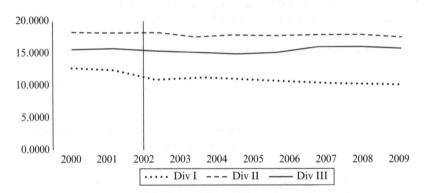

Figure 9.4   Proportionality gap by division

decreased slightly over time for all schools, especially schools belonging to the NCAA. Figure 9.4 shows that, among NCAA schools, the proportionality gap has decreased over the last part of the decade among Division I and Division II schools, but it may have increased slightly in Division III.

The stories at the margin of noncompliance, however, are different. When gauging noncompliance as a proportionality gap exceeding 3 percent (Figures 9.5 and 9.6) or 5 percent (Figures 9.7 and 9.8) there are no obvious declines in noncompliance after 2002–03 among non-NCAA and NCAA schools. However, there appears to have been a decline in Division I (save the outlier year of 2003–04) and Division II in recent years. Overall, we observe very minor downward trends in noncompliance.

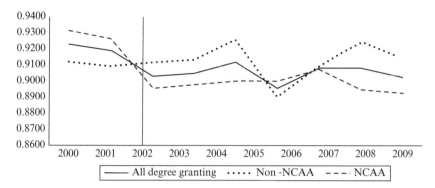

Figure 9.5   Proportionality gap over 3 percent indicator by NCAA membership

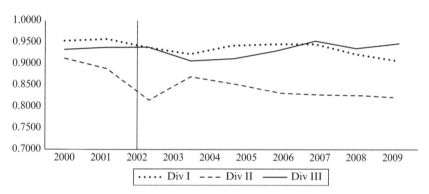

Figure 9.6   Proportionality gap over 3 percent indicator by division

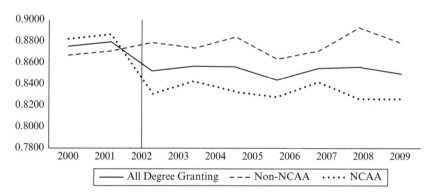

Figure 9.7   Proportionality gap over 5 percent indicator by NCAA membership

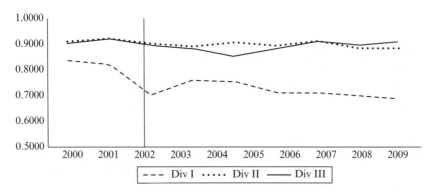

Figure 9.8   Proportionality gap over 5 percent indicator by division

Table 9.1   Persistence of noncompliance

	If X proportionality gap in 2000, what percent always have a gap Z?			Average years out of compliance	
	$Z \geq 0\%$	$Z > 3\%$	$Z > 5\%$	3% Criterion	5% Criterion
$X =$ Any	84.80	74.93	66.38	8.1750	7.7246
$X > 0\%$	88.82	78.49	69.53	8.4039	7.9724
$X > 3\%$	89.74	81.22	71.95	8.5236	8.1356
$X > 5\%$	90.83	83.81	75.82	8.6219	8.3493

We now turn to the important question of whether an individual institution that achieves compliance remains compliant or soon reverts to noncompliance. In Table 9.1, we provide some descriptive statistics of the compliance patterns of schools over the decade. Of the 1,743 schools in our panel data, only 265 (15 percent) ever experience reverse proportionality gaps (that is, negative gaps) during the decade. The complement of this is that 85 percent of schools over the decade *always* had a positive proportionality gap. Additionally, 75 percent of schools were always noncompliant by at least 3 percent and 66 percent of schools by at least 5 percent. The proportion of schools that were always noncompliant was even greater among schools that began the decade with positive proportionality gaps or were 'noncompliant' by 3 or 5 percent. In the most extreme subsample of schools whose proportionality gaps exceeded 5 percent in 2000–01, nearly 91 percent always experienced a positive proportionality gap and 76 percent were always noncompliant by the loosest measure in every year.

Another way of viewing compliance information is to consider the

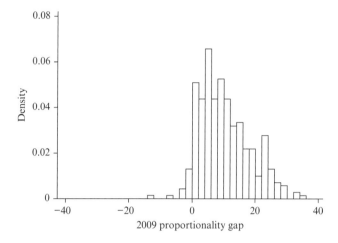

Figure 9.9   NCAA Division I

average number of years that schools are noncompliant by our two bench-marks, which is about eight out of 10 years. Schools that start with greater average proportionality gaps have longer than average periods of non-compliance. Altogether, we observe a great deal of noncompliance, even at the end of the decade. What might be of even more concern to policy makers is that compliance in one year is no guarantee of future compli-ance. Of the 586 schools that are ever compliant by our loosest standard, a 5 percent proportionality gap, almost 80 percent revert to a proportional-ity gap of more than 5 percent in at least one year. This suggests that there is considerable 'transitory compliance' in which colleges comply occasion-ally but not regularly.

We also examine the distribution of the proportionality gaps across NCAA divisions over time in Figures 9.9 to 9.11. These figures make it clear that, while Divisions II and III have the greatest difficulty in meeting proportionality, all NCAA institutions are far from being in compliance. Clearly, the norm is for institutions not to be in compliance in terms of the proportionality gap. Furthermore, only a handful of NCAA institutions have negative proportionality gaps. While it is striking that any school has a *negative* gap, exploring this is outside the scope of our chapter.

9.5.3   Proportionality Gaps and Compliance in 2009–2010

We have established that there is a degree of persistence, in the aggregate, for noncompliant schools to stay noncompliant and that even schools that do comply at some point are at substantial risk of noncompliance in the

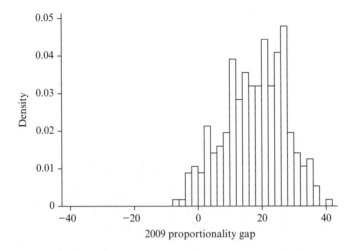

Figure 9.10   NCAA Division II

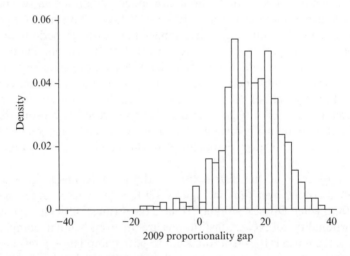

Figure 9.11   NCAA Division III

future.[12] To determine what factors predict noncompliance, we shift to considering all 1,990 schools with complete data in 2009–10. We begin by examining the mean differences between schools that belong to the NCAA and those that do not. Table 9.2 presents summary statistics by each subset (not mutually exclusive) of our data as described above.

The proportions of schools across all divisions that exhibit positive

Table 9.2   2009 proportionality gap and compliance status by classification

	Mean	Std dev.	Min	Max
All degree granting, $N = 1990$				
Proportionality gap	15.6680	10.2174	−29.7817	54.2192
Proportionality gap > 0%	0.9543	0.2089	0	1
Proportionality gap > 3%	0.9020	0.2974	0	1
Proportionality gap > 5%	0.8513	0.3559	0	1
Non-NCAA, $N = 969$				
Proportionality gap	16.9710	11.0477	−29.7817	54.2192
Proportionality gap > 0%	0.9515	0.2149	0	1
Proportionality gap > 3%	0.9112	0.2845	0	1
Proportionality gap > 5%	0.8782	0.3272	0	1
NCAA, $N = 1021$				
Proportionality gap	14.4313	9.1978	−16.2723	41.2191
Proportionality gap > 0%	0.9569	0.2032	0	1
Proportionality gap > 3%	0.8932	0.3090	0	1
Proportionality gap > 5%	0.8257	0.3796	0	1
Division I, $N = 342$				
Proportionality gap	10.2610	7.9514	−13.9674	34.5069
Proportionality gap > 0%	0.9591	0.1984	0	1
Proportionality gap > 3%	0.8216	0.3834	0	1
Proportionality gap > 5%	0.6901	0.4631	0	1
Division II, $N = 281$				
Proportionality gap	17.8098	9.6791	−7.3245	41.2191
Proportionality gap > 0%	0.9537	0.2104	0	1
Proportionality gap > 3%	0.9146	0.2800	0	1
Proportionality gap > 5%	0.8861	0.3182	0	1
Division III, $N = 398$				
Proportionality gap	15.6296	8.5135	−16.2723	37.4112
Proportionality gap > 0%	0.9573	0.2025	0	1
Proportionality gap > 3%	0.9397	0.2383	0	1
Proportionality gap > 5%	0.8995	0.3010	0	1

proportionality gaps are statistically indistinguishable. However, the size of the gap varies systematically. Non-NCAA schools have a larger average proportionality gap with a larger standard deviation than NCAA schools. Non-NCAA schools are also more likely to be noncompliant at the margins of noncompliance, the 3 or 5 percent proportionality gap. NCAA Division I schools are more likely to be compliant than Divisions II and III; they have a smaller average proportionality gap and standard deviation as well. While Division III has a smaller average proportionality gap than Division II, a greater proportion of Division III schools are noncompliant than Division II schools. Thus, while previous studies examine only the size of proportionality gaps, it is also important to consider their variance. We build on the existing literature by analyzing the variance below.

9.5.4   Regression Analysis

To understand the factors underlying an institution's proportionality gap, we estimate reduced form regressions using several independent variables to explain the size of the proportionality gap, the dependent variable.[13] For each of our six (non-mutually exclusive) subsamples we estimate separate OLS regressions to allow the effect of the explanatory variables to vary with the school's classification (for example, NCAA or non-NCAA). We limit the observations in these regression equations to schools with positive proportionality gaps in 2009–10, so we have a non-random sample, similar to Anderson et al. (2006). The estimates from these equations, therefore, should be applied only to institutions that do not have proportional representation of females in athletics. The equations take the form:

$$Y_i = \alpha + \beta FE_i + \theta FB_i + \delta^1 P_i + \varepsilon \qquad (9.1)$$

where Y represents the proportionality gap for institution i; FE_i measures the percent female enrollment for the ith institution, FB_i is a binary variable equal to one if the ith school has a football program, and P_i is a vector of variables describing the institution and its preferences. Included in the vector P_i are binary indicators for the division (Division I is the default), and the availability of an occupational curriculum (in addition to academic courses) at the institution. The vector P_i also contains, where relevant (for example, not in NCAA Division III), an indicator of whether the institution is a historically black college or university (HBC). HBCs may face unique challenges in achieving gender equity because in the past they largely fielded only a few sports including football, basketball, and track.

P_i also has indicators for geographical region to control for social climate (South, West, and East, so that Midwest is the default); the highest degree offered (where less than a bachelor's degree is the default for the samples that include non-NCAA schools, and a bachelor's degree is the default for the sample containing only NCAA schools, all of which offer at least four-year degrees); private school (public schools may face more pressure to comply with Title IX); for-profit institution; urban and rural location; and the total enrollment of undergraduates.

For four-year NCAA schools, we also include several variables from IPEDS: the school's six-year graduation rate, the percent of applicants admitted, and the percent of admitted students who enroll (the admissions yield). We expect these variables to capture important dimensions of school quality, which may be important for compliance, as more selective schools may put less emphasis on athletics and may attract students who participate in less traditional sports such as fencing or equestrian. Because these variables are available only for four-year schools and are missing for a small percentage of those, we include them in alternate specifications of the model and only in closer examination of NCAA member institutions.

Data limitations preclude our estimation of the structural theoretical model we presented earlier. Thus, this choice of independent variables is only loosely predicated on the theoretical model and is motivated in large part by the empirical work of others discussed above, particularly Anderson et al. (2006). We extend the data over both time and school classification and thus provide the most up-to-date analysis of compliance and an additional perspective on the understudied non-NCAA institutions.[14]

Table 9.3 presents separate results for NCAA and non-NCAA institutions, as well as the overall regression on all 1,899 schools with positive proportionality gaps. The percent of female enrollment is consistently statistically significant and positive. The magnitudes of the coefficients suggest that, depending on the sample, a one percentage point increase in the proportion of female undergraduates increases the proportionality gap by between one-half and two-thirds of a percentage point, with a significantly stronger impact on NCAA schools than non-NCAA schools ($p < 0.001$). A larger student body is associated with lower proportionality gaps. There are at least three possible explanations for this finding: increasing returns to scale that allow a larger institution to offer more sports, a more diverse set of tastes for athletics among female students, and a greater emphasis on extracurricular activities in larger schools, which implies more sports and other activities.

As expected, given that HBCs enroll much larger percentages of women they have larger proportionality gaps, at least in the NCAA (Sander, 2008). It also appears that geographical region is more predictive in the NCAA sample and in ways that are consistent with the findings of previous research: Southern schools have larger proportionality gaps (relative to the Midwest), while schools in the East and West have smaller proportionality gaps.[15] Conferring more-advanced degrees reduces the proportionality gap in non-NCAA schools, as does status as a private school. For-profit status, however, outweighs the private school status in the non-NCAA sample, implying that for-profit private schools have proportionality gaps roughly seven percentage points higher than otherwise identical schools.

Table 9.3   OLS regressions of 2009 proportionality gaps

	All degree-granting N = 1899		Non-NCAA N = 922		NCAA N = 977	
	Coef.	Std err.	Coef.	Std err.	Coef.	Std err.
% Female enrollment	0.4780	0.0261***	0.4991	0.0408***	0.6701	0.0282***
Football					7.6316	0.4073***
NCAA	−2.2343	0.6974***				
Division II	4.5426	0.6526***			4.6629	0.5422***
Division III	4.0872	0.5921***			4.4549	0.5245***
Total undergrad enrollment (1000s)	−0.1215	0.0299***	−0.0941	0.0430**	−0.1642	0.0341***
Occupational offerings	0.4862	0.5268	−3.9470	1.1689***	1.7520	0.4585***
Historically black college	2.8445	1.0411***	−2.2033	1.8172	2.7522	0.8501***
South	0.7305	0.4725	0.0471	0.6959	2.4118	0.4988***
West	−3.0381	0.5680***	−1.4309	0.8141*	−3.2827	0.6333***
East	−2.8078	0.4604***	0.1436	0.8794	−2.2769	0.4541***
Bachelor's degree	−4.3399	0.8832***	−4.5196	1.1482***		
Master's degree	−4.2211	0.7799***	−5.5533	1.1754***	0.8781	0.5736
Doctorate	−4.5882	0.8534***	−4.4390	1.6156***	−0.0436	0.6298
Private	0.0612	0.4988	−2.3951	1.2344*	0.7061	0.4550
For profit	7.2405	2.9364**	9.0262	3.4140***	2.4010	2.7228
Urban	−0.6694	0.4014*	−0.4344	0.6770	0.0602	0.3729
Rural	−0.0559	0.5574	−0.0542	0.7345	1.0194	0.6421
Constant	−6.2865	1.6624***	−4.1399	2.6093	−30.4912	1.8080***

Note: Robust standard errors. *** $p < 0.01$, ** $p < 0.05$, * $p < 0.1$.

Table 9.4 presents results from similar regressions for NCAA institutions, both aggregated and partitioned by division. The columns labeled (B) show the results of an alternatively-specified model that includes three measures of quality – the six-year graduation rate, percent of applicants admitted, and the percent enrolled of those admitted. We present both models for comparison, especially since the addition of these explanatory variables reduces each sample size. Some strong results hold, in sign and significance if not in magnitude, across model specification and sub-sample of the data. Percent female enrollment and presence of a football program increase the proportionality gap. In models where it is included, a higher six-year graduation rate reduces the proportionality gap. The quality factors included in column B eliminate the statistical significance of HBCs, suggesting that the indicator of HBC status in the more parsimonious model may have been a proxy for (lesser) quality, other things held constant.

The effect of geographical region is mostly the same as in the other subsample, but the statistical strength of these estimated coefficients is reduced in some of the division-specific models. Though magnitudes vary across divisions, very little is qualitatively different between the division-specific models or different from the aggregate NCAA model. For this reason, we continue to focus on the NCAA/non-NCAA comparison.

In addition to standard regressions, we estimate analogous quantile regressions of proportionality gaps for each subsample of institutions. While OLS regressions fit a line through the data to predict the *mean* value of dependent variable given a set of explanatory variables, quantile regression (QR) estimates the relationships between explanatory variables and the value of the dependent variable at the *p*th percentile. These results are particularly useful for understanding the influence of each independent variable on the proportionality gap of those schools that are closer to proportionality (lower quantiles) compared to those who are further from proportional representation (higher quantiles) conditional on the value of the other explanatory variables. Since we are estimating relationships in the data of only noncompliant schools, the nonparametric approach of quantile regression is useful in light of the likelihood that the error distribution is non-normal.

In the interest of space, we present a limited set of results from the quantile regressions in Figures 9.12 and 9.13. The estimated coefficients on percent female enrollment shown in Figure 9.12 demonstrate the generally stronger influence of this factor on the schools that, conditional on all other factors, exhibit especially large proportionality gaps. Thus, schools that are inclined to ignore Title IX are particularly affected by higher female enrollments. Each of the coefficients represented in the line chart is significant at the 1 percent level. We also see that percent female enrollment has a greater effect in NCAA schools than in non-NCAA schools. Across all classifications, the estimated effect of female enrollment is greater at higher percentiles. This suggests that the proportion of female students is an even bigger concern for schools that are furthest from proportional representation.

Figure 9.13 reports the estimated coefficients for the undergraduate enrollment of the institution (measured in thousands). Where statistically significant, it reduces the proportionality gap. It is particularly strong at

Table 9.4   OLS regressions of 2009 proportionality gaps, by NCAA division

	All NCAA				Division I			
	N = 977 (A)		*N* = 936 (B)		*N* = 328 (A)		*N* = 315 (B)	
	Coef.	Std err.	Coef.	Std err.	Coef.	Std err.	Coef.	Std err.
% Female enroll- ment	0.6701	0.0282***	0.6358	0.0276***	0.6939	0.0586***	0.6575	0.0594***
Football	7.6316	0.4073***	8.1496	0.3923***	5.6544	0.7587***	5.5834	0.8418***
Division II	4.6629	0.5422***	2.9521	0.5278***				
Division III	4.4549	0.5245***	3.7918	0.4814***				
Total und. enroll. (1000s)	−0.1642	0.0341***	−0.1294	0.0312***	−0.1449	0.0367***	−0.1206	0.0341***
Occupa- tional offerings	1.7520	0.4585***	1.3139	0.4620***	1.1881	0.7195*	1.6059	0.7268**
Histori- cally black college	2.7522	0.8501***	1.2394	0.9109	3.7268	1.0686***	1.9553	1.2353
South	2.4118	0.4988***	1.8599	0.5015***	2.5401	0.7949***	1.8986	0.8001**
West	−3.2827	0.6333***	−2.9320	0.6319***	−1.6511	0.8678*	−1.6085	0.9239*
East	−2.2769	0.4541***	−1.7349	0.4474***	−2.1605	0.8228***	−1.7752	0.8564**
Master's degree	0.8781	0.5736	0.8394	0.5504	1.4969	2.9912	−4.0433	2.2866*
Doctorate	−0.0436	0.6298	0.0051	0.5876	0.2242	2.9306	−5.0287	2.1835**
Private	0.7061	0.4550	2.5053	0.4990***	0.1479	0.8102	1.6707	0.9400*
For profit	2.4010	2.7228	4.7682	3.7857				
Urban	0.0602	0.3729	−0.0077	0.3625	0.0899	0.6321	0.0431	0.6266
Rural	1.0194	0.6421	0.7198	0.6253	2.0525	1.0729*	1.8201	0.9698*
6-year gradua- tion rate			−0.1121	0.0136***			−0.0900	0.0225***
Total percent admitted			−0.0004	0.0109			−0.0093	0.0165
Total admis- sion yield			0.0094	0.0141			0.0351	0.0203*
Constant	−30.4912	1.8080***	−23.2462	2.3756***	−31.1285	4.4647***	−19.6421	5.1010***

Note: Robust standard errors. *** $p < 0.01$, ** $p < 0.05$, * $p < 0.1$.

	Division II				Division III			
	N = 268 (A)		N = 247 (B)		N = 381 (A)		N = 374 (B)	
	Coef.	Std err.	Coef.	Std err.	Coef.	Std err.	Coef.	Std err.
	0.7252	0.0559***	0.7063	0.0561***	0.6433	0.0402***	0.6104	0.0402***
	10.3322	0.7755***	10.6609	0.7712***	7.5788	0.6259***	7.9421	0.5799***
	−0.2417	0.1247*	−0.1361	0.1228	0.1186	0.1289	0.1661	0.1153
	3.1153	0.8211***	2.4632	0.8809***	1.4625	0.8174*	0.2566	0.8124
	0.6728	1.3132	0.3031	1.5068				
	2.7325	1.0127***	2.6451	1.0414**	1.9474	0.9832**	1.2543	0.9055
	−3.2450	1.3654**	−2.9592	1.3794**	−4.5478	1.0670***	−3.5600	1.0744***
	−3.8232	1.1540***	−2.8226	1.1587**	−1.7331	0.6850**	−1.3562	0.6315**
	−0.9506	1.2266	−0.2728	1.2377	1.3366	0.6660**	1.2306	0.6583*
	−1.1588	1.3599	−0.8417	1.2767	0.1594	0.7898	0.3754	0.7618
	2.0616	0.9342**	3.5722	1.0727***	1.9331	0.8749**	3.9705	0.8332***
	−0.4905	0.7712	−0.6860	0.7994	0.2329	0.6005	0.0317	0.5626
	2.2650	1.1999*	2.5320	1.2752**	−0.3537	0.9419	−1.1488	0.8414
			−0.1106	0.0284***			−0.1249	0.0240***
			0.0221	0.0275			−0.0024	0.0184
			0.0124	0.0245			−0.0082	0.0265
	−29.3191	3.9246***	−27.3477	4.8541***	−26.6559	2.5546***	−18.5942	3.9395***

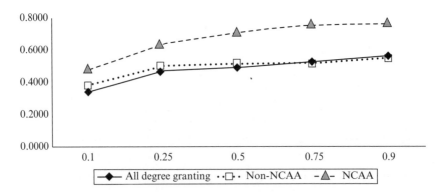

Figure 9.12   Coefficients on percent female

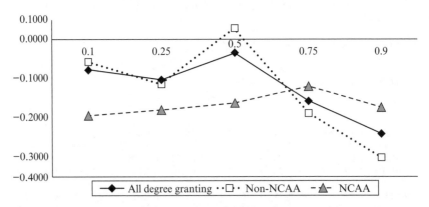

Figure 9.13   Coefficients on total undergraduate enrollment

the lower and upper percentiles of the conditional distribution of the proportionality gap for the NCAA sample but only for the upper tail of the proportionality gap for schools not in the NCAA.

9.5.5 Probit Analysis of Noncompliance

Tables 9.3 and 9.4 show the determinants of the proportionality gaps. However, as we have seen, a positive proportionality gap does not mean that a college is out of compliance if the gap is less than the tolerated threshold. We now examine what determines whether a school falls within the proportionality threshold and hence is considered compliant. Because the decision to comply with Title IX is a qualitative decision – that is, a question that can be answered yes or no – the dependent variable is now a binary variable. When the dependent variable takes on discrete values of 0 or 1, OLS estimation can create problems. For example, because the error term is no longer normally distributed, we cannot use the standard hypothesis tests to analyze the coefficients. Instead of OLS, we use probit analysis to estimate the equation:

$$C_i = \alpha + \beta FE_i + \theta FB_i + \delta' \mathbf{P_i} + \varepsilon_i. \tag{9.2}$$

The dependent variable, C_i, is equal to one if the school is noncompliant (by favoring men) and zero if it is in compliance, where compliance is alternately defined as within to 3 or 5 percentage points of the representation of women on campus, as in Anderson et al. (2006). Thus, positive (negative) coefficients should still be interpreted as hindrances (contributors) to proportionality. The other variables are the same as for model (9.1) and are described above. Because probit coefficients have no intuitive interpretation, Table 9.5 also includes estimated marginal effects, which show the impact of a one-unit increase in an independent variable on the probability that the institution is in compliance ($C_i = 1$). The estimation uses all 1,990 schools with complete data in 2009–10, not just those with positive proportionality gaps.

As in the proportionality gap models, the percent female enrollment is consistently positive across samples and highly significant, indicating that schools more heavily populated by women are more likely not to be in compliance. Conferring more advanced degrees reduces the probability of noncompliance in non-NCAA schools, showing that more academically oriented schools are less likely to violate Title IX. NCAA schools with football programs are 10 or 20 percentage points more likely to be noncompliant, depending on whether one uses a 3 or 5 percent threshold.

Other probit estimates differ from the proportionality gap estimates, possibly due to the fact we are not using a sample that has been selected based on noncompliance. The results from the probit estimation thus reveal what factors are important at the compliance margin, that is, what factors determine whether a school is within the threshold. In contrast, the results for equation (9.1) show what factors affect the degree of noncompliance as measured by the magnitude of the proportionality gap. For example, HBCs are no more or less likely than other colleges, other factors held constant, to be noncompliant, despite the higher proportionality gaps for HBCs in the NCAA. Geographical region is also less predictive of noncompliance than of the magnitude of proportionality gap, though a Southern location is significant and positive for NCAA schools. Status as a private college does not affect the probability of noncompliance in any

Table 9.5 Probit analyses of 2009 compliance, 3 and 5 percent thresholds

	Gap exceeding 3 percent				Gap exceeding 5 percent			
	Coef.	Std err.	Marg.	Std err.	Coef.	Std err.	Marg.	Std err.
All degree-granting, N = 1990								
% Female enrollment	0.0876	0.0065***	0.0086	0.0007***	0.0792	0.0057***	0.0130	0.0010***
NCAA	0.1288	0.1930	0.0126	0.0190	-0.0110	0.1550	-0.0018	0.0254
Division II	-0.0179	0.1716	-0.0018	0.0171	0.2624	0.1467*	0.0378	0.0186**
Division III	0.4471	0.1866**	0.0352	0.0121***	0.5687	0.1556***	0.0743	0.0163***
Total undergrad enrollment	-0.0186	0.0073**	-0.0018	0.0007**	-0.0200	0.0068***	-0.0033	0.0011***
Occupational offerings	-0.0030	0.1262	-0.0003	0.0123	-0.0027	0.1151	-0.0004	0.0189
Historically black college	-0.3536	0.2409	-0.0450	0.0387	-0.1521	0.2227	-0.0273	0.0435
South	0.1651	0.1257	0.0154	0.0111	0.1596	0.1127	0.0252	0.0170
West	-0.2240	0.1391	-0.0249	0.0174	-0.3371	0.1241***	-0.0641	0.0269**
East	-0.0134	0.1283	-0.0013	0.0127	-0.2487	0.1086**	-0.0442	0.0210**
Bachelor's degree	-0.3855	0.2022*	-0.0470	0.0301	-0.6369	0.1790***	-0.1368	0.0477***
Master's degree	-0.4805	0.1982**	-0.0566	0.0277**	-0.6504	0.1730***	-0.1287	0.0401***
Doctorate	-0.6791	0.2238***	-0.0873	0.0363***	-0.8541	0.1867***	-0.1798	0.0479***
Private	0.1423	0.1283	0.0137	0.0123	0.1380	0.1124	0.0224	0.0181
Urban	-0.1103	0.1061	-0.0110	0.0108	-0.1106	0.0923	-0.0184	0.0157
Rural	-0.2797	0.1412**	-0.0321	0.0189*	-0.2118	0.1272*	-0.0382	0.0251
Constant	-2.8983	0.3999***			-2.5547	0.3504***		
Non-NCAA, N = 969								
% Female enrollment	0.0822	0.0085***	0.0078	0.0010***	0.0768	0.0080***	0.0108	0.0012***
Total undergrad enrollment	-0.0104	0.0105	-0.0010	0.0010	-0.0191	0.0095**	-0.0027	0.0013**
Occupational offerings	-0.6869	0.2528***	-0.0556	0.0181***	-0.5253	0.2209**	-0.0654	0.0243***
Historically black college	-0.5210	0.3644	-0.0735	0.0708	-0.2394	0.3484	-0.0393	0.0657
South	0.0009	0.1610	0.0001	0.0153	0.0071	0.1454	0.0010	0.0203
West	0.0088	0.1999	0.0008	0.0189	0.0080	0.1750	0.0011	0.0244
East	0.6044	0.2632**	0.0411	0.0120***	0.6234	0.2506**	0.0643	0.0174***

Bachelor's degree	−0.6651	0.2126***	−0.0916	0.0397**	−0.8168	0.1990***	−0.1649	0.0524***
Master's degree	−0.7704	0.2505***	−0.1109	0.0498**	−0.7798	0.2278***	−0.1537	0.0578***
Doctorate	−1.2729	0.3391***	−0.2745	0.1134**	−1.0374	0.3007***	−0.2552	0.1022**
Private	0.0465	0.2559	0.0044	0.0237	−0.0531	0.2119	−0.0075	0.0305
Urban	−0.0495	0.1578	−0.0048	0.0155	−0.1000	0.1442	−0.0144	0.0214
Rural	−0.3084	0.1712*	−0.0338	0.0216	−0.2800	0.1596*	−0.0437	0.0278
Constant	−2.1440	0.5027***			−2.0931	0.4497***		
NCAA, N = 1021								
% Female enrollment	0.1473	0.0127***	0.0072	0.0013***	0.1264	0.0105***	0.0167	0.0018***
Football	1.3594	0.1861***	0.1078	0.0216***	1.2044	0.1413***	0.2019	0.0295***
Division II	0.0985	0.1997	0.0046	0.0091	0.3690	0.1682**	0.0432	0.0175**
Division III	0.8302	0.2176***	0.0370	0.0112***	0.8630	0.1939***	0.1027	0.0209***
Total undergrad enrollment	−0.0389	0.0113***	−0.0019	0.0007***	−0.0275	0.0098***	−0.0036	0.0013***
Occupational offerings	0.2804	0.1928	0.0115	0.0064*	0.1271	0.1569	0.0157	0.0181
Historically black college	−0.9067	0.3546**	−0.0990	0.0668	−0.5395	0.3190*	−0.0995	0.0776
South	0.4158	0.2042***	0.0179	0.0084**	0.3242	0.1791*	0.0393	0.0202*
West	−0.2733	0.2247	−0.0167	0.0172	−0.5776	0.2026***	−0.1046	0.0481**
East	−0.0061	0.2094	−0.0003	0.0103	−0.4598	0.1695***	−0.0681	0.0280**
Master's degree	−0.0722	0.2856	−0.0036	0.0145	−0.0465	0.2229	−0.0062	0.0299
Doctorate	−0.1897	0.2769	−0.0094	0.0137	−0.3599	0.2293	−0.0483	0.0320
Private	0.0683	0.1833	0.0034	0.0091	0.1916	0.1524	0.0257	0.0205
For profit	1.1948	0.4050***	0.0200	0.0052***	1.3166	0.3876***	0.0666	0.0104***
Urban	0.1004	0.1697	0.0049	0.0083	0.0915	0.1365	0.0120	0.0178
Rural	0.0284	0.3150	0.0014	0.0147	0.0144	0.2569	0.0019	0.0332
Constant	−7.2263	0.7792***			−6.4532	0.6919***		

Notes:

Robust standard errors. Marginal effects (Marg.) are calculated at the mean of the variable except in the case of dummy variables where the marginal effect represents a change in the indicator from 0 to 1.

*** $p < 0.01$, ** $p < 0.05$, * $p < 0.1$.

sample, although private, non-NCAA colleges have smaller proportionality gaps, other things held constant.

We interpret these probit results with caution. Because compliance in the twenty-first century is relatively rare, there is little variation in the dependent variable. Furthermore, the persistence results we presented earlier suggest that noncompliance is the normal state of being, so even if a school is currently compliant, it will typically revert to being noncompliant. Because we have limited our analyses to a cross-section, we leave it for future research to consider the dynamics of compliance more fully.

9.6   CONCLUSION

This chapter thoroughly examines the history of and compliance with Title IX, as it applies to college athletics. We have focused on whether schools meet the compliance standard of substantial proportionality. Our most striking conclusion is that, although Title IX has increased women's opportunities to participate in athletics, most postsecondary schools have been and remain noncompliant. In our total sample, we also find that larger schools with fewer women in the student body, smaller athletic programs, and no football team are more likely to comply with Title IX. The same is true for schools that offer graduate degrees.

The long-term failure of postsecondary schools to comply with Title IX is not equivalent to failing women. Widespread and persistent noncompliance (combined with instances of fleeting compliance) may indicate that schools face a binding constraint – perhaps demand by female students for college athletic opportunities. Rising female enrollment in college naturally increases the target percentage of female athletes, making it harder for schools to be in compliance (Thomas, 2011a). This can be particularly difficult if women choose not to play sports in college because the professional offerings they face after graduation are limited or if women simply value other activities in college more than they value athletics. Perhaps limited opportunities for sports in high school disproportionately affect women and limit the grooming of would-be college athletes. The question of whether differences in opportunities at the secondary- or primary-school level affect participation at the college level deserves greater study.

On the other hand, persistent noncompliance might result from a nonbinding constraint, namely the lack of enforcement of Title IX. The OCR's pursuit of relatively few cases against noncomplying institutions over the decades since Title IX's implementation signals that the probability of investigation is low. This, in turn, influences the calculation of the expected cost of noncompliance. Any school that is found to be violating Title IX risks losing its federal funding, although this punishment has never been used. Further, OCR cannot cite any cases of suspected discrimination against female athletes it referred to the Justice Department for additional action. The situation has led many to conclude that Title IX has failed due to lack of enforcement. The examination of these issues lies beyond the scope of this chapter.

NOTES

*   We thank Heidi Verheggan for her research assistance. John J. Cheslock generously answered questions we had about the data and provided his own data so we could check our updated numbers.
1. Although our focus is on intercollegiate athletics, it is worth remembering that Title IX applies to all educational programs. In a recent study of high-school athletic participation, Betsey Stevenson concludes that 'compliance with Title IX largely involved an increase in girls' access to sports with little change in the opportunities available to boys' (Stevenson, 2007: 504).
2. Cheslock and Eckes (2008) provide an excellent overview of the evolution of Title IX.
3. Gender differences in financial aid and in athletic facilities and equipment are also worthy of study and are part of Title IX compliance as well, though they receive considerably less media attention. See Zimbalist (1997) for further clarification of these issues.
4. NCAA certification is a process schools undergo to ensure integrity in the institutions' athletic program. Certification is typically done every 10 years at an institution. Certification requires that each school complete a year-long self-study of the institution's athletics program. After completing the self-study, a team of outside evaluators visits the department and, among other things, determines whether the institution has established plans for making or maintaining progress in gender equity. However, the NCAA put a moratorium on the program in April 2011 to evaluate its cost-effectiveness (NCAA, 2011).
5. The OCR does not encourage or require that schools cut men's sports to be compliant with Title IX although this is a criticism often leveled at the law (Thomas, 2011b). Marburger and Hogshead-Makar (2003) argue that it is profit-motivated athletics departments rather than Title IX that is usually behind the decision to cut men's sports.
6. An important contribution made by Anderson and Cheslock is how to use the EADA data in a consistent manner over time since there have been substantial changes to the questionnaire over time such that in some years institutions report unduplicated figures in one year (an unduplicated figure means that an athlete who plays multiple sports is counted only once) and duplicated figures in other years (a duplicated figure means that an athlete who plays multiple sports is counted once for each sports). They note that they use duplicated participation figures that are adjusted for differences in reporting over time, an improvement over previous work.
7. While this possibility has not been examined by other researchers in this area, Monks cites a report in the *Chronicle of Higher Education* that indicates that this approach is clearly on the mind of at least some university presidents.
8. In 1992, the Big Ten Conference approved a resolution promising that within five years 40 percent of the varsity athletes at each of its schools would be women. At the time, the prevailing average was 30 percent (Sigelman and Wahlbeck, 1999).
9. Current NCAA rules allow 85 scholarship players in football and 105 total players for home games.
10. Cheslock (2007, 2008) discusses in detail the changes in NCAA membership over time and the practical implications for longitudinal comparisons. In our context, if new

members of a sanctioning body exhibit a different distribution of proportionality-gap influencing characteristics than the incumbent schools, it may be these differences that come through in a naive longitudinal analysis (apples to oranges) rather than the question of more likely importance – the change in the average proportionality gap over time within a given set of schools over time.

11. EADA has attempted to calculate unduplicated data for years prior to 2003 but has not made them public.

12. This persistence may reflect heterogeneity across schools (observed or unobserved) and/ or state dependence (that is, inertia). Separately identifying these sources of persistent noncompliance is best addressed within a dynamic framework, an important avenue for future research.

13. Our analysis is largely descriptive, so we do not compare our results to those of previous empirical studies. We do not attempt to model the underlying decision-making process of colleges or the dynamic nature of the problem. As all of these covariates are to some degree choice variables as well, we view our analysis as correlational.

14. Partially because of the structure of the EADA data at the time, Anderson et al. (2006) must supplement the EADA data and IPEDS with information provided by other organizations including the NCAA, Barron's, and the National Association of College and University Business Officers. We use fewer data sources, but examine a similarly broad set of explanatory variables in our work.

15. This persistent finding in the literature that schools located in the Southern US are less likely to be compliant all else equal is puzzling and to date no explanation has emerged.

REFERENCES

Anderson, Deborah J. and John J. Cheslock (2004), 'Institutional Strategies to Achieve Gender Equity in Intercollegiate Athletics: Does Title IX Harm Male Athletes?', *American Economic Review*, **94**(2), May: 307–11.

Anderson, Deborah J., John J. Cheslock and Ronald G. Ehrenberg (2006), 'Gender Equity in Intercollegiate Athletics: Determinants of Title IX Compliance', *Journal of Higher Education*, **77**(2), March–April: 225–50.

Beveridge, Charles P. (1996), 'Title IX and Intercollegiate Athletics: When Schools Cut Men's Athletic Teams', *University of Illinois Law Review*, **1996**(3): 809–42.

Carroll, Kathleen A. and Brad R. Humphreys (2000), 'Nonprofit Decision Making and Social Regulation: The Intended and Unintended Consequences of Title IX', *Journal of Economic Behavior and Organization*, **43**(3), November: 359–76.

Cheslock, John J. (2007), *Who's Playing College Sports? Trends in Participation*, East Meadow, NY: Women's Sports Foundation.

Cheslock, John J. (2008), *Who's Playing College Sports? Money, Race and Gender*, East Meadow, NY: Women's Sports Foundation.

Cheslock, John J. and Suzanne E. Eckes (2008), 'Statistical Evidence and Compliance with Title IX', in *Legal Issues and Institutional Research*, edited by A. Luna, New Directions for Institutional Research Number 138, San Francisco, CA: Jossey-Bass, pp. 31–45.

Findlay, Leanne C. and Anne Bowker (2009), 'The Link between Competitive Sport Participation and Self-concept in Early Adolescence: A Consideration of Gender and Sport Orientation', *Journal of Youth and Adolescence*, **38**(1), January: 29–40.

Fox, Claudia K., Daheia Barr-Anderson, Dianne Neumark-Sztainer and Melanie Wall (2010), 'Physical Activity and Sports Team Participation: Associations with Academic Outcomes in Middle School and High School Students', *Journal of School Health*, **80**(1), January: 31–7.

Habel, Melissa A., Patricia J. Dittus, Christine J. De Rosa, Emily Q. Chung and Peter R. Kerndt (2010), 'Daily Participation in Sports and Students' Sexual Activity', *Perspectives on Sexual and Reproductive Health*, **42**(2), February: 244–50.

Irick, Erin (2011), '1981–82 to 2010–2011 NCAA Sports Sponsorship and Participation Rates Report', online at: http://ncaapublications.com/p-4243-student-athlete-participation-1981-82-2010-11-ncaa-sports-sponsorship-and-participation-rates-report.aspx (accessed January 27, 2012).

Kaestner, Robert and Xin Xu (2006), 'Effects of Title IX and Sports Participation on Girls' Physical Activity and Weight', *Advances in Health Economics and Health Services Research*, **17**: 79–111.

Leeds, Michael A., Yelena Suris and Jennifer Durkin (2004), 'College Football and Title IX', in *Economics of College Sports*, edited by John Fizel and Rodney Fort, Studies in Sports Economics, Westport, CT and London: Greenwood, Praeger, pp. 137–51.

Marburger, Daniel P. and Nancy Hogshead-Makar (2003), 'Is Title IX Really to Blame for the Decline in Intercollegiate Men's Non-Revenue Sports?', *Marquette Sports Law Review*, **14**(1), Fall: 65–93.

Miller, Kathleen E., Donald F. Sabo, Merrill J. Melnick, Michael P. Farrell and Grace M. Barnes (2000), *The Women's Sports Foundation Report: Health Risks and the Teen Athlete*, East Meadow, NY: Women's Sports Foundation.

Mitchell, Nicole and Lisa A. Ennis (2007), *Encyclopedia of Title Nine and Sports*, Westport, CT: Greenwood.

Monks, James (2005), 'Title IX Compliance and Preference for Men in College Admissions', Cornell Higher Education Research Institute (CHERI), Paper 30, online at: http://digital-commons.ilr.cornell.edu/cheri/30 (accessed July 11, 2011).

National Collegiate Athletic Association (NCAA) (2011), 'Board Directs Alternative Approach to Division 1 Certification', online at: http://www.ncaa.org/wps/wcm/connect/public/NCAA/Resources/Latest+News/2011/April/Board+directs+alternative+approach+to+Division+I+certification (accessed July 11, 2011).

President's Council on Physical Fitness (1997), 'Physical Activity & Sport in the Lives of Girls', online at: http://www.fitness.gov/girlssports.pdf (accessed July 29, 2011).

Rishe, Patrick James (1999), 'Gender Gaps and the Presence and Profitability of College Football', *Social Science Quarterly*, **80**(4), December: 702–17.

Sander, Libby (2008), 'Historically Black Colleges Are Not in Compliance With Title IX, Study Finds', *Chronicle of Higher Education*, February 27th.

Sigelman, Lee and Paul J. Wahlbeck (1999), 'Gender Proportionality in Intercollegiate Athletics: The Mathematics of Title IX Compliance', *Social Science Quarterly*, **80**(3), September: 518–38.

Stafford, Sarah L. (2004), 'Progress Toward Title IX Compliance: The Effect of Formal and Informal Enforcement Mechanisms', *Social Science Quarterly*, **85**(5), December: 1469–86.

Stevenson, Betsey (2007), 'Title IX and the Evolution of High School Sports', *Contemporary Economic Policy*, **25**(4), October: 486–505.

Stevenson, Betsey (2010), 'Beyond the Classroom: Using Title IX to Measure the Return to High School Sports', *Review of Economics and Statistics*, **92**(2), May: 284–301.

Suggs, Welch (2005), *A Place on the Team: The Triumph and Tragedy of Title IX*, Princeton, NJ: Princeton University Press.

Taliaferro, Lindsay A., Barbra A. Rienzo and Kristine A. Donovan (2010), 'Relationships Between Youth Sport Participation and Selected Health Risk Behaviors from 1999 to 2007', *Journal of School Health*, **80**(8), July: 399–410.

Terry, Neil and Crecencio Ramirez (2005), 'Gender Equity Regulation and Profitability in College Athletics', *Academy of Educational Research Journal* (Report), **9**, September.

Thomas, Katie (2011a), 'College Teams, Relying on Deception, Undermine Gender Equity', *New York Times*, April 25.

Thomas, Katie (2011b), 'Colleges Cut Men's Programs to Satisfy Title IX', *New York Times*, May 1.

US Department of Education Office of Postsecondary Education (2010), 'User's Guide for the Equity in Athletics Disclosure Act Web-Based Data Collection', online at: https://surveys.ope.ed.gov/athletics (accessed June 20, 2011).

Wushanley, Ying (2004), 'Equality Over Power: The Impact of Title IX on Intercollegiate Athletics for Women', Chap. 7, in *Playing Nice and Losing: The Struggle for Control of Women's Intercollegiate Athletics, 1960–2000*, Syracuse, NY: Syracuse University Press.

Zimbalist, Andrew (1997), 'Gender Equity and the Economics of College Sports', *Advances in the Economics of Sport*, **2**: 203–23.

Zimbalist, Andrew (2003), 'What to do about Title IX', *Gender Issues*, **21**(2), 55–9.

10. Revenues and subsidies in collegiate sports: an analysis of NCAA Division I women's basketball
*Robert W. Brown and R. Todd Jewell**

10.1 INTRODUCTION

In the nearly 40 years since it was passed and signed into law by President Richard Nixon, Title IX of the Educational Amendments of 1972 has required colleges and universities to offer female student-athletes opportunities comparable to male student-athletes. Partly as a result, the number of women participating in intercollegiate sports has increased from around 30,000 in 1971 to over 165,000 in 2005 (National Coalition for Women and Girls in Education, 2008). Controversy has surrounded Title IX since its inception, primarily because athletic administrators view Title IX as an additional economic constraint within which they must operate. Administrators at schools with large 'revenue-producing' football or men's basketball teams, which have traditionally subsidized non-revenue sports, may be forced to transfer revenue from non-revenue men's sports to women's sports. The size of the transfer depends on the size of the surplus revenues generated across all athletic teams as well as the women's sports teams in particular.

Revenue-producing inter-collegiate athletic programs often rely on football or men's basketball to subsidize non-revenue sports and general athletic expenses (Leeds et al., 2004). The National Collegiate Athletic Association (NCAA), the umbrella organization that establishes rules for colleges with the most prestigious sports programs, restricts the mobility of athletes between schools and controls recruiting of and compensation for these student-athletes. Currently, compensation to NCAA student-athletes is limited to the value of an athletic scholarship (tuition, fees, room, board, and books) plus a small amount of income that a player can earn, which is less than the revenues produced by the best student-athletes. As a result, revenue-producing players generate economic rents that can subsidize non-revenue athletic programs and other recipients. The NCAA recently rejected paying athletes directly, in the form of a $2,000 stipend (Associated Press, 2011; Eichelberger, 2011). While $40 a week would clearly help student-athletes with incidental expenditures such as gasoline or entertainment, it would not compensate the best athletes for the revenues they generate. On the other hand, a $2,000 stipend to athletes in non-revenue-producing sports would amount to an additional transfer from revenue producers.

There are few empirical estimates of the revenues generated by college athletes because of the lack of reliable data on athletic revenues and the lack of direct measures of player skills and productivity. Brown (1993, 1994) and Brown and Jewell (2004) estimate the marginal revenue product (MRP) of NCAA football and men's basketball players by regressing a college team's revenues on the number of 'premium players' on the team, where a premium player is defined as a college player who is eventually drafted into the National Football League (NFL) or the National Basketball Association (NBA), holding constant other factors that influence revenues. Since only the best college players are drafted, professional draft data proxy for the skill level of an individual college football or basketball player. Brown (1993) shows that the MRP of a premium college football player (that is, a future NFL draftee) exceeds $500,000 in 1988–89 revenues for his college team, while Brown and Jewell (2004) find a value closer to $400,000 when considering a larger sample of schools.

More recent estimates indicate that a premium college football player's MRP exceeded $1,000,000 during the 2004–05 season (Brown, 2011). A premium men's college basketball player (that is, a future NBA draftee) generated approximately $1,000,000 in 1988–89 revenues for his college team (Brown, 1994), as confirmed in Brown and Jewell (2004). From an economic perspective, the excess revenues above the maximum NCAA-mandated payment to student-athletes constitute monopsony rents that are transferred to other parties. These include administrative and coaching salaries, athletic facilities, and unprofitable sports teams (Kahn, 2007).

Brown and Jewell (2006) use the methodology from earlier studies to estimate the MRP of a premium college women's basketball player using 2000–01 data, where a premium player is defined as one who is eventually drafted into the Women's National Basketball Association (WNBA). Team revenue data were from Equity and Athletic Disclosure Act (EADA), where total revenues were aggregated across ticket sales, guarantees/options, concessions, radio and television, government support, student fees, and institutional support, among other sources. The authors' results indicate that a premium women's college basketball player generates approximately $300,000 per year in revenues for her school.

However, their quantile regression estimates show that these effects vary considerably across schools, with premium players at the best programs generating well in excess of the average, as might be expected. It appears that, by the dawn of the twenty-first century, at least some NCAA women's basketball teams required lower subsidies from the athletic department or the university budget and that a few teams had become net-revenue producers and, thus, net subsidizers of other sports. Specifically, premium women players at elite basketball programs generate rents that, like rents from revenue-producing football and men's basketball programs, may be transferred to non-revenue-producing programs.

The aggregate nature of the 2000–01 EADA data used by Brown and Jewell (2006) confound the marginal revenue estimates by including revenue sources that are likely to be independent of a team's current players, such as student fees and institutional and government support. In the present chapter, we update and improve the 2000–01 estimates using data on team revenues from 2004–05 comprising 15 separate revenue categories. To give a more complete picture of the value of current star players, we estimate players' MRP using disaggregated team revenue data.

In Section 10.2, we present a model of the revenues generated by the most-talented female basketball players, using Brown's (1993) methodology and detailed data from the 2004–05 basketball season. In Section 10.3, we estimate the model using quantile regressions, and we discuss the implications of these results. We find, for example, that the value of a premium player varies widely, depending on the percentile of the estimation. She can bring as little as $22,000 or as much as $200,000 in revenue to her program. In Section 10.4, we briefly review the literature on the funding of women's programs. We differentiate between women's basketball programs that directly generate revenues and those that require transfers (implicit or explicit) from other revenue sources, such as student fees and institutional support. We sketch the flow of revenues between women's basketball programs and other entities, such as institutional support, student fees, and other athletic programs. We find that, although there are wide differences in revenues, costs, and subsidies across NCAA Division I women's basketball programs, these programs cannot completely fund themselves and must receive some sort of subsidy. Section 10.5 concludes.

10.2   DATA ANALYSIS AND MODEL

Past research on revenues in college sports has generally looked at the earning potential of student-athletes as indicated by *total* athletic revenues. However, aggregate revenue data come from many different sources. Some of the revenues allocated to women's basketball, such as student fees, government and institutional aid, or endowment and investment income, are likely to be independent of the skill levels of current team members. As a result, aggregate revenue data do not allow us to track the flow of athletic monies across the university, athletic department, and third-party sources, or across programs within the athletic department.

This chapter supplements previous research with more detailed financial information collected by the *Indianapolis Star* from the NCAA through public information requests. Biannually, the NCAA requires member schools to complete a survey detailing all sources of revenues and all expenses on football, men's basketball, and women's basketball. These data identify 15 revenue categories for 160 Division I women's basketball teams during the 2004–05 basketball season, approximately half of the 328 schools competing in NCAA Division I that year. Since these data were collected via public information requests, they include only public universities. There were 31 conferences plus independents (that is, schools not affiliated with a conference) in Division I during the 2004–05 basketball season, and our dataset covers 27 conferences and independents. Because the Ivy League, the Metro-Atlantic Athletic Conference, the Patriot League, and the West Coast Conference consist largely of private colleges, which do not have to disclose their data, we exclude these conferences from the analysis.

Table 10.1 summarizes our sample of NCAA Division I women's basketball programs by revenue category. Details of the types of revenues included in each category appear in Appendix 10A. Many categories of women's basketball revenues may be unrelated to the quality of the team's current players. For example, we expect premium *current* players to directly increase the demand for ticket sales, game day concessions and parking fees, contributions (that is, direct contributions and those required in excess of a ticket value), advertising and sponsorships, and perhaps guarantees from away-game attendance. However, these 'direct revenues' average only 47 percent of all revenues in women's basketball. The remaining 53 percent of revenues come from sources independent of the current team's quality, such as student fees, government and institutional aid, and endowment/investment income. Among these revenue sources, student fees and direct institutional support are the largest shares, together averaging about 40 percent of revenues for women's basketball programs.

Table 10.1 shows that an average NCAA women's basketball team produced $494,840 in revenues in the 2004–05 season, with a wide dispersion across teams. The standard deviation is over $300,000, with the highest revenues exceeding $5.5 million and the lowest just over $5,500. On average, ticket sales comprised 25 percent of revenues, followed closely by 24 percent from institutional support, 15 percent from student fees, and 13 percent from contributions. Each of the remaining categories totaled less than 5 percent of total revenues. The distribution of total revenues across teams is highly skewed to the right, so the mean is greater than the median.

*Table 10.1   Women's basketball revenues and expenses (*n = 160*) ($)*

Revenue category	Mean	Median	Std dev.	Max.	Min.
Ticket sales	124,503	17,313	537,619	4,227,145	510
Student fees	73,703	0	544,563	1,145,908	0
Guarantees	6,187	2,000	551,779	53,959	0
Contributions	64,646	11,112	559,304	1,334,497	0
Third party support	5,709	0	567,175	153,488	0
Direct government support	7,460	0	575,341	249,640	0
Direct institutional support	120,867	334	583,871	1,522,310	0
Indirect support	10,815	0	592,791	366,543	0
NCAA/conf. distributions	11,492	0	602,134	224,850	0
Broadcast rights	10,987	0	611,933	836,870	0
Game day sales	11,379	149	622,226	252,775	0
Royalties and advertising	13,106	0	633,058	405,003	0
Sports camps	23,684	0	644,475	644,475	0
Investment income	6,913	0	656,560	272,072	0
Other revenues	3,390	0	669,324	120,861	0
Total revenues	494,840	316,213	682,863	5,555,758	5,510
Total expenses	907,264	1,184,835	748,334	5,582,514	240,250
Revenues minus expenses	−620,752	−689,994	595,873	1,475,661	−2,282,708

Source: Indianapolis Star.

Table 10.2   Deciles of total revenues

Percentile (%)	10	20	30	40	50	60	70	80	90
Revenues ($)	27,069	67,882	109,467	182,391	316,213	479,503	574,855	799,467	1,086,809

Source: Indianapolis Star.

Before developing a model based on these disaggregated data, we examine the distribution of revenue across colleges. Table 10.2 lists deciles for total revenues of women's basketball teams in the 2004–05 season. The data suggest that total revenue from women's basketball is skewed to the right. This conclusion is supported by our calculation that 62 percent of

Table 10.3   Revenue category comparisons

	Teams ≤ 35th%	Teams ≥ 50th%
Ticket sales	23	26
Student fees	0	16
Guarantees	12	1
Contributions	16	13
Third party support	2	1
Direct government support	1	1
Direct institutional support	16	24
Indirect support	5	2
NCAA/conf. distributions	3	2
Broadcast rights	0	2
Game day sales	2	2
Royalties and advertising	4	2
Sports camps	11	5
Investment income	2	1
Other revenues	3	1

Source: Indianapolis Star.

teams report less than the $494,840 mean team revenues in 2004–05. Fifty percent of the teams in the sample earned revenues under $316,213, with 38 percent of teams producing revenues over $500,000, four of which had over $2 million in total revenues.

Table 10.3 disaggregates total revenue by source and shows how much each source contributed for teams at or below the 35th percentile and teams at or above the median. Teams in the upper half of the *Total Revenues* distribution receive a slightly higher proportion of revenues from ticket revenues and a much higher proportion from student fees and direct institutional support. On the other hand, teams in the bottom 35 percent generate 12 percent of their revenue from away-game guarantees, while teams in the upper half generate only 1 percent. Strong teams in search of an easy win often use such guaranteed payments as a way to attract weak competition. The bottom 35 percent also receive a slightly larger percentage of their revenue from contributions.

Next, we compare disaggregated revenues across revenue quintiles for NCAA Division I women's basketball teams. Table 10.4 lists the averages for all revenue categories in dollar amounts for each of the five quintiles of total revenue. The trends that we discern below from Table 10.4 motivate us to investigate the relationship between revenue source and revenue quintile more closely in Section 10.4.

Table 10.4   *Average revenues by category within each quintile of total revenues(%)*

	1st quintile	2nd quintile	3rd quintile	4th quintile	5th quintile
Ticket sales	9,990	28,602	49,883	91,139	429,985
Student fees	0	4,223	31,011	130,990	208,313
Guarantees	9,813	4,603	6,538	6,078	3,941
Contributions	3,788	15,442	59,023	69,594	171,133
Third party support	335	5,693	2,041	2,854	17,089
Direct government support	0	1,078	6,966	21,066	14,130
Direct institutional support	2,511	22,714	78,849	186,239	308,066
Indirect support	0	5,491	7,416	20,669	19,877
NCAA/conf. distributions	804	3,446	13,773	12,027	26,577
Broadcast rights	0	135	6,209	5,875	41,419
Game day sales	694	3,945	7,242	11,969	32,042
Royalties/advertising	963	3,119	15,889	14,717	29,906
Sports camps	2,657	12,690	29,694	23,936	48,431
Investment income	360	1,812	5,360	2,438	23,850
Total revenues	32,515	115,583	321,046	606,810	1,379,985

Source: Indianapolis Star.

Several patterns regarding ticket sales and total revenues emerge from these disaggregated data. First, average total revenues increase at a decreasing rate moving from the first to the fourth quintiles but then jump at a higher rate from the fourth to the fifth quintile. Second, ticket revenues increase at a decreasing rate over quintiles one to three and then at an increasing rate from quintiles three to five. Third, the percentage of total revenue that comes from ticket sales falls from quintiles one through four, and then rises in the fifth quintile. Taken together, these observations suggest that teams rely less on ticket revenues as their overall revenues rise, but ticket revenue spikes for the most successful programs.

To gain a deeper understanding of the determinants of team revenue and its components, we develop an empirical model. We use the disaggregated revenue data to distinguish revenues that are closely tied to the quality of current players from revenues that are, arguably, independent of player quality. To generate estimates of MRP for women's basketball players, we employ three measures of revenues. The first dependent variable includes only *Ticket Revenues*, which is presumably most directly correlated with the performance and skill levels of current players. Estimates of the MRP of female college basketball players using *Ticket Revenues* evaluate their impact on game-day demand. The second dependent variable (*Direct Revenues*) is the sum of ticket revenues, contributions, game-day concessions, away-game guarantees, conference distributions, royalties, advertisements, and sponsorships. This broader measure of revenues is closely tied to current players, so MRP estimates using *Direct Revenues* reflect the ability of female student-athletes to generate revenues from a range of sources beyond game attendance. The third dependent variable (*Total Revenues*) aggregates all 15 categories of revenues. MRP estimates using *Total Revenues* are comparable to existing estimates in the literature and include many revenue sources that may be independent of a team's current players.

Following the methodology detailed in Brown (1993, 1994), we estimate a women's college basketball player's marginal revenue product by regressing a team's 2004–05 revenues on the number of its players drafted from its 2004–05 roster into the WNBA, and on other control variables. We assume that a college basketball team's revenues are a function of the quality of the team, the quality of its opponents, and its market demand characteristics. The basic revenue relationship is given in equation (10.1), where *i* indexes team, *j* indexes opponent, *Q* indicates team quality as the sum of its players' skill levels, *M* represents market characteristics, and *R* is a function that maps team quality, opponent quality, and market characteristics onto revenues:

$$Revenues_i = R(Q_i, Q_j, M_i). \tag{10.1}$$

Using Brown's methodology, player skill is proxied by whether a player is drafted by a professional team. In the case of women's basketball, the WNBA, established in 1997, provides the necessary professional-draft data. A player is a 'premium player' if she is drafted into the WNBA at the end of her college career. Team quality (Q_i) is the sum of all premium players (that is, future WNBA draftees) on a school's squad during the 2004–05 season. Players who were on a college team's 2004–05 roster could have been drafted into the WNBA in 2005, 2006, 2007, or 2008. For example, a premium junior player contributes to her 2004–05 college team revenues but cannot be drafted until 2006. Following Brown and Jewell (2006), we disregard players who were freshmen in 2004–05. Freshman players are unlikely to have much of an impact on team skill, especially in women's basketball, where nearly all student-athletes play for their entire four-year eligibility period. Thus, the WNBA-draft measure, *Draft*, includes only those players who were sophomores, juniors, or seniors in 2004–05.

The number of premium players may not measure the overall quality of a team, especially a team that has no premium players. In order to measure Q_i more completely, we include a measure of overall team quality based on the ratings performance index (RPI) of women's basketball teams. RPI is a weighted average of a team's winning percentage and that of its opponents; thus, it measures team quality conditional on schedule strength. RPI is often used to rank NCAA teams, especially in basketball, and the NCAA uses it to determine the participating teams and seeding for postseason basketball tournaments. We use the RPI-based ranking of all women's college basketball teams produced by *Collegiate Basketball News* (www.rpiratings.com) as of the end of the 2004–05 regular season. The variable *Rank* reports these RPI rankings. The top-ranked team for the regular season 2004–05 is given a value of 1, the second-ranked team is assigned 2, and so on until the last-ranked team has a value of 328. Given the reverse ordering of the ranking numbers, we expect the coefficient on *Rank* to be negative, since a higher rank (a lower number) should result in higher revenues.

The revenues that any school attracts are also a function of the quality of its opponents. Because college basketball teams play the majority of their games against conference opponents, we proxy for Q_j with a vector of dummy variables for conference (*Conference*), which accounts for unobservable conference effects. Following Brown and Jewell (2006), metro statistical area (MSA) population (*MSA*) measures market potential (M_j). The predicted sign on *MSA* is ambiguous, since a larger population implies a larger potential demand, but larger MSAs also tend to have more substitutes in terms of entertainment for sports fans and marketing opportunities for companies looking to sponsor athletic events. Table 10.5 presents summary statistics for the estimation sample.

Under the assumption that R is a linear function, our empirical model is given by equation (10.2):

$$Revenues_i = \alpha + \beta_1 \times Draft + \beta_2 \times Rank + \gamma \times Conference_i + \delta \times$$
$$MSA_i + \varepsilon_i. \tag{10.2}$$

The parameters α, β_1, β_2, and δ and the vector γ are coefficients to be estimated, and ε is the random error term. The coefficient β_1 is interpreted as the MRP of a premium women's basketball player. Recall that β_2 is expected to be negative, since *Rank* is ordered so that a lower number indicates a higher ranking.

The data in Tables 10.1 and 10.2 indicate a skewed distribution of team revenues, with the mean driven above the median by a few high-revenue teams. Standard OLS estimates around the conditional mean may be

*Table 10.5   Summary statistics (*n = *160)*

Variable	Description	Mean	Std dev.
Ticket Revenues	Ticket sales for home games (2004–05)	$ 124,503	$ 399,112
Direct Revenues	Revenues from ticket sales, contributions, game-day concessions, away-game guarantees, conference distributions, and royalties, advertisements, and sponsorships (2004–05)	$ 166,667	$ 427,360
Total Revenues	Revenues from all sources (2004–05)	$ 494,840	$ 669,490
Draft	Number of WNBA draft picks (2005 to 2007)	0.481	0.978
Rank	End of regular season ranking (March 2005)	146.2	92.23
MSA	Population of metro statistical area (2000)	1,234,354	2,022,637

Sources: Indianapolis Star; wnba.com; rpiratings.com; census.gov.

sensitive to the existence of outliers in skewed data. Unlike OLS, which estimates the mean of the dependent variable, quantile regression (Koenker and Bassett, 1978) estimates the conditional median and other conditional percentiles of the dependent variable. As a result, it is particularly useful when the error term is not symmetrically distributed. Quantile regression estimators are robust to the presence of outliers, as in our data, while OLS estimators are generally not. In addition, quantile regression techniques allow us to analyze different parts of the conditional distribution of the dependent variable, while OLS estimates are conditional means. Thus, we also evaluate MRP at different points in the conditional distribution.

10.3   RESULTS AND DISCUSSION

Tables 10.6, 10.7, and 10.8 present MRP quantile regression estimates using *Ticket Revenues, Direct Revenues*, and *Total Revenues*, respectively, for the 20th, 35th, 50th (median), 65th, and 80th percentiles. Each reported estimation includes a complete set of conference dummies, which we suppress for the sake of brevity. Before discussing the results, we present two caveats. First, the estimates presented in the following tables may *overstate* MRP, given a potential endogeneity problem. Brown and Jewell (2006) point out that premium players are generally attracted to better programs,

Table 10.6   *Estimates using* Ticket Revenues *(*n = *160)*

Variable	20%	35%	Median	65%	80%
Draft	**12,427**	**29,857**	**102,316**	**96,593**	**169,217**
	(0.00)	**(0.00)**	**(0.00)**	**(0.00)**	**(0.00)**
Rank	**−36.32**	−43.87	−65.90	**−124.71**	**−236.72**
	(0.00)	(0.32)	(0.15)	**(0.00)**	**(0.00)**
MSA	**−0.0014**	−0.0014	−0.0021	**−0.0030**	−0.0037
	(0.00)	(0.45)	(0.20)	**(0.00)**	(0.14)
Constant	**10,295**	13,548	23,232	**44,789**	**78,566**
	(0.00)	(0.35)	**(0.09)**	**(0.00)**	**(0.00)**
Adjusted R^2	0.10	0.13	0.19	0.26	0.34

Note: p-values in parentheses; coefficients at lower than 10% level in bold; estimations include complete set of conference dummies.

so the number of premium players may be correlated with unobservable factors, such as the quality of coaching or facilities, factors that also lead to greater revenues. Second, the estimates may *understate* the MRP of current players if the success of current players increases future women's basketball revenues or increases donations to the university's general fund.

Table 10.6 shows that a future WNBA draftee has a larger impact on ticket revenues at higher conditional percentiles of the dependent variable. For example, the median regression implies that an additional premium women's basketball player increases *Ticket Revenues* by $102,316, over three times the size of the coefficient at the 35th percentile. The impact of star players stalls at the 65th percentile, as the coefficient on *Draft* is smaller than at the median, but the two coefficients are not statistically different from each other. The upward trend in MRP reappears when one moves from the 65th to the 80th percentile.

As expected, the coefficient on *Rank* is negative for all percentiles because a higher rank number implies a worse rank. The impact, though, is insignificant at the 35th and 50th percentiles. As with star players, the impact of team quality, measured by the coefficient on *Rank*, is greater at higher conditional percentiles. These results indicate that the impact of star players and team quality on ticket revenue is greater for teams whose ticket revenue is unusually high given the number of players drafted, the team's rank, and the rest of the explanatory variables.

The coefficient on *MSA* is consistently negative, but, like *Rank*, it is not significant for all percentiles. This resolves the theoretical ambiguity of the impact of *MSA*. The negative *MSA* coefficient implies that the negative effect of local competition for sports entertainment in areas with larger

Table 10.7   Estimates using Direct Revenues *(tickets, contributions, game-day concessions, away-game guarantees, NCAA/ conference distributions, royalties/advertisements/ sponsorships) (*n = 160*)*

Variable	20%	35%	Median	65%	80%
Draft	**21,713**	**51,650**	**113,697**	**134,328**	**200,273**
	(0.00)	**(0.00)**	**(0.00)**	**(0.00)**	**(0.00)**
Rank	**−62.19**	**−66.81**	**−157.00**	**−171.29**	−323.30
	(0.02)	**(0.01)**	**(0.00)**	**(0.01)**	(0.15)
MSA	**−0.0025**	**−0.0032**	**−0.0057**	**−0.0070**	−0.0091
	(0.01)	**(0.00)**	**(0.00)**	**(0.00)**	(0.25)
Constant	**19,662**	**34,401**	**65,127**	**82,179**	**131,259**
	(0.03)	**(0.00)**	**(0.00)**	**(0.00)**	**(0.04)**
Adjusted R^2	0.11	0.15	0.22	0.30	0.40

Note: *p*-values in parentheses; coefficients at lower than 10% level in bold; estimations include complete set of conference dummies.

populations outweighs any positive impact on revenues from having more potential women's basketball fans.

In Table 10.7, we present estimates using *Direct Revenues*, a broader measure of revenues that are directly related to current players. The signs of the coefficients on *Draft*, *Rank*, and *MSA* are largely consistent with those reported in Table 10.6. As above, *Draft* is consistently significant. *Rank* is significant at all but the highest percentile, as is *MSA*. A comparison of the MRP of a premium player on *Ticket Revenues* and on *Direct Revenues* suggests that most of the revenue-generating potential for a premium women's college basketball player comes from ticket sales, which suggests that additional revenue sources do not increase as much as gate revenue at each percentile.

At the lower percentiles, an additional future draftee adds relatively more to *Direct Revenues* compared to *Ticket Revenues* than at higher percentiles. This implies that teams in the lower conditional percentiles of revenues see a relatively higher contribution of other factors, such as away-game guarantees. The higher contribution of such factors makes intuitive sense, as teams that do unusually poorly will see a greater contribution from other schools, which are likely to do less poorly.

Estimates in Table 10.8 have much lower significance than in either of the preceding tables. *Draft* is significant only at the lowest two percentiles, *Rank* is significant only at the 35th percentile (and has the wrong sign), and *MSA* is significant only at the 35th and 50th percentiles. The lack of

Table 10.8   Estimates using Total Revenues *(n = 160)*

Variable	20%	35%	Median	65%	80%
Draft	**77,031**	**111,345**	103,452	133,886	146,280
	(0.00)	**(0.00)**	(0.13)	(0.15)	(0.31)
Rank	381.71	**520.69**	928.26	1,153.45	1,849.91
	(0.24)	**(0.00)**	(0.45)	(0.19)	(0.19)
MSA	−0.0061	**−0.0314**	**−0.0411**	−0.0487	−0.0124
	(0.55)	**(0.00)**	**(0.09)**	(0.12)	(0.72)
Constant	143,922	**226,965**	**390,896**	**553,293**	**773,121**
	(0.15)	**(0.00)**	**(0.08)**	**(0.04)**	**(0.06)**
Adjusted R^2	0.10	0.13	0.17	0.15	0.23

Note: *p*-values in parentheses; coefficients at lower than 10% level in bold; estimations include complete set of conference dummies.

significance makes intuitive sense, as total revenue includes a variety of items that are not related to the current performance of the team or its individual players. The significance of *Draft* at the lowest percentiles suggests that teams that have low revenues conditional on the independent variables rely more heavily on the drawing power of star players than do teams with unusually high conditional revenues.

10.4   SUBSIDIES AND TRANSFERS IN WOMEN's NCAA BASKETBALL

Subsidies form an important part of revenues for women's intercollegiate sports. The subsidies are transfers from other parties, such as the student body, the university budget, or other profitable sports. The literature on the subsidization of women's college sports programs generally concentrates on the connection between women's programs and football programs. Leeds et al. (2004) show that a small amount of net revenues flow from college football to women's sports, while expenditures on football come at the expense of women's programs. The authors suggest that the net impact of a football program on women's sports expenditures is negative, unless the net revenues from football are extremely high. Specifically, schools tend to underfund women's programs, and even the most profitable football programs provide only small subsidies to women's sports programs.

Rishe (1999) shows that profits from college football increase expenditures per female student-athlete but reduce the proportion of all expenditures on women athletes because the vast majority of football profit is funneled into men's sports. Agathe and Billings (2000) find evidence supporting a positive spillover of football success to other intercollegiate sports. Depken et al. (2011) show that very small and very large colleges with Division I football programs have greater women's college basketball attendance than schools that do not have them, with the greatest effect being for very small schools. If women's basketball attendance and revenues are positively correlated, this result implies that a football program augments women's basketball revenues for very small and very large schools.

In Table 10.4, which shows revenue by source for the unconditional quintiles, the two largest categories of indirect revenues are student fees and direct institutional support. Together, these sources constitute nearly 40 percent of team revenues in our sample. Table 10.4 shows that student fees and direct institutional support increase at an increasing rate at least up to the fourth quintile, both in absolute amount and as a percentage of total revenues. Teams in the first quintile depend heavily on ticket sales and away-game guarantees to fund their programs, averaging over 60 percent of their revenues from these sources; however, these two categories generate less than $20,000 per team on average. None of the teams in the first quintile received revenues from student fees, and direct support made up only 8 percent of total revenues. Therefore, operational losses incurred by these teams would have been offset by other athletic funds, such as revenue from football or men's basketball.

Teams in the second quintile receive much more revenue from student fees and direct institutional support than teams in the first quintile. The sum of these two categories averages $26,937 (23 percent of team revenues), slightly less than revenue from ticket sales ($28,602) for this quintile. Third-quintile teams generate more in ticket revenues than second-quintile teams, but, again, much of the overall increase in revenue comes from outside the women's basketball program in the form of student fees and institutional support. On average, teams in the third quintile generate 34 percent of total revenues from student fees and direct institutional support. Teams in the fourth quintile receive over 50 percent of their total revenue from these outside sources. Teams in the highest quintile averaged $208,313 in student fees and $308,000 in institutional support, together comprising 37 percent of their total revenues. Although this percentage is considerably less than for fourth-quintile teams, it remains a large amount of resources transferred from non-women's-basketball sources.

We ran quintile regressions to assess the impact of premium women's basketball players on student fees and direct support. We do not present the results because the coefficients on *Draft* in all these regressions were insignificant. The lack of significance suggests that student fees and institutional support are independent of a team's premium players, perhaps because the revenue was allocated prior to the 2004–05 season. Further, both of these revenue sources are generally determined through collective decision-making processes at the university, such as student referenda or decisions within the administration.[1] Given the complexity of collective decision-making processes, we cannot identify whether the revenues from student fees and institutional support represent non-market subsidies or a university's preferences towards women's basketball. For example, let us assume that student-fee allocations are determined through a student vote. On the one hand, student-fee revenues may represent the value that students (or the median student-voter) place on athletic programs. Alternatively, student-fee revenues may be the outcome of rent-seeking activities by special-interest groups. Similar reasoning pertains to the decision-making processes by which direct institutional support is allocated to particular programs; these revenues may be allocated based on the preferences of administrators or committees – appointed or elected – that reflect the preferences of interest groups.

Although it is difficult to determine whether student fees and institutional support for women's college basketball programs represent consumer demand or rent seeking, there is no doubt that these revenues represent transfers from one group to another. Furthermore, as Table 10.1 shows, the average women's basketball program had negative net revenues of over $600,000, and nearly all women's 2004–05 NCAA Division I basketball programs were subsidized in some way. The lone exception was the University of Connecticut, a perennial women's basketball powerhouse.[2] Even considering student fees and institutional support as revenue rather than a subsidy, only 18 teams broke even or made a profit, with only four (Connecticut, Missouri State, South Alabama, and Eastern Kentucky) earning more than $50,000. Thus, despite subsidies from students and universities, most NCAA Division I women's basketball programs lose money, even those programs that are successful on the court. If the 2004–05 season is representative of other years, it is reasonable to conclude that women's basketball programs are not self-supporting.

We now identify the ultimate recipients of the subsidies when a women's basketball program cannot support itself. Some of the subsidies flow to the current players as scholarships and athletic and academic support. Only 21 of the 160 schools in our data had direct revenue large enough to cover scholarships for women's basketball. The majority of women's basketball scholarship recipients receive scholarships in excess of what their teams generate in revenues. Thus, female college basketball players are subsidized as a group, even though the best of them (that is, premium players) may generate excess revenues that are allocated to their peers.

As many studies point out (for example, Kahn, 2007), the monopsony structure of the market for college athletes allows for excess athletic revenues to be funneled to coaches. Only eight schools generate sufficient direct revenue to cover the median coaching salary of $384,113: Connecticut, Texas Tech, Tennessee, Minnesota, Missouri State, Texas, New Mexico, and Kansas State.

We finish this section by peeling back the revenue breakdown for top-revenue teams, defined as those programs at or above the 95th percentile of the revenue distribution. On average, 48 percent of these teams' revenues were from ticket sales and contributions, 10 percent were from student fees, and 25 percent were from (direct and indirect) institutional support. Even the top teams exhibit wide differences across revenue categories. Nevertheless, the relatively high proportion of revenues from student fees and institutional support indicate that these top teams do not all produce sufficient revenue.

To illustrate, consider the revenue sources for some high-revenue teams. Eastern Michigan, the lowest-revenue team in this group with $1,311,594 in total revenues, earned a mere 1 percent of its revenues from ticket sales. Student fees contributed 22.5 percent, with direct institutional support adding 44.5 percent, and indirect institutional support generating another 22 percent. SUNY-Binghamton earned slightly more in total revenues than Eastern Michigan, but it still received less than 5 percent of total revenue from ticket sales. Student fees comprised nearly 40 percent of SUNY-Binghamton's revenues, direct institutional support added over 18 percent, indirect institutional support added 28 percent, and government entities contributed nearly 7 percent. Missouri State, approximately in the middle of total revenues for these high-revenue schools, generated nearly 50 percent of its revenues from ticket sales and contributions, with another 31 percent from direct institutional support. The University of Texas, just above Missouri State in total revenues, produced over 60 percent of its revenues from tickets and contributions alone, illustrating that even high-revenue teams generate revenue in very different ways.

The University of Connecticut is in a league of its own. UConn generated nearly all of its $5.5 million in revenue from ticket sales (76 percent); contributions (8 percent) and media rights (15 percent) were small by comparison. The next highest in total revenues was Texas Tech University, which took in just over $4.1 million, 84 percent of which came from tickets sales and contributions, with student fees making up almost 10 percent. Clearly, UConn and Texas Tech can self-fund women's basketball. On the other hand, Rutgers University's women's basketball team was number three on the total revenue list at over \$2.7 million, but it was also arguably the most highly subsidized program with over \$1.5 million (56 percent of its revenues) coming from direct institutional support; ticket sales and contributions comprised less than 20 percent of its total revenues.

10.5 CONCLUSION

This chapter adds to existing research on women's basketball by analyzing the components of women's basketball revenues. It investigates how the play of current student-athletes, the revenues they generate, and the revenues that can be attributed to other factors are interconnected. The MRP estimates in this chapter improve upon existing estimates because they demonstrate the revenue-generating potential of elite-level women's college basketball players more directly.

NCAA rules limit the amount of money that student-athletes can 'earn' on campus. Past research indicates that the best student-athletes in the revenue-producing sports of football and men's basketball generate extensive revenues for their schools' athletic programs, far in excess of what they receive during their four years of college eligibility. This chapter analyzes recent data on revenues and expenditures for NCAA Division I women's basketball programs. We find that premium women's basketball players generate revenues for their schools that are a fraction of those produced by the premium football and men's basketball players, thus validating past research. Specifically, we find that a premium female player generated between \$12,000 and \$200,000 in revenue in 2004–05, depending on the definition of revenue and the conditional percentile of the team's revenue.

The finding that the best women's basketball players generate revenues for their schools is not novel, nor is the finding that women generate less revenue than men. However, this study is the first to perform a deeper analysis of revenues and revenue sources in women's college basketball. We find that, in 2004–05, most programs in our sample (nearly 87 percent) did not generate enough revenues associated with current players (termed 'direct revenues' in this chapter) to fund the scholarships of those players. Thus, in a purely monetary sense, having women's basketball programs at these schools came at the expense of another group; whether it was students, other athletic programs, or academic programs, someone had to subsidize women's basketball scholarships at most NCAA Division I schools in 2004–05. The conclusion becomes stronger when coaches' salaries are taken into account. In that case, only eight programs funded themselves out of direct revenues in 2004–05. The remaining 95 percent of schools used other revenue sources to fund their women's basketball programs.

The recent suggestion by the NCAA to pay student-athletes a $2,000 stipend has led to a renewed debate of the merits of the pay-for-play model in college athletics. Although the issue of amateurism may be the thorniest part of the discussion (with the possible legal problems associated with categorizing student-athletes as employees), the concept of the 'revenue-generating student-athlete' forms the core of the argument for paying college athletes. The NCAA reports that a full athletic scholarship in 2009 was worth approximately $15,000 for an in-state student at a public university, $25,000 for an out-of-state student at a public university, and $35,000 at a private university (NCAA, 2011). In men's basketball and football, the best players generate well in excess of these amounts, and paying athletes in the revenue-generating sports would imply a seismic shift in the business model of college athletics. Finding adequate sources for funding pay-for-play in non-revenue sports could prove an even bigger adjustment. Given that men's basketball and football subsidize other sports, administrators would have to find new sources of support for non-revenue sports.

This chapter shows that most Division I women's basketball programs are implicitly or explicitly subsidized and do not generate sufficient revenues to support themselves. Thus, any policy that increases the payment to women's basketball players must consider the source of existing subsidies. If teams in revenue-producing sports begin to pay their own players an amount based on their MRPs, then rents to fund subsidies from athletic budgets to women's basketball programs would necessarily be reduced. In order for schools to maintain compliance with Title IX, subsidies from other sources (such as student fees) would likely be increased for women's basketball to offset a decrease in athletic transfers. But at least women's basketball generates some revenues; the impact of a reduction in transfers from revenue-producing sports would have a much greater effect on sports that generate little or no revenues.

NOTES

*   The authors thank Cameron Tubbs for excellent research assistance. In addition, we acknowledge the help of Jim Sukup of *Collegiate Basketball News* for providing the RPI-based ranking data.
1.   Students at three California universities voted against higher student fees to support intercollegiate athletics (Clotfelter, 2011).
2.   For more on the dominance of some women's basketball programs, see Chapter 12 in this volume.

REFERENCES

Agthe, Donald E. and R. Bruce Billings (2000), 'The Role of Football Profits in Meeting Title IX Gender Equity and Policy', *Journal of Sports Management*, **14**(1), January: 28–40.

Associated Press (2011), 'NCAA Shelves $2,000 Athlete Stipend', *ESPN.com* online at: http://espn.go.com/college-sports/story/_/id/7357868/ncaa-puts-2000-stipend-athletes-hold (accessed December 16, 2011).

Brown, Robert W. (1993), 'An Estimate of the Rent Generated by a Premium College Football Player', *Economic Inquiry*, **31**(4), October: 671–84.

Brown, Robert W. (1994), 'Measuring Cartel Rents in the College Basketball Player Recruitment Market', *Applied Economics*, **26**(1), January: 27–34.

Brown, Robert W. (1996), 'The Revenues Associated with Relaxing Admission Standards at Division I-A Colleges', *Applied Economics*, **28**(7), July: 807–14.

Brown, Robert W. (2011), 'Estimates of College Football Player Rents', *Journal of Sports Economics*, **12**(2), April: 200–212.

Brown, Robert W. and R. Todd Jewell (2004), 'Measuring Marginal Revenue Product in College Athletics: Updated Estimates', in John Fizel and Rodney Fort (eds), *Economics of College Sports*, Westport, CT: Praeger, pp. 153–62.

Brown, Robert W. and R. Todd Jewell (2006), 'The Marginal Revenue Product of a Women's College Basketball Player', *Industrial Relations*, **45**(1), January: 96–101.

Clotfelter, Charles T. (2011), *Big-Time Sports in American Universities*, Cambridge: Cambridge University Press.

Depken, Craig A., Courtney Williams and Dennis P. Wilson (2011), 'From the Hardwood to the Gridiron to the Dorm: Influences on Attendance to Women's College Basketball', *International Journal of Sport Finance*, **6**(1), February: 3–22.

Eichelberger, Curtis (2011), 'NCAA Board Approves $2,000 Payments to Athletes', *Bloomberg News*, online at: www.bloomberg.com/news/2011-10-27/ncaa-board-approves-2-000-payments-to-athletes-postseason-academic-ban.html (accessed January 8, 2012).

Kahn, Lawrence M. (2007), 'Cartel Behavior and Amateurism in College Sports', *Journal of Economic Perspectives*, **21**(1), Winter: 209–26.

Koenker, Roger and Gilbert Bassett (1978), 'Regression Quantiles', *Econometrica*, **46**(1), January: 33–50.

Leeds, Michael A., Yelena Suris and Jennifer Durkin (2004), 'College Football and Title IX', in John Fizel and Rodney Fort (eds), *Economics of College Sports*, Westport, CT: Praeger pp. 137–52.

National Coalition for Women and Girls in Education (2008), 'Title IX at 35: Beyond the Headlines', online at: www.ncwge.org/PDF/TitleIXat35.pdf

National Collegiate Athletic Association (NCAA) (2011), 'How Do Athletic Scholarships Work?', online at: www.ncaa.org/wpswcm/connect/public/NCAA/Resources/Behind+the +Blue+Disk/How+Do+Athletic+Scholarships+Work (accessed June 9, 2012).

Rishe, Patrick James, (1999), 'Gender Gaps and the Presence and Profitability of College Football', *Social Science Quarterly*, **80**(4), December: 702–17.

APPENDIX 10A

Table 10A.1   Revenue category definitions

Category	Definition
Ticket sales	Sales of admissions to athletics events, including ticket sales to the public, faculty and students, and money received for shipping and handling of tickets
Student fees	Student fees assessed for support of (or that portion of overall fees allocated to) intercollegiate athletics
Guarantees	Revenues received from participation in away games
Contributions	Amount received (in cash or in kind) from any individual or group that is designated, restricted, or unrestricted by the donor for the operation of the athletics program. Also, amounts paid in excess of a ticket's value
Third party support	Amount provided by a third party and contractually guaranteed by the institution, but not included on the institution's W–2 (e.g., car stipend, country club membership, entertainment allowance, clothing allowance, speaking fees, housing allowance, compensation from camps, radio income, television income, or shoe and apparel income)
Direct government support	State, municipal, federal, and other government appropriations made in support of the operations of intercollegiate athletics
Direct institutional support	Amount of institutional resources used for the current operations of intercollegiate athletics, including all unrestricted funds allocated to the athletics department by the university
Indirect support	Value of facilities and services provided by the institution not charged to athletics
NCAA/conf. distributions	Revenues received from participation in bowl games and tournaments, and from all NCAA distributions, including amounts received for direct participation or through a sharing arrangement with a conference
Broadcast rights	Revenues received directly for radio/TV broadcasts, Internet, and e-commerce rights
Game day sales	Revenues from game programs, novelties, food or other concessions, and parking
Royalties and advertising	Revenues (both in cash and in kind) from corporate sponsorships, sales of advertisements, trademarks, and royalties
Sports camps	Revenues received by the athletics department for sports camps and clinics
Investment income	Endowment distributions and other investment income in support of the operations of intercollegiate athletics
Other revenues	Miscellaneous revenues (less than 5% of total revenues may appear on this line)

Source: Indianapolis Star, April 1, 2006.

11. The impact of increased academic standards of Proposition 16 on the graduation rates of women and men in Division IA intercollegiate athletics
B. Erin Fairweather

11.1 INTRODUCTION

The academic achievement of student-athletes has been the subject of much public debate. The National Collegiate Athletic Association (NCAA) has claimed that student-athletes have an 'excellent experience' in college and that student-athletes in even the NCAA's most competitive divisions graduate at higher rates than non-athletes. If true, this implies that intercollegiate athletics actually benefit student-athletes academically (NCAA Research Staff, 2009).[1] However, there is little agreement on whether intercollegiate athletics make student-athletes better-rounded individuals or whether they simply make student-athletes 'unpaid professionals' (Zimbalist, 1999).

The NCAA's implementation of Proposition 16 added to the debate, as it contradicted the NCAA's own claim that student-athletes graduate at a higher rate than the overall student population. In August 1995, Proposition 16 began to impose more-stringent academic standards for student-athletes, which raises the following question: if student-athletes were already reaching higher levels of academic achievement than the overall student population, why did the NCAA need to raise the scholastic bar for incoming freshmen?

One explanation might be that the NCAA implemented Proposition 16 for all student-athletes when in reality the NCAA was targeting specific subgroups. For example, the NCAA might have expected Proposition 16 to present a binding constraint for men, but not for women. In this chapter, I test whether Proposition 16's changes in the eligibility requirements facing student-athletes had different impacts on male and female student-athletes.

In Section 11.2, I explain Proposition 16, which implemented more rigorous academic standards for student-athletes beginning in 1995, and I present a brief review of the literature.[2] In Section 11.3, I discuss the data, which I gathered from various sources. The data show that women have higher graduation rates than men whether or not they participate in sports. In Section 11.4, I introduce the 'difference-in-differences' (DiD) estimator as a way to test the impact of Proposition 16 on male and female student-athletes. In Section 11.5, I present the results of this estimation. While women are more likely to graduate than men, I find no evidence that Proposition 16 had a significant impact on the graduation rates of either student-athletes or non-athletes, regardless of gender. Section 11.6 concludes.

11.2   THE NCAA's PROPOSITION 16 IN CONTEXT

From the 1986–87 academic year through 1994–95, incoming freshman student-athletes at NCAA institutions were subject to academic eligibility requirements as laid out in Proposition 48.[3] The NCAA enacted Proposition 48 to compel prospective student-athletes to prepare for the academic rigors of college (Temkin and Young, 1990). Proposition 48 specified that students had to meet two criteria to be eligible for intercollegiate athletics and athletic grants-in-aid: they had to obtain a minimum score of 700 on their Standard Aptitude Tests (SATs) or 17 on their American College Testing (ACTs), and they had to earn a minimum 2.0 grade point average in 11 core high-school courses.

To further tighten academic requirements, the NCAA implemented Proposition 16 beginning in August 1995. Colleges phased in the higher standards in two steps in 1995–96 and 1996–97. The first cohort (1995–96) of student-athletes was required to have a 2.0 grade point average in 13 core courses in high school rather than 11, but it did not face a higher SAT/ACT requirement. The second cohort (1996–97) was subject to both the stricter course requirements and a higher SAT requirement. The revision created a 'sliding scale' in which 'a student athlete with an SAT score of 700 (ACT of 17) [needed] a GPA of at least 2.5; alternatively, a student athlete with an SAT score of 900 (ACT score of 21) [needed] a GPA of at least 2.0' (IES, 1995).

While standardized tests are highly controversial and hence draw more attention, a student's high-school course load might be a better predictor of success in college than standardized test scores (Adelman, 1999). The fact that Proposition 16 was implemented in two stages, one of which left the SAT requirements unchanged, allows me to study the effect of course requirements and SAT scores separately. I therefore separately test the impact of both stages of Proposition 16 on the graduation rates of men and women in Section 11.4.

NCAA policies that impose stricter academic standards for student-athletes often face political resistance. Many critics claim that the more stringent standards disproportionately impact students of different races. The divisiveness of this issue was evidenced by the class action federal lawsuit brought by Cureton and Shaw (United States Court of Appeals, 1999), who argued that Proposition 16 constituted discrimination against prospective students who were African American. Their lawsuit was overturned when the Court ruled that the NCAA did not directly receive federal funds and was not subject to Title VI of the Civil Rights Act (Anderson and Hauser, 2000).

In contrast to the controversy over differential racial impacts, the differing gender impacts of such policies have received little attention despite evidence that such a difference exists. For example, a higher percentage of male than female prospective student-athletes was barred from participating in intercollegiate athletics in 1995 and 1996 for not meeting the NCAA's eligibility requirements.[4] This may have occurred because male and female student-athletes have different priorities. Alternatively, the difference might reflect differences in academic talent. In either scenario, it is plausible that tighter academic standards for student-athletes create a binding constraint for men but not for women.

This chapter examines whether Proposition 16 affected male and female student-athletes differently. It therefore resembles the analysis by Amato et al. (2001), which studies the impact of Proposition 48 on the relationship between the success of a school's football program and the graduation rates of its football players. They find a negative relationship prior to Proposition 48 but no relationship after its implementation. These findings suggest that Proposition 48 imposed a binding constraint on prospective football players.

While the literature on the academic achievement of student-athletes is deep, it has yet to reach a consensus. The lack of consistency is largely due to the failure of the studies to account for unobserved heterogeneity in the sample. My use of the DiD technique accounts for this heterogeneity and provides a more reliable analysis of Proposition 16.

When examining this subject, many researchers have focused on variations in grade point average. For example, Lang and Rossi (1991) find that, for a weighted sample of Division I schools, the grade point averages of student-athletes do not differ significantly from those of the general student population, although they find that athletes are not as likely to make the Dean's List. Maloney and McCormick (1993) conclude that athletic participation has an insignificant impact on grade point average for all students except those involved in a revenue sport (that is, football and men's basketball) in-season, in which case the relationship is negative.[5]

Another measure of academic success is college graduation. Long and Caudill (1991) find that varsity athletes were more likely to graduate than their non-varsity counterparts in 1971. However, the cohort of students that they examine entered college before the enactment of Title IX, so women comprised a mere 5 percent of athletes at the time. This chapter adds to Long and Caudill by using a sample that includes a larger number of women, which allows me to contrast the academic success of athletes by gender.

Debrock et al. (1996) find that male student-athletes at successful Division I athletic programs have significantly lower graduation rates; they also find that overall graduation rates are unaffected by athletic participation. However, their sample includes only members of the women's basketball and men's football and basketball teams, which is a small percentage of the total number of student-athletes. It is not likely to be representative of all student-athletes, given that it includes only the two revenue-generating men's sports and the most popular women's sport.

Finally, Stevenson (2006: 16) finds that Title IX-induced athletic participation has a positive 'large and statistically significant effect on female educational attainment'. Unlike previous studies, such as Debrock et al., this chapter compares the graduation rates of athletes to those of non-athletes rather than the overall graduation rates. Since overall graduation rates include student-athletes, comparisons that do not separate athletes from non-athletes can be misleading. Separating the two allows me to make an unbiased comparison of the student groups.

11.3   DATA

Ideally, I would have performed my estimations using individual-level data, but that information is not publicly accessible. As a result, I collected university-level data for all Division IA institutions for the 2000–01, 2001–02, and 2002–03 academic years. The panel dataset has as its dependent variable the graduation rates taken from the NCAA's publications. Since the graduation rates published by the NCAA are calculated by dividing the total freshman enrollment of an institution by the number of students who graduated within six years, this panel dataset uses the entering freshman classes of 1994–95, 1995–96 and 1996–97.[6]

The NCAA website, www.ncaa.org, provided the overall graduation rates for each member institution, as well as graduation rates for many subsets of the student population. Those graduation rates are for 'the most recent graduating class for which the required 6 years of information is available'. Because the first stage of Proposition 16 (hereafter 'Stage One') took effect in the 1995–96 academic year, the first cohort of students subjected to these newly implemented regulations is included in the 2001–02 graduation rates reported by the NCAA. Accordingly, the first cohort of students subjected to the second stage of Proposition 16 (hereafter 'Stage Two'), which was implemented starting in the 1996–97 academic year, are included in the NCAA's 2002–03 graduation rates. The NCAA graduation rates examined for this study do not account for the fact that students who transferred from their original college may have gone on to graduate from another institution. While the NCAA has recently addressed this issue by instituting a new methodology for calculating graduation rates, these data are not available for the period during which Proposition 16 was implemented.[7]

Finally, I include only universities that have Division IA football programs.[8] Institutions that support Division IA football programs, now known officially as the 'Football Bowl Subdivision', tend to have larger athletic programs. Despite their Division IA status, I excluded the US Naval Academy, the US Military Academy, and the US Air Force Academy since they do not offer scholarships based solely upon athletic ability.[9]

I gathered graduation rates for the total student population, graduation rates for athletes, the size of the total undergraduate population, and the total numbers of athletes from the NCAA website, and I created separate subsamples for men and women. Comparing athletes and non-athletes is more appropriate than comparing athletes and the overall student population, of which athletes are a subset. I used Bayes' theorem to calculate the graduation rates for male non-athletes and female non-athletes, which allows me to compare the outcomes of athletes and non-athletes across gender.[10]

While it would be useful to analyze the graduation rates for specific sports, rather than for all athletes, the data required to do so are not available. To comply with the Family Education Right and Privacy Act (FERPA), the NCAA suppresses graduation rates for subgroups that contain fewer than three students, thus generating too many empty cells to permit an analysis of individual sports. In particular, NCAA does not reveal data regarding men's and women's basketball program because of the relatively small number of players per team (Silver, 2004).[11]

I gathered the total number of students, the proportion of incoming freshmen who are women, and the proportion of incoming freshmen who are black from the NCAA website. I incorporate these control variables in the next section. The *Chronicle of Higher Education* website (www. chronicle.com) provides the following information for each of the three

Table 11.1   Graduation rates of all students

Type	Mean	Std dev.
Athletes	0.5828	0.1275
Non-athletes	0.5703	0.1682
Total	0.5775	0.1491

Table 11.2   Graduation rates by gender

Gender	Student athletes		Non-athletes	
	Mean	Std dev.	Mean	Std dev.
Men	0.5125	0.1472	0.5440	0.1805
Women	0.6930	0.1372	0.6025	0.1669
Total	0.5828	0.1275	0.5703	0.1682

years of interest for men's and women's programs: number of sports teams, athletic scholarship budgets, athletic recruiting budgets, athletic program revenues, and the average salary of the head coaches.

Lastly, the Princeton Review's *Complete Book of Colleges* (2001, 2002, and 2003) and the College Board's *College Handbook* (2001, 2002, and 2003) provide profiles of the incoming freshman classes of each class considered, which includes the average ACT score of incoming freshmen.[12] They also provide information regarding the athletic conference for each institution, and whether the school is a public or private school.

One argument often used by supporters of intercollegiate athletics is that the mean graduation rate for student-athletes is greater than that of the overall student population. Table 11.1 confirms this by showing that the mean institutional graduate rate for student-athletes is higher than that of the general student body and non-athletes.

When the data are separated by gender, a very different picture emerges. For example, the average graduation rate for male athletes is approximately 51 percent, 3 percentage points less than for male non-athletes and 6.5 percent less than the overall graduation rate (Tables 11.1 and 11.2). However, the average graduation rate for female athletes is 9 percent higher than that of non-athletes and 11.5 percent above the overall mean. The difference for women is statistically significant at the 1 percent level. This examination of the data suggests that there are large differences in academic achievement between men and women in Division IA athletics.

11.4 EMPIRICAL MODEL: THE DID ESTIMATOR

The DiD estimator enables me to take advantage of the natural experiment that occurred when the NCAA altered the environment facing student athletes. It succeeds where other techniques fail because it avoids a trap into which more standard techniques fall. For example, one might think that one could measure the impact of Proposition 16 by running a regression of graduation rates for student-athletes over time. One would identify the impact of Proposition 16 with a dummy variable equal to one for all years after its implementation. The resulting estimates, however, could be biased because the passage of Proposition 16 might have been the result of changing attitudes toward the importance of academic performance that would have led to higher graduation rates anyway.[13] Moreover, these changes in attitudes might affect the behavior of non-athletes as well so that one could mistakenly ascribe higher graduation rates among student athletes to Proposition 16 when they are actually the result of broad secular changes in attitudes and behavior.

DiD does not estimate how a treated group behaves pre- and post-treatment. Instead, it compares the change in the behavior of the treated group with the change in the behavior of an untreated group over the same period. This comparison of the two differences gives the technique its name, 'difference in differences'. Comparing the two differences also cancels the impact of unobserved characteristics on the two groups over the two time periods. (For more on DiD, see Buckley and Stang, 2003.)

DiD is a natural fit for this estimation for two reasons. First, I have data that span the years in which the NCAA enacted Proposition 16. This allows me to estimate the impact of each stage of Proposition 16's implementation. Second, since only student-athletes were subject to the NCAA's policy change, the implementation of Proposition 16 creates a natural experiment, with the non-athlete student population serving as the control group. I split the sample, running separate sets of regressions for men and women to determine whether the impact of Proposition 16 on the graduation rates of student-athletes varies by gender.

The basic DiD format for estimating the impact of Stage One of Proposition 16 (which increases only the core high-school course requirements of student-athletes) on athletes and non-athletes appears in equation (11.1):

$$GR_{ist}^{j} = \alpha^{j} + \lambda_{1}^{j} A_{is} + \lambda_{2}^{j} YR02_{t} + \lambda_{DD}^{j} (A_{is} * YR02_{t}) + \varepsilon_{ist}^{j}, \quad (11.1)$$

where GR_{ist}^{j} is the likelihood that a student of sex j (j = Male, Female) at institution i with student-athlete status s in cohort t will graduate. A_{is} is a dummy variable equal to 1 if student i is an athlete. $YR02_t$ is a dummy variable equal to 1 for the cohort that entered in 1995–96 (and should have graduated by 2001–02). $A_{is}*YR02_t$ is an interaction term equal to the product of A_{is} and $YR02_t$. For example, all three variables equal one for a student who played a varsity sport and entered college in fall 1995.

It is not hard to interpret the values of the coefficients of equation (11.1). (See Angrist and Pischke (2009) for a general derivation or Leeds and McCormick (2006) for an application to the sports literature.) In particular, the constant term (α^j) is the likelihood that a non-athlete in the pre-Proposition 16 cohort graduates. λ_1^j is the impact of being an athlete on graduating in the pre-Proposition 16 cohort. It is an alternative way of expressing the difference:

$$\Delta_1 = (GR1_A^{Yr01} - GR1_N^{Yr01}), \tag{11.2}$$

where the subscript A denotes student athletes and N denotes non-athletes, the superscript $Yr01$ indicates graduation by academic year 2000–01 (that is, prior to the implementation of Proposition 16), and the gender dummy is suppressed. Recall that the graduation rate for 2000–01 corresponds to the incoming class of 1994–95, and the 2001–02 rates are for the cohort that entered in 1995–96. λ_2^j is the impact of Proposition 16 on the likelihood that a non-athlete of sex j would graduate, as expressed by the difference:

$$\Delta_N^1 = (GR1_N^{Yr02} - GR1_N^{Yr01}). \tag{11.3}$$

Finally, λ_{DD}^j (Δ_N^1) is the DiD, that is, the impact of Proposition 16 on athletes of sex j minus the impact of Proposition 16 on non-athletes of the same sex:

$$\Delta^1 = (GR1_A^{Yr02} - GR1_A^{Yr01}) - (GR1_N^{Yr02} - GR1_N^{Yr01}). \tag{11.4}$$

Thus, if λ_{DD}^j is statistically significant, Proposition 16 had a different impact on athletes of sex j than it had on non-athletes of the same sex. Similar regressions can show the impact of Stage Two of Proposition 16 (see equations (11.7) and (11.8)).

Estimating equation (11.1) is complicated because I had data on graduation rates for institutions rather than graduation likelihoods for individual students. I therefore estimated equation (11.4) using logit regression. Card and Sullivan (1988) recommend using the logit model when the dependent variable is a probability, as this estimation framework allows the independent variables to have a nonlinear effect on the outcome. In a logit framework, the probability of graduating approaches 1 at a decreasing rate as the values of the explanatory variables grow. This is more reasonable than assuming that the graduation rate approaches 1 at a constant rate.

I also added a vector of control variables for the type of school to the following logits:

$$\ln\left(\frac{GR_{ist}^M}{1 - GR_{ist}^M}\right) = \alpha_{ist}^M + \varphi_1^M \mathbf{SCHOOL}_{it}^M + \lambda_1^M A_{is} + \lambda_2^M YR02_t$$

$$+ \lambda_{DD}^M (A_{is} * YR02_t) + \varepsilon_{ist}^M, \quad (11.5)$$

$$\ln\left(\frac{GR_{ist}^F}{1 - GR_{ist}^F}\right) = \alpha_{ist}^F + \varphi_1^F \mathbf{SCHOOL}_{it}^F + \lambda_1^F A_{is} + \lambda_2^F YR02_t$$

$$+ \lambda_{DD}^F (A_{is} * YR02_t) + \varepsilon_{ist}^F, \quad (11.6)$$

where M and F indicate males and females. The gender-specific $\mathbf{SCHOOL}_{it}$ vectors contain variables that control for institutional emphasis on athletics. Specifically, they are: recruiting budget, scholarship budget, average head coaching salary, athletic department revenues, presence of the men's and women's basketball teams in the NCAA basketball tournament's Sweet Sixteen (an indicator of a program's competitiveness), and whether 50 percent or more of the conference's members were invited to participate in the NCAA Basketball tournament (an indicator of the relative strength of a program's conference).

To analyze the impact of Stage Two of Proposition 16, I run the analogous logits:

$$\ln\left(\frac{GR_{ist}^M}{1 - GR_{ist}^M}\right) = \alpha_{ist}^M + \varphi_1^M \mathbf{SCHOOL}_{it}^M + \lambda_1^M A_{is} + \lambda_2^M YR03_t$$

$$+ \lambda_{DD}^M (A_{is} * YR03_t) + \varepsilon_{ist}^M, \quad (11.7)$$

$$\ln\left(\frac{GR_{ist}^F}{1 - GR_{ist}^F}\right) = \alpha_{ist}^F + \varphi_1^F \mathbf{SCHOOL}_{it}^F + \lambda_1^F A_{is} + \lambda_2^F YR03_t$$

$$+ \lambda_{DD}^F (A_{is} * YR03_t) + \varepsilon_{ist}^F. \quad (11.8)$$

The indicator variable $YR03_t$ specifies the cohort, where $YR03_t = 1$ if the graduation rate is for the 2002–03 academic year and $YR03_t = 0$ if it is for the 2000–01 academic year. The interaction variable $(A_{is} * YR03_t) = 1$ if the graduation rate is for student-athletes in 2002–03, and 0 otherwise. Again, λ_{DD} is the DiD estimator.

Summary statistics for all independent variables appear in Table 11.3. I expect some of the control variables – athletic recruiting budgets,

Table 11.3 Summary statistics

Independent variables	2001 Mean	2001 Std dev.	2002 Mean	2002 Std dev.	2003 Mean	2003 Std dev.
Men's Sweet Sixteen	0.1308	0.3380	0.1284	0.3353	0.1193	0.3248
Women's Sweet Sixteen	0.1101	0.3137	0.1005	0.3013	0.1284	0.3353
ACT/SAT Converted	24.5047	2.8815	24.5646	2.9754	24.1449	2.8110
Men's Conference Strength	0.4771	0.5006	0.2936	0.4564	0.3028	0.4605
Women's Conference Strength	0.3028	0.4605	0.3761	0.4855	0.2661	0.4429
Public University	0.8624	0.3453	0.8624	0.3453	0.8630	0.3446
Number of Men's Teams	9.2385	2.3196	9.2844	2.3124	7.5596	2.1356
Number of Women's Teams	10.6239	2.1155	10.7215	2.1439	8.9541	2.0155
Men's Scholarship Budget*	22.6991	10.1537	24.4585	10.5502	26.4543	11.4687
Women's Scholarship Budget*	15.5928	7.5359	17.2770	8.4935	19.1337	9.4955
Men's Recruiting Budget*	3.7243	1.9343	3.6920	2.0103	3.8481	2.1205
Women's Recruiting Budget*	1.5562	0.7381	1.5955	0.7524	1.6814	0.7636
Men's Program Revenues*	158.2761	129.3751	168.4989	131.1660	188.1736	143.1677
Women's Program Revenues*	14.0564	17.4303	15.3263	18.2392	18.6585	22.0631
Salary of Men's Head Coach*	1.1596	0.7608	1.3090	0.9452	1.5777	1.1376
Salary of Women's Head Coach*	0.5705	0.1914	0.6202	0.2235	0.6568	0.2277
Proportion Female	0.5203	0.0483	0.5216	0.0489	0.5227	0.0508
Proportion Black	0.0768	0.0621	0.0776	0.0647	0.0794	0.0673
Proportion Athlete	0.0256	0.0146	0.0247	0.0151	0.0240	0.0151
Number of Students	14,655	6,753	15,305	6,971	15,755	7,055

Note: * US$ thousands.

242

numbers of teams, proportion of students who are athletes, head coaching salaries, athletic department revenues,[14] competitiveness of programs, and strengths of the conferences – to have a negative impact on graduation rates for both student-athletes and non-athletes since they indicate that resources are being invested in athletics instead of academics. For historical reasons, I also expect the proportion of students who are black to lower graduation rates of both student types. Similarly, I expect the proportion of women to increase graduation rates. Finally, I expect average ACT/SAT scores to have a positive effect on graduation rates, as higher scores are supposed to indicate greater academic aptitude.

Two control variables have no clear impact *a priori*. Public universities are typically less expensive than private institutions, so, *ceteris paribus*, public university students do not need to work as much to pay for school. However, it is also likely that public university students have less financial support from their families and have fewer academic resources than those who attend more expensive private universities. Thus, the impact of public university status on graduation rates is unclear. The second ambiguous variable is the university's student population. Although larger institutions may be able to exploit economies of scale and provide better facilities for their students, it is possible that students have better access to teachers and administrators at smaller institutions.

Finally, some control variables could push the graduation rates of student-athletes in one direction and the graduation rates of non-athletes in the other. For example, to the extent that the athletic scholarship budget indicates an institution's focus on athletics over academics, it could negatively impact the graduation rates of non-athletes. But the budget could positively impact the graduation rates of student-athletes, insofar as student-athletes feel less financial pressure if they have more scholarship funds.

11.5 EMPIRICAL RESULTS

Table 11.4 presents the sign and the significance of the coefficients in equations (11.5), (11.6), (11.7), and (11.8). It shows that, holding all other factors constant, the graduation rates of male student-athletes (*Athlete*) are significantly lower than those of male non-athletes at both stages of Proposition 16's implementation.[15] In contrast, equations (11.7) and (11.8) show that the graduation rates of female student athletes (*Athlete*) are, all else equal, significantly higher than those of their non-athlete counterparts in both stages. These findings are all significant at the 1 percent level. Analogous OLS estimation using the DiD technique, as well as

Table 11.4   Sign and significance of independent variables

Variable	Stage One of Proposition 16		Stage Two of Proposition 16	
	Men	Women	Men	Women
Athlete Cohort	Negative (1%)	Positive (1%)	Negative (1%)	Positive (1%)
	–	–	–	–
Athlete & Cohort	–	–	–	–
Sweet Sixteen	–	–	–	–
ACT/SAT	Positive (1%)	Positive (1%)	Positive (1%)	Positive (1%)
Public University	Negative (1%)	–	Negative (5%)	–
Conference Strength	–	–	–	–
Number of Teams	–	–	–	–
Recruiting Budget	Positive (1%)	–	Positive (1%)	Positive (1%)
Program Revenues	–	–	–	–
Scholarship Budget	–	Positive (1%)	Negative (1%)	–
Salary of Head Coach	Negative (1%)	–	Negative (1%)	–
Proportion Female	–	–	–	–
Proportion Black	Negative (1%)	Negative (1%)	Negative (1%)	Negative (1%)
Proportion Athlete	Positive (5%)	–	Positive (5%)	–
Number of Students	Positive (1%)	–	Positive (1%)	Positive (5%)

cross-sectional OLS and logit regressions for each of the stages (not presented here), showed similar results. Thus, I find that there are differences in academic achievement between men and women in Division IA intercollegiate athletics, and these findings are robust to model specification.

While athletes graduate at different rates, I find no evidence that Proposition 16 had any impact on graduation rates of either student-athletes or non-athletes, regardless of gender. Both the cohort effect and the interaction effect were statistically insignificant. This implies that the reform changed neither the level of graduation rates nor the spread in graduation rates between athletes and non-athletes.

Several of the other independent variables are statistically significant at the 1 percent and 5 percent levels. The average ACT score of incoming freshmen is positive and significant for all estimations, as expected. The proportion of students who are black has a significant, negative impact for all regressions. The size of an institution, as measured by student enrollment, is significant and positive for men in both stages and for women only in Stage Two.

The impact of the average head coach's salary in the men's athletic program is negative and significant for men but insignificant for women. The proportion of total enrollment that comprises student-athletes is significant and positive for men but insignificant for women. These two findings could be interpreted to mean that the breadth of an institution's commitment to athletics positively influences graduation rates, while its depth of commitment to one or more revenue sports negatively affects graduation rates. Also, the athletic department's recruiting budgets for men and women are positive and significant in Stage Two. Thus, I find that investment in a successful athletic program has an ambiguous impact on a university's graduation rates.

11.6   CONCLUSION

This chapter contributes to the literature on athletic participation and academic performance in three ways. First, it establishes that the graduation rates of female athletes at NCAA Division IA institutions are significantly higher than those of female non-athletes, while the graduation rates of male athletes are likely to be lower than those of male non-athletes. Second, the DiD technique makes it possible to leverage the natural experiment created when the NCAA implemented Proposition 16 to test the hypothesis that more rigorous academic standards impacted student-athletes at Division IA universities. Moreover, DiD eliminates potential omitted variable bias that might result from using data at the university level. My results are therefore more reliable than those of studies that do not use DiD. Third, the chapter tests the hypothesis that Proposition 16 imposed a binding constraint on men but not on women.

I find no evidence that Proposition 16 had a statistically significant impact on either male or female student-athletes. The result comes as no surprise for women, as female student-athletes graduated at a higher rate than non-athletes even before Proposition 16. The finding that Proposition 16 did not affect the relative graduation rate for men is a surprise. It might result from the fact that I had to use overall graduation rates rather than graduation rates for specific sports, which are not available. This effectively combined the graduation rates of student-athletes in non-revenue sports, such as tennis and gymnastics, with those in the revenue sports of football and basketball, for whom Proposition 16 was intended.

Since the main argument leveled against Proposition 16 was that it would disproportionately punish black student-athletes, a natural next step would be to further subdivide the sample by race. However, given that the graduation rates of black male and female student-athletes appear to be significantly higher than the overall graduation rates of black male and female students, I do not expect Proposition 16 to have had a significant impact on either race or gender. If Proposition 16 has not had a positive impact on the graduation rates of any student-athlete subgroups, then the NCAA could have found a better use for the time and effort it spent implementing it.

NOTES

1. Dr Myles Brand's lecture notes from his speech entitled, 'Money, Motive and March Madness', which he presented March 18, 2005, at the Union League in Philadelphia when he was President of the NCAA.
2. The NCAA is divided into three Divisions based on availability of athletic scholarships, minimum number of athletic programs by gender, and so on. Proposition 16 applies only to Division I schools. I further restrict my analysis to institutions which support Division IA football programs (now known as the 'Football Bowl Subdivision'). Given that these institutions tend to involve more elaborate athletic programs, a priori one would expect the impact of Proposition 16 on these institutions to be greater. See www.ncaa.org/wps/portal/ncaahome?WCM_GLOBAL_CONTEXT=/ncaa/NCAA/About+The+NCAA/Membership/div_criteria.html.
3. In 1983 the NCAA adopted Proposition 48, the organization's first policy which set forth minimum academic requirements for incoming freshmen student-athletes. See www.ncaa.org/wps/wcm/connect/public/NCAA/Academics/academics+history.
4. In 1995 the NCAA ruled that 4 percent of prospective female student-athletes, 5.9 percent of men in Olympic sports, and 10.5 percent of men in revenue sports were academically ineligible. The numbers rose in 1996 to 6.3 percent of females, 9.8 percent of men in Olympic sports, and 17.2 percent of men in revenue sports. See www.ncaa.org/news/1998/19980126/active/3504n01.html.
5. The only two sports that have consistently produced positive net revenues at the Division IA level are men's football and men's basketball. Hence, these sports are known as 'revenue sports'.
6. For additional information regarding the NCAA's graduation rate calculation methodology for the relevant period, see http://fs.ncaa.org/Docs/grad_rates/2003/d1/information.html.
7. The NCAA began publishing Graduation Success Rates (GSRs), which are calculated using a distinctly different methodology, starting in the 2004–05 academic year. GSRs have not been calculated retrospectively, and thus GSR data are available only for freshman cohorts who started college in the 1998–99 academic year and beyond. There is no a priori reason to believe that the NCAA's methodology would produce biases across gender or across time.
8. Institutions that were not classified as Division IA for both academic years of observation were also excluded.

9. These institutions also may differ fundamentally from the other Division IA members given their status as military training grounds.

10. Bayes' theorem provides a useful formula for calculating conditional probabilities. Using Bayes' theorem, I am able to estimate the graduation rates of men and women, respectively, conditional on their being non-student-athletes. In other words, assuming that a set of men are not student-athletes, I can use Bayes' theorem to estimate their graduation rate using the data provided by the NCAA.

11. For example, see the following NCAA graduation rate report regarding the University of South Florida's 1996–97 freshman cohort, which suppresses the graduation rates for its men's and women's basketball programs, see http://usfweb2.usf.edu/assessment/SACS%202005%20Report/reaffirmation/docs/3.3.1-64.pdf.

12. For institutions that reported only average SAT scores, I use the College Board's 2000 SAT I-ACT Score Comparison Table (2004) to convert the composite SAT score to the appropriate ACT score.

13. Alternatively, it could have been passed as a result of a growing recognition of a worsening crisis, in which case the estimates would falsely reveal a negative impact.

14. While at first glance one might expect that higher athletic department revenues would translate to more resources for the entire institution, in most cases even if the athletic department agreed to 'share the wealth', revenues garnered are too small to have a positive impact on a school's academic resources.

15. See Appendix 11A for all applicable coefficients and *p*-values for each regression.

REFERENCES

Adelman, Clifford (1999), *Answers in the Tool Box: Academic Intensity, Attendance Patterns, and Bachelor's Degree Attainment*, Washington, DC: United States Department of Education.

Amato, Louis H., John M. Gandar and Richard A. Zuber (2001), 'The Impact of Proposition 48 on the Relationship between Football Success and Football Player Graduation Rates', *Journal of Sport Economics*, **2**(2), May: 101–12.

Anderson, Paul M. and Kirsten Hauser (eds) (2000), 'Third Circuit Holds NCAA Is Not Subject to Title VI', *You Make the Call . . .*, **2**(3), Winter, online at: http://sports.findlaw.com/sports_law/makethecall/winter2000/cure/index.html (accessed February 18, 2012).

Angrist, Joshua D. and Jörn-Steffen Pischke (2009), *Mostly Harmless Econometrics: An Empiricist's Companion*, Princeton, NJ: Princeton University Press.

Buckley, Jack and Yi Shang (2003), 'Estimating Policy and Program Effects with Observational Data: The Differences-in-Differences Estimator', *Practical Assessment, Research and Evaluation*, online at: www.pareonline.net/Home.htm (accessed November 3, 2004).

Card, David and Daniel Sullivan (1988), 'Measuring the Effect of Subsidized Training Programs on Movements in and out of Employment', *Econometrica*, **56**(3), May: 497–530.

'College Board 2000 SAT I-ACT Score Comparisons Table' (2004), online at: www.college-board.com/sat/cbsenior/html/stat00f.html (accessed November 19, 2004).

College Handbook (2001), New York: The College Board.

College Handbook (2002), New York: The College Board.

College Handbook (2003), New York: The College Board.

Complete Book of Colleges (2001), The Princeton Review, New York: Random House.

Complete Book of Colleges (2002), The Princeton Review, New York: Random House.

Complete Book of Colleges (2003), The Princeton Review, New York: Random House.

Debrock, Lawrence, Wallace Hendricks and Roger Koenker (1996), 'The Economics of Persistence: Graduation Rates of Athletes as Labor Market Choice', *Journal of Human Resources*, **31**(3), Summer: 299–306.

Institute of Education Sciences (IES): National Center for Education Statistics (1995), 'Who

Can Play? An Examination of NCAA's Proposition 16', Statistics in Brief, Washington DC: US Department of Education, online at: nces.ed.gov/pubs/web/95763.asp (accessed January 10, 2012).

Lang, Eric L. and Robert J. Rossi (1991), 'Understanding Academic Performance: 1987–1988 National Study of Intercollegiate Athletes', paper presented at the Annual Meeting of the American Research Association, Chicago, IL, April 3–7.

Leeds, Michael A. and Barbara Erin McCormick (2006), 'Econometric Issues in Sports Economics', in *Handbook of Sports Economics Research*, edited by J. Fizel, Armonk, NY: M.E. Sharpe, pp. 221–36.

Long, James E. and Steven B. Caudill (1991), 'The Impact of Participation in Intercollegiate Athletics on Income and Graduation', *Review of Economics and Statistics*, **73**(3), August: 525–31.

Maloney, Michael T. and Robert E. McCormick (1993), 'An Examination of the Role that Intercollegiate Athletic Participation Plays in Academic Achievement: Athletes' Feats in the Classroom', *Journal of Human Resources*, **28**(3), Summer: 555–70.

NCAA Research Staff (2009), 'NCAA Research Related to Graduation Rates of Division I Student-Athletes 1984–2002', *NCAA Research*, November, online at: www.ncaa.org/wps/wcm/connect/babb88004058023db423b5a8eaf4dbca/Federal+Graduation+Rates+Summary+19+Year+11_09.pdf?MOD=AJPERES&CACHEID=babb88004058023db423b5a8eaf4dbca (accessed January 10, 2012).

Silver, Rebecca (2004), 'Daniel McQuade: Colleges Fail Their Basketball Players', *The Daily Pennsylvanian*, April, online at: http://www.thedp.com/index.php/article/2004/04/daniel_mcquade_colleges_fail_their_basketball_players.

Stevenson, Betsey (2006), 'Beyond the Classroom: Using Title IX to Measure the Return to High School Sports', Wharton Business School Working Paper, Philadelphia, PA, March.

Temkin, Barry and Linda Young (1990), 'Prop 48 Gets Mixed Grades: Athletes Paying More Attention', *Chicago Tribune*, October, online at: http://articles.chicagotribune.com/1990-10-19/sports/9003290394_1_force-athletes-scholastic-aptitude-test-american-college-test.

United States Court of Appeals, Third Circuit (1999), *Cureton v. National Collegiate Athletic Association*, No. 99–1222, December, online at: http://www.caselaw.findlaw.com/us-3rd-circuit/1116586.html (accessed January 11, 2012).

Zimbalist, Andrew (1999), *Unpaid Professionals: Commercialism and Conflict in Big-Time College Sports*, Princeton, NJ: Princeton University Press.

APPENDIX 11A

Table 11A.1   Stage One Proposition 16 – men's program estimates
differences-in-differences logit

Variable	Parameter estimate	Standard error	Wald Chi-square	Pr > ChiSq
Athlete	−0.6735	0.2407	7.8262	0.0051
Cohort	0.1890	0.2439	0.6003	0.4384
Athlete & Cohort	0.0553	0.3390	0.0266	0.8705
Sweet Sixteen	−0.2540	0.2643	0.9239	0.3365
ACT/SAT	0.4082	0.0495	67.9207	<0.0001
Public University	−0.7026	0.2651	7.0234	0.0080
Conference Strength	0.0950	0.1878	0.2559	0.6130
Number of Teams	−0.0117	0.0523	0.0498	0.8234
Recruiting Budget	0.1038	0.0149	48.5997	<0.0001
Program Revenues	0.0714	0.0743	0.9224	0.3368
Scholarship Budget	−0.00196	0.00113	2.9978	0.0834
Salary of Head Coach	−0.5043	0.1305	14.9328	0.0001
Proportion Female	0.1198	2.0037	0.0036	0.9523
Proportion Black	−6.1060	1.5106	16.3396	<0.0001
Proportion Athlete	24.0868	9.6311	6.2547	0.0124
Number of Students	0.000059	0.000022	7.2886	0.0069

Table 11A.2   Stage One Proposition 16 – women's program estimates
differences-in-differences logit

Variable	Parameter estimate	Standard error	Wald Chi-square	Pr > ChiSq
Athlete	1.7440	0.2490	49.0697	<0.0001
Cohort	0.2632	0.2420	1.1828	0.2768
Athlete & Cohort	−0.5580	0.3393	2.7050	0.1000
Sweet Sixteen	0.3596	0.2866	1.5746	0.2095
ACT/SAT	0.4892	0.0496	97.4273	<0.0001
Public University	0.2078	0.3293	0.3983	0.5280
Conference Strength	−0.0136	0.2104	0.0042	0.9484
Number of Teams	−0.0167	0.0604	0.0769	0.7815
Recruiting Budget	−0.1677	0.1719	0.9518	0.3293
Program Revenues	−0.00266	0.00531	0.2512	0.6163
Scholarship Budget	0.0860	0.0197	19.1124	<0.0001
Salary of Head Coach	−0.9279	0.5326	3.0354	0.0815
Proportion Female	−0.6206	2.0370	0.0928	0.7606
Proportion Black	−4.3323	1.4980	8.3645	0.0038
Proportion Athlete	17.9362	9.8773	3.2975	0.0694
Number of Students	0.000038	0.000020	3.4833	0.0620

Table 11A.3   *Stage One Proposition 16 – men's program estimates differences-in-differences logit*

Variable	Parameter estimate	Standard error	Wald Chi-square	Pr > ChiSq
Athlete	−0.6972	0.2408	8.3810	0.0038
Cohort	0.00727	0.2735	0.0007	0.9788
Athlete & Cohort	0.2274	0.3367	0.4560	0.4995
Sweet Sixteen	−0.2024	0.2702	0.5612	0.4538
ACT/SAT	0.4348	0.0513	71.8049	<0.0001
Public University	−0.5887	0.2524	5.4409	0.0197
Conference Strength	0.1994	0.1963	1.0325	0.3096
Number of Teams	0.0183	0.0545	0.1127	0.7371
Recruiting Budget	0.1084	0.0142	58.5392	<0.0001
Program Revenues	0.1412	0.0740	3.6374	0.0565
Scholarship Budget	−0.00383	0.00119	10.2990	0.0013
Salary of Head Coach	−0.3144	0.1060	8.7923	0.0030
Proportion Female	2.0158	1.9588	1.0591	0.3034
Proportion Black	−7.2918	1.4912	23.9115	<0.0001
Proportion Athlete	18.4594	8.7373	4.4635	0.0346
Number of Students	0.000052	0.000021	6.3004	0.0121

Table 11A.4   *Stage One Proposition 16 – women's program estimates DiD logit*

Variable	Parameter estimate	Standard error	Wald Chi-square	Pr > ChiSq
Athlete	1.8208	0.2496	53.2102	<0.0001
Cohort	0.1912	0.2848	0.4510	0.5019
Athlete & Cohort	−0.3315	0.3361	0.9729	0.3240
Sweet Sixteen	0.4103	0.2825	2.1101	0.1463
ACT/SAT	0.4927	0.0499	97.6265	<0.0001
Public University	−0.1080	0.2708	0.1591	0.6900
Conference Strength	0.2254	0.2161	1.0878	0.2970
Number of Teams	0.0322	0.0606	0.2831	0.5947
Recruiting Budget	0.0759	0.0174	19.1219	<0.0001
Program Revenues	−0.2217	0.1943	1.3020	0.2538
Scholarship Budget	−0.00081	0.00453	0.0319	0.8582
Salary of Head Coach	−0.9395	0.5950	2.4931	0.1143
Proportion Female	−0.6835	2.0919	0.1068	0.7439
Proportion Black	−6.0819	1.5003	16.4321	<0.0001
Proportion Athlete	16.2725	8.8423	3.3867	0.0657
Number of Students	0.000039	0.000020	3.9185	0.0478

12. Gender differences in competitive balance in intercollegiate basketball
Jaret Treber, Rachel Levy and Victor A. Matheson*

12.1 INTRODUCTION

Over the 2008–09 and 2009–10 seasons, the University of Connecticut (UConn) women's basketball team went 78–0 and captured two National Collegiate Athletic Association (NCAA) championships.[1] The UConn Huskies exhibited unprecedented dominance, winning every game but one by at least 10 points, with an average margin of victory of more than 30 points,[2] assuring themselves of a place in the pantheon of team sports. Their dominance also spawned debate about their impact on women's college basketball. Some believe that UConn's streak attracted more fans to women's college basketball, while others argue that fan interest waned as UConn's run greatly diminished the drama associated with the chase for a national championship. Attendance data provide limited insight. During the 2008–09 and 2009–10 seasons, average attendance at NCAA Division I women's basketball games fell by 1.7 and 1.6 percent from the previous year, suggesting that UConn's reign may have adversely affected interest in the game. Such a conclusion is somewhat contradicted by the fact that these two seasons registered the third- and fourth-highest per game attendance since the inception of the women's NCAA tournament in 1982.[3]

The underlying issue in this debate is a fundamental topic in sports – the relationship between relative team quality and fan demand. Do fans prefer teams to be evenly matched or do they prefer dominant teams? The very first paper in modern sports economics, Simon Rottenberg's seminal paper on baseball labor markets, notes in its introduction that spectator sport is a unique industry in that 'competitors must be of approximately equal "size" if any are to be successful' (Rottenberg, 1956: 242). This notion was echoed a decade later by Walter Neale, who stated that 'the economics of professional sports is that receipts depend upon competition among . . . the teams. "Oh Lord, make us good, but not that good," must be their prayer' (Neale, 1964: 2). Since these early origins, sports economists have continued to study competitive balance.

Numerous authors provide excellent overviews of competitive balance, including Zimbalist (2002), Fort and Maxcy (2003), and Sanderson and Siegfried (2003). Studies of competitive balance typically analyze one of three basic issues: methods for calculating competitive balance, the effect of competitive balance on attendance and revenues, and the effect of league rules or other factors on competitive balance. This chapter addresses the last issue.

Most studies of the determinants of competitive balance have focused on league rules, such as free agency, revenue sharing, salary caps and floors, reverse-order drafts, and unbalanced scheduling. Furthermore, the existing literature has examined professional sports, with only a handful of studies of competitive balance in college athletics.[4] Consequently, much remains to be learned about competitive balance at the intercollegiate level.

Until the mid-2000s, the literature on competitive balance in college sports focused solely on college football. Berri (2004) has expanded the scope of the literature with a comparison of competitive balance in college football, baseball, and basketball. He identifies differences in competitive balance across these sports and argues that they can be largely attributed to variation in how professional basketball impacts the pool of players available to colleges. Building on Stephen Jay Gould's idea (1986, 1996), Berri concludes that 'the underlying population of players the sport can employ primarily determines competitive balance' (2004: 221). Identifying and explaining trends and patterns in competitive balance in college sports, both within a given sport and across multiple sports, is important for improving our understanding of its underlying determinants. This chapter focuses on the determinants of competitive balance in a single sport: women's basketball.

We expand the scope of the literature on competitive balance in college sports by analyzing the effects of gender on competitive balance in inter-collegiate basketball in the United States. In Section 12.2, we use the concentration of championships and performance in the NCAA Division I basketball tournament to show that women's college basketball is less competitively balanced than men's. In Section 12.3, similar to Berri (2004), we draw on Gould's work (1986, 1996) to explain this difference in competitive balance across genders. We argue that competitive balance in men's college basketball improved naturally over time and that the women's game should follow a similar pattern. Given the ever-increasing popularity of men's college basketball, this should be welcome news for those concerned with the long-term success of women's college basketball. We also discuss how the absence of a lucrative women's professional basketball league may prevent women's college basketball from reaching the same level of balance as men's. Section 12.4 concludes with suggestions for further work.

12.2 MEASURING COMPETITIVE BALANCE IN COLLEGE BASKETBALL

The NCAA is the largest governing body in intercollegiate sports and serves as a rule-making body for its 1,100 member schools. Schools are categorized into one of three divisions in the NCAA based on school size, recruiting rules, athlete eligibility, and the availability of scholarship money for athletes. The highest level of competition is in Division I, which is made up of 335 schools, including large state universities, most of the largest private non-profit universities, and many smaller private and state colleges. The NCAA sponsors 38 championships for male and female athletes in Division I. Men's and women's basketball are the most commonly offered sports at Division I schools, with all Division I schools offering men's basketball and all but two schools sponsoring women's basketball.[5] Basketball is also the most popular women's spectator sport at the collegiate level, attracting over 8 million fans at the Division I level in 2011. On the men's side, basketball is second only to football, attracting over 27 million fans in 2011 and generating significant media revenues.[6]

The NCAA has sponsored a national championship in men's basketball since 1939 and in women's basketball since 1982. The tournaments have taken a variety of formats. Most observers consider 1985 the start of the 'modern era' in the men's college basketball tournament, as the NCAA expanded the tournament to a 64-team, nationally seeded, single elimination tournament. The tournament also experienced a dramatic rise in popularity in the 1980s. The NCAA kept this format until 2001, at which time it added an additional play-in game, increasing the field to 65 teams. The men's tournament added three play-in games in 2011, increasing the field to 68 teams. The women's championship grew to a 64-team, regionally seeded field in 1994, and by 1996 it had evolved into a 64-team nationally seeded single-elimination tournament, just like the men's championship. In both the men's and women's basketball tournaments, each conference champion receives an automatic bid. A selection committee fills the remaining tournament slots based on each team's perceived quality.

There are many methods to measure competitive balance, in part because at least two distinct types of competitive balance exist.[7] Intra-season competitive balance refers to the closeness of competition within a particular season, while inter-season balance refers to the uncertainty of outcome between seasons. For example, in soccer, the English Premier

League title hunt frequently comes down to the final day of competition, with many teams in the chase until late in the season, suggesting a strong degree of intra-season balance. In the 16 seasons since 1995, however, only three teams, Manchester United, Chelsea, and Arsenal, have won the championship. Along with Liverpool, these 'big four' have accounted for 45 of the 48 top three league finishes over this period, indicating a remarkably low level of inter-season balance.

The most commonly used method of measuring intra-season balance in team sports is the standard deviation of win percentage, which measures the variability of win percentages among teams in a league. A league with low competitive balance is typically characterized by a large number of teams with either very high or very low win percentages, leading to a high standard deviation. This method is both intellectually appealing and easy to apply. In addition, the standard deviation of win percentage can be used to compare the relative competitive balance of leagues with different numbers of teams and, with only slight modification, leagues with different season lengths.

Unfortunately, the standard deviation of win percentage measure is of only limited use in college basketball because of the stratification of teams by conference and the limited interaction among teams from different conferences. In the NCAA, teams are typically organized into conferences with other teams of similar ability, and they play roughly half their games within their conference, thus limiting the amount of contact with teams in different conferences. The standard deviation of winning percentage may simply capture the fact that teams are relatively balanced within their own conferences while failing to identify wide discrepancies in talent between conferences.

Analyzing the results of the NCAA tournament avoids the problem of stratification by conference. In the NCAA tournament, the overwhelming majority of matchups involve teams from different conferences. If the talent disparity between a low seed and a high seed is small, then the margin of victory should be low and the probability of an upset correspondingly high. Conversely, an unbalanced tournament should exhibit wide margins of victory between any pair of seeds as well as relatively few upsets. In addition, since both the men's and women's tournaments follow similar formats, comparing their results allows one to draw conclusions regarding the relative competitive balance in men's and women's basketball.

Table 12.1 presents the average first-round margin of victory and the win percentage for each seed in the men's tournament between 1985 and 2011 and in the women's tournament between 1994 and 2011. The data indicate that first-round games in the women's tournament are far less bal-

Table 12.1   First round NCAA tournament results

Seed	Men's tournament, 1985–2011		Women's tournament, 1994–2011	
	Win margin	Win %	Win margin	Win %
1	25.84***	100.0	39.97***	98.6
2	16.77***	96.2*	27.50***	100.0*
3	11.53***	84.6***	19.76***	100.0***
4	9.49***	78.8**	16.00***	93.1**
5	4.54	66.3*	7.61	77.8*
6	3.94	68.3	7.22	70.8
7	2.20	58.7	5.36	65.3
8	−0.16	48.1	0.39	47.2
9	0.16	51.9	−0.39	52.8
10	−2.20	41.3	−5.36	34.7
11	−3.94	31.7	−7.22	29.2
12	−4.54	33.7*	−7.61	22.2*
13	−9.49***	21.2**	−16.00***	6.9**
14	−11.53***	15.4***	−19.76***	0.0***
15	−16.77***	3.8*	−27.50***	0.0*
16	−25.84***	0.0	−39.97***	1.4

Note: *, **, and *** denote statistical significance between the men's tournament and the women's tournament at the 10%, 5%, and 1% levels, respectively.

anced than in the men's tournament. Comparing win percentages for men and women shows that upsets occur less frequently at nearly every seed-pairing in the women's tournament, with the difference in percentages being statistically significant in half of the seed pairings in the first round. Moreover, higher-seeded women's teams win by larger margins than do the favorites in the men's tournament. The difference in the margin of victory is also statistically significant for half the pairings.

Because upsets in earlier rounds have cascading effects in subsequent rounds, analysis of results in later rounds is problematic; however, the prevalence of upsets can be measured by averaging the values of the remaining seeds at each round. If better seeds win, then the average of the seed numbers at each successive round will remain low while upsets will cause lower-ranked seeds to advance, increasing the average of the seed numbers in each round. Table 12.2 contains the seed averages for the men's and women's tournament for each round along with an 'idealized' average of seeds, which assumes no upsets. Again, the data show that upsets are less likely throughout the entire women's tournament than in the men's tournament. Overall, the women's NCAA

Table 12.2   Round by round average seed remaining

Round	Average of remaining seeds		
	Men	Women	Idealized
1	8.50	8.50	8.5
2	5.73	5.18	4.5
3	4.39	3.42	2.5
4	3.18	2.42	1.5
5	2.55	2.07	1.0
6	2.23	1.69	1.0

basketball tournament exhibits fewer upsets and more lopsided games, suggesting less overall intra-season competitive balance than the men's tournament.

Inter-season competitive balance can be examined by measuring the concentration of NCAA championships. When national championships are concentrated among only a few teams, inter-season competitive balance is low; when many different schools win national titles, inter-season competitive balance is high.[8] To measure championship concentration we utilize the Herfindahl–Hirschman index (HHI), which is used to measure market concentration. We calculate the HHI by squaring each school's share of the championships, adding these figures together, and multiplying by 10,000. Perfect balance for this measure occurs if no team wins multiple titles. To account for the fact that the 'perfect balance' HHI varies with the number of years under consideration, we focus on the ratio of the actual to the perfect Herfindahl–Hirschman Index Ratio (HHIR). This is quantitatively equivalent to summing the squares of the number of championships won by each school and dividing by the number of seasons under consideration. The lower the HHIR, the more balanced the distribution of championships. The HHIR should allow for straightforward comparisons across leagues.

Our initial analysis covers the period over which there was both a men's and women's NCAA Division I basketball tournament (1982 through 2011). Tables 12.3 and 12.4, listing the men's and women's champions for these years, provide evidence of greater championship concentration in the women's game. Nineteen men's teams won at least one title, compared to 14 teams on the women's side. While no men's team won more than four titles, both the Tennessee women and Connecticut women surpassed this mark by winning eight and seven titles, respectively. Table 12.5 further confirms that championships were more concentrated in women's college basketball. Over this period, the HHIR was 2.20 in the men's

Table 12.3   Men's NCAA Division I champions (1982–2011)

University	Year
Arizona	1997
Arkansas	1994
Connecticut	1999, 2004, 2011
Duke	1991, 1992, 2001, 2010
Florida	2006, 2007
Georgetown	1984
Indiana	1987
Kansas	1988, 2008
Kentucky	1996, 1998
Louisville	1986
Maryland	2002
Michigan	1989
Michigan St.	2000
North Carolina	1982, 1993, 2005, 2009
North Carolina St.	1983
Syracuse	2003
UCLA	1995
UNLV	1990
Villanova	1985

Source: Aggregated from the listing of champions on the NCAA webpage (http://www. ncaa.com/history/basketball-men/d1).

game and 4.47 in the women's game. These numbers indicate that the men's actual HHI was slightly more than twice the 'perfect balance' HHI, whereas the women's actual HHI was approximately four and a half times greater than the 'perfect balance' HHI. This evidence of greater championship concentration in women's college basketball is consistent with the perception that men's college basketball is more competitively balanced than women's.

Further examination of men's college basketball suggests that the game has grown more balanced over time. For the 30 years prior to 1982, the HHIR for men's Division I basketball was 4.40, twice as high as the more recent 30-year period and nearly identical to the value for women's NCAA Division I basketball during its first 30 years of existence. Extending the period back to 1939, the first year of the men's NCAA tournament, only slightly reduces the HHIR to 3.98. In the next section, we suggest that the evolution of competitive balance in men's college basketball provides insight into the future of competitive balance in women's college basketball.

Table 12.4   Women's NCAA Division I champions (1982–2011)

University	Year
Baylor	2005
Connecticut	1995, 2000, 2002, 2003, 2004, 2009, 2010
Louisiana Tech	1982, 1988
Maryland	2006
North Carolina	1994
Notre Dame	2001
Old Dominion	1985
Purdue	1999
Southern California	1983, 1984
Stanford	1990, 1992
Tennessee	1987, 1989, 1991, 1996, 1997, 1998, 2007, 2008
Texas	1986
Texas A&M	2011
Texas Tech	1993

Source: Aggregated from the listing of champions on the NCAA webpage (http://www.ncaa.com/history/basketball-women/d1).

Table 12.5   Herfindahl–Hirschman index ratios (HHIRs) (only Division I)

Division	1982–2011	1952–1981	1939–1981
Men's NCAA Division I	2.20	4.40	3.98
Women's NCAA Division I	4.47	n.a.	n.a.

Note: For each time period the HHI was calculated by squaring the share of championships won by each school, adding these squared values together, and multiplying by 10,000. The HHIR represents the difference between this HHI and the HHI that would be obtained if no team won more than one title. Data on championships were obtained from the listing of champions on the NCAA webpages http://www.ncaa.com/history/basketball-women/d1 and http://www.ncaa.com/history/basketball-men/d1.

12.3   AN EXPLANATION OF IMPROVEMENT: CHANGES IN THE DISTRIBUTION OF PLAYER ABILITY

In 1986, renowned paleontologist and baseball aficionado Stephen Jay Gould offered an evolution-based explanation for the disappearance of the 0.400-hitter in Major League Baseball (MLB). Gould argued that player ability in any sport is initially widely dispersed. A small number of naturally gifted athletes are near the limit of human capability, while the

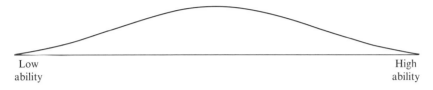

Source: Adapted from Gould (1986, 1996).

Figure 12.1   Initial distribution of player ability

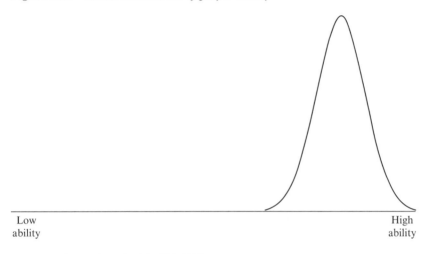

Source: Adapted from Gould (1986, 1996).

Figure 12.2   Distribution of player ability after years of growth in the popularity of the sport has generated greater practice and training

average player is much farther to the left in the distribution. As a sport's popularity grows and practice and training intensify, more and more players move closer to the limit of human capability, and the distribution of player ability becomes more compressed.

This process is illustrated in Figures 12.1 and 12.2. As the distribution of ability compresses and shifts to the right, the gap between great and average players diminishes (Gould, 1986). Anecdotal evidence from many sports supports this idea. Twenty-two of the 35 batters to hit 0.400 or better for an entire season did so in the nineteenth century. No one has batted 0.400 since Ted Williams did so in 1941. In the National Basketball Association (NBA), eight of the top 10 single-game individual point totals occurred prior to 1980, and no player has come within 13 points of the single-season

scoring record of 50.4 points per game that Wilt Chamberlain established in 1961. Over a National Football League (NFL) career spanning
1957–65, Jim Brown averaged 100 yards rushing per game and 5.2 yards
per attempt, records that still stand.[9] While today's elite athletes continue
to produce impressive performances, their accomplishments are neither as
rare nor as enduring as those of the superstars who preceded them.

Gould's theory of the evolution of player ability has implications for
competitive balance in professional sports. If team owners do not differ
significantly in their ability to attract and retain talented players and
if all owners are equally motivated to field the best possible teams, the
decreasing divide between good and great players allows more teams to
compete effectively. There is some evidence that this has occurred over
time in professional sports. Chatterjee and Yilmaz (1991) found increasing parity in MLB over time, a result confirmed by Zimbalist (1992) and
several others.[10] Similar to Chatterjee and Yilmaz, Zimbalist credited 'the
compression of baseball talent' as the 'powerful leveling force' (1992: 97).
Somewhat counterintuitively, the continuing imbalance in the NBA may
also be evidence of Gould's theory at work. Berri et al. (2005) argue that
because height is an important determinant of ability in professional basketball, the compression of player ability is limited by the persistence of a
relatively 'short supply of tall people' (p. 1037).

Competitive balance might be increasing even faster at the collegiate
level than at the professional level. The limits that the NCAA places on
intercollegiate athletic programs reinforce the natural compression of
player abilities. For example, the NCAA fixes player compensation at the
value of a college education. It has also reduced the number of scholarships that schools can offer in some sports. Both of these factors can accel-
erate the compression of player ability across teams. If colleges cannot pay
their athletes, schools with greater revenue potential cannot attract elite
players with higher salaries. Meanwhile, their ability to hoard talent has
been diminished by reductions in scholarship limits.[11] These restrictions
on college behavior may make the playing field more level in college sports
than in professional sports.

Differences in the dispersion of player ability may account for the differences in competitive balance in men's and women's college basketball.
Opportunities to engage in competitive basketball have been greater for
men than for women. For example, the first women's tournament came
40 years after the first men's Olympic basketball tournament was held
in 1936. The first men's national collegiate championship, the National
Invitational Tournament, took place in 1938. It was another 34 years
before the newly formed Association for Intercollegiate Athletics for
Women (AIAW) crowned the first women's national collegiate champion.

At the professional level, more than 50 years passed between the founding of the Basketball Association of America in 1946[12] and the Women's National Basketball Association (WNBA) in 1997. With more opportunities to play basketball at various levels, men should be further along in the process of compressing player ability. Therefore, we expect a greater divide between elite and average players in the women's than in the men's game. This implies that acquiring an elite player should provide a greater advantage in the women's than in the men's game.

Recent experience is consistent with this idea. Since 1983, the Naismith Award has been presented to the player of the year in men's and women's college basketball. Of the 29 female recipients, 23 were on teams that made it to the Final Four and 12 came from championship teams. On the men's side, only 12 of the 29 recipients made it to the Final Four and just three were from championship teams. If Gould's idea of the evolution of player ability holds, the advantage of landing elite players should dissipate over time, making women's college basketball more competitively balanced.

One could be more confident about predicting greater balance in the women's game if one could find evidence of Gould's argument in the men's game. The short history of the Naismith Award is insufficient to make such an assessment possible, but the Associated Press (AP) has been naming a player of the year since 1961. Of the first 25 winners of this award, 14 came from a Final Four team, and 11 played in the championship game. Over the last 26 years, just six AP award winners have made it to the Final Four and only three played in the championship game. It appears that the potential for a great player to carry a team to the elite stage in men's basketball has diminished over time.

Examining the concentration of NCAA Divisions II and III basketball championships provides another test of Gould's hypothesis. In general, we expect Division I schools to select players in the right tail of the player ability distribution and schools from Divisions II and III to select players in the middle and in the left tail.[13] As illustrated in Figure 12.3, this implies that Division II schools are likely to select from a more narrowly dispersed

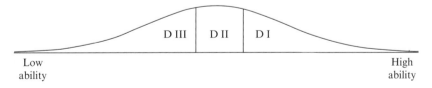

Source: Adapted from Gould (1986, 1996).

Figure 12.3   Initial distribution of player ability by NCAA division

Table 12.6   Herfindahl–Hirschman index ratios (HHIRs) (all divisions)

Division	1982–2011	1957–1981
Men's NCAA Division I	2.20	4.84
Men's NCAA Division II	1.80	2.28
Men's NCAA Division III	1.87	n.a.
Women's NCAA Division I	4.47	n.a.
Women's NCAA Division II	2.80	n.a.
Women's NCAA Division III	1.93	n.a.

Note: For each time period the HHI was calculated by squaring the share of championships won by each school, adding these squared values together, and multiplying by 10,000. The HHIR represents the difference between this HHI and the HHI that would be obtained if no team won more than one title. Data on championships were obtained from the listing of champions on the NCAA webpages http://www.ncaa.com/history/basketball-women/d1 and http://www.ncaa.com/history/basketball-men/d1.

talent pool than Divisions I and III schools. However, the best players in Division III are drawn from the middle of the distribution, whereas the best players in Division I are drawn from the far right tail of the distribution. In other words, for any given interval of talent, there is a larger supply of top Division III players than top Division I players. Consequently, we expect greater competitive balance in both Divisions II and III than in Division I. Furthermore, while the quality of play in all divisions is likely to increase as the distribution of player ability compresses towards the biological limit, the impact on competitive balance should be greatest in Division I.

Table 12.6 lists the HHIR for all three NCAA divisions in men's and women's basketball. As expected, Division I is slightly less balanced than Divisions II and III on the men's side. A similar ordering is observed in the women's game, though it appears that Division I is far less balanced than Division II, which in turn is somewhat less balanced than Division III. Examining changes over time reveals that men's Division I experienced greater improvement in competitive balance over time than men's Division II.[14] These observations all conform to predictions derived from Gould's idea of the evolution of player ability.

A complementary factor contributing to the increasing competitive balance in men's college basketball has been the tremendous growth in the popularity of professional basketball. From 1970 to 2008, total attendance increased from roughly 5.5 million to approximately 21.5 million, and the average NBA salary grew twentyfold from $213 thousand to $4.8 million.[15] The increasing financial returns of the NBA may have hastened the compression of talent in men's college basketball in two ways. First, the potential for future fame and fortune likely increased the number of

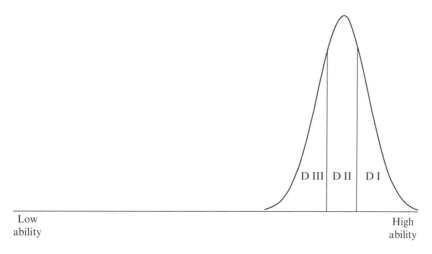

Low
ability

High
ability

Source: Adapted from Gould (1986, 1996).

*Figure 12.4   Distribution of player ability by NCAA division after years
of growth in the popularity of the sport has generated greater
practice and training*

male athletes pursuing basketball at the youth, high-school, and collegiate
levels, which would have pushed the distribution of talent towards the
human limit. Second, as the potential gains from playing professional
basketball have escalated, so too has the number of players choosing to
forgo years of college eligibility to enter the NBA draft. Since 1996, 520
players have entered the NBA draft before exhausting their college eligibility, triple the annual average over the preceding 20 years.[16] By luring away
an increasing number of elite underclassmen, the NBA further compresses
the distribution of player ability in men's college basketball by reducing
the right tail of the talent distribution.[17] Therefore, it is likely that the
NBA has accelerated the increase in competitive balance in men's NCAA
Division I basketball. As Berri (2004: 221) notes, 'the ability of teams to
consistently dominate college basketball is diminished'.

Women's NCAA Division I basketball lacks a similar stimulant. The
WNBA does not have the same appeal in women's college basketball
for three reasons. First, the financial rewards associated with becoming
a professional women's basketball player are not large.[18] In 2009, the
maximum rookie salary in the WNBA was $44,945 and the maximum
salary was only $99,500.[19] Since the WNBA does not offer the fame
or financial security afforded by the NBA, fewer girls are likely to be
attracted to the sport, slowing the natural progression to the limit of

human ability. Second, low salaries in the WNBA and professional women's basketball leagues in Europe mean that forgoing a college degree to begin a professional basketball career brings lower benefits to women. Lacking an attractive, plausible alternative, elite players in women's college basketball stay in school longer than their male counterparts. Finally, the collective bargaining agreement in the WNBA bars women from entering the draft before exhausting their collegiate eligibility or turning 22 years of age, further restricting the movement of elite women's players out of the collegiate ranks. Without the allure of large salaries in professional basketball, women's NCAA Division I basketball may never reach the same level of competitive balance as men's NCAA Division I basketball.

This section has argued that competitive balance follows a natural progression. In a sport's early years, the wide dispersion of talent leads to competitive imbalance. As the sport's popularity grows, the imbalance diminishes as greater investment in practice and training compresses the distribution of player ability. Based on changes in the HHIR, it appears that men's NCAA Division I basketball has followed this pattern. It seems reasonable to expect that women's NCAA Division I basketball will follow a similar pattern, though the lack of a highly lucrative women's professional basketball league suggests that the change will be more protracted.

12.4   CONCLUSION

Sports economists have devoted considerable effort to measuring and explaining competitive balance. Given the substantial revenues generated by major professional sports, much of the literature has focused on professional sports, with particular attention to MLB. Despite concerns about competitive balance in intercollegiate athletics, it has received far less attention from sports economists. This chapter contributes to the limited literature on the topic. Using several measures of competitive balance, we find evidence of greater balance in men's than in women's Division I college basketball. Given the relative infancy of women's college basketball, there is reason to believe that women's Division I basketball will become more balanced as the distribution of athletic talent compresses over time. However, absent considerable growth in the popularity of women's professional basketball, competitive balance in women's Division I basketball will continue to lag behind men's.

This chapter constructs a framework for analyzing competitive balance in college basketball and college sports more generally, yet much remains to be done within this framework. A cursory examination of championships in other college sports reveals patterns of persistent imbalance, perhaps most noticeably in swimming and diving, and track and field.[20] These patterns of imbalance raise numerous questions. How widespread is persistent imbalance in college sports? Why has the trend toward increased balance observed in men's college basketball failed to materialize in other intercollegiate sports? Why are women's teams less competitively balanced than men's teams in some sports (such as basketball and soccer) but not in others (such as track and swimming)? Does the individual nature of sports such as swimming and track play a role? Finally, are there alternative explanations for variations in competitive balance that might include the ability of dominant programs to attract top athletes? Future work should address these issues, beginning with analyzing the degree of imbalance in intercollegiate sports more completely and then explaining why trends in competitive balance vary across sports.

The effects of imbalance in college sports are also not well understood. For example, the extent to which fan interest in women's college basketball has been affected by the University of Tennessee and University of Connecticut dynasties is unclear. Perhaps these dynasties have drawn attention to a sport in its relative infancy, or perhaps they threaten to undermine its popularity. Men's college basketball faced a similar situation with the UCLA dynasty, and it is likely that this scenario has played out in other college sports. Subsequent research should address the extent to which fans of college athletics respond to changes in competitive balance and the degree to which the response varies across sports. A better understanding of the evolution of competitive balance in college athletics, and the response of fans, would help assess the efficacy of NCAA policies to promote competitive balance.

NOTES

*   The authors thank Stacey Hochkins for excellent research assistance. This research was also supported by generous funding from the May and Stanley Smith Charitable Trust.
1.   UConn won the first 12 games of the 2010–11 season to stretch their win streak to 90 games, establishing the longest winning streak in the history of men's and women's NCAA basketball.
2.   By comparison, during their 88-game win streak in the early 1970s the UCLA Bruins men's basketball teams won 16 games by less than 10 points, and their average margin of victory was 23 points. Scores from each game in UCLA's and UConn's streaks were retrieved from http://www.ncaa.com/news/basketball-women/2010-12-20/ucla-uconn-road-88-wins on May 20, 2011.
3.   Per game attendance figures are based on attendance at all regular season and tournament games. The 2007–08 season registered the highest per game attendance in NCAA Division I women's college basketball, followed by the 2006–07 season.
4.   Bennett and Fizel (1995), Eckard (1998), Sutter and Winkler (2003), and Depken and

Wilson (2004, 2006) examined how changes in various factors including telecast rights and NCAA rules and regulations influenced competitive balance in college football. Quirk (2004) provided evidence suggesting that competitive imbalance may be a determinant of conference realignment in college football. Berri (2004) investigated whether the population of players affects competitive balance in NCAA football, basketball, and baseball. Perline and Stoldt (2007) examined competitive balance in college basketball for the Missouri Valley Conference.

5. The Citadel and the Virginia Military Institute (VMI) are the only two schools that offer Division I men's basketball but do not offer Division I women's basketball. Both schools only began admitting women in the mid-1990s and remain predominantly male.

6. Total attendance for women's Division I basketball was obtained from http://fs.ncaa. org/Docs/stats/w_basketball_RB/reports/Attend/11att.pdf on September 26, 2011. Total attendance for men's Division I basketball was obtained from http://fs.ncaa.org/ Docs/stats/m_basketball_RB/Reports/attend/2011.pdf on September 26, 2011.

7. See Humphreys (2002) for a more detailed discussion.

8. Focusing only on championships ignores other potential indicators of changes in competitive balance. For instance, Butler University's back-to-back runner-up finishes in the men's NCAA Tournament, cited as evidence of increasing parity (Bolch, 2011 and Weiss, 2010) would not be reflected in analysis focused on championship concentration. Nevertheless, championships are a primary focus of team sports and thus the concentration of championships is likely to be one, though certainly not the only, important indicator of competitive balance.

9. Bo Jackson averaged 5.5 yards per rushing attempt over his career. However, he played only four seasons and thus is not credited with breaking the mark set by Jim Brown.

10. See, for example, Balfour and Porter (1991), Butler (1995), Horowitz (1997), Quirk and Fort (1997), Depken (1999), and Schmidt and Berri (2001).

11. See Berri (2004) for greater discussion on fundamental differences between college and professional sports.

12. The NBA resulted from the merger of the Basketball Association of America with the National Basketball League in 1949.

13. Exceptions would occur, as a player's position in the distribution is not known with certainty before entering college. It seems reasonable to assume that quality of play generally increases with division. Assuming that absolute quality is a determinant of fan demand, attendance data may provide some insight. Per game attendance in women's Division I basketball is nearly four times higher than in Division II and roughly seven times higher than in Division III. A similar gap exists between Divisions II and III in men's college basketball. The gap in per game attendance between Divisions I and II is even larger in the men's game.

14. The 1957–81 period was used to compare improvement in competitive balance between men's NCAA Division I and II because 1957 was the first year in which the Division II tournament was held. The NCAA Division III tournament began in 1975, which did not provide enough observations to make reasonable comparisons.

15. All figures are in 2008 dollars.

16. Data on early entrants in the NBA draft were compiled from www.nbahoopsonline. com.

17. Berri (2004) makes the same argument.

18. For more on compensation in the WNBA, see Chapter 7 in this volume.

19. For more on salaries in the WNBA, see Articles V and VIII of the WNBA Collective Bargaining Agreement (Hunter and Orender, 2008).

20. In Division I swimming and diving, three schools have accounted for 24 of the last 30 titles on the men's side and four schools have accounted for 24 titles on the women's side. Imbalance is even greater at the Division III level where Kenyon College won 29 men's titles and 22 women's titles in the last 30 years. In track and field, Louisiana State University has won 14 of the last 30 women's titles and the University of Arkansas has claimed 12 men's titles over that period.

REFERENCES

Balfour, Alan and Phillip K. Porter (1991), 'The Reserve Clause and Professional Sports: Legality and Effect on Competitive Balance', *Labor Law Journal*, **42**(1), January: 8–18.

Bennett, Randall W. and John L. Fizel (1995), 'Telecast Deregulation and Competitive Balance: Regarding NCAA Division I Football', *American Journal of Economics and Sociology*, **54**(2), April: 183–9.

Berri, David J. (2004), 'Is There a Short Supply of Tall People in the College Game?', in J. Fizel and R. Fort (eds), *Economics of College Sports*, Westport, CT: Praeger, pp. 211–23.

Berri, David J., Stacey L. Brook, Bernd Frick, Aju J. Fenn and Roberto Vicente-Mayoral (2005), 'The Short Supply of Tall People: Competitive Imbalance and the National Basketball Association', *Journal of Economics Issues*, **39**(4), December: 1029–41.

Bolch, Ben (2011), 'Basketball's Controversial One-and-Done Rule gives College Coaches Fits, but Changing It Doesn't Appear Likely to Be on the Table at NBA Labor Talks', *Los Angeles Times*, Home Edition: Sports, May 18.

Butler, Michael R. (1995), 'Competitive Balance in Major League Baseball', *American Economist*, **39**(2), Fall: 46–52.

Chatterjee, Sanjit and Mustafa R. Yilmaz (1991), 'Parity in Baseball: Stability of Evolving Systems?', *Chance*, **4**(3), Summer: 37–42.

Depken, Craig A. (1999), 'Free Agency and Competitiveness of Major League Baseball', *Review of Industrial Organization*, **14**(3), May: 205–17.

Depken, Craig A. and Dennis P. Wilson (2004), 'Institutional Change in the NCAA and Competitive Balance in Intercollegiate Football', in J. Fizel and R. Fort (eds), *Economics of College Sports*, Westport, CT: Praeger pp 197–209.

Depken, Craig A. and Dennis P. Wilson (2006), 'NCAA Enforcement and Competitive Balance in College Football', *Southern Economic Journal*, **72**(4), April: 826–45.

Eckard, E. Woodrow (1998), 'The NCAA Cartel and Competitive Balance in College Football', *Review of Industrial Organization*, **13**(3), June: 347–69.

Fort, Rodney and Joel Maxcy (2003), 'Competitive Balance in Sports Leagues: An Introduction', *Journal of Sports Economics*, **4**(2), May: 154–60.

Gould, Stephen J. (1986), 'Entopic Homogeneity Isn't Why No One Hits .400 Any More', *Discover Magazine*, **7**(8), August: 60–66.

Gould, Stephen J. (1996), *Full House: The Spread of Excellence from Plato to Darwin*, New York: Three Rivers.

Horowitz, Ira (1997), 'The Increasing Competitive Balance in Major League Baseball', *Review of Industrial Organization*, **12**(3), June: 373–87.

Humphreys, Brad R. (2002), 'Alternative Measures of Competitive Balance in Sports Leagues', *Journal of Sports Economics*, **3**(2), May: 133–48.

Hunter, William and Donna Orender (2008), 'WNBA Collective Bargaining Agreement', online at: http://www.womensbasketballonline.com/wnba/wnbacba08.pdf (accessed November 5, 2011).

Neale, Walter C. (1964), 'The Peculiar Economics of Professional Sports', *Quarterly Journal of Economics*, **78**(1), February: 1–14.

Perline, Martin M. and G. Clayton Stoldt (2007), 'Competitive Balance in Men's and Women's Basketball: The Cast of the Missouri Valley Conference', *The Sport Journal*, **10**(4), October.

Quirk, James (2004), 'College Football Conferences and Competitive Balance', *Managerial and Decision Science*, **25**(2), February: 63–75.

Quirk, James and Rodney Fort (1997), *Pay Dirt: The Business of Professional Team Sports*, Princeton, NJ: Princeton University Press.

Rottenberg, Simon (1956), 'The Baseball Players' Labor Market', *Journal of Political Economy*, **64**(3), June: 242–58.

Sanderson, Allen R. and John J. Siegfried (2003), 'Thinking About Competitive Balance', *Journal of Sports Economics*, **4**(4), November: 255–91.

Schmidt, Martin B. and David J. Berri (2001), 'Competition and Attendance: The Case of Major League Baseball', *Journal of Sports Economics*, **2**(2), May: 147–67.

Sutter, Daniel and Stephen Winkler (2003), 'NCAA Scholarship Limits and Competitive Balance in College Football', *Journal of Sports Economics*, **4**(1), February: 3–18.

Weiss, Dick (2010), 'Thank Heaven Devils Are in the Semis', *Daily News* (New York), Sports Final Edition, March 29.

Zimbalist, Andrew (1992), *Baseball and Billions: A Probing Look Inside the Big Business of Our National Pastime*, Boston, MA: Basic Books.

Zimbalist, Andrew (2002), 'Competitive Balance in Sports Leagues – An Introduction', *Journal of Sports Economics*, **3**(2), May: 111–21.

13. Coaching women and women coaching: pay differentials in the Title IX era
*Peter von Allmen**

13.1 INTRODUCTION

Title IX changed the landscape of intercollegiate sports for female high-school and college athletes. Prior to Title IX, colleges and universities averaged just 2.5 women's teams per institution, and total participation was fewer than 20,000 students.[1] By 2010, schools fielded an average of 8.64 women's teams (over 9,000 teams in total), with over 1,500 additions in the last ten years alone. The number of female athletes now exceeds 180,000 (Acosta and Carpenter, 2010).

Opportunities to coach women's teams have grown with the number of female athletes. Ironically, the percentage of women employed as college coaches of women's teams has declined almost continuously since 1972. As Figure 13.1 shows, approximately 90 percent of women's teams were coached by women prior to Title IX. In the years immediately following

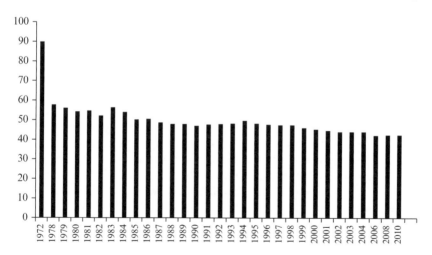

Source: Acosta and Carpenter (2010), at: http://www.acostacarpenter.org/2010pdf%20 combined%20final.pdf.

Figure 13.1 Percentage of NCAA women's teams coached by women

the implementation of Title IX, that figure fell to less than 60 percent. By 2010, just over 40 percent of women's teams were coached by women. In Division II, fewer than 35 percent of women's teams were coached by women.

Because the number of women's teams increased rapidly following the passage of Title IX, the initial increase in the number of teams coached by men may be simply a function of the supply of coaches with sufficient experience to coach at the college level. However, such reasoning cannot explain why the percentage of women coaches has continued to fall. Over 1,700 women's teams have been added since 1998, but the number of women coaches has increased by only about half that amount, and most of those gains were between 1998 and 2000. While 685 teams have been added since 2004, only 169 of them are coached by a woman (ibid.). Thus, the trend may well be worsening. In addition, average head and assistant coaching salaries at all levels, but particularly in Division I-A, are substantially higher for men's teams than for women's.

There are many possible explanations for the divergence between the number of women's teams and athletes and the number of women coaches. It may be the result of demand differences due to discrimination by employers (as investigated in Humphreys, 2000 and Brook and Foster, 2010). It may also be the result of employee discrimination by coworkers or role discrimination that discourages women from entering the coaching profession. Women's programs in general may also face differential treatment due to discrimination by employers. As a result, demand-side discrimination across gender lines may take the form of systematic differential treatment of either the women who coach (or would like to coach), women's programs, or both.

It could also be that the observed differences are not due to demand-side discrimination but to differences in supply-side factors, such as the difficulties in managing work–home life balance (as discussed in Fazioli, 2004 and Rhode and Walker, 2008). Coaching at the college level involves long and variable hours as well as significant travel. The challenges of balancing such a career with family have led even highly successful female coaches to quit. Gregory (2007) recounts the stories of coaches like Dena Evans, head cross-country coach at Stanford, and Karen Tessmer at Worcester State College (now Worcester State University) who often brought their infant children to practice with them. Despite winning a national championship, Evans decided to leave coaching. While these supply-side factors may play a role in observed gender differences in coaching, to fully address both supply- and demand-side considerations would require more space than a single chapter allows.

This chapter is one of the first to examine the dynamics of the labor market for coaches of women's teams at the college level from an economic perspective. The results of this study have important policy implications. If women are systematically discouraged from entering the coaching profession or treated differentially if they do, the National Collegiate Athletic Association (NCAA) and its member institutions should act to eliminate this problem. If women are discouraged at a societal level from coaching, the problem is no less troubling, but the solution is much more complex.

The issues surrounding women and coaching are multi-dimensional. To shed light on several of these dimensions, I analyze expenditures, performance, and salaries across team and coach gender lines. Section 13.2 looks across sports by gender. It compares coaching salaries at different divisions and subdivisions of the NCAA as well as operating expenses and total expenses for men's and women's teams without regard to the gender of the coach. Section 13.3 estimates the role of the coach's gender on the performance of top-ranked Division I softball teams. Section 13.4 estimates the relationship between the coach's gender on the salary of men's and women's golf coaches. Section 13.5 points out policy implications and offers suggestions for future research.

13.2 RESOURCES DEVOTED TO SPORTS BY GENDER

Changes in women's sports have been tracked extensively since the passage of Title IX, most notably through two comprehensive datasets. Acosta and Carpenter have detailed the progress of women's athletics for over 30 years in their annually updated 'Women in Intercollegiate Sport: A Longitudinal National Study'. This extraordinary work provides an excellent set of descriptive statistics that detail the changes in women's sports participation since Title IX. 'The Equity in Athletics Data Analysis Cutting Tool' (hereafter, Equity in Athletics Data), published by the Office of Post-Secondary Education (2011) of the US Department of Education, contains detailed information at the institution level on the number of coaches employed, revenues, and expenditures by institution by sport. In this section, I use the Equity in Athletics Data to analyze and compare the allocation of resources at various institutions and for selected sports.

13.2.1 Coaching Salaries by Institution Type

This subsection focuses on the question of equal pay for equal work. There are two questions of interest: do male and female coaches earn equal

Table 13.1   2007 average head coaching salaries by institution type

Group	Category	Men	Women	ratio
DIA	Unadj.	336,611	112,533	2.99
	n	864	1,071	
	per FTE	371,182	122,575	3.03
	n	783.53	983.26	
DIAA	Unadj.	80,063	51,550	1.55
	n	926	1,069	
	per FTE	99,251	62,346	1.59
	n	746.68	883.89	
DIAAA	Unadj.	85,666	55,638	1.54
	n	647	752	
	per FTE	110,435	69,149	1.60
	n	507.16	605.06	
DII w/Football	Unadj.	38,948	30,370	1.28
	n	966	1,058	
	per FTE	58,678	47,513	1.23
	n	641.18	676.27	
DII no Football	Unadj.	29,885	27,663	1.08
	n	743	865	
	per FTE	47,874	44,462	1.08
	n	463.82	537.59	
DIII w/Football	Unadj.	28,458	23,554	1.21
	n	2001	1,998	
	per FTE	53,799	46,586	1.15
	n	1058.45	1,010.19	
DIII no Football	Unadj.	18,332	16,945	1.08
	n	1,117	1,323	
	per FTE	40,014	37,358	1.07
	n	511.75	600.11	

Source: 'The Equity in Athletics Data Analysis Cutting Tool', http://ope.ed.gov/athletics/.

salaries for equal work, and, do coaches of men's and women's teams, regardless of their gender, earn equal salaries?

Table 13.1 shows the average head coaching salaries for men's and women's teams by institution type for 2007.[2] In this case, we do not know the gender of the coach and so are comparing salaries across men's and women's teams. Because over 97 percent of men's teams are coached by men, the averages for men's teams correspond closely to salaries for male coaches. However, Figure 13.1 shows that only about 45 percent of women's teams are coached by women, making it impossible to draw conclusions from these data on the salaries of coaches by gender. (The Equity in Athletics Data do not provide the salaries of individual coaches.) I consider these questions in Section 13.4.

The NCAA divides Division I schools into several subcategories based on their football programs. The Football Bowl Subdivision (FBS, formerly Division IA) comprises 120 universities with very large football programs. These schools must offer at least 16 sports and must meet minimum attendance standards for football. The Football Championship Division (FCS, formerly known as Division IAA) consists of colleges and universities that sponsor Division I football at a lower level of commitment than FBS schools. FCS schools must offer 14 varsity sports rather than 16 and determine their football championship through a season-ending tournament rather than though bowl play and polling, as in the FBS. Division I (formerly Division IAAA) comprises schools that compete at the Division I level but do not sponsor football.[3] To maintain consistency with the Equity in Athletics Data and avoid confusion with the generic use of the term 'Division' I, the former nomenclature for subdivisions is used throughout the chapter. Table 13.1 shows the unadjusted average salaries, the number of coaches in that subdivision, and the average annual salary adjusted to a full-time equivalent for each subdivision. Salaries shown do not include external income, such as income from endorsements. The means in the table are striking in two ways. First, the salaries of coaches of men's teams in Division IA are roughly three times those of coaches of women's teams. This differential is not surprising, given that average head coaching salary for Division IA football teams exceeded $1 million for 2007 (AAUP, 2007–08 Table B). Second, salaries are much more equal at lower divisions, particularly in divisions that do not sponsor football, though the average salaries of the head coaches of men's teams are always higher.

Table 13.2 shows the same data as Table 13.1 but for assistant coaches. While the ratio of the salaries of the coaches of men's and women's teams is not as large as for head coaches, assistant coaches of men's teams in Division IA earn more than twice as much as women's assistant coaches. In all divisions that offer football except IAA, the unadjusted average for men's assistants is at least 50 percent more than the average for women's assistants. Although football may be driving this result, the ratio of men's teams' assistant salaries to women's teams' assistant salaries is 1.25 even in Division IAAA schools, which have no football program.[4] Because many assistant coaches are part-time, it is important to consider the salary per full-time equivalent (per FTE). On this basis, assistants' salaries in men's sports are about 25 percent greater than assistants' salaries in women's sports in divisions below IA.

There are a number of possible reasons why these differences might

Table 13.2   2007 average assistant coaching salaries by institution type

Group	Category	Men	Women	ratio
DIA	Unadj.	101,303	47,424	2.14
	n	2,648	2,054	
	per FTE	116,013	56,312	2.06
	n	2,312.24	1,729.8	
DIAA	Unadj.	34,597	24,855	1.39
	n	2,341	1,559	
	per FTE	46,954	37,390	1.26
	n	1,724.9	1,036.36	
DIAAA	Unadj.	33,463	26,975	1.24
	n	1,067	1,170	
	per FTE	51,046	41,239	1.24
	n	699.47	765.31	
DII w/Football	Unadj.	17,665	11,239	1.57
	n	2,024	1,094	
	per FTE	33,979	27,923	1.22
	n	1,052.22	440.35	
DII no Football	Unadj.	9,962	8,227	1.21
	n	868	903	
	per FTE	25,880	23,560	1.10
	n	334.14	315.31	
DIII w/Football	Unadj.	8,072	4,847	1.67
	n	4,507	2,856	
	per FTE	26,964	21,002	1.28
	n	1,350.39	659.1	
DIII no Football	Unadj.	3,977	3,650	1.09
	n	1,463	1,597	
	per FTE	18,521	16,986	1.09
	n	314.15	343.12	

Source: 'The Equity in Athletics Data Analysis Cutting Tool', http://ope.ed.gov/athletics/.

exist. At a fundamental level, if the labor markets were otherwise competitive and characterized by a single salary, differences would be due to
differential demand or supply. Alternatively, it could be that the supply
of coaches for women's teams is greater than the supply of coaches for
men's because women are systematically shut out of the men's market but
not vice versa. If this is so, then the salaries of coaches of women's teams
would be lower. In this case, discrimination in the form of unequal access
to employment creates salary differences. We might also observe such a
difference in supply if women did not want to coach men's teams, but

the converse was not true. It that case, the difference in supply would not be due to discrimination. Given that less than half of women's teams are coached by women, it does appear that supply-side forces are responsible for some of the difference in salaries.

It could also be that salary differences are due to differences in demand. As noted above, this may imply that some form of discrimination is at work. In the absence of discrimination, demand is determined solely by marginal revenue product (MRP), which equals the extra output attributable to a worker (marginal product) times the additional revenue that a small increase in output brings (marginal revenue). Thus, salaries might differ due to differences in marginal revenue across men's and women's sports. While men's programs at Division I schools, particularly football and basketball programs, generate far greater revenue than women's programs, the difference in marginal revenue is much smaller at schools without these large revenue-producing sports, making revenue differences unlikely as a source of salary differences. I return to this discussion in Section 13.4. If differences in salaries are due instead to differences in marginal product, women's teams must be receiving lower-quality coaching than men's. This would easily explain salary differences if women were inferior coaches to men (given that virtually no women coach men's sports). I investigate this possibility further in Section 13.3.

The effects of either unequal access to work or unequal pay for equal work on both female student athletes and their coaches are far reaching. If colleges discriminate against women's teams by paying their coaches less, these jobs are less desirable than men's jobs, all else equal. As a result, male athletes may receive better coaching than women if the best coaches are attracted to and are hired for the highest-paying jobs. If female coaches are shut out of coaching men's teams but women's team salaries exceed the reservation salary for these women, female athletes may still receive high-quality coaching, but the coach suffers wage discrimination.

13.2.2   Total Expenditures on Selected Sports by Division

Many sports played at the collegiate level are essentially the same for men and women. For these sports, which include golf, tennis, soccer, baseball/softball, basketball, and volleyball, there is no reason to assume that the resources required to field a team of women are different from those required to field a team of men.[5] Tables 13.3 and 13.4 break down operating expenses (that is, game-day expenses) and total expenses for these sports as well as for all sports and for football, where applicable, for all subdivisions within Division I.[6] They also show the ratios of men's to women's team expenses. Table 13.3 also shows average expenditures per

Table 13.3 2007 operating expenses by institution type selected sports

Sport	Category	DIA			DIAA			DIAAA		
		Men	Women	Ratio	Men	Women	Ratio	Men	Women	Ratio
Golf	Average total expend.	90,086	83,278	1.08	38,935	37,255	1.05	49,138	43,960	1.12
	n	110	99	1.11	102	89	1.15	81	58	1.40
	Average per participant	8,513	9,246	0.92	4,062	4,630	0.88	5,386	5,863	0.92
Tennis	Average total expend.	105,266	87,079	1.21	31,310	30,054	1.04	33,190	30,743	1.08
	n	87	113	0.77	100	115	0.87	78	90	0.87
	Average per participant	10,067	9,231	1.09	3,330	3,372	0.99	3,577	3,459	1.03
Soccer	Average total expend.	128,548	140,344	0.92	73,934	66,578	1.11	82,260	80,115	1.03
	n	50	112	0.45	66	114	0.58	84	87	0.97
	Average per participant	4,576	5,295	0.86	2,803	2,783	1.01	3,023	3,140	0.96
Baseball/ softball	Average total expend.	325,411	183,606	1.77	130,131	83,635	1.56	161,475	88,137	1.83
	n	105	100	1.05	106	108	0.98	82	77	1.06
	Average per participant	8,638	9,254	0.93	4,015	4,543	0.88	4,837	4,726	1.02
Basketball	Average total expend.	794,141	476,172	1.67	253,486	159,945	1.58	336,680	199,095	1.69
	n	120	120	1.00	124	122	1.02	98	98	1.00
	Average per participant	52,423	34,191	1.53	16,983	11,141	1.52	23,270	13,995	1.66
Volleyball	Average total expend.	153,470	168,330	0.91	22,831	68,473	0.33	86,856	76,000	1.14
	n	8	117	0.07	4	118	0.03	10	90	0.11
	Average per participant	7,047	10,860	0.65	1,607	5,038	0.32	4,129	5,383	0.77
All sports	Average total expend.	3,912,482	1,573,538	2.49	1,015,972	630,472	1.61	757,967	613,833	1.23
	n	120	120	1.00	124	124	124.00	98	98	1.00
Football	Average total expend.	2,319,593			371,151					
	n	117			120					
	Average per participant	20,381			3,853					

Note: n = no. of schools reporting.

Source: Author calculations based on data from 'The Equity in Athletics Data Analysis Cutting Tool', http://ope.ed.gov/athletics/.

276

Table 13.4 2007 total expenses by institution type selected sports

Sport	Category	DIA			DIAA			DIAAA		
		Men	Women	Ratio	Men	Women	Ratio	Men	Women	Ratio
Golf	Average total expend.	380,835	390,590	0.98	141,990	152,959	0.93	191,278	191,972	1.00
	n	110	99		102	89		81	58	
Tennis	Average total expend.	442,482	478,318	0.93	153,111	183,162	0.84	178,229	213,194	0.84
	n	87	113		100	115		78	90	
Soccer	Average total expend.	701,973	819,501	0.86	424,268	414,594	1.02	508,047	540,753	0.94
	n	50	112		66	114		84	87	
Baseball/ softball	Average total expend.	1,204,405	814,081	1.48	508,364	395,302	1.29	645,226	450,621	1.43
	n	105	100		106	108		82	77	
Basketball	Average total expend.	3,653,421	1,971,311	1.85	1,167,397	833,243	1.40	1,627,664	1,046,193	1.56
	n	120	120		124	122		98	98	
Volleyball	Average total expend.	571,262	854,882	0.67	870,92	410,825	0.21	378,565	496,035	0.76
	n	8	117		4	118		10	89	
All sports	Average total expend.	18,160,071	7,598,321	2.39	5,120,649	3,298,055	1.55	3,691,979	3,462,090	1.07
	n	121	121		124	124		98	98	
Football	Average total expend.	11,107,681			2,330,487					
	n	117			120					

Note: n = no. of schools reporting

Source: Author calculations based on data from 'The Equity in Athletics Data Analysis Cutting Tool', http://ope.ed.gov/athletics/.

participant. All calculations are based on data from the Equity in Athletics Data for the 2006–07 season.

Table 13.3 shows that golf, tennis, and soccer have game-day expenses that are very similar across gender lines. At the participant level, expenses in golf, tennis, soccer, and baseball/softball are nearly all within 10 percent of one another, and expenses are more likely to be greater for women than for men. While the expense ratios for golf, tennis and soccer are quite similar, the ratios for basketball and volleyball are markedly different, though in opposite directions.

In basketball, operating expenses for men's teams are roughly 60 percent greater than for women's teams. Even at the participant level, the difference is greater than 50 percent at all levels. Such differences seem odd given that men's and women's basketball are identical games played on the same surface and that operating expenses do not include recruiting expenses, coaches' salaries, or athletically related student aid. One possible explanation is cost differences related to attendance, as men's basketball produces large revenues, in part due to high attendance levels, while women's games have much lower attendance. For example, average home attendance for men's basketball in 2007 was 5,327 per game while for women's games, it was just 1,586.[7] The differences in volleyball's operating expenses go in the opposite direction, particularly in Division IAA, where men's operating expenses are only about a third of those for the women's teams. I return to this point below.

Table 13.4 shows that across all sports, differences in total expenses are substantially greater in subdivisions with football, particularly Division IA, where the ratio of expenditures on men's sports to women's sports is 2.39. By contrast, in Division IAAA, that same ratio is just 1.07. At the individual sport level, the ratio of total expenses for men and women is again very close to 1.0 for golf, tennis, and soccer, and for most of these sports, men's total expenses are less than women's. This is particularly true again for volleyball, where the expenses for women are much greater than those for men. It is notable that none of these sports is a 'revenue sport' (that is, not basketball or football) for either gender.

There are two possible explanations for these systematic differences. First, women's teams might receive more non-scholarship resources than men's in the form of better equipment, better facilities, higher coaching salaries, or any other category of expenses included in the total. Second, there might be significant differences in scholarships. For example, in women's volleyball, Division I institutions may offer up to 12 scholarships (which are not divisible across athletes). Men's volleyball teams, however, are allotted only 4.5 scholarships (which may be given as partial scholarships among more than five players). The Equity in Athletics Data do not include scholarships or aid broken down by sport. At the aggregate level (across all sports), they report that average aid to men exceeds aid to women by approximately $900,000 and $350,000, respectively, in Division IA and IAA, but Division IAAA schools, which do not offer football, offer women $360,000 more in aid than they offer men. Thus, in Divisions IA and IAA, the large number of football scholarships clearly masks differences in other sports.

The total expense ratios are quite different for basketball. In all three subdivisions of Division I, men's expenses exceed women's by at least 40 percent. Basketball differs from the other sports in Table 13.4 in that men's Division I basketball is a large revenue-producing sport. Thus, the best men's coaches command extraordinary salaries for reasons that do not hinge on discrimination.

In summary, while men's and women's teams of like sports may receive substantially different resources, the sources of these differences are difficult to pinpoint, particularly in Divisions IA and IAA (though football and basketball coaching salaries at major programs are responsible for some of those differences). A closer look at specific non-revenue sports and sports at institutions without football reveals that funding is much more equal (particularly in the case of operating expenses) and that funding for women is often as much as or greater than funding for men.

13.3   COACHING PERFORMANCE BY GENDER IN SOFTBALL

As Figure 13.1 showed, more than half of all women's teams are now coached by men. Three factors might lead to lower representation of women in the coaching ranks. The first is a lack of desire by women to coach (as noted in the Introduction), which affects the supply side of the market. Second, discrimination against women could affect the demand side of the market. Finally, it could be that men are systematically more productive than women. In this case, there would be differences in demand across gender, but not because of discrimination. This section investigates productivity differences as a potential source of differential demand.

Casual observation indicates that women are at least as likely to coach highly successful women's athletic teams as men are. Women hold many head coaching positions at top-ranked programs in softball and in women's basketball and soccer. Based on end-of-season rankings for 2006–07, 60 percent of women's basketball teams (AP poll) teams, 32 percent of women's soccer teams (Soccer America ranking), and 60 percent of softball teams (RPI ranking) in the top 25 had female coaches. Taken together, these 75 top-ranked teams were just as likely to be coached by a woman as by a man.[8]

To investigate the success of female coaches more thoroughly, I examine a single sport in greater detail. The analysis below focuses on Division I softball. The NCAA publishes team rankings using an index known as RPI (rating percentage index), which is calculated based on team performance and strength of schedule (the opponent's winning percentage and the winning percentage of the opponent's opponents). This index is available for all Division I teams. While other ranking systems exist, they are not conducive to econometric study, as polls, such as USA Softball, do not extend beyond the top 25 teams. The model below includes the top 100 teams in the final 2007 rankings. Of these programs, 71 percent are coached by women.

If women and men are equally skilled at coaching, we should not observe a systematic relationship between the gender of the coach and the RPI ranking of the team. To test this hypothesis, it is important to control for other factors that influence team ranking. One such factor is program expenditures because team performance is likely to be influenced by program expenses relative to competing programs. To control for this, I construct the ratio of expenditures of each program to the expenses of all programs in the sample (*SHAREEXP*). The expected sign of the coefficient for this variable is negative in that greater expenses relative to opponents should lead to a higher ranking (that is, a lower-ranking number).

In addition to controlling for expenses, a program's history of success will likely influence its ability to attract top recruits. Thus, the model should control for program reputation. To do so, I construct a variable (*WS10*) equal to the number of World Series appearances over the 10-year period, 1996–2005.[9] The expected sign of this coefficient is also negative, as a better program reputation should lead to higher ranking.

Given that strength of schedule is an important determinant of RPI, the model also includes a dummy variable for the *PAC-10*, which is the dominant conference in women's softball. Of the 74 World Series appearances by teams included in *WS10*, 37 are by schools in the *PAC-10*. No other conference has more than 10 appearances over the same period.

Finally, the model includes a dummy variable for the gender of the coach (male coach = 0). As noted above, if men and women are equally skilled at coaching, gender should not be a significant determinant of team rank. The complete specification is shown in equation (13.1). Results appear in Table 13.5.

$$RPI = f(SHAREEXP,\ WS10,\ PAC\text{-}10,\ GENDER). \qquad (13.1)$$

Table 13.5 Coaching productivity in women's softball

Variable	Coefficient	Std err.	*t*-value	$P > |t|$
Constant	92.01	7.91	11.63	0.000
GENDER	4.14	5.17	0.80	0.425
SHAREEXP	−3933.81	650.44	−6.05	0.000
WS10	−3.11	1.58	−1.97	0.052
PAC-10	−9.56	10.78	−0.89	0.378
Adj. $R^2 = 0.41$				

Note: Dependent variable is women's softball rank ($n = 100$).

The results for individual coefficients reveal much about successful softball teams. The model explains the data rather well, with an adjusted-R^2 of 0.41. Relative expenditure by team is strongly significant in the expected direction. Teams that spend more achieve a higher end-of-season rank. In addition, program reputation, as measured by *WS10*, is significant in the expected direction. *PAC-10* is not significant, though this may be due to its relatively strong correlation with *WS10* ($r = 0.60$). Most importantly, the coefficient on the gender of the coach is not significantly different from zero, indicating that male and female softball coaches do not perform differently. This result provides substantial evidence that female coaches have skills equal to those of their male counterparts.

13.4 THE DETERMINANTS OF COACHING SALARIES

Because data on athletic performance are so widely available, studies of the salaries of professional athletes are very common. Research on coaching salaries is much less common. Two important examples are the work of Humphreys (2000) and Brook and Foster (2010), both of whom studied the salaries of college basketball coaches.

Using data from 1990 to 1991, Humphreys finds that coaches of men's teams earn substantially more than coaches of women's teams (regardless of the gender of the women's team coach). Among women's teams, the median salary of female coaches is about 9 percent more than that of male coaches. He estimates several salary models for different samples and specifications. In specifications that include only women's teams, Humphreys finds that female coaches earn significantly more than male coaches do, even after controlling for other factors, though the margin falls to approximately 7 percent. He also finds that career-winning percentage is positively related to salary, as are basketball revenue and the size of the institution.

Humphreys shows that if one considers only the head coaches of women's teams, as the percentage of other coaches in the program that are women increases, the salaries of women's basketball coaches rise. Using a combined sample that includes both men's and women's programs, he finds that women's head coaching salaries are about half those of men even after controlling for institutional factors (including revenue). He concludes that the large gender gap may be attributable to one of three forces: the differential effects of program prestige on athletic director decisions, possible tastes for discrimination by athletic directors or consumers, and a greater ability of men's head coaches to capture monopoly rents.

Brook and Foster also analyze Division I men's and women's basketball. Their data and approach differ from Humphreys' in that they use total program compensation (that is, head and assistant coaches), actual rather than estimated revenues, and more recent data than Humphreys. They conclude that differences in wages across team-gender lines are most likely due to revenue differences – that is, that coaching men's and women's teams are two distinct labor markets.

13.4.1 Golf Salary Model

To build on the above work, this subsection considers coaching salaries in a very different sport. Like basketball, golf is essentially the same game for men and women. Unlike basketball, neither men's nor women's golf is a large revenue-producing sport. Thus, it provides a very different perspective on differences across team-gender lines. As Brook and Foster (2010) report, in *Stanley v. University of Southern California*, the Court of Appeals rejected the claim of gender discrimination because men's basketball revenues were 90 times those of women's. In golf, no such dramatic difference exists. According to Equity in Athletics Data, for the 96 Division IA schools that offer both men's and women's golf, almost half of golf-related revenues come from women's teams. In Division IA, men's teams average under $25,000 more in revenue than women's teams. This small difference in revenue makes it more difficult to explain why data published in *Golfweek* show that coaches of men's teams earned about $72,200 in 2006–07, while coaches of women's teams averaged just $61,100. It seems clear that such differences are not due to inferior coaching by women, as 18 of the top 25 programs in the sample are coached by women.

To determine what factors determine the salaries of golf coaches, I estimate separate equations for men's and women's teams. For women's teams, a key variable of interest is the gender of the coach (*GENDER*). Of the 76 teams in the women's sample, 55 were coached by women and 21 were coached by men. This variable is absent from the men's specification, as all men's teams had male coaches. Other variables are measures of experience and productivity: the tenure of the coach (*TENURE*), tenure squared (*TENURESQ*), and the number of conference championships won by that coach (*CONFCH*). I also include a dummy variable equal to 1 if the individual was coach of both the men's and women's teams (*MANDW*). Total athletic revenue at the institution (*ATHREV*) and a dummy variable equal to 1 if the school had a football program (*FOOTBALL*) measure the athletic program's resources and prestige. To control for the overall emphasis on sports of a given gender at each institution, *EXPRATIOFT* is the share of total athletic expenses devoted to women's programs and *EXPRATIOMT* is the share of total athletic expenses devoted to men's programs. For the women's programs, one additional independent variable captures the gender climate at the institutions (following Humphreys, 2000): the percentage of coaches at the school that are women (*PCTFEMALE*). Total enrollment at the institution (*TOTPOP*) controls for the effects of school size. Consistent with standard practice in salary estimation, the dependent variable is the natural logarithm of salary (*LNSALARY*). Thus the coefficients approximate the percentage change in salary given a one-unit change in the independent variable. The full specification of the men's salary equation is shown in equation (13.2). The women's salary equation is shown in equation (13.3).

$$LNSALARY_M = f(TOTPOP, ATHREV, EXPRATIOMT, FOOTBALL, \\ TENURE, TENURESQ, CONFCH, \\ GOLFWEEKRANK, MANDW) \qquad (13.2)$$

$$LNSALARY_W = f(TOTPOP, ATHREV, EXPRATIOFT, FOOTBALL, \\ PCTFEMALE, GENDER, TENURE, TENURESQ, \\ CONFCH, CONFCH, GOLFWEEKRANK, \\ MANDW) \qquad (13.3)$$

The data for coaching salaries come from *Golfweek* magazine, which published the head coach salaries by institution of the top 100 men's and women's teams for that year (less a few missing observations for which they did not have data).[10] Salaries represent base pay only and do not include additional income earned from camps, bonuses or equipment contracts. As such, they do not represent the full returns to productivity, but they still provide useful information on differences across team and gender lines. Additional data on individual coaches and the percentage of teams

Table 13.6   Wage determination in NCAA men's golf coaches, 2006–07

Dependent variable is ln*salary*   *N* = 74

Variable	Model 1	Model 2
TOTPOP	8.94e-06**	8.83e-06
	(2.03)	(1.94)
ATHREV	−2.14e-08	−2.43e-08
	(−0.88)	(−0.97)
EXPRATIOMT	0.606	0.499
	(1.58)	(1.10)
FOOTBALL	0.141	0.146
	(1.01)	(0.99)
TENURE	–	0.005
	–	(0.34)
TENURESQ	–	−0.00008
	–	(−0.17)
CONFCH	0.019	0.0145
	(1.73)***	(1.07)
GOLFWEEKRANK	−0.0005*	−0.0049*
	(−3.84)	(−3.57)
MANDW	–	−0.0937
	–	(−0.52)
Constant	10.643*	10.687*
	(41.25)	(33.20)
R-squared	0.416	0.422
Adj R-sq.	0.364	0.341

Note: *t*-values in parentheses. * indicates significance at 1% level; ** indicates significance at 5% level; *** indicates significance at 10% level.

coached by women are from institution and conference websites. Revenue and expenses data are from Equity in Athletics Data and are recorded in thousands of dollars. The final sample includes 76 women's team coaches and 74 men's team coaches, all from Division I.

The results for the men's equation are in Table 13.6. The results for women's teams are in Table 13.7. The original specification is shown as Model 2 in both tables. In each case, variables that had virtually no influence on the dependent variable were dropped to arrive at the final specification, which is shown as Model 1 in both tables. For men's teams, the primary drivers of salaries are the size of the institution and the performance of the team as measured by rank. Interestingly, the other experience measures, the productivity variables (that is, *TENURE* and *CONFCH*), and the presence of a football team do not impact salaries. The overall

Table 13.7   Wage determination in NCAA women's golf coaches, 2006–07

Dependent variable is ln*salary*   N = 76

Variable	Model 1	Model 2
TOTALPOP	–	7.30e-08
	–	(0.02)
EXPRATIOFT	0.455**	0.448**
	(2.04)	(1.86)
ATHREV	3.28e-06*	3.25e-06**
	(2.75)	(2.57)
FOOTBALL	0.180**	0.176***
	2.13	(2.07)
PCTFEMALE	–	0.032
	–	(0.17)
GENDER	0.130**	0.128***
	1.96	(1.74)
TENURE	−0.029***	−0.029***
	(−1.88)	(−1.86)
TENURESQ	0.001**	0014**
	(2.26)	(2.10)
CONFCH	–	−0.0009
	–	(0.08)
MANDW	0.116	0.117
	(1.36)	(1.38)
GOLFWEEKRANK	−0.008*	−0.008*
	(−6.42)	(−6.36)
Constant	10.90*	10.90*
	(95.51)	(73.45)
R-squared	0.701	0.701
Root MSE	0.199	0.203

Note: *t*-values in parentheses. * indicates significance at 1% level; ** indicates significance at 5% level; *** indicates significance at 10% level. Estimated using robust standard errors.

fit of the equation is good, with an adjusted R^2 of about 0.36 in the final specification.

For women's teams (shown in Table 13.7), the overall performance of the final specification is even better, as the R^2 is 0.70. Greater total athletic revenue at the institution increases coaches' salaries. All else equal, female coaches earn about 13 percent more than male coaches. Increases in expenditures on women's sports (*EXPRATIOFT*) result in increased wages for coaches. In contrast to the results for men's teams, the existence of a football program increases salaries for coaches of women's teams

– a result that appears to run counter to the often-stated argument that Division I football teams do not subsidize other programs. It is possible, however, that *FOOTBALL* is a proxy for an overall commitment to athletics at those institutions that pay higher salaries to coaches of women's teams. The coefficient for *PCTFEMALE* is not significant. This result, related to the gender balance of the overall athletic department, contradicts Humphreys, who found evidence that having more female coaches on staff increased female coaches' salaries. The remaining results are similar to those of men, in that tenure and the number of conference championships do not appear to impact salary, nor does having joint responsibility for both men's and women's teams (though this result should be interpreted with caution, as the incidence of joint coaching responsibilities was only true for a small number of coaches in the sample). Finally, the rank of the program strongly impacts salaries in the expected direction, indicating that coaches are compensated for current team quality.

13.5   CONCLUSION

This chapter contributes to research on how colleges treat women's teams and female coaches by evaluating salaries and expenses at an aggregate level and productivity and wages at an individual sport level. Aggregate data indicate that coaches of women's programs earn less than coaches of men's programs at both the head and assistant coach levels. These differences are particularly pronounced at larger institutions, and data here generally reinforce the often-cited notion that large, revenue-producing sports drive much of this difference. Resources at the individual sport level tend to be distributed much more equally. With the exception of basketball and baseball/softball, the operating expenses and total expenses for sports played by both men and women are similar, and the resources of women's programs frequently exceed those of men's programs. Thus, a familiar theme emerges – the existence of large football programs creates a large disparity in resources.

Evidence from women's softball indicates that women are no less skilled than men at coaching. At the individual program level, casual observation shows that analysis of Division I softball programs shows that women perform just as well as their male counterparts. From a policy perspective, it is important for athletic directors to be aware of this result. If women are discriminated against in the form of unequal access to these positions due to perceived differences in quality, these results can help to educate institutions regarding their misperceptions.

The analysis of salaries for men's and women's golf – a non-revenue sport – indicate that female coaches earn more than male coaches, even after adjusting for the performance of the team. In women's programs, there are increasing returns to tenure, though the benefit of experience takes many years to accrue. In general, given the similarities in responsibilities, differences in the base salaries in men's team and women's team labor markets are difficult to explain and so represent a fruitful opportunity for further research.

Taken together, the results indicate that, at the aggregate level, large athletics programs still have significant work to do to equalize athletics expenditures across gender lines. Results from the softball and golf analyses indicate that there are also supply-side issues at work. Women should be encouraged to coach, and athletic directors should provide the opportunity to do so. Based on the results here, women who choose coaching as a career perform just as well as men. Given that women coach less than half the women's teams – and that the percentage is falling – colleges should do more to encourage coaching as a career among women. Institutions should also develop programs to help coaches overcome the kinds of work–life balance barriers identified in Rhode and Walker (2008) and Fazioli (2004). While institutions will not be able to eliminate the stresses of the home–work balance problem for coaches – male or female – additional resources aimed at easing this constraint would likely be well spent.

NOTES

*   A previous version of this chapter was presented at the 2011 Meetings of the Western Economic Association, San Diego, California. The author gratefully acknowledges helpful comments from David Berri, the participants at the conference session, and the editors of this volume.
1. For an extended treatment of Title IX, see Chapter 9 of this volume.
2. To maintain consistency across sections of the chapter, data in all tables is from the 2006–07 academic years. Salaries represent '(A)ll wages and bonuses the institution pays a coach as compensation attributable to coaching', 'Equity in Athletics Data Analysis Cutting Tool, Glossary of Terms' at: http://ope.ed.gov/athletics/glossary-Popup.aspx?idlink=16 (accessed November 23, 2011).
3. For additional details on the breakdown of the subdivisions of Division I, see 'Differences Among the Three Divisions: Division I', at: http://www.ncaa.org/wps/wcm/connect/public/ncaa/about+the+ncaa/who+we+are/differences+among+the+divisions/division+i/about+division+i (accessed November 23, 2011).
4. A few Division IAAA schools do offer football, though they play that sport in lower divisions.
5. Baseball and softball are somewhat of an anomaly in that, although they are similar games, men's rosters are much larger than women's on average due to differences in pitching staff size. According to the Equity in Athletics Data, men's Division IA baseball rosters average over 37 players, while softball rosters in the same division average just over 20 players.

6. Operating expenses include '(A)ll expenses an institution incurs attributable to home, away, and neutral-site intercollegiate athletic contests (commonly known as game-day expenses), for (A) Lodging, meals, transportation, uniforms, and equipment for coaches, team members, support staff (including, but not limited to team managers and trainers), and others; and (B) Officials'. Total expenses include '(A)ll expenses attributable to intercollegiate athletic activities. This includes appearance guarantees and options, athletically related student aid, contract services, equipment, fundraising activities, operating expenses, promotional activities, recruiting expenses, salaries and benefits, supplies, travel, and any other expenses attributable to intercollegiate athletic activities', Equity in Athletics Glossary, at: http://ope.ed.gov/athletics/glossaryPopup. aspx (accessed June 7, 2011).

7. Sources: NCAA.org. 'Men's 2007 Basketball Attendance' at: http://fs.ncaa.org/Docs/ stats/m_basketball_RB/Reports/attend/2007.pdf and NCAA.org. 'Women's 2007 Basketball Attendance', at: http://fs.ncaa.org/Docs/stats/w_basketball_RB/reports/ Attend/07att.pdf (accessed December 1, 2011).

8. Rankings are from Soccer America's College Soccer Reporter. 'Soccer America Women's Top 25: Final Rankings', at: http://www.socceramerica.com/article/1614/5-soccer-america-womens-top-25-final-rankings.html; NCAA.org. '2007 Women's Softball RPI', at: http://web1.ncaa.org/app_data/weeklyrpi/2007WSBrpi1.html; and ESPN Women's Basketball, '2007 NCAA Women's Basketball Rankings – Postseason', at: http://espn.go.com/womens-college-basketball/rankings/_/year/2007. Data on gender of head coaches are from the individual institution websites. Data on the gender of the coaches are from each institution's website.

9. Eight teams advance to the College World Series each year. The 1996–2005 period was chosen to capture the recent history of the program. The year 2006 was omitted to reduce undue emphasis on current player quality (that is 2007 ranking is likely to be strongly affected by players already at the institution in 2006.)

10. *Golfweek* ('College Coaching Salaries: Who Makes What?', 2009) indicated that most salaries were from 2006–07 but does not specifically identify the year for every institution. In a few cases, salaries were reported from 2007–08 (and were eliminated from the sample). In order to test the robustness of the estimates, all observations for which the coach had less than one full year of tenure prior to 2006–07 were dropped from both the men's and women's equations, and the final specification (model 1) was re-estimated (results not shown). The resulting sample sizes were 71 for women and 69 for men. The results were very similar with an average change in statistically signifi-cant coefficients in the men's equation of 8.3 percent and 3.5 percent in the women's equation. Particularly in the women's equation, many of the key coefficients remained virtually constant. As a result, the results for the full sample are shown in Tables 13.6 and 13.7.

REFERENCES

Acosta, R. Vivian and Linda Jean Carpenter (2010), 'Women in Intercollegiate Sport: A Longitudinal, National Study, Thirty Year Update', online at: www.acostacarpenter.org (accessed May 21, 2011).

American Association of University Professors (AAUP) (2007–08), 'Report on the Economic Status of the Profession', online at: http://www.aaup.org/AAUP/comm/rep/Z/ ecstatreport2007–08 (accessed April 19, 2011).

Brook, Stacey L. and Sarah Foster (2010), 'Does Gender Affect Compensation Among NCAA Basketball Coaches?', *International Journal of Sport Finance*, 5(2), May: 96–106.

'College Coaching Salaries: Who Makes What?' (2009), *Golfweek*, November 24. Original publication date: September 8, 2007. online at: http://www.golfweek.com/news/2009/ nov/24/look-who-makes-what-college-coaching/ (accessed June 21, 2011).

ESPN Women's Basketball, '2007 NCAA Women's Basketball Rankings – Postseason', online at: http://espn.go.com/womens-college-basketball/rankings/_/year/2007 (accessed December 1, 2011).

Fazioli, Jennifer K. (2004),'The Advancement of Female Coaches in Intercollegiate Athletics', Background paper for the Coaching and Gender Equity project, April.

Gregory, Sean (2007), 'Where are the Women Coaches?', *Time*, August 16.

Humphreys, Brad R (2000), 'Equal Pay on the Hardwood: The Earnings Gap Between Male and Female NCAA Division I Basketball Coaches', *Journal of Sports Economics*, **1**(3), May: 299–307.

NCAA.org, 'Men's 2007 Basketball Attendance', online at: http://fs.ncaa.org/Docs/stats/m_basketball_RB/Reports/attend/2007.pdf (accessed December 1, 2011).

NCAA.org, 'Women's 2007 Basketball Attendance', online at: http://fs.ncaa.org/Docs/stats/w_basketball_RB/reports/Attend/07att.pdf (accessed December 1, 2011).

NCAA.org, '2007 Women's Softball RPI', online at: http://web1.ncaa.org/app_data/weeklyrpi/2007WSBrpi1.html (accessed December 1, 2011).

Office of Post-Secondary Education (2011), 'The Equity in Athletics Data Analysis Cutting Tool', online at: http://ope.ed.gov/athletics/ (accessed November 23, 2011).

Rhode, Deborah L. and Christopher J. Walker (2008), 'Gender Equity in College Athletics: Women Coaches as a Case Study', *Stanford Journal of Civil Liberties*, **4**, February: 1–50.

Soccer America's College Soccer Reporter, 'Soccer America Women's Top 25: Final Rankings', online at: http://www.socceramerica.com/article/1614/5-soccer-america-womens-top-25-final-rankings.html (accessed December 1, 2011).

PART IV

WOMEN IN OLYMPIC AND INTERNATIONAL SPORTS

14. Gender differences in competitiveness: empirical evidence from 100m races

Bernd Frick and Friedrich Scheel

14.1 INTRODUCTION

In recent years a broad consensus has emerged among social scientists about the existence of a considerable gender gap in competitiveness. We define 'competitiveness' as the willingness and ability to perform in a setting in which the payoff is explicitly based on the rank order of one's performance. The reasons for the emergence and persistence of the gap remain highly contested. Researchers in different social sciences have proposed four explanations for the observed differences in behavior. To some degree these theories complement one another, and to some degree they compete with one another.

First, evolutionary psychologists posit that gender differences in competitiveness reflect predispositions that evolved because of men's longer and more intense training and greater competitive motivation (for example, Deaner 2006a, 2006b, 2011). Second, medical experts and sports scientists claim that the observed pattern has its roots in physical differences between men and women, such as hormonally regulated variations in body fat and the cardiovascular system, a lower oxygen uptake capacity, greater susceptibility to injuries, and a weaker response to training efforts by women (see, *inter alia*, Cheuvront et al., 2005). Third, sociologists assert that gender differences in competitiveness result from socio-cultural conditions fostering differences in socialization of boys and girls (for example, Henslin, 1999). Finally, economists argue that behavioral differences of humans are largely motivated by differences in opportunities and incentive structures (for example, Becker, 1993).

In this chapter, we use cross-sectional and longitudinal data from 100-meter races (ranging from world-class competitions, such as the finals of the Olympic Games and the International Amateur Athletic Federation (IAAF) World Championships, to national and regional races) to empirically discriminate among these four approaches. By analyzing the performance of male and female sprinters at both the top level of competition and at less elite, albeit highly select, levels, we shed light on the controversial question of whether men and women perform differently under competitive pressure.

Section 14.2 provides a selective review of the recent experimental and non-experimental literature. Section 14.3 describes the data and methodology and offers some descriptive statistics. Section 14.4 presents the econometric evidence, and Section 14.5 concludes with a brief summary and some implications for further research.

14.2 PREVIOUS EMPIRICAL RESEARCH

Although the literature on gender differences in competitiveness has recently grown rapidly, there is as yet no consensus concerning the reasons for its emergence and persistence. Moreover, the more fundamental question of whether the observed gender differences are due to genetic differences or behavioral characteristics is still open. A number of empirical studies suggest that a gender gap in competitiveness is likely to emerge in particular circumstances, such as a promotion tournament, where the pressure to succeed is high. An equally large number of studies using data from 'real-life experiments' find no statistically significant gender differences. These studies argue that controlled laboratory experiments provide an ideal setting to obtain undistorted measures of behavioral differences between men and women in competitive environments.

Finally, an already large and still increasing number of publications use data from professional sports to analyze and explain gender differences of highly self-selected athletes with similar aspirations and 'competitive motivations'. Sports data are particularly useful as they are available in the form of byproducts of today's comprehensive sports coverage (see Frick, 2004). Notwithstanding their respective merits, all three strands of literature suffer from major shortcomings, which, in turn, might explain the difficulties to reach a consensus in answering one of the presumably most pertinent questions in the field of gender economics.

14.2.1 Real-life Evidence

Using real-world data drawn from 'natural experiments' a number of studies find considerable gender differences in risk taking and performance under competitive pressure. Analyzing quantitative data obtained from test scores of Czech students applying to tuition-free selective universities, Jurajda and Münnich (2008, 2011) find that women perform significantly worse than equally able men in competitive situations. Since the women in their sample do not shy away from self-selecting into highly competitive admissions programs, the authors reject differences in risk aversion as a possible explanation for the gender gap in test performance.

In a similar study, Ors et al. (2008) reach the same conclusion by showing that the performance of female applicants on admission tests at an elite French university is significantly lower than the performance of male applicants. Again, differences in risk aversion and ability cannot explain the observable pattern, because women perform significantly better in high-school exams as well as during their first year at the university, suggesting that women tend to 'choke' in competitive environments.

Attali et al. (2010) compare the performance in a standardized test (the Graduate Record Examination: GRE) that is used by many graduate schools in the US as a selection tool, with the performance in an experimentally designed second GRE taking place immediately after the 'real' test. The authors document a greater gender gap in performance in the competitive 'real' GRE than in the experimental GRE, which they attribute to men's performing better 'when it counts', that is, when the stakes are particularly high.

Price (2008) examines how students at various high-ranked academic institutions in the US respond to the Mellon Foundation's Graduate Education Initiative, a competitive scholarship program that was initially designed to encourage students to make quick progress towards their degree. As a result, the time to candidacy was statistically significantly reduced for male, but not for female students. Moreover, the reduction in time to candidacy was greater for both males and females when a larger fraction of the competing cohort was female.

In a different type of study, Hogarth et al. (2012) find gender differences in competitive situations which they attribute to differences in risk tolerance. Exploiting the natural experiment of a TV game show, where candidates answer questions similar to the ones that are known from the board game Trivial Pursuit in multiple rounds, the authors reveal that women earn 40 percent less than male contestants and exit the game voluntarily and earlier than men, particularly when women are in the minority.[1] Corroborating the latter result, Neelakantan (2010) finds that approximately 10 percent of the gender gap in accumulated wealth of elderly Americans ($194,000 for men and $95,000 for women) can be attributed to differences in risk taking, as women prove to be more conservative investors with a significantly lower probability to invest in stocks.

However, a number of studies find no persistent behavioral gender differences in competitive behavior and thus stand in stark contrast to the findings presented so far. Using data from the British Workplace Employees Relations Survey, Manning and Saidi (2010) analyze earnings and work effort under performance pay and find very modest (if any) evidence for gender differences with respect to sorting into performance pay. Moreover, they find only a small effect of performance pay on earnings, which does not significantly differ by gender. Delfgaauw et al. (2009) conduct a field experiment in a Dutch retail chain consisting of 128 stores. Following the introduction of short-term sales competitions among randomly chosen subsamples of these stores, they find large positive effects on sales growth, but only in stores where the manager and a large fraction of the workforce are of the same gender. That is, shops with mostly female staff and a female manager improve their performance under competitive pressure to the same extent as male-dominated shops with a male manager. Interestingly enough, these results hold true even in the absence of any monetary rewards, suggesting a high symbolic value of winning a tournament.[2]

In a similar academic setting as in the studies by Jurajda and Münnich (2008, 2011) and Ors et al. (2008), documenting the existence of a considerable gender performance gap in highly competitive and stressful situations, Leuven et al. (2011) find no gender differences in either sorting or performance among male and female students in an introductory microeconomics course. In a study of teachers in Israel, Lavy (2008) finds that the performance of mathematics and language teachers is affected by neither the introduction of competitive elements in the remuneration process nor the gender composition of the group of teachers at a particular school. Following the introduction of a performance-related bonus system, neither the average rank nor the probability of winning a prize or the size of the prize differs by gender. Moreover, the gender composition of the groups of teachers competing with each other does not affect the performance of female teachers.

Exploring gender differences in risk aversion and negotiating practices, Feidakis and Tsaoussi (2009) compare the behavior of Greek attorneys, Greek business students and a control group consisting of young employees in public and private organizations. They find no statistically significant gender differences among attorneys and conclude that gender differences are unlikely to occur in groups of employees with a distinct professional culture.

14.2.2   Laboratory Experiments

Recently, the general finding that women perform worse under pressure than men has been challenged in a number of laboratory experiments. Shurchkov (2008) asked students to perform a verbal task (generally considered to favor women) under different conditions. The participants were divided in groups of four and required to solve word-in-word puzzles in a limited amount of time.[3] To examine the influence of competitive pressure on participants, the experiment was conducted in two stages. In the first round, a piece-rate scheme was used to reward the participants. Participants solved their tasks in a non-competitive environment, as their compensation was determined by their absolute rather than their relative performance. In the second round, a winner-take-all tournament rewarded only the winner of each group, while the other group members did not receive any compensation for their efforts. The behavior of male and female participants proved to be similar in the non-competitive as well as in the tournament setting. Moreover, neither men nor women improved their performance as a result of competitive pressure. Hence, Shurchkov (2008) finds no evidence that women underperform relative to men in a competitive environment. In a more recent study, Shurchkov (2012) examines two task stereotypes (math exercises versus verbal tasks) under different competitive regimes and time constraints and finds that men outperform women in a high-pressure math tournament while women succeed in a low-pressure verbal test.

Much in line with these latter results, Dreber et al. (2011) find no difference in performance under competitive pressure of 7–10-year-old boys and girls in Sweden. Following the initial research conducted with 9–10-year-old schoolchildren in Israel by Gneezy and Rustichini (2004),[4] Dreber et al. replicated the field experiment with children from 11 primary schools in the Stockholm area. In addition to competing in a short distance race, the children engaged in rope skipping and modern dancing, two tasks that were deliberately chosen as they are perceived to be advantageous for girls. In the first round of the experiment, the children performed the task alone with no direct competition. In the second round, the children were matched in pairs according to their performance in the first round. As expected, the boys on average ran faster while the girls performed better in rope skipping and dancing. However, Dreber et al. found no differences in the performance under competitive pressure between boys and girls.

A possible explanation for the contradictory results of the two studies is that children in rather male-dominated societies (for example, Israel) experience different socialization and nurture than children in a more gender-equal society (as in Sweden). In a similar spirit, Cárdenas et al. (2011) examine gender differences in competitiveness and risk taking among children aged 9–12 in Colombia and Sweden, two countries ranked 55th and 4th in terms of gender equality according to various macroeconomic indicators. Surprisingly, boys and girls proved to be equally competitive in all tasks in Colombia whereas the results for Sweden were mixed. However, girls are more risk averse in both countries, with a smaller gender gap in Sweden. Finally, Ivanova-Stenzel and Kübler (2011) examine whether the gender gap in performance depends on the gender composition of teams by introducing a real-effort task with wages either based on the teams' absolute performance or on the teams' relative performance in a competitive setting. The results suggest that, relative to a single-sex setting, gender diversity decreases the gender gap in performance in a competitive environment, while the gap increases in a non-competitive setting.

Another finding that emerges from a number of experimental studies is that women shy away from competition. Niederle and Vesterlund (2007) find that, when having the choice between performing a real task in a competitive setting in which the reward is based on one's relative performance (as in a rank-order tournament) versus a non-competitive environment, such as a piece-rate scheme that rewards one's absolute performance regardless of the performance of others, twice as many men as women self-select into the tournament (for similar findings, see Kamas and Preston, 2009; Vandegrift and Yavas, 2009; and Datta Gupta et al., 2011). Since the performances of men and women in the two different settings are similar, men apparently tend to enter tournaments too often while equally able women shy away from them too often.[5]

Examining the competitive choices of girls from single-sex and coeducational schools, Booth and Nolen (2012) find that girls from single-sex schools behave more like boys when randomly assigned to mixed-sex experimental groups, providing evidence for socially caused gender differences rather than inherent gender traits. Drawing on the allegedly immense differences in matrilineal and patriarchal societies, a number of studies have examined gender differences in competitiveness within these natural settings. Gneezy et al. (2009) examine the competitiveness of men and women in two societies, the Massai, a patriarchal society in Tanzania, and the Khasi, a matrilineal society in Northeast India. They find that in the patriarchal Massai society the gender gap is similar to that in Western societies. However, the gender gap is reversed in the matrilineal society, as women are found to be more competitive than men. Andersen et al. (2011) compare the competitiveness of children in patriarchal and matrilineal societies and show that the gender differences in competitiveness start to evolve around puberty, with the more pronounced changes occurring in the patriarchal society. For additional studies using data from matrilineal and patriarchal societies see, for example, Andersen et al. (2008), Gong and Yang (2011), and Hoffman et al. (2011).

14.2.3 Sports Data

Sports data are particularly well suited to explore gender differences in competitive behavior. First, professional athletes represent a highly self-selected sample of persons with competitive motivation, enabling researchers to analyze gender differences among homogeneous individuals with a distinct professional attitude. Second, since the contestants have very specific *ex ante* information about prize structures and their opponents' abilities, the self-selection process as well as the incentive effects of tournaments can be examined in detail. Moreover, the high degree of transparency of the athletes' performances and capabilities is likely to reduce gender differences in overconfidence, which, in turn, might lead to a reduction in the gender gap in competitiveness (Frick 2011a, 2011b).

Garratt et al. (2011) examine the self-selection process of male and female runners in the 'State Street Mile', a running event that offers its participants the choice between a less competitive race without any prize money and a more competitive one with prize money. The authors find that qualified women and older runners are less likely to choose the competitive race than qualified young men. The fastest younger women, however, being aware of their abilities, do not shy away from competition, as they always enter the more competitive race. These results are consistent with Nekby et al. (2008) who find that, in an elite 10,000-meter race in Sweden, women are at least as likely as men to self-select into starting groups that are beyond their current physical abilities, suggesting that within the latter groups, overconfidence is equally likely for men and women.

Frick and Klaeren (1997) and Frick (1998) examine how male and female professional marathon runners respond to changes in prize money and prize structure. They find that women respond more to an increase of the total purse as well as to changes in its distribution, while their performance (that is, their finish time) is unaffected by bonus payments.[6]

These behavioral differences can be explained by the fact that the elite female marathon runners at that time (in the 1980s and early 1990s) were more heterogeneous (that is, less balanced) than the male elite runners. Due to that heterogeneity and an equal number of lucrative races for men and women, the top female athletes were initially able to avoid competing against each other by strategically entering certain events only. Thus, it was possible for a woman, but not for a man (who, due to the greater homogeneity in the field, always faced competitors of similar strength) to win a marathon with a 'suboptimal' performance (that is, a time that is well above the world record). However, over time, the gender gap in competitive balance has considerably narrowed, especially in long-distance and ultramarathon running. It appears that the most prestigious (and most lucrative) women's races (5,000m track, 10,000m road, half marathon and marathon) have been particularly 'balanced' throughout the period of observation of nearly 40 years (see, for example, Frick 2011a, 2011b).

Using a similar approach but different data, several studies explore the response of professional tennis players to 'competitive pressure'. Paserman (2007) analyzes set-level data from Grand Slam tournaments and finds that, for both men and women, the quality of the game deteriorates with increasing stakes. This deterioration in performance is greater for women in the decisive set, albeit not statistically significant. Yet, when examining point-by-point data, Paserman (2010) finds that women, but not men, are more likely to produce 'unforced errors' at crucial points of the match. Hence, there is evidence of a statistically significant gender gap in performance under pressure, even among highly self-selected persons. Sunde (2009) uses data from the final two rounds of all ATP (Association of Tennis Professionals) Master and Grand Slam tournaments in the years between 1990 and 2002 to analyze the behavior of male tennis professionals. He finds that in uneven contests both the favorite and the underdog perform worse than in 'balanced' contests, supporting the incentive hypothesis. Lallemand et al. (2008) find exactly the opposite result for female tennis players, as a greater difference between the two contestants results in a larger number of wins by the favorite and a larger number of losses by the underdog, which is in line with the capability hypothesis.[7]

Ehrenberg and Bognanno (1990a, 1990b) find that the overall prize money as well as its distribution have a significant impact on player performance in professional golf. The higher the total purse and the larger the prize differential, the lower are the scores and thus the better is the performance of an individual golfer. In addition, it appears that a golfer's performance during the last round is positively correlated with the marginal returns to effort (that is, the higher the rewards for improving one's rank) the smaller the number of strokes required to finish that particular round. However, replicating that study with comparable data from the Ladies' Professional Golf Association (LPGA) Tour in the year 2000, Matthews et al. (2007) are unable to confirm the results of Ehrenberg and Bognanno for female players. They show that an increase of the total purse leads to higher scores, signifying weaker performance. A possible explanation for the observed gender differences in performance is that women are likely to succumb to the pressure that comes with large prizes at stake (that is, 'choking under pressure'), whereas men respond positively to an increase of prizes by delivering a better performance.

Table 14.1   Overview of the datasets

Type of data	Performance level		
	International	National	Regional
Annual Top 100 Best Lists 2001–2010	X		
Annual Top 50 Best Lists 2001–2010	X	X	
Finishing Times in Finals (Top 5) 2001–2010	X	X	X

14.3   DATA AND DESCRIPTIVE EVIDENCE

Our estimation uses four different datasets. The first one includes the top 100 male and top 100 female athletes worldwide in the years 2001–10 at the 100m distance, the most popular short-distance race in the world. The size and the structure of the datasets are displayed in Table 14.1. The data are assembled and constantly updated by a group of formerly competitive long-distance runners who are also devoted statisticians. The data can be accessed on their website (www.arrs.net). Since all relevant information on these top-100 male and female performers (name, date of birth, nationality, finish time, date and place of competition) is available for 10 years, the total number of observations is 2,000. The second dataset is very similar to the first one and includes the top 50 male and female German sprinters at the same distance during the same time period (*n* = 1,000). The data for Germany are assembled and constantly updated by the German Track and Field Association and can be retrieved from their website (www.deutscher-leichtathletik-verband.de). In our third dataset we merge the top 50 international athletes with the top 50 national athletes of both genders, again yielding 2,000 observations.

Using the first two datasets, we calculate the time difference between men and women of the same rank for each of the ten years.[8] To ensure comparability, we calculate the difference not in seconds, but the percentage difference of the respective man and woman's performances (for an illustration see Table 14.2):

$$PD = [(FFT_{ij} - MFT_{ij})/MFT_{ij}]*100, \qquad (14.1)$$

where:

PD: percentage difference in finishing times;
FFT: female finishing time in year *i* and on rank *j*; and
MFT: male finishing time in year *i* and on rank *j*.

Table 14.2 An illustration of dataset 1

Year	Category	Rank	Male athlete	Time	Time difference (in %)	Female athlete	Time
2008	Intern'tl	1	Usain Bolt	9.69	11.25	Torri Edwards	10.78
		2	Asafa Powell	9.72	10.91	Shelly-Ann Fraser-Price	10.78
		3	Tyson Gay	9.77	10.54	Kerron Stewart	10.80
		: :					
		98	Rolando Palacios	10.22	11.15	Monique Henderson	11.36
		99	Justyn Warner	10.23	11.05	Chalonda Goodman	11.36
		100	Peimeng Zhang	10.23	11.05	Tahesia Harrigan	11.36
: :							
2010	National	1	Tobias Unger	10.14	9.47	Verena Sailer	11.10
		2	Alex. Kosenkow	10.26	10.43	Anne Möllinger	11.33
		3	Marius Broening	10.26	10.43	Yasmin Kwadwo	11.33
		: :					
		48	Korbinian Greding	10.76	11.52	Katharina Grompe	12.00
		49	Eric Franke	10.76	11.71	Franziska Dobler	12.02
		50	Timo Stinski	10.76	11.80	Sinje Florczak	12.03

Source: Association of Road Running Statisticians (www.arrs.net) and own calculations.

Table 14.3 An illustration of dataset 2

Category	Rank	Name	Time	Year	Event	Sex	Var. coeff.
International	1	Usain Bolt	9.58	2009	World Championship	1	0.013835
International	2	Tyson Gay	9.71	2009	World Championship	1	
International	3	Asafa Powell	9.84	2009	World Championship	1	
International	4	Daniel Bailey	9.93	2009	World Championship	1	
International	5	Richard Thompson	9.93	2009	World Championship	1	
International	1	Shelly-Ann Fraser	10.73	2009	World Championship	0	0.010153
International	2	Kerron Stewart	10.75	2009	World Championship	0	
International	3	Carmelita Jeter	10.90	2009	World Championship	0	
International	4	Veronica Campbell-Brown	10.95	2009	World Championship	0	
International	5	Lauryn Williams	11.01	2009	World Championship	0	
⋮							
National	1	Tobias Unger	10.20	2008	Nat. Championship	1	0.004783
National	2	Stefan Schwab	10.29	2008	Nat. Championship	1	
National	3	Martin Keller	10.32	2008	Nat. Championship	1	
National	4	Alexander Kosenkow	10.33	2008	Nat. Championship	1	
National	5	Ronny Ostwald	10.33	2008	Nat. Championship	1	
National	1	Verena Sailer	11.28	2008	Nat. Championship	0	0.008837
National	2	Cathleen Tschirch	11.45	2008	Nat. Championship	0	
National	3	Anne Möllinger	11.48	2008	Nat. Championship	0	
National	4	Marion Wagner	11.54	2008	Nat. Championship	0	
National	5	Karoline Köhler	11.57	2008	Nat. Championship	0	
⋮							

Table 14.3 (continued)

Category	Rank	Name	Time	Year	Event	Sex	Var. coeff.
Regional	1	Christian Blum	10.40	2007	Bavarian Championship	1	0.021153
Regional	2	Marco Thomann	10.81	2007	Bavarian Championship	1	
Regional	3	Lasse Zunker	10.88	2007	Bavarian Championship	1	
Regional	4	Gerald Stürzenhof	10.96	2007	Bavarian Championship	1	
Regional	5	Florian Prockl	11.07	2007	Bavarian Championship	1	
Regional	1	Susi Zimanyi	11.93	2007	Bavarian Championship	0	0.013561
Regional	2	Franziska Bertenbr	11.97	2007	Bavarian Championship	0	
Regional	3	Hacker Hanne	12.05	2007	Bavarian Championship	0	
Regional	4	Stefanie Staudacher	12.19	2007	Bavarian Championship	0	
Regional	5	Pamela Spindler	12.38	2007	Bavarian Championship	0	

Sources: the-sports.org (http://www.the-sports.org/athletics-s5-c0-b0.html), as well as leichtathletik.de (http://www.leichtathletik.de/index. php?SiteID=16) and own calculations.

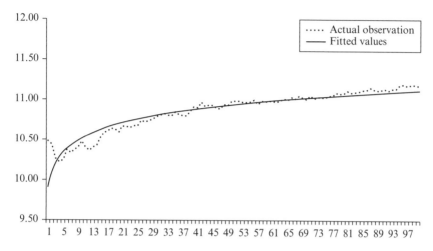

Source: Global Annual Ranking, 2001–2010.

Figure 14.1 *Percentage difference in finish times between male and female athletes by rank*

In our estimations – presented in Section 14.4, below – we use the percentage time difference between a male and a female runner at the same rank in the annual (international or German) best list as the dependent variable. If – as suggested by most of the available literature from Section 14.2 – female athletes exhibit a lower degree of competitiveness, the time difference will increase from rank to rank. If, on the other hand, women exhibit a similar degree of competitiveness, the time difference will be more or less constant across the ranking.

Figures 14.1 and 14.2 illustrate equation (14.1) for international and German athletes. The broken lines in the figures show the actual (averaged) observations for the years 2001 to 2010, while the black lines show the fitted values. They reveal that a concave trend represents the observable pattern quite well: the percentage difference in the top performances of male and female sprinters increases monotonically, but with a lower slope in the international data than in the national (German) data. Interestingly, the percentage difference in finish times in the global ranking decreases in the top ranks, suggesting that the performance of the top five of the female elite is more homogeneous than the top five of the male elite. This may be because of the dominance of a single runner among men, the 'Usain Bolt effect'.

Apart from the observable differences in the degree of competitiveness between men and women, the size of the population of male and female

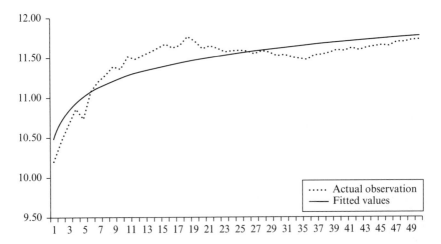

Source: German Annual Ranking, 2001–2010.

Figure 14.2   Percentage difference in finish times between male and female athletes by rank

runners is likely to affect the average performance of those making it into the 'Top 50', as measured by the mean finish times in Figures 14.1 and 14.2. Population size is also likely to affect the dispersion of the performances of the top athletes, which we measure with the coefficient of variation of the top 50 performers in both a small country like Germany and the world. It appears from Figures 14.3 and 14.4 that the dispersion in the large international population is far smaller than in the small national population and that this difference is much larger in the case of women. The fact that the difference in average performance and in performance dispersion between the small and the large pool is far lower for men than for women has two implications. First, the histories of professional track and field athletics are quite different for men and for women (a phenomenon that is usually referred to as 'path dependency'; for a detailed discussion in the sports context, see Frick, 2011b). Second, certain thresholds may exist, beyond which an increase in the number of competitors is unlikely to increase the average quality of the contestants significantly.[9]

Our fourth dataset is different from the first three. It includes the five top finishers in the 100m finals at international,[10] national, and regional championships[11] over the 2001–10 period both for men and women (Table 14.4). Using the finish times of the five top performers we first calculate the coefficient of variation to determine the 'closeness' or the

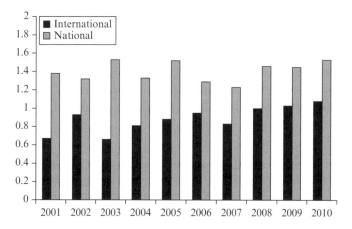

Figure 14.3   Coefficient of variation of the performance of male sprinters, 2001–2010

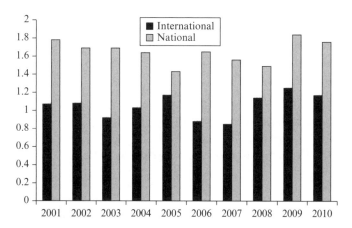

Figure 14.4   Coefficient of variation of the performance of female sprinters, 2001–2010

'competitive balance' of these races. We then use these figures in an analysis of variance to check whether competitiveness among male and female athletes differs among the three levels.[12]

It appears from Table 14.4 that – as expected – the coefficient of variation is much lower for men than for women and far higher at the regional and – to a lesser extent – the national level. These results are consistent with the ones reported above and lend further support to the hypothesis that women exhibit a lower degree of competitiveness than men.

Table 14.4   Analysis of variance of male and female athletic performance

	Var. coef.	Std dev.	No. of observations	*F*-value
International				
Women	0.84	0.36	59	1.45[+]
Men	0.76	0.34	59	
National				
Women	1.02	0.30	9	10.31***
Men	0.63	0.21	9	
Regional				
Women	1.94	0.85	54	13.93***
Men	1.42	0.56	54	

Note: [+] Not significant; *** $p < 0.01$.

14.4   ECONOMETRIC FINDINGS

Figures 14.1 and 14.2 suggest a relationship between rank and competitiveness, but they do not give the precise relationship, nor do they account for other factors that might affect competitiveness. To state the relationship between rank and competitiveness more precisely, we estimate the following regression model separately for international and national runners, using our first two datasets separately (to ensure robustness of standard errors, we always bootstrap with 200 replications):

$$PD_{ij} = \alpha_0 + \alpha_1 \, RANK_{ij} + \alpha_2 \, RANK_{ij}^2 + \alpha_3 \, TT + \varepsilon_{ij}, \qquad (14.2)$$

where:

PD_{ij}:   percentage difference in finishing time between female and male runner on rank i in year j;

$RANK$:   position of runner i in year j in annual ranking; and

TT: linear time trend ($2001 = 1, \ldots, 2010 = 10$).

The second regression model uses both datasets simultaneously and includes in the estimation two interaction terms to account for possible differences between the international and national levels as well as a multiplicative combination (that is, an interaction term) of the national dummy and the linear time trend:

$$PD_{ij} = \alpha_0 + \alpha_1 \, RANK_{ij} + \alpha_2 \, RANK_{ij}^2 + \alpha_3 \, NAT\_RANK_{ij} + \alpha_4 \, NAT\_RANK_{ij}^2 + \alpha_5 \, TT + \alpha_6 \, NAT\_TT + \varepsilon_{ij}, \qquad (14.3)$$

where:

PD_{ij}:	percentage difference in finishing time between female and male runner on rank *i* in year *j*;
$RANK_{ij}$:	position of runner *i* in year *j* in annual ranking (ranging from 1 to 50; including squared term);
TT:	linear time trend (2001 = 1, . . ., 2010 = 10);
NAT_RANK:	multiplicative combination of German dummy and rank (including squared term); and
NAT_TT:	multiplicative combination of German dummy and linear time trend.

It appears from Table 14.5 that – corroborating the impression generated by Figures 14.1 and 14.2 – the percentage difference in the finish times between men and women at the same rank increases with rank, albeit at a declining rate, suggesting that the pool of female runners is still more heterogeneous than the pool of male runners. Moreover, the coefficient of the linear time trend is positive and statistically significant in both estimations, which implies that the performance differential between men and women increases as time progresses. Finally, these effects are far stronger in the national (German) sample than in the international sample. Thus, the evidence presented so far is not consistent with any of the hypotheses held by psychologists, medical scientists, sociologists, or economists, as all four suggest that differences between the sexes should be declining over time, albeit for different reasons.

These results are completely at odds with the findings reported in two companion papers using data from long- and ultra-distance running (Frick 2011a, 2011b), which document a significant decrease in the performance differential over time. We cannot rule out the possibility that these different developments are caused by the frequency and rigor of drug-testing. On the one hand, women benefit far more from using steroids and testosterone than men. On the other hand, these substances are far easier to detect than, for example, very small doses of EPO, a drug that is preferred by long-distance runners. Thus, the increasing performance differential is most likely caused by the recent decline in the use of performance-enhancing drugs by top female athletes (for a similar argument, see, for example, Seiler et al., 2007).[13]

Given the increasing performance differential between male and female sprinters, ordinary least squares (OLS) may not be the appropriate estimation technique if the impact of the position in the annual ranking is not constant across the distribution. Since this problem has been acknowledged in the sports economics literature by many researchers, some of

Table 14.5   Estimation results

	Coefficient	Std error	t	P
Model 1: International Sample (Worldwide)				
RANK	0.01752	0.00128	13.65	***
RANK²#	−0.00911	0.00123	−7.40	***
TT	0.19282	0.00302	−6.39	***
Constant	−28.37846	6.05049	−4.69	***
No. of obs.		1,000		
Replications		200		
Wald Chi²		220.8		
$R^2 * 100$		43.8		
Model 1: National Sample (Germany)				
RANK	0.06099	0.00677	9.00	***
RANK²#	−0.09047	0.00114	−7.91	***
TT	0.01545	0.00605	2.55	**
Constant	−20.29035	12.14130	−1.67	*
No. of obs.		500		
Replications		200		
Wald Chi²		117.1		
$R^2 * 100$		33.0		
Model 2 (Pooled Data including International and National Top 50)				
RANK	0.02066	0.00465	3.52	***
RANK²#	−0.01253	0.00884	−1.25	+
NAT_RANK	0.04036	0.00657	4.43	***
NAT_RANK²	−0.00078	0.00013	−5.08	***
TT	0.02734	0.00393	6.93	***
NAT_TT #	0.02170	0.00363	5.98	***
Constant	−44.58343	7.89106	−5.65	***
No. of obs.		1,000		
Replications		200		
Wald Chi²		1,894.2		
$R^2 * 100$		62.3		

Note: +Not significant; * $p < 0.10$; ** $p < 0.05$; *** $p < 0.01$.

them now use quantile regression estimation (see, for example, Hamilton, 1997; Berri and Simmons, 2009; and Vincent and Eastman, 2009) in the case that the dependent variable (for example, log of player salary) has a particularly large kurtosis.[14] Of course, OLS is the best linear unbiased estimator provided that the error distribution is homoskedastic, and OLS parameters tend to a normal distribution around true values even if the individual residuals are not normally distributed. However, OLS constrains the marginal effects of covariates to be the same throughout the conditional distribution of the performance, which is not necessarily the case. Therefore, we investigate the impacts of rank at various quantiles of the conditional performance distribution, not just the conditional mean. To ensure robustness of standard errors, we again bootstrap with 200 replications.

It appears from Table 14.6 that the impact of *RANK* on the performance differential between male and female athletes is decreasing across the quantiles of the distribution. Again, this finding is at odds with the results reported in Frick (2011a, 2011b), where the coefficients appear to be remarkably constant. We are tempted to attribute this somewhat unexpected result to the different costs and returns to using illegal substances. It is particularly worth noting that the coefficients of the trend variable differ considerably across the quantiles as well as between the international and national samples. This suggests that the observable increase in the gender gap in performance has been much stronger in the small pool (that is, in Germany). It also suggests that this increase has been particularly large among the less talented athletes. These findings are again neither consistent with the 'culture-and-incentives hypothesis' nor with the 'biology-and-predispositions hypothesis'.

14.5   CONCLUSIONS AND IMPLICATIONS FOR FUTURE RESEARCH

The evidence from 100m races presented in this chapter is not fully compatible with any of the four competing explanations. However, competitive pressure seems to affect performance equally for men and women. Irrespective of gender, the coefficient of variation in the annual top performances is smaller in a large (world) population than in a small population (Germany). As a result, we favor the sociological and economic 'culture-and-incentives' hypotheses, according to which athletes become more competitive if they are socialized and incentivized to compete and have opportunities to do so. Perhaps surprisingly, competitiveness has decreased among women in recent years, which is at odds with all four hypotheses and seems to imply that the use of illegal substances has declined more among women than among men.

These results notwithstanding, additional tests of the 'culture-and-incentives' hypothesis can – and should – be performed to add further support. First, the increasing 'cultural heterogeneity' of the top runners is

Table 14.6   Quantile regression

	Quantile				
	0.10	0.25	0.50	0.75	0.90
International (Top 100)					
RANK	0.0303***	0.0234***	0.0142***	0.0123***	0.0091***
	(13.85)	(12.60)	(9.50)	(4.45)	(3.86)
RANK²#	−0.0192***	−0.0132***	−0.0068***	−0.0053*	−0.0023⁺
	(−10.04)	(−8.69)	(−5.51)	(−1.81)	(−1.19)
TT	0.0222***	0.0044*	0.0004⁺	0.0270***	0.0314***
	(3.55)	(1.93)	(0.12)	(3.75)	(9.53)
Constant	−34.790**	1.215⁺	9.630*	−43.540***	−52.070***
	(−2.78)	(0.27)	(1.67)	(−3.02)	(−7.86)
National (Top 50)					
RANK	0.0440***	0.0347***	0.0181**	0.0130*	−0.0022⁺
	(7.37)	(5.96)	(2.10)	(1.93)	(−0.34)
RANK²#	−0.0410***	−0.0279***	−0.0130⁺	−0.0057⁺	0.0188*
	(−4.04)	(−3.02)	(−0.88)	(−0.48)	(1.71)
TT	0.0419***	0.0251***	0.0093⁺	0.0383***	0.0480***
	(4.77)	(6.10)	(0.89)	(5.29)	(8.20)
Constant	−74.48***	−40.53***	−8.36⁺	−66.11***	−85.32***
	(−4.24)	(−4.91)	(−0.40)	(−4.56)	(−7.27)
Pooled (Top 50)					
RANK	0.0440***	0.0347***	0.0181**	0.0130*	−0.0022⁺
	(6.79)	(5.52)	(2.34)	(1.88)	(−0.29)
RANK²#	−0.0410***	−0.0279***	−0.0130⁺	−0.0057⁺	0.0188⁺
	(−3.69)	(−2.77)	(−0.95)	(−0.49)	(1.43)
NAT_ RANK	0.0380***	0.0311***	0.0268***	0.0043⁺	0.0086⁺
	(3.73)	(3.11)	(2.64)	(0.43)	(0.81)
NAT_ RANK²#	−0.0672***	−0.0603***	−0.0533***	−0.0154⁺	−0.0250⁺
	(−3.79)	(−3.76)	(−3.02)	(−0.93)	(−1.43)
TT	0.0419***	0.0251***	0.0093⁺	0.0383***	0.0480***
	(4.85)	(6.33)	(0.98)	(5.43)	(9.31)
NAT_TT	0.0036⁺	−0.0031⁺	−0.0054⁺	−0.0398***	−0.0467***
	(0.30)	(−0.29)	(−0.47)	(−3.99)	(−5.98)
Constant	−74.48***	−40.53***	−8.37⁺	−66.11***	−85.32***
	(−4.30)	(−5.09)	(−0.44)	(−4.67)	(−8.27)

Note: ⁺ Not significant; * $p < 0.10$; ** $p < 0.05$; *** $p < 0.01$; # Multiplied by 100 for presentational purposes.

likely to affect the degree of competitiveness of both men and women, as it increases both the size and the composition of the pool of athletes. Male sprinters from the US ceased dominating international competition in the 1980s, but US women held sway for a longer period. In the last several decades, the percentage of world-class athletes has increased considerably among both sexes, particularly from the Caribbean and among women.

Thus, the disproportional increase in the number of athletes from Central and South America may have intensified the competition among women more than among men. Second, since comparable data are available for other events in track and field, the empirical analyses can – and should – be extended. Apart from middle- and long-distance races that have already been analyzed in detail, track and field events include a number of other disciplines – such as throwing and jumping – where the gender gap in world records is considerably larger (at 15–18 percent compared to 10–12 percent in distance running).

So far, there has been no comparable empirical analysis of gender differences in competitiveness in such field events as shot put, discus, javelin and hammer throw, high jump, pole vault, long jump, and triple jump. The observable differences in competitiveness between the track events on the one hand and the field events on the other may be due to biological factors that make women relatively better at running. Another possible explanation is that fewer women choose to engage in field disciplines which, in turn, are likely to result in a lower degree of competitiveness. Unfortunately, the data that are available on the top performers and/or the top performances in the throwing and the jumping disciplines are not as complete as they are for the running disciplines (see, for example, www.iaaf.org). It does appear, however, that, with the exception of long jump, far fewer female athletes are responsible for the 100 best performances in a given year as well as the all-time best performances than the respective number of male athletes. This suggests that there is a higher degree of 'performance concentration' and a lower level of competitiveness among women.

NOTES

1. Using data from the TV game show 'The Weakest Link', Antonovics et al. (2009) find that women's likelihood of correctly answering a question is unaffected by the opponent's gender whereas men are more likely to give a correct answer when competing against a woman. Säve-Söderbergh and Lindquist (2011) analyze the behavior of women in the game show 'Jeopardy' and find that irrespective of any strategic gains, women play more conservatively when facing male competitors only.
2. Furthermore, this assumption is supported by the fact that despite the considerable variation in team size the authors are unable to find any evidence for free riding.
3. In a word-in-word puzzle, the objective is to form as many words as possible from the letters of another long word.
4. The children had to run a distance of 40 meters twice, first alone and then matched with a child of equal ability. While boys increased their effort (that is, ran faster) in a competition, the girls' performance was unaffected by the setting.
5. See also Price (2009), Balafoutas and Sutter (2010), Cason et al. (2010), Niederle et al. (2010), Sutter and Rützler (2010), Wozniak et al. (2010), Healy and Pate (2011), and, using data from professional tennis players, Wozniak (2012). A notable exception is Price (2010) who uses a similar experimental design but fails to find gender differences

in competition aversion. This is mainly because the participants in this study did not display any gender difference in confidence, which is considered more important in explaining gender differences in competitiveness than differences in risk preferences, as examined in numerous experimental studies (for example, Halko et al., 2008; Charness and Gneezy, 2010, and Garcia-Gallego et al., 2010, or, for a summary, Croson and Gneezy, 2009). A nice example for men's overconfidence is presented in Reuben et al. (2012). In a two-stage real effort task groups select a leader to compete against other group leaders. It is found that men are selected significantly more often as leaders than is suggested by their individual performance in the first stage and that this is mainly driven by men's overconfidence.

6. Bonus payments are typically rewards for beating certain finish times, such as the world or course record or pre-specified thresholds.

7. The capability hypothesis posits that differences in talent and abilities result in a high (low) probability of the favorite (the underdog) to win a contest. The incentive hypothesis states that greater heterogeneity among the players' *ex ante* abilities results in worse performance by both the favorite and the underdog, who assume that the outcome of the match is largely predetermined.

8. The kernel density estimation of the time difference is available from the authors upon request.

9. For a different approach to such gender differences, see, for example, Chapter 12 in this volume.

10. Here we include the Olympic Games, the IAAF World Championships as well as the Golden League and the Diamond League Meetings.

11. By 'regional championships' we mean the finals in the respective competition at the level of the federal states.

12. Since in some of the regional championships only five athletes participated in the finals, we had to restrict our analysis to the top five finishers.

13. This does not imply that the use of illegal substances has declined in general, but that the 'old stuff' has been replaced by more effective and more difficult to detect performance-enhancing drugs.

14. Presence of non-normality in the dependent variable is indicated by a large kurtosis value and in our case the D'Agostino et al. (1990) test is performed by the sktest command in Stata 11. In the two datasets used here the kurtosis of the dependent variable (percentage difference in finishing times between female and male runner on the same rank in the annual top 100 and top 50) is 3.74 (national) and 3.39 (international).

REFERENCES

Andersen, Steffen, Erwin Bulte, Uri Gneezy and John A. List (2008), 'Do Women Supply More Public Goods than Men? Preliminary Experimental Evidence from Matrilineal and Patriarchal Societies', *American Economic Review*, **98**(2), May: 376–81.

Andersen, Seffen, Seda Ertac, Uri Gneezy, John A. List and Sandra Maximiano (2011), 'Gender, Competitiveness and Socialization at a Young Age: Evidence from a Matrilineal and a Patriarchal Society', Working Paper, Copenhagen Business School.

Antonovics, Kate, Peter Arcidiacono and Randall Walsh (2009), 'The Effects of Gender Interactions in the Lab and in the Field', *Review of Economics and Statistics*, **91**(1), February: 152–62.

Attali, Yigal, Zvika Neeman and Analia Schlosser (2010), 'Rise to the Challenge or not Give a Damn: Differential Performance in High vs. Low Stakes Tests', unpublished manuscript, Tel Aviv University.

Balafoutas, Loukas and Matthias Sutter (2010), 'Gender, Competition and the Efficiency of Policy Interventions', Discussion Paper 4955, Institute for the Study of Labor, Bonn.

Becker, Gary S (1993), 'Nobel Lecture: The Economic Way of Looking at Behavior', *Journal of Political Economy*, **101**(3), June: 385–409.

Berri, David J. and Rob Simmons (2009), 'Race and the Evaluation of Signal Callers in the National Football League', *Journal of Sports Economics*, **10**(1), February: 23–43.

Booth, Alison and Patrick Nolen (2012), 'Choosing to Compete: How Different Are Girls and Boys?', *Journal of Economic Behavior and Organization*, **81**(2), February: 542–55.

Cárdenas, Juan-Camilo, Anna Dreber, Emma von Essen and Eva Ranehill (2011), 'Gender Differences in Competitiveness and Risk Taking: Comparing Children in Colombia and Sweden', *Journal of Economic Behavior and Organization*, **83**(1), June: 11–23.

Cason, Timothy N., William A. Masters and Roman M. Sheremeta (2010), 'Entry into Winner-take-all and Proportional-prize Contests: An Experimental Study', *Journal of Public Economics*, **94**(9–10), October: 604–11.

Charness, Gary and Uri Gneezy (2010), 'Strong Evidence for Gender Differences in Experimental Investment', *Journal of Economic Behavior and Organization*, **83**(1), June: 50–58.

Cheuvront, Samuel N., Robert Carter III, Keith C. DeRuisseau and Robert J. Moffatt (2005), 'Running Performance Differences between Men and Women: An Update', *Sports Medicine*, **35**(12): 1017–24.

Croson, Rachel and Uri Gneezy (2009), 'Gender Differences in Preferences', *Journal of Economic Literature*, **47**(2): 1–27.

D'Agostino, Ralph B., Albert Belanger and Ralph B. D'Agostino, Jr (1990), 'A Suggestion for Using Powerful and Informative Tests of Normality', *The American Statistician*, **44**(4), November: 316–21.

Datta Gupta, Nabanita, Anders Poulsen and Marie Claire Villeval (2011), 'Gender Matching and Competitiveness: Experimental Evidence', *Economic Inquiry*, doi: 10.1111/j.1465-7295.2011. 00378.x.

Deaner, Robert O. (2006a), 'More Males Run Relatively Fast in U.S. Road Races: Further Evidence of a Sex Difference in Competitiveness', *Evolutionary Psychology*, **4**: 303–14.

Deaner, Robert O. (2006b), 'More Males Run Fast: A Stable Sex Difference in Competitiveness in U.S. Distance Runners', *Evolution and Human Behavior*, **27**(1), January: 63–84.

Deaner, Robert O. (2011), 'Distance Running as an Ideal Domain for Demonstrating a Sex Difference in Enduring Competitiveness', Working Paper online at: http://faculty.gvsu.edu/deanerr/Deaner%202012%20Distance%20running%20as%20an%20ideal%20domain%20for%20showing%20a%20sex%20difference%20in%20competitiveness.pdf.

Delfgaauw, Josse, Robert Dur, Joeri Sol and Willem Verbeke (2009), 'Tournament Incentives in the Field: Gender Differences in the Workplace', Discussion Paper 4395, Institute for the Study of Labor, Bonn.

Dreber, Anna, Emma von Essen and Eva Ranehill (2011), 'Outrunning the Gender Gap – Boys and Girls Compete Equally', SSE/EFI Working Paper Series in Economics and Finance No. 709, Department of Economics, Stockholm University.

Ehrenberg, Ronald G. and Michael L. Bognanno (1990a), 'Do Tournaments Have Incentive Effects?', *Journal of Political Economy*, **98**(6), December: 1307–24.

Ehrenberg, Ronald G. and Michael L. Bognanno (1990b), 'The Incentive Effects of Tournaments Revisited: Evidence from the European PGA Tour', *Industrial and Labor Relations Review*, **43**(3), February: 74–88.

Feidakis, Andreas and Aspasia Tsaoussi (2009), 'Competitiveness, Gender and Ethics in Legal Negotiations: Some Empirical Evidence', *International Negotiation: A Journal of Theory and Practice*, **14**(3), Fall: 537–70.

Frick, Bernd (1998), 'Lohn und Leistung im professionellen Sport: Das Beispiel Stadt-Marathon', *Konjunkturpolitik*, **44**: 114–40.

Frick, B. (2004), 'Warum laufen die denn so schnell? Die Anreizwirkungen von Prämien bei professionellen Marathonläufern', in Dieter H. Jütting (ed.), *Die Laufbewegung in Deutschland – interdisziplinär betrachtet*, Münster: Waxmann, pp 33–48.

Frick, Bernd (2011a), 'Gender Differences in Competitiveness: Empirical Evidence from Professional Distance Running', *Labour Economics*, **18**(3), June: 389–98.

Frick, Bernd (2011b), 'Gender Differences in Competitive Orientations: Empirical Evidence from Ultramarathon Running', *Journal of Sports Economics*, **12**(3), June: 317–40.

Frick, Bernd and Rainer Klaeren (1997), 'Die Anreizwirkungen leistungsabhängiger Entgelte: Theoretische Überlegungen und empirische Befunde aus dem Bereich des professionellen Sports', *Zeitschrift für Betriebswirtschaft*, **67**: 1117–38.

Garcia-Gallego, Aurora, Nickolaos Georgantzis and Ainhoa Jaramillo-Gutierrez (2010), 'Gender Differences in Ultimatum Games: Despite Rather than Due to Risk Attitudes', *Journal of Economic Behavior and Organization*, **83**(1), June: 42–9.

Garratt, Rodney J., Catherine Weinberger and Nicholas Johnson (2011), 'The State Street Mile: Age and Gender Differences in Competition Aversion in the Field', *Economic Inquiry*, doi: 10.1111/ j.1465-7295.2011.00370.x.

Gneezy, Uri, Kenneth L. Leonard and John A. List (2009), 'Gender Differences in Competition: Evidence from a Matrilineal and a Patriarchal Society', *Econometrica*, **77**(5), September: 1637–64.

Gneezy, Uri and Aldo Rustichini (2004), 'Gender and Competition at a Young Age', *American Economic Review*, **94**(2), May: 377–81.

Gong, Binglin and Chun-Lei Yang (2011), 'Gender Differences in Risk Attitudes: Field Experiments on the Matrilineal Mosuo and the Patriarchal Yi', *Journal of Economic Behavior and Organization*, **83**(1), June: 59–65.

Halko, MarjaLiisa, Markku Kaustia and Elias Alanko (2008), 'The Gender Effect in Risky Asset Holdings', *Journal of Economic Behavior and Organization*, **83**(1), February: 66–81.

Hamilton, Barton Hughes (1997), 'Racial Discrimination and Basketball Salaries in the 1990s', *Applied Economics*, **29**(3), October: 287–96.

Healy, Andrew and Jennifer Pate (2011), 'Can Teams Help to Close the Gender Competition Gap?', *Economic Journal*, **121**(555), January: 1192–204.

Henslin, James M. (1999), *Sociology: A Down-To-Earth Approach*, 4th edn, Boston, MA: Allyn & Bacon.

Hoffman, Moshe, Uri Gneezy and John A. List (2011), 'Nurture Affects Gender Differences in Spatial Abilities', *Proceedings of the National Academy of Sciences of the United States of America*, **108**(36): 14786–8.

Hogarth, Robin M., Natalia Karelaia and Carlos Andrés Trujillo (2012), 'When Should I Quit? Gender Differences in Exiting Competitions', *Journal of Economic Behavior and Organization*, **83**(1), June: 136–50.

Ivanova-Stenzel, Radosveta and Dorothea Kübler (2011), 'Gender Differences in Team Work and Team Competition', *Journal of Economic Psychology*, **32**(5), October: 797–808.

Jurajda, Štěpán and Daniel Münnich (2008), 'Gender Gap in Admission Performance Under Competitive Pressure', Working Paper 371, Center for Economic Research and Graduate Education, Charles University, Prague.

Jurajda, Štěpán and Daniel Münnich (2011), 'Gender Gap in Performance Under Competitive Pressure: Admission to Czech Universities', *American Economic Review*, **101**(3), May: 514–18.

Kamas, Linda and Anne Preston (2009), 'Social Preferences, Competitiveness and Compensation: Are there Gender Differences?', Working Paper, Santa Clara University, Santa Clara, CA.

Lallemand, Thierry, Robert Plasman and Francois Rycx (2008), 'Women and Competition in Elimination Tournaments: Evidence from Professional Tennis Data', *Journal of Sports Economics*, **9**(1), November: 3–19.

Lavy, Victor (2008), 'Gender Differences in Market Competitiveness in a Real Workplace: Evidence from Performance-Based Pay Tournaments among Teachers', Working Paper 14338, National Bureau of Economic Research, Cambridge, MA.

Leuven, Edwin, Hessel Oosterbeek, Joep Sonnemans and Bas van der Klaauw (2011), 'Incentives versus Sorting in Tournaments: Evidence from a Field Experiment', *Journal of Labor Economics*, **29**(3), January: 637–58.

Manning, Alan and Farzad Saidi (2010), 'Understanding the Gender Pay Gap: What's

Competition Got to Do with It?', *Industrial and Labor Relations Review*, **63**(4), November: 681–98.

Matthews, Peter H., Paul M. Somers and Francisco J. Peschiera (2007), 'Incentives and Superstars on the LPGA Tour', *Applied Economics*, **39**(1), June: 87–94.

Neelakantan, Urvi (2010), 'Estimation and Impact of Gender Differences in Risk Tolerance', *Economic Inquiry*, **48**(1), January: 228–33.

Nekby, Lena, Peter Thoursie and Lars Vahtrik (2008), 'Gender and Self-selection into a Competitive Environment: Are Women more Overconfident than Men?', *Economics Letters*, **100**(3), September: 405–7.

Niederle, Muriel, Carmit Segal and Lise Vesterlund (2010), 'How Costly is Diversity? Affirmative Action in Light of Gender Differences in Competitiveness', Working Paper, Stanford University, Stanford, CA.

Niederle, Muriel and Lise Vesterlund (2007), 'Do Women Shy away from Competition? Do Men Compete too Much?', *Quarterly Journal of Economics*, **122**(3): 1067–101.

Niederle, Muriel and Lise Vesterlund (2011), 'Gender and Competition', *Annual Review of Economics*, **3**, September: 601–30.

Ors, Evren, Frédéric Palomino and Elöic Peyrache (2008), 'Performance Gender-Gap: Does Competition Matter?', Discussion Paper No. 6891, Centre for Economic Policy Research, London.

Paserman, Daniele (2007), 'Gender Differences in Performance in Competitive Environments: Evidence from Professional Tennis Players', Discussion Paper 2834, Institute for the Study of Labor, Bonn.

Paserman, Daniele (2010), 'Gender Differences in Performance in Competitive Environments: Evidence from Professional Tennis Players', Working Paper, Boston University, Cambridge, MA and Hebrew University, Jerusalem.

Price, Curtis R. (2009), 'Gender, Competition, and Managerial Decisions', Working Paper, University of Southern Indiana, Evansville, IN.

Price, Curtis R. (2010), 'Do Women Shy away from Competition? Do Men Compete too Much? A (Failed) Replication', Working Paper, University of Southern Indiana, Evansville, IN.

Price, Joseph (2008), 'Gender Differences in the Response to Competition', *Industrial and Labor Relations Review*, **61**(3), April: 320–33.

Reuben, Ernesto, Pedro Rey-Biel, Paola Sapienza and Luigi Zingales (2012), 'The Emergence of Male Leadership in Competitive Environments', *Journal of Economic Behavior and Organization*, **83**(1), June: 111–17.

Säve-Söderbergh, Jenny and Gabriella Sjögren Lindquist (2011), '"Girls will be Girls", Especially among Boys: Risk-taking in the "Daily Double" on "*Jeopardy*"', *Economics Letters*, **112**(2), August: 158–60.

Seiler, Stephen, Jos J. de Koning and Carl Foster (2007), 'The Fall and Rise of the Gender Difference in Elite Anaerobic Performance 1952–2006', *Medicine and Science in Sports and Exercise*, **39**(3), March: 534–40.

Shurchkov, Olga (2008), 'Performance in Competitive Environments: Are Women Really Different?', Department of Economics, Wellesley College Discussion Paper, Wellesley, MA.

Shurchkov, Olga (2012), 'Under Pressure: Gender Differences in Output Quality and Quantity under Competition and Time Constraints', *Journal of the European Economic Association*, **10**(5), October: 1189–213.

Sunde, Uwe (2009), 'Heterogeneity and Performance in Tournaments: A Test for Incentive Effects Using Professional Tennis Data', *Applied Economics*, **41**(25): 3199–208.

Sutter, Matthias and Daniela Rützler (2010), 'Gender Differences in Competition Emerge Early in Life', Discussion Paper 5015, Institute for the Study of Labor, Bonn.

Vandegrift, Donald and Abdullah Yavas (2009), 'Men, Women, and Competition: An Experimental Test of Behavior', *Journal of Economic Behavior and Organization*, **72**(1), October: 554–70.

Vincent, Claude and Byron Eastman (2009), 'Determinants of Pay in the NHL: A Quantile Regression Approach', *Journal of Sports Economics*, **10**(3), June: 256–77.

Wozniak, David (2012), 'Gender Differences in a Market with Relative Performance Feedback: Professional Tennis Players', *Journal of Economic Behavior and Organization*, **83**(1), June: 158–71.
Wozniak, David., William T. Harbaugh and Ulrich Mayr (2010), 'Choices about Competition: Differences by Gender and Hormonal Fluctuations, and the Role of Relative Performance Feedback', Working Paper, University of Oregon, Eugene, OR.

15. Do men and women respond differently to economic contests? The case of men's and ladies' figure skating

Eva Marikova Leeds and Michael A. Leeds[*]

15.1 INTRODUCTION

A consensus has developed in the economics literature that economic contests can elicit efficient levels of effort from the participants. This occurs in both the corporate world (for example, Bognanno, 2001) and the realm of sports. Economic contests base rewards on a participant's rank rather than marginal product. As a result, small improvements in productivity bring discrete changes in rewards if they change a participant's rank, while large improvements bring no change in reward if the participant's rank is unchanged.

Because of the detailed data on performance and compensation that exist for professional athletes, sports provide a particularly appropriate setting to analyze the incentive effects of economic contests, which are also known as rank order tournaments (ROTs). A broad literature now applies ROT theory to a variety of sports. At first, almost all applications of ROT theory to sports– like the sports economics literature in general – pertained solely to men's sports. Increasingly, however, sports data are used to test the hypothesis that women and girls are more hesitant to join a rank-order event and that they perform worse in competitive environments than men and boys. Numerous papers using experimental data have supported this hypothesis. If these experimental findings can be confirmed using 'real-world' data, then reward structures based on economic contests could place women at a distinct disadvantage to men in the labor market.

This chapter compares the impact of a particular economic contest on the performance of male and female figure skaters. Using data from the 2009–10 figure skating season, we test three hypotheses that have been raised by the experimental literature regarding the behavior of men and women. First, we ask whether men and women respond differently to the incentives provided by the competition. Second, we test whether women respond more negatively than men to disappointing performance in the early rounds of the competition. Finally, we test whether women avoid competition more than men do.

Our results largely contradict the experimental literature. We find that women respond more positively than men to the incentives posed by the economic contest presented by figure skating competitions. Similarly, female figure skaters are more resilient in the face of negative feedback than their male counterparts, and they do not avoid competing with other elite skaters. These results suggest that the findings of the experimental literature do not apply to elite female figure skaters. Further research is therefore needed before one can conclude that female executives, who, like figure skaters, have self-selected into a given occupation, are at a disadvantage in competitive settings.

Section 15.2 provides background on the theory of economic contests with specific application to sporting events. Section 15.3 explores the literature regarding differences in how men and women respond to economic contests. Section 15.4 shows how figure skating can be modeled as an economic contest. It also presents the estimating equation and describes our data set. Section 15.5 contains the estimation results, and Section 15.6 concludes.

15.2   ECONOMIC CONTESTS

The literature on economic contests begins with the seminal paper by Lazear and Rosen (1981). Lazear and Rosen note that analyses of labor markets typically assume that workers are paid their marginal revenue product, the value of their effort. A system of compensation that ties workers' pay directly to their contributions to firm revenues, often called 'piece rate', generates the efficient level of effort by workers, who exert effort until the compensation for a little more effort (producing one more piece) equals the marginal disutility of effort. The piece-rate system, however, works only if employers can observe the marginal physical product (MPP) of their employees. Unfortunately, such close monitoring of workers is either impossible or prohibitively costly for any but the simplest tasks. Thus, while it might be easy for employers to pay a piece rate if their workers sell cars or pick fruit, a piece-rate system becomes far less practical when the workers produce a less tangible, less easily counted good or service. As a result, according to Lazear and Rosen, many firms reward slightly more productive workers with wages and salaries that are much higher than the pay of their less productive coworkers, even if the absolute differences in productivity are small.

Lazear and Rosen develop a two-period model in which employers wish to elicit the optimal amount of effort from two identical employees.[1] In the first period, the employer specifies a reward structure, with the more productive employee receiving a high wage (w_1) and the less productive employee receiving a low wage (w_2). The two wages are set so that the expected profits of the firm (assumed to operate in a competitive market) are zero. In the second period, the workers effectively compete for the high wage, with the more productive employee being declared the winner. Under a set of relatively general conditions, Lazear and Rosen show that setting the appropriate spread between w_1 and w_2 elicits the efficient amount of effort by both workers. The ROT thus bases workers' rewards on their productivity relative to other workers, rather than on the absolute level of their productivity. The winner of the tournament receives a reward that exceeds his/her MRP, while the loser receives a reward that is lower than his/her MRP. The firm can elicit more effort from its workers by increasing the difference in rewards or less effort by reducing the difference in rewards. An appropriately designed ROT can reproduce the results of a piece-rate system without the costly monitoring needed for a piece-rate system.

In separate papers, Lazear and Rosen modify their basic model. Lazear (1989) notes that workplace relations can affect workers' responses to pay disparities. In particular, activities that require workers to cooperate ('teamwork') might suffer when workers focus on their individual contributions. Worse still, workers might attempt to undermine the performance of their coworkers. Rosen (1986) extends the original model to the multi-period setting of an elimination tournament. In an elimination tournament, losers at stage s of a tournament receive compensation w_s, while winners at stage s get the right to compete at stage $s + 1$, where the loser receives $w_{s+1} > w_s$. Rosen shows that the more talented participants do not exert maximal effort unless the ultimate prize is disproportionately large. Thus, as the reward for winning the tournament, w_N, rises, the chance of an upset in the tournament falls, as the more talented performers exert increasing effort.

O'Keeffe et al. (1984) extend the model by accounting for global, rather than marginal, incentives. In particular, they analyze incentives when the contest involves such unequally talented contestants that a marginal increase in effort has no impact on rank outcome. They conclude that individuals who have little chance of winning the contest maximize their utility exerting the minimum possible amount of effort required to stay in the tournament.

Ehrenberg and Bognanno (1990a and 1990b) were the first to view sports competitions as economic contests, forming the basis for the ensuing literature. They make two key observations regarding tournaments in the US and European Professional Golf Association (PGA) Tours. First, the percentage of the purse awarded to each participant follows a fixed, predetermined distribution across all tournaments. This fixed distribution of prize money awards much more of the purse to the first-place finisher than to the second-place finisher (18 versus 10 percent), and the differential falls until the reward for moving up one spot approaches zero. For example, the incentive to move from second to first place is much greater than the incentive to move from 22nd place to 21st place. Second, the size of the purse differs across tournaments so that the absolute size of the reward differential varies across tournaments even if the percentage of the purse is constant.

Ehrenberg and Bognanno (1990a and 1990b) use the above observations to formulate two hypotheses. First, they posit that golfers who enter the fourth (final) round of a tournament higher up the leader board have a greater incentive to play well than players who are farther down because the reward to improving their position is much greater. Therefore, scores for leading golfers will be better than for those who are farther behind, all else equal. Second, because larger purses lead to larger rewards to moving up the leader board, players have a greater incentive to play well in tournaments in which the total prize is greater. Thus, scores will be lower in tournaments with greater prizes, all else equal.

Ehrenberg and Bognanno test the above hypotheses by estimating the equation:

$$s_{ji} = \alpha_0 + \alpha_1 TPRIZE_i + \alpha_2 \mathbf{x_i} + \alpha_3 \mathbf{y_j} + \alpha_4 \mathbf{z_i} + v_{ij}. \qquad (15.1)$$

The explanatory variables in equation (15.1) consist of the total amount of prize money awarded in tournament i ($TPRIZE_i$) and three vectors: the first vector contains variables related to the difficulty of the course in tournament i ($\mathbf{x_i}$), the second contains variables related to the ability of golfer j ($\mathbf{y_j}$), and the third contains variables related to the ability of the other golfers in tournament i ($\mathbf{z_i}$). Equation (15.1) remains the basis for current empirical research on the impact of tournament settings.

Ehrenberg and Bognanno specify the dependent variable (s_{ji}) in three different ways. To test for the impact of the prize differential on a player's overall performance, they define the dependent variable as the total number of strokes by player j in tournament i. To test whether the differential affects all rounds of the tournament equally, they also run two separate regressions. In the first, they define s_{ji} as the number of strokes in the first two rounds ('before the cut'). In the second, they define s_{ji} as the number of strokes in the final round.

Ehrenberg and Bognanno (1990a and 1990b) obtain similar results for the US and European professional golf tours. They find that the size of the purse reduces the overall number of strokes, indicating that larger prize differentials elicit better performances. However, they find no impact on the score in the first two rounds, which suggests that the distribution and size of prize money does not affect performance when the impact of effort is still unclear. This is confirmed in the final specification. In this estimation, Ehrenberg and Bognanno use the ranking of the player headed into the final round as well as the total size of the purse to find the monetary impact of an improvement in ranking. They find that these incentives have a strong impact on golfers' scores in the final round. The link between the reward to improved standing and performance remains at the heart of empirical analyses of tournament settings.

In their study of professional road racing, Lynch and Zax (2000) explicitly consider the role of the purse on the field of competitors. When they do not control for the underlying ability of the participants, Lynch and Zax find that larger purses lead to superior performances. When they control for underlying ability, their results show that the faster times result from the fact that larger purses attract better runners. The superior performance could thus result from self-selection by potential participants rather than stronger incentives for those who do participate.

Gilsdorf and Sukhatme (2008a and 2008b) test Rosen's theory of elimination tournaments in women's and men's professional tennis. They find evidence supporting Rosen's (1986) theory that greater mismatches result in lower effort for both men and women. They also find that larger purses, and hence larger monetary differences in prize money for the winner and loser, increase the probability that the favored player wins at each stage of the tournament.

Frick et al. (2003) test Lazear's hypothesis that teamwork limits the power of pay differentials to stimulate performance. They specify team performance for the four major North American sports leagues (Major League Baseball: MLB; the National Baseball Association: NBA; the National Football League: NFL; and the National Hockey League: NHL) and find that salary differentials among teammates, as measured by the Gini coefficient, have an uneven impact on team performance. In particular, they find that pay spreads have a positive impact on performance in the NBA, a statistically insignificant impact in the NFL and NHL, and a negative impact in MLB.

15.3 GENDER DIFFERENCES IN THE RESPONSE TO ECONOMIC CONTESTS AND COMPETITIVESS IN SPORTS

15.3.1 Economic Contests

There is now a large literature detailing the different ways in which men and women respond to economic contests. The broad conclusions of this literature (excellently summarized by Croson and Gneezy, 2009) are that women do not respond as well as men when the reward is determined competitively, with the winner taking a disproportionate reward. Consistent with this finding, women are more reluctant than men to enter such competitions. Such aversion to competition could put women at a disadvantage in the corporate world and in other settings where rewards are set by competition among workers. Much of this literature, however, is based on experiments, whose results are often contradicted by studies using non-experimental data.

In one of the first tests of gender differences in contests, Gneezy et al. (2003) conducted a controlled experiment in which students at the Technion, an engineering university in Israel, were asked to solve mazes. Some of the students were told that they would be rewarded based on the number of mazes they solved in a given time period (a piece-rate scheme), while others were told that the person who solved the most mazes in their group would receive the prize. They found no difference, on average, in the number of mazes men and women solved in the piece-rate setting. However, when faced with a competitive setting, men's performance improved but women's performance was unchanged, resulting in a gender gap. They found that the gap was greatest in mixed-gender groups.

Gneezy and Rustichini's (2004) results largely support the earlier findings. They had Israeli fourth graders run in timed, individual settings and then in head-to-head competitions. They found that girls ran more slowly in the head-to-head competition than in the non-competitive settings, while boys ran faster. Their results were independent of the gender composition of the race (same-sex or mixed) or the relative abilities of the competitors, as measured by their results in the non-competitive race.

Booth and Nolen (2012) note one potential consequence of the gender difference in performance. They randomly sorted a sample of English high-school students into single-sex and mixed groups and then, like Gneezy et al. (2003), had the students solve mazes under piece rates in one round and in tournament settings in another round. In the third round, they allowed the students to choose either a piece rate or tournament reward system. They found that girls were more likely than boys to choose the piece-rate setting, though the gap was smaller for girls who attended single-sex high schools.

Gill and Prowse (2010) provide an important insight into why women perform relatively poorly in economic contests and seek to avoid them more than men. In their experiment, men and women were randomly assigned to groups of two, though the identity of the partner was kept secret. All participants were asked to position a 'slider' on a computer screen using a mouse. They were scored based on how many sliders they were able to place at exactly 50 on a scale of 0 to 100 in two minutes. The prize for the round was then awarded to a single winner, based on a lottery. The likelihood of winning the lottery rose with the participant's performance of the task.[2] Performance was thus not the sole determinant of whether a person won the prize, as the luck of the draw also played a significant role in determining the winner. Gill and Prowse find that women respond to not winning as a result of bad luck by reducing their effort in later rounds of the experiment. The gender difference in the response to bad luck is so pronounced that the 'differential responses to luck account for about half of the gender performance gap that we observe in our experiment' (p. 1).

15.3.2 Competitiveness

There is a small but growing literature concerning gender differences in the response to competitive settings in sports. The evidence of these studies is decidedly mixed. Some studies find differences in behavior of men and women, but the stark contrast of the experimental studies is generally not supported. This contradiction between experimental and non-experimental settings might reflect the fact that labor markets do not have random assignments of workers. Instead, individuals – ranging from professional athletes to corporate executives – self-select into specific occupations, which could result in behavior that differs from that in a laboratory setting.

Matthews et al. (2007) apply Ehrenberg and Bognanno's (1990a and 1990b) model to women's golf on the LPGA Tour. They find evidence that women respond negatively to incentives by shooting higher scores in tournaments that offer higher purses.[3] There are, however, two weaknesses with this argument. First, the evidence of a perverse effect is not strong, as the key coefficients are frequently statistically insignificant. Second, the results might be affected by selection bias because Matthews et al. include only golfers who were among the top 50 money winners in 2000.

Gilsdorf and Sukhatme (2008a and 2008b) find little difference in the behavior of male and female tennis players. Using probit estimation, they show that purse size is positively related to the likelihood that higher-seeded players win in both men's and women's tennis tournaments, as predicted by Rosen (1986). Because each match in an elimination tournament must have a winner and a loser, Gilsdorf and Sukhatme's results are necessarily measures of relative outcomes. By construction, the study cannot address whether the overall quality of play increases or decreases with the size of the purse or how this change compares with the quality of play in men's competition.

Paserman (2010) also finds no support for gender differences in competitive situations. He uses stroke-by-stroke data from seven Grand Slam tennis tournaments to analyze how men and women respond to pressure situations. He finds that both men and women play more cautiously and hence make fewer unforced errors at key points in the match. The drop in unforced errors by men and women is statistically indistinguishable.

Unlike the other studies in sports, Frick (2011) addresses gender differences in participation decisions rather than in performance. His results support Booth and Nolen's (2012) hypothesis that women avoid competitive situations. To do this, he matches the finishing times for the top 200 male and female runners at each distance from 3,000m to the marathon, using data from 1973 through 2009. Frick computes the percentage difference in times by the man and woman at each rank and finds that the percentage difference between men's and women's times grows as the numerical rank rises (meaning the rank worsens). He concludes from this finding that the field of women runners was less balanced than the men's field, in that poorly ranked men are closer to the top-ranked men than is the case for women. Because men and women have the same number of lucrative races, Frick concludes that the top female athletes were able to avoid competing against each other by strategically entering certain events. He finds, however, that this avoidance has declined over time.

15.4   FIGURE SKATING AS AN ECONOMIC CONTEST

We have shown above that the experimental literature and the non-experimental studies that use sports competitions frequently yield contradictory results. One reason for this inconsistency is the failure of the non-experimental literature to screen out factors that could confound the results of the contest. Figure skating competitions provide a more perfect 'laboratory' because they avoid two important pitfalls that confront most previous studies of sports contests.

First, many previous studies of economic contests in sports involve head-to-head competition. In some cases, as in tennis, the studies look only at relative performance. They therefore cannot say whether the outcome results from one player's elevating her game or the other player's falling back.[4] Even unforced errors, as measured by Paserman (2010), could be a response to an opponent who is dominating the match or simply playing unexpectedly well. The same could be true in competitions that are not explicitly confrontational, such as racing or golf. In these supposedly individual sports, one performs simultaneously with one or more opponents, so one's performance could be a direct response to what they do. A runner, for example, could respond to an unusually fast or slow pace set by her competitors, or a golfer could attempt a particularly risky shot after seeing a golfer in her group make a spectacular shot.

In figure skating, the competitors perform sequentially, and, as a result, cannot be affected by the skaters who come after them. The impact of earlier skaters is only indirect, as skaters perform routines that are generally known in advance and offer little room for spontaneity. Thus, skaters can react only to the knowledge that the earlier skaters have performed particularly well or particularly poorly. Hence, one skater's performance is less likely to have a direct impact on the performance of another skater than is the case in most other athletic competitions. In addition, we have access to the scores of all skaters, so we can measure the absolute level of performance of each woman, not just her relative performance.

Second, the other sports are exposed to the elements. Studies of performance must therefore take account of such outside forces as the weather or the difficulty of a course. Even the most comprehensive of datasets cannot fully account for all such factors, as they can change from one moment to the next. The best one can do is hope that the omitted variables have a random effect on performance. In contrast, figure skating competitions take place on a uniform surface over a fixed period of time. There is therefore little chance that outside factors beyond the competitors' control will affect the quality of the performance.

Figure skating also enables us to look beyond how men and women respond to tournament conditions and test how men and women respond to positive or negative feedback. Because the competition takes place in two stages, skaters enter the Free Skate knowing how they had been judged in the Short Program. (The segments of figure skating competition are described in detail below.) They skate in groups of six, with the six skaters with the worst Short Program scores skating first and the six skaters with the best Short Program scores skating last. The order within each group of six is determined by a random draw. The results of the Free Skate (also known as the 'Long Program') allow us to test whether men women and men respond to relatively poor performances by reducing their effort, as suggested by Booth and Nolen (2012) and by Gill and Prowse (2010).

Finally, we can test whether Frick's (2011) claim – that elite women avoid head-to-head competition with one another while men do not – extends to figure skating. Our data from the 2009–10 figure skating season allow us to identify the participants in each of the competitions. We can combine these data with skaters' points from the previous season to test whether the women's field in any given competition is more or less homogeneous than the field in the men's side of the same competition.

15.4.1   Figure Skating as an Economic Contest

Like the golf tournaments studied by Ehrenberg and Bognanno (1990a and 1990b), figure skating competitions involve multiple rounds. Skaters typically participate in two rounds, each of which is evaluated by a panel of judges.[5] As in golf, a skater's rank is determined by the sum of the two scores. Unlike golfers, figure skaters win by receiving the highest (as opposed to the lowest) score. In addition, while golf consists of playing the same set of 18 holes four times, a skating competition consists of two very different stages.

The first portion of a skating competition is known as the 'Short Program'. The Men's and Ladies Short Programs both last two minutes and fifty seconds, with a penalty assessed against skaters who exceed their allotted times. In 2009–10, the Ladies' Short Program contained eight required elements, consisting of three types of jumps, three types of spins, a step sequence, and a spiral sequence.[6] The Men's Short Program also required three jumps and spins, but the spiral sequence was replaced with another step sequences. For a detailed listing of the elements, see Appendix 15A1. Skaters perform the Short Program in random order and are then divided into groups of six based on their scores. The group with the lowest (worst) six scores performs the Free Skate first. Subsequent groups contain better-ranked skaters until the group with the highest (best) six scores skates last. (There is a maximum of four groups.) The order within each group of six in the Free Skate is randomly determined.

As its name suggests, the Free Skate gives competitors more freedom over the individual components of their performances than the Short Program does. The Ladies' Free Skate lasts four minutes and must contain seven jump elements, three combinations, three spins, one step sequence, and one spiral sequence. The Men's Free Skate lasts a half-minute longer. The men may perform up to eight jump elements, three spins, three combinations, and two step sequences. For a detailed explanation of how judges score skating routines, see Appendix 15A2.

The reward structure in figure skating is based on a skater's final standing rather than on the total number of points she is awarded. We include several different types of figure skating competitions. The 2010 Olympics and the 2010 World Championship are by far the two most prestigious events in our sample. Although neither competition carries an explicit monetary award, a skater's fame and chances for outside income typically depend on finishing 'on the podium', among the top three skaters.[7]

The European Championship is not on the same level as the World Championship, but it is a major international competition that assembles many of the world's top figure skaters. The European Championship was prestigious enough that the International Skating Union (ISU) – the body that oversees figure skating, synchronized skating, speed skating, and short-track speed skating – created the Four Continents Championship for skaters from Africa, the Americas, Asia, and the Americas in 1999 to serve as an equivalent competition. Finally, we include the ISU Grand Prix events. The skaters with the top cumulative scores in the season's Grand Prix competitions meet in the ISU Grand Prix Final. In Grand Prix events themselves, monetary prizes depend on the skaters' order of finish rather than on the number of points she accumulated.

15.4.2 Estimation and Data

Our estimating equation closely resembles that of Ehrenberg and Bognanno (1990a and 1990b):

$$s_{ij} = \beta_0 + \beta_1 x_i + \beta_2 y_j + \beta_3 z_{ij} + \varepsilon_{ij} \qquad (15.2)$$

In Equation (15.2), s_{ij} is the Free Skate score by skater i in competition j, x_i is a vector of variables pertaining to the ability of skater i, y_j is a vector of variables describing competition j, and z_{ij} is a vector of variables reflecting the performance of skater i in the Short Program of competition j. (Because prize money is not always awarded, we have left out the prize variable.) The vector x_i contains variables relating the skater's age and the number of points he/she accumulated in 2008–09 competitions. We have no clear prediction as to the impact of a skater's age, but we do expect a higher score in 2008–09 to imply that a skater is more inherently talented and will perform better in 2009–10 competitions.

Unlike Ehrenberg and Bognanno, we do not have to account for many external factors that would affect an athlete's performance, such as differences in course size or weather conditions, as each skating competition takes place under uniform physical conditions. However, there are a number of competition-specific factors that could affect the final score. First, it is possible that the judging in some competitions is harsher than the judging in others. To capture the fact that all scores might be higher or lower in some competitions, the vector y_j contains the mean score of all skaters in the competition's Short Program and whether the competition took place in the skater's home country. In addition, while the Olympics and the World Championships do not have a monetary prize structure, they are better known than the other competitions, and success in them is likely to have a greater impact on a skater's lifetime income than success in any other competition. We therefore include dummy variables that indicate whether the competition was the Olympics or the World Championship.

The average level of judging in the Short Program could reflect easier judging overall or could lead judges to 'make up' for the high scores by judging the Free Skate more harshly. We have no clear prediction regarding its effect. We do expect a 'home ice' advantage thanks to less travel and a more supportive audience. In addition, studies of basketball have shown that home fans affect the judgment of referees (Moskowitz and Wertheim, 2011). While such an impact would add to the home ice advantage, the judging system described above was instituted in part to minimize subjectivity in judging, thereby reducing the impact of a home crowd on judges. The total score is determined by a randomly selected subset of the judges marking the event.

If figure skating competitions had the same incentive effects as the golf tournaments analyzed by Ehrenberg and Bognanno (1990a and 1990b), a skater's performance should be better in the more highly valued events, even after controlling for the quality of the competitors. We therefore expect the dummy variables for the Olympics and World Championships to have a positive effect on Free Skate scores.

Finally, we include a set of variables that capture the individual skater's performance going into the Free Skate. These variables consist of the skater's score in the Short Program, the skater's rank after the Short Program, the number of points by which the skater trails the leading skater after the Short Program, and whether the skater is among the best six skaters entering the Free Skate and thus skates in the last group.

A performance in the Short Program that places a skater closer to the leader increases the likelihood that the skater could win the competition – or at least end up on the podium with a good performance in the Free Skate. We expect all measures of individual performance in the Short Program to be directly related to the skater's score in the Free Skate.

Unfortunately, these variables do not capture only incentive effects. Even the best of skaters can have a subpar competition, and sometimes a lesser skater can have the competition of a lifetime to upset otherwise more accomplished skaters. A positive coefficient on the variables related to a skater's score in the Short Program could reflect either the response to incentives or the continuation of a positive or negative 'shock' in that competition.

One variable, however, explicitly captures the incentive effect. In addition to the absolute performance as measured by the Short Program score and the relative position given by the placement entering the Free Skate, we have a dummy variable that indicates whether the skater was in the final group of skaters for the Free Skate. As noted above, the group in which skaters perform their Free Skate is determined by their performance in the Short Program. A skater's appearing in the final group provides no new information on skill or incentives once one controls for the variables described above. However, skating in the final six, with the top skaters in the competition, changes the 'atmospherics' surrounding the skater. If, as hypothesized by Booth and Nolen (2012) and Gill and Prowse (2010), women respond more negatively to disappointment than men do, then skating in the final six should have a stronger impact on women than on men.

In a second regression we add an interaction term that equals the product of the skater's point total in 2008–09 and a dummy variable that equals one if the competition was the Olympics or the World Championship. We include this variable to determine whether more talented skaters perform better in the more prestigious competitions. This test is analogous to that performed by Gilsdorf and Sukhatme (2008a and 2008b) when they test whether favored tennis players are more likely to win a match when the match has a greater monetary reward.

We collected data for competition results of seven ISU 'Grand Prix' events plus four championship events: the European and Four Continents Championships, the 2010 Olympics, and the 2010 World Championships (ISU 2009a–g, 2010a–c).[8] The websites for these events provided detailed information on the skaters' performances as well as their ages and home countries. We obtained data on the skater's performance in the 2008–09 season from figure skating world rankings (ISU 2011). The ISU calculates this performance measure by adding the skaters' scores in the Olympics and/or World Championships and their top and second-best scores in Grand Prix and other international competitions. We used the total points for the 2008–09 season as a measure of a skater's ability entering the 2009–10 season. Evgeny Plushenko presented something of a problem, as he did not skate competitively during the 2008–09 season but was a dominant skater in the following season. Rather than delete him from the sample, we gave him a score that was equal to the highest men's point total in 2008–09.

The means for the variables appear in Table 15.1. Men were, on average, about a year and a half older than women. Men's scores in the Free Skate were about 32.5 points higher, in part reflecting the greater length of the program and the greater number of permitted jumps. Partly because the Short Program is the same length and because the routines are more precisely delineated, the difference between the mean scores of men and women was only 6.5 points. Average total points in 2008–09 were lower for men, probably because we had data for more men, which means that

Table 15.1   Means of key variables

Variable	Men	Women
Age of Competitor	22.14	20.41
Score in the Short Program	69.10	54.11
Rank after Short Program	9.07	9.03
Mean Score of Short Program	60.32	53.88
Skated on Home Ice (% of total)	0.14	0.14
In Last Group of Skaters (% of total)	0.40	0.42
Olympic Competition (% of total)	0.14	0.16
World Championship (% of total)	0.14	0.16
Points in 2008–2009	545.50	690.07
Points Behind Top Skater	16.48	13.62
Score in Free Skate	128.25	95.65

our men's sample had more marginal skaters. The only other difference of note was that, on average, men trailed the leading skater by almost three points more than the average woman did in 2009–10, though this could be due to the larger sample of men.

15.5   RESULTS

Before running regressions to analyze skaters' responses to tournament settings, we checked the data to see whether elite female figure skaters avoided head-to-head competition, as Frick (2012) claims is the case for elite female distance runners. Unlike Frick, we collected only one year of data, so we could not compare results by rank, as he did for runners. Instead, we computed the coefficient of variation of the 2008–09 point totals for each competition in our sample. If competitive balance is worse among women than among men, we would expect the variance (standardized by the mean point total) to be greater for women.

The first two columns of Table 15.2 show the coefficient of variation for the tournaments included in this study. While the values for men and women are fairly close, the coefficient of variation is consistently larger for women. This need not indicate, however, that women strategically enter tournaments, as the coefficient of variation for women is higher in the four championship tournaments, which are highly unlikely to be subject to strategic entry (the Four Continents Championship, the European Championship, the World Championship, and the Olympics). It is almost certain that every eligible man and woman would take part in these com-

Table 15.2 Coefficient of variation of 2008–2009, points for men's and ladies' competitions

Tournament	CV – men	CV – women	Ratio – men	Ratio – women
Trophée Eric Bompard	0.529	0.652	0.859	0.842
Skate Canada	0.496	0.671	0.805	0.867
Skate America	0.521	0.712	0.846	0.920
Rostelecom Cup	0.580	0.691	0.940	0.893
NHK Trophy	0.565	0.562	0.916	0.725
Cup of China	0.614	0.796	0.995	1.029
Grand Prix Finals	0.556	0.322	N/A	N/A
Four Continents	1.184	1.432	N/A	N/A
European Championships	0.639	0.987	N/A	N/A
World Championships	0.648	0.890	N/A	N/A
Olympics	0.617	0.774	N/A	N/A

petitions. A higher coefficient of variation may indicate a greater spread of abilities among women. We therefore treat the coefficient of variation for the Olympics as a baseline measure of competitive balance and compute the ratio of the coefficient of variation in each of the Grand Prix tournaments to the coefficient of variation in the Olympics. (We do not include the Grand Prix Final, as the participants in the final event are determined based on the results of the previous six events.) When we do that, we see even less difference between men and women, with the ratio being greater for women in three tournaments and greater for men in three tournaments as well.

The results of the OLS regressions appear in Table 15.3. Overall, the regressions fit the data very well, with adjusted R^2s of just below 0.7 for men and just over 0.7 for women. Our findings in the first two columns of the table generally show that figure skaters respond to incentives, though their responses differ from what the existing literature would lead one to expect. The results show that the economic contest structure has a slightly negative impact on the performance of men but generally has a positive impact on the performance of women.

Two control variables have no effect on either men or women. As age has no clear a priori effect, we were not surprised that it had no significant impact.[9] Similarly, the results show no 'home ice' advantage. Apparently, a friendly crowd does not have the same impact in figure skating that Moskowitz and Wertheim (2011) claim it has in other sports.

Table 15.3   Determinants of free skate score

Variable	Baseline regression		Interaction	
	Men	Women	Men	Women
Age of Competitor	0.073	−0.321	0.073	−0.322
	(0.24)	(1.33)	(0.24)	(1.33)
Points in 2008–2009	0.010***	0.0112***	0.009***	0.109***
	(3.71)	(4.71)	(2.97)	(3.92)
Mean Score of Short	−0.362	−0.2039	−0.325	−0.190
Program	(1.22)	(0.60)	(1.07)	(0.55)
Skated on Home Ice	−2.683	−1.0221	−2.649	−1.079
	(0.99)	(0.44)	(0.98)	(0.47)
Olympic Competition	1.247	18.6915***	−0.837	17.730***
	(0.31)	(5.08)	(0.15)	(3.25)
World Championship	1.763	11.2342***	0.132	10.375**
	(0.49)	(3.78)	(0.132)	(2.22)
Score in the Short	1.334***	0.3900	1.309***	0.398
Program	(3.80)	(1.42)	(3.67)	(1.43)
Rank after Short	0.171	−0.9473***	0.272	−0.922***
Program	(0.29)	(2.99)	(0.44)	(2.75)
In Last Group of	−4.990*	0.0225	−4.839	0.156
Skaters	(1.66)	(0.01)	(1.60)	(0.06)
Points Behind Top	−0.305	−0.308*	−0.372	−0.308*
Skater	(0.66)	(1.69)	(0.77)	(1.69)
Points × Major	N/A	N/A	0.003	0.001
Championship			(0.55)	(0.24)
Constant	59.545***	92.520***	59.616***	91.366***
	(2.75)	(5.51)	(2.74)	(5.21)
Adjusted R^2	0.672	0.711	0.671	0.709
Number of observations	165	145	165	145

Note: *t*-statistics in parentheses; * significant at 10 percent; ** significant at 5 percent; *** significant at 1 percent.

A third control variable, the points a skater accrued in 2008–09, had a statistically significant, positive impact for both sexes. This finding leads to the reassuring conclusion that better skaters got higher scores in the 2009–10 season. For both men and women, every additional 100 total points in the previous season led to a little more than 1.1 additional points in a 2009–10 Free Skate. It is the only variable to have a statistically significant result for both men and women.

The dummy variables that indicated whether the competition was the Olympics or the World Championships had a statistically significant, positive impact on women's but not on men's performances. Women's scores were far higher in both the Olympics and the World Championship than in the other competitions, even after we accounted for the quality of the skater. It is also possible that the stakes for men – in terms of endorsements and exhibitions – are lower for men than for women, but that lies beyond the scope of this study. Because these competitions are the most widely publicized and lead to greater professional and commercial opportunities than the other competitions, we take these results as indicating that female figure skaters respond positively to the greater incentives provided by these events.

Skaters' performance in the Short Program had a mixed impact on their performance in the Free Skate. The first measure of Short Program performance, the overall mean score of the Short Program, had no impact for either men or women. This suggests that high overall scores in the Short Program did not indicate that judges were generally lenient, nor did they indicate that judges would 'make up' for high scores by being particularly strict in their scoring of the Free Skate.

Skaters' individual performances in the Short Program had significant effects, but they differed for men and women. In fact, no variable had a significant impact for both sexes. A skater's score in the Short Program had a positive impact on men's score in the Free Skate, but it had no impact for women. The fact that the impact did not hold for women leads us to believe that this coefficient does not reflect behavior by the judges. A skater's absolute score does not reflect his or her likelihood of winning the overall competition, as it says nothing about where this score falls relative to the competition. We therefore cannot conclude anything about a skater's response to incentives from this coefficient. It could simply show that a male skater was having a good week.

The two variables that most closely reflect the incentives laid out by Ehrenberg and Bognanno (1990a and 1990b) are a skater's rank after the short program and the number of points by which a skater trails the leader after the Short Program. In both cases, a higher value of the variable reduces the chance that the skater will win the competition and that he or she will be on the podium at all. A higher rank number means that the skater must pass more competitors to catch the leading skater, and a greater point differential means that the skater has to skate that much better to catch the leaders. Thus, negative coefficients for these two variables imply that a skater has a worse Free Skate if her rank after the Short Program is worse and that she also has a worse Free Skate if she trails the leading skater by more points. Conversely, a skater who is closer to leader will perform better in the Free Skate. These responses are consistent with the incentive effects first laid out by Ehrenberg and Bognanno. Both of these variables have a negative impact on a woman's Free Skate score but have no impact on a man's score. Female figure skaters therefore respond consistently with the predictions of the Ehrenberg–Bognanno framework, but male figure skaters do not.

The final Short Program variable, whether the skater is placed in the best group of six skaters, who perform last, fails to support the hypothesis that women respond poorly to setbacks. In fact, it suggests just the opposite. The coefficient is insignificant for women, which implies that the atmospherics surrounding being in the final group of skaters have no impact on their scores. Men, on the other hand, respond negatively to being in the final group, suggesting that they are more likely to succumb to jitters than women are.

The last two columns of Table 15.3 add an interaction effect between the major competitions – the World Championships and the Olympics – and the players' rank in 2008–09. This variable captures the interplay of rank and incentives noted in Gilsdorf and Sukhatme (2008a and 2008b). They found that more highly seeded tennis players were more likely to win a match when more prize money was at stake. While the World Championships and Olympics do not offer a direct payoff, they clearly are the most lucrative skating competitions in terms of prestige and lifetime earnings. If figure skaters behaved like tennis players, one would expect this variable to have a positive impact, as better skaters will have higher Free Skate scores in the major competitions. We find no such impact, as the coefficient on this variable is statistically insignificant, and including this variable has minimal impact on the other coefficients.

15.6   CONCLUSION

As with many other areas of economic theory, sports provide an excellent 'laboratory' for the study of how women and men respond to economic contests. Ironically, the results from this laboratory frequently contradict the findings of truly experimental studies. The experimental literature consistently finds that women respond worse than men to tournament settings. Non-experimental studies using data from tennis (Gilsdorf and Sukhatme, 2008a and 2008b) and golf (Paserman, 2010) find no difference in how men and women respond. Studies of golf and tennis, however, cannot control perfectly for weather conditions or for interactions among the participants. Our study of figure skating builds on previous sports studies by controlling for the conditions under which the participants perform and minimizing the interaction between the participants.

Using data from 11 skating contests from the 2009–10 skating season, we find that women respond positively to incentives. Our results support previous non-experimental findings and contradict much of the experimental literature. We go beyond the previous literature in showing that female figure skaters respond more positively to incentives than male skaters do.

Because the most important figure skating events do not offer an explicit prize, we cannot directly measure how monetary incentives affect performance. However, we show that women respond very strongly to being on the big stage provided by the Olympics and World Championships, while men do not respond at all. Because winning at the Olympics and World Championships is far more prestigious and more lucrative (albeit indirectly) than the other tournaments, one can interpret this result as saying that women respond positively to a higher overall purse, as Ehrenberg and Bognanno (1990a and 1990b) found for male golfers.

We also find that women who are more highly ranked and closer to the leader after the Short Program score more highly in the Free Skate. These results show that skaters who are higher up the reward gradient entering the Free Skate respond positively to the greater incentive to perform well. This result is again analogous to Ehrenberg and Bognanno's findings for male golfers.

Contrary to Ehrenberg and Bognanno's findings for golfers, male skaters do not respond to either the purse size or their position on the reward gradient. A better absolute score in the Short Program leads to a better score in the Free Skate, but the absolute score says nothing about the skater's position relative to his competitors. Moreover, we find that male skaters respond negatively to the pressure of being among the final six skaters – those who have the best chance of finishing 'on the podium'.

We also have two results that contradict previous non-experimental findings. Unlike Gilsdorf and Sukhatme (2008a and 2008b), who find that favorites in elimination tournaments are more likely to win a match when greater rewards are on the line, we find that the better skaters (as measured by total points in the previous season) do no better in the Olympics and World Championships than in the ISU tour events.

Finally, we find no evidence that female figure skaters enter events strategically in order to avoid competing with one another. If women sought out less-competitive fields, then the coefficient of variation of the skaters' ISU points earned in the 2008–09 season (our measure of the talent of the skater in the 2009–10 season) for the six ISU Grand Prix events in 2009–10 should be higher for women than for men. Instead, we find that the coefficient of variation is greater for men in three of the six events. This finding suggests either that female figure skaters behave differently from the female distance runners studied by Frick (2011) or that female figure skaters do not have enough events to be able avoid other elite competitors.

When combined with the results from other sports, our key findings indicate that economic contests might not place women at the severe disadvantage that the experimental studies suggest in either sports or broader labor markets. The conflict between the two sets of results is puzzling until one recognizes that an experimental setting fails to capture an important aspect of the job market. Experimental studies rightly take great care in randomly assigning people to tasks, but the labor market is hardly random. Workers – like athletes – self-select into activities for which they are particularly well-suited and strongly motivated. We find – and many of the other results that use data from sports indicate – that such women respond at least as well as men to the incentives that ROTs provide. Further work will show whether this finding extends to women in the corporate world as well.

NOTES

*   We thank Jane Ruseski for her helpful comments on an earlier draft of this chapter and Melanie Leeds for her able research assistance.
1.   Their findings can be extended to a larger workforce.
2.   The probability of winning the prize was $(50 + \Delta)/100$, where Δ is the differential in the scores of the two participants.
3.   For evidence that reinforces this result and finds a similar result for men on the PGA tour, see Chapter 5 in this volume.
4.   Technically, one could try to get at this by looking at such measures as unforced errors and winning shots.
5.   Some of the large competitions also have a preliminary round, though we ignore that here.
6.   The spiral sequence was deleted from the Short Program starting in the 2010–11 season.
7.   Some nations provide supplemental payments and other benefits, such as exemption from otherwise mandatory military service (in the case of South Korea) for world champions or Olympic medalists. In addition, a country's representation in the next year's World Championships depends on the placement of its skaters in the current championships.
8.   The Grand Prix events were the Cancer.net Skate America, the Cup of China, HomeSense Skate Canada, the NHK Trophy, the Rostelecom Cup, the Trophée Eric Bompard, and the Grand Prix Final. The regional events were the European Championships and the Four Continents Championship.
9.   We had wanted to use age squared as well, but, because the ages of the competitors are from such a narrow range, age and age squared were too highly correlated to use in the same regression.

REFERENCES

Bognanno, Michael L. (2001). 'Corporate Tournaments', *Journal of Labor Economics*, **19**(2), April: 290–315.

Booth, Alison and Patrick Nolen (2012), 'Choosing to Compete: How Different Are Girls and Boys?', *Journal of Economic Behavior and Organization*, **81**(2), February: 542–55.

Croson, Rachel and Uri Gneezy (2009), 'Gender Differences in Preferences', *Journal of Economic Literature*, **47**(2), June: 1–27.

Ehrenberg, Ronald G. and Michael L. Bognanno (1990a), 'The Incentive Effects of Tournaments Revisited: Evidence from the European PGA Tour', *Industrial and Labor Relations Review*, **43**(3), February: S74–88.

Ehrenberg, Ronald G. and Michael L. Bognanno (1990b), 'Do Tournaments Have Incentive Effects?', *Journal of Political Economy*, **98**(6), December: 1307–24.

Frick, Bernd (2011), 'Gender Difference in Competitiveness: Empirical Evidence from Professional Distance Running', *Labour Economics*, **18**(3), June: 389–98.

Frick, Bernd, Joachim Prinz and Karina Winkelmann (2003), 'Pay Inequality and Team Performance: Empirical Evidence from the North American Major Leagues', *International Journal of Manpower*, **24**(4): 472–88.

Gill, David and Victoria Prowse (2010), 'Gender Differences and Dynamics in Competition: The Role of Luck', IZA Discussion Paper Series, No. 5022, June.

Gilsdorf, Keith F. and Vasant A. Sukhatme (2008a), 'Tournament Incentives and Match Outcomes in Women's Professional Tennis', *Applied Economics*, **40**(18), September: 2405–12.

Gilsdorf, Keith F. and Vasant A. Sukhatme (2008b), 'Testing Rosen's Sequential Elimination Tournament Model: Incentives and Player Performance in Professional Tennis', *Journal of Sports Economics*, **9**(3), June: 287–303.

Gneezy, Uri, Muriel Niederle and Aldo Rustichini (2003), 'Performance in Competitive Environments: Gender Difference', *Quarterly Journal of Economics,* **118**(3), August: 1049–74.

Gneezy, Uri and Aldo Rustichini (2004), 'Gender and Competition at a Young Age', *American Economic Review*, **94**(2), May: 377–81.

International Skating Union (ISU) (2009a), 'Cancer.net Skate America', *ISU Grand Prix of Figure Skating 2009/2010*, online at:http://www.isuresults.com/results/gpusa09/index.htm (accessed September 15, 2010).

International Skating Union (2009b), 'Cup of China', *ISU Grand Prix of Figure Skating 2009/2010*, online at: http://www.isuresults.com/results/gpchn09/index.htm (accessed September 15, 2010).

International Skating Union (ISU) (2009c), 'HomeSense Skate Canada', *ISU Grand Prix of Figure Skating 2009/2010*, online at: http://www.isuresults.com/results/gpcan09/index.htm (accessed September 15, 2010).

International Skating Union (ISU) (2009d), *ISU Grand Prix of Figure Skating Final 2009/2010*, online at: http://www.isuresults.com/results/gpf0910/index.htm) (accessed September 15, 2010).

International Skating Union (ISU) (2009e), 'NHK Trophy', *ISU Grand Prix of Figure Skating 2009/2010*, online at: http://www.isuresults.com/results/gpjpn09/index.htm (accessed September 15, 2010).

International Skating Union (ISU) (2009f), 'Rostelecom Cup', *ISU Grand Prix of Figure Skating 2009/2010*, online at: http://www.isuresults.com/results/gprus09/index.htm (accessed September 15, 2010).

International Skating Union (ISU) (2009g), 'Trophée Eric Bompard', *ISU Grand Prix of Figure Skating 2009/2010*, online at: http://www.isuresults.com/results/gpfra09/index.htm (accessed September 15, 2010).

International Skating Union (ISU) (2010a), *ISU European Figure Skating Championships 2010*, online at: http://www.isuresults.com/results/ec2010/index.htm (accessed September 15, 2010).

International Skating Union (ISU) (2010b), *ISU Four Continents Figure Skating Championships 2010*, online at: http://www.isuresults.com/results/fc2010/index.htm (accessed September 15, 2010).

International Skating Union (ISU) (2010c), *ISU Four Continents Figure Skating Championships 2010*, online at http://www.isuresults.com/results/wc2010/index.htm (accessed September 15, 2010).

International Skating Union (ISU) (2011), *ISU World Standings for Single and Pair Skating and Ice Dance*, online at: http://www.isuresults.com/ws/ws/wsladies.htm (accessed March 14, 2011).

Lazear, Edwin P. (1989), 'Pay Equality and Industrial Politics', *Journal of Political Economy*, **97**(3), June: 561–80.

Lazear, Edwin P. and Sherwin Rosen (1981), 'Rank Order Tournaments as Optimum Labor Contracts', *Journal of Political Economy*, **89**(5), October: 841–64.

Lynch, James G. and Jeffrey S. Zax (2000), 'The Rewards to Running: Prize Structure and Performance in Professional Road Racing', *Journal of Sports Economics*, **1**(4), November: 323–40.

Matthews, Peter, Paul Sommers and Francisco Peschiera (2007), 'Incentives and Superstars on the LPGA Tour', *Applied Economics*, **39**(1–3), January: 87–94.

Moskowitz, Tobias J. and L. Jon Wertheim (2011), *Scorecasting*, New York: Crown Archetype.

O'Keeffe, Mary, W. Kip Viscusi and Richard J. Zeckhauser (1984), 'Economic Contests: Comparative Reward Schemes', *Journal of Labor Economics*, **2**(1), January: 27–56.

Paserman, M. Daniele (2010), 'Gender Difference in Competitive Environments? Evidence from Professional Tennis Players', Boston University Working Paper WP2010-047, Boston, MA, January.

Rosen, Sherwin (1986), 'Prizes and Incentives in Elimination Tournaments', *American Economic Review*, **76**(4), September: 701–15.

US Figure Skating (2010), 'International Judging System (IJS)', *Welcome to U.S. Figure Skating*, online at: http://www.usfigureskating.org/New_Judging.asp?id=289 (accessed May 20, 2011).

APPENDIX 15A1 THE COMPOSITION OF THE MEN'S AND LADIES' SHORT PROGRAM AND FREE SKATE

Men's Short Program required elements:

- Lasts 2:50
- Three Jump Elements
  A double or triple axel jump
  A triple or quadruple jump immediately preceded by connecting steps
  A jump combination consisting of a double jump and a triple jump, two triple jumps, or a quadruple jump and a double or triple jump
- Three Spin Elements
  A flying spin
  A camel or sit spin with one change of foot
  A spin combination with one change of foot
- Two different step sequences (Changed to one in 2010)
  Two of: straight line, circular, or serpentine

Ladies' Short Program required elements:

- Lasts 2:50
- Three Jump Elements
  A double or triple axel
  A triple jump preceded by connecting steps
  A jump combination (one double and one triple or two triple jumps)
- Three Spin Elements
  A flying spin
  A layback spin
  A spin combination with one change of foot
- Two Sequences
  One step sequence (straight, circular, or serpentine)
  One spiral sequence

Men's Free Skate required elements:

- Lasts 4:30
- Jumps:
  Up to eight jump elements

At least one – but no more than three – must be an axel
- Combinations
  No more than three combinations/sequences
  No more than one three-jump combination
- Spins
  No more than three spins
  All spins must be of a different nature
- Step Sequence
  At most two sequences
  May be straight-line, circular, or serpentine

Ladies' Free Skate required elements:

- Lasts 4:00
- Jumps:
  Up to seven jump elements
  At least one – but no more than three – must be an axel
- Combinations
  No more than three combinations/sequences
  No more than one three-jump combination
- Spins
  No more than three spins
  All spins must be of a different nature
- Sequences
  At most two step sequences
  One step sequence
  One spiral sequence

APPENDIX 15A2   THE FIGURE SKATING SCORING SYSTEM

The International Skating Union (ISU) reformed the way judges scored figure skating performances in the wake of allegations that the results of the 2002 Olympic figure skating competition had been rigged.[1] For many years, commentators had accused judges of favoring competitors from their own countries. The 2002 Winter Olympics went beyond jingoism to score-trading in which a French judge agreed to rate a Russian pairs team highly if a Russian judge gave high scores to a French ice dancing team.

The ISU tried to remedy the problem of inappropriate scoring with several changes. First, judges are now anonymous, which reduces the ability of judges to trade scores or of political authorities to influence their countries' judges. Second, judges are no longer bound by the 6.0 scale. Judges evaluate the quality of each element according to a fixed scale. For example, a successful triple axel is worth 8.5 points (with a 10 percent bonus for those performed more than halfway through a performance). Judges assign the axel a grade of execution (GOE), which can range from +3 to −3. Rather than allowing each judge to apply his/her own GOE, the competition computes a group GOE by randomly selecting nine of the 12 judges, deleting the high and low score, and computing the average of the remaining seven scores. Previously, nine identifiable judges entered their score directly, with all nine scores counting. The grade is then applied to the base score according to a predetermined weighting system. A technical panel assists the judges by identifying each element in real time and providing instant replay, should it be needed.

As before, the technical score is supplemented by a more subjective measure, now called the program component score. This evaluation is based on skating skills, execution, interpretation, and timing. The judges have less room for subjectivity, however, as they must assign scores to a predetermined set of components in increments of 0.25.

In addition to reducing the role played by subjective judgment and hence the chance to rig scores, the new system more directly links a skater's rank to his or her own performance. Under the old system, skaters were evaluated ordinally. As a result, a skater who was several places below another after the short program could not possibly catch up unless the other skater performed poorly and fell several places in the free skate. Now, skaters can make up any difference after the short program if they skate well enough in the free skate.

Note

1. For a detailed description of the ISU scoring system, see US Figure Skating (2010).

16. International women's soccer and gender inequality: revisited
Joshua Congdon-Hohman and
Victor A. Matheson

16.1 INTRODUCTION

While most research in sports economics has focused on the microeconomic aspects of sport, such as the demand for sports, market structure, the sports labor market, and competitive balance, a number of papers have examined the influence of macroeconomic factors, such as GDP, population, or political organization on international sporting achievement. There are several reasons to study the effect of macroeconomic variables on national sporting success beyond simple economic curiosity or as an exercise in forecasting. First, there may be important links between a nation's sporting performance and the economic value of its sports industry. Every four years, for example, enrollment in gymnastics and figure skating classes boom in countries that have reached the Olympic podium in these sports. Similar effects likely occur in team sports, such as basketball or soccer. Second, since the factors that determine performance are largely economic, it may be possible to use sports success as a proxy for overall economic development. Prosperity may generate sporting success through superior sports infrastructure and athletes' earnings. In addition, greater national income may promote individual sports participation by making leisure time more available.

As in the rest of sports economics, studies of international sporting success have generally focused on men's sports, particularly soccer. This chapter examines the factors that lead to success in women's soccer. Women's sports are relatively neglected in the literature, and the results for men do not necessarily generalize to women. Moreover, international success in *women's* sports may be a reflection of both the level of gender equality in a country and overall economic development.

A number of studies have investigated national success in the Olympic Games (Hoffmann et al., 2002a, 2004; Bernard and Busse, 2004; Johnson and Ali, 2004) and in international soccer (Hoffmann et al., 2002b; Houston and Wilson, 2002; Leeds and Leeds, 2009). Hoffmann et al. (2006) and Torgler (2008) specifically examine the economic factors that predict success in international women's soccer (or women's football, as it is referred to in many parts of the world). As in Hoffmann et al. (2006), this chapter studies women's international soccer and seeks to ascertain: '(a) whether the same factors explain the performance of both men's and women's national teams; and if not, (b) which alternative variables can help explain female international success' (ibid.: 999). In addition, this chapter clarifies and extends the results of previous work by taking advantage of the development of the international women's game.

After a historical description of women's soccer (Section 16.2), we describe and compare the Fédération Internationale de Football Association (FIFA) rankings for men and women (Section 16.3). Section 16.4 presents the empirical model and estimation results. Section 16.5 concludes and places the results in the broader context of development.

16.2   WOMEN'S SOCCER

Soccer is a predominantly male sport in terms of both participation and support. This is partly due to the masculine image of sports in general and soccer in particular. Female participation, however, has existed nearly as long as soccer itself, as noted by Murray (1996), Williams (2002), and FIFA (2003).[1] Indeed, in the 1920s some women's soccer matches in England drew over 50,000 spectators (BBC, 2005). Perhaps fearing competition for fans, the English Football Association (FA) banned women from playing at all grounds it controlled until 1970. Women's soccer leagues were formed in Italy and Germany in the 1930s, and Italy created the first women's national team in 1950. In the subsequent 30 years, numerous countries, particularly in northern Europe, followed the Italian lead by forming their own amateur domestic leagues and international teams. Formal international competitions began in Europe in the early 1980s, and, in 1991, nearly 60 years after the first Men's World Cup, FIFA held the first Women's World Cup. The first women's Olympic competition followed in 1996.

While the success of women's soccer does not rival that of the men's game worldwide, the game has many fans. The gold medal match of the 1996 Olympics was played in front of a sold-out crowd of 75,000 in Athens, Georgia. The 1999 Women's World Cup drew 658,000 fans to 17 matches in the United States. The average attendance of over 38,000 per game compared favorably to attendance in the men's English Premier League, which averaged just over 30,000 fans per game during the same year.[2] A live audience of 92,000 watched the American victory in the championship match at the Rose Bowl, which remains the largest live audience for a women's sporting event. The television audience in the United States for the final match exceeded 40 million viewers. This is the largest audience for any soccer match ever shown on US television and a number comparable to the television ratings for a typical World Series baseball game or National Basketball Association Finals game. The success of the United States' national team in the 1999 Woman's World Cup propelled stars, such as Mia Hamm and Brandi Chastain, to national prominence.

The popular success of the 1999 Women's World Cup led, two years later, to the formation of the Women's United Soccer Association (WUSA) in the US, the first fully professional women's soccer league in the world. WUSA drew 8,300 fans per game in its inaugural season. Though this number is substantially lower than attendance in the world's major men's leagues, it rivals that of many teams in the smaller soccer-playing nations or the average team in the lower divisions of larger countries. For example, 48 of the 72 teams in England's 1st, 2nd, and 3rd Divisions (representing the 2nd, 3rd and 4th highest divisions of play) averaged less than 8,300 fans per match in 1999–2000. (We collected attendance numbers from various league websites, box scores, FIFA, and public data sources.) WUSA collapsed after only three seasons in September 2003 (ironically during the US-hosted World Cup tournament) due to 'a shortfall in sponsorship revenue and insufficient revenue from other core areas of the business', according to WUSA chairman John Hendricks (BBC, 2003).

Other professional women's teams and leagues have followed the lead of WUSA. Women's Professional Soccer (WPS) resurrected professional women's soccer in the United States in 2009 and attracted average attendance of 3,500 to 4,500 per game, with peak matches drawing as many as 15,000 fans (SoccerAmericaDaily, 2011). The players in WPS were fully professional with league-wide player salaries averaging about $35,000 per year in 2011 (Leighton, 2010). Like WUSA before it, the league has struggled financially, and the long-term sustainability of the league is in doubt. In early 2012, the league, which had fallen to only five teams, announced that it was suspending play for the 2012 season but expressed hope that games would resume in 2013.

The Union of European Football Associations (UEFA), the governing body for soccer in Europe, has sponsored a continent-wide women's club championship since 2000–01. In 2009–10, UEFA rebranded the competition as the UEFA Women's Champions League, which attracted 54 clubs from 46 nations in 2011–12. The clubs participating in this event range from fully amateur to fully professional. In England, the FA has sponsored the Women's Premier League since 1991, with many of the men's English Premier League teams fielding a side (team) in the women's league. In 2011, the eight-team FA Women's Super League (WSL) supplanted the Women's Premier League as the top women's league in the country. With operating budgets roughly one-tenth those of the WPS in the US and top player salaries of £25,000 for only a handful of players, the WSL is only a semi-professional league, but one in which some female athletes can earn full-time salaries. Similarly, the Women's Bundesliga in Germany has existed since 1990, again with largely semi-professional players sprinkled with a handful of top players who earn higher salaries. Attendance at Women's Bundesliga matches are a fraction of that of the WPS, with top clubs averaging only about 1,000 spectators per game, but top matches have occasionally attracted crowds of 20,000 to 30,000 (FFC Frankfurt, 2011).

Subsequent Women's World Cup competitions have also been quite successful. Roughly 10 million Germans watched their team on TV win the championships in both 2003 and 2007 (Welt, 2007). The 2011 Women's World Cup hosted by Germany averaged over 26,000 fans per game and generated strong television ratings. The final match between the US and Japan had 14.1 million and 10.1 million viewers in the two countries, respectively, and matches involving the host country averaged roughly 16 million viewers in Germany, one-fifth of the country's total population (FIFA, 2011).

Despite the success of professional women's soccer teams in several countries and the strong ratings for international competitions, women's soccer has so far remained largely an amateur sport. According to FIFA, 'soccer for young girls in many parts of the world is often considered . . . a solely recreational activity [owing to] cultural barriers, social mores and the lack of any financial hope for a future in the game' (FIFA, 2003). As a result, one may expect different factors to drive international success in the women's game compared with men's international soccer.

16.3   FIFA RANKINGS

FIFA regularly calculates a ranking of men's and women's national soccer teams. The men's rankings have been published since 1993 and are updated monthly, while the women's rankings have been published since 2003 and are updated roughly quarterly. For both ranking systems, FIFA calculates a points total for each country on the basis of international senior games, weighted by match result, home advantage, importance of the match, ranking of the opponent, and time since the match. Full details of the ranking procedure are available from the FIFA website. As of July 2011, FIFA ranks 206 men's national teams that have played a sufficient number of games. These national teams typically represent recognized independent countries. They also include a handful of quasi-independent territories, such as Guam and the Faroe Islands, and, for historical reasons, the four countries comprising the United Kingdom: England, Scotland, Wales, and Northern Ireland. On the women's side, FIFA fully ranks 129 countries. It ranks another 43 countries provisionally either because they have played fewer than five full international matches or because the team has been inactive for more than 18 months. The 172 countries with an active or provisional women's ranking represent a substantial increase since 2003. The original 2003 ranking had only 113 teams, and Hoffmann et al.'s (2006) study of women's soccer analyzed only 88 countries.

The small number of countries examined is the greatest limitation of the earlier studies. Hoffmann et al. dealt with missing data by excluding the countries from their econometric analysis. Unfortunately, this decision results in the loss of important information. In 2003, socioeconomic and cultural factors played a significant role in a nation's decision to field a national team and its resulting rank. For example, even a cursory look at 2003 data revealed that few predominantly Muslim countries had a women's soccer program. Since Hoffmann et al. examined only existing programs, they were unable to comment on the role that religion may have played in a country's strength in women's international soccer. The development of the international women's game now allows many more countries to be examined.

We assign countries without a ranked women's program a point value equal to 500, a convenient round figure that is just below the lowest point value of any of the currently ranked women's teams (Comoros at 534 points). Assigning a point value of 500 instead of 0 eliminates the sharp jump that would otherwise occur in reported points between countries that have played a handful of games and those that have played none. Although assigning a point value of 500 is arbitrary, we feel that a value of 500 better reflects the differences in quality between countries with no women's soccer program and those with a 'token' program.

Table 16.1 shows the point totals of the top 20 women's teams as of July 2011 as well as the FIFA ranks of their corresponding men's national teams and their placings (that is, tournament results) in the four women's Olympics and six Women's World Cup tournaments held to date. The table reveals that there are three apparent women's soccer hubs in the world, North America (USA and Canada), Northern Europe (Norway, Sweden, Denmark, Germany, England, the Netherlands, Iceland, and Finland) and East Asia (China, Japan, and North Korea). With the exception of Brazil, the traditional Latin American powerhouses on the men's side do not appear near the top of the women's rankings. Additionally, predominantly Islamic nations participate in international women's soccer

Table 16.1   *FIFA points, men's FIFA rank, and tournament placements*
for the top 20 women's soccer teams[a]

Country	FIFA rank (women's)	FIFA points (women's)	FIFA rank (men's)	1st	2nd	3rd	4th
USA	1	2,162	30	5	2	3	0
Germany (DEU)	2	2,146	3	2	1	3	1
Brazil (BRA)	3	2,121	4	0	3	1	2
Japan (JAP)	4	2,101	16	1	1	0	1
Sweden (SWE)	5	2,085	19	0	0	2	1
England (ENG)	6	1,997	6	0	0	0	0
France (FRA)	7	1,981	15	0	0	0	1
Canada (CAN)	8	1,953	105	0	0	0	1
Australia (AUS)	9	1,946	23	0	0	0	0
Norway (NOR)	10	1,940	12	2	1	1	2
Italy (ITA)	11	1,934	8	0	0	0	0
North Korea (PRK)	12	1,927	115	0	0	0	0
Denmark (DNK)	13	1,888	21	0	0	0	0
Netherlands (NLD)	14	1,888	2	0	0	0	0
China (CHN)	15	1,870	73	0	2	0	1
South Korea (KOR)	16	1,851	28	0	0	0	0
Iceland (ISL)	17	1,848	121	0	0	0	0
Spain (SPA)	18	1,816	1	0	0	0	0
Finland (FIN)	19	1,811	75	0	0	0	0
Russia (RUS)	20	1,809	18	0	0	0	0

Notes:
FIFA rankings based on the FIFA World Rankings in July 2011.
a.   Tournament results are from positions in the previous four Olympics and previous six
  World Cup tournaments.

at a much lower rate than other countries, as only 69 percent of Islamic
nations with a men's team also have a women's team, compared to 87
percent of non-Islamic nations. These observations point to clear political,
economic, and cultural forces behind women's soccer.

Figure 16.1 shows the relative performance of women's teams compared with their male counterparts. We gave three-letter identifiers to
each pairing based on the country codes provided by the World Bank
(with additional codes given to non-national teams including the British
Virgin Islands (country code 'BVI'), Cook Islands (COO), England
(ENG), Northern Ireland (NIR), Palestine (PST), Scotland (SCT), Tahiti
(TAH), Taiwan (TWN), and Wales (WAL)). For clarity, only countries
with ranked women's and men's programs are displayed. Overall soccer

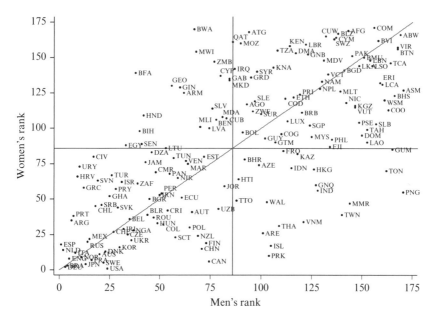

Source: FIFA website.

Figure 16.1 Performance of women's versus men's teams

strength decreases as one moves away from the origin. Nations in the south-west quadrant have above-average international soccer performance for both men's and women's teams and typically include most developed countries and those with large populations. Conversely, smaller and developing nations with below-par men's and women's soccer performance, such as Afghanistan (AFG), Aruba (ABW), Bhutan (BTN), Comoros (COM), and the US Virgin Islands (VIR), are located in the north-east quadrant. Teams tend to be loosely clustered along the 45-degree line, indicating that success in the men's game is correlated with success in the women's game. The 45-degree line measures the relative quality of men's versus women's soccer in a country. Countries below the diagonal exhibit stronger performance in women's soccer than in men's. This group includes such countries as the United States (USA), Canada (CAN), China (CHN), Iceland (ISL), Myanmar (MMR), North Korea (PRK), and Papua New Guinea (PNG). Above the diagonal are countries with relatively stronger men's teams, which includes such notable teams as Portugal (PRT), Uruguay (URY), Côte d'Ivoire (CIV), Argentina (ARG), Croatia (HRV), Honduras (HND), Burkina Faso (BFA), Botswana (BWA), and Malawi (MWI).

16.4   EMPIRICAL MODEL AND RESULTS

The implicit model underlying all studies of international sporting success is that countries with more economic resources are able to direct these resources towards athletic success. We model success by using the FIFA points attained by both women and men (y_i) using the following regression model:

$$y_i = \beta_0 + \beta \mathbf{X_i} + \varepsilon_i. \tag{16.1}$$

In equation (16.1), $\mathbf{X_i}$ represents a vector of independent variables for each country i. Some of the variables have been used in previous papers, and the others provide new explanations for success for both men's and women's sides. Unless otherwise noted, data are from the *Central Intelligence Agency Factbook*, which reports the most recently available data for each country based on the CIA's own estimates and other reputable sources. The vector $\mathbf{X_i}$ includes purchasing power parity GDP per capita (in thousands of dollars), the population of the country (in millions), and indicators for whether a majority of the country's citizens identify themselves as Muslim, whether the country is ruled by a communist regime, and whether it has a Latin heritage.

GDP per capita is a proxy for a country's level of economic development, which is associated with the availability of better sporting infrastructure as well as leisure time for athletes. In addition, affluent nations can afford to offer larger financial incentives for sports participation. Countries with larger populations have a larger talent pool from which to draw players. We include an indicator variable for Communist countries based on the findings of the prior literature. We define a Communist country as one that is controlled by a single political party that identifies itself as Communist. In 2011, this group includes China, North Korea, Cuba, Vietnam, and Laos. We did not include an indicator for formerly Communist countries because it has been a generation since many of these nations ended Communist rule. Moreover, identifying the impact of the transition from Communism is often complicated by the splintering of many of these formerly Communist countries into smaller nations. Latin heritage is identified by whether the country is majority Spanish, Portuguese, or Italian speaking. Latin cultural origin captures the special status of soccer in these countries, which is rooted in the particular conceptions of gender roles and the significance of masculinity in these societies (Bar-On, 1997; Archetti, 1999).

Based on earlier findings by Hoffman et al. (2002b, 2006), we also include the squared value of the deviation of a country's average Celsius temperature (as computed by Mitchell et al., 2003) from the 'ideal' temperature of 14 degrees Celsius (approximately 57 degrees Fahrenheit)). Given the fact that soccer is generally played outside, climates that are either too hot or too cold limit the ability of players to participate in the game. Therefore, researchers frequently hypothesize that soccer success falls as the deviation from the ideal temperature rises.

The ε_i term represents unobserved error for each country and is assumed to be distributed with a mean of zero and finite variance. We estimate equation (16.1) using OLS. To correct for heteroskedasticity, we use robust standard errors (also known as Huber/White estimators) to calculate robust *p*-values for each coefficient reported below.

We estimate four variants of equation (16.1). It is reasonable to presume that some countries have a greater affinity for soccer for unobserved cultural reasons that will lead to success for both the men's and women's teams. We use FIFA points of the other gender's soccer team to control for this affinity. Because socioeconomic factors that drive success in men's and women's international soccer might be correlated with underlying cultural factors, the FIFA points of the other gender's soccer team could be highly correlated with the other variables in the equation. As a result, the inclusion of the other gender's FIFA points might obscure or diminish the effects of the other variables. For this reason, we estimate the relevant equation for each model separately both including and omitting the other gender's FIFA points in the regression. Given the broader popularity of the men's game and its longer history, men's points almost certainly serve as a better reflection of 'love for soccer' than women's points. Thus, we expect the inclusion of men's points to have greater explanatory power as a predictor of women's points than the inclusion of women's points as a predictor of men's points. For the sake of completeness and symmetry, we present both.

Columns 1 and 2 of Table 16.2 present the results from equation (16.1) when we do not include the performance of the other gender's team. While per capita income has a positive effect on FIFA points for men but not for women, population has a positive effect for women but not for men. As found in previous work, Latin heritage is associated with higher points for men but not women. While Hoffman et al. (2006) found that deviations from the ideal temperature had a negative effect only on men's rankings when using 2003 data, we find that temperature has a negative effect on both genders' points. This finding makes more sense than Hoffman et al.'s, as there is no a priori reason to believe that temperature should affect men more than women. Communism has a negative impact for men but not for women. Due to the relatively large coefficients displaying opposite signs for men's and women's teams, the hypothesis that Communism has an equal impact on men and women can be rejected with 99 percent confidence.

Table 16.2   OLS regression results for base model

Variable	1 Women's points	2 Men's points	3 Women's points	4 Men's points
GDP/Capita	3.69	2.56	1.7	0.96
	(0.141)	(0.053)*	(0.328)	(0.120)
Communist	212.02	−204.92	370.75	−297.04
	(0.234)	(0.005)***	(0.018)**	(0.000)***
Muslim	−195.02	−35.96	−167.16	48.78
	(0.008)***	(0.415)	(0.011)**	(0.245)
Latin	118.33	209.07	−43.62	157.66
	(0.131)	(0.010)***	(0.475)	(0.013)**
Population	0.66	0.23	0.48	−0.06
	(0.014)**	(0.255)	(0.003)***	(0.632)
Temperature	−1.05	−1.41	0.04	−0.95
	(0.093)*	(0.003)***	(0.923)	(0.005)***
Men's Points			0.77	
			(0.000)***	
Women's Points				0.43
				(0.000)***
Constant	1,229.20	460.64	872.39	−73.47
	(0.000)***	(0.000)***	(0.000)***	(0.317)
Observations	196	196	196	196
Adjusted R-squared	0.139	0.152	0.426	0.435

Note: Robust p-values in parentheses; * significant at 10%; ** significant at 5%; *** significant at 1%.

The inclusion of an indicator for strong Muslim affiliation in a country proves to be an important addition to the literature. This indicator has a negative impact on the FIFA points for women while having no effect on the men's points. The difference between the coefficients is significant at the 98 percent level. This result is most likely rooted in the cultural differences in freedoms of men and women in many Muslim countries.

The results change slightly when we control for a country's cultural affinity for soccer. Columns 3 and 4 of Table 16.2 show that the success of a country's men's team strongly predicts success of a women's team and vice versa. While the significance and sign of most independent variables do not change, the inclusion of the other sex's soccer success reduces the impact of per capita income below standard significance thresholds. Additionally, the role of Communism is amplified and now has a positive impact on women's FIFA points and a negative impact on men's performance.

The results for Communist regimes have a compelling explanation. The labor market for men's soccer is much larger than that for women's soccer. The high salaries of top male soccer players in free-market economies provide strong incentives for men to develop their talent. Women's soccer stars, however, earn only a fraction of their male counterparts, and even top players have difficulty supporting themselves as professional players. Communist nations, especially those that severely limit the ability of their players to emigrate, such as North Korea or Cuba, do not traditionally offer such disparate rewards to top performers (in sports or other activities). The low and compressed rewards limit the incentive for men to develop their skills. While market forces provide strong incentives for men but not women to develop their talents, Communist nations may be better able to subsidize the development of women's soccer. Communist countries' advantages in excelling in non-revenue sports in the Olympics have been widely identified in the existing literature (Hoffmann et al., 2002a, 2004; Bernard and Busse, 2004; Johnson and Ali, 2004).

Looking beyond the baseline model, we now examine the role of women's cultural position in each country in soccer success. Sports sociologists have asserted that men view soccer as an expression of masculinity and have therefore been hostile to women's making inroads into the sport (Giulianotti, 1999). Such hostility has hampered the development of women's sport (Williams, 2002). As a result, gender inequality, as reflected in a country's economic variables, should negatively impact women's soccer performance.

Hoffmann et al. (2006) included the ratio of women's to men's earnings in their original study, concluding that countries with relatively equal earnings across gender perform better in women's soccer. While current data on relative income shares are not available, we examine two other measures of gender equality: the percentage of women in parliament and the ratio of women's to men's secondary school enrollment rates. We do not use the ratio of women's to men's labor force participation rates as suggested by Klein (2002) due to the unclear link between labor participation and gender equality. Though the United Nations Development Programme's (UNDP) composite gender inequality index (GDI) would also be a good measure of gender equality, it is calculated for only two-thirds of the countries with ranked men's soccer national teams. The two measures we have chosen should capture both the role of women in society as reflected by representation in government and the opportunities provided to women relative to men through education.

Specifically, we estimate two versions of equation (16.1), each with a different measure of gender equality:

$$y_i = \beta_0' + \beta_1'*Gender\_Equality_i + \beta_2'*Missing_i + \beta'*\mathbf{X}_i + \varepsilon_i. \quad (16.2)$$

Like most available measures of gender equality, data on the female share of members of parliament and the female-to-male enrollment ratio are not available for all countries. Twelve countries are missing values for parliamentary share, and 22 are missing enrollment ratios. Though these countries tend to be small and underdeveloped nations, whose exclusion does not impact the results, we include them by replacing the missing values with zeros and including an indicator (*Missing*) to identify countries that do not report the percentage of female parliamentarians or the enroll-ment ratio. By identifying and replacing the unreported values, we are able to continue to use the full sample of countries and expand our ability to compare results across specifications.

The results for using the percentage of national parliamentary seats held by women (*Parliament Share*) as a proxy for gender equality are presented in Table 16.3. Data on the percentage of seats held by women are available for each country through the World Bank and are from the most recent year available, with the majority from 2010. The results in columns 1 and 2 show that as the share of women in a country's parliament rises, so does success in the women's game when men's FIFA points are not included. Interestingly, the greater representation of women leads to improved success in the men's game. One possible interpretation of these findings is that many measures of gender equality reflect overall economic development rather than the relative status of men and women in the economy. This argument is bol-stered by the fact that the impact of the share of female parliamentarians decreases in both magnitude and significance when FIFA points for the other gender are included. The decline is consistent with our conclusion that economic development is a key determinant of FIFA points for each gender. However, not all measures of gender equality exhibit this tendency.

Table 16.4 shows that the above results do not extend to the enrollment ratio. The table presents the result of using the ratio of women's to men's secondary school enrollment rates (*Enrollment_ratio*) to measure gender equality rather than the share of women in a nation's parliament. The enrollment rates are the most recent values reported by the United Nations Educational, Scientific, and Cultural Organization (UNESCO) Institute for Statistics, with most from 2009. For this measure, a value of 100 repre-sents equal enrollment rates for men and women. We believe that this ratio captures a country's educational opportunities for women relative to men and should be an important determinant of success for female athletes.

The gender ratio of enrollment has a strongly significant, positive impact on women's success regardless of whether men's points are included. Countries that provide women with academic opportunities

Table 16.3   *OLS regression results including female share of parliament*

Variable	1 Women's points	2 Men's points	3 Women's points	4 Men's points
Parliament	6.17	4.53	2.71	2.03
Share	(0.080)*	(0.059)*	(0.356)	(0.276)
GDP/Capita	3.68	2.77	1.56	1.27
	(0.147)	(0.043)**	(0.368)	(0.040)**
Communist	147.72	−258.31	345.41	−318.22
	(0.466)	(0.001)***	(0.045)**	(0.000)***
Muslim	−176.58	−31.01	−152.85	40.61
	(0.014)**	(0.482)	(0.021)**	(0.345)
Latin	100.12	190.4	−45.6	149.8
	(0.206)	(0.016)**	(0.456)	(0.016)**
Population	0.67	0.22	0.5	−0.05
	(0.011)**	(0.254)	(0.003)***	(0.696)
Temperature	−0.78	−1.17	0.12	−0.86
	(0.198)	(0.007)***	(0.798)	(0.010)**
Men's Points			0.77	
			(0.000)***	
Women's				0.41
Points				(0.000)***
Missing	−137.08	−266.42	66.8	−210.82
	(0.289)	(0.000)***	(0.575)	(0.000)***
Constant	1,109.95	379.57	819.47	−70.59
	(0.000)***	(0.000)***	(0.000)***	(0.423)
Observations	196	196	196	196
Adjusted *R*-squared	0.168	0.226	0.423	0.464

Note: Robust *p*-values in parentheses; * significant at 10%; ** significant at 5%; *** significant at 1%.

closer to those given to men have more success in women's sports. The impact for men is starkly different. Though gender equality in education does not significantly impact the success of men when women's points are not included, it does have a highly significant, negative impact on men's success when they are included. It would appear that the gender equality in a country increases the resources for a women's program at the expense of the men's program. Additionally, the inclusion of either gender equality measure slightly improves the quality of fit of the model as reflected by the higher adjusted *R*-squared values.

While the United States has been far and away the most successful nation in women's soccer (see Table 16.1), its success on the women's side stands

Table 16.4   OLS regression results including enrollment ratio

Variable	1 Women's points	2 Men's points	3 Women's points	4 Men's points
Enrollment_	4.59	−1.4	5.69	−3.46
ratio	(0.029)**	(0.333)	(0.001)***	(0.005)***
GDP/Capita	2.47	2.84	0.23	1.73
	(0.345)	(0.057)*	(0.899)	(0.025)**
Communist	239.27	−178.12	379.93	−285.49
	(0.186)	(0.038)**	(0.012)**	(0.000)***
Muslim	−174.42	−53.05	−132.52	25.22
	(0.024)**	(0.242)	(0.052)*	(0.545)
Latin	58.2	211.44	−108.78	185.32
	(0.489)	(0.014)**	(0.089)*	(0.005)***
Population	0.63	0.21	0.46	−0.07
	(0.019)**	(0.304)	(0.007)***	(0.569)
Temperature	−0.86	−1.41	0.25	−1.02
	(0.174)	(0.004)***	(0.579)	(0.004)***
Men's Points			0.79	
			(0.000)***	
Women's				0.45
Points				(0.000)***
Missing	373.9	−214.56	543.34	−382.34
	(0.079)*	(0.152)	(0.002)***	(0.003)***
Constant	800.21	604.13	323.13	245.03
	(0.000)***	(0.000)***	(0.071)*	(0.050)*
Observations	196	196	196	196
Adjusted R-squared	0.15	0.152	0.448	0.45

Note: Robust p-values in parentheses; * significant at 10%; ** significant at 5%; *** significant at 1%.

in stark contrast to its relatively modest success on the men's side. The US, however, is unique among industrialized nations in promoting athletics in its public school system and at the collegiate level. The connection between schooling and athletics results in wholesale subsidization of sports in what is otherwise a strongly free-market economy. Furthermore, Title IX of the Education Amendments of 1972 prohibits gender discrimination in federally funded educational programs. The provision of athletic opportunities for women has been among the most visible outcomes of the Title IX legislation. In effect, the success of the United States in low-revenue sports, such as women's soccer, is at least in part the result of the non-market provision of athletic opportunities through the educational system.

If the US experience is similar to that in other countries, we might expect the level of education (as opposed to the relative opportunities afforded men and women) in a country to affect the success of women's athletic teams. Specifically, education may be a complement to team athletics for women, as the alternative to formal education may be home responsibilities. This may be different for men who have more freedom outside of school to meet and play with others. To examine this question, we modify equation (16.1) to include the gross enrollment rates at all levels for young men (*Male_rate*) and women (*Female_rate*) as reported by the UNESCO Institute for Statistics. We include both rates in each specification in order to capture both a country's investment in the gender of interest and its overall investment in education. The resulting model is represented by the following equation:

$$y_i = \beta_0'' + \beta_1''*Female\_rate_i + \beta_2''*Male\_rate_i + \beta_3''*Missing_i + \beta''*\mathbf{X_i} + \varepsilon_i.$$
$$(16.3)$$

As in equation (16.2), we set enrollment equal to zero and include an indicator for any country missing an enrollment value for either gender, which allows us to keep our full complement of countries. Though 52 countries have at least one missing value, the results are broadly similar when those countries are excluded rather than given values and missing indicators.

The inclusion of separate school enrollment rates of men and women reveals an interesting difference in their impact on the success of men's and women's soccer. Table 16.5 shows that women's success is strongly related to their enrollment rate, but is not significantly affected by the general level of education as measured by the enrollment rate of men. The enrollment rate of neither gender is significantly related to the men's soccer success. These results suggest that education may be a key determinant of women's performance. Specifically, we see that the ratio of enrollment rates does not change the effect of Islam, but the level of education does. We conclude that the unequal treatment of women in a society and the lack of interaction with other women outside the home both hinder the development of a strong national women's soccer team. This finding may also imply that women's soccer depends more on formal soccer training in educational environments than men's soccer does, possibly due to the differences in non-institutional opportunities afforded each gender, such as youth soccer and the freedom to play informally.

To separate the role of education as a proxy for gender equality from its role as a distinct source of soccer skills, we include both a proxy for gender equality and gross rates of enrollment for men and women. Because the

Table 16.5   OLS regression results including men's and women's enrollment rates

Variable	1 Women's points	2 Men's points	3 Women's points	4 Men's points
Female_rate	10.58	3.34	8.52	−0.82
	(0.032)**	(0.293)	(0.030)**	(0.738)
Male_rate	4.9	6.03	1.19	4.1
	(0.408)	(0.131)	(0.806)	(0.183)
GDP/Capita	−0.43	0.4	−0.67	0.56
	(0.824)	(0.737)	(0.642)	(0.467)
Communist	188.03	−202.8	313.11	−276.74
	(0.448)	(0.014)**	(0.134)	(0.000)***
Muslim	−38.23	50.67	−69.48	65.7
	(0.587)	(0.283)	(0.289)	(0.141)
Latin	28.76	161.32	−70.74	150.01
	(0.680)	(0.025)**	(0.245)	(0.016)**
Population	0.72	0.24	0.57	−0.04
	(0.003)***	(0.180)	(0.001)***	(0.760)
Temperature	0.02	−0.72	0.47	−0.73
	(0.970)	(0.104)	(0.313)	(0.036)**
Men's Points			0.62	
			(0.000)***	
Women's Points				0.39
				(0.000)***
Missing	1,063.45	607.7	688.64	189.5
	(0.000)***	(0.000)***	(0.000)***	(0.139)
Constant	33.86	−257.43	192.63	−270.75
	(0.869)	(0.092)*	(0.283)	(0.039)**
Observations	196	196	196	196
Adjusted *R*-squared	0.341	0.262	0.498	0.438

Note: Robust *p*-values in parentheses; * significant at 10%; ** significant at 5%; *** significant at 1%.

gender enrollment ratio and the gross enrollment rates are closely related, we use the percentage of parliamentary seats held by women as our measure of gender equality here. The resulting equation is therefore:

$$y_i = \beta_0''' + \beta_1''' * Parliament\ Share_i + \beta_2''' * Female\_rate_i + \beta_3''' * Male\_rate_i$$
$$+ \beta_4''' * Missing_i + \beta''' * X_i + \varepsilon_i \qquad (16.4)$$

Here, *Missing* is an indicator for any country that does not have available data for the gender equality measure or one of the enrollment rates. This category now includes 58 of the 196 countries in the initial analysis.

Table 16.6   *OLS regression results including female share of parliament and men's and women's enrollment rates*

Variable	1 Women points	2 Men points	3 Women points	4 Men points
Parliament Share	7.13	6.28	2.79	3.37
	(0.022)**	(0.007)***	(0.281)	(0.059)*
Female_rate	15.04	6.08	10.84	−0.04
	(0.003)***	(0.055)*	(0.007)***	(0.986)
Male_rate	−10.04	−3.73	−7.46	0.36
	(0.118)	(0.314)	(0.126)	(0.893)
GDP/Capita	0.12	0.89	−0.49	0.84
	(0.953)	(0.453)	(0.746)	(0.241)
Communist	120.5	−263	302.18	−312.05
	(0.648)	(0.009)***	(0.154)	(0.000)***
Muslim	−86.87	22.83	−102.65	58.19
	(0.195)	(0.638)	(0.106)	(0.211)
Latin	47.51	167.98	−68.54	148.64
	(0.522)	(0.023)**	(0.272)	(0.016)**
Population	0.71	0.24	0.54	−0.05
	(0.006)***	(0.203)	(0.002)***	(0.681)
Temperature	−0.28	−0.88	0.32	−0.76
	(0.655)	(0.056)*	(0.500)	(0.033)**
Men's Points			0.69	
			(0.000)***	
Women's Points				0.41
				(0.000)***
Missing	264.92	76.54	212.04	−31.3
	(0.149)	(0.479)	(0.129)	(0.670)
Constant	717.73	171.25	599.42	−120.91
	(0.001)***	(0.222)	(0.001)***	(0.332)
Observations	196	196	196	196
Adjusted *R*-squared	0.255	0.229	0.461	0.443

Note: Robust *p*-values in parentheses; * significant at 10%; ** significant at 5%;
*** significant at 1%.

The results in Table 16.6 show a pattern similar to those in Tables 16.3 and 16.5, which included female parliamentary representation and enrollment rates separately. Women's share of parliamentary seats continues to have a positive impact on both male and female success, but this effect decreases when the other sex's FIFA points are included in columns 3 and 4. Women's gross enrollment rate continues to have a positive impact on women's soccer success regardless of whether men's success is included. We interpret these results as strong evidence that opportunities for young women to gather and interact in school affect women's soccer success, regardless of the level of gender equality.

16.5   CONCLUSION

Sports success represents a type of human development not reflected in GDP per capita. In particular, it reflects the freedom of individuals to participate in leisure activities. As Anand and Sen (1995: 1) argue, 'a great deal has been achieved . . . in shifting the focus of attention of the world community from such mechanical indicators of economic progress . . . to indicators that come closer to reflecting the well-being and freedoms actually enjoyed by populations'. Non-material indices of economic development and individual well-being, such as the United Nation's Development Programme's (UNDP) Human Development Index (HDI), combine income per capita with quality of life indicators, such as life expectancy, health, education and political freedom. Sports success reflects another aspect of well-being.

This line of reasoning has implications for the analysis of women's soccer. The results in this chapter suggest that the performance of the men's national team alone may not be a good indicator of human development in a country if women's sporting success is driven by a different set of factors. In Anand and Sen's (1995: 5) words, a 'simple arithmetic average of achievement . . . overlooks systematic and potentially large differences between distinct groups of people, in particular women and men'. In recognition of this very fact, in 2008, UNDP produced a modified form of its own HDI, the Gender Inequality Index (GII). The GII resembles the HDI, but it accounts for differences in the distribution of achievements between men and women. Similarly, a comparative look at women's sport sheds light on human development as well as the extent of gender inequalities in the countries under investigation. Women's soccer success may therefore provide a useful indicator of the ability of women to realize their potential in different societies.

NOTES

1. For more on women's soccer, see Chapter 17 in this volume.
2. *Editors' Note*: The attendance figures for the Women's World Cup vary depending upon whether one considers 'doubleheader' games one event or two. The figures used here consider each game a separate event. The figures in Chapter 17 consider the doubleheaders a single event and result in slightly lower attendance.

REFERENCES

Anand, Sudhir and Amartya Sen (1995), 'Gender Inequality in Human Development: Theories and Measurement', Occasional Paper 19, Human Development Office, United Nations Development Programme.

Archetti, Eduardo P. (1999), *Masculinities: Soccer, Polo and the Tango in Argentina*, Oxford: Berg.

Bar-On, Tamir (1997), 'The Ambiguities of Soccer, Politics, Culture, and Social Transformation in Latin America', *Sociological Research Online*, **2**(4).

BBC (2003), 'US Women's Soccer League Folds', online at: news.bbc.co.uk (accessed 16 September 2003).

BBC (2005), 'Trail-blazers who Pioneered Women's Football', online at: http://news.bbc.co.uk/sport2/hi/football/women/4603149.stm (accessed June 3, 2005).

Bernard, Andrew B. and Meghan R. Busse (2004), 'Who Wins the Olympic Games: Economic Development and Medal Totals', *Review of Economics and Statistics*, **86**(1): 413–17.

Fédération Internationale de Football Association (FIFA) (2003), online at: http://www.fifa.com (accessed May 20, 2011).

Fédération Internationale de Football Association (FIFA) (2011), 'FIFA Women's World Cup Germany 2011 sets new TV viewing records', online at: http://www.fifa.com (accessed November 21, 2011).

FFC Frankfurt (2011), 'Die Erfolgsstory des 1', FFC Frankfurt, online at: http://www.ffc-frankfurt.de/c/cms/front_content.php?idcat=8 (accessed August 26, 2011).

Giulianotti, Richard (1999), *Soccer: A Sociology of the Global Game*, Cambridge: Polity.

Hoffmann, Robert, Lee Chew Ging, Victor Matheson and Bala Ramasamy (2002a), 'Public Policy and Olympic Success', *Applied Economics Letters*, **9**(8), October: 545–8.

Hoffmann, Robert, Lee Chew Ging, Victor Matheson and Bala Ramasamy (2002b), 'The Socio-Economic Determinants of International Football Performance', *Journal of Applied Economics*, **5**(2), November: 253–72.

Hoffmann, Robert, Lee Chew Ging, Victor Matheson and Bala Ramasamy (2004), 'Olympics Success and ASEAN Countries: Analysis and Policy Implications', *Journal of Sports Economics*, **5**(3), August: 262–76.

Hoffmann, Robert, Lee Chew Ging, Victor Matheson and Bala Ramasamy (2006), 'International Women's Football and Gender Inequality', *Applied Economics Letters*, **13**(15), December: 999–1001.

Houston, Robert G. and Dennis P. Wilson (2002), 'Income, Leisure and Proficiency: An Economic Study of Football Performance', *Applied Economics Letters*, **9**(14), October: 939–43.

Johnson, Daniel K.N. and Ayfer Ali (2004), 'A Tale of Two Seasons: Participation and Success at the Summer and Winter Olympic Games', *Social Science Quarterly*, **85**(4), December: 974–93.

Klein, Michael W. (2002), 'Work and Play: International Evidence of Gender Equality in Employment and Sports', NBER Working Paper 9081, Cambridge, MA.

Leeds, Michael A. and Eva Marikova Leeds (2009), 'International Soccer Success and National Institutions', *Journal of Sports Economics*, **10**(4), January: 369–90.

Leighton, Tony (2010), 'FA Confident "Super League" Will Not Suffer Financial Meltdown', *The Guardian*, online at: http://www.guardian.co.uk/football/2010/nov/14/fa-womens-super-league (accessed November 14, 2010).

Mitchell, Timothy D., Timothy R. Carter, Phillip D. Jones, Mike Hulme and Mark New (2003), 'A Comprehensive Set of High-resolution Grids of Monthly Climate for Europe and the Globe: The Observed Record (1901–2000) and 16 Scenarios (2001–2100)', *Journal of Climate*: submitted.

Murray, Bill (1996), *The Word's Game: A History of Soccer*, Urbana, IL: University of Illinois Press.

SoccerAmericaDaily (2011), 'Average attendance drops despite Women's World Cup bump', online at: http://www.socceramerica.com (acessed November 12, 2011).

Torgler, Benno (2008), 'The Determinants of Women's International Soccer Performances', *International Journal of Sport Management and Marketing*, **3**(4): 305–18.

Welt (2007), '50,5 Prozent Marktanteil beim WM-Finale', online at: http://www.welt. de/sport/article1226616/50_5_Prozent_Marktanteil_beim_WM_Finale.html   (accessed October 1, 2007).

Williams, John (2002), 'Women and Soccer', Factsheet 5, Sir Norman Chester Centre for Soccer Research, University of Leicester.

17. The economic impact of the Women's World Cup
Dennis Coates

17.1 INTRODUCTION

> A good run at the World Cup, it creates a lot of interest, it certainly creates a
> lot of interest amongst non-soccer folks, but I'm not sure it makes all that much
> change on the soccer horizon.
>> ('Mike & Mike in the Morning', ESPN Radio, July 18, 2011)

The Women's World Cup is arguably the most prominent international women's sporting contest. This prominence comes despite having begun in only 1991. Since then, it has enjoyed robust growth. At the first event, held in China, 12 teams competed in six venues, four of which had seating capacity of 15,000 or less. The largest venue had a seating capacity of 60,000, but the second largest could hold only 25,000. When Germany hosted the World Cup in 2011, 16 teams played in nine host cities in much larger facilities. Only two of the stadiums had a capacity of less than 25,000 and none seated fewer than 20,000.

Attendance at the two events is difficult to compare because the 1991 figures look suspicious. All the official attendance figures are reported in thousands and are too similar to the reported capacities of the venues and sometimes even exceed them.[1] Even accepting the apparently inflated Chinese figures, FIFA (Fédération internationale de football association) documents show that average attendance at the first Women's World Cup was less than 20,000. In the 1999 tournament, held in the United States, average attendance was 37,319 in eight venues, half of which had a capacity of more than 80,000. The 2007 tournament, which was again in China, had an average attendance of 37,218 in five venues, the smallest of which had a capacity of 33,000. Average attendance in Germany 2011 was 26,428. The decline in attendance between 2007 and 2011 might be the result of generally smaller stadiums and a far weaker global economy.

Total attendance was greatest for the 1999 World Cup, followed closely by attendance at the 2007 event, both of which drew over 1.190 million spectators to 32 matches. The 1999 World Cup was the first to feature 16 rather than 12 teams; it also increased the number of matches to 32 from 26. In Germany, total attendance exceeded 845,000.

The television audience has grown since the inception of the event, and the production of the broadcast has become more sophisticated. For the 2011 event, FIFA had 18 cameras for some matches, including in-goal cameras, overhead cameras, and even cameras capturing the arrival of the teams to the stadium. FIFA announced that 'Virtual graphics will also be provided to support broadcasters and ultimately ensure fans enjoy a viewing experience *on a par with the men's game*' (FIFA, 2011a, italics added; see also FIFA, 2011b).

The literature on the economics of large-scale sporting events (mega-events) focuses on the impact of the event on the host country or city (see, for example, Humphreys and Prokopowicz, 2007; Leeds, 2008; Porter and Fletcher, 2008; Fourie and Santana-Gallego, 2010; Coates and Depken, 2011; and Maennig and Zimbalist, 2012). This focus is understandable given that such mega-events as the Olympic Games or the FIFA (Men's) World Cup are generally touted as a means of boosting the host country's economy through income and job creation, through enhanced prestige, and as a signal of the host country's intent to open itself to international trade. The focus is also understandable because the host country provides both explicit and implicit financial support for the events.

This chapter adds to the literature in two ways. First, it analyzes the impact of the Women's World Cup on the host country. In addition, it examines the impact of the Women's World Cup on the state of women's soccer. In most countries, the impact of a country's performance in the Women's World Cup is likely to have a much bigger impact on the overall health of the women's league than the success of the men's team will have on the men's league. For team sports, such as soccer, cricket, and rugby, which have well-established men's professional leagues outside the US, and for baseball, basketball, football, and hockey, which have well-established men's professional leagues within the US, there are few long-standing and high-profile women's professional sports leagues. Additionally, women athletes have lagged far behind men in terms of compensation and, especially, endorsements. This chapter argues that some of the success of women's professional soccer leagues and of rising endorsement deals for women athletes is linked to the success of the US women's soccer team, particularly in the FIFA Women's World Cup in 1999.

Section 17.2 briefly reviews the literature. In Section 17.3, I use data from Rose and Spiegel (2011) to estimate the impact of the Women's World Cup on exports and GDP growth, and I contrast my results with estimates of the impact of the Men's World Cup. The results show that hosting the Women's World Cup has no effect on either international trade or the growth rate of gross domestic product. The findings do not mean that event had no economic impact, but they do mean that one needs to look elsewhere to find it. Section 17.4 looks at the effect of the World Cup on the development of professional women's soccer. This section also presents a brief history of women's soccer leagues and traces the impact of the 1999 Women's World Cup on the growth and development of women's professional soccer leagues. Section 17.5 examines endorsement deals for soccer players and other prominent women athletes. Section 17.6 concludes.

17.2 BRIEF REVIEW OF THE LITERATURE

In one of their many contributions, Baade and Matheson (2004) warn that cities overestimate the economic impact of mega events. Specifically, they show that the 1994 World Cup generated losses for the US cities that hosted the matches. According to their estimates, the cities sustained combined cumulative losses that were larger than the expected gain from the events (over $5.5 billion). Hagn and Maennig (2007) show that the 1974 World Cup had neither a short- nor a long-run effect on employment in 75 German municipalities.

Porter and Fletcher (2008) use data from the 1996 Summer Olympic Games and 2002 Winter Olympic Games to show that input–output models provide unreliable predictions of the impact of sporting events because these models assume constant factor prices. In fact, 'factor price increases absorb the impact of real increases in demand' (p. 1). Leeds (2008) shows that during the Salt Lake City Olympic Games, taxable sales revenue increased in Colorado, thus suggesting that the Olympics displaced tourists that would otherwise have gone to Utah.

Coates and Depken (2011: 601) examine the impact on tax revenue 'of various sporting and entertainment events . . . for 23 cities in Texas between January 1990 and December 2008'. They find that, while regular-season games (as well as the NFL (National Football League) Super Bowl and the NBA (National Basketball Association) All-Star game) increase local sales tax revenues, post-season college games reduce them. Fourie and Santana-Gallego (2010: 1), in a rare departure from the typical results of the literature, find a positive effect of hosting sporting events, including the World Cup. 'Using a standard gravity model of bilateral tourism flows between 200 countries from 1995 to 2006', which is derived from Rose and Spiegel (2011), they find that tourist arrivals increase by 7.6 percent. The results are larger for participants and statistically insignificant for nonparticipants.

Rose and Spiegel's study of the impact of the Olympics on bilateral trade patterns forms the basis of the framework I use to study the impact of the Women's World Cup. They base their estimation on the commonly used gravity model of trade. The gravity model applies Newtonian mechanics to bilateral trade flows by linking the volume of trade directly to the 'mass' of the two economies and inversely to the distance between them. Their estimation model can thus be expressed as:

$$\ln(X_{ijt}) = \alpha_0 + \alpha_{ij}D_{ij} + \beta'\mathbf{M_{ijt}} + \gamma'\mathbf{Z_{ijt}} + \delta_{it}\mathbf{S_{it}} + \varepsilon_{ijt} \quad (17.1)$$

where X_{ijt} is the volume of trade between country i and country j at time t, D_{ij} is the distance between countries i and j, $\mathbf{M_{ijt}}$ is a vector of variables that capture the mass of the two countries, $\mathbf{Z_{ijt}}$ is a vector of variables (explained below) that reflect the figurative distance between the two countries, and $\mathbf{S_{it}}$ is a vector of dummy variables that indicates whether country i hosted an event in year t.

Rose and Spiegel measure mass in three ways, using the countries' population, land area, and GDP per capita. In addition to physical distance, they use cultural, historical, and financial measures of distance. Specifically, they account for whether the countries share a common language, belong to a regional trade agreement, were both colonized by the same country, were colonies of one another, or were ever part of the same country. Rose and Spiegel also include whether the two countries share a border and the number of countries in each pair that is an island (0, 1, or 2).

Rose and Spiegel hypothesize that some nations bid to host the Olympics as part of a broader strategy of globalization. Starting with the 1960 Summer Games in Rome and continuing through the 2008 Summer Games in Beijing, many host countries have simultaneously engaged in economic and sometimes political openness. One sign of greater economic openness is a significant expansion of international trade. Rose and Spiegel incorporate variables that indicate the year in which a country hosted the Summer or Winter Olympics, and the Men's World Cup and all subsequent years, hypothesizing that bidding to host these events serves as a signal to the world that the country intends to be more open to trade.

Rose and Spiegel estimate a variety of equations to assess the sensitivity of their results to alternative approaches and alternative subsets of the data. In alternative specifications they allow for year fixed effects, trading-partner fixed effects, originating-country fixed effects, destination-country fixed effects, and, where possible, combinations of these fixed effects. For example, in some specifications they have year and originating-country dummy variables and destination-country fixed effects. They also allow for originating-country-specific time trends. To test for influential observations, they estimate the model on a variety of geographical and temporal subsamples of the data. Their resulting estimates of the impact of the Olympics are consistent across these alternatives.

17.3 THE IMPACT OF THE WOMEN'S WORLD CUP ON TRADE AND INCOME PER CAPITA

I extend Rose and Spiegel's analysis in three ways. First, and most importantly, I add the Women's World Cup variables to the regressions. These variables are constructed in the same way that Rose and Spiegel construct the variables for the Olympics and the Men's World Cup, but I report only regressions that include permanent effects as opposed to year-of-the-event effects.[2] Second, I improve upon Rose and Spiegel's specification by adding the lagged value of exports from country k to country j as a regressor. This modification captures the multi-year relationships between trading partners, which produce substantial inertia, or serial correlation, in the exports from one country to another. Rose and Spiegel do not account for this characteristic of trade. Third, following Coates (2012) who identified Japan as a potentially influential observation, particularly in a growth equation, I include a separate Summer Olympic effect for Japan, which expanded its trade dramatically in the post-Second World War era and hosted a Summer Olympics very early in the sample's time period, and a separate effect for the inaugural Women's World Cup hosted by China. Rose and Spiegel hypothesize that bidding for and hosting major international sporting events is a means by which countries signal their intent to be open to international trade.

In the time period analyzed here and by Rose and Spiegel, only China, the United States, and Sweden hosted a Women's World Cup. It seems unlikely that the US and Sweden were sending an openness signal, but it is clearly possible that China was. One can dispute whether one can attribute much of China's economic growth to the inaugural Women's World Cup in 1991. While the World Cup was a major international sporting event, it occurred only seven years after the People's Republic of China returned to the Summer Olympics in 1984 and 11 years after it returned to the Winter Olympics. This period also coincides with rapid growth in Chinese exports and imports following market-based reforms initiated in the late 1970s.

Results for the parameters of interest are presented in Table 17.1. Country fixed effects, country-specific time trends, and year fixed effects are not reported. Also not reported are variables on income and population of each country in the pair, membership in a customs region, common language, common colonizer, distance between countries, island nations, and similar variables included by Rose and Spiegel. The table reports only

Table 17.1   Bilateral trade effects of Women's World Cup

Variable	Model 1	Model 2	Model 3	Model 4	Model 5
Women's WC	0.561	−0.178	−0.247		−0.046
	0.000	0.000	0.000		0.002
Summer Olympics	0.263	0.230	0.235		0.025
	0.000	0.000	0.000		0.012
Winter Olympics	0.201	−0.027	−0.028		−0.031
	0.000	0.588	0.578		0.013
Men's World Cup	0.313	0.275	0.279		0.055
	0.000	0.000	0.000		0.000
China Women's WC			0.238		0.053
			0.039		0.116
Lagged log exports				0.809	0.757
				0.000	0.000
Constant	−20.523	−18.404	−18.386	−4.075	−2.610
	0.000	0.000	0.000	0.000	0.000
R-squared	0.613	0.695	0.695	0.869	0.873
Observations	449,220	449,220	449,220	409,746	409,746

Notes:
All regressions include: log of distance between trading partners, log of population and log of GDP per capita of both countries, whether or not the countries share a currency, have a common language, are parties to a regional trade agreement, share a border, were ever part of the same country, had a common colonizer, whether the importer is now or ever was a colony of the exporter, the log of the area of the exporter, and the number of island nations in the trading pair. The regressions also include exporting country fixed effects and year effects.
p-values below coefficient estimates.
Model 1: Rose and Spiegel (2011) with Women's World Cup Host added.
Model 2: R–S country fixed effects with Women's World Cup Host added.
Model 3: Model 2 plus China Women's World Cup Host added.
Model 4: Introducing lagged log of bilateral exports, no sport events.
Model 5: Model 4 plus sports events.

the coefficients from the sports event variables. Models 1 and 2 are identical to models reported by Rose and Spiegel except for the inclusion of the Women's World Cup variable. Model 3 adds a dummy variable indicating Chinese observations after that country hosted the Women's World Cup for the first time. Model 4 adds the lagged value of log exports to the basic Rose and Spiegel model but omits indicators of sports events, and Model 5 expands that model to include the sports event variables and the country and year effects. All models are estimated using errors clustered on trading pairs.

Model 1 produces results for the Summer and Winter Olympic variables and the Men's World Cup variable that resemble those reported by Rose and Spiegel, effects for the Summer Games and the World Cup that seem far too large to be plausible. Indeed, this model also finds an astonishingly large impact of hosting the Women's World Cup. Every year after and including the year a country hosts the Women's World Cup, that country's exports are 75 percent larger than they would otherwise have been.[3] The Summer Games' effect is about 30 percent and the Men's World Cup effect is about 37 percent. All of the coefficients are statistically significant at the 1 percent level or better.

The puzzling results for the impact of the Women's World Cup and Winter Olympic effects are not robust to alternative specifications. Model 2 introduces year and country effects. The Women's World Cup coefficient is now negative and statistically significant. The implied impact of hosting the event under this specification is a reduction of exports of about 16 percent (the coefficient is −0.178). Regressions not reported here that control for trading-partner fixed effects also find the Women's World Cup results in a statistically significant reduction in exports similar in size to that of Model 2. These results imply that the more reliable models consistently show that hosting the Women's World Cup is linked to a permanent reduction in export volume. This estimated impact, which is quite similar to the pattern of impacts of the Winter Olympics variable, leads to the next modification of the model.

While hosting a mega event might signal a growing openness to international trade, not all host nations send the same signal. Both the United States and Sweden (which hosted the Women's World Cup in 1995) were well integrated into the global community long before they hosted the Women's World Cup. The impact of the Women's World Cup on China might be far different, because, in 1991, when it hosted the Women's World Cup for the first time, it was in the midst of integrating itself into the world community. Based on this reasoning, I added a Chinese Women's World Cup variable to the analysis, the results of which are shown as Model 3 in Table 17.1. The inclusion of a China Women's World Cup dummy variable has little impact on the Summer and Winter Olympics or the Men's World Cup variables but it does lead the overall Women's World Cup variable to be slightly more negative (−0.178 versus −0.247). The Women's World Cup variable remains statistically significant at better than the 1 percent level. The China Women's World Cup variable is significant at the 5 percent level and positive. The Women's World Cup and Chinese Women's World Cup variables are essentially equal except for opposite signs. The estimated coefficients imply, therefore, that hosting the Women's World Cup is connected to about a 22 percent reduction in exports for the US and Sweden and essentially no impact on exports for China.

The coefficients on the Summer Olympics and the Men's World Cup variables remain large and significant throughout these specifications. Hosting the Summer Olympics raises exports by about 27 percent, while hosting the Men's World Cup raises exports by 32 percent in Model 3. Many readers may find this impact implausibly large. Coates (2012) addresses this question by including lagged exports as an explanatory variable in the model. Model 4 shows the estimated effect of the lagged export variable in a regression with no sports events variables and no country or year effects. Model 5 reports the sports event coefficients from a model that includes a lagged export variable. Including this variable in the analysis reduces the estimated Summer Olympics coefficient to 0.025 and the Men's World Cup coefficient to 0.055. These are far lower and more plausible than the effects reported for Model 3. The harmful impact of hosting the Women's World Cup in the United States and Sweden is also far smaller once lagged exports are in the model, a coefficient of −0.046 compared to −0.247. The positive coefficient on the Chinese Women's World Cup is similarly reduced so that the net impact, the sum of the Women's and Chinese Women's World Cup variables, is again essentially zero.

The evidence of this section strongly implies that hosting the Women's World Cup has little or no beneficial impact on a country's international trade. Having no impact on trade does not mean that hosting the event has no impact on the economy of the host country. An alternative question is the extent to which hosting the event affects the rate of economic growth. Using the income data from Rose and Spiegel (2011), I estimate a growth equation that includes hosting the Women's World Cup as an explanatory variable. Coates (2012) estimates a similar model that includes the Summer and Winter Olympics and variables indicating whether a country hosted either the Commonwealth Games or the Pan American Games. The model includes the log of population and country fixed effects and country-specific time trends.

Equation (17.2) is adapted from Barro and Sala-i-Martin (1999). Their model assumes that every country has the same steady-state, or long-run equilibrium, levels of GDP per capita and capital–labor ratio. This implies that poorer countries grow faster than richer ones, but that these growth rates will also converge over time. The parameter β_1 is a function of the speed of convergence. If countries do not have the same steady state, then the model does not hold. If one wants to test for convergence, the empirical analysis should be done on a homogeneous group of countries. The goal is to assess whether hosting the Women's World Cup influences a country's growth rate of GDP per capita. Consequently, the discussion and analysis focus on the event effects and not on estimating the rate of convergence. The estimating equation is:

Table 17.2   Growth regression

Variable	Base model	China	Japan	China and Japan
Summer Olympics	0.026	0.026	0.015	0.015
	0.060	0.060	0.305	0.307
Winter Olympics	0.015	0.015	0.009	0.009
	0.446	0.449	0.640	0.645
Women's World Cup	0.009	0.008	0.008	0.006
	0.675	0.763	0.721	0.816
Japan Summer Olympics			0.071	0.071
			0.070	0.070
China Women's World		0.011		0.013
Cup		0.854		0.830
Men's World Cup	−0.015	−0.015	−0.013	−0.013
	0.213	0.216	0.256	0.259
Lagged real GDP per	−0.149	−0.149	−0.151	−0.151
capita	0.000	0.000	0.000	0.000
R-squared	0.158	0.158	0.159	0.159
N	4,431	4,431	4,431	4,431
Null: Event coefficients all zero F-statistic	1.47	1.18	1.19	1.53
Prob-values	0.209	0.316	0.104	0.163

$$\ln rgdppc_{it} - \ln rgdppc_{it-1} = \beta_0 + \beta_1 \ln rgdppc_{it-1} + \beta_2 \ln population_{it} +$$

$$\sum_k \delta_k m_{itk} + \sum_j \gamma_j D_{itj} + \mu_{it}, \qquad (17.2)$$

where $\ln rgdppc_{it}$ is the log of real GDP per capita in country i at time t, and $\ln population$ is the log of the population of the ith country in year t, the βs, γs, and δs are parameters to be estimated, and μ is a random error term with mean zero and variance that may differ by country i. The D_{itj} capture city- and year-specific effects and city-specific time trends; m_{itk} are the event dummy variables, which take a value of 1 in every year from the first time a country hosts an event through the end of the sample, and zero for all prior years. There are four events in the analysis, the Summer and Winter Olympics, the Men's World Cup, and the Women's World Cup. The δ_k are the parameters of interest, particularly those pertaining to the Women's World Cup.

Table 17.2 shows the estimation results for the variables of interest in the growth equation. None of the event variables is individually significant at the 5 percent level, though the Summer Olympics variable is significant at the 10 percent level. Even that weak significance disappears when one controls for the Tokyo Summer Olympics of 1964 separately, as is done in the third column of Table 17.2. Those results show that the impact of hosting the Summer Olympics is largely driven by one country, Japan. Nonetheless, the coefficient on the Women's World Cup is not statistically significant in any of the four growth regressions. In other words, there is no evidence that hosting the Women's World Cup had any impact on the level of economic growth in any of the first three countries to host it.

The analysis of this section has shown that hosting the Women's World Cup did not materially affect the level of exports by the host country, nor did it cause that country to experience more rapid growth in real output per person. Such findings are not surprising. As seen earlier in the chapter, there is little evidence that events like the Olympics (Porter and Fletcher, 2008) or the Men's World Cup (Baade and Matheson, 2004; Hagn and Maennig, 2007; Maennig, 2007) have large impacts on the overall economic circumstances of the host country, so for the Women's World Cup, which is far smaller than either, to generate them would be surprising. As mentioned earlier, average attendance at the 2011 FIFA Women's World Cup held in Germany was 26,428; the most highly attended Women's World Cups, those in the US in 1999 and in China in 2007, each had average attendance of over 37,000 (37,319 and 37,218, respectively). By contrast, the last Men's World Cup with average attendance below 30,000 (24,250) was in Chile in 1962, and every Men's World Cup since then, except Spain in 1982, averaged more than 42,000 per game in attendance. Each Men's World Cup has involved more than 32 matches since 1958, and it changed to a 64-match format starting in France in 1998, while the Women's World Cup expanded to 32 matches only in 1999.

17.4   OTHER IMPACTS OF THE WOMEN'S WORLD CUP

The evidence above indicates that hosting the Women's World Cup has little impact on either the volume of international trade or the rate of economic growth in the host country. The event is both quite new and suffers from the relative underdevelopment of women's sports in general and women's soccer in particular. That relative underdevelopment has historical roots, which I describe below. At the same time, it may be that the Women's World Cup has accelerated the growth of women's soccer both in the United States and around the world.[4] This section examines the scant information available on women's soccer to assess the impact of the World Cup on the expansion of the game.

One dramatic difference between the women's and men's events is their connection to professional leagues. The Women's United Soccer Association (WUSA), the first women's professional soccer league in the United States, started in 2000 and folded in September 2003. Nonetheless, during its short existence, the WUSA attracted over 8,000 fans per game, a number on a par with the top-tier men's leagues in some small countries and with lower division teams in some larger countries. A more apt comparison is the average attendance for the clubs in Major League Soccer (MLS), the top men's soccer division in the United States, during 2000–03. Average attendance for all MLS clubs in the period was about 14,800. Two of the clubs, the now-defunct Miami Fusion in 2000 and FC Dallas in 2003, averaged below 8,000 in one season. All other clubs averaged over 9,000, and most averaged over 10,000 in every season. Thus, the WUSA drew well compared to the men's league, which is evidence that there was a relatively strong market for women's soccer in the United States.

The interest in women's soccer in the early 2000s might have been a short-lived response to the dramatic US win in the 1999 Women's World Cup in Los Angeles. The league started well with respect to attendance. The league's financial plan called for breaking even by the fifth season, with attendance of 7,000 per game projected for the first year, a television deal, and between $14 and $20 million in corporate sponsorships (Lee, 2001). Lee (2003a) reported that five of the eight teams in the WUSA had lower average attendance in 2003 than in 2002. In addition, television and corporate sponsorships fell short of expectations (Lee, 2003a, 2003b). Turner Broadcasting agreed to broadcast 22 WUSA games, hoping to achieve ratings of 0.5 to 1.0, which would match the initial ratings of the Women's NBA and MLS (Lee, 2001). Unfortunately, the ratings for the WUSA were far lower, about 0.1 on Pax TV.

A new league, Women's Professional Soccer (WPS), formed in 2007 with plans to begin play in 2009.[5] Several of its clubs struggled financially throughout its existence. For example, the 2010 champion, FC Gold Pride, folded shortly after winning the championship. Despite greater-than-anticipated losses in their first year, many teams promised to continue operating. According to a news release on the WPS website,[6] 'The league average salary is expected to be around $32,000 for the 2009 season under a seven-month playing contract'. However, *Sports Illustrated* reported that[7] 'The average WPS player salary in 2010 was about $27,000, with U.S. Women's national team players and top internationals earning around double that'. The *New York Times'* Jere Longman reported that the average WPS salary in 2011 was $25,000. The disparities in pay presented another difficulty. WPS clubs were required to pay US National team players at least $40,000, with star players and foreign nationals making $60,000 to $80,000 per season. Brazilian star Marta reportedly made $500,000 per year, while other players earned less than $10,000. Some reportedly were paid $200 per game.[8]

WPS attendance dropped from an average of about 4,700 in its inaugural season to about 3,600 in the second year.[9] Attendance for the 2011 season was mixed, ending down slightly from 2010. From the start of the season through the date of the Women's World Cup Final on July 17, 2011, WPS average attendance was 2,881; after the World Cup, average attendance rose to 5,126, excluding WPS playoff games. The Women's World Cup apparently sparked interest in the WPS, at least through the end of the 2011 season. In May of 2012, the league folded, in part because of poor attendance and weak television ratings. Three WPS teams began playing in the WPSL, which is a mix of professional and amateur teams.[10] Christie Rampone, a US national team player, 'suggested WPS consider a semipro model that exists in Germany and other European countries'.[11]

Women's association football outside the United States began to grow in the 1970s, but even now few countries have fully professional women's leagues. A better description of most of the existing professional women's leagues is that they are semi-professional, as some players earn a living playing the game, while many, perhaps most, do not.[12] The discussion that follows focuses on leagues in England, with some attention paid to France, Germany, Sweden, and Japan, for three reasons. First, I had ready access to information in English and colleagues from non-English-speaking countries, who were willing to share their knowledge. Second, Germany has consistently competed for the championship, winning it in 2003 and 2007; Sweden's women have been highly competitive on the world stage and Sweden hosted the Women's World Cup; and Japan was a surprise winner of the 2011 World Cup championship. Finally, France, Germany, and England have well-developed, and in the cases of Germany and England, enormously successful and highly competitive men's professional football leagues.

The men's soccer leagues in England are well developed and highly functioning. Players for English Premier League teams are among the most highly compensated footballers in the world. By contrast, English women's soccer is just beginning to organize. In August 2011, the website for England's FA announced 'a new elite, summer league for women's football', the Women's Super League (WSL).[13] This would supplement the men's leagues which run from August through May. The article says that '(t)he WSL concept was developed to enable players in this country to earn a good living from the game whilst allowing WSL clubs to develop new revenue streams and support for women's football'.

The intent to promote the development of women's football and to enable women players to earn a living from the game is quite a remarkable turnaround from the position of the FA in 1921. Contemporary accounts were highly critical of the women's game, game conditions, and the use of game revenues:

> Complaints having been made as to football being played by women, the Council feel impelled to express their strong opinion that the game of football is quite unsuitable for females and ought not to be encouraged.
>
> Complaints have been made as to the conditions under which some of these matches have been arranged and played, and the appropriation of the receipts to other than Charitable objects.
>
> The Council are further of the opinion that an excessive proportion of the receipts are absorbed in expenses and an inadequate percentage devoted to Charitable objects.
>
> For these reasons the Council requests the clubs belonging to the Association refuse the use of their grounds for such matches. (Simkin, 2012b)

The request not to let women use the facilities was in response to a series of matches in 1920 between England and France. Four matches played in England raised money for disabled and discharged veterans of the First World War. The first match had an attendance of 25,000; the attendance at the third and fourth matches was 12,000 and 10,000, respectively. The teams then met for matches in France, where attendance was 22,000, 16,000, and 14,000, respectively. The English team returned home and continued playing matches. On December 26, a match drew an attendance of 53,000, 'with an estimated 14,000 disappointed fans locked outside'. In 1921, despite turning down over 100 matches, the team played in matches with total attendance reported at 900,000. The club played matches whose proceeds were to benefit miners during the 1921 Miners' Lock-out, and this involvement in politics may have been the reason that the Football Association moved to forbid use of club facilities for women's football, though the stated objection was concern for the women's health. As recently as 1962, the Football Association 'stopped a match from taking place at the British Legion ground at Newton between Preston Ladies and Oldham Ladies in aid of the Wigan Society for the Blind. The Wigan Rovers rented the ground from the British Legion and the FA told them that they faced suspension if they allowed the game to go ahead' (ibid.).

The Women's Football Association (WFA) formed in 1969 and established a national cup competition in 1971 (Simkin, 2012a). Twelve years later, the WFA associated with the FA. The English team reached the final in the first ever Union of European Football Associations (UEFA) women's tournament in 1984 and won the tournament in 1985. In 1991, the WFA established a 24-team league. Despite the existence of this league, the ability of English women to compete on the international level did not proceed sufficiently rapidly for the WFA and the FA. For example, the England side did not qualify for the 1991 Women's World Cup and exited the 1995 competition in the first round of the knockout stage, having come in second in their group. England did not qualify for the 1999 or 2003 World Cups and was eliminated from both the 2007 and 2011 events in the first stage of the knockout round. The announcement of the new women's league with the goal of allowing women to earn a living from the game came less than two months after the England side was eliminated from the 2011 tournament.

France and Germany have also had a long tradition of women's soccer. *Championnat de France de football feminine* was established in 1974. Since 2004–05 it has had 12 teams, the bottom two of which are relegated. Yet the league is not firmly established. Marie-Georges Buffet, Sports Minister in France from 1997 through 2002, in a July 4, 2012 interview with Adrien Pecout for *SoFoot*, said, 'women's football is not well developed yet. There are a lot of amateur clubs without a women's section'. Some clubs try to create women's teams but fail because there are not enough girls, who then end up playing against boys, failing, and quitting. Minister Buffet says the French Football Federation needs to make a major effort to help the clubs, something that requires political will.[14] She also suggests that trying to create a women's professional league artificially by having female counterparts to the male teams will not work because of a shortage of players. Instead, she indicates that local amateur clubs should form teams, even if it means working together to have enough players.[15]

The lack of players for the women's professional league in France may explain why American teenager Lindsey Horan withdrew from a commitment to play soccer at the University of North Carolina to sign a two-year professional contract with Paris-Saint Germaine.[16] Yet it was only in 2009 that the French Bureau du Conseil Fédéral created professional status for women soccer players.[17] Apparently, the intent was to enable French clubs to receive compensation should their players wish to leave, as in the cases of Sonia Bompastor and Camille Abily who had been contacted by American teams in the WPS. Apparently, the rule, which was intended to prevent French players from leaving for the United States, has attracted American players to France.

The German Women's Bundesliga was formed in 1990 by the German Football Association (DFB). The league has 12 teams and, like its French counterpart, the 11th and 12th place teams suffer relegation to the second division. The structure was modified in 1997 to make a single national league from two regional leagues. A unique feature of German women's football is the close link between the clubs and the national team. 'Germany understands that a strong national team benefits the clubs, and that strong clubs benefit the national team', according to Shek Borkowski, former coach of Russian champions Zvezda 2005 Perm.[18] It could also reflect the relatively weak international structure of women's soccer, as the German club teams consist almost entirely of German players. The integration includes 'weekly communication between club coaches and the national team coaching staff'. Many of the clubs even employ the same game tactics as the national team.

While the Women's Bundesliga has a structure similar to the fully professional men's league, it uses a semi-professional model. Most players for the Women's Bundesliga must have a second source of income, and many are also students. As in the US, national team players have higher salaries than other players, but across the league salaries are low. Despite low salaries, the league requires funding from the DFB to survive. Recall that average attendance in WPS games was 3,500 or higher; the best clubs in the Women's Bundesliga average even less, around 1,000.

Like the German and the French leagues, the 12-team Nadeshiko women's soccer league in Japan is best described as semi-professional. Soccer got a late start in Japan, where the J League (men) began very recently, in 1993. Despite Japan's victory in the 2011 Women's World Cup, women's soccer still faces many hurdles. The *Asahi Shimbun* reports that 'the excitement that gripped the nation after Japan's World Cup victory may not automatically lead to more funding or popularity in women's professional soccer', where teams in the Nadeshiko League average under 800 fans per match. Moreover, The *Asahi Shimbun* article (World Cup Victory Unlikely to Boost Nadeshiko League, 2011) also reports that former president of the Japan Football Association Saburo Kawabuchi attributes some of Japan's success on the international level to Japanese women playing abroad. Under a program begun in 2010, players were provided with funds to assist them in transferring to teams outside Japan.[19]

Sweden, a perennial world power in women's soccer, also has only a semi-professional women's league. It held a national championship for women's teams in 1973 and formed a top division nationwide league in 1988 by gathering clubs from around the country (http://svenskfotboll.se/in-english/domestic-football/). The top division, Damallsvenskan, has 12 teams, the bottom two of which are relegated to Division 1 which consists of two leagues. Salary data are not generally available, but in September of 2007 some salaries for Swedish athletes for 2005 and 2006 were published in the newspaper *Expressen*. It reports salaries for both men's and women's soccer teams and for some club officials. Unfortunately, there is no uniformity as to the officials included in the dataset. It generally provides information for the team's trainer, but some teams also include information for the club director, '*sportchef*', president, and in some cases 'president and CEO'. Moreover, in a handful of instances, both the women's and men's soccer teams from the same sport club are listed.[20] For all the individuals listed, the average salary for men is 282,623 kroner (n = 679), about \$42,400; for women, the average is 125,479 kroner (n = 199), about \$18,820.[21] Removing coaches and club officials from the men's salary average drops it to 258,257 kroner (\$38,742); making a similar adjustment on the women's side produces an average of 108,502 kroner (\$16,277).

The Swedish data include far more men's than women's teams, and the men's teams list more players than do the women's teams. Only one men's team fails to include a trainer in the salary list, and several include an assistant trainer. Altogether there are 27 trainers or assistant trainers for the 23 men's squads. By contrast, only six of the 10 women's teams list a trainer. Not too much should be made of this disparity because the salary information was taken from tax records and put together by the newspaper staff. Nonetheless, it suggests the relative underdevelopment of the women's game, even in a country that is a perennial power. Moreover, only one player, Brazilian forward Marta da Silva, a five-time FIFA World Player of the Year, was more highly paid than the team's trainer. At the time the salary data were collected, Marta was in the midst of leading the Swedish league in scoring for three consecutive years. On the men's side, most clubs have several players whose salaries exceed the pay of the trainer.

17.5   ENDORSEMENTS IN WOMEN'S SOCCER

The previous section makes clear that women's soccer has struggled for fan interest and commercial success. Similarly, women professional soccer players earn much less for playing soccer than their male counterparts, and top women's leagues around the world usually include both professionals and amateurs. However, the Women's World Cup may have helped women soccer players to succeed in a different way: through endorsements.

The success of women's soccer has led to endorsement deals for many of the American women from the 1996 Olympic and 1999 World Cup championship squads, though these deals were small in comparison to those garnered by other women athletes. The Forbes list of the 100 highest-paid athletes reveals that the highest-paid female athlete in every year since 1990 has been a tennis player.[22] In no year does a soccer player appear on the list. In fact, no woman from a team sport is ever on the list, which is dominated by tennis players. A list of the top-25 female endorsers in the *Sports Business Journal* (May 11, 1998) lists Mia Hamm as tied for 13th, with deals valued at $1 million. Several women basketball players and one volleyball player appeared on the list, but all the rest were individual sport athletes, predominantly from tennis and golf.

Hamm's shoe line at Nike, and the related ads featuring her with Michael Jordan, was the most prominent deal involving a member of the US women's soccer team. Nike even named a large building after her on its Oregon campus. Other women from the team signed endorsement deals between the 1996 Olympic and 1999 World Cup successes. For example, Carla Overbeck signed a shoe deal with Fila, and Kristine Lilly with Adidas. However, few of these deals lasted long. Overbeck's deal expired in 2001, and the endorsements had little carryover into new opportunities for women.

Ellen Zavian, a sports lawyer and agent who represented many of the women on the US national team, commenting on a draft of this chapter, has claimed that the largest economic impact of all women's sports participation and success is probably through the apparel and fashion markets, a result she described as 'sad' (Zavian, 2011). Specifically, Zavian explained that 'the money female athletes earn from their governing bodies/leagues is very small, compared to their sponsorship money. Most of the sponsorship money comes from their apparel/footwear deal' (Zavian, 2012). The growth of women's participation in sports and even their success in the competitions has not translated into economically viable women's professional leagues. And without these leagues, the opportunity to build a professional athletic career is still much weaker for the women than for the men.

Ms. Zavian is not alone in her assessment of women's endorsement possibilities. Evidence suggests that success in athletic competition alone does not bring endorsements for women. Other attributes, particularly physical attractiveness rather than athletic prowess, may still be the key to endorsement success for women athletes.[23]

Michelle Kaufman, writing in the 1998 *Sports Business Journal*, claimed that 'a female athlete's looks are still a factor in securing endorsements – much more so than male athletes' looks'. She went on to quote Tom George, the senior vice president for athlete marketing at Advantage International, the company that represented star basketball player Sheryl Swoopes:

> I'll probably take heat for saying this, but when I'm pitching Sheryl Swoopes I bring up the fact that she's not only a wonderful athlete, but she's a mom and she's very attractive. . . . How a woman looks still matters in endorsements and

just about everything else. It's not right, but it's reality. Pretty women are more marketable. (Kaufman, 1998)

Perhaps the best example of the importance of appearance is tennis player Anna Kournikova, an attractive young blonde who appeared in men's magazines including the *Sports Illustrated* swimsuit issue in 2004 and was voted as the 'hottest female athlete' on the ESPN.com website. While Ms. Kournikova ranked in the top five in female athlete earnings, she never won a major tournament and never ranked higher than eighth best female tennis player in the world. There can be little doubt that these attitudes remain. Kiefer and Scharfenkamp (2012) study the popularity of female tennis players and find that the more attractive the player, the more popular she is, and popularity is important for endorsements.

This claim is further supported by recent evidence. Consider the 2011 US Women's World Cup team, which featured goalkeeper Hope Solo and forward Abby Wambach.[24] James (2011) commented: 'Since the end of the World Cup, Solo has signed multiyear endorsement deals, with Gatorade, Bank of America, BlackBerry, Ubisoft, and Electronic Arts, which are believed to exceed seven figures'.[25] Solo also was more in the public eye than Wambach. She drove a pace car at the Brickyard 500, posed nude for *ESPN the Magazine* (The Body Issue, 2011), and competed on 'Dancing with the Stars'. Speaking on 'The Dan Patrick Show' (August 22, 2011), she said, 'post-tournament of course there's those opportunities out there for many of us, not just me, and it is our duty to capitalize on whatever we can do to bring attention to the game and to the sport, but being true to ourselves as athletes'. While Solo denies using nudity to promote herself,[26] she has also said, 'Hopefully, in selling the sex symbol persona, at the end of the day we'll gain more viewership and more long-term fans' ('Hope Solo Talks about Effect of Sex Appeal in Marketing Female Athletes', 2011).

Not just physical attractiveness matters for success as an endorser. Doug Shabelman, president of Burns Entertainment, emphasizes personality. 'Every time you see Hope Solo, she's pumping her fist and clapping her hands and she's got a really great demeanor and a great smile and everything about it is positive'.[27] By contrast, Wambach is 'more understated personally and professionally' than Solo.[28]

Abby Wambach had numerous endorsement deals prior to the World Cup, including with Nike since 2002 and Gatorade since 2004, and has starred in ad campaigns since the games, especially leading up to the 2012 Summer Olympics. She also signed a deal with Bank of America. While Wambach's marketing image has emphasized her athletic prowess, and she is often depicted in her soccer uniform, dripping with sweat, she has recently followed Solo's lead, posing nude for *ESPN the Magazine* (The Body Issue, 2012). In a video on the ESPN the Magazine website, Wambach says that she is proud of her body and that she wants to show people 'that no matter who you are, no matter what shapes you are, that's still beautiful'.[29]

17.6 CONCLUSION

This chapter has examined the economic impact of the Women's Football World Cup from two perspectives. The first is the traditional approach to mega events, examining the impact of hosting the event on two macro-economic variables, international trade and growth of GDP. Using bilateral trade data and the empirical model of Rose and Spiegel (2011), I find that hosting the Women's World Cup does not have a positive effect on trade. It appears that hosting the Cup worked out well for China, where the estimated impact of hosting has no effect. This is an improvement over the negative and statistically significant effect estimated for the United States and Sweden. The evidence is strong that hosting the Women's World Cup has no impact on the rate of economic growth.

A different approach to examining the impact of the Women's World Cup is to find how women's soccer and women soccer players have fared since the tournament began in 1991. The great success of the US women in winning the 1999 Women's World Cup in dramatic fashion spurred the creation of a women's professional soccer league in the United States. Despite initial success, that league folded after three years. Women's professional soccer in the rest of the world is no more developed as most leagues are semi-professional, combining both paid and unpaid players. Evidence indicates that women's leagues do not draw large crowds even when the players are among the best in the world. Moreover, while the women's professional soccer league in the US from 2000 to 2003 drew average attendance of around 8,000, it folded after three seasons. Its successor league also operated for only three seasons and rarely drew a crowd of 8,000 except for the championship match, with average attendance less than 4,800, the peak reached in the first season. Leagues outside the United States draw even less well. Despite its success, the Women's World Cup does not appear to have produced a large or lasting effect on the growth of women's professional soccer.

In contrast, the effects of the great success of the early women's teams led to some of the players' getting impressive endorsement deals and becoming celebrities. However, the financial rewards and celebrity of these exceptional athletes pale in comparison to the queens of endorsements from tennis and golf. The evidence also raises questions about the durability of the endorsement deals. As Ellen Zavian laments, the lasting impact may have been predominantly for women to earn endorsements through the athletic apparel and fashion industry rather than through sport careers. Finally, endorsements may be disproportionately linked to appearance, or sex appeal, rather than athletic success.

NOTES

1. The attendance figures for China 2007 are less dubious, as they are rarely equal to facility capacity and are generally not nice, round numbers.
2. I am grateful to Rose and Spiegel for providing both their data and programs.
3. Percentage change is calculated as $100*[\exp(0.561)-1]$, where 0.561 is the estimated coefficient on the Women's World Cup variable.
4. A related literature asks what makes women's teams successful in international competitions and if the factors are the same for both men's and women's teams. See Hoffmann et al. (2006), Torgler (2008), and Matheson and Congdon-Hohman (2011).
5. The league folded in spring 2012 but discussions about a new league had begun by summer of 2012.
6. See http://www.womensprosoccer.com/news/press_releases/090216-player-contract-finalized.
7. See http://sportsillustrated.cnn.com/2010/writers/jeff_kassouf/12/06/wps.salary/index.html#ixzz1YF7z7rxr.
8. See http://www.nytimes.com/2011/08/09/sports/soccer/unsteady-financial-footing-for-womens-soccer-league.html?pagewanted=all.
9. See http://www.sportsbusinessdaily.com/Daily/Issues/2011/08/16/Research-and-Ratings/WPS-gate.aspx?hl=WPS%20attendance&sc=0.
10. See http://www.sportsbusinessdaily.com/Daily/Issues/2012/05/21/Leagues-and-Governing-Bodies/WPS.aspx?hl=WPS%20attendance&sc=0.
11. See http://www.nytimes.com/2011/08/09/sports/soccer/unsteady-financial-footing-for-womens-soccer-league.html?pagewanted=all (Longman, 2011).
    In the aftermath of the United States winning the gold medal in Women's Soccer at the 2012 London Olympic Games, there is a renewed push for a women's professional soccer league in the United States. See http://goal.blogs.nytimes.com/2012/08/11/for-womens-leagues-strike-1-strike-2-strike-3/.
12. Kassouf (2010) wrote, 'The fully professional status of WPS is truly still a rarity in women's soccer. . . . Players in most of the better European leagues work additional jobs in the offseason (and even during the season) to make the dream of playing top-flight soccer come true'. See http://sportsillustrated.cnn.com/2010/writers/jeff_kassouf/12/06/wps.salary/index.html.
13. The article may be found at: http://www.thefa.com/GetIntoFootball/Players/Players Pages/WomensAndGirls.
14. Minister Buffet also supported a petition to get the French government to acknowledge the Women's World Cup as a major sport event which would give the opportunity to watch it freely on television. See http://www.womenssoccerunited.com/profiles/blogs/french-feminine-football-former-minister-of-sports-interview.
15. See http://www.womenssoccerunited.com/profiles/blogs/french-feminine-football-former-minister-of-sports-interview. French original at: http://www.sofoot.com/buffet-le-sport-reflete-le-sexisme-de-la-societe-159006.html (Pecout, 2012).
16. See http://www.ourcoloradonews.com/golden/sports/horan-breaks-new-ground-with-pro-contract/article_0598366e-d753-11e1-a390-0019bb2963f4.html (Miller, 2012).

17. See http://www2.lequipe.fr/redirect-v6/homes/Football/breves2009/20090306_081943_statut-pro-pour-ces-dames.html.
18. See http://espn.go.com/news-opinion/6670374/women-world-cup-german-pro-league-brings-success (Pel, 2011).
19. See http://www.asahi.com/english/TKY201107210380.html (accessed September 7, 2011).
20. It is important to remember that European sports clubs are quite different from franchises in the US professional leagues. An individual club may have teams in several sports, both men's and women's, and teams in multiple divisions of the same sport.
21. A kroner is roughly equal to $0.15.
22. The information is available at the Topendsports website at: http://www.topendsports.com/world/lists/earnings/women-paid.htm (accessed October 3 2011).
23. For more on the importance of body image in women's sports, see Chapter 10 in this volume.
24. Other players from that World Cup team also had endorsement deals. For example, prior to the competition, Under Armour, a sports apparel company, had signed three women, Heather Mitts, Lauren Cheney, and Becky Sauerbrunn (Walker, 2011). Winning is also important. Susan Berfield (2011) noted the commercial success of Solo and Wambach but then wrote, 'Yet most others on the team remain anonymous – a reminder that for American soccer players public exposure is usually ephemeral. "It would have been amazing if this team won," says Hamm, who led the U.S. team to a World Cup championship in 1999. "So many more players would have been included in the celebration".' See http://www.businessweek.com/magazine/selling-abby-wambach-10202011.html.
25. See http://espn.go.com/espnw/more-sports/7144750/hope-solo-abby-wambach-take-different-paths-soccer.
26. Ibid.
27. Ibid.
28. Ibid.
29. See http://espn.go.com/espn/story/_/id/8094534/us-national-soccer-team-forward-abby-wambach-strips-2012-body-issue-espn-magazine.

REFERENCES

Baade, Robert A. and Victor A. Matheson (2004), 'The Quest for the Cup: Assessing the Economic Impact of the World Cup', *Regional Studies*, **38**(4), June: 343–54.
Barro, Robert and Xavier Sala-i-Martin (1999), *Economic Growth*, Cambridge, MA: MIT Press.
Berfield, Susan (2011), 'Selling Abby Wambach', online at: http://www.businessweek.com/magazine/selling-abby-wambach-10202011.html (accessed July 25, 2012).
Coates, Dennis (2012), 'Not-so-Mega Events', in Maennig and Zimbalist (eds), pp. 401–33.
Coates, Dennis and Craig A. Depken, II (2011), 'Mega-events: Is Baylor Football to Waco What the Super Bowl Is to Houston?', *Journal of Sports Economics*, **12**(6), December: 599–620.
FIFA.com, (2011a), 'Unprecedented TV Coverage of FIFA Women's World Cup 2011', online at: http://www.fifa.com/womensworldcup/organisation/media/newsid=1376651/index.html (accessed September 23, 2011).
FIFA.com (2011b) 'FIFA Women's World Cup Germany 2011 Sets New TV Viewing Records', online at: http://www.fifa.com/womensworldcup/organisation/media/newsid=1477957/index.html (accessed September 23, 2011).
Fourie, Johan and Maria Santana-Gallego (2010), 'The Impact of Mega-Events on Tourist Arrivals', Stellenbosch University Working Paper 171.
Hagn, Florian and Wolfgang Maennig, (2007), 'Short-term to Long-term Employment

Effects of the Football World Cup 1974 in Germany', IASE/NAASE Working Paper Series, No. 07–21.

Hoffmann, Robert, Lee Chew Ging, Victor Matheson and Bala Ramasamy (2006), 'International Women's Football and Gender Inequality', *Applied Economics Letters*, **13**(15), December: 999–1001.

'Hope Solo Talks About Effect of Sex Appeal in Marketing Female Athletes' (2011), *Sports Business Journal*, online at: http://www.sportsbusinessdaily.com/Daily/Issues/2011/08/24/Marketing-and-Sponsorship/Hope-Solo.aspx? (accessed August 24, 2011).

Humphreys, Brad R. and Szymon Prokopowicz (2007), 'Assessing the Impact of Sport Mega Events in Transition Economies: Euro 2012 in Poland and Ukraine', *International Journal of Sport Management and Marketing*, **2**(5–6), June: 496–509.

James, Brant (2011), 'Hope Solo, Abby Wambach Take Different Paths', *ESPNW*, October 24, online at: http://espn.go.com/espnw/more-sports/7144750/hope-solo-abby-wambach-take-different-paths-soccer (accessed July 17, 2012).

Kassouf, Jeff (2010), 'Player wages the hot topic in WPS', online at: http://sportsillus-trated cnn.com/2010/writers/jeff_kassouf/12/06/wps.salary/index.html (accessed July 12, 2012).

Kaufman, Michelle (1998), 'Women Take Their Place at the Table', *Sports Business Journal*, May, online at: http://www.sportsbusinessdaily.com/Journal/Issues/1998/05/19980511/No-Topic-Name/Women-Take-Their-Place-At-The-Table.aspx (accessed October 3, 2011).

Kiefer, Stephanie and Katrin Scharfenkamp (2012), 'The Impact of Physical Attractiveness on Popularity of Female Tennis Players on Online Media', Discussion Paper 6/2012, Institute of Organizational Economics, University of Münster, online at: http://econstor.eu/bitstream/10419/59593/1/71895341X.pdf (accessed July 20, 2012).

Lee, Jennifer (2001), 'WUSA's Goals within Reach', *Sports Business Journal*, April 9–15, online at: http://www.sportsbusinessdaily.com/Journal/Issues/2001/04/20010409/No-Topic-Name/Wusas-Goals-Within_Reach.aspx (accessed December 4, 2010).

Lee, Jennifer (2003a), 'WUSA to Seek Individual Owners', *Sport Business Journal*, August 11–17, online at: http://www.sportbusinessdaily.com/Journal/Issues/2003/08/2003081/This-Weeks-Issue/WUSA-To-Seek-Individual-Owners.aspx (accessed December 4, 2012).

Lee, Jennifer (2003b), 'WUSA's Third Season Posts Mixed Results', *Sports Business Journal*, August 18–24, online at: http://www.sportbusinessdaily.com/Journal/Issues/2003/08/20030818/This-Weeks-Issue/Wusas-3Rd-Season-Posts-Mixed-Results.aspx (accessed December 4, 2012).

Leeds, Michael (2008), 'Do Good Olympics Make Good Neighbors?', *Contemporary Economic Policy*, **26**(3), July: 460–67.

Longman, Jere (2011), 'After World Cup Thrills, Players Return to Unstable Women's League', *New York Times*, August 9, online at: http://www.nytimes.com/2011/08/09/sports/soccer/unsteady-financial-footing-for-womens-soccer-league.html?pagewanted=all (accessed July 24, 2012).

Maennig, Wolfgang (2007), 'One Year Later: A Re-appraisal of the Economics of the 2006 Soccer World Cup', IASE/NAASE Working Paper Series, No. 07-25.

Maennig, Wolfgang and Andrew Zimbalist (2012), *International Handbook on the Economics of Sporting Mega Events*, Cheltenham, UK and Northampton, MA, USA: Edward Elgar.

Matheson, Victor A. and Joshua Congdon-Hohman (2011), 'International Women's Soccer and Gender Inequality: Revisited', Faculty Research Series No. 11-07, Department of Economics, College of the Holy Cross, Worcester, MA.

Miller, Brian (2012), 'Horan Breaks New Ground with Pro Contract', online at: http://www.ourcoloradonews.com/golden/sports/horan-breaks-new-ground-with-pro-contract/article_0598366e-d753-11e1-a390-0019bb2963f4.html (accessed July 20, 2012).

Pecout, Adrien (2012), 'Buffet: "Le sport reflète le sexisme de la société"', online at: http://www.sofoot.com/buffet-le-sport-reflete-le-sexisme-de-la-societe-159006.html (accessed July 24, 2012).

Pel, Jenna (2011), 'German Pro League Brings Success', online at: http://espn.go.com/espnw/news-opinion/6670374/women-world-cup-german-pro-league-brings-success   (accessed July 21, 2012).

Porter, Phillip K. and Deborah Fletcher (2008), 'The Economic Impact of the Olympic Games: Ex Ante Predictions and Ex Post Reality', *Journal of Sports Management*, **22**(4), July: 470–86.

Rose, Andrew K. and Mark M. Spiegel (2011), 'The Olympic Effect', *Economic Journal*, **121**(553), June: 652–77.

Simkin, John (2012a), 'English Ladies Football Association', *The Encylopedia of British Football*, online at: http://www.spartacus.schoolnet.co.uk/Felfa.htm (accessed August 10, 2012).

Simkin, John (2012b), 'Women and Football', online at: http://www.spartacus.schoolnet.co.uk/Fwomen.htm (accessed August 10, 2012).

'Soccer as a Popular Sport: Putting Down Roots in Japan' (2006), *The Japan Forum*, online at: http://www.tjf.or.jp/eng/content/japaneseculture/32soccer.htm (accessed September 17, 2011).

Torgler, Benno (2008), 'The Determinants of Women's International Soccer Performances', *International Journal of Sport Management and Marketing*, **3–4**, July: 305–18.

Walker, Andrea K. (2011), 'Under Armour's Rookie Strategy for Endorsement Deals', online at: http://articles.baltimoresun.com/2011-07-25/business/bs-bz-under-armour-endorsement-20110725_1_endorsement-deals-sports-apparel-endorsements (accessed July 19, 2012).

'World Cup Victory Unlikely to Boost Nadeshiko League' (2011), *The Asahi Shimbum*, English Web Edition, July 22, online at: http://www.asahi.com/english/TKY201107210380.html (accessed August 11, 2012).

Zavian, Ellen (2011), Personal correspondence.

Zavian, Ellen (2012), Personal correspondence.

18. An economic analysis of the sudden influx of Korean female golfers into the LPGA

Young Hoon Lee, Ilhyeok Park, Joon-Ho Kang and Younghan Lee*

18.1 INTRODUCTION

The US Ladies Professional Golf Association (LPGA) tour was founded in 1950 and has since developed into one of the most popular golf events in the world. Its annual purse is the largest among women's golf tours. Historically, most LPGA members have been American and, until 1980, 90 percent of total tournaments were won by American golfers. Since then, the LPGA Tour has been experiencing rapid globalization, especially in the 2000s. Female golfers from various countries have earned LPGA Tour cards and non-US golfers have now won more tournaments than US golfers.

At first, the number of foreign golfers increased slowly, with most of them coming from Europe and Australia. In contrast, in the last decade, Asian women have flooded into the LPGA Tour. As a result, in 2010, approximately half of the top-10 golfers in most tournaments were Asian, and most of these were Korean.

The influx of Korean golfers may signal a significant shift in the revenue structure of the LPGA, which is a critical concern for the LPGA's business model. In particular, the success of Korean women in the LPGA has increased the proportion of its revenues that come from Korea. Since Se Ri Pak won her first championship at the McDonald's LPGA Championship in 1998, every LPGA tournament has been televised live in Korea. The value of Korean broadcasting rights has increased accordingly. In 1994, Korean LPGA broadcasting rights were valued at only \$60,000, but they rose to \$2.25 million in 2009 and to more than \$4.0 million in 2010 (Yonhap News, 2009).

Korean companies began to sponsor LPGA events in 1995 (for example, Samsung World Championship), and they have since sponsored two or three events every year. Should this trend continue, it may cause the LPGA to lose a significant portion of its US-derived revenue. As the number of tournaments won by US golfers falls, the number of LPGA fans in the US might fall as well. Among the 25 tournaments comprising the 2011 LPGA Tour, only 13 are held in the US. This reflects a large decrease from the 2008 tour, which consisted of 34 tournaments, almost all of which were held in the US. The recession is a clear cause of this change (though the number of the PGA tournaments has remained constant throughout the Great Recession), but the influx of Korean golfers into the LPGA is at least a partial cause. Therefore, the overall effect of the influx of Korean golfers on the LPGA revenue may prove, in the aggregate, to be negative.

One rationale for the revenue decline in the United States is consumer discrimination. Studies of several sports have found evidence of fan discrimination based on nationality or race (for example, Medoff, 1986; Nardelli and Simon, 1990; Hamilton, 1997). Forley and Smith (2007) show that Major League Baseball fans engage in consumer discrimination. In particular, fans of the Boston Red Sox attend fewer baseball games when Hispanic players are added to the roster. Kanazawa and Funk (2001) analyze Nielsen ratings for National Basketball Association games and find strong evidence that greater participation by white players causes viewership to increase and that the marginal revenue product of white players exceeds that of comparable black players. If golf fans in the US also discriminate on the basis of race or nationality, demand for the LPGA Tour must also decrease, *ceteris paribus*. (See Greenhaus et al., 1990, and Arrow, 1998, for a discussion of discrimination in a broader context.)

The principal objective of this chapter is to analyze the possible causes of the influx of Korean women golfers into the LPGA. We also address two related questions. The first question is why the influx of Korean golfers is so much larger in the LPGA than in the men's Professional Golf Association (PGA). The second question is why Japanese women have not also entered the LPGA in large numbers. The Japanese Ladies' Professional Golf Association (JLPGA) tour has grown into the second-richest women's professional tour. This indicates that many Japanese women have world-class skills, but – for some reason – they have largely stayed in Japan. We assess the incentives of Korean and Japanese golfers to switch labor markets from their homeland's golf tours to the LPGA Tour. Many have argued that the influx can be explained by the success of Se Ri Pak, which encouraged young Korean golfers to follow in her footsteps. Jiyai Shin, another star Korean golfer, stated in an interview:

> I saw Se Ri Pak winning the 1998 (US open) event. It was amazing for me, because before Se Ri Pak's wonderful performance, I never knew that the sport of golf even existed. I watched it on TV and thought that golf seems to be a very

interesting game. Since the Se Ri Pak syndrome, my friends, Inbee Park and many others pursued a career in golf. Actually, Se Ri Pak is our idol. (USGA, US Women's Open Website, 2009)

Taking Jiyai Shin's statement into consideration, we briefly discuss the effect of Se Ri Pak's success on the influx of Korean women in LPGA.

A seminal paper by Roy (1951) discussed occupational choice with heterogeneous skills. In his discussion regarding self-selection between fishing and hunting, Roy demonstrated that workers self-select the sector that provides them with the highest expected earnings. Borjas (1987, 1994) used Roy's framework to lay out a simple two-sector model of immigration. We use the Borjas model to explain the switch from the Korean Ladies' Professional Golf Association (KLPGA) to the LPGA. According to the decision rule in Borjas (1987), the difference in the average earnings in the two countries is not the only factor that potential migrants consider. The earning distributions are also critical. For example, a top golfer in the KLPGA would be reluctant to move into the LPGA even though the average earnings in the LPGA are greater than in the KLPGA if the variance of earnings in the LPGA is very small or the correlation of random factors between two tours is negative. We assess the labor market switch by comparing all the relevant determinants of migration from the KLPGA to the LPGA.

Section 18.2 provides a historical overview of Korean women players' performance in the LPGA. Section 18.3 discusses possible causes of their move to the LPGA and explains why similar moves did not occur in Japan. We also review the immigration decision model of Borjas (1987) and apply it to LPGA and KLPGA data, most of which are obtained from the official websites of US LPGA and KLPGA. In Section 18.4, we assess the competition levels for both genders' golf tours in Korea and the US and the implications for migration patterns. We then evaluate the unique skills of Korean golfers who migrate. Section 18.5 concludes. We predict that the influx of Korean golfers will ultimately decline and that some Korean golfers will return to the KLPGA or move to the Japanese tour.

18.2   HISTORICAL OVERVIEW OF KOREAN WOMEN GOLFERS IN THE LPGA

The LPGA Tour is one of the most popular golf events in the world, attracting the world's best female golfers. They are drawn by the tour's long history, the prestige of the association, and the large purses. The first foreigner to win an LPGA title was Fay Crocker from Uruguay, in the

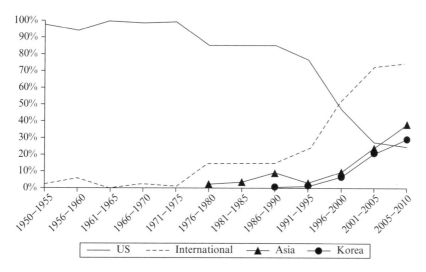

Source: Created by the authors based on the data from the official US LPGA website.

Figure 18.1   LPGA titles earned by US, international, Asian, and Korean golfers

1955 Serbin Open. A Japanese golfer, Hisako Higuchi became the first Asian golfer to ever win an LPGA tournament when she won the 1976 Colgate European Open. Since then, Asian players have won 143 titles (7.7 percent), with most of those wins occurring within the past decade. China, Japan, South Korea, the Philippines, Taiwan, and Thailand have all produced female golfers who have won at least one LPGA title, but most wins have been secured by Korean women. Koreans won a total of 93 titles, corresponding to 5 percent of all tournaments and to 65 percent of all Asian wins between 1950 and 2010.

Figure 18.1 shows the recent change in the number of titles won by players of different nationalities. It presents the percentage of titles won by US, international (non-US), Asian, and Korean players in five-year blocks. Until 1995, there were no significant changes, except that non-Asian international golfers (which, in this case, means European and Australian golfers) won about 10 percent of tournaments in the 1976–90 period. In 1996, the percentage of titles won by international (non-US) players started to increase rapidly. Between 2005 and 2010, more Asian players than US players won LPGA titles. Since 1998, the year in which Se Ri Pak won her first LPGA title, most of the titles won by Asians have gone to Koreans (80.4 percent of Asian wins).

Because a high percentage of titles can be won by a few superstars, we

Table 18.1   Percentage of top 10 LPGA finishes by nationality

Year	No. of tournaments	US	Korea	Sweden	Australia	Others
2001	34	54.5 (218/58)	8.8 (35/7)	11.0 (44/7)	6.0 (24/6)	19.8 (79/25)
2002	31	44.7 (156/52)	15.5 (54/8)	12.0 (42/9)	8.3 (29/8)	19.5 (68/21)
2003	31	40.4 (137/49)	24.2 (82/14)	7.4 (25/9)	8.8 (30/9)	19.2 (65/18)
2004	32	36.9 (130/48)	23.9 (84/14)	8.8 (31/6)	5.6 (20/5)	24.7 (87/10)
2005	30	37.2 (132/33)	25.6 (91/16)	12.1 (43/8)	5.4 (19/7)	19.7 (70/20)
2006	33	39.0 (143/35)	28.3 (104/23)	9.3 (34/8)	5.4 (20/5)	18.0 (66/21)
2007	31	36.7 (119/27)	25.0 (81/22)	10.8 (35/7)	6.5 (21/6)	21.0 (68/17)
2008	34	33.7 (123/35)	29.9 (109/23)	9.6 (35/9)	5.8 (21/6)	21.1 (77/17)
2009	28	29.0 (86/25)	31.6 (94/27)	9.8 (29/7)	4.4 (13/3)	25.3 (75/16)
2010	24	26.6 (71/21)	39.7 (106/19)	3.7 (10/4)	4.9 (13/4)	25.1 (67/19)

Note: Numbers include only official tournaments and exclude match play games. The total numbers of top 10 exceed the 'number of tournament × 10' because many players were tied for 10th place. The numbers in columns 3–7 are the number of top 10 finishes by a given country divided by the total number of top 10 finishes. For example 218/400 = 0.545. The numbers in parentheses are (number of top 10/number of players).

report the percentages of top 10 finishes in Table 18.1 to illustrate the recent success of Korean players more completely. The percentage of top 10 finishes (incidence count, not head count) by Koreans has increased steadily over the past decade. In the 2001 Tour, 54.5 percent of all top 10 scores were by US golfers; Korean women golfers accounted for only 8.8 percent. On the 2010 tour, the percentage of Korean golfers in the top 10 rose to 39.7 percent, whereas US golfers secured only 26.6 percent of the top 10 finishes. During these 10 seasons, the percentages of the Korean and US golfers increased by 450 percent and decreased by 50 percent, respectively.

Table 18.2 shows the top 10 money winners in selected years. In 2001, Annika Sorenstam was the top prize winner, earning $2.1 million. The US and Korea put three and two golfers, respectively, in the top 10 in that year. In 2010, there were two Americans (Cristie Kerr and Michelle Wie) and four Koreans in the top 10 money winners. Moreover, many Korean women are succeeding on the LPGA Tour, while most other countries have only one or two standout players, such as Annika Sorenstam of Sweden, Karrie Webb of Australia, and Lorena Ochoa of Mexico. The US and Korea are the only two countries with more than 20 players in the list of top 10 finishers; no other country has had more than 10 players on the list (see the numbers after the slash in the brackets of Table 18.1).

The influx of Korean players is also evident in Figure 18.2, which shows the total number of qualified Korean players in the LPGA. The

Table 18.2 Top 10 prize winners

Ranking	2001			2004			2007			2010		
	Name	Country	Prize	Name	Country	Prize	Name	Country	Prize	Name	Country	Prize
1	A. Sorenstam	Sweden	2,106*	A. Sorenstam	Sweden	2,545	L. Ochoa	Mexico	4,365	N.Y. Choi	Korea	1,871
2	S.R. Pak	Korea	1,623	G. Park	Korea	1,525	S. Pettersen	Norway	1,802	J. Shin	Korea	1,783
3	K. Webb	Australia	1,535	L. Ochoa	Mexico	1,451	P. Creamer	USA	1,385	C. Kerr	USA	1,602
4	L. Kane	Canada	947	M. Mallon	USA	1,359	M.H. Kim	Korea	1,274	Y. Tseng	Taiwan	1,574
5	M. Hjorth	Sweden	848	C. Kerr	USA	1,190	S.H. Lee	Korea	1,100	S. Pettersen	Norway	1,557
6	R. Jones	USA	785	K. Stupples	USA	969	C. Kerr	USA	1,099	A. Miyazato	Japan	1,457
7	D. Pepper	USA	776	M.H. Kim	Korea	932	J. Jang	Korea	1,039	I.K. Kim	Korea	1,210
8	M.H. Kim	Korea	762	H.W. Han	Korea	841	A. Park	Brazil	984	S.H. Kim	Korea	1,209
9	L. Diaz	USA	751	K. Webb	Australia	748	M. Pressel	USA	972	M. Wie	USA	888
10	C. Matthew	UK	748	J. Rosales	Phillipines	694	J.Y. Lee	Korea	966	P. Creamer	USA	884

Note: * Thousand US dollars.

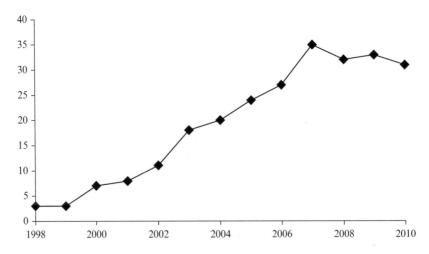

Source: Created by the authors based on the data from the official US LPGA website.

Figure 18.2   Number of Korean players in LPGA Tour by year

total number increased steadily from 1998 to 2007, when it reached the maximum of 35 players. The data confirm the flood of Korean golfers into the LPGA.

18.3   POSSIBLE CAUSES OF THE INFLUX

In order to uncover the possible causes of the influx of Korean women into the LPGA, we discuss the maturity of the KLPGA, compare prize money and competition level in the LPGA and KLPGA, and contrast the KLPGA with the JLPGA. We analyze the above factors in the framework of the Borjas self-selection model of immigration. Therefore, we first present the Borjas model and then apply it to the issues we examine.

18.3.1   The Immigration Decision Model

Borjas (1987) lays out a simple, two-sector Roy model to analyze immigration. He shows that immigrants differ systematically from the overall populations of both their native and new countries. In particular, people whose earnings are either artificially suppressed in their home country or whose skills are particularly well-suited to their destination country are more likely to immigrate. We apply this model to the golfers' decision to switch from the KLPGA to the LPGA. The earnings in KLPGA and LPGA are:

$$w_K = \mu_K + \varepsilon_K, \tag{18.1}$$

$$w_{US} = \mu_{US} + \varepsilon_{US}, \tag{18.2}$$

where μ_K is the average earnings for all Korean women in KLPGA and μ_{US} is what their average earnings would be if they all moved to the LPGA. The random 'error' terms refer to individual-specific abilities in the KLPGA and LPGA. They are distributed $\varepsilon_k \sim N(0, \sigma_k)$ and $\varepsilon_{us} \sim N(0, \sigma_{us})$ and have the correlation coefficient ρ. Korean women who are active in the KLPGA migrate to the LPGA when the net impact on pay, given by the index function I, is positive:

$$I = (\mu_{US} - \mu_K - \pi) + (\varepsilon_{US} - \varepsilon_K), \tag{18.3}$$

where π is a time-invariant measure of the cost of moving to LPGA. Therefore, the probability that a golfer moves from the KLPGA to the LPGA is given by:

$$P = \Pr[I > 0] = 1 - \Phi(z), \tag{18.4}$$

where $z = -(\mu_{US} - \mu_K - \pi)/\sigma_v$, $v = \varepsilon_{US} - \varepsilon_K$, and Φ is the standard normal distribution function. Equation (18.4) implies that the migration decision depends on both the average earnings gap $(\mu_{US} - \mu_K - \pi)$ and the earnings distributions of the two Tours. Specifically, migrants are likely to fall in the upper tail of the distribution $\Phi(z)$. Migrants are therefore more likely to succeed in the LPGA than the average Korean member of the KLPGA. This self-selection means that the conditional expected earnings of migrants is greater than w_k. Equation (18.5) gives the counterfactual expectation of what Korean golfers would earn had they not moved to the LPGA, while equation (18.6) shows the expected earnings of Korean golfers in the LPGA:

$$E[w_K|I > 0] = \mu_K + \frac{\sigma_K \sigma_{US}}{\sigma_v}\left(\rho - \frac{\sigma_K}{\sigma_{US}}\right)\lambda, \tag{18.5}$$

$$E[w_{US}|I > 0] = \mu_{US} + \frac{\sigma_K \sigma_{US}}{\sigma_v}\left(\frac{\sigma_{US}}{\sigma_K} - \rho\right)\lambda, \tag{18.6}$$

where $\lambda = \phi(z)/[1 - \Phi(z)]$, and ϕ is the probability density function of the standard normal distribution.

The second terms in equations (18.5) and (18.6) reflect self-selection, which depends upon the variances and correlation coefficient in the earning distributions of KLPGA and LPGA as well as the net average difference in earnings. The expected increase in earnings by Korean golfers who move to the LPGA is particularly large if any of three conditions holds. First, the expected gain in earnings grows as the average earnings gap, $w_{US} - w_K$, grows. That is, a Korean migrant will earn more if she moved. Second, she expects to gain more as the earning variance in LPGA (σ_{US}^2) grows. This occurs because, due to self-selection, a woman who migrates expects to be in the upper end of the distribution of the LPGA. The greater the variance of earnings in the LPGA, the greater her gain will be. Finally, a migrant expects to gain more as the earning variance in KLPGA (σ_K^2) shrinks. This condition is the flipside of the previous condition. As the distribution of earnings in Korea condenses, the winnings of those who are in the upper tail fall, reducing the benefits of staying in Korea.

We analyze the distributions of prize earnings in the KLPGA and LPGA by using data from the 2000s. Unlike averages and variances of earnings in KLPGA and LPGA, the correlation coefficient of ε_K and ε_{US} is not observed. The correlation is a critical factor in the migration decision since it determines where a golfer who is currently in the KLPGA would be located in the earning distribution in the LPGA. For example, a golfer in the top 5 percent of the KLPGA prize money may be reluctant to move to the LPGA without knowing ρ even if the average and variance of earnings in the LPGA are greater than those in KLPGA because she fears that even top Korean golfers will not do well in the LPGA. Therefore, we need to address Korean golfers' expectations of ρ.

18.3.2   The Growing Maturity of the KLPGA

As can be noted from Jiyai Shin's remarks, Se Ri Pak was a catalyst for the influx of Korean women into the LPGA. However, such motivation itself could not have produced so many competitive golfers unless the KLPGA was already mature – that is, unless its members were sufficiently skilled. Therefore, a necessary condition for the influx is that the KLPGA Tour produces golfers who can compete in the LPGA.

When the KLPGA was founded in 1978 with only eight professional golfers, it staged very few events. Table 18.3 shows the number of members and tournaments in the KLPGA by five-year intervals. By 1995, only 119 members had passed the qualifying test. However, beginning in the mid-

Table 18.3   Number of KLPGA members and KLPGA tournaments

Year	New members	Cumulative no. of members	Annual no. of tournaments
1978–1985	29	29	5.0
1986–1990	29	58	8.6
1991–1995	61	119	9.0
1996–2000	114	233	12.2
2001–2005	223	456	14.2
2006–2010	329	785	21.6

1990s, this number increased greatly. Some 114 new members joined the KLPGA in 1996–2000, 223 joined in 2001–05, and 329 joined in 2005–10. The 237 percent increase in membership over the past decade means that the golfers who entered the KLPGA during this millennium represent 75 percent of its total membership. The number of tournaments was only in the one-digit range until the early 1990s, but the average number grew to 12.2 in the late 1990s and 14.2 in the early 2000s. While the KLPGA Tour had less than half the number of events of the LPGA Tour during this period, most Korean golfers who are now in the LPGA played in the KLPGA Tour.

Figure 18.3 compares the number of tournaments in the four major women's golf Tours. The LPGA and JLPGA hold the most tournaments. The number of tournaments of the KLPGA is approximately half that of the LPGA, but it is comparable to that in the Ladies European Tour (LET). The fact that the Rolex world rankings of women golfers include performance in the KLPGA also supports the argument that the KLPGA is sufficiently mature to produce competitive golfers. The Rolex rankings began in 2006 and include the US LPGA, JLPGA, KLPGA, LET, and Australian LPG Tours in its calculations. Therefore, despite its short history, the KLPGA Tour provides a sufficiently competitive environment for participating golfers to develop their skills and to acquire experience. The existence of the second division of the KLPGA Tour demonstrates its depth and shows that Korean teenagers now have an opportunity to grow as golfers.

18.3.3   Prize Money, Sponsorship, and the JLPGA

Se Ri Pak's success in the LPGA made teenage Korean golfers aware of their potential as professional golfers in the LPGA and the lucrative rewards available in the LPGA. That is, Pak's performance helped Korean

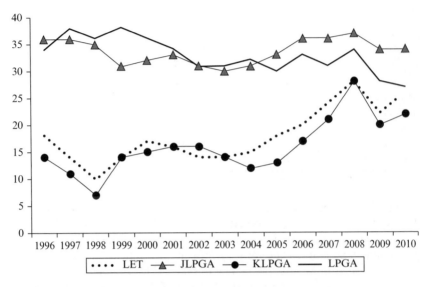

Figure 18.3   Number of tournaments in four different golf Tours

golfers form a large, positive expectation of ρ (the correlation coefficient of ε_K and ε_{US}). Figure 18.4 compares the annual prize money of the four major women's golf Tours: the LPGA, JLPGA, KLPGA and Ladies' European Tour (LET). The four tours offer widely varying prize money. The LPGA has the largest purse, and the KLPGA has the smallest. In particular, the LPGA's total purse ($45.1 million) was approximately 10 times that of the KLPGA's ($4.4 million) in the 2005 season. Table 18.4 shows that mean prize money of the LPGA was more than 10 times larger than that of the KLPGA in 2004. The difference in expected earnings is even larger in the top 5 and 10 percent of players (Table 18.5). The top 5 and 10 percent of LPGA players earned 11.43 and 11.41 times more than analogous KPLGA players did in 2001. Table 18.4 also shows that, since 2007, the earnings on the two Tours have begun to converge. However, the mean earnings on the LPGA Tour remain almost four times those on the KLPGA Tour. Table 18.5 shows that a similar pattern holds for the expected earnings of the most successful golfers on the Tours.

For simplicity, we assume that ρ = 1 and the immigration cost is $100,000, and we consider the immigration decision in 2010. Setting ρ = 1 implies that a golfer who is in the 95th percentile in the prize money list of the KLPGA would also be in the 95th percentile of the LPGA. Using data for the top 5 percent (Table 18.5) of players in prize money from the LPGA and the KLPGA, we calculate the index value (equation (18.3))

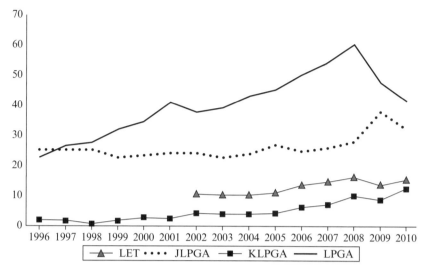

Figure 18.4   Total purse (million US$) of LPGA, KLPGA, JLPGA and LET

for a golfer on the 95th percentile. The expected net gain for the average golfer is $(\mu_{US} - \mu_K - \pi) = (230,118 - 74,591 - 100,000) = 54,474$, and we approximate the difference in error terms given by the difference in average earnings of players in the 95th percentile, $(\varepsilon_{US} - \varepsilon_K) = (1,532,837 - 387,963) = 993,081$. This results in the index value $I = 1,047,555$.

The variation in prize money in each Tour is another factor in the migration decision. The variation in the LPGA, as represented by the coefficient of variation (CV), was larger than that in the KLPGA until 2006 (see Table 18.4). For example, the CV of the LPGA in 2003 was about 50 percent larger than that of the KLPGA. This means that the LPGA prize money distribution had larger tails at both ends than KLPGA prize money distribution in the early 2000s. As in Borjas (1987, 1994), higher expected earnings and greater variation of expected earnings in the LPGA Tour motivated Korean women to migrate. From the professional golfer's perspective, the LPGA is a more lucrative labor market than the KLPGA. If the competition levels are more or less equal then ρ is positive and close to one. Unlike the expected values, the coefficients of variation have neither converged nor diverged over time. The difference between LPGA and KLPGA started to diminish since around 2007 in terms of both mean prize money and within-Tour variation.

Based on the information in Table 18.4, we calculate the ratio of the variances and the conditional expected earnings (18.5) and (18.6) for a

Table 18.4   Mean, standard deviation and coefficient of variation of prize money by year

Year	LPGA				KLPGA				LPGA–KLPGA ratio (means)
	N*	Mean**	SD	CV***	N	Mean	SD	CV	
2001	203	$171,805	278,507	1.62	102	$17,331	22,723	1.31	9.91
2002	200	$170,316	307,171	1.80	95	$19,590	25,937	1.32	8.69
2003	258	$142,212	267,844	1.88	103	$17,207	21,733	1.26	8.26
2004	193	$200,561	315,724	1.57	103	$19,871	24,113	1.21	10.09
2005	192	$204,245	324,254	1.59	97	$26,950	34,644	1.28	7.58
2006	197	$226,344	385,389	1.70	107	$39,365	56,346	1.43	5.75
2007	190	$237,598	430,671	1.81	116	$46,972	87,750	1.87	5.06
2008	188	$282,694	404,520	1.43	120	$58,994	98,028	1.66	4.79
2009	161	$267,665	367,106	1.37	104	$46,524	74,839	1.61	5.75
2010	161	$230,118	363,928	1.58	105	$74,591	91,973	1.23	3.09

Notes:
*   Number of players included in the calculation. Only LPGA members who earn more than $0 are included.
** ($N \times$ Mean) is less than actual total purse of each year because only the registered LPGA members are included in the calculation. Part of prize money was earned by non-LPGA members in the tournaments that were co-hosted by LPGA and other countries' association. For example, the 2005 CJ Nine Bridge Classic was held in Korea, and co-hosted by LPGA and KLPGA. Many non-LPGA members won prize money in the tournament.
*** Coefficient of variation (standard deviation/mean).

Table 18.5   Mean of top 5 percent and 10 percent of prize money by year

Year	Mean of top 5%			Mean of top 10%		
	LPGA	KLPGA	LPGA–KLPGA ratio	LPGA	KLPGA	LPGA–KLPGA ratio
2001	$1,088,326	$95,245	11.43	$839,113	$73,550	11.41
2002	$1,179,358	$111,447	10.58	$873,313	$81,433	10.72
2003	$1,066,603	$94,519	11.28	$809,453	$72,932	11.10
2004	$1,225,271	$95,547	12.82	$926,140	$78,607	11.78
2005	$1,217,071	$141,654	8.59	$950,871	$110,039	8.64
2006	$1,595,277	$244,172	6.53	$1,180,702	$182,173	6.48
2007	$1,498,639	$338,434	4.43	$1,159,133	$228,064	5.08
2008	$1,571,646	$410,121	3.83	$1,276,148	$293,717	4.34
2009	$1,447,068	$308,195	4.70	$1,209,648	$214,529	5.64
2010	$1,532,837	$387,963	3.95	$1,156,656	$306,597	3.77

Table 18.6 *Conditional mean earnings in KLPGA and LPGA for golfers moving in LPGA*

Year	$E(w_{US}/I > 0)$	$E(w_K/I > 0)$	$k = \sigma_{US}/\sigma_K$	$1/k = \sigma_K/\sigma_{US}$
2001	375.183	37.065	11.472	0.087
2002	406.660	42.887	11.226	0.089
2003	347.745	33.163	12.981	0.077
2004	400.968	37.080	12.670	0.079
2005	398.185	50.170	9.005	0.111
2006	455.980	77.116	6.514	0.154
2007	484.017	102.268	4.660	0.215
2008	447.507	103.200	3.951	0.253
2009	413.743	77.113	4.845	0.206
2010	413.137	120.844	3.957	0.253

golfer who has moved to LPGA from KLPGA, as displayed in Table 18.6. The necessary and sufficient condition for positive selection, in which the best golfers leave the KLPGA (the home country) for the LPGA (the host country) and outperform the native (US) golfers, is: $\rho > \min(1/k, k)$ where $k = \sigma_{US}/\sigma_K > 1$. Recall that σ_j is the variance of abilities in country *j*. In 2001, the positive selection condition was satisfied if ρ is greater than 0.087 since $k = 11.472$ already satisfies $k > 1$. Therefore, the condition for top Korean golfers to switch to the LPGA would have been satisfied in 2001. However, the condition became tighter in 2010, as ρ should be greater than 0.253 and k was only 3.957. The two left-most columns display the conditional expectation of earnings for golfers with $I > 0$.

The expected earnings for Korean golfers who moved to the LPGA were $375,183 in 2001, while their expected earnings if they stayed in the KLPGA were only $37,065. This difference was large enough to induce top Korean golfers to the LPGA, even if there was a large switching cost. However, the difference in earnings has decreased continuously, and the ratio of expected earnings was only 3.4 in 2010, far less than the ratio of 10 in 2001 (see Table 18.6). Therefore, the incentive to switch tours has fallen in recent years.

The migration model also needs information about the cost of moving and the correlation of earnings in the two countries. If Korean golfers have confidence in their golfing skills, which implies a high expected correlation coefficient, the large payoff gap should motivate them to switch Tours, even in the face of language and cultural barriers. However, moving to the LPGA Tour induces various risks. For example, language difficulties and cultural misunderstanding in the US might undermine what Fried and Tauer (2011) call a golfer's 'mental fortitude', her ability to perform under pressure. This introduces an element of risk on the LPGA Tour that would not exist on the KLPGA Tour and can prevent a golfer from playing up to her potential. Additionally, a professional golfer travels on a weekly basis, and the average traveling distance in the LPGA Tour is much greater than in Korea. Travel thus adds to the mental strain of performing on the LPGA Tour and to the risk Korean golfers face when they move to the LPGA from the KLPGA.

Travel also adds a monetary cost to migration. According to Crosset (1995), the average annual traveling cost was between $30,000 and $40,000 for a golfer who participated in the 1994 LPGA Tour. This amount is approximately equal to the prize money of the 90th ranked player. However, the enormous expected payoff dominates the added risks and costs and leads Korean women to try the LPGA Tour.

Sponsorship is another incentive for Korean golfers to switch to the LPGA, since a successful career in the LPGA Tour brings lucrative sponsorships from Korean companies. According to news reports, Se Ri Pak received approximately $3 million per year in sponsorship money from a Korean company called 'CJ Group' between 2002 and 2007. However, this incentive has diminished in recent years. For example, Shin, who contracted with a security company in 2009, receives approximately $1.5 million per year.

The JLPGA has a longer history than the KLPGA, and it held 34 Tours in 2010, about 55 percent more than the KLPGA. More than 250 players participated in the JLPGA Tour each year for last decade, which means that the JLPGA is quite mature and has many good golfers. The total purse in the JLPGA had been approximately half of that in the LPGA until 2008. With the decline of the LPGA purse since 2008, the total purses on the two Tours have become roughly equal. The difference in purses between the JLPGA and KLPGA Tours explains why Korean golfers, but not Japanese golfers, entered the LPGA in large numbers. Considering the various costs incurred on the LPGA Tour, a doubling of the total purse may not be sufficient to lead Japanese women golfers into the LPGA.

18.4   MIGRATION INTO THE LPGA AND GOLF SKILLS

18.4.1   The Difference in Migration Patterns between the PGA and the LPGA

This subsection explains why many Korean women have moved from the KLPGA to the LPGA, but relatively few Korean men have moved to the

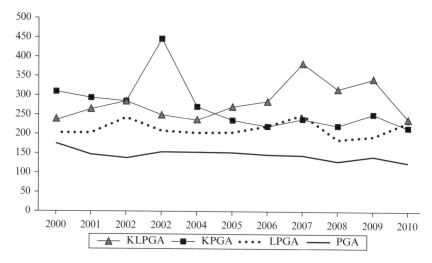

Figure 18.5   Herfindahl–Hirschman index of prize money

PGA, even though the prize money gap between the PGA and the KPGA is even wider than that between the LPGA and the KLPGA. While a handful of Korean golfers have been regular members of the PGA and a few of them have enjoyed successful careers, the performance of Korean men in the PGA has been far below the performance of Korean women in the LPGA. We show below that this disparity might result from differences in the intensity of competition on the two Tours.

Figure 18.5 compares the competition level of the men's and women's golf Tours in the US and Korea using temporal variations in the Herfindahl–Hirschman index (HHI) for the four golf Tours. The HHI is a measure of the concentration of firms in an industry, which reflects the degree of competition in the industry. To measure competition on the golf Tours, we calculate the concentration of prize money for individual golfers. We assume that a golf Tour and an individual golfer resemble an industry and a firm, respectively, and that each Tour consists of 100 golfers. We collected the data of the top 100 prize money winners and calculated the HHI as follows:

$$HHI = \frac{\sum_{i=1}^{100} s_i^2}{T}, \; s_i = 100 \cdot \frac{M_i}{T}, \tag{18.7}$$

where M_i is golfer i's prize money and T is the sum of the prize money for the top 100 golfers. The HHI ranges from 0 to 10,000, with larger numbers reflecting less competition.

From 2000 to 2010, the HHI of the PGA was the lowest of the four Tours, and there has been little temporal variation in this figure. This implies that the PGA Tour is the most competitive of the four, and that its competition level has remained relatively constant over the 2000s. Aside from the competition of the professional Tours, the probability of earning a PGA Tour card is also much slimmer than the probability of earning an LPGA Tour card. For example, 1,389 players applied for the 2010 PGA Tour qualifying tournament, while only 330 players applied for the 2010 LPGA Tour qualifying tournament. In Korea, the KLPGA evidences tighter competition than KPGA in the first half of the 2000s, even though the KPGA has grown increasingly competitive over the past five seasons.

On the women's Tours, Figure 18.5 shows that the HHI gap between the LPGA and the KLPGA was very narrow in 2000–06 and became slightly wider in 2007–09. However, the levels of competition were more or less equal to one another in the 2010 season. The similarity in the HHIs implies that the entry barrier was not high for Korean women who had already been successful in the KLPGA. Still, the uncertain benefits and costs of moving from her homeland to the LPGA Tour might make a risk-averse woman reluctant to transfer to the LPGA unless she has a high expectation of a successful career there.

Among women, the relatively unbalanced competition for prize money in the LPGA helps successful Koreans anticipate a high probability of success in the US. In contrast, the PGA is much more competitive than the KPGA, though this gap has narrowed somewhat in the second half of the 2000s. The tight competition in the PGA Tour and the difficulty inherent in passing the qualifying tournament has set a high entry barrier for foreign golfers. As the KPGA Tour was the least balanced of the four Tours in the first half of the 2000s, top Korean men enjoyed monopoly earning power in the KPGA, and were thus less likely to pursue professional careers in the PGA. Additionally, some LPGA tournaments, but no PGA tournaments, are held in Korea. This implies that Korean women have greater access to the LPGA. In fact, several Korean golfers earned their LPGA Tour cards solely by winning LPGA tournaments held in Korea.

In the context of the immigration model, Korean golfers have information on all the variables except ε_{US} in the index function (equation (18.3)). The insignificant difference in the level of competition between the LPGA and the KLPGA leads top Korean female golfers, whose ε_K are positive and large, to expect $\varepsilon_{US} > 0$, which implies a high probability of migrating. On the other hand, tight competition in the PGA leads top Korean men to expect that $\varepsilon_{US} < 0$, suggesting a low probability of migrating.

18.4.2　Golf Skills of Korean Women in the LPGA

The success of migrants to the LPGA in the late 1990s opened the door for many young Korean women to switch their affiliation to the LPGA in the 2000s. This raises the question, 'What are the main sources of their success?' Korean women may simply have better golf skills, the result of training and natural talent. Alternatively, they may be more efficient at earning prize money than other golfers with comparable skills. In this subsection, we limit ourselves to comparing golf skills. We apply the estimation results from previous studies to our data to analyze how the different aspects of the game translate into an advantage or disadvantage for Korean golfers.

We show below that Korean women can drive more accurately and putt better than the league average, but their driving distance is less than the league average. Greater accuracy with less power is thus a characteristic of the average Korean women golfer. The three left-most columns in Table 18.7 compare four variables showing the golf skills of Korean and non-Korean golfers. These statistics are based on all LPGA members who participated in at least one tournament each year from 2004 to 2010. The average number of players included in the calculation is about 150 per year.

From 2004 to 2010, we calculate annual averages of driving distance (DD), driving accuracy (DA, the percentage of times a driven ball lands on the fairway), green-in-regulation (GIR), and the number of putts ($PUTT$). Over the period, the average driving distance of Koreans is consistently shorter than that of non-Koreans. This may be attributable to the physical differences between Asian and Western golfers, as Western players are generally larger than Asian players, even though this physical gap has narrowed somewhat. The average height of Western women who are the top 20 of the 2010 Rolex ranking list is 170.5cm, corresponding to an approximate 4cm height advantage over Korean women.

Table 18.7　Golf skills and their effects on score and prize money in 2004–
2010: comparison between Koreans and non-Koreans (Others)

Variables	Korean: A	Others: B	A – B	Effects on score	Effects on prize money
DD	247.270	248.790	−1.520	−0.046	−9.804*
DA	70.179	68.106	2.073	0.053	11.387
GIR	63.833	63.787	0.046	0.004	0.955
PUTT	29.503	29.989	−0.486	0.334	71.754

Note:　* Thousand US dollars.

Korean women have an edge in driving accuracy. The difference between Koreans and Others is about 2 percent throughout the 2004–10 period. *GIR*, which is determined by driving and iron shot skills, remains fairly steady over time. Therefore, the relative iron shot performance of Koreans is indeterminate, since the abilities of driving power and accuracy counteract one another, and the *GIR* is close to the league average. However, Koreans appear to retain a significant edge in putting. The average number of putts per round for Koreans is consistently smaller (by about 0.5) than that of Others.

Park and Lee (2011) evaluate the effects of various golf skills on score and prize money earned using panel data for 132 female golfers in the LPGA and determine that driving shots, iron shots, sand bunker shots, and putting skills all significantly influence scoring and prize money. We apply the estimates in Tables 2 and 4 of Park and Lee to the difference of average skills between Koreans and Others to calculate the effect of each skill on both score and prize money. These impacts appear in the last two columns in Table 18.7. Our calculation demonstrates that the putting advantage is a principal source of successful performance by Korean golfers in the LPGA. The advantage in *PUTT* allows Korean golfers to earn $71,754 more in prize money on average.

18.5   CONCLUSION

In this chapter, we have discussed the reasons for the sudden influx of Korean women into the LPGA in the 2000s. We also place the influx in the broader context of international migration using the analytical framework of Borjas (1987, 1994). Because Korean women have higher expected earnings than Japanese women relative to the earnings in their home country, they are more likely to migrate. Analogously, Korean woman expect higher earnings from playing on the LPGA than Korean men expect from playing on the PGA, so they are more likely to migrate than Korean men.

The KLPGA has grown to become one of the five major ladies' professional golf Tours upon which the Rolex World Rankings are based. The mature KLPGA has allowed young women to apply their golf skills in competitive settings and to accumulate experience and ability as professional golfers. The huge difference in total prize money and in the number of tournaments between the KLPGA and the LPGA provided the best Korean golfers with an incentive to migrate. Moreover, success as an LPGA golfer led to enormous publicity and lucrative sponsorships in Korea. The incentives for Korean women to switch from the KLPGA to LPGA were sufficiently large to compensate for the possible risks and costs of playing in the LPGA. We show that competitive balance in the LPGA is more or less similar to that in the KLPGA, which implies that there is a high probability that a golfer who is successful in the KLPGA will perform well in the LPGA.

The relatively unbalanced competition in the LPGA Tour stands in stark contrast to the tightly balanced competition in the PGA Tour, in which Asian golfers have proven less successful, and provides an added incentive for migration to Korean women. Finally, Korean women's golf skills of accuracy and putting are advantages for the average Korean woman, while her weak driving power is a disadvantage. Putting ability appears to be a significant factor contributing to the competitiveness of Korean golfers in the LPGA.

We can now speculate what the future will bring. The payoff difference between the two ladies' golf Tours has narrowed dramatically in recent years, owing to a sizable decline of the total purse in the LPGA after the 2008 season and a steady increase in the KLPGA's purse. Between 2001 and 2010, the total prize money on the KLPGA Tour has risen from 10 percent to approximately 30 percent of the LPGA's prize money. As shown in Figure 18.3, the KLPGA has offered at least 20 tournaments per year since 2007. The same trend can be observed in mean prize money and within-Tour variations (see Tables 18.4 and 18.5).

As the popularity of the KLPGA has grown, sponsorship has generally followed. According to a news release from May 2008, the TV ratings of live KLPGA tournaments have increased gradually, whereas the viewing ratings of the LPGA in Korea have decreased, reflecting the increasing popularity of the KLPGA and the decreasing popularity of the LPGA in Korea (Jungang Daily News, 2008). In addition, we have shown that the earning variance ratio, k, has consistently decreased, from 11.47 in 2001 to 3.96 in 2010. Therefore, the likelihood that talented golfers will migrate has fallen.

In Japan, the JLPGA's purse reached 75 percent of the LPGA's, and the number of tournaments surpassed that of the LPGA by seven in 2010. Therefore, the sum of prize money in the JLPGA and KLPGA combined exceeded that of the LPGA in 2010. Because Japan is so close to Korea, Korean and Japanese golfers can participate in tournaments in both the KLPGA and the JLPGA if they hold both Tour cards. About 20 Korean golfers have participated in the JLPGA Tour since 2005. Korean players contributed only about 4 percent of players in JLPGA in the early 2000s, but this percentage has doubled in the late 2000s (8.5 percent in 2010).

Since Korean women's incentives for switching from the KLPGA to the LPGA are smaller than in previous years, we expect the number of new

Korean entrants into the LPGA to decline in the future; we also anticipate that some less-successful Korean golfers will return to the KLPGA Tour. In 2006, 20 Korean women ranked among the top 150 but did not play in the LPGA, and this number increased to 32 in 2010. If the LPGA hopes to encourage this trend, it might consider lengthening golf courses in order to exploit the Western women's relative advantage of driving power over Korean women, which might ultimately bring more American fans to the LPGA.

NOTE

*   We thank two research assistants, Hansol Hwang and Woohyung Lee of Seoul National University, for their time and effort in collecting data and preparing tables and figures. The very detailed and helpful comments of the editors are gratefully acknowledged.

REFERENCES

Arrow, Kenneth J. (1998), 'What Has Economics to Say about Discrimination?', *Journal of Economic Perspectives*, **12**(2), Spring: 91–100.

Borjas, George J. (1987), 'Self-Selection and the Earnings of Immigrants', *American Economic Review*, **77**(4), September: 531–53.

Borjas, George J. (1994), 'The Economics of Immigration', *Journal of Economic Literature*, **32**(4), December: 1667–717.

Crosset, Todd W. (1995), *Outsiders in the Clubhouse: The World of Women's Professional Golf*, Albany, NY: State University of New York Press.

Foley, Mark and Fred H. Smith (2007), 'Consumer Discrimination in Professional Sports: New Evidence from Major League Baseball', *Applied Economics Letters*, **14**(13), October: 951–5.

Fried, Harold O. and Loren W. Tauer (2011), 'The Impact of Age on the Ability to Perform under Pressure: Golfers on the PGA Tour', *Journal of Productivity Analysis*, **35**(1), October: 51–9.

Greenhaus, Jeffrey H., Saroj Parasuraman and Wayne M. Wormley (1990), 'Effects of Race on Organizational Experiences, Job Performance Evaluations, and Career Outcomes', *Academy of Management Journal*, **33**(1), March: 64–86.

Hamilton, Barton Hughes (1997), 'Racial Discrimination and Professional Basketball Salaries in the 1990s', *Applied Economics*, **29**(3), March: 287–96.

Jungang Daily News (2008), 'Sinking LPGA and Rising KLPGA: KLPGA Viewing Rating is 3 Times Higher than That of LPGA', May 16.

Kanazawa, Mark T. and Jonas P. Funk (2001), 'Racial Discrimination in Professional Basketball: Evidence from Nielsen Ratings', *Economic Inquiry*, **39**(4), October: 599–608.

Medoff, Marshall H. (1986), 'Baseball Attendance and Fan Discrimination', *Journal of Behavioral Economics*, **15**(1–2), Spring–Summer: 149–55.

Nardinelli, Clark and Curtis Simon (1990), 'Consumer Racial Discrimination in the Market for Memorabilia: The Case of Baseball', *Quarterly Journal of Economics*, **105**(3), August: 575–95.

Park, Ilhyeok and Young Hoon Lee (2011), 'Efficiency Comparison of International Golfers in LPGA', Paper presented at the annual conference of the Western Economic Association, San Diego, CA, July.

Roy, Andrew D. (1951), 'Some Thoughts on the Distribution of Earnings', *Oxford Economic Papers*, **3**(2), June: 135–46.
Yonhap News (2009), 'Increase of Broadcasting Right Fee of LPGA Due to an Overly Heated Competition between Korean Broadcasting Companies', February 12.

19. Media coverage and pay in women's basketball and netball in Australia
Ross Booth

19.1 INTRODUCTION

Women's sport in Australia does not receive the same amount of media coverage or the same sponsorship levels as men's sport. The low coverage stems from what Jobling calls 'the circular problem' of sponsorship and popularity. Because potential sponsors see low turnout and little reward, they have little reason to support women's sports. The lack of sponsorship, in turn, limits the media coverage of the sport and depresses attendance and viewership (Jobling, 1994: 169). As a result, despite achievements on the international stage that often outshine those of Australian men, Australian women frequently toil in relative obscurity and receive pay that is a small fraction of that earned by men in the same sport.

Unlike most countries, Australia has two counterparts to men's basketball: women's basketball and netball. Today, women's basketball is essentially identical to the men's version of the game. The most noticeable difference is that women use a slightly smaller ball to facilitate ball handling and shooting. For most of its history, however, women's basketball bore little resemblance to men's basketball. This version of the game quickly died in most countries – particularly in the United States – after men's rules became the norm in the early 1970s. In the Commonwealth of Nations (formerly the British Commonwealth), however, the distinctly female version of the sport, known as 'netball', has continued to thrive.

Australia is perhaps the only nation to enjoy international success in both women's basketball and netball. Australian women are well represented in the Women's National Basketball Association (WNBA) and won the bronze medal in women's basketball at the 2012 Summer Olympics. At the same time, Australia has dominated international play in netball, having won five of the last six world championships.[1]

Women's basketball and netball have also enjoyed considerable commercial success in Australia, particularly when compared with other women's sports. Australia supports professional leagues in both sports. Each of the leagues has experienced, for women's sports, significant television coverage, though disparities continue to exist in both media coverage and pay when compared to men's sports in Australia.

This chapter examines the development of women's basketball and netball in Australia and compares the media coverage and pay in both sports. In addition, it compares the coverage and pay of men's and women's basketball, soccer, and field hockey in Australia. Section 19.2 provides an overview of media coverage of women's sports in Australia. Section 19.3 examines media coverage and salaries in basketball. Because Australian women have been much more successful in this sport internationally than Australian men have been, one might expect gender pay differentials in basketball to be much lower than in other sports. However, good media coverage in Australia has not translated into good salaries, so the best women's basketball players play professionally overseas. This section also briefly discusses other Olympic sports in Australia. Section 19.4 describes the historical development of women's basketball and netball, the latter of which has become the most popular women's sport in Australia. Section 19.5 turns to media coverage and pay in netball, which has become a semi-professional league in Australia and New Zealand. We show that both coverage and pay is considerably higher for netball than for women's basketball. Section 19.6 concludes.

19.2   AN OVERVIEW OF MEDIA COVERAGE OF WOMEN'S SPORT IN AUSTRALIA

The 2006 Senate Estimates Committee inquiry into women in sport and recreation in Australia reported that the Committee was disappointed at the continuing poor coverage of women's sport by all media, and it recommended that the government fund the Australian Sports Commission (ASC) to replicate in 2008–09 the surveys and analysis that the ASC performed in its 1996 report, *An Illusory Image* (the report was published in 1997; see Phillips, 1997). In response, the Australian government has identified the promotion of women in sport as a key focus area, and the ASC, through its Women and Sport unit, is working toward improving leadership opportunities as well as achieving greater recognition of women's sport and female athletes in the media.

The ASC commissioned research into how much coverage there is of women's sport and female athletes in radio, television, and print media relative to the coverage of male sport, male athletes, and mixed sport. The research, conducted between January 2009 and July 2009, also focused on how the media portray women's sport and female athletes. It examined whether female athletes are routinely stereotyped, sexualized or trivialized in the media, and how they are depicted relative to male athletes[2] (Lumby et al., 2010: v).

The ASC report reached three main conclusions. First, it found that men's sports received vastly disproportional coverage compared to women's sports. In particular, women's sports received only 9 percent of all sports coverage, while men's sports received 81 percent (Lumby et al., 2010: v).

The ASC report also noted that the media do not just report less on women's sports, they also report on fewer women's sports. The news coverage of women's sports primarily extended from the individual sports of tennis (where women were discussed almost as frequently as men – 182 mentions of men versus 163 mentions of women), surfing, cycling and golf to the team-based sport of netball. In non-news programming, tennis had the most equal gender split in terms of both participants and audiences. The report saw the focus on individual women's sports as unsurprising for two reasons. First, team sports require greater infrastructure, which is more of a barrier for women's sports than for men's. Second, the presence of a few exceptional individuals might be enough to attract sponsors and other funding to individual sports (ibid., 2010: vi).

Second, despite the extreme disparity in attention paid to men's and women's sport across all media surveyed, the report found that the tone and content of reports on female athletes and female sport have greatly improved compared to previous studies. In the print and television commentary and reporting, analyzed in depth in this research, the stereotyping of female athletes was remarkably absent.

Third, the report found the coverage of female sport to be more favorable than that of male sport, both in year-round and Olympic reporting. This can largely be attributed to unfavorable coverage of the behavior of some male athletes and to the media's presentation of female Olympians as more successful (or at least, less unsuccessful) than their male counterparts.

The report noted that there was no bias in Australia's coverage of the Olympics in part because women have been successful on the international stage. Australian women have won more medals than Australian men at three of the last four Summer Olympics. In the 2012 London Games, Australian women won 20 medals (three of them gold) while Australian men won only 15 medals (four gold). While Australia won fewer medals overall, the gender breakdown in 2012 is very similar to that of the 2008 Beijing Games, where Australian women won 24 medals (eight gold) and Australian men won 21 (six gold) ('Australia – Medals', 2012; IOC, 2012). The same pattern held at the 2010 New Delhi Commonwealth Games. In New Delhi, despite fielding a team comprising fewer women than men

(149 as against 182), Australian women won more gold (39 versus 33 for men and one mixed), silver (28 versus 27 for men) and bronze (26 versus 22 for men). At the 2006 Melbourne Commonwealth Games women won more gold and silver medals (men won more bronze medals), even though once more there were fewer women than men on the team (Australian Womensport & Recreation Association, 2010a).

The report also points to television news coverage of the Beijing Olympic Games as an example of how equal year-round sporting coverage could be, quantitatively and qualitatively. In Beijing, women received the same quantity of television coverage, and 'were more likely to be discussed in contexts beyond simply results (such as training and preparation, and in a sporting industry context)' (Lumby et al., 2010: vi). The report indicated that the coverage in Beijing was much more favorable than the coverage of both the 1992 and 1996 Olympic Games. These earlier games had featured women in traditionally female sports, such as gymnastics, but ignored their participation in sports traditionally associated with men, such as judo (ibid.: 7).[3]

To summarize, the report provided a mixed review of current coverage of women's sports in Australia. It cited significant improvement in coverage since the 1990s, particularly in the media's growing emphasis on women's athleticism and their declining gender stereotyping. It found that women now receive more favorable TV coverage than men, though they receive far less coverage overall. The lack of coverage is particularly lamentable, given the disproportionate success of Australian women on the international stage and the high representation of Australian women as both participants and spectators of sport (ibid.: vii).[4]

While the report addressed the state of women's sports in general, one sport has stood out. Thanks to a set of fortuitous circumstances, women's soccer has received more media coverage than other women's sports in Australia. Unlike other women's sports, women soccer teams benefit from their affiliation with men's teams and from the social obligations of the Australian Broadcasting Company (ABC). Australian clubs in the men's A-League field and help fund affiliated women's teams in the W-League. The W-League is also backed by the property group Westfield, which is owned by Frank Lowy, the chairman of the Football Federation Australia (FFA). Unlike many sports leagues in Australia (including the A-League and national men's team, the Socceroos), women's soccer clubs get free-to-air television coverage on the ABC, the national broadcaster. According to Lynch (2011), the ABC makes this free coverage available because of the network's social responsibility charter and its commitment to women's sport. Although women's soccer receives considerable media attention, the Australian Womensport &

Recreation Association notes (2010b) that its coverage by the ABC is limited to only one game a week.

Nevertheless, the coverage soccer receives appears to have affected the sport's popularity. While there are little or no rights fees paid by the ABC, Lynch (2011) believes that the exposure on free-to-air television is very important for the future of the sport. Lynch quotes FFA statistics, which show that there are 396,000 female players in Australia. Participation in girls and women's soccer grew by 8.4 percent in the eight years between 2000 and 2009, making it the fastest-growing female participation sport in the country. In contrast, netball (which has a larger player base) grew by only 0.9 per cent in the same period.

19.3   MEDIA COVERAGE AND PAY IN WOMEN's BASKETBALL

Australian women have been highly successful both individually and as a team – much more successful than Australian men. The 'Opals' – a nickname based on a gem found in Australia – won Olympic silver medals in 2000, 2004, and 2008 and an Olympic bronze in 2012. In 2006, the Opals won the International Basketball Federation (known by the acronym of its French name, FIBA) World Championship for Women. Australian women are also successful individually. In the 2011–12 season, seven of them played in the WNBA. Since the inception of WNBA, Australia has been the most heavily represented 'foreign' nation, with 21 women having played in the league, more than twice as many as any nation other than the US. In contrast, only 10 Australian men have ever played in the National Basketball Association (NBA) (two of whom were native-born Americans who became naturalized Australian citizens after playing in Australia), and, during the 2011–12 season, only two Australian men played in the NBA. Women's relative success, however, has translated into neither extensive media coverage nor high salaries, as women's professional basketball lags far behind men's basketball in Australia in both areas.

Until relatively recently, women's basketball was mostly a local affair, with club teams playing intrastate competition. In 1981, two years after the successful launch of the men's National Basketball League (NBL), eight women's teams paid A$25 apiece to create the Women's Interstate Basketball Conference. The resulting central fund of A$200 indicates that financing was a major constraint facing the new league. With financial considerations in mind, the league turned away several potential teams from New South Wales because it felt that they were too far away from the other teams to justify the cost of travel. Over the next few years, the league slowly expanded, and, in 1986, it was renamed the Women's National Basketball League (WNBL). The WNBL currently consists of 10 teams, nine in Australia and one – the Christchurch Sirens – located in New Zealand (WNBL, 2011).

In 1989 the WNBL gained its first major sponsorship, a A$258,000 deal with the Pony sports apparel company. In addition, the ABC agreed to broadcast the league's championship series. In 1993, the WNBL teams decided to contribute enough money to have the game televised on a weekly basis by the ABC. However, there were anxious times during 2001 when the ABC contemplated changing its televising of sport and dropping its coverage of the WNBL, as well as netball. (A more complete treatment appears in the next section.) A successful lobbying effort resulted in both sports being retained by the ABC. In 2006–07, the ABC increased its coverage by broadcasting WNBL games live on Friday nights as part of its digital television sports coverage as well as replaying a game in the regular Saturday afternoon slot. Over the years, both the NBL and the WNBL have struggled to attract and retain major sponsors as a way to maintain free-to-air coverage. In 2010, the NBL returned to live, free-to-air television for the first time in nine years when the new Australian network One HD started broadcasting 2–3 games a week, while the ABC continued its coverage of the WNBL.

The lure of higher salaries overseas has made it difficult for both men's and women's basketball teams to retain their best players. The NBL salary cap for the 2009–10 season was A$1,000,000 for a roster of 10. In 2009, the average salary in the NBL was about A$74,000 (Basketball Australia, 2009; NBL, 2011). There is no salary cap in the WNBL, though one is currently being discussed (Cameron, 2012). While some WNBL players can now earn between A$50,000 and A$150,000 per year, the average annual salary in 2009 was between A$5,000 and A$10,000. As a result, only a handful of players can afford to make playing in the WNBL their full-time job (Basketball Australia, 2009; Sully, 2011).

In addition to salaries for league play, payment for representing Australia on its national team is reported as low, but similar for men and women. Matt Nielson, the captain of the Australian men's basketball team (the Boomers) also plays in Europe. His playing contract pays him about A$250 per game for Australia and about half that for every day at a training camp. Lauren Jackson, captain of the Australian women's national basketball team (the Opals), is reported to have the same contract as Nielson. Jackson also plays in the WNBA in the United States. The equality for these two star players is somewhat surprising, given the general inequality for other players and other sports.

The inequality that we see in the pay of male and female basketball players exists in other sports as well. Nader (2011) examines pay inequality between individual Australian male and female athletes who play the same sports.[5] First, Nader compares the salary of Melissa Barbieri, captain of the Australian women's soccer team (the Matildas), who also plays for Melbourne Victory's women's team, with that of Lucas Neill, captain of the Australian men's soccer team (the Socceroos). Again, the Matildas' performance outshone that of the Socceroos. In late 2010, the Matildas won the women's Asian Cup tournament, while the Socceroos lost the men's Asian Cup tournament final in January 2011.

Under the collective bargaining agreement, Barbieri's playing contract pays her about A$32,000 plus a share of prize money awarded to the Matildas. Barbieri is also captain of the Melbourne Victory, whose players receive A$150 per match. In contrast, Neill received about A$200,000 for appearing in the 2010 World Cup. He also received about A$80,000 for playing in the Asia Cup final. In 2012, Neill made US$1.5 million playing for Al Jazira in the United Arab Emirates. However, Al Jazira released him at the end of the season, and he has yet to join a new club (Fox Staff Writers, 2012).

In the case of field hockey, Nader notes that Madonna Blyth, the captain of Australia's women's field hockey team (the Hockeyroos) receives only about A$22,000 a year. Blyth recognizes that women's hockey suffers from the circular problem, as the Hockeyroos have no major sponsor. Mark Knowles, Jamie Dwyer, and Liam de Young, the co-captains of the Australian men's field hockey team (the Kookaburras), do not receive much more than Blyth, as they are paid only about A$39,000 a year, though Knowles also plays professionally for Australia's Queensland Blades and Dwyer plays for Bloemendaal, H.C. in the Netherlands.

19.4   THE ORIGINS OF NETBALL

Netball is a direct descendant of basketball, and, like basketball, has a more directly traceable lineage than most other modern sports. In this section, I explain the origins of netball. Because most American readers are unfamiliar with netball, I also provide a brief overview of the game and its place in Australian sport.

James Naismith created basketball by writing down 13 rules for a new game at the Springfield (Massachusetts) YMCA Training Institute in 1891. Within weeks, Senda Berenson, a 24-year-old Jewish immigrant from Lithuania who had recently become the director of 'physical culture' at nearby Smith College, had adapted the game for women.

Berenson divided the court into three sections, with each team designating two players to its offensive section of the court, two players to its defensive section, and one player to the middle section. The stationing reflects the names of the positions, as the forwards played in the forward, offensive section; the guards protected the goal in the defensive section; and the center played in the middle. The court design and positioning stayed unchanged in the US until 1934, when the court was divided into two sections, with three women stationed in each half. As with the men's game, neither physical contact nor movement while holding the ball was permitted. These limitations are present in some form in the modern game, as physical contact results in a 'foul' charged to the player who initiated the contact, and players are permitted to move only one step with the ball unless they dribble (bounce) it (see Taylor, 2001; Grundy and Shackleford, 2005).

Some of the differences between the women's and the men's game developed over time as the rules slowly became codified. For example, both the men's and the women's game initially disallowed all movement with the ball. While the men's game soon allowed unlimited movement with the ball as long as the player continuously dribbled it, the women's was slower to adapt. At first, women were allowed only three dribbles with the ball before they had to stop moving. Unlimited dribbling was not permitted in the women's game until 1966 (Hult and Trekel, 1991).

Differences in the rules governing men's and women's basketball reflected the underlying conditions, beliefs, and prejudices of the time. For many college-age women – the initial focus of the women's basketball – basketball was the first team sport they had ever played. To attract women to participate and to placate college administrators who often opposed any physical activity for women, Berenson limited aggressive play and other 'unladylike' behavior. Even this was not enough for those who believed women to be fragile creatures whose reproductive functions could be damaged by physical exertion. Such notions led Stanford University to ban all women's intercollegiate athletic competition from 1899 to 1904. It also led to the creation of a short-lived rival game, known as 'Basquette', which placed even greater limits on the movements of players[6] (Taylor, 2001; Grundy Shackleford, 2005; Treagus, 2005).

Berenson's version of women's basketball moved to England in 1895, when an American educator visited Marina Bergman-Osterberg's Physical Training College. The number of players in the English version increased from five to seven or nine (the number varied). The English version of the game used more players because of the different attire worn by its players. American women wore 'bloomers', an early version of women's gym clothes, to play basketball, while English women initially played the game in long skirts and thus were much less mobile. Partly for this reason, all dribbling

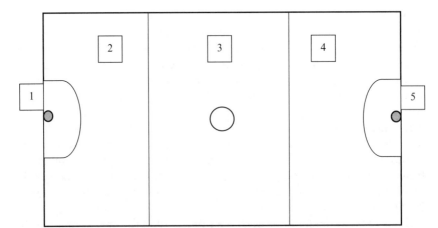

Notes
1.   Team A's shooting circle (Team A moves from right to left).
2.   Team A's attacking third.
3.   The centre third.
4.   Team B's attacking third (Team B moves from left to right).
5.   Team B's shooting circle.

Figure 19.1   The netball court

was prohibited in the English game. Another key addition was borrowed from field hockey: all shots in the English variant of women's basketball had to come from within a 'shooting circle'. This circle was actually a semi-circle set along each endline, with the net along the diameter (see Figure 19.1). The English game was codified and given the name 'netball' in 1901, as the English added a net to what had been a plain hoop in order to clarify when a ball had gone through the hoop (Taylor, 2001; Treagus, 2005).

English educators brought netball to Australia in 1897, before the English rules had been formally codified, so the rules continued to evolve in Australia even after the game had been codified in England. As a result, the Australian game varied from place to place. For example, some areas used nine players per side instead of the normal seven. Even the name of the sport was different in Australia, as the All-Australia Women's Basket Ball Association (AAWBBA) was formed in 1927, in part to codify the uniquely Australian rules for the game. The AAWBBA rules were reconciled with those in New Zealand and England in 1939, but full international standardization did not occur until the first world championship in 1963. The AAWBBA finally changed its name to All-Australia Netball Association in 1970 and is now known as Netball Australia (Jobling, 1994; Taylor, 2001; Treagus, 2005).

Netball spread rapidly in Australia for two reasons: it was cheap, and it did not conflict with traditional notions of womanly behavior. All one needed were hoops and a flat surface, which could range from urban asphalt to rural fields. In addition to encouraging participation by women, the low cost reduced opposition by male members of sports associations, who frequently viewed themselves as involved in a zero-sum game with women. Moreover, netball did not directly challenge any of the stereotypes of the day, which greatly reduced any opposition by sports authorities. Men and many women were happy to see that netball's restrictive rules and ladylike attire reflected traditional notions of femininity (Taylor, 2001; Grundy and Shackleford, 2005; Treagus, 2005).

Today, netball is the most popular women's sport in both Australia and New Zealand. According to the ABS (2009), about 5 per cent of Australian women participate in netball, roughly the same percentage as play tennis. It is by far the most popular team sport, as only half as many women play soccer, the next-most popular sport. Despite its popularity in Australia and the rest of the Commonwealth, netball is little known throughout the rest of the world.

Netball is played on a court that is 30.5 metres long and 15.25 metres wide, divided into three zones, as in Figure 19.1. The ball looks like more like a volleyball than a basketball, as it is smaller than a standard women's basketball and is white. Each team now has seven players, and – unlike basketball, in which the positions flow into one another – each netball player has a distinct position, which limits where she may go on the court. A player who strays outside of the area designated for the position is deemed 'offside' and the opposing team is given a 'free pass', which is a pass taken from the spot of the infraction.

To help the umpires identify who can play where, each player wears letters on her jersey that identify her position (for example, 'C' for centre or 'WD' for wing defence). A goal shooter must move anywhere in the attacking third of the court illustrated in Figure 19.1, but she must stay in that third. A goal attack must play in the attacking third or centre third of the court. A wing attack can move in the attacking or centre third, but she may not go into the shooting circle, which is a subsection of the attacking third of the court. The centre can play anywhere except in either shooting circle. The wing defence can move within the centre and defensive thirds of the course, with the exception of the shooting circle. The goal defence can move anywhere within the defensive and centre thirds of the court. Finally, the goal keeper must play in the defensive third of the court.

The rules of netball continue to reflect the restrictions of early women's basketball. Only the goal shooter and the goal attack are allowed to shoot the ball, and they can do so only inside the shooting circle. Unlike contemporary women's basketball players, netball players may still not dribble the ball. Similar to basketball players, netball players may advance the ball only 1.5 steps before passing. Even when not moving, netball players may not hold the ball indefinitely. They may hold the ball for no more than three seconds before passing or shooting it. Basketball has a similar but more complicated rule in which the player must pass or shoot within five seconds, but only when she is pressured by a defensive player.[7] 'Pressure' occurs when a defensive player is within three feet of the player with the ball. This kind of pressure cannot occur in netball, as defenders are not allowed to move within three feet of the player with the ball. In netball, players can advance the ball by passing, with each pass being at least a body-width long, so a player may not simply hand the ball off to a teammate. No such restriction on passing exists in basketball (Teach PE, 2012). Even the attire of netball players is distinctly more 'feminine' than those of basketball players, as netball players continue to wear skirts rather than shorts. As the numerous knee and ankle injuries to netball players suggest, however, netball play is an intense, physical sport (Treagus, 2005).

In the United States, as well as in much of the rest of the world, the adoption of men's rules effectively killed the distinctly female version of basketball, though it persisted in a few areas, most notably in Iowa, for several years. A likely reason for the failure of women's basketball to evolve into the parallel sport of netball can be found in the degree of commitment to the sport in the early 1970s. Title IX, which changed the face of women's sports in the United States by requiring that they receive as much funding as men's sports,[8] came one year after women's basketball adopted men's rules. Prior to Title IX, women's basketball had received so little attention that many states did not have a uniform set of rules by which schools played (Grundy and Shackleford, 2005). The lack of commitment resulted in the relatively poor performance of the US in international play prior to that time. American women did not win a medal in the FIBA Women's World Championships after they had won the first two championships in 1953 and 1957 (and would not win a medal again until 1979). This contrasts sharply with American women's strong performance in Olympic sports in general and may be explained by the fact that women's basketball was not an Olympic sport until 1976, and so there was relatively little incentive to create strong teams. Thus, the adoption of men's rules occurred at roughly the same time that sports authorities in the United States began to take women's sports seriously.

In contrast, netball had been firmly established in Australia long before the United States and the IOC began to emphasize the new version of women's basketball. Partly because of their long history with netball,

Australia and New Zealand have dominated international play and have won every World Championship in netball since 1963. On the club level, Australia has fully integrated play with New Zealand. The Trans-Tasman Netball League Ltd (TTNL), a joint venture of Netball Australia and Netball New Zealand, began play in 2008. Like the WNBL, the TTNL has 10 teams. Unlike the WNBL, the TTNL is an international league, with five teams located in Australia and five in New Zealand. The TTNL is the first semi-professional netball competition in Australasia, having succeeded two national leagues: Australia's Commonwealth Bank Trophy (1997–2007), and New Zealand's National Bank Cup (1998–2007).

19.5   MEDIA COVERAGE AND PAY IN NETBALL

Netball receives substantial television coverage in Australia, much more than the limited time allotted to the WNBL. Channel ONE HD screens all games live or near-live, subject to programming commitments, while Network Ten screens every Sunday afternoon game live wherever possible. In addition Telstra, a leading provider of internet broadband and mobile devices, has become TTNL's major sponsor. Telstra now streams all matches through its Big Pond Sport News TV Channel on a slightly delayed schedule throughout Australia (ANZ Championship, 2011).

Sully (2011) argues that digital free-to-air television has provided the platform for sponsors and the television networks to invest in women's sport. In a national first, netball is now shown live 10 hours a week over a 19-week season, compared with the one-hour highlights shown on ABC television once a week prior to introduction of the TTNL. As netball is the top participation sport for women, games are sold out, and the television networks are beginning to benefit from the sport's broad popularity. David White, former general manager of sport at Network Ten says:

> The rise in netball's popularity, its commercial appeal and general professionalism of the top level domestically and internationally has been massive in the last three years. And while the girls aren't earning as much as AFL [Australian Football League] players, certainly in time their salaries and sponsorship appeal will grow substantially and I think they'll blaze a trail.

Indeed, television ratings have been very strong. The TV audience for the 2010 Commonwealth Games final between archrivals Australia and New Zealand peaked at 1.67 million viewers in five major cities, and with another 30 per cent to account for viewers in the rest of Australia, the peak audience was around 2.2 million. According to White, this figure 'puts it right up there in terms of one of the most watched sports of the year' (Sully, 2011).

The TTNL strictly limits the salaries its players can earn, but the salaries are still well above those paid to WNBL players. TTNL team payrolls are set at A$262,000, which comes to almost A$23,000 per player for a roster of 12, plus bonuses and incentives worth A$50,000. While more established players earn A$35,000–45,000 a year, rookies can make only A$12,000 (Wu, 2011). This compares very well with the average salary of less than A$10,000 in the WNBL.

The Australian Netball Players' Association (ANPA), the players' union, estimates that there are no more than two full-time players per club, though even this small number would not have been possible prior to the TTNL. The ANPA reports that players are divided as to whether netball should become fully professional. Some players like to improve their long-term career prospects through continuing employment. The TTNL aims to increase salaries so that more players can earn a full-time living playing netball, but it fears that rising labor costs could threaten the long-term viability of the league. The captain of the Australian national netball team (known as the Diamonds), Sharelle McMahon, is reported to have a contract of about A$25,000 to play for the national team and about A$50,000 to play for the Vixens in the local championship.

While women trail behind men in their earnings as professional athletes, there is evidence that the gap may be closing, especially in netball and basketball. Craig Kelly, CEO of sports marketing and management company Elite Sports Properties, feels that the women's arena is on the verge of experiencing unprecedented growth. He has identified women's basketball and netball as growth areas, saying of the women in these sports, '[F]or us they're just as important as the men on our books. They're starting to earn decent enough money for us to warrant putting the time and effort into it' (Sully, 2011).

19.6   CONCLUSION

This chapter has presented information about media coverage and pay in women's sports in Australia with a focus on basketball and netball. It showed that, according to the 2010 ASC Report, while the quantity of coverage accorded women's sports in Australia is only a small fraction of the coverage of men's sports, the quality of coverage may exceed that of men's sports. Australia's female athletes are no longer presented in stereotypical fashion, and women's sports are portrayed more favorably in part because women behave more professionally. What women lose in terms of the extent of coverage, they gain in terms of quality.

Media coverage of women's basketball has been improving as well, in part because Australia's national team has been so successful internationally. Women's pay has been increasing since the inception of the semi-professional league, the WNBL, in 1986. While individual players benefit from playing opportunities abroad, the league has been hurt by their departure. On the other hand, the experience abroad has made the Opals a contender in international competition.

While the notion of 'separate but equal' has dubious connotations in the United States because segregation has so often been instrumental in providing unequal treatment, separateness in sports has proved beneficial to female athletes in Australia. Netball, a sport played only by women, developed in Australia more fully than in the rest of the world. It gained such a strong identity that it has continued to thrive despite the growing popularity of women's basketball after the sport adopted men's rules in the 1970s. While virtually unheard of in the United States, netball is the most popular women's sport in Australia both in attendance and in participation. It is so popular that it has its own semi-professional league, has a sponsorship agreement with Telstra and is well represented in the media. The Commonwealth Games championship match is one of the most watched sports events in Australia.

Prospects for future media coverage for women's sports are good in Australia. Soccer has been adopted as a leading women's sport by the ABC and is partially sponsored by the men's league. The ABC has also covered women's basketball since 1993. Finally, the 'circular problem' of many sports (low media coverage, poor popularity, and weak sponsorship) is not present in netball. The sport's popularity has led to a strong league and extensive media coverage, which will help to maintain its popularity.

NOTES

1. Like the World Cup in soccer, the netball championship is played quadrennially, with the latest championships taking place in 2011. Australia took the silver medal in the 2003 championships, which were won by New Zealand.
2. For more on images of women in sports, see Stull, Chapter 3 in this volume.
3. For more on gender stereotypes in sports, see Stull, Chapter 3 in this volume.
4. For more on the participation of Australian women in sport, see Booth and Leeds, Chapter 2 in this volume.
5. These payments do not include sponsorships or what they are paid overseas or for playing in smaller leagues. Nader's (2011) sources were sponsorships, payments from overseas or payment for playing in smaller leagues.
6. Basquette had nine players, each restricted to a particular zone on the court.

7. This rule applies whether the player is holding or dribbling the ball.
8. For more on Title IX, see Chapter 9 in this volume.

REFERENCES

ANZ Championship (2011), 'Broadcast FAQs', 'Netball: Change the Game', online at: http://www.anz-championship.com/matches/broadcast/ (accessed October 8, 2012).

'Australia – Medals' (2012), Official London 2012 Website, online at: http://www.london2012.com/country/australia/medals/index.html (accessed September 1, 2012).

Australian Bureau of Statistics (2009), 'Perspectives on Sport', Feature Article 3, Women in Sport, Canberra, online at: http://www.abs.gov.au/AUSSTATS/abs@.nsf/Previousprodu cts/4156.0.55.001Feature%20Article3May%202009?opendocument&tabname=Summary &prodno=4156.0.55.001&issue=May%202009&num=&view= (accessed May 29, 2011).

Australian Womensport & Recreation Association (2010a), 'Gold, Silver and Bronze to the Women!', Media Release, 1 November.

Australian Womensport & Research Association (2010b), 'How to Spend $45 Million on Women's Sport!', Media Release, December 7.

Basketball Australia (2009), 'Making Your Career in Basketball: A Guide to the Australian Basketball Pathway', online at: http://www.tams.act.gov.au/__data/assets/pdf_file/0006/158208/Making_Your_Career_In_Basketball.pdf (accessed June 7, 2012).

Cameron, Ben (2012), 'Salary Cap on Agenda', Bendigo Weekly, online at: http://www.bendigoweekly.com.au/news/salary-cap-on-agenda (accessed April 12, 2012).

Fox Staff Writers (2012), 'Lucas Neil on the lookout for a new team after being released by UAE Pro League club Al Jazira', Fox Sports, online at: http://www.foxsports.com.au/football/lucas-neill-on-the-lookout-for-new-team-after-being-released-by-uae-pro-league-club-al-jazira/story-e6frf423-1226381249673 (accessed June 2, 2012).

Grundy, Pamela and Susan Shackelford (2005), *Shattering the Glass: The Remarkable History of Women's Basketbal*, New York: New Press.

Hult, Joan S. and Marianna Trekell (1991), *A Century of Women's Basketball*, Reston, VA: American Alliance for Health, Physical Recreation and Dance.

International Olympic Committee (IOC) (2012), 'Search All Olympic Medalists', olympic.org, online at: at http://www.olympic.org/medallists-results?athletename=&category=1 &games=30769&sport=&event=&mengender=true&womengender=false&mixedgende r=false&teamclassification=false&individualclassification=false&continent=5&country =30785&goldmedal=false&silvermedal=false&bronzemedal=false&worldrecord=false &olympicrecord=false&targetresults=false (accessed June 22, 2012).

Jobling, Ian F. (1994), 'Netball', in *Sport in Australia: A Social History*, edited by Wray Vamplew and Brian Stoddart, Cambridge: Cambridge University Press pp. 154–71.

Lumby, Catharine, Helen Caple and Kate Greenwood (2010), *Towards a Level Playing Field: Sport and Gender in Australian Media*, Canberra: Australian Sports Commission.

Lynch, Michael (2011), 'Women Kick Goals', The Age, 18 June.

Nader, Carol (2011), 'Working-Class Champions', The Age, 5 March.

National Basketball League (NBL) (2011), 'Salary Cap/Points Cap', online at: http://www.nbl.com.au/nbl-hq/salary-cap-player-points (accessed October 8, 2011).

Phillips Murray (1997), *An Illusory Image: A Report on the Media Coverage and Portrayal of Women's Sport in Australia*, Canberra: Australian Sports Commission.

Sully, Sandra (2011), 'Fighting Back', Australian Women's Health, online at: http://au.lifestyle.yahoo.com/womens-health/article/-/9503061/fighting-back/ (accessed October 8, 2011).

Taylor, Tracy (2001), 'Gendering Sport: The Development of Netball in Australia', *Sporting Traditions*, **18**(1), November: 57–74.

Teach PE (2012), 'Netball Rules', online at: http://www.teachpe.com/netball/rules.php (accessed June 19, 2012).

Treagus, Mandy (2005), 'Playing Like Ladies: Basketball, Netball, and Feminine Restraint', *International Journal of the History of Sport*, **22**(1), January: 88–105.

Women's National Basketball League (WNBL) (2011), 'History of the WNBL', online at: http://www.wnbl.com.au/index.php?id=64 (accessed October 8, 2011).

Wu, Andrew (2011), 'Gerrard Slams Salary Cap – Netball', *The Age*, 7 May, Sport 4.

Index

Abily, Camille 378
abuse, physical, emotional and sexual
  7, 65, 157
academic requirements and graduation
  rates 2, 159, 161, 355–61
  see also National Collegiate Athletic
    Association (NCAA) Division
    IA and Proposition 16
age restrictions in sports 2, 7, 156–67,
  171–2
  ability 163
  abuse, physical and sexual 157
  age fraud 160
  antitrust and/or labor law 161–2
  Association of Tennis Professionals
    (ATP) World Tour 161
  baseball 162
  basketball 159, 162, 165–6
  boxing 162
  burnout prevention 160
  child labor laws 163
  collective bargaining agreement
    (CBA) 159, 161, 162–3, 165
  corruption 160
  cycling 163
  economic impact 163–6
  education requirement 159, 161
  Fédération Internationale de
    Gymnastique (FIG) 157, 160
  figure skating 156–7
  football 162
  golf 156–7, 159–60
  governing bodies 171–2
  grand slam 158
  gymnastics 156–7, 159, 160
  hockey 162
  injuries, career-ending, prevention
    of 164
  International Tennis Federation
    (ITF) Age Eligibility
    Commission 158
  Ironman Triathlon World
    Championships 163
  Junior Tour 158
  Ladies Professional Golf
    Association (LPGA) 157, 159
  legal, cultural and ethical criticism
    159
  legal status 160–63
  Major League Baseball (MLB) 161,
    162
  muscular and skeletal development
    160
  National Basketball Association
    (NBA) 159, 161, 165–6
  National Football League (NFL)
    161, 162–3
  National Hockey League (NHL) 161
  ordinary least squares (OLS)
    regression 164
  overwork, vulnerability to 157
  playing ability, intelligence, maturity
    and financial stability 160
  Professional Golf Association
    (PGA) Tour 161
  public image 160
  reserve clause 162
  running 163
  self-selection 165–6
  social benefits 159
  stochastic frontier analysis 163
  swimming 163
  tennis 156–7, 158, 159, 162, 164
  Women's National Basketball
    Association (WNBA) 7, 157,
    159
  Women's National Basketball
    Players' Association (WNBPA)
    159
  Women's Tennis Association
    (WTA) Tour 157, 158, 163–5,
    166–7
American Junnior Golf Association
  (AJGA) Tournaments 97
antitrust and/or labor law 161–2
Ashe, Arthur 115

Association of Tennis Professionals
     (ATP) World Tour 161
assortative mating 3
athletics 62–5
attendance at sports events 3, 21–38
     Australia 49, 410
     basketball 133–5
     by marital status and spouse's sports
          capital 30
     by sports participation 26
     data 28–30
     econometric results 30–37
     marriage and attendance 27–8,
          29–30, 37
     model 24–8
     participation 26
     previous research 22–4
     probit model 34–5
     sports capital 25–7, 31–2
     Women's World Cup 365–6, 375–6,
          382
attire, modest 4
Augustus, Seimone 147
Austin, Tracy 156, 158
Australia 163, 397
Australia: basketball and netball *see*
     basketball and netball in
     Australia
Australia: participation in women's
     sport 3, 40–54
     aerobics/fitness 41, 42, 47
     attendance patterns 49
     Australian Olympic Committee
          (AOC) 51–2
     Australian Rules Football 49, 50
     basketball 49, 50
     business deals ('grass ceiling') and
          networking 48, 51
     competition/challenge 44, 46–8, 50,
          51, 53, 54
     composite commodity consumption
          46
     cricket 49
     cycling 41, 42
     dog racing 49
     family-unfriendly demands 52–3
     gender differences 47, 51
     gender roles in the family 48
     golf 41, 42, 48, 49
     harness racing 49

health/fitness/well-being (including
     weight loss) 42, 43–4, 46–8, 51,
     53, 54
home production function 46–7
horse racing 49
income 46–7, 48
life cycle changes in activities 42, 47
lowering barriers to participation
     51–3
macho culture 52
marginal utility of consumption 48
model 45–51
motivations 40
motor sports 49
national sporting organizations
     (NSOs) 51, 52
netball 41, 42, 49, 50
non-participation and constraints
     40, 44–5, 48
'old-boy' network 52
participation by age and gender 43
patterns of sports and physical
     recreation activities 41–5
role models and mentors, lack of
     52, 54
rugby league 49, 50
rugby union 49, 50
running 42
soccer 42, 49
socialization and enjoyment 43–4,
     46–8, 50, 51, 53, 54
Sport Leadership Grants and
     Scholarships for Women
     Program (ASC) 53
swimming 42
tennis 42, 49, 50
time allocation and constraints 45,
     46, 49, 53
transport 44
underrepresentation 52, 54
utility function 46
walking 41, 42, 44, 47, 53
Women in Sport Leadership
     Register (ASC) 53
work responsibilities 48
avoidance behaviour 13

Barbieri, Melissa 416
baseball 11
     age restrictions 162

coaching 276–8, 286
basketball 9–11, 12
  age restrictions 159, 162, 165–6
  coaching 275, 276–9, 282, 286
  collective bargaining agreement
    (CBA) 264, 416
  endorsements 381
  Proposition 16 236
  and quantile regression 2
  Title IX 175, 420
  see also revenues and subsidies in
    National Collegiate Athletic
    Association (NCAA) Division I
    women's basketball
basketball and gender differences in
  competitive balance 10–11, 135–7,
    251–66
  Associated Press (AP) player-of-the-
    year award 261
  average first-round results 254–5
  collective bargaining agreement
    (CBA) 264
  Herfindahl-Hirschman index (HHI)
    256–7
  Herfindahl-Hirschman Index Ratio
    (HHIR) 256–8, 262, 264
  inter-season competitive balance
    253–4, 256
  intra-season competitive balance
    253–4
  measurement 253–8
  Naismith Award 261
  National Basketball Association
    (NBA) 259, 262–3
  National Collegiate Athletic
    Association (NCAA) 254–5,
    256, 260, 264
  National Collegiate Athletic
    Association (NCAA) Division I
    251, 253, 257–8, 262, 263
  National Collegiate Athletic
    Association (NCAA) Division
    II 262
  National Collegiate Athletic
    Association (NCAA) Division
    III 262
  player ability distribution changes
    258–64
  round by round average seed
    remaining 256

standard deviation of win
    percentage 254
  Women's National Basketball
    Association (WNBA) 263–4
basketball and netball in Australia:
  media coverage and pay 16, 49,
    50, 410–24
  All-Australia Women's Basket Ball
    Association (AAWBBA) 418
  attendance 410
  Australian Broadcasting Company
    (ABC) 413–14, 415, 421
  Australian Netball Players'
    Association (ANPA) 422
  Australian Sports Commission
    (ASC): Women and Sport unit
    411–12
  collective bargaining agreement
    (CBA) 416
  International Basketball Federation
    (FIBA) 414
  media coverage 411–14
  media coverage in basketball
    414–16
  media coverage and pay in netball
    421–2
  National Basketball Association
    (NBA) 414
  National Basketball League (NBL)
    414, 415
  Netball Australia 418
  netball court design and positioning
    417–19
  netball, origins of 416–21
  netball rules 417–20
  pay inequalities 415–16
  popularity 410
  salaries 415, 422
  Senate Estimates Committee inquiry
    (2006) 411
  sponsorship 410
  Trans-Tasman Netball League
    (TTNL) 421–2
  TV viewership 410
  Women's National Basketball
    Association (WNBA) 410, 414
  Women's National Basketball
    League (WNBL) 415, 421–2,
    423
behavioral conflict 64–5

behavioral differences in
    competitiveness 293–4, 299
Berenson, Senda 416–17
Bergman-Osterberg, Marina 417
biological factors and competitiveness
    92, 313
Blyth, Madonna 416
body image 60–61, 67
Bompastor, Sonia 378
bone density, low 64
Borkowski, Shek 379
boxing 162
Brazil 349
British Commonwealth 16
British Open 102
Brown, Jim 260
Brunson, Rebekkah 147
Buffet, Marie-Georges 378
burnout prevention 160
business deals ('grass ceiling') and
    networking 48, 51
Buss, Jerry 134

capability effect 99
capability hypothesis 300
Capriati, Jennifer 156, 158
Caribbean 312
Catchings, Tamika 147
Central America 313
Chamberlain, Wilt 260
Champions Tour 5, 74, 76, 80, 82–3
Chastain, Brandi 347
child labor laws 163
Chile 374
China 160
    Women's World Cup 365, 369–71,
        373–4, 383
'choking under pressure' 300
Civil Rights Act 177
Civil Rights Restoration Act (1988)
    179
Clarett, Maurice 162
coaching women and women
    coaching: pay differentials 11–12,
        269–88
    average assistant coaching salaries
        by institution type 274
    average head coaching salaries by
        institution type 272
    baseball 276–8, 286

basketball 275, 276–9, 286
    Division I 275, 284
    Division IA 272–4, 276–9, 282
    Division IAA 272–4, 276–9
    Division IAAA 272–4, 276–9
    Equity in Athletics Data 271, 273,
        278–9, 282, 284
    football 275, 276–9, 286
        Division II 272–4
        Division III 272–4
    golf 276–8, 286–7
        salary model 282–6
    institution type, coaching salaries by
        271–5
    marginal revenue product (MRP)
        275
    National Collegiate Athletic
        Association (NCAA) 271
        percentage of womens' teams
            coached by women 269
        wage determination for men's golf
            coaches 284
        wage determination for women's
            golf coaches 285
    operating expenses 275–6, 278, 286
    program expenditures 280–81
    program reputation 280–81
    rating percentage index (RPI) 280
    salary determinants 281–6
    scholarships 278–9
    soccer 276–8
    softball 276–8, 286, 287
        coaching performance by gender
            279–81
        coaching productivity 281
        Division I 280, 286
    tennis 276–8
    total expenditures on selected sports
        by division 275–9
    total expenses 275, 277, 286
    volleyball 276–8
    work–life balance barriers 270, 287
Coates, John 52
collective bargaining agreement
    (CBA)
    age restrictions 159, 161, 162–3, 165
    basketball 137, 139, 264, 416
    netball 416
Colombia 297
Commonwealth Games 372, 412–13

Communist countries 352–5, 357–8, 360–61
competition avoidance/aversion
figure skating 319–20, 324, 326, 327, 332
sprinting 13
competitive balance *see* basketball and gender differences in competitive balance
competitiveness and gender differences 293–314, 325–6
ability 295
analysis of variance 308
behavioral differences 293–4, 299
biological factors 313
capability hypothesis 300
'choking under pressure' 300
closeness or competitive balance 306–7
cultural heterogeneity 311–12
culture-and-incentives hypothesis 300, 311
data and descriptive evidence 301–8
drug-testing and performance-enhancing drugs 309, 311
econometric findings 308–11
estimation results 310
finish times, percentage difference in 305, 306
genetic differences 294
Germany and 100m distance race 301–8, 309–12
golf 300
Graduate Record Examination (GRE) 295
implications for future research 311–13
incentive structures 293
international athletes sample 301–8, 309–12
matrilineal and patriarchal societies 298
Mellon Foundation Graduate Education Initiative 295
negotiating practices 296
nurture 297
opportunities 293
ordinary least squares (OLS) regression 310–11
overconfidence 299

path dependency 306
performance 307
physical differences 293
population size 305–6
predispositions 293
previous empirical research 294–301
laboratory experiments 296–8
real-life evidence 294–6
sports data 298–301
quantile regression 310, 312
regression model 308
risk aversion and risk taking 295, 296, 297
running 299
self-selection 299–300
socialization 293, 297, 311
socio-cultural conditions 293
tennis 300
thresholds 306
'Usain Bolt effect' 305
corporate branding 134–5
corporate sponsorships 375
corruption 160
Crocker, Fay 390–91
cultural factors 57, 58, 92
golf 92
soccer 350, 353–5
cultural heterogeneity 311–12
cultural lag 4, 56, 59, 64–5, 67
culture-and-incentives hypothesis 300, 311
cycling 41, 42, 163
Czechoslovakia 294

da Silva, Marta 380
Diaz, L. 393
difference-in-differences (DiD) technique 10, 235, 239–43, 245, 249–50
disordered eating 4, 62, 63–4, 68
Djokovic, Novak 115
drug-testing and performance-enhancing drugs 13, 309, 311
Dwyer, Jamie 416

earnings
basketball 16, 139, 153
coaching 281–6
golf 5–6, 94, 96, 100, 103, 105, 108–9, 111, 390, 395, 397–402

Women's World Cup 375–6, 379
see also basketball and netball in
Australia; coaching; prize
money; skiing: earnings and
performance
East Asia 349
eating disorders 4, 62, 63–4, 68
economic contests *see* figure skating:
gender-differential responses to
economic contests
economic impact of Women's World
Cup 365–85
apparel and fashion markets 381,
384
attendance 365–6, 375–6, 382
bilateral trade patterns 367–8, 370,
382
Chile 374
China 365, 369–71, 373–4, 383
corporate sponsorship 375
endorsements 380–84
England 376–8
FIFA (Fédération International de
Football Association) 365–6
Football Association (FA) 377–8
France 374, 376, 378
GDP 372–3, 382
Germany 365, 367, 374, 376, 378–9
gravity model of trade 368
growth regression 373
impact on trade and income per
capita 369–74
Japan 369, 373–4, 376, 379
literature review 367–9
losses (revenue) 367
Major League Soccer (MLS) 375
personality 382
physical attractiveness 381–4
professional leagues, connection to
375
salaries 375–6, 379
semi-professionals 376, 379
Sweden 369, 371–2, 376, 379–80,
383
television audiences 366
television deals 375
Union of European Football
Associations (UEFA) 377
United States 365, 367, 369, 371–2,
374–5, 380, 383

Women's Football Association
(WFA) 377–8
Women's Professional Soccer (WPS)
375–6
Women's Super League (WSL) 376
Women's United Soccer Association
(WUSA) 375
WPSL 376
education requirement 159, 161
endorsements 380–84
EPO (drug) 309
equal opportunities *see* Title IX
Equity in Athletics Disclosure Act
(EADA) 9, 179, 180, 189–90, 191
Europe 346
European Championships 329, 331–2
European Tour 96
Evans, Dena 270
exercise, excessive 68

Family Education Right and Privacy
Act (FERPA) 237
Fédération Internationale de
Gymnastique (FIG) 157, 160
Fédération Internationale de Ski (FIS)
Alpine Ski World Cup 6, 116,
117–19
'Female Athletic Triad' 64
FIFA (Fédération International de
Football Association) 14, 346,
348–51, 352, 353, 354, 365–6
figure skating and age restrictions
156–7
figure skating: gender-differential
responses to economic contests
12, 13–14, 319–38, 341–4
'atmospherics' 331
coefficient of variation for men's and
ladies' competitions 333
competition avoidance/aversion
319–20, 324, 326, 327, 332
competitiveness 325–6
estimation and data 329
European Championships 329,
331–2
Four Continents Championship 329,
331–2
Free Skate 13–14, 327–31, 334–7,
341–2
'home ice' advantage 330

incentives 319–20, 333, 335–6, 337
individual performance 335
International Skating Union (ISU)
    343
    Grand Prix events 329, 331, 333,
        337
    marginal physical product (MPP)
        320
    marginal revenue product (MRP)
        321
    means of key variables 332
    negative feedback 319–20, 327, 331
    negative impact 333, 336, 337
    Olympics 328–37, 343
    ordinary least squares (OLS)
        regression 333
    participation decisions 326
    piece rate 320
    point differential 335
    rank number 335, 336
    rank-order tournaments (ROTs)
        319, 321, 338
    results 332–6
    reward structure 328
    score 335
    scoring system 343
    selection bias 325
    self-selection 338
    Short Program 327–31, 335–7,
        341–2
    team performance 323
    World Championships 328–32,
        334–7
football 8, 12
    age restrictions 162
    coaching 272–4, 275, 276–9, 286
    Proposition 16 235–6
    revenues and subsidies 225–6
    Title IX 175, 183–4
    see also soccer
Football Association (FA) 346, 377–8
    Women's Premier League 347
    Women's Super League (WSL)
        347–8
Four Continents Championship 329,
    331–2
France 295
    Bureau du Conseil Fédèral 378
    football 374, 376, 378
    Football Association 378

gender differences 10, 116
    Australia 47, 51
    competitive balance 11
    golf 5, 102, 105
    skiing 117, 122, 129
    see also basketball and gender
        differences; competitiveness
        and gender differences; golf:
        gender differences in response
        to incentives; international
        women's soccer and gender
        inequality
gender gap 13
genetic differences and competitiveness
    294
George, Tom 381–2
Germany
    and 100m distance race 301–8
    football 346, 365, 367, 374, 376,
        378–9
    Football Association (DFB) 378
    Women's Budesliga 348, 378–9
GII 362
golf 12, 116
golf: gender differences in response to
    incentives 5–6, 92–112
    affirmative action 95
    American Junior Golf Association
        (AJGA) Tournaments 97
    biological factors 92
    British Open 102
    capability effect 99
    coefficient estimates 102, 104
    competition, reaction to 92, 93
    course difficulty 102, 103, 105
    course distance 105
    course ratings 105–7
    cultural factors 92
    empirical results 102–11
    endogeneity 109
    European Tour 96
    experimental studies 93–6
    final-round scores 100, 110, 111–12
    fixed-effects model 312
    gender differences 102, 105
    Hausman specification tests 109
    'hot hand' performance streaks 97
    Ladies Professional Golf
        Association (LPGA) Tour 96,
        100, 102–7, 109–11

marginal prize money variables 109, 111
marginal return measures 111–12
means and standard deviation 102, 104, 109
multicollinearity 105
new model of incentives 100–102
nonexempt players 108
nurture 95
opponent ability 100, 102, 105, 109, 112
ordinary least squares (OLS) regression 104, 110
par 103, 105
par distance 103
par values 105–6
pay schemes (piece-rate, tournament and revenue-sharing contracts) 94
player ability 100, 109
prize money and financial incentives 96, 100, 103, 105, 108, 109, 111
Professional Golf Association (PGA) tour 96–7, 100, 102–5, 107–11
risk preferences 92
sample selection bias 312
sample tournaments 103
self-selection bias 101
social preferences 92
superstar effects 108, 312
t-statistics 102, 104, 106, 107
team-work 293–4
total score approach 100, 111
tournament characteristics 100, 109
tournament theory 111
two-stage least squares regression (2SLS) 109–11
weather 312
White's heteroskedasticity corrected standard errors 102
golf: gender and skill convergence (United States) 73–89
age and driving distance 82–3
age and earnings 75, 80
Champions Tour 74, 76, 80, 82–3
data envelopment analysis 80
driving distance 74, 76, 80–81, 82–8
gender-based earnings decomposition 80
golf production function (literature review) 75–82
Granger causality 85–8, 89
Ladies Professional Golf Association (LPGA) 73–4, 76–89
performance before and after childbirth 75
Professional Golf Association (PGA) 73–4, 76–89
professional golf production and earnings 77–9
purse size and performance 75, 85–8
putting performance 81–2
quantile regression 81
race and nationality 75
Senior Professional Golf Association (SPGA) Tour 77–9, 82
skill convergence 84
structural model 80–81
technology in golf equipment 74
United States Golf Association (USGA) 73
value of the marginal product (VMP) 76
Women's Professional Golf Association (WPGA) 73
golf
age restrictions 156–7, 159–60
Australia 41, 42, 48, 49
coaching 276–8, 282–7
competitiveness and gender differences 300
gender-differential responses to economic contests 326–7, 336, 337
and immigration theory 2
self-selection 2
governing bodies 171–2
graduation rates *see* National Collegiate Athletic Association (NCAA) Division IA and Proposition 16 impact on academic standards and graduation rates
Graf, Steffi 156
Granger causality 5, 85–8, 89
Greece 296
Greene, Nance 117

gymnastics and age restrictions 156–7,
    159, 160

Hamm, Mia 347, 381
Hausman specification tests 109
health and physical well-being 3–4
hegemonic femininity 65, 66
Hendricks, John 347
Herfindahl–Hirschman index (HHI)
    11, 256–8, 262, 264, 403–4
Higuchi, Hisako 391
Hingis, Martina 156, 158
Hjorth, M. 393
hockey 162, 416
Horan, Lindsey 378
'hot hand' performance streaks 97
human development index (HDI) 362

illegal substances *see* drug-testing
immigration theory and golf 2
incentives
    and competitiveness 293
    figure skating 319–20, 333, 335–6,
        337
    see also golf: gender differences in
        response to incentives
injuries, career-ending, prevention of
    164
Integrated Postsecondary Education
    Data System (IPEDS) 189–90,
    198
International Basketball Federation
    (FIBA) 414
International Gymnastics Federation
    (FIG) 7
International Olympic Committee 66
International Skating Union (ISU) 343
    Grand Prix events 329, 331, 333, 337
International Tennis Federation (ITF)
    Age Eligibility Commission 158
international women's soccer and
    gender inequality 345–62
    Brazil 349
    climate 352–3, 357–8, 360–61
    Communist countries 352–5, 357–8,
        360–61
    cultural factors 350, 353–5
    East Asia 349
    economic factors 345, 350
    empirical model and results 352–62

enrollment ratios and education
        level 355–61
    Europe 346
    FIFA 346, 348–51, 352, 353, 354
    Football Association (FA) 346
        Women's Premier League 347
        Women's Super League (WSL)
            347–8
    GDP per capita 352–4, 357–8,
        360–61
    Germany 346, 348
    GII 362
    Huber/White estimators 353
    human development index (HDI)
        362
    Islamic countries 349–50, 354,
        357–8, 359–61
    Italy 346
    Latin countries 352–3, 354, 357–8,
        360–61
    men's points 354, 357–8, 360–61
    North America 349
    Northern Europe 349
    Olympics 345, 346, 349
    ordinary least squares (OLS)
        regression 353, 354
    parliamentary share 355–7, 360
    per capita income 353
    performance of women's versus
        men's teams 351
    political factors 350
    population 353, 354, 357–8, 360–61
    religious factors 349
    socioeconomic factors 353
    Union of European Football
        Associations (UEFA) Women's
        Champions League 347
    United States 346–7, 357–9
    Women's Professional Soccer (WPS)
        347
    Women's Soccer Association
        (WUSA) 347
    Women's World Cup 346–7, 349
Iran 67
Ironman Triathlon World
    Championships 163
Islamic countries and soccer 4, 349–50,
    354, 357–8, 359–61
Islamic culture, barriers caused by
    65–7

Israel 296, 297, 324
Italy 346

Jackson, Lauren 415
Jaeger, Andrea 158
Japan
    football 369, 373–4, 376, 379
    Japanese women in United States
        golf 15
    Nadeshiko women's soccer league
        379
Javits Amendment (1974) 178
Johnson, Lyndon 177
Jones, R. 393

Kane, L. 393
Kaufman, Michelle 381–2
Kawabuchi, Saburo 379
Kelly, Craig 422
Kerr, Christie 392
Khasi (matrilineal society) (India)
    298
Killy, Jean-Claude 117
Kim, M.H. 393
Knowles, Mark 416
Korean Ladies Professional Golf
    Association (KLPGA) 390, 394–5,
    396–9, 400–403, 404, 407–8
Kournikova, Anna 156, 382

lacrosse 182
Ladies European Tour (LET) 397–9
Ladies Professional Golf Association
    (LPGA): economic analysis of
    influx of Korean female golfers
    12, 388–408
    annual travelling costs 402
    Australian Ladies Professional Golf
        397
    broadcasting rights 388
    consumer discrimination 389
    driving accuracy 405–6, 407
    driving distance 405
    earnings 390, 395, 401
    golf skills 405–6
    green-in-regulation 405–6
    Herfindahl–Hirschman index (HHI)
        403–4
    historical overview 390–94
    immigration decision model 394–6

Japanese Ladies Professional Golf
    Association (JLPGA) 389, 394,
    397–402, 407
Korean Ladies Professional Golf
    Association (KLPGA) 390,
    394–5, 396–9, 400–403, 404,
    407–8
Ladies European Tour (LET) 397–9
mental fortitude 401–2
migration patterns 402–5
number of Korean players in tour by
    year 394
number of tournaments in four
    different golf tours 398
payoff difference 407
percentage of top 10 finishes by
    nationality 392
prize money 397–402
putting 405–6, 407
self-selection 390, 396
sponsorship 397–402, 407
titles earned by US, international,
    Asian and Korean golfers 391
top 10 prize winners 393
total purse of four different golf
    tours 399
TV ratings 407
Ladies Professional Golf Association
    (LPGA) data 5, 6
Ladies Professional Golf Association
    (LPGA) Tour 96, 100, 102–7,
    109–11
    age restrictions 7, 157, 159
    gender-differential responses to
        economic contests 325
    Korean women 15–16
    skill convergence and gender 73–4,
        76–89
Latin countries 352–3, 354, 357–8,
    360–61
Lee, Young Hoon 15–16
lesbianism stigmatization 65
Lilly, Kristine 381
Loehr, Jim 158
'Looking-Glass Self Model' 59
low-energy availability (LEA) 64, 68
Lucic, Mirjana 163

McCoughtry, Angel 147
McMahon, Sharelle 422

Major League Baseball (MLB) 258, 264
  age restrictions 161, 162
  consumer discrimination 389
  gender-differential responses to economic contests 323
Major League Soccer (MLS) 375
marathons 98–9, 121–2, 326
marginal physical product (MPP) 320
marginal revenue product (MRP) 214–15, 219–24, 229–30, 275, 321
marriage and sports attendance 3
Marta 376
Massai (patriarchal society) (Tanzania) 298
matrilineal and patriarchal societies 298
Matthew, C. 393
media coverage *see* basketball and netball in Australia
Mellon Foundation Graduate Education Initiative 295
Men's World Cup 368–74
menstrual cycle disruption 64
Montsho, Amantle 65
Moore, Maya 147
muscular and skeletal development 160

Naismith, James 416
NASCAR racing 124–5
National Basketball Association (NBA) 147, 150–53, 414
  age restrictions 159, 161, 165–6
  consumer discrimination 389
  gender differences in competitive balance 259, 262–3
  overstatement of scoring value 7
  revenues and subsidies 214
  and the Women's National Basketball Association (WNBA) 133–7, 139–40, 142–4
National Basketball League (NBL) 414, 415
National Collegiate Athletic Association (NCAA) 9, 11, 12
  coaching 269, 271, 284, 285
  see also basketball and gender differences in competitive balance; revenues and subsidies; Title IX
National Collegiate Athletic Association (NCAA) Division IA and Proposition 16 impact on academic standards and graduation rates 10, 233–47, 249–50
  American College Testing (ACTs) scores 234, 243, 245
  basketball 236
  Bayes' theorem 237
  data 236–8
  difference-in-differences (DiD) technique 235, 239–43, 245, 249–50
  empirical results 243–5
  federal action lawsuit (Cureton and Shaw) 235
  football program 235–6
  graduation rates 238
  independent variables, sign and significance of 244
  logit regressions 240–41, 244
  ordinary least squares (OLS) regression 243–4
  racial impacts 235
  Stage One of Proposition 16 237, 249, 250
  Stage Two of Proposition 16 237
  Standard Aptitude Tests (SATs) scores 234, 243
  summary statistics 242
National Football League (NFL) 161, 162–3, 214, 323
National Hockey League (NHL) 161, 323
negative feedback and impact on performance 319–20, 327, 331, 333, 336, 337
negotiating practices and competitiveness 296
Neill, Lucas 416
netball 2, 12
  collective bargaining agreement (CBA) 416
  see also basketball and netball in Australia
Netherlands 296
New Zealand 418, 420, 421
Nielsen, Matt 415
Nigeria 65

Nixon, Richard 177, 213
North America 349
North Korea 160
Northern Europe 349
nurture 95, 297

Ochoa, Lorena 392
Office for Civil Rights (OCR) 179,
	208–9
'old-boy' network 52
Olympics 8, 14, 367–74, 413
	basketball 410, 412
	figure skating 328–37, 343
	soccer 336, 345, 349
ordinary least squares (OLS)
		regression 9, 13, 81
	age restrictions 164
	basketball 221–2, 243–4
	competitiveness and gender
		differences 310–11
	figure skating 333
	golf 104, 110
	skiing 125, 126–9
	soccer 353, 354
	Title IX 198, 200, 201–3, 205
Overbeck, Carla 381
overconfidence 299
overwork, vulnerability to 157

Pak, Se Ri 388, 389–90, 391, 393, 396,
	397–8, 402
Pan American Games 372
pay *see* earnings
Pecout, Adrien 378
peer groups 62–3
Pepper, D. 393
performance-enhancing drugs *see*
	drug-testing
physical differences and
	competitiveness 293
Plushenko, Evgeny 331
political factors 350
predispositions and competitiveness
	293
Pressel, Morgan 160
prize money
	golf 94, 96, 100, 103, 105, 108, 109,
		111
	skiing 120, 121, 122, 124–5, 126,
		128–9

probit models 34–5, 204–8
Professional Golf Association (PGA)
	406
	data 5, 6
	gender and skill convergence 73–4,
		76–89
	gender-differential responses to
		economic contests 321–3
Professional Golf Association (PGA)
	Tour 96–7, 100, 102–5, 107–11
	age restrictions 161
	Asian men 15
proportionality *see* Title IX
Proposition 16 *see* National Collegiate
	Athletic Association (NCAA)
	Division IA and Proposition 16
Proposition 48 234–5
public image 160

quantile regression 9, 13, 81, 201
	basketball 2, 214–15, 222
	competitiveness 310, 312

racing *see* running
Rampone, Christie 376
rank-order tournaments (ROTs) 5–6,
	12, 319, 321
	figure skating 319, 321, 338
	skiing 115, 116–17
rating percentage index (RPI) 280
reaction to competition 92
regression analysis 198–204
	see also ordinary least squares
		regression; quantile regression
religious factors 349
revenues and subsidies in National
	Collegiate Athletic Association
	(NCAA) Division I women's
	basketball 213–30, 232, 236
	average revenues by category 219
	away-game guarantees 226
	broadcast rights 217–19, 232
	contributions 216–19, 228–9, 232
	data analysis and model 215–22
	direct revenues 216, 220, 222, 224
	draft 222–7
	Equity and Athletic Dislosure Act
		(EADA) data 214–15
	game day sales 217–19, 232
	government support 217–19, 232

guarantees 232
indirect revenues 226
indirect support 217–19, 232
institutional support 216–19, 226–9,
    232
investment income 217–19, 232
marginal revenue product (MRP)
    214–15, 219–24, 229–30
metrostatistical area (MSA)
    population 221, 222–5
NCAA/conf. distributions 217–19,
    232
ordinary least squares (OLS)
    regression 221–2
professional draft 220–21
quantile regression 214–15, 222
rank 221–5
ratings performance index (RPI) 221
results 222–5
revenues and expenses 217, 232
royalties and advertising 217–19,
    232
sports camps 217–19, 232
student fees 216–19, 226–8
subsidies and transfers 225–9
summary statistics 222
third party support 217–19, 232
ticket sales 216–19, 222–4, 226,
    228–9, 232
total revenues 216–20, 222, 225, 226,
    229
reward structures 4
risk aversion and risk taking 295, 296,
    297
risk preferences 92
role conflict/strain 4, 57–60, 62–5, 67,
    68
role models and mentors, lack of 52, 54
Rubens, Paul 61
running/racing 299–300
    100m distance race 301–8
    age restrictions 163
    Australia 42
    competitiveness and gender
        differences 299, 301–8
    distance running/racing 98–9, 116,
        122
    foot races 116, 121
    gender differences in response to
        incentives 97–9

gender-differential responses to
    economic contests 326–7
half marathons 121
long-distance 299
road 98–9, 128, 323
sprinting 12–13
ultramarathons 98, 299

salaries *see* earnings
Saudi Arabia 66, 67
scholarships 278–9
Scott, Larry 158
Seles, Monica 156
self-esteem 63
self-image 62–3
self-selection 185
    age restrictions 165–6
    competitiveness and gender
        differences 299–300
    figure skating 338
    golf 2, 101, 390, 396
    skiing 129
semi-professionals in football 376, 379
Senior Professional Golf Association
    (SPGA) Tour 77–9, 82
sex discrimination elimination *see* Title
    IX
sexualization of women's sport 65,
    381–4
Shabelman, Doug 382
Shalala, Donna 175
Sherman Antitrust Act (1890) 7, 161–2
Shin, Jiyai 389–90, 402
skiing: earnings and performance 2, 6,
    115–30
    data 122–5
    Downhill 117–18, 122–5, 126–9
    effort 120, 121, 122, 123
    empirical analysis 125–8
    Fédération Internationale de Ski
        (FIS) Alpine Ski World Cup
        116, 117–19
    gender differences 129
    gender gap 122
    gender preferences 117
    Giant Slalom 117–18, 122–4, 126–9
    heteroskedasticity correction 126
    interquartile range 126, 128–9
    ordinary least squares (OLS)
        regression 125, 126–9

prediction, empirical tests of 120
prize structure 120, 121, 122, 124–5,
    126, 128–9
race time 123
rank-order tournaments with
    nonlinear payoffs 115, 116–17
scoring system 119
self-selection 129
Slalom 117–18, 129
speed events *see* Downhill; Super-G
standard deviation 126, 128–9
STATA 126
summary statistics 123
Super-combined 117–18
Super-G 117–18, 129
talent and ability 120, 121
technical events *see* Giant Slalom;
    Slalom
tournament theory 116, 119–22, 124,
    126
unobservable heterogeneity 125, 129
White–Huber 'sandwich' correction
    126
soccer 1, 12, 14–15, 182
    Australia 42, 49
    coaching 276–8
    media coverage 413–14
    see also economic impact of
        Women's World Cup; football;
        international women's soccer
        and gender inequality
social preferences 92
socialization 61, 293, 297, 311
socialization and enjoyment of sport
    43–4, 46–8, 50, 51, 53, 54
socio-cultural factors and
    competitiveness 293
socioeconomic factors 353
sociological determinants of
    participation 56–68
    athletics 62–5
    behavioral conflict 64–5
    body images: visual representation
        of status 60–61, 67
    body types 60–61
    bone density, low 64
    cultural factors 57, 58
    cultural lag 56, 59, 64–5, 67
    disordered eating 62, 63–4, 68
    exercise, excessive 68

'Female Athletic Triad' 64
    gender distinctions 64
    Islamic culture, barriers caused by
        65–7, 68
    judged sports 63
    lean sports 63–4, 68
    'Looking-Glass Self Model' 59
    low-energy availability (LEA) 64, 68
    material culture 56
    menstrual cycle disruption 64
    non-lean sports 64–5
    non-material culture 56
    norms 58
    peer groups 62–3
    role conflict/strain 57–60, 62–5, 67,
        68
    self-esteem 63
    self-image 62–3
    socialization 61
    statuses, achieved/ascribed 57–60
    subcultures 57–8
    United States 62–5
    values 58
softball 1, 12
    see also under coaching
Solo, Hope 382
Song, Aree 160
Sorenstam, Annika 392, 393
South Africa 65
South America 313
sponsorship 375
    basketball and netball 410
    golf 397–402, 407
sports capital 3, 25–7, 31–2
*Stanley v. University of Southern
    California* 282
Stosur, Samantha 115
superstar effects 108, 312
Sweden 297, 299
    football 369, 371–2, 376, 379–80,
        383
swimming 42, 163
Swoopes, Sheryl 381–2

team-work 293–4
tennis 7, 116, 121
    age restrictions 156–7, 158, 159, 162,
        164
    Australia 42, 49, 50
    coaching 276–8

competitiveness and gender
differences 300
endorsements 380–82
gender differences in response to
incentives 97, 99–100
gender-differential responses to
economic contests 323, 325–6,
336
Tessmer, Karen 270
Thompson, Alexis (Lexi) 157, 160
Title IX 8–9, 11, 175–210, 213, 236,
358
accommodation of interests 178
admission preferences 183
applicants admitted, percentage of
200
basketball 175, 420
budget constraints 188–9
compliance 3 and 5 percent
thresholds 206–7
continued program expansion 178
data and estimation 189–208
probit analysis of noncompliance
204–8
proportionality and compliance,
time trends in 191–5
proportionality gaps and
compliance 195–8
regression analysis 198–204
sample selection 190–91
enforcement and compliance rules
180
enrolled of those admitted,
percentage of 200
Equity in Athletics Disclosure Act
(EADA) 179, 180, 189–90, 191
evolution of the law 177–9
football 175, 183–4
funding 175, 182
geographical region 201, 205
health-care costs 182
historically black college or
university (HBC) 198–9, 201,
205
inception 177
Integrated Postsecondary Education
Data System (IPEDS) 189–90,
198
National Collegiate Athletic
Association (NCAA) 176, 179,

180–82, 186, 191, 192, 198–9,
200–205
National Collegiate Athletic
Association (NCAA) Division I
181, 183–4, 191–5, 197–8
National Collegiate Athletic
Association (NCAA) Division
II 181, 191–5, 196, 197–8, 200,
202–3, 206–7
National Collegiate Athletic
Association (NCAA) Division
III 181, 191–6, 197–8, 200,
202–3, 206–7
non-National Collegiate Athletic
Association (NCAA) schools
190–91, 197, 199, 201, 205,
208
noncompliance 189, 192, 194, 195
noncompliance, impact of penalties
of 188
noncompliance, persistence of 194
noncompliance as utility-maximizing
choice 187
ordinary least squares (OLS)
regression 198, 200, 201–3, 205
positive outcomes 185
positive proportionality gap 194
previous empirical work 180–87
proportionality 205
proportionality compliance 180–84
proportionality gap 179, 180–82,
184, 191, 192, 193–4, 198–204
quantile regressions 201
revenues and subsidies 230
reverse discrimination 175
reverse proportionality gaps 194
self-selection 185
six-year graduation rate 200–201
sociological determinants of
participation 62
sports offerings and proportionality
compliance 180
substantial proportionality 178–9,
208
substitution effect 189
theoretical model of institutional
response 186–9
trends in high school sports 182
undergraduate enrollment
coefficients 204

tournament theory 5, 111, 116, 119–22, 124, 126
Tower Amendment (1974) 178, 183
Trans-Tasman Netball League (TTNL) 421–2
trivialization of women's sport 65

Union of European Football Associations (UEFA) 377
Women's Champions League 347
United Kingdom 295–6, 324, 376–8, 417–18
United States 12
basketball 116, 410, 420
competitiveness and gender differences 312
Golf Association (USGA) 73
London Olympics 8
netball 116, 417
Open 115
soccer 346–7, 357–9
sociological determinants of participation 62–5
trends in high school sports 182
Women's World Cup 365, 367, 369, 371–2, 374–5, 380, 383
see also in particular golf: gender and skill convergence; Women's National Basketball Association (WNBA)
'Usain Bolt effect' 305

volleyball 276–8, 381

Wade, Virginia 115
Wambach, Abby 382–3
Webb, Karrie 96–7, 392, 393
Whalen, Lindsay 142–7
White, David 421–2
Wie, Michelle 392
Williams, Venus 156
Women's Football Association (WFA) 377–8
Women's National Basketball Association (WNBA) 6–7, 9, 11, 132–54
Adj.P40 value across positions 145
age restrictions 7, 157, 159
assists 142–3, 146, 150, 151
attendance 133–5

blocked shots 142–3, 145, 150
broadcast coverage 134
broadcast revenues 153
collective bargaining agreement (CBA) 137, 139
competitive balance 135–7
core players 139
corporate branding 134–5
defensive efficiency 140–41, 142
defensive rebounds 141
dispersal draft 137
draft position 151
field goals 140–41, 142–3, 145
foul shots 141
Fourth Year Option 138
free agency 137
free throws 141, 142
gender differences 263–4
historical background 137
inter-seasonal balance 153
labor market 137–9
media coverage and pay 410, 414
minutes per game, determinants of 151, 152
modeling wins 139–44
Noll–Scully ratio 135–6
offensive efficiency 140–41, 142
offensive rebound 141
offer sheet 138
Pareto principle 147
personal fouls 142, 150, 151
playoff appearances 136–8
points scored 143, 153
points surrendered 143
points-per-shot 140–41
possession 141, 143, 150, 153
profits 133–5
rebounds 141, 150, 153
Reserved Players 137–8
Restricted Free Agents 137–8
revenues 133–5, 152–3, 214
reverse-order draft 137
salary capping 153
salary scale 139
scoring 150, 151
shooting efficiency 150, 153
standard deviation 135–6
steals 150, 153
subsidies 214
top 40 players 148–9

traded players 150
turnovers 141, 145, 150, 153
Unrestricted Free Agents 137–8
value of player and team statistics
144
winning percentage determinants
142
wins 144–7
Women's National Basketball League
(WNBL) 415, 421–2, 423
Women's National Basketball Players'
Association (WNBPA) 159
Women's Professional Golf
Association (WPGA) 73
Women's Professional Soccer (WPS)
347, 375–6

Women's Super League (WSL) 376
Women's Tennis Association (WTA)
1, 7, 116, 157, 158, 163–5, 166–7
Women's United Soccer Association
(WUSA) 347, 375
Women's World Cup 14–15, 346–7,
349
see also economic impact of
Women's World Cup
work–life balance 270
WPSL 376

Young, Liam de 416

Zavian, Ellen 381, 384